MIDWEST HOME

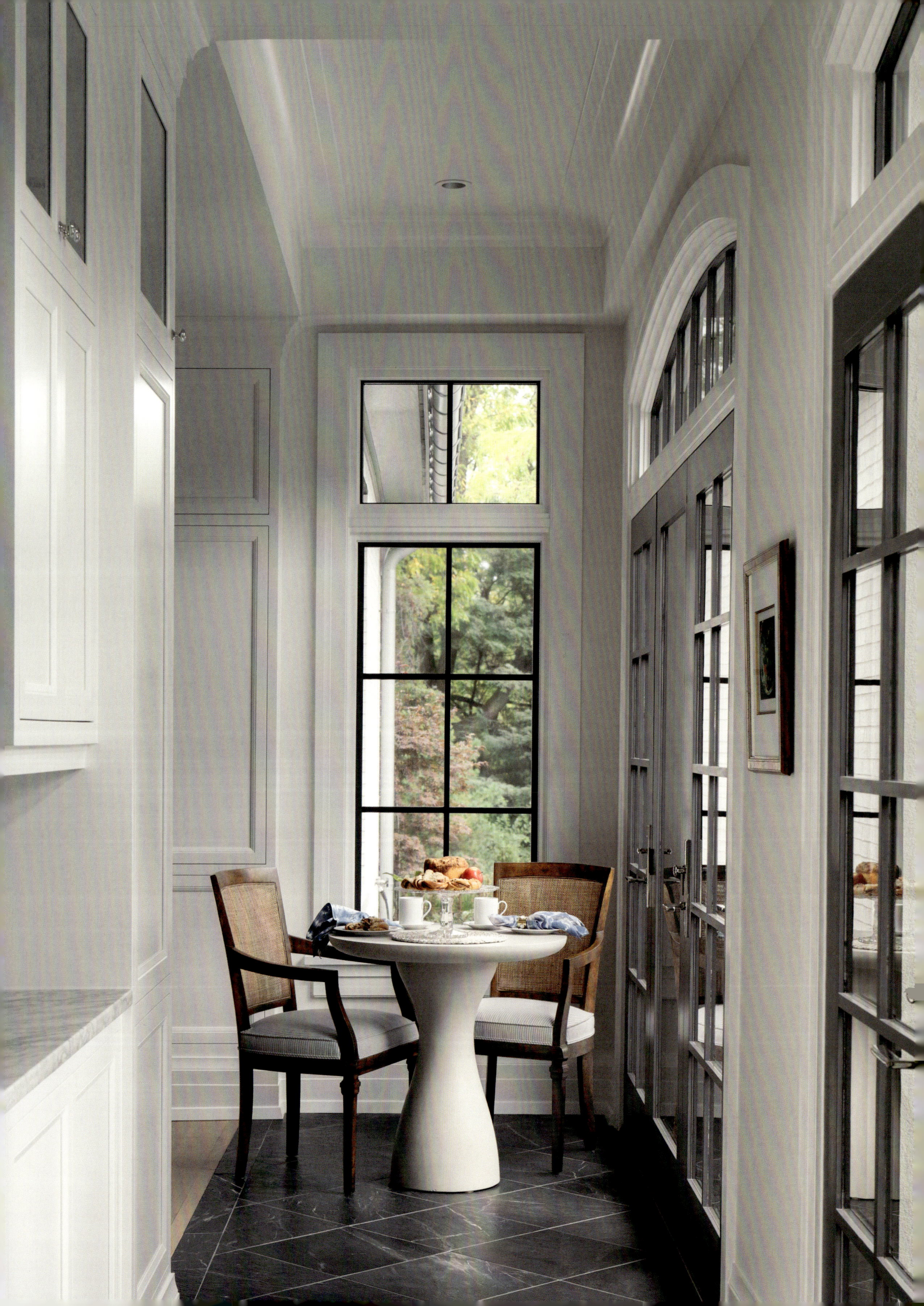

MIDWEST HOME

Interior Design in America's Heartland

RYAN HAINEY

Foreword by Carl Dellatore

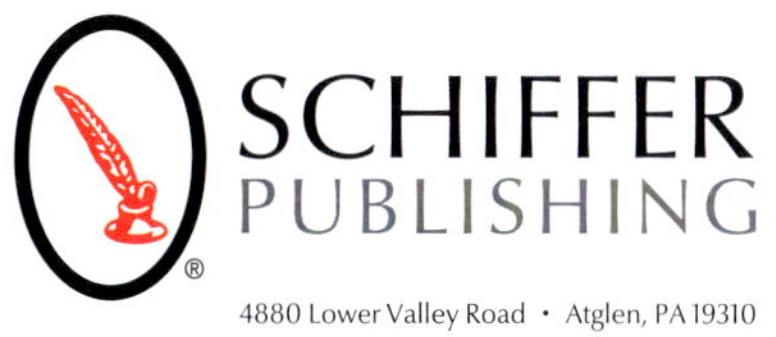

4880 Lower Valley Road • Atglen, PA 19310

Other Schiffer Books on Related Subjects:
Interior Designers at Home: Inspiration, Aesthetic, and Function with 20 Top Global Designers, Stephen Crafti, 978-0-7643-6738-0
PowerHouse: Interior Designs for Self, Style, and Sanctuary, Penny Drue Baird, 978-0-7643-6980-3
It's All in the Mix: Design Ideas for Living Well, Dann Foley, 978-0-7643-6721-2

Library of Congress Control Number: 2025939975

Design by Ryan Hainey

Photography by Ryan Hainey Photography LLC
For more information, please visit www.ryanhainey.com.
Photograph retouching by Slaven Gabric

Type set in Museo Sans/Mrs Eaves XL Serif Narrow

ISBN: 978-0-7643-7110-3
ePub: 978-1-5073-0669-7

Printed in China

10 9 8 7 6 5 4 3 2 1

Published by Schiffer Publishing, Ltd.
4880 Lower Valley Road
Atglen, PA 19310
Phone: (610) 593-1777; Fax: (610) 593-2002
Email: info@schifferbooks.com
Web: www.schifferbooks.com

To the transformative power of our environments,
where every corner whispers our story.
May this book ignite your passion
to craft spaces that unveil the layers of your true self.

With deep admiration for the Midwestern design community,
whose support and collaboration have nurtured our growth,
I dedicate this work to my parents,
whose unwavering belief pushed me to chase my dreams,
and to my wife and kids,
who inspire me to embrace my fullest self with unyielding passion.

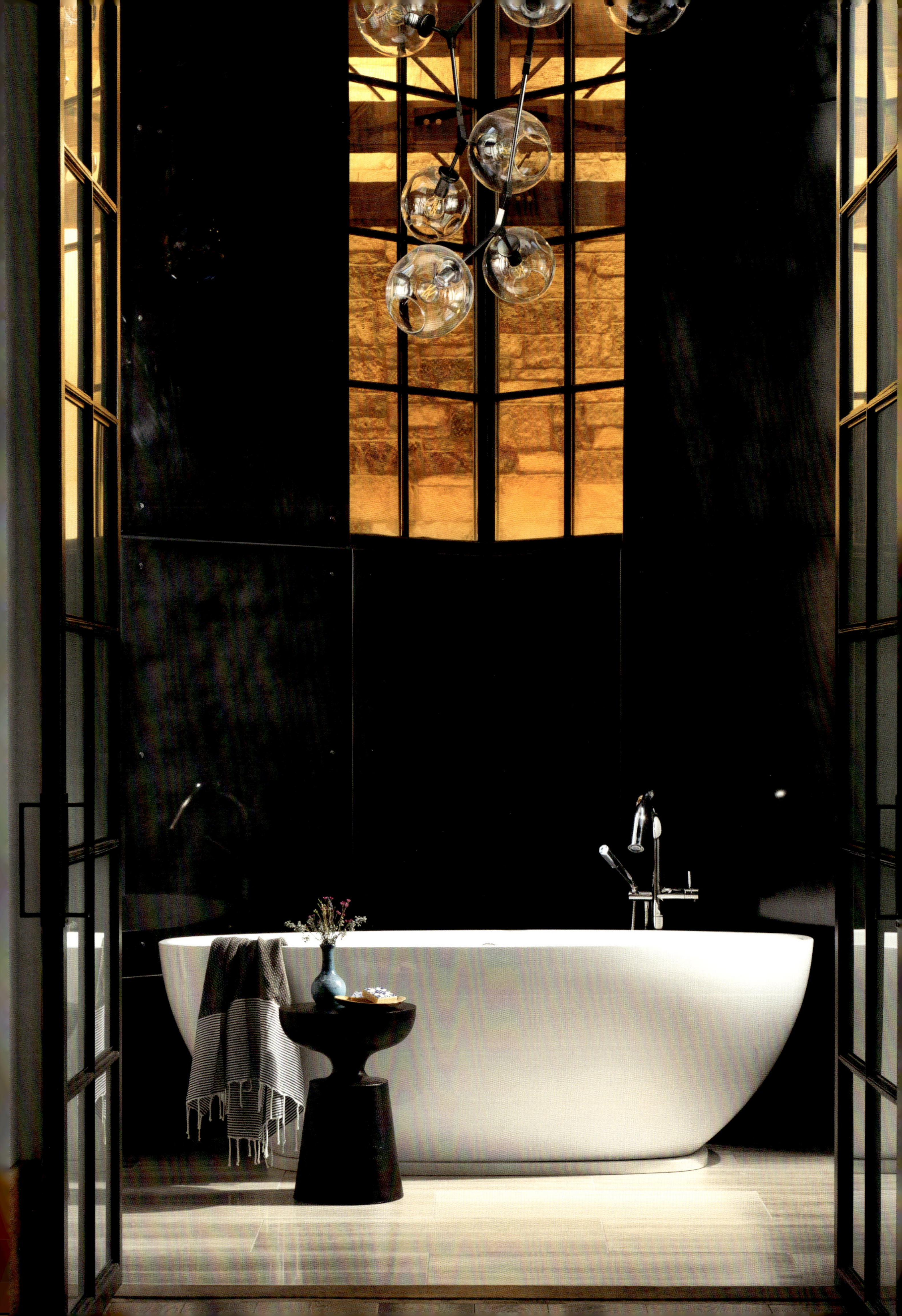

CONTENTS

FOREWORD

For decades, American interior design discourse has been dominated by bicoastal perspectives. Design media have often focused their lenses on New York's cosmopolitan abodes or California's sun-drenched multicultural spaces, creating a significant blind spot in our appreciation of design diversity—particularly regarding America's heartland contributions.

As a journalist documenting interiors nationwide, I've witnessed a renaissance away from the spotlight. Midwestern design isn't simply adapting coastal trends with a regional accent—it's speaking an entirely different language that deserves its chapter in the American design lexicon.

What makes this oversight particularly striking is how the Midwestern design ethos anticipates many of today's most progressive design conversations. Midwestern interiors embodied a waste-not philosophy long before sustainability became a buzzword, with furnishings selected for generational longevity rather than seasonal relevance. Before "adaptive reuse" entered the architectural vocabulary, Midwestern designers thoughtfully repurposed industrial spaces, agricultural structures, and historic buildings with ingenious respect for their origins.

The Midwestern sensibility offers a refreshing counterpoint to the often-homogenized spaces in distant cities across the globe, which are often virtually indistinguishable. In contrast, the Midwest preserves its distinct character, not as some folksy relic but through an ongoing conversation between its people and the land they inhabit.

As we enter an era where concerns about overconsumption and environmental impact increasingly influence design choices, the Midwestern tradition of thoughtful restraint and material honesty provides valuable lessons. These spaces aren't defined by what they contain but by what they convey—warmth, history, belonging, and an abiding sense of place.

This book invites you to reconsider what we value in interior design, and to discover the extraordinary in what has been too often dismissed as ordinary. The Midwestern design story reminds us that true innovation usually occurs not in the spotlight but in the steady, thoughtful work in the spaces between.

—CARL DELLATORE

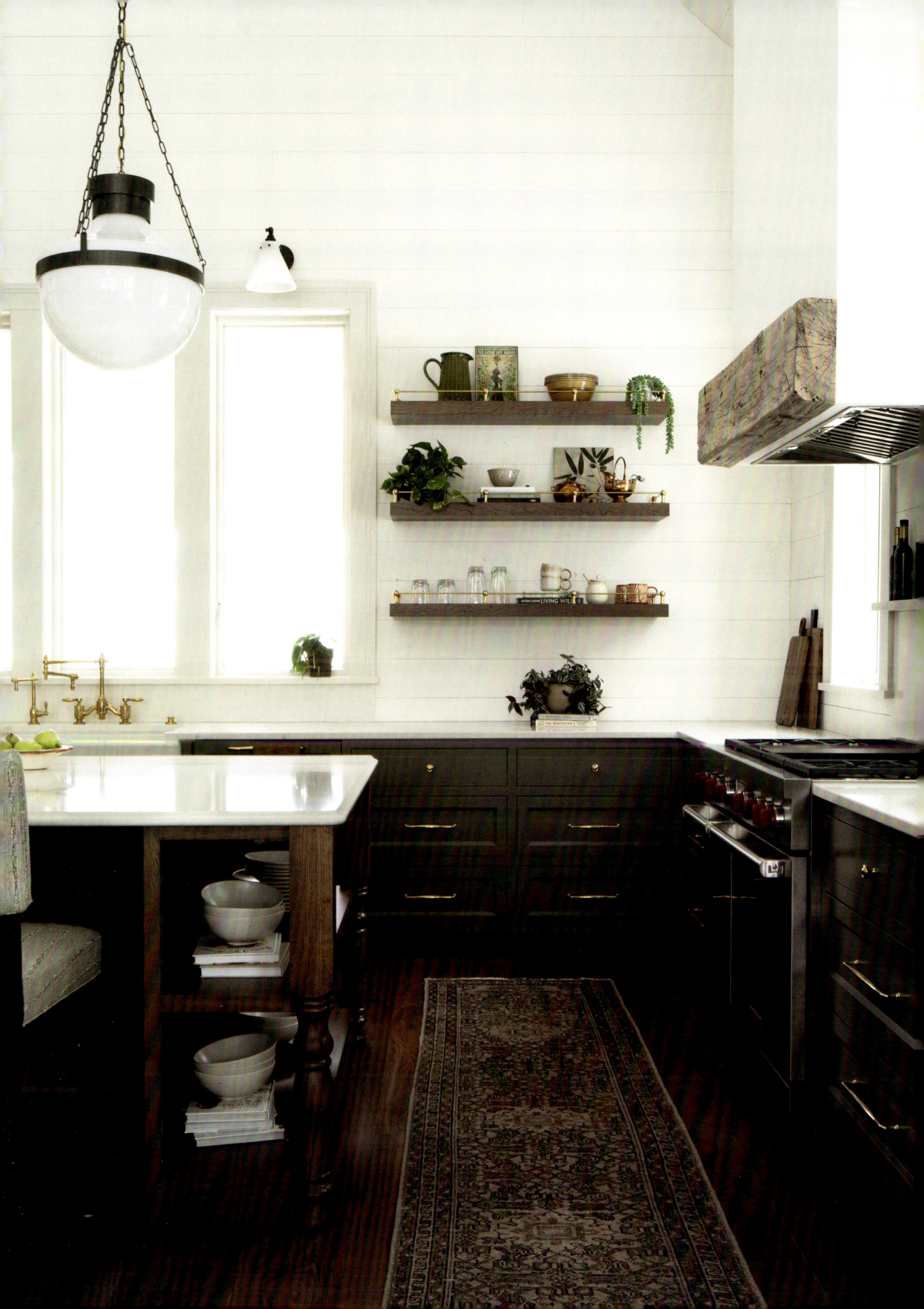
TO LOSE MY MIND
LIVING WIL
DEFINED DISH
THE MEATEATER

INTRODUCTION

In the Midwest, design is not an abstract concept but a physical reality that develops with intention. Throughout America's heartland, interiors and architecture take shape with the measured pace of seasonal change. In contrast with coastal cities, which can chase fads, Midwestern spaces stay attuned to the stories contained within their structures—narratives as complex and multifaceted as the deep, fertile soil beneath them.

Though sometimes overlooked in contemporary design discourse, this region's steadfast character nurtures creativity in its most authentic form. Here, aesthetic value doesn't announce itself with grandiosity; rather, it permeates spaces like morning light filtering through gently parted curtains—subtle yet undeniably present.

Within these pages, you'll discover homes that reveal the remarkable diversity of Midwestern-designed environments. From the industrial heritage of repurposed warehouses to the intimate warmth of rural homesteads, from historical restorations to clean-lined contemporary interventions, these works span time and sensibilities. Yet, beneath their varied expressions lies a shared foundation: a genuine connection to place. Each project resonates with its surroundings—interiors that reflect the regional vernacular, color palettes drawn from native landscapes, and materials harvested from local resources.

What distinguishes these spaces is their quiet assurance—a confidence that requires no declaration, much like the Midwestern temperament itself. The design is as unpretentious and enduring as a handbuilt stone wall that has weathered decades of harsh winters. Here, substance precedes style; function informs form. The raw honesty of exposed timber beams, the tactile satisfaction of hand-troweled plaster, and the purposeful simplicity of crafted furnishings speak to historical continuity and modern relevance.

Walk through a Midwestern sunroom and notice how the light falls across wide-planked floors patinated over time, or observe how a contemporary kitchen is inflected with classical references while accommodating modern needs—much like the region itself, standing with one foot planted firmly in tradition while the other steps confidently toward innovation. As such, these interiors feel like a conversation between past and present, between the practical pioneering spirit that built these communities and the present-day sensibilities that now refine them. And you'll find gardens that extend this dialogue outdoors with thoughtful plantings that respect seasonal rhythms and celebrate regional flora and fauna.

Like a well-worn quilt handed down through generations, these homes combine utility with beauty, comfort, and sophistication. The designers in this book understand that true luxury isn't found in extravagance but in spaces that welcome you home, surround you with beauty, and support the business of living.

—RYAN HAINEY

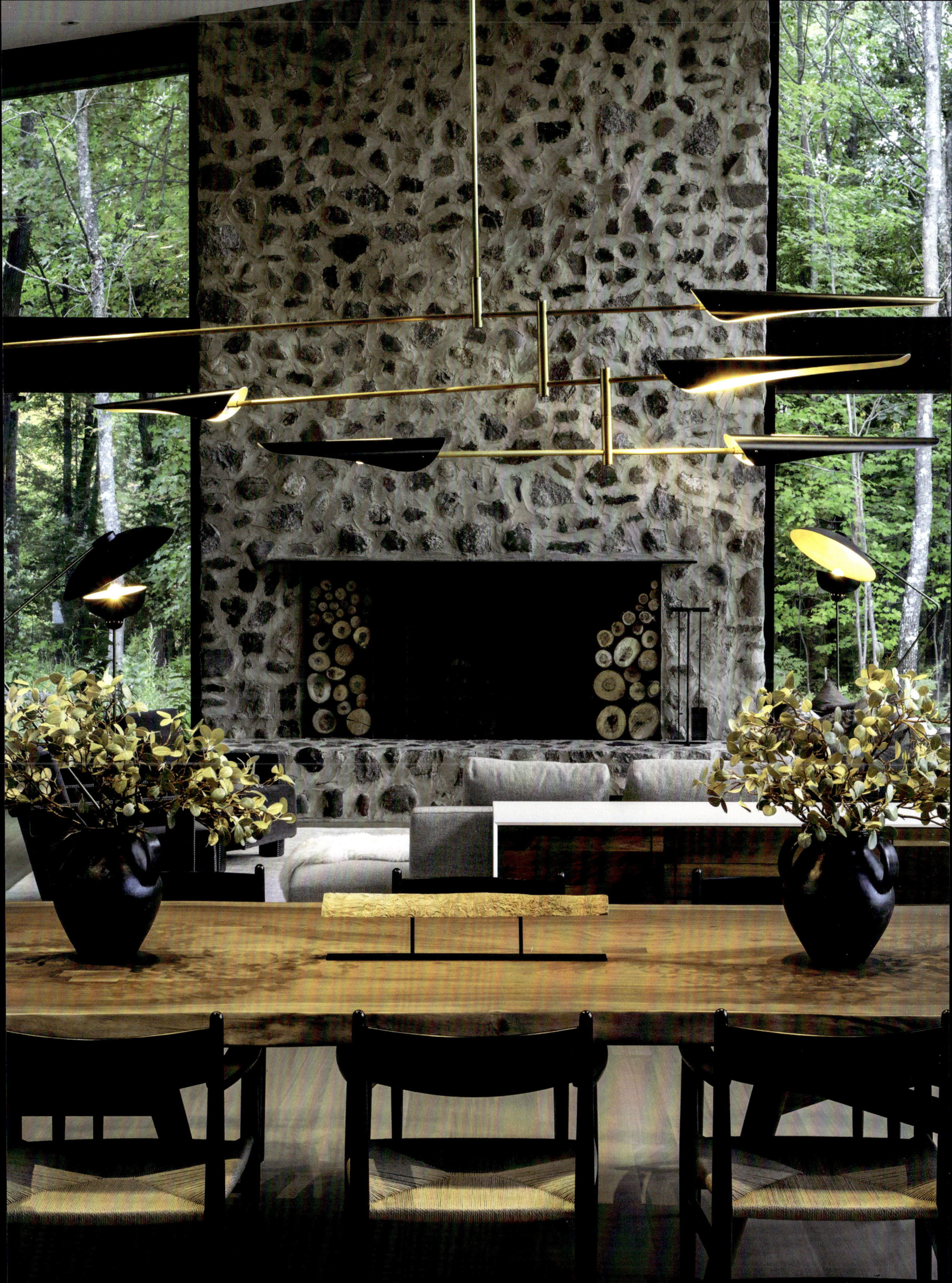

CRAFTSMAN ESTATE

Richard Sherer / Deep River Partners

Located in north-central Wisconsin where the pristine waters of Pine Lake meet the expansive woodland-framed sky, this elegant Craftsman-style home epitomizes the tenets of Midwestern style: a focus on honest materials, the incorporation of handcrafted structural elements, and a reverence for the surrounding topography.

Conceived by Richard Sherer of Deep River Partners, who has a trained eye for traditional building artistry that incorporates modern creature comforts, the completed home creates a relaxing haven for a multigenerational family that appreciates all that lake life offers.

The storied Craftsman ethos of building with indigenous materials is evidenced in the home's lower facade, fashioned from locally quarried Lannon stone, and the wooden shingles of the upper facade and roof. While structurally robust, the exterior's tiered terraces and artfully designed walls blend harmoniously with the bordering landscape, as though the home has risen organically on the shoreline.

Entering the main house, one is instantly struck by the Craftsman hallmarks: exposed beams, millwork bracketry, tongue-and-groove ceiling panels, and bluestone floors. The ground-level floor plan, with its expansive living room, enveloping library, and sumptuous dining space, clearly speaks to the homeowner's penchant for entertaining. On the second floor, beautifully appointed suites provide a quiet retreat away from the communal rooms below.

While Sherer and his team's design is undeniably timeless, it also anticipates the family's future needs with a primary bedroom suite on the first floor—an architectural insight whose accessibility will be valued well into the decades ahead.

The same caring thoughtfulness placed on accommodating the future is shown in honoring the past. The antique boathouse was carefully preserved, which is a tangible link to the property's rich history.

As the seasons change on Pine Lake, this home's character changes too. Radiant heating meets the brisk Midwestern climate in winter, and well-placed windows afford breathtaking views of the snow-swept landscape. In warmer months, family and friends venture onto terraces and docks to embrace the lake's timeless allure.

A broad covered porch welcomes visitors and is central to this Wisconsin Craftsman home's elevation. The lower roofline focuses on the main entrance while establishing a comfortable human scale. A substantial mahogany-paneled front door provides security, complemented by charming small-paned sidelights and transom windows that introduce natural light and ventilation to the foyer beyond. Large, locally sourced limestone steppers transition to refined thermal limestone borders containing multicolored natural bluestone.

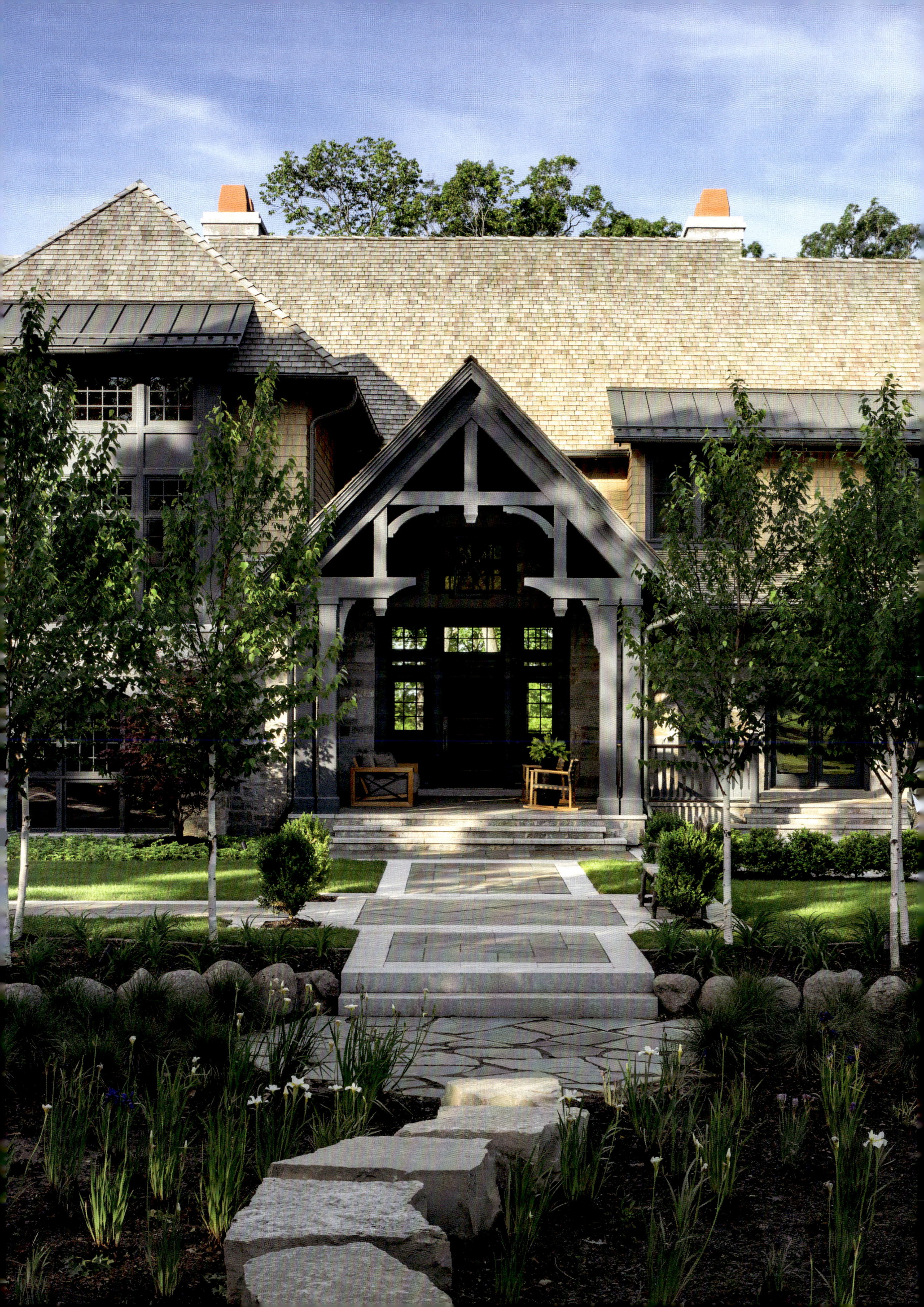

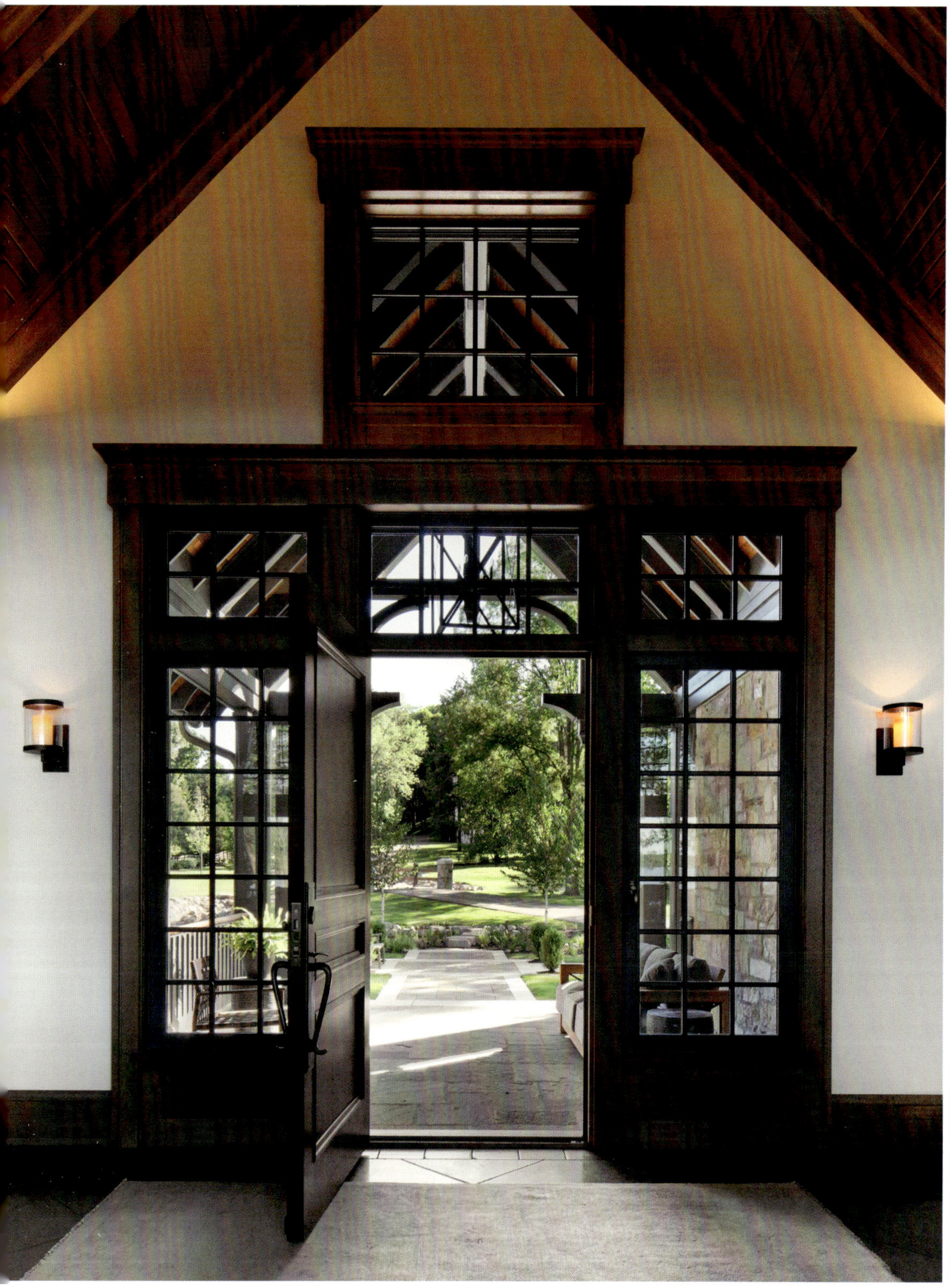

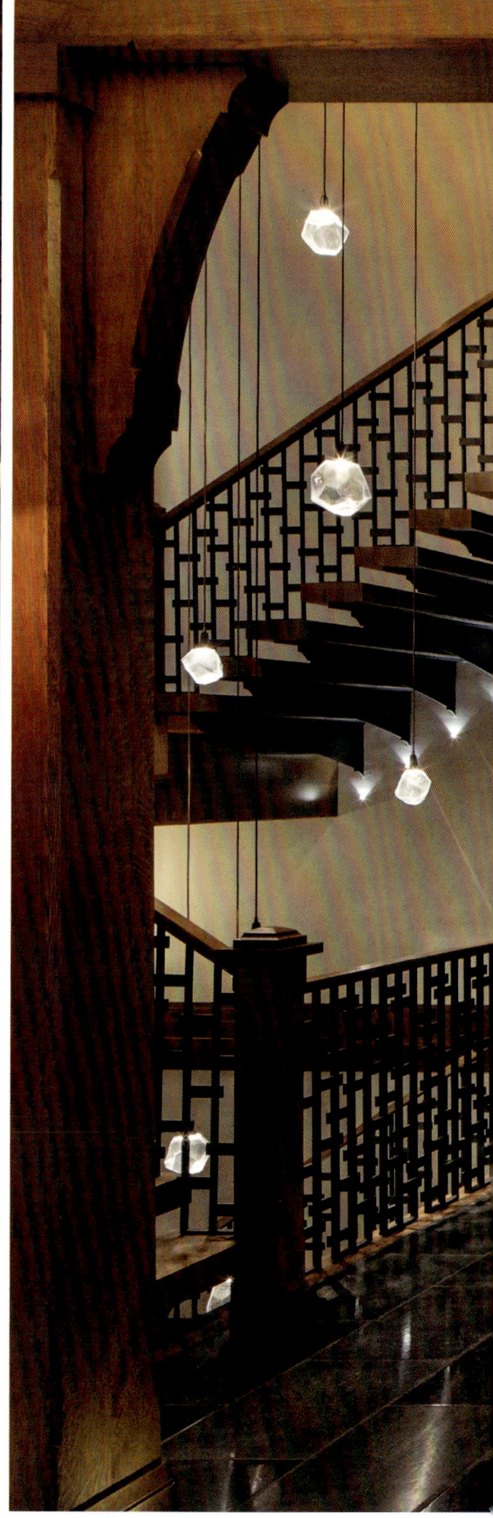

Select plain-sawn white oak defines this Craftsman home, harmonizing with stone, metal, tile, and glass. The striking staircase features cantilevered oak treads supported by rhythmic steel fins, while the metal balustrade creates an artistic framework around suspended cast-glass lighting.

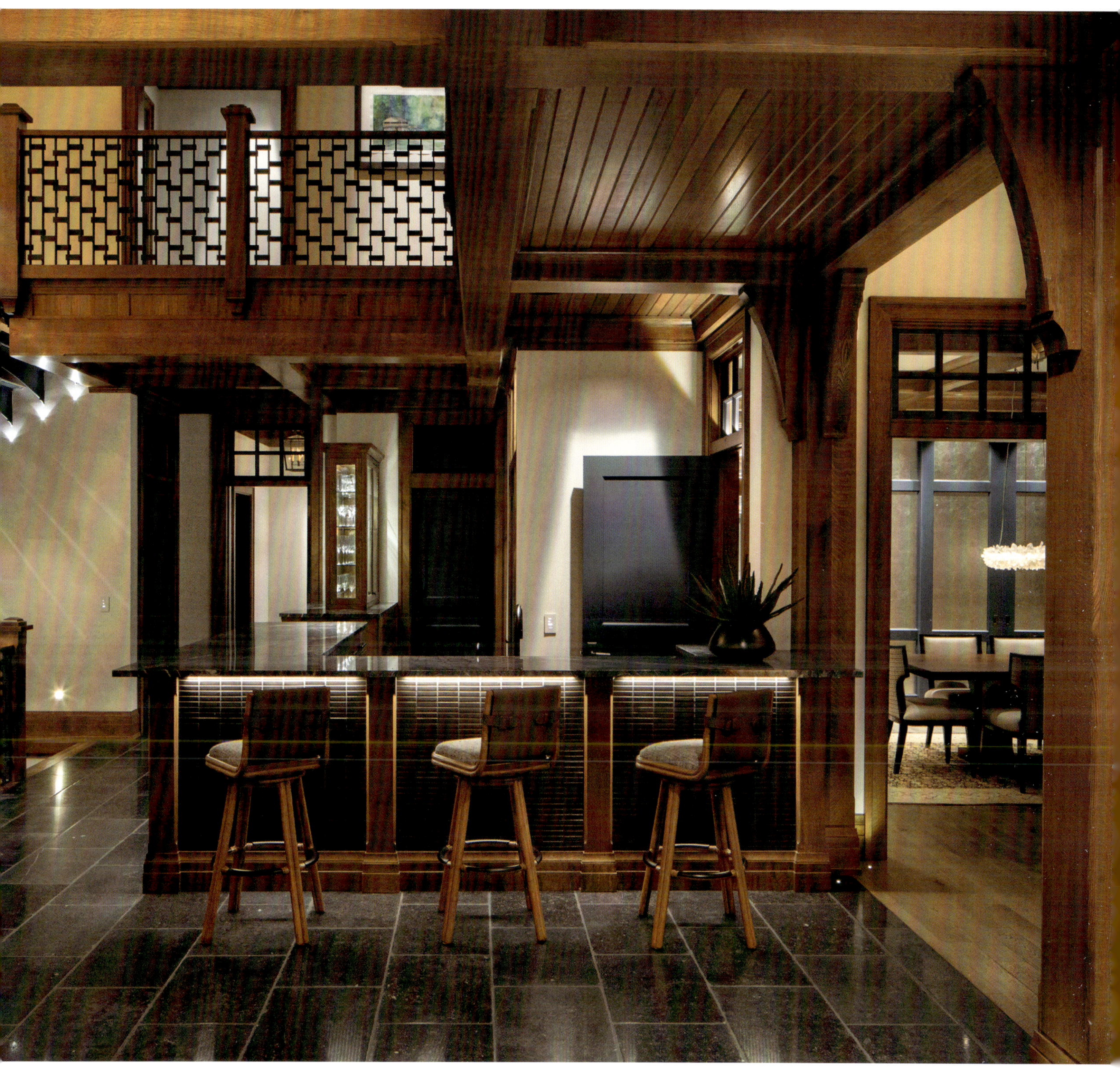

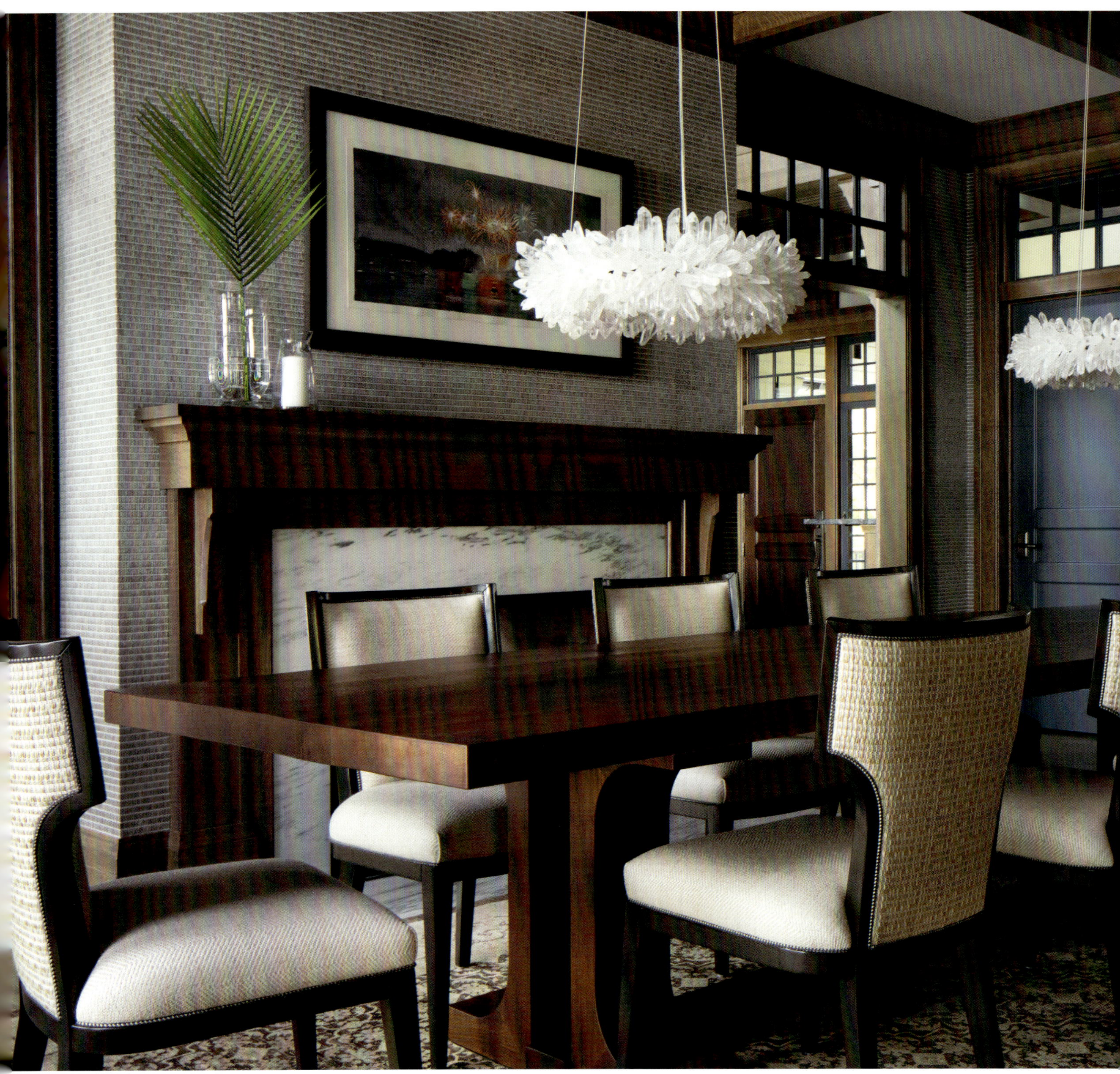

The home features three distinct gathering spaces: a comfortable dining room for shared meals, a dramatic great room with soaring ceilings, and an intimate library retreat. Throughout these spaces, clear, select plain-sawn white oak exposed rafters and tongue-and-groove ceiling panels with transparent stain showcase the home's meticulous artistry and authentic materials, creating a seamless design aesthetic.

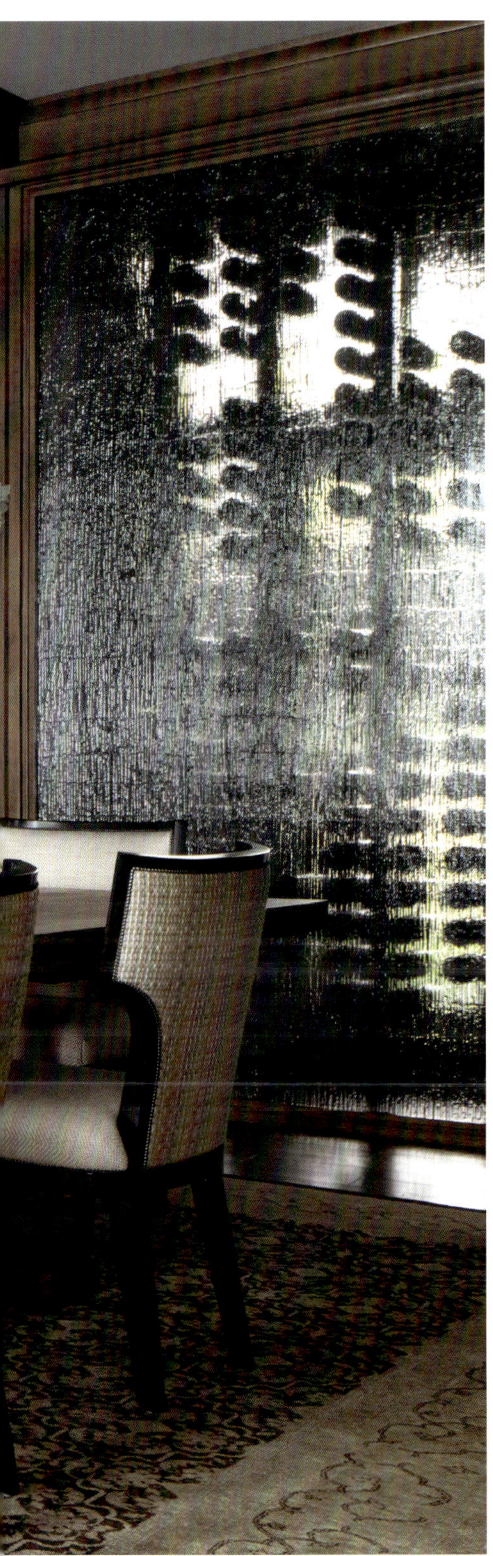
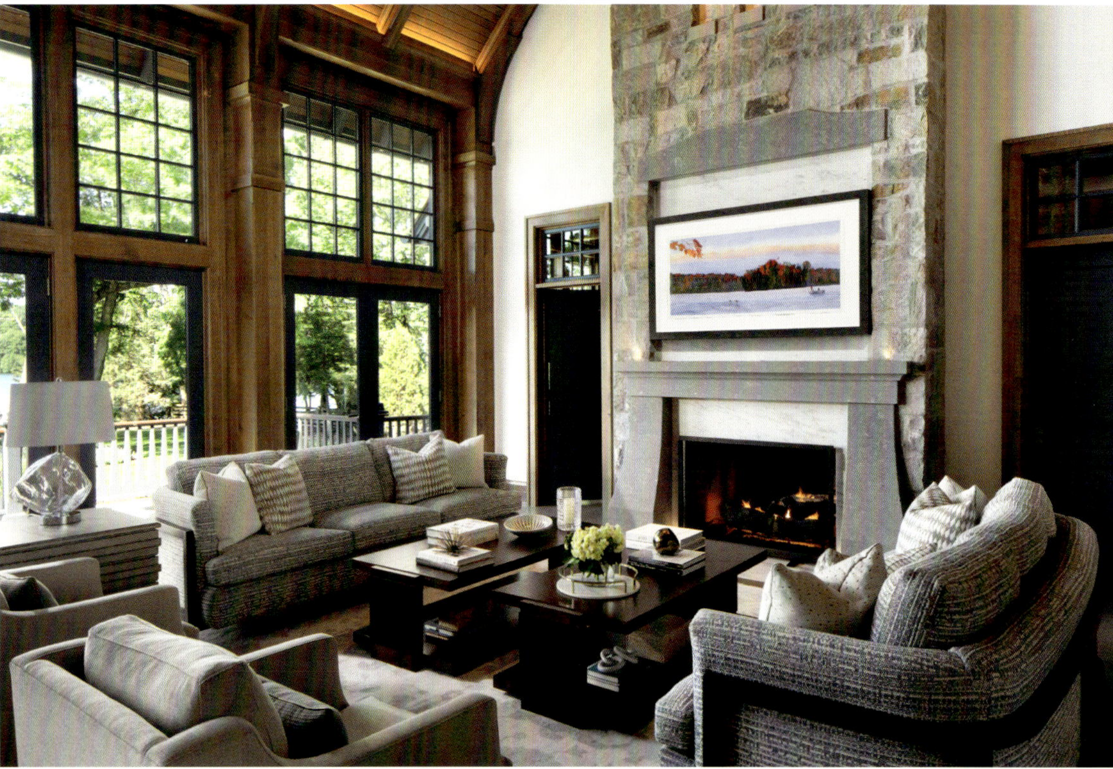
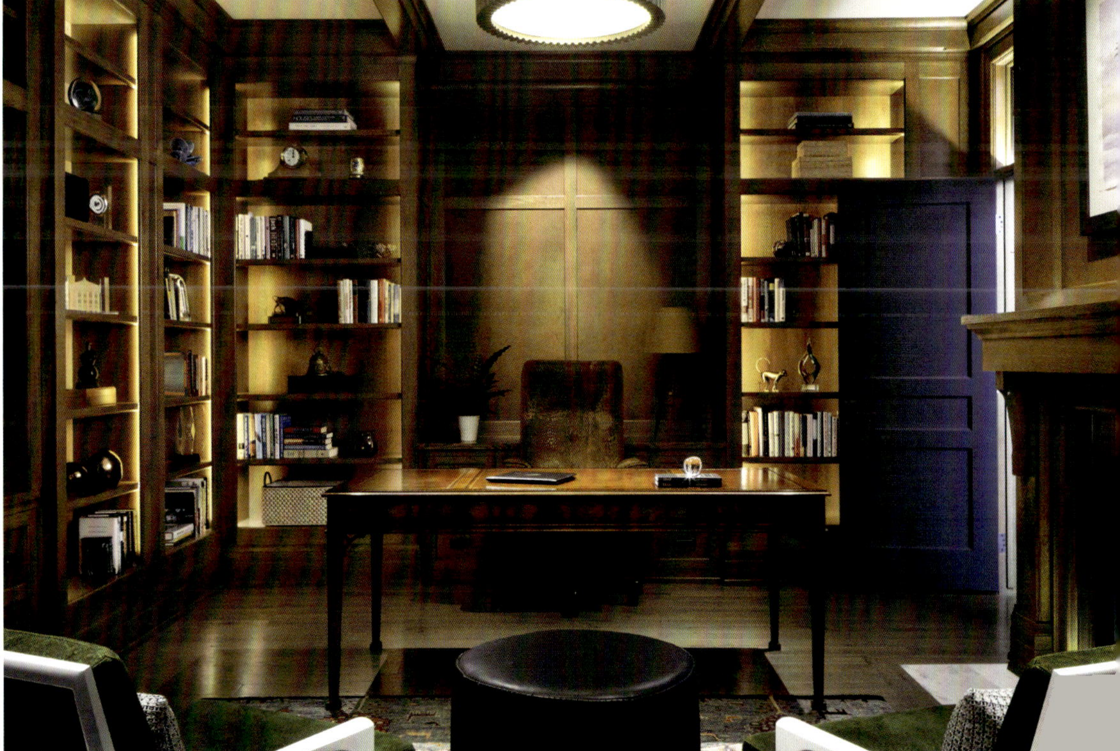

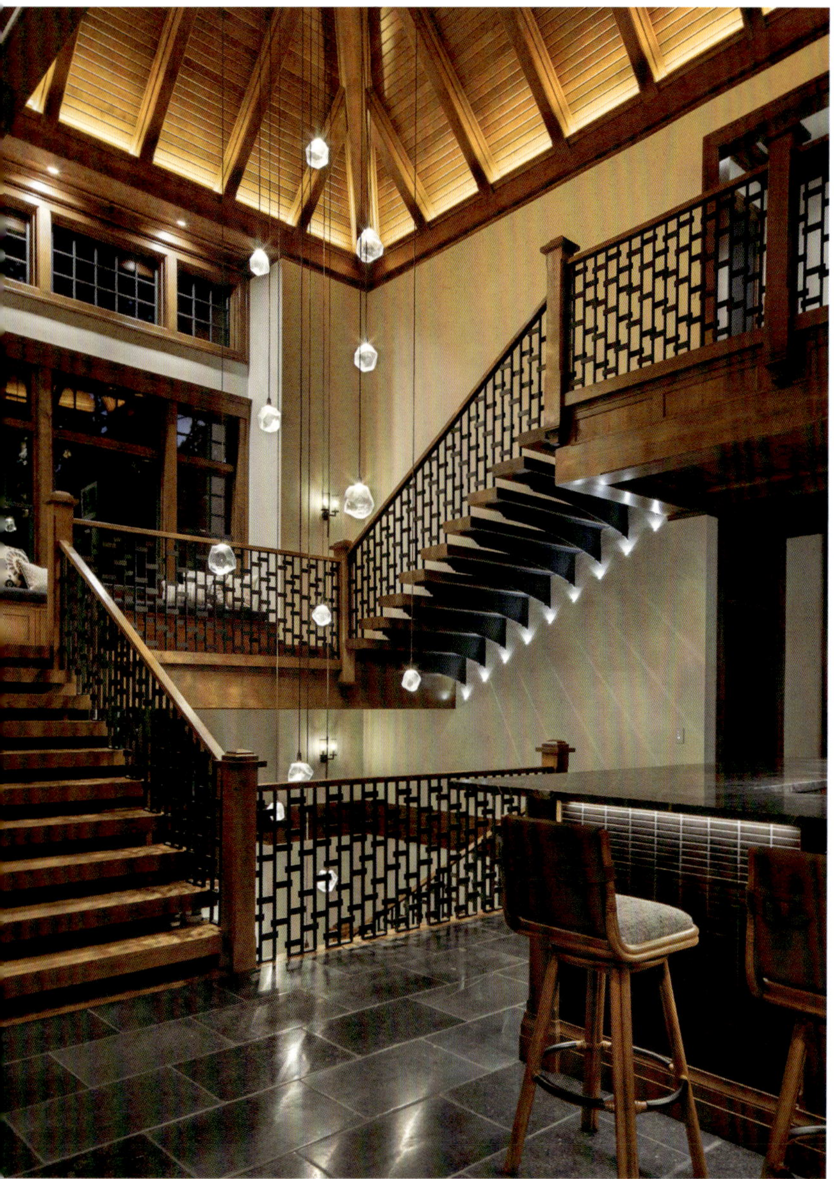

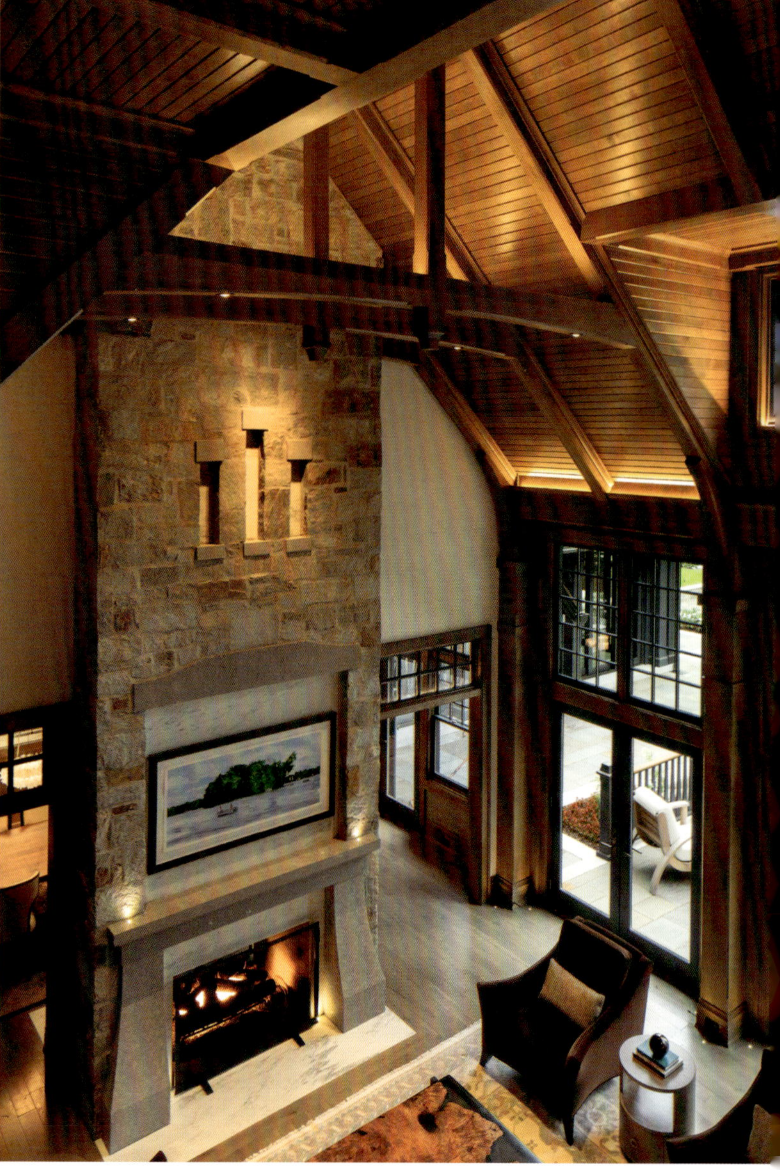

As seen in these images, breathtaking spatial drama reveals itself through honest structural expression. The great room ceiling peaks 25 feet above the first floor, while the stair hall soars 40 feet from the lower level. Open trusswork, exposed rafters, and tongue-and-groove ceiling panels celebrate authentic Craftsman principles.

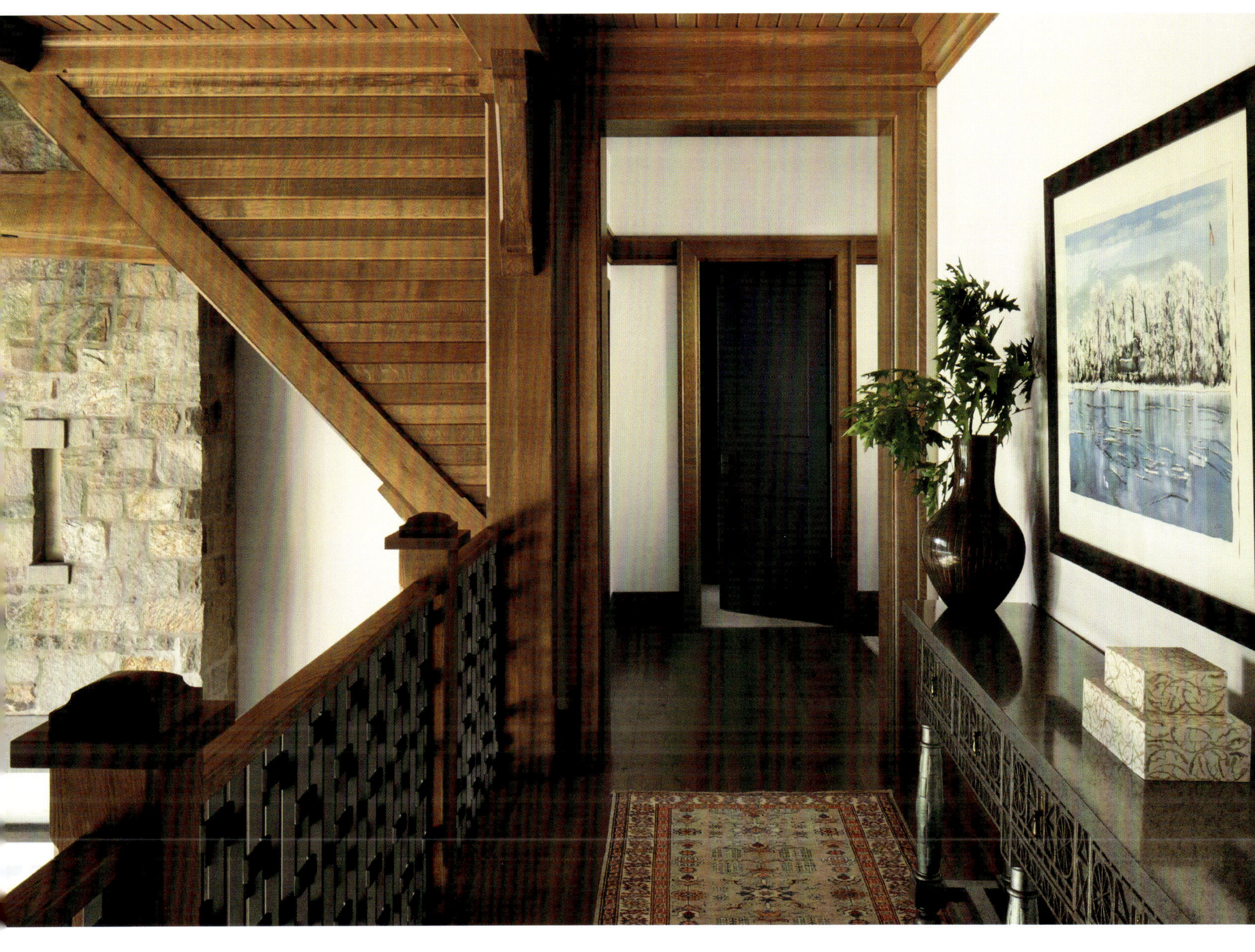

Elegant accommodations span three levels of this thoughtfully designed home. The first floor houses the main bedroom, with an en suite bath, while the second floor features a guest bedroom with a private bath and a dedicated family suite combining a bedroom, a charming bunk room, and a shared bathroom. A convenient full bath serves the lower level.

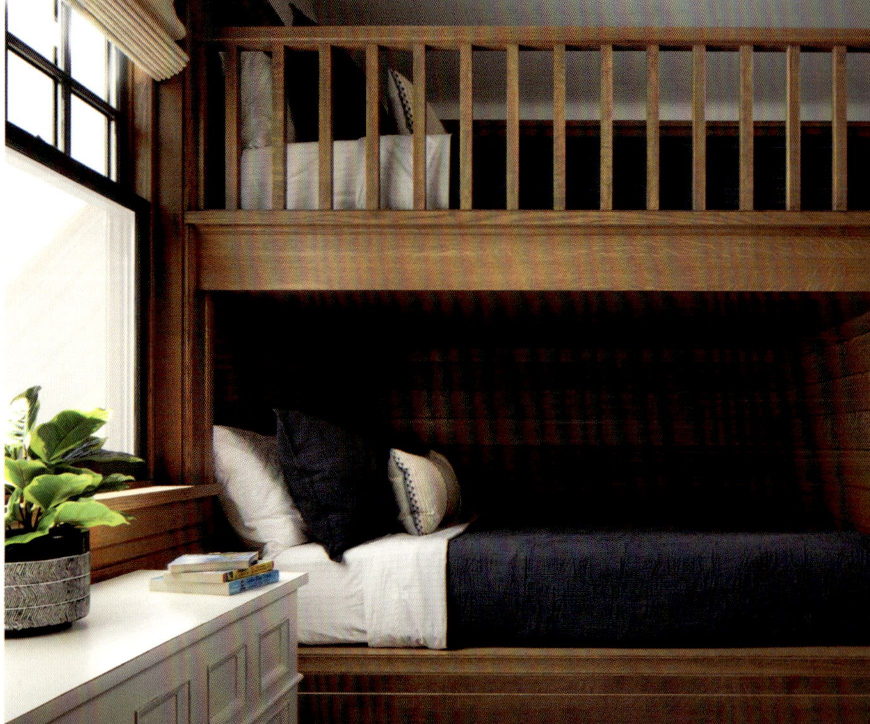

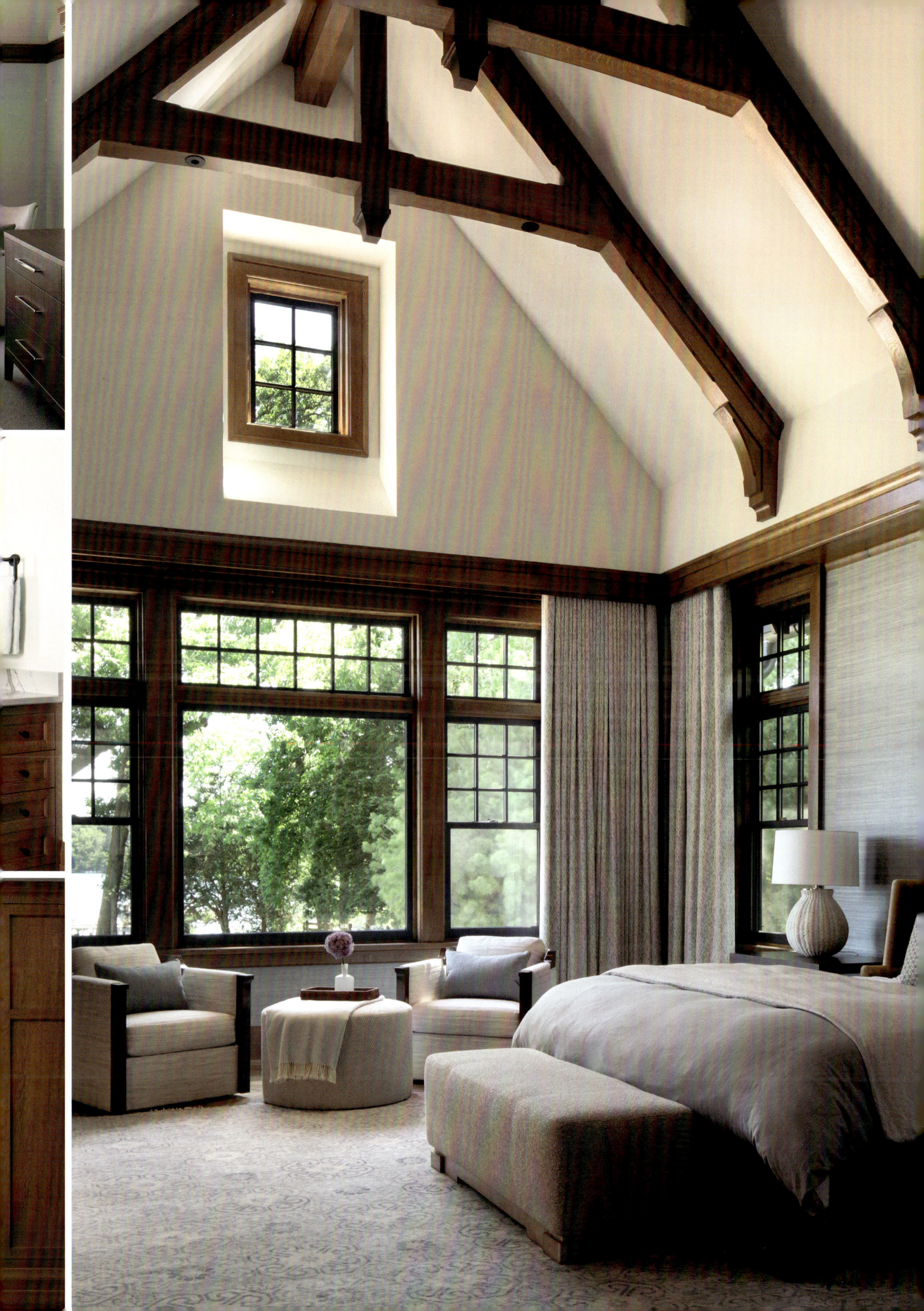

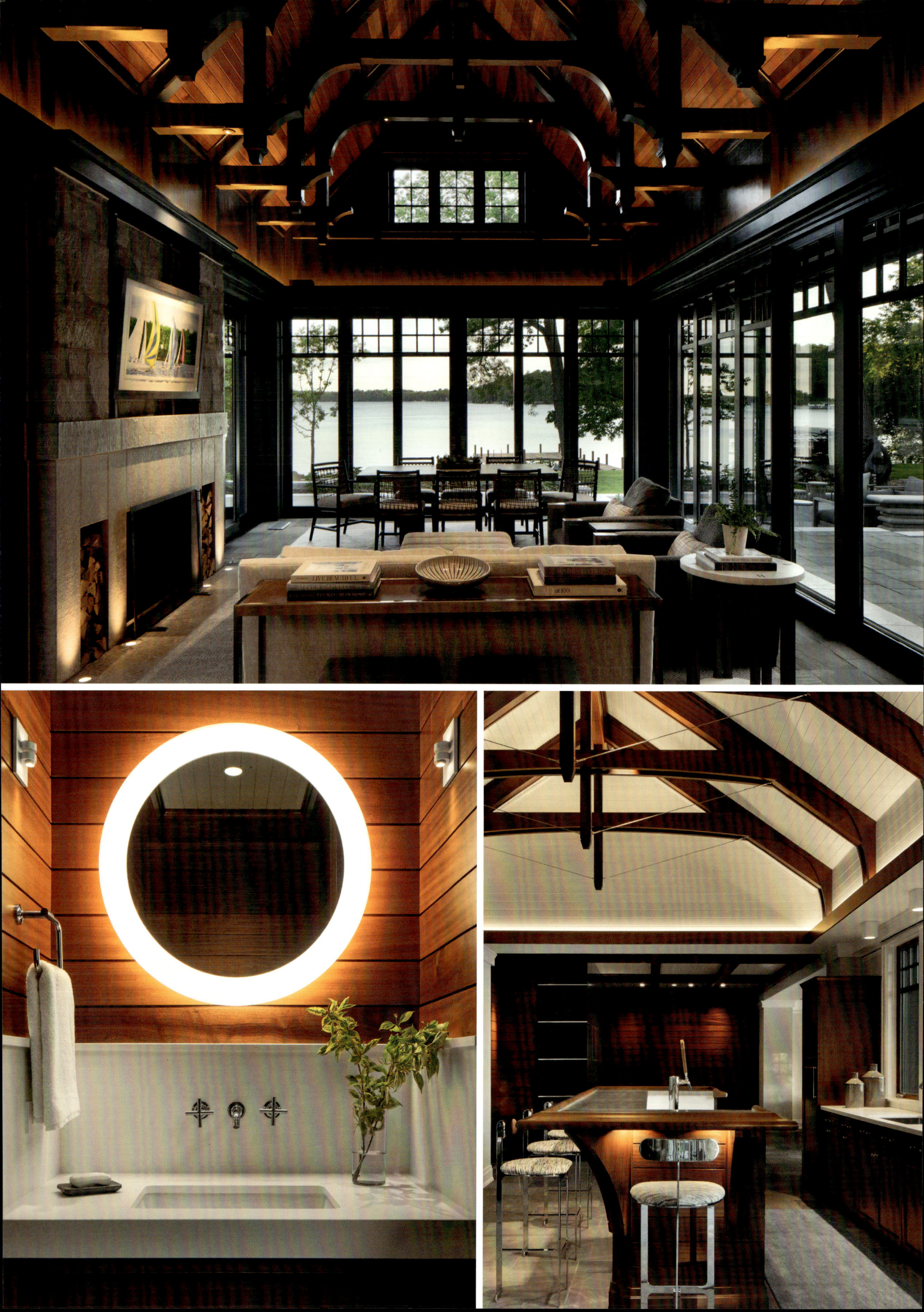

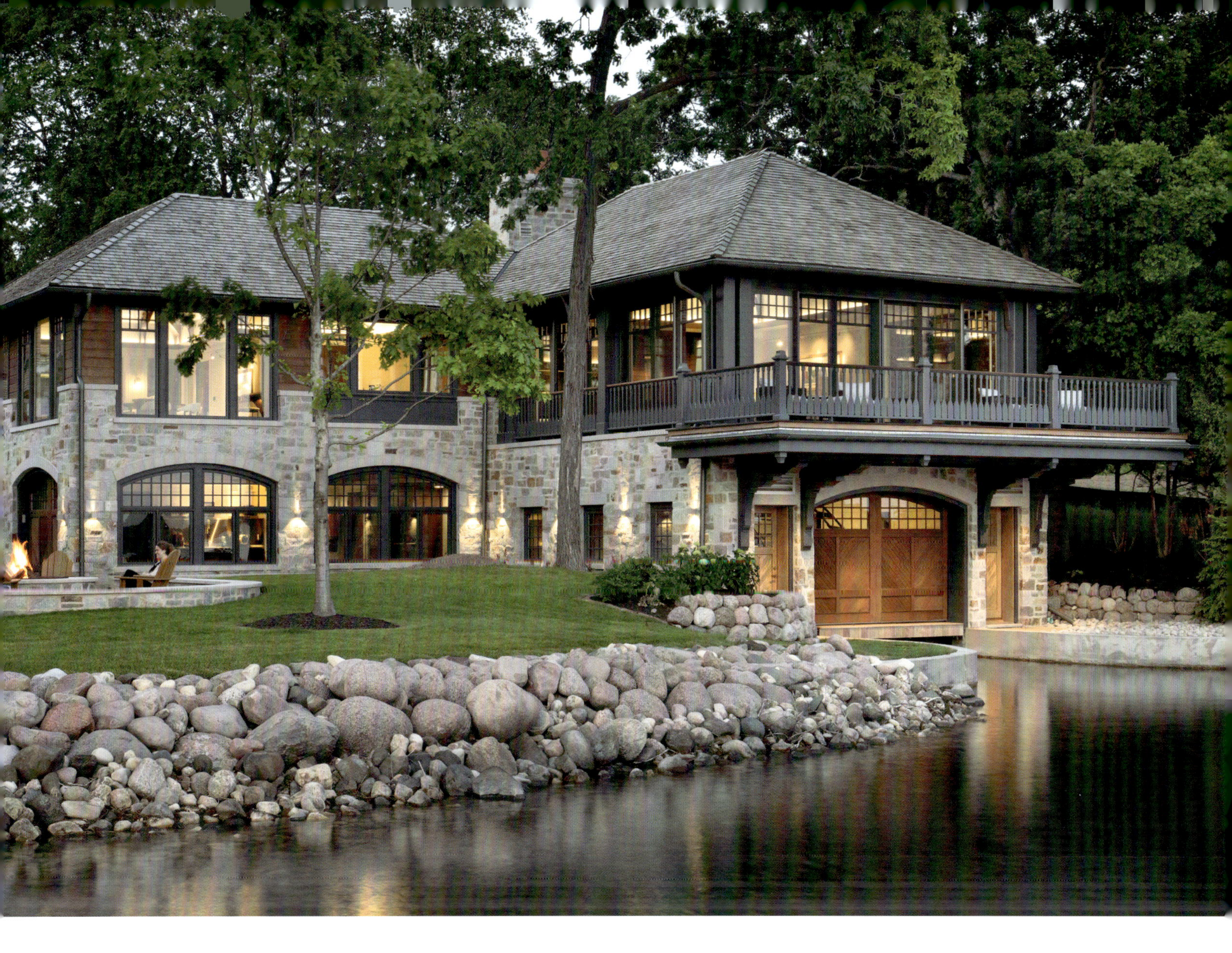

The main house pavilion extends gracefully toward the lakefront boathouse, creating a visual connection to the water. Interior spaces—including the lake bath, shower, changing area, beverage center, and lake lounge—frame stunning water views. The boathouse's cantilevered deck and large-format sliding doors blur indoor-outdoor boundaries, while exterior shots showcase the home's integrated lakeside presence.

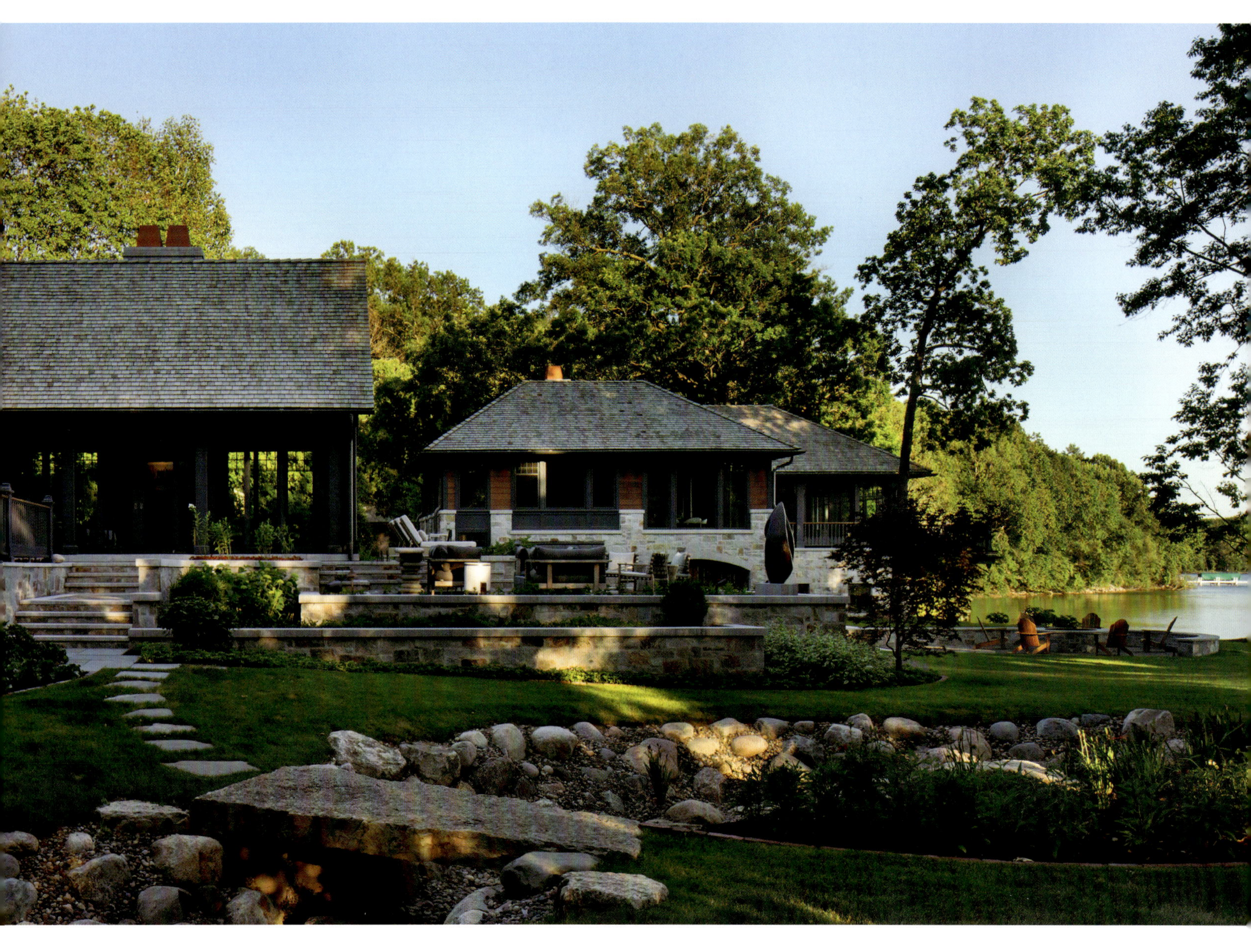

In the boathouse sitting room, every element is considered—from the embrace of its circular seating to the balustrade, where slender paddles form a rhythmic ode to the lake outside.

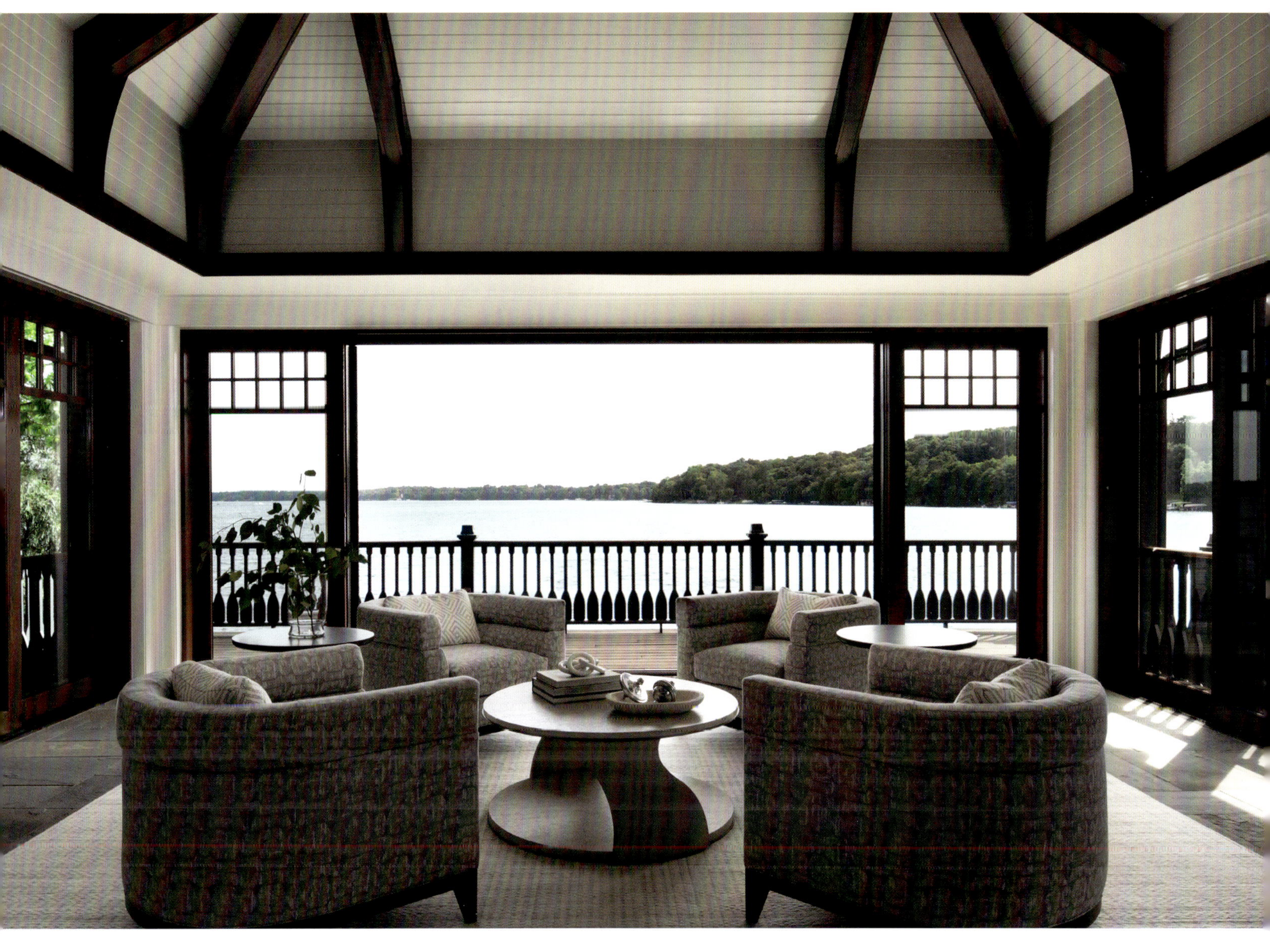

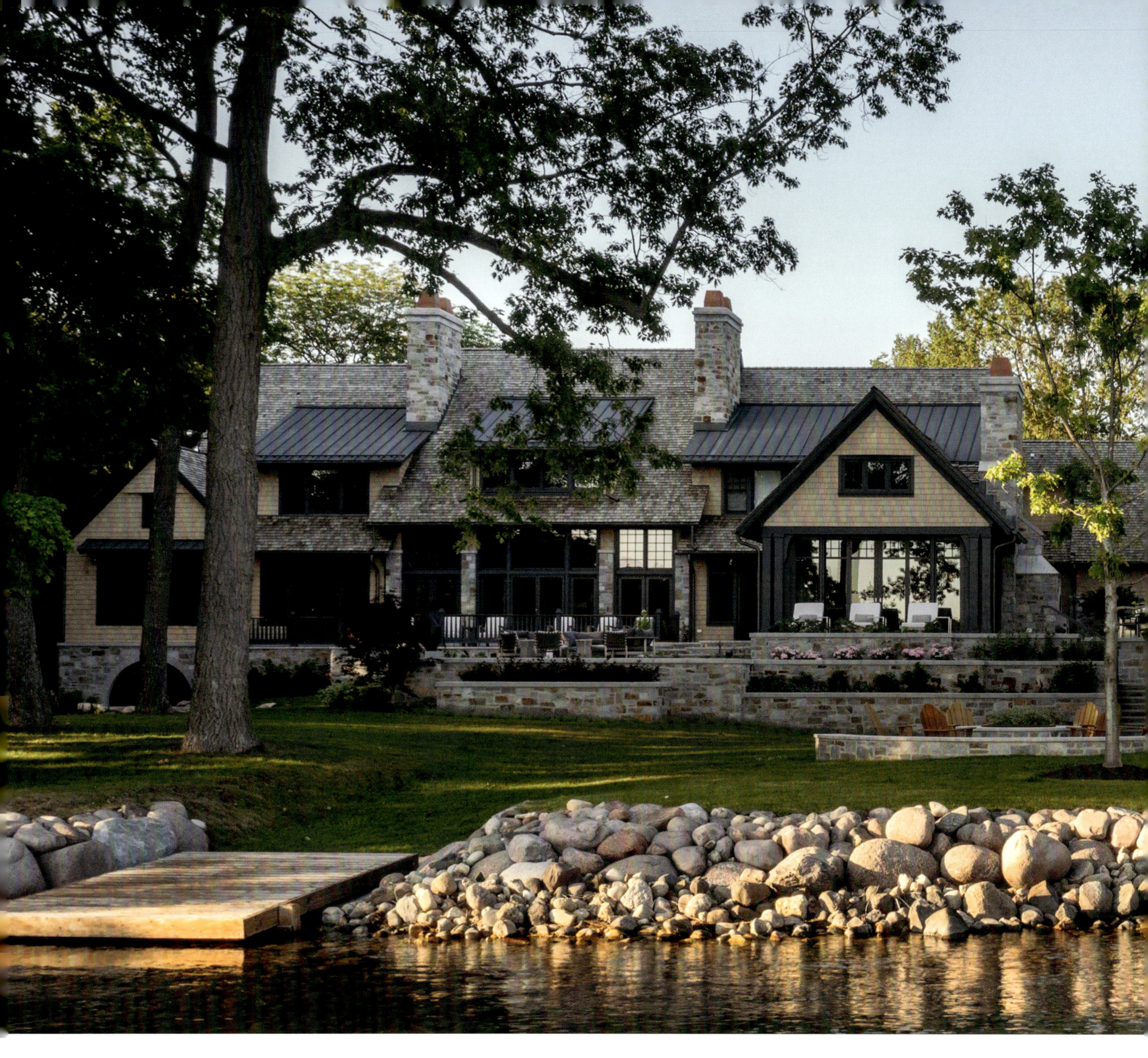

Fieldstones excavated from the original farmstead create a natural boundary at the water's edge of the south-facing lakefront. The property honors its agricultural heritage by repurposing the original barn, now integrated into the sweeping facade. It also embraces lake living through the boathouse's wooden doors, which open directly onto the water.

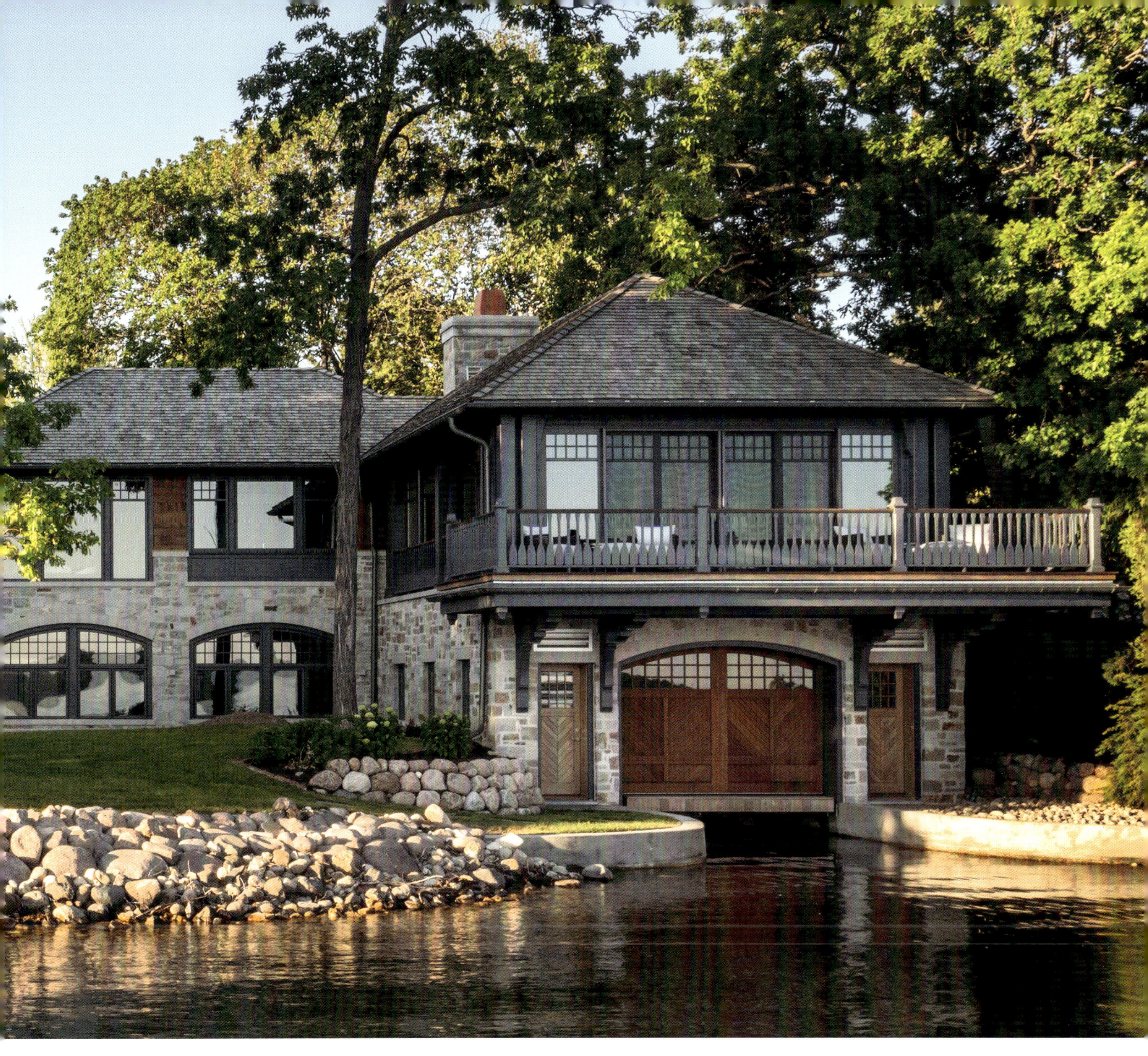

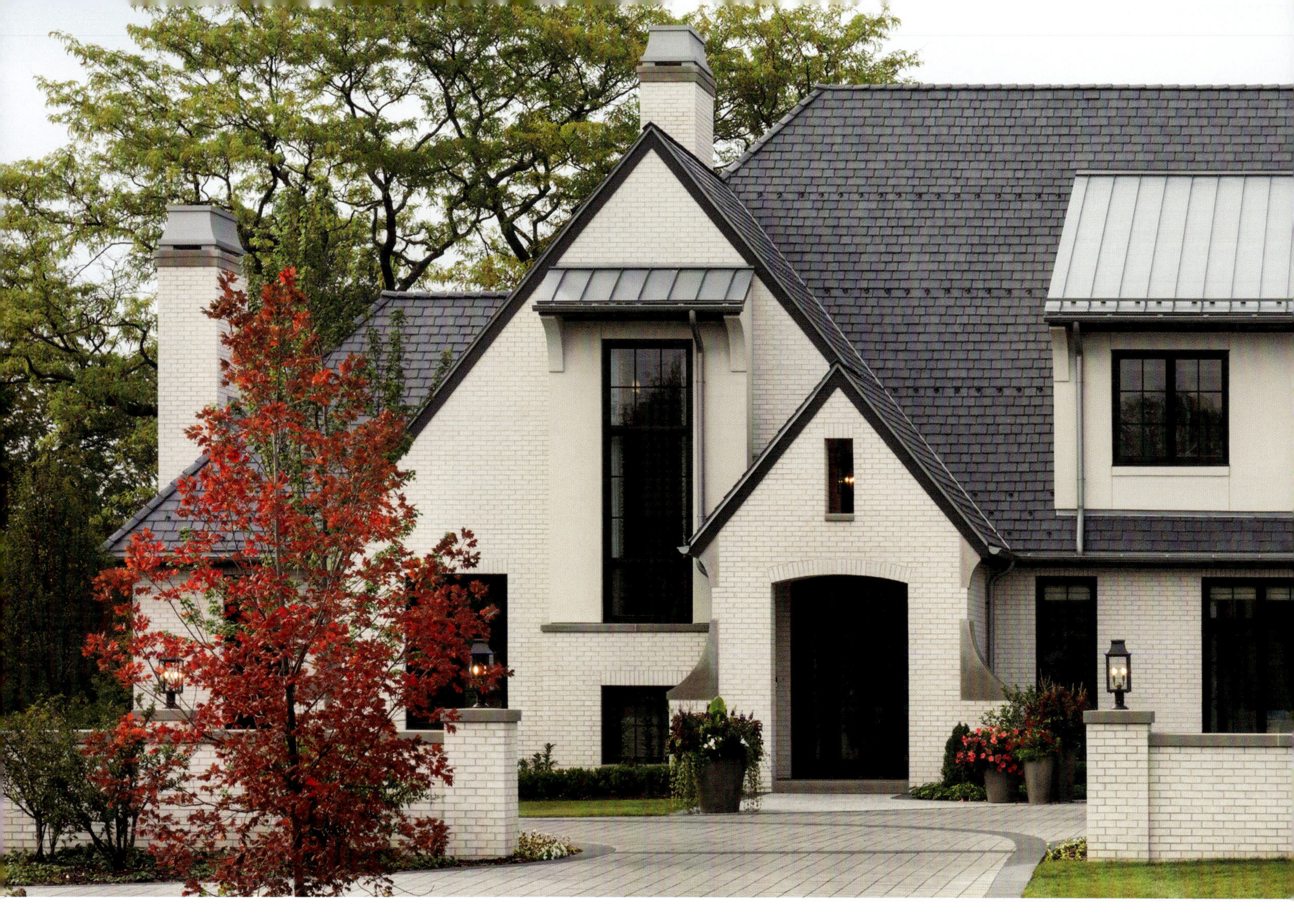

MIDWEST EUROPEAN MANOR

Richard Sherer / Deep River Partners

Rising on a picturesque hilltop in Elm Grove, Wisconsin, located 10 miles from Milwaukee and pristine Lake Michigan, this contemporary residence reflects the nuanced architectural vernacular of European country houses reimagined for the Midwest. It was commissioned by the founder of a national development firm and his wife, whose affinity for late-nineteenth- and early-twentieth-century craftsmanship set the tone for the home's design.

To turn their wishes into a reality, the couple enlisted Richard Sherer and his team at Deep River Partners, who crafted a seamless blend of materials, finishes, and furnishings that reflect the American heartland.

The approach to the home's 3.5-acre parcel is a meandering drive flanked by graceful garden walls. As you arrive at the patterned granite cobblestone auto court, the home's sloping facade reveals a stately blend of white-fired brick, stone, and zinc that nods to continental sensibilities asserted in twenty-first-century style.

Beyond the home's front door, you're enveloped in an inviting ambiance, with exposed ceiling beams, a soft white color palette, patterned hardwood floors, and sumptuous carpets underfoot. To extend the welcoming quality, Sherer's floor plan showcases an open, effortless flow between the

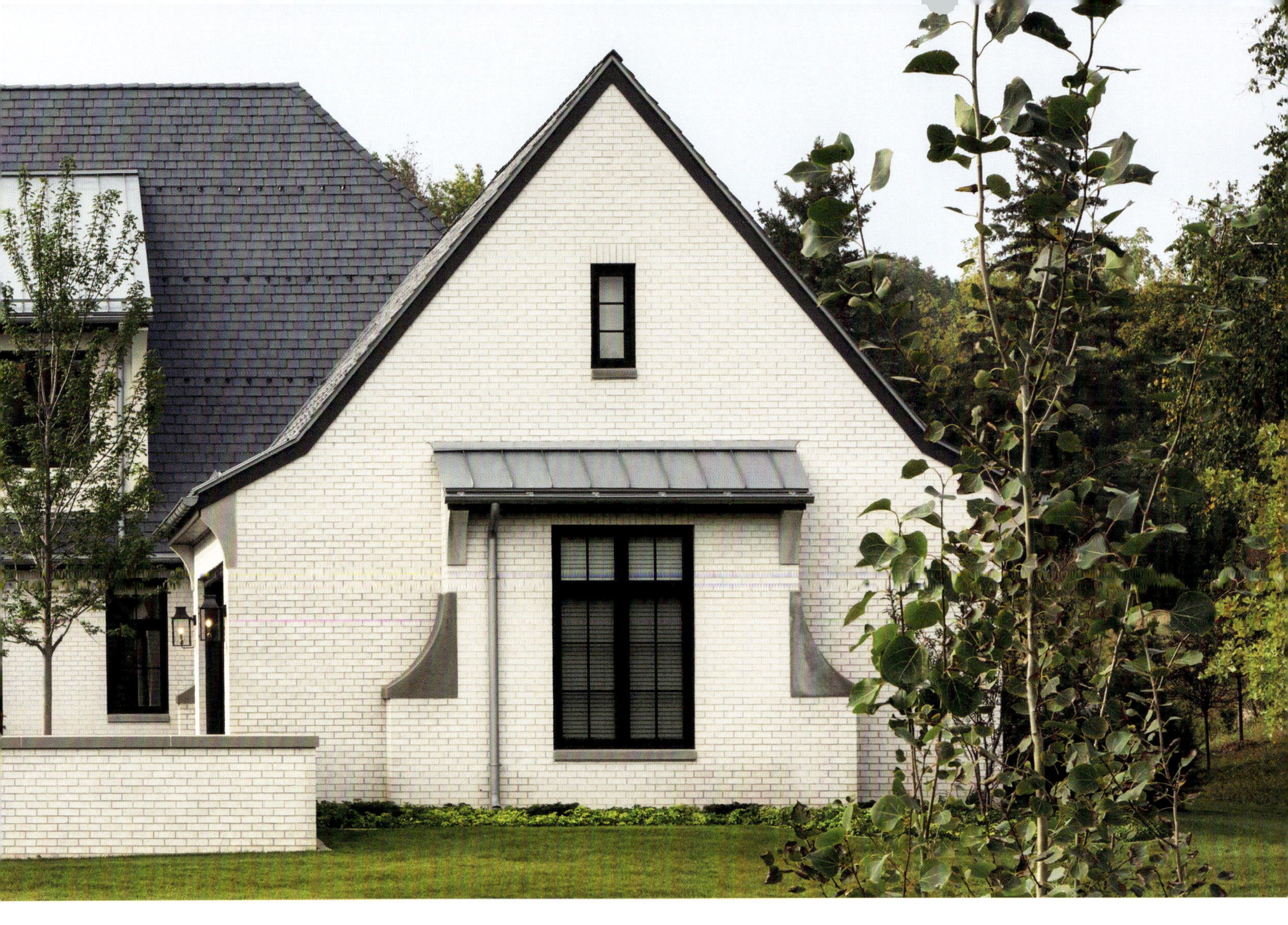

expansive living room, the dining room, and an all-white kitchen with integrated appliances and ample storage space—an ideal layout for modern cooking and entertaining.

In the summer months, French doors open to a raised terrace and pergola for alfresco dining. A stone fireplace surrounded by patio furniture is ideal for pre- and post-dinner conversation. The terrace also features a small formal garden, visually connecting the home to the surrounding woodland with its mature trees.

With an eye on the horizon, Sherer's team has incorporated a first-floor primary suite with a library and a salon, a foresight that will accommodate future generations. Like the most storied European estates, the home is destined to become part of the family's legacy.

The home features an Old World European farmhouse-inspired design. Its exterior showcases Alaska white brick from the Belden Brick Company in Canton, Ohio, with mortar specially selected to match the brick color for a unified appearance. The shingled roof is accented with standing-seam zinc window overhangs. The entry drive and auto court are paved with granite cobblestone.

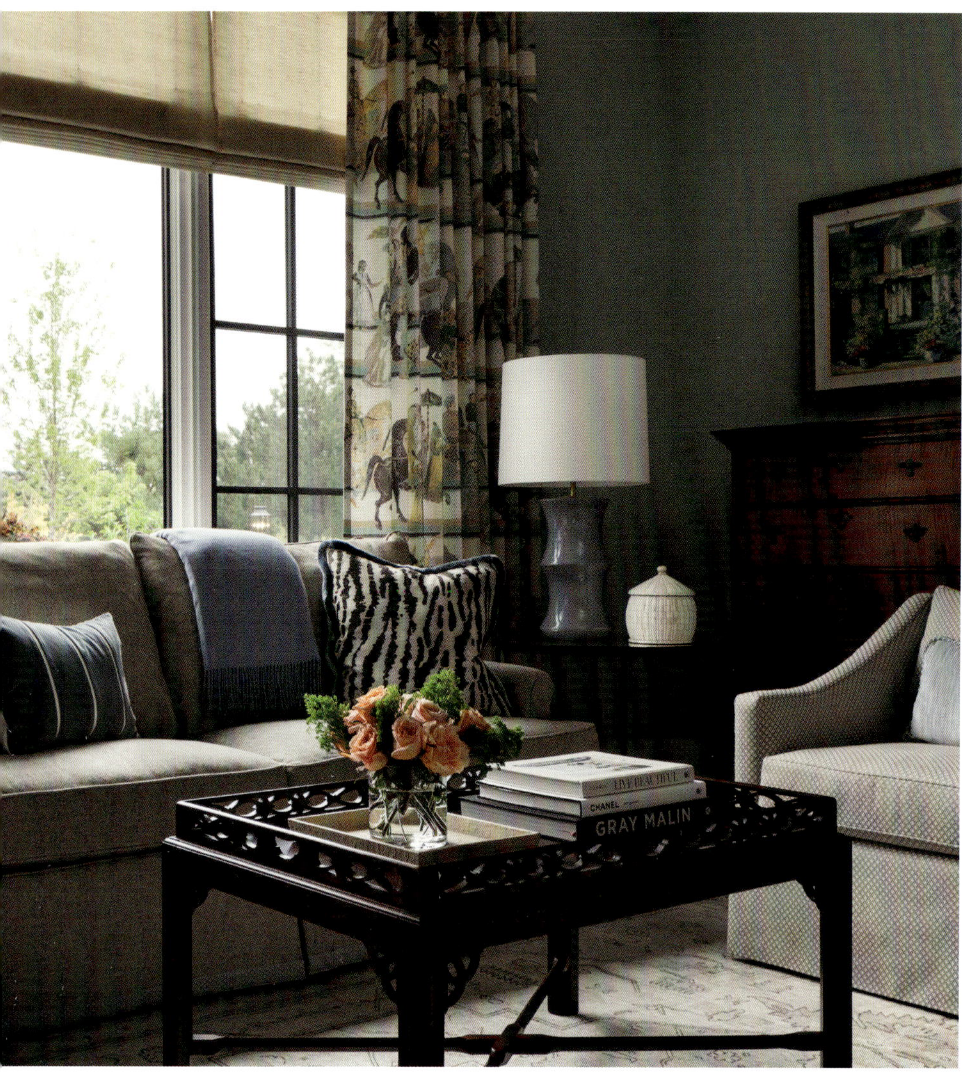

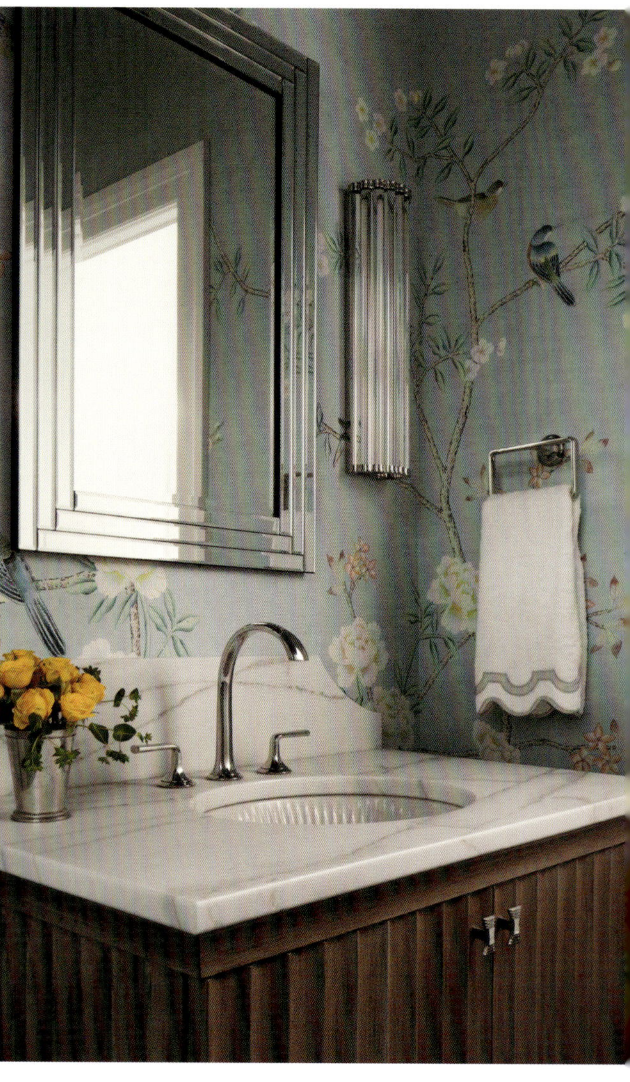

A refreshing palette shifts from the client's former home, which had a darker interior, to a light, airy aesthetic here. Subtle contrasts between elements create a thoughtfully curated space that appears assembled over time. Walls in Benjamin Moore OC-45 Swiss Coffee and trim in OC-117 Simply White provide gentle definition to architectural details.

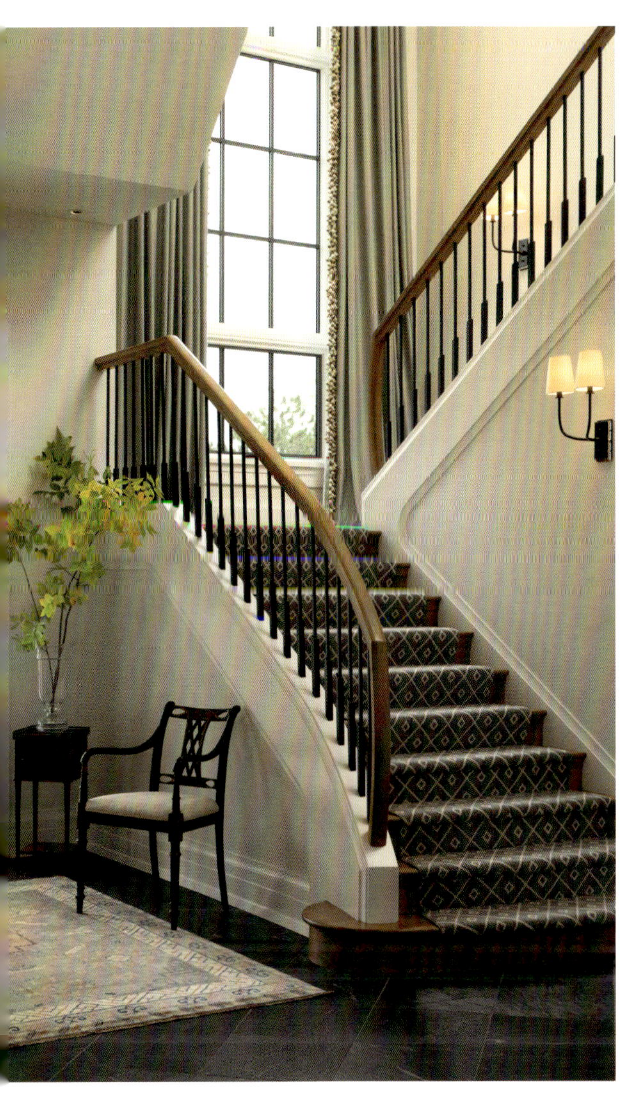

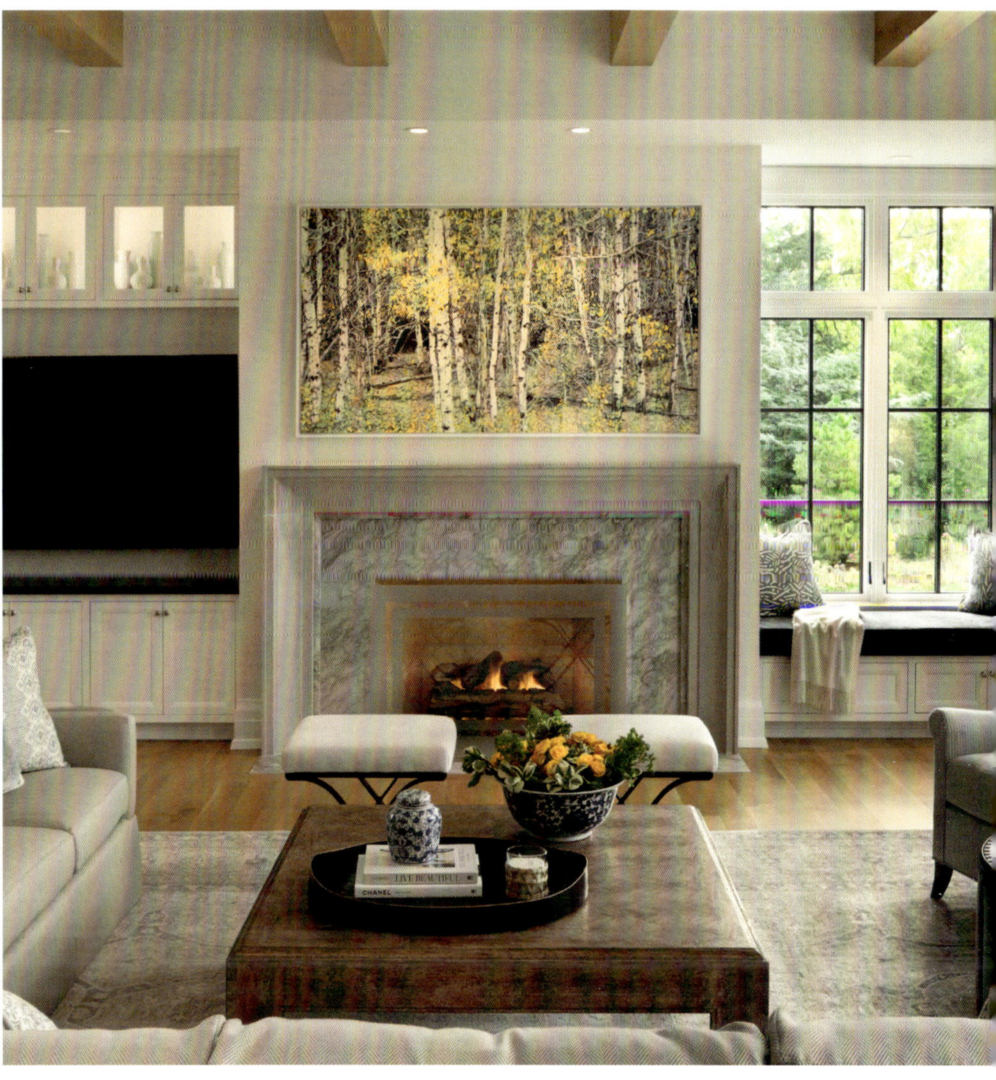

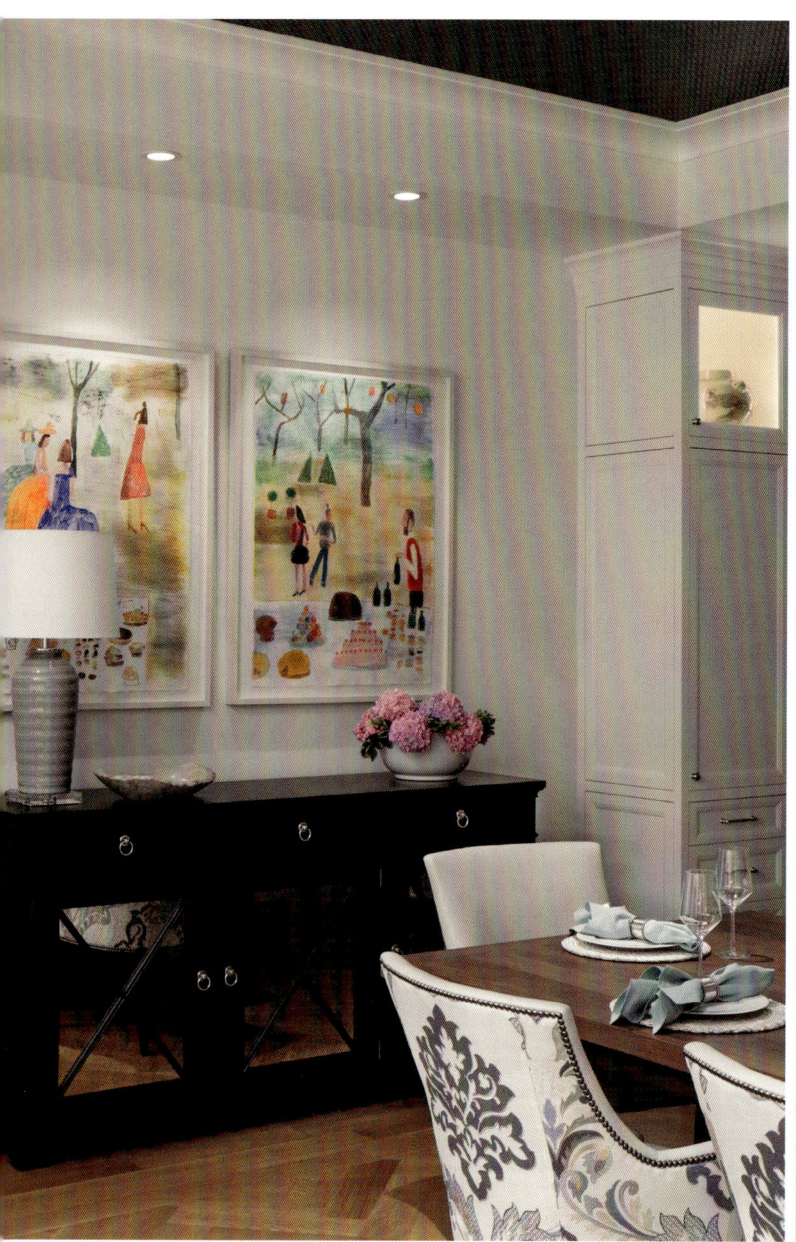

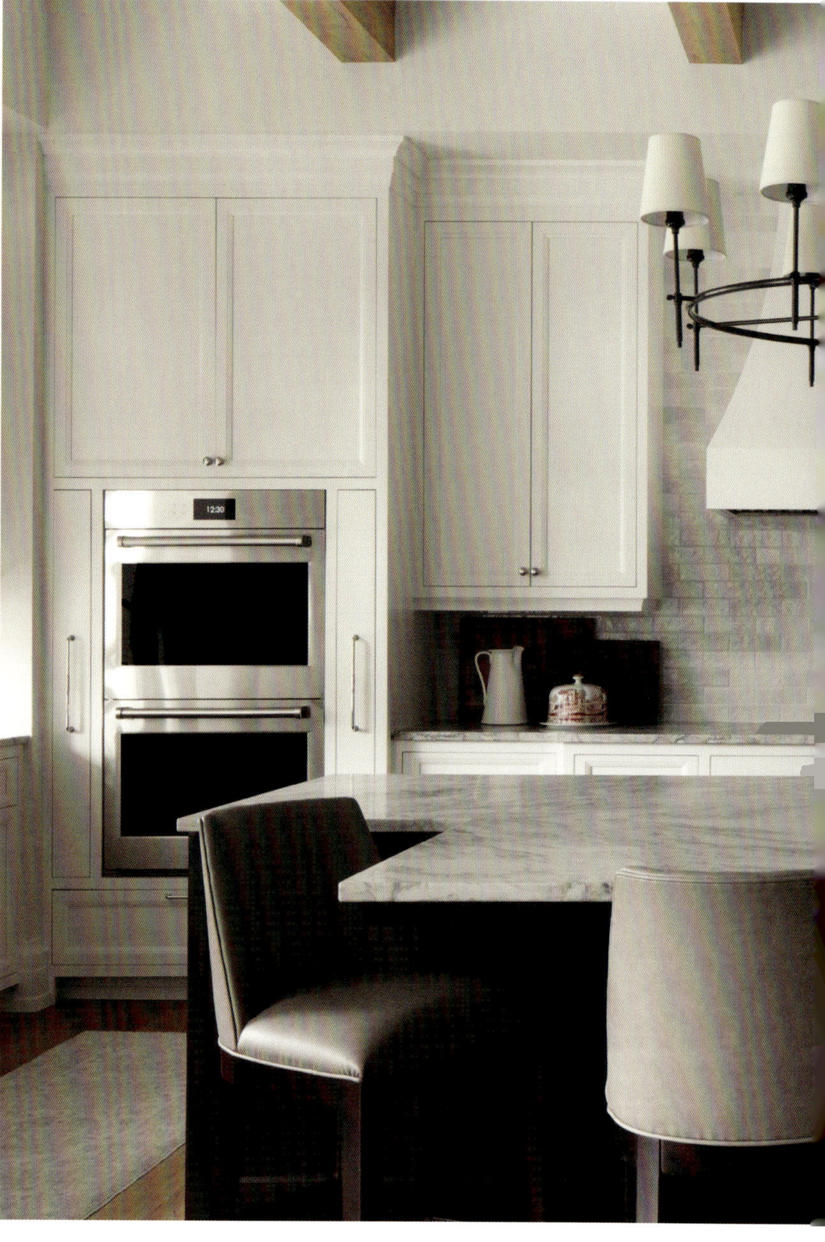

The home offers three distinct dining areas: an elegant formal dining room adjacent to the kitchen and great room, a central breakfast bar integrated into the kitchen island for casual meals, and a sun-filled breakfast nook connecting the kitchen and dining room for a seamless flow. The latter also functions as a game table or workspace for study.

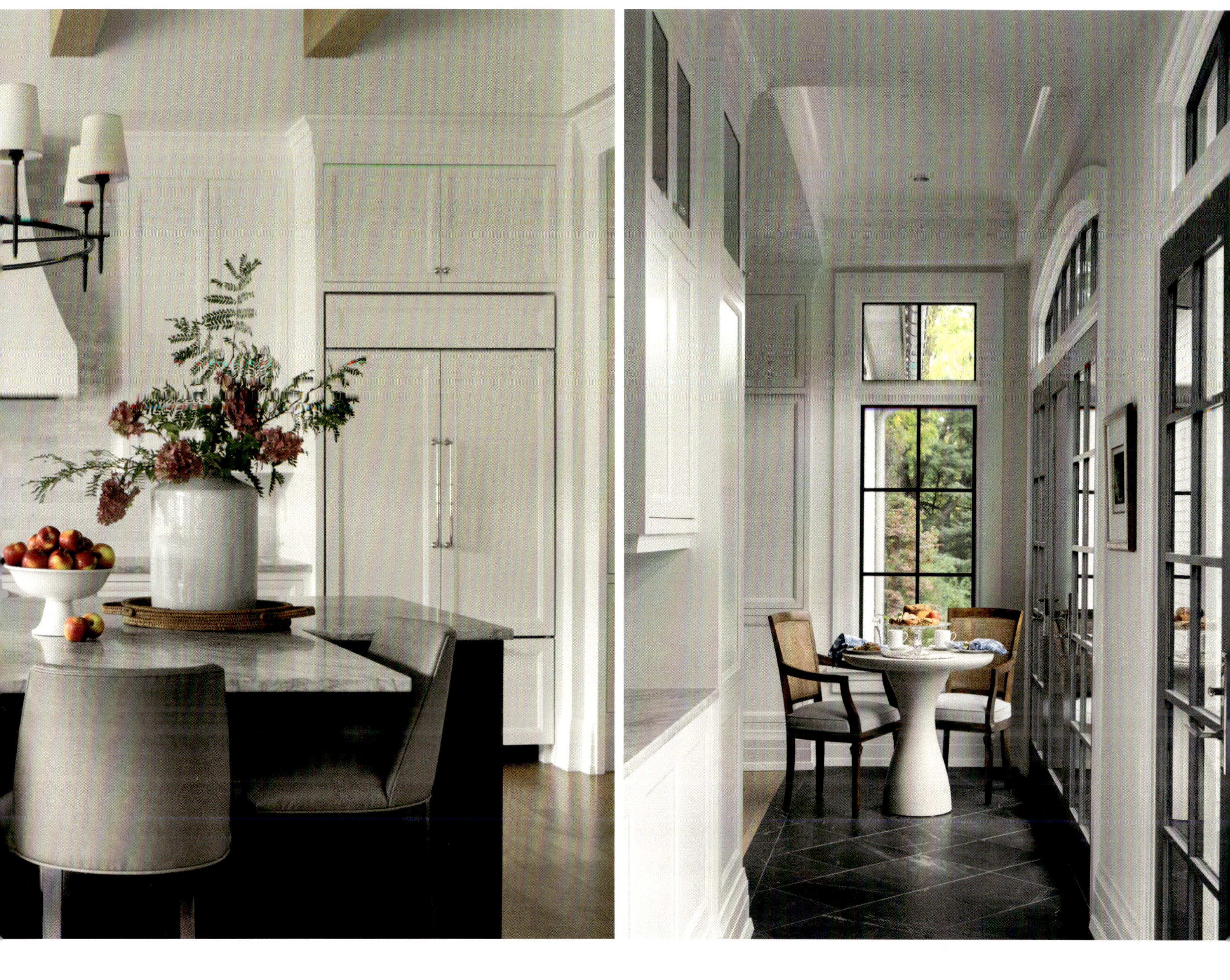

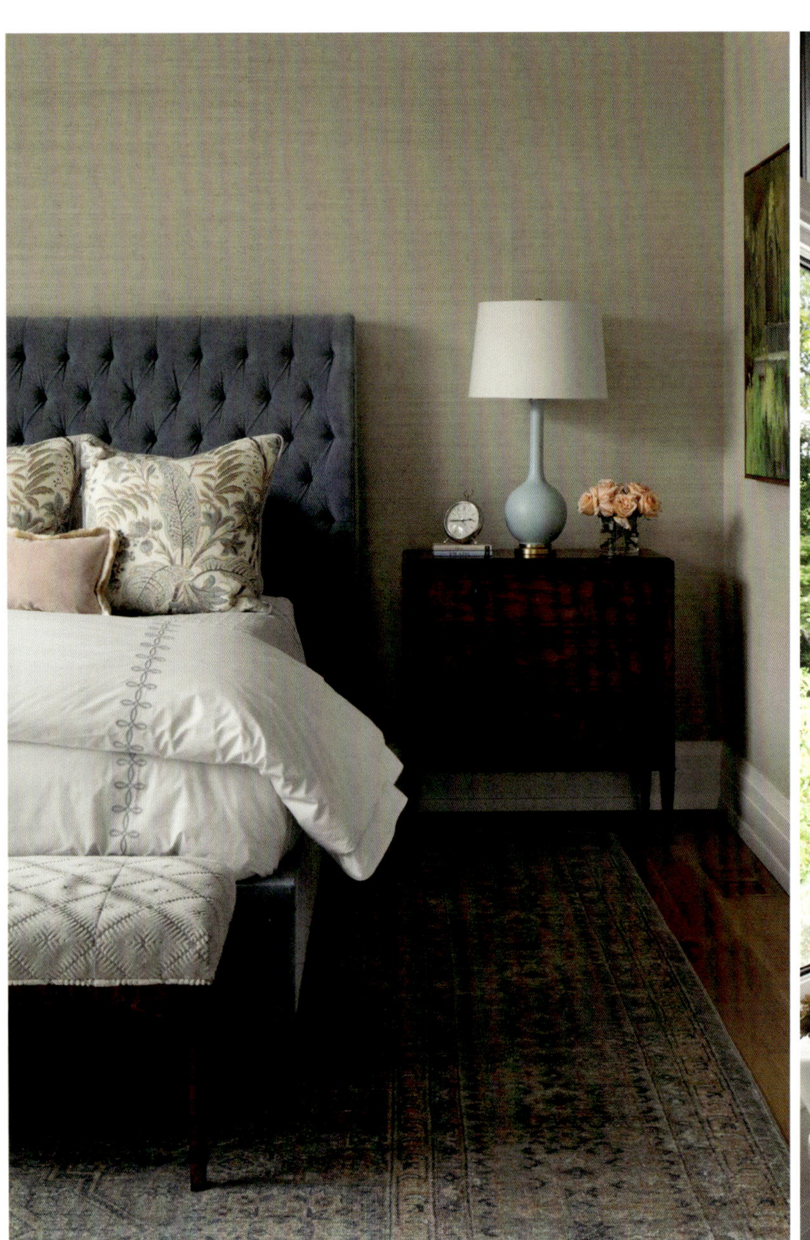

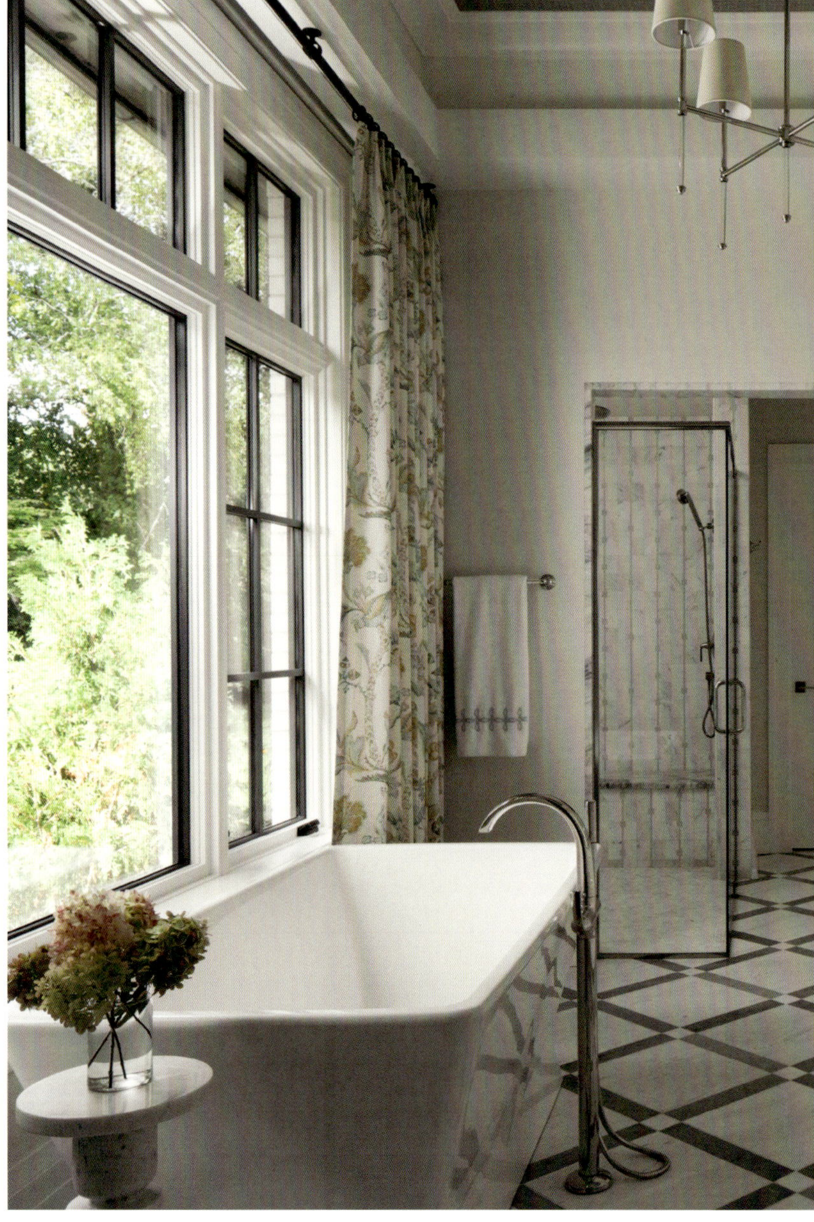

The serene primary bedroom features a luxurious deep-tufted headboard that establishes an elegant focal point. Its spacious en suite bathroom showcases refined details, including a thoughtfully positioned soaking tub nestled against a window that frames peaceful garden views. The countertops and custom-patterned flooring are crafted from exquisite marble, creating a cohesive and sophisticated aesthetic throughout the private retreat.

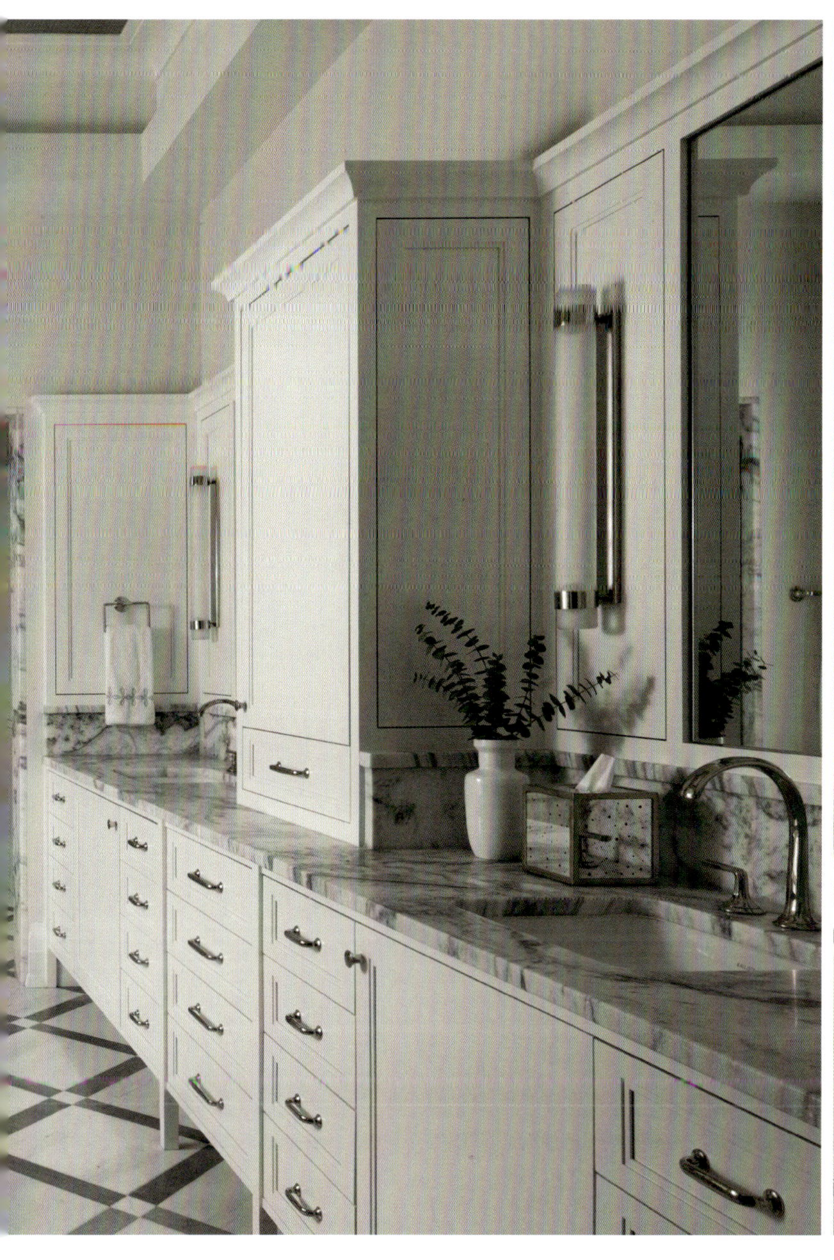

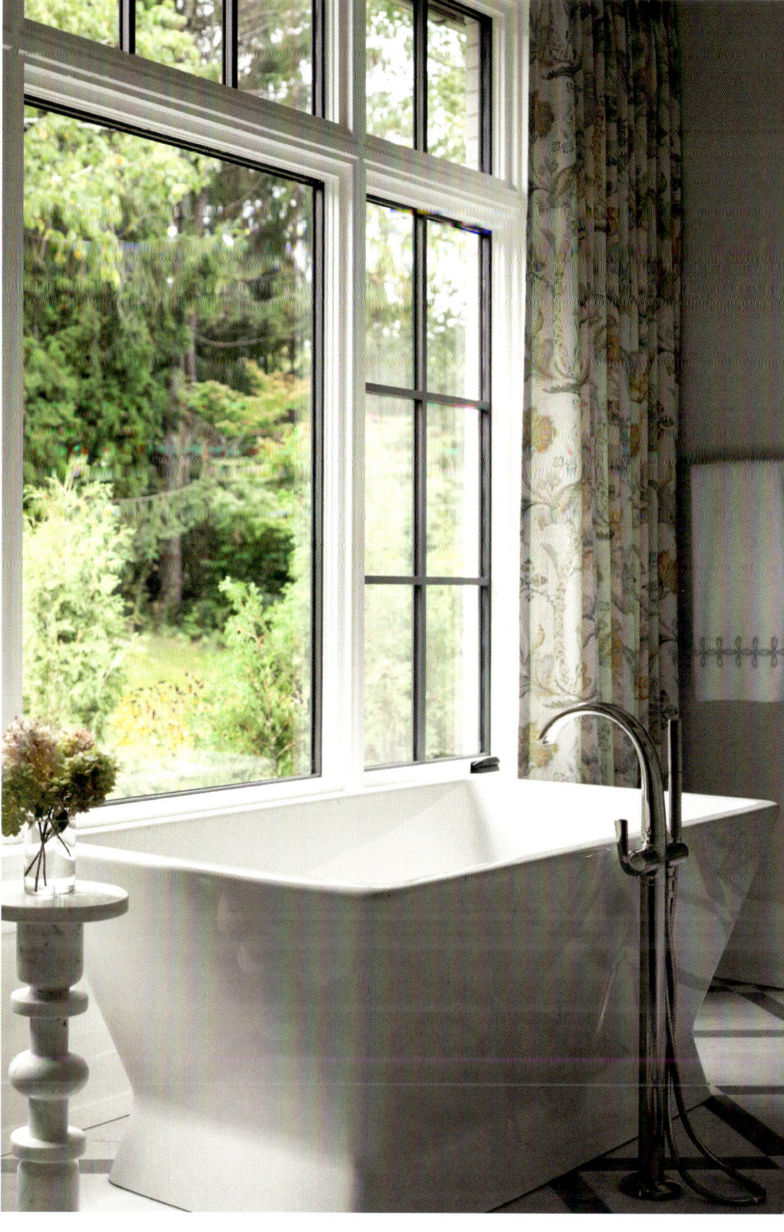

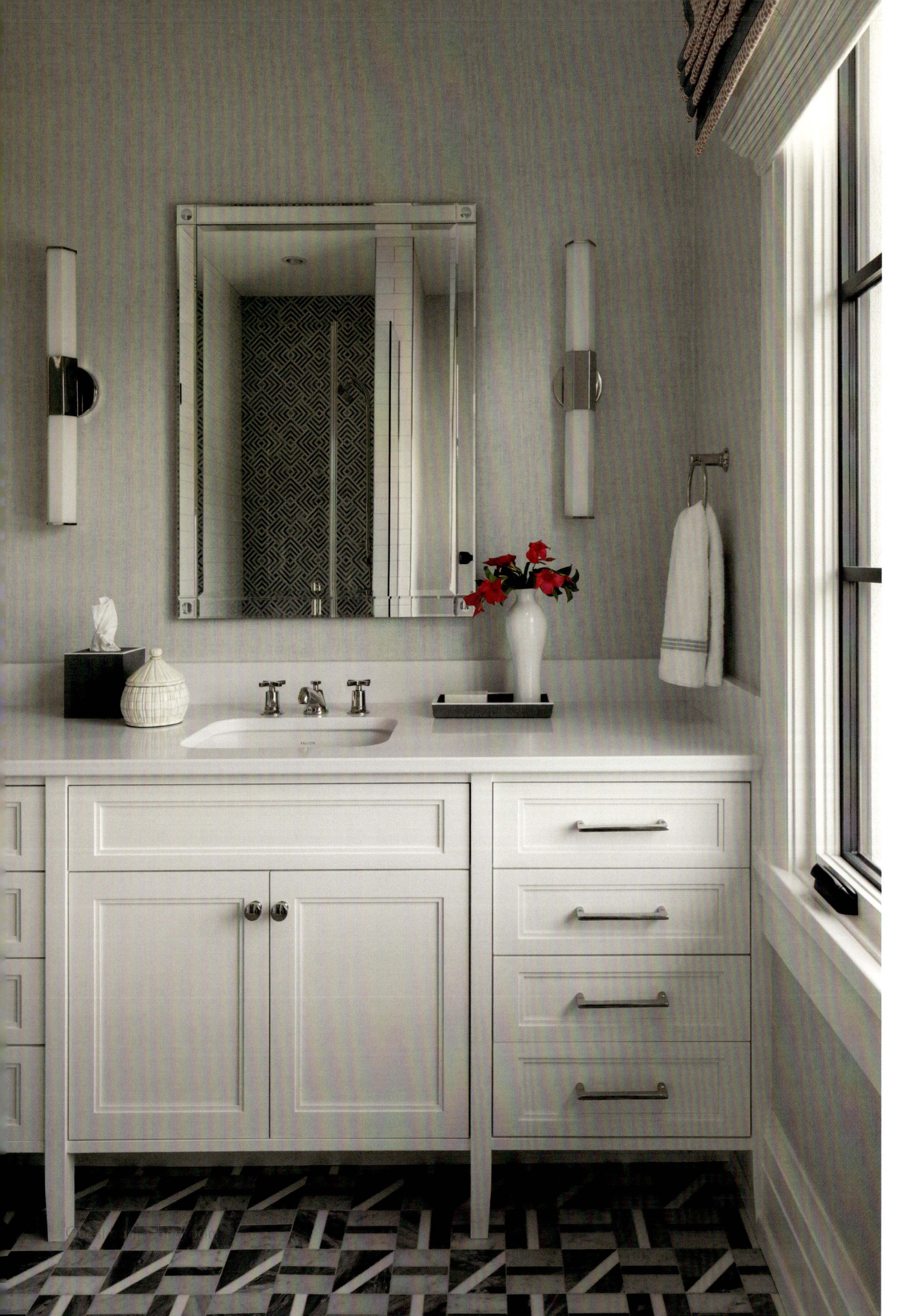

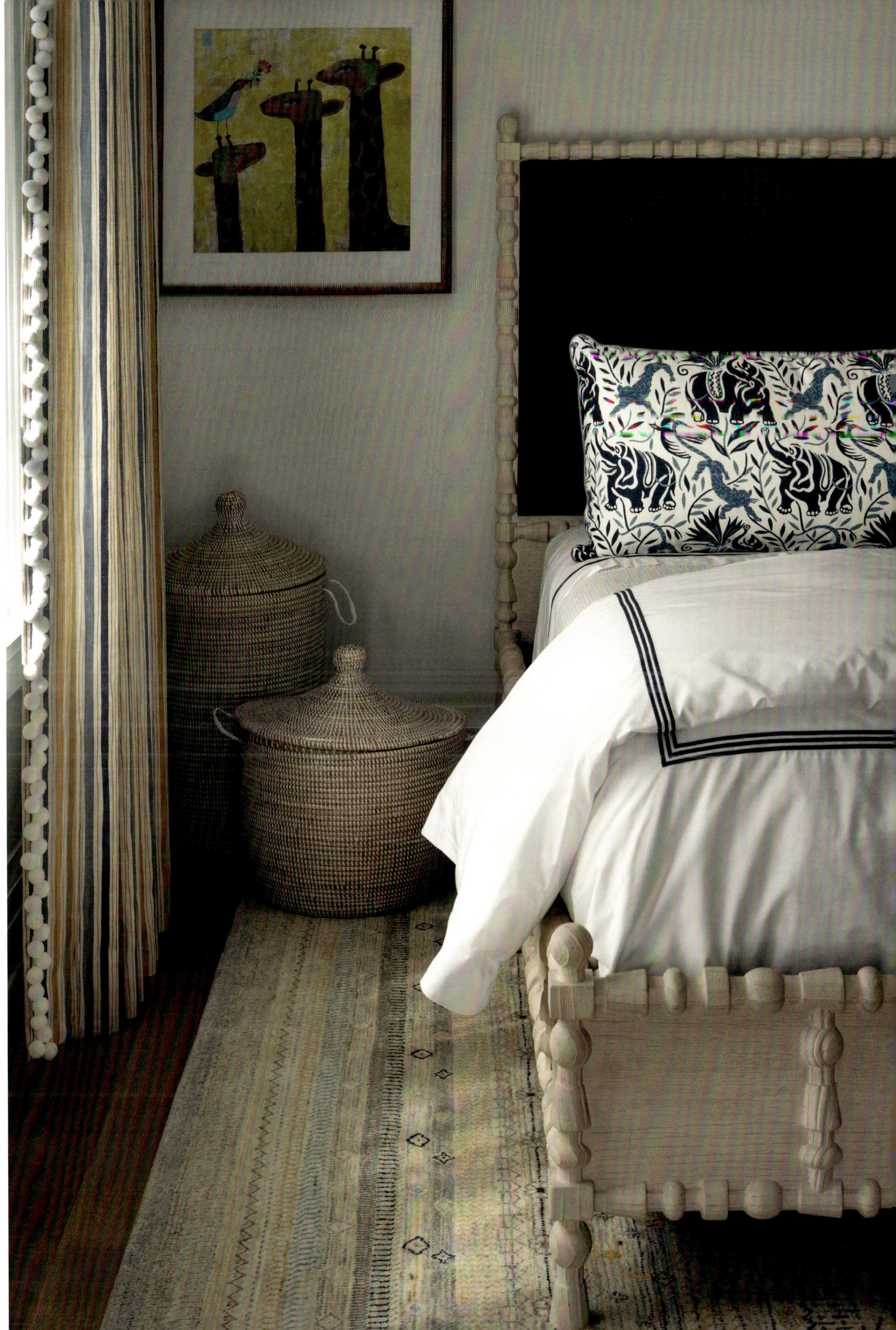

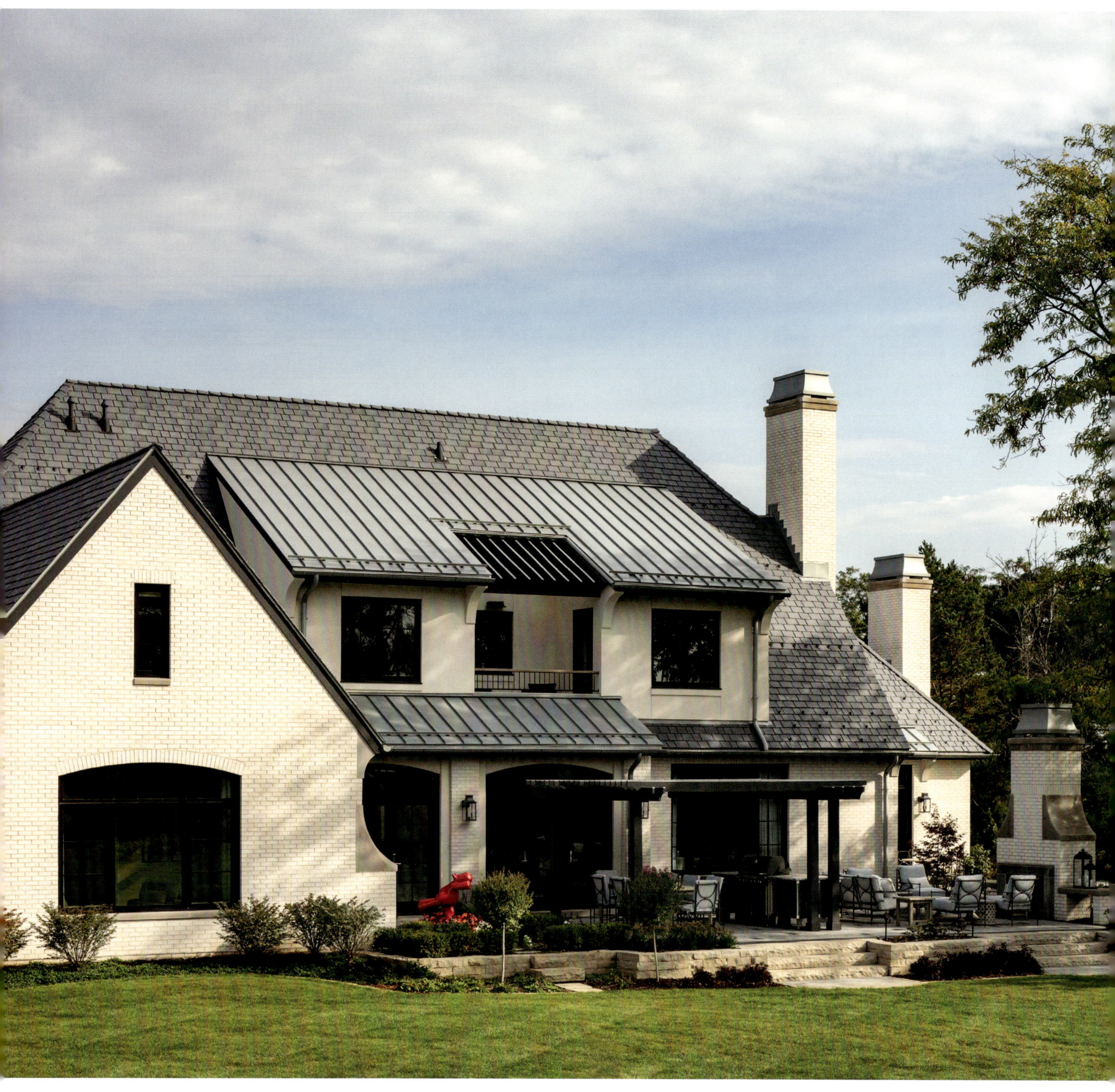

PREVIOUS: This refined guest bedroom invites guests to experience gracious hospitality. It showcases a distinguished carved wooden bed and elegant floor-to-ceiling curtains adorned with tasteful tassels. The adjoining bathroom continues the welcoming ambiance, with creamy white surfaces complemented by an intricate mosaic marble floor.

ABOVE: The home's rear elevation opens to an expansive patio, partially shaded by a majestic mature locust tree. A pergola-covered dining area adjoins an inviting outdoor fireplace with comfortable seating that invites conversation. Beyond this versatile entertainment space sits a private tennis court, completing the property's recreational amenities.

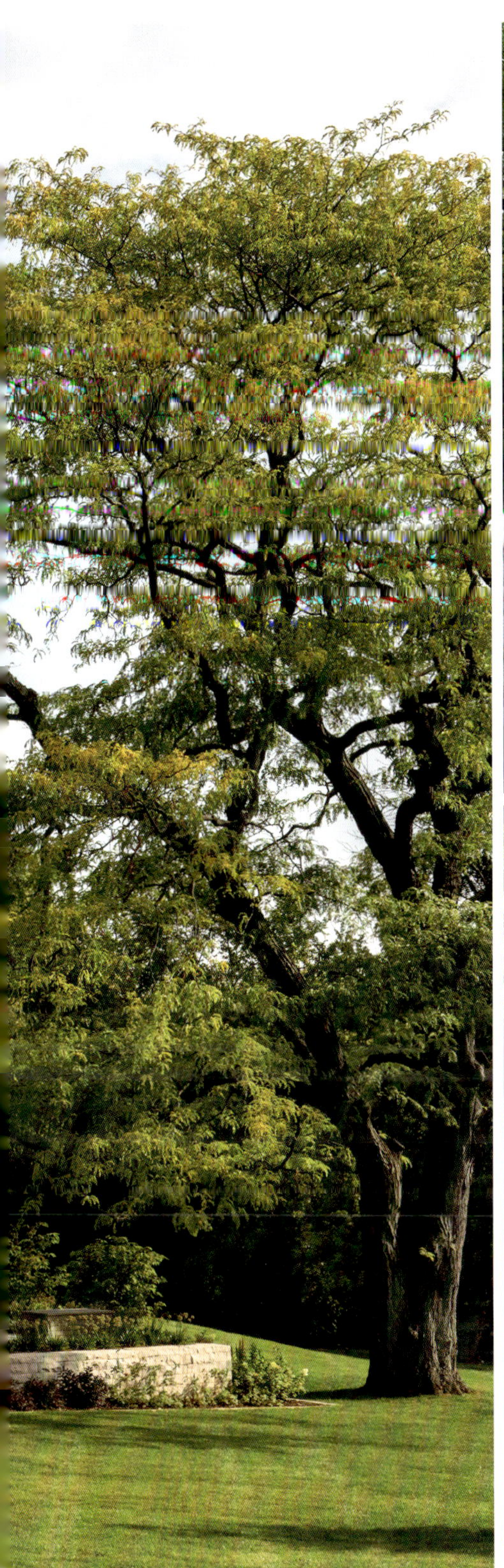

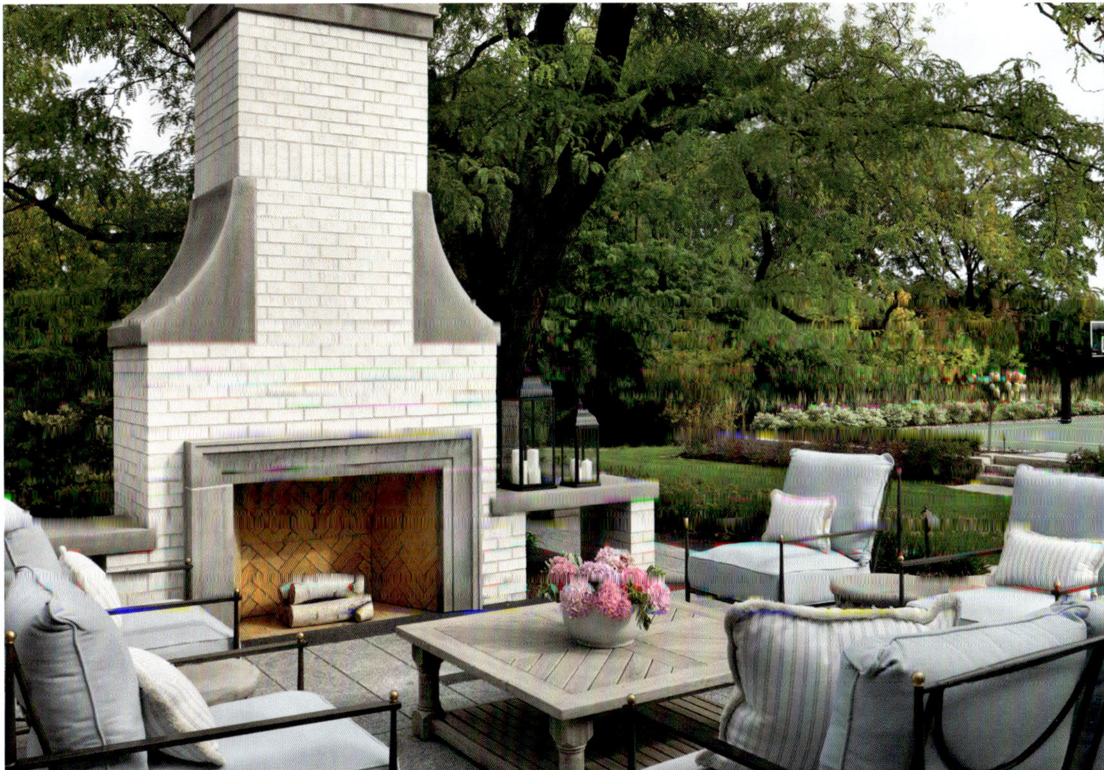

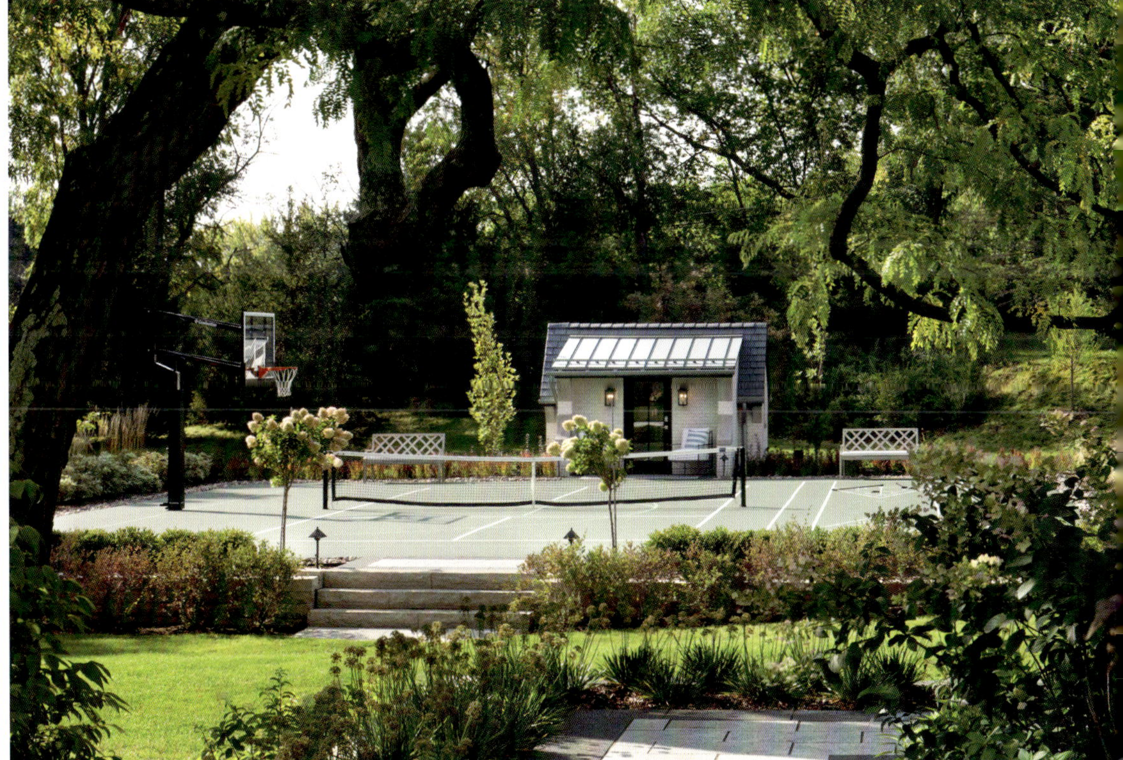

HISTORIC MILWAUKEE MANSION

Donna Sweet / Haven Interiors

Nestled along Milwaukee's lakefront, this residence on North Lake Drive was designed by architect Alexander C. Eschweiler and built between 1917 and 1919 for beer executive Joseph Uihlein Sr. The mansion remained in the Uihlein family until the 1970s, when it was reimagined as condominiums, bridging the city's early-twentieth-century architectural vernacular with modern life.

Crossing the threshold of this 3,347-square-foot abode, you are transported to an era of unparalleled craftsmanship. Details such as linenfold paneling, stone arches, and intricate plaster ceilings showcase early-twentieth-century splendor. Stained glass windows bathe interiors in vivid light and, at sunset, warm the rooms with a golden glow. The centerpiece of the home is a two-story oak staircase that beams with opulent splendor.

The new owners of this particular unit—a couple in their sixties who embrace urban life—and designer Donna Sweet of Haven Interiors faced the challenge of revitalizing the home without erasing its character. Their solution? A deft merger of respect and reinvention that exemplifies the careful balance between architectural preservation and modernity.

At the start, Sweet introduced a palette harmonizing with the home's patinated dark oak: lush green, soft beige, and warm gray. Textures were layered thoughtfully, creating a dialogue between historical elements—antique furniture pieces—and modern upholstered and case-good silhouettes. The resulting rooms feel timeless and contemporary.

Sweet updated the lighting by replacing select chandeliers with new ones that improved functionality without disrupting design integrity. Outside, an acre of ground is enclosed by brick walls and iron gates, evoking the allure of private grandeur. In the back, an English garden blossoms before the waves of Lake Michigan, a private Eden for the owners and their dogs.

With the last design details attended to, this townhome illustrates how historic residences can evolve without losing their essence. It's a personalized sanctuary honoring its past, celebrating its present, and looking confidently to the future—a testament to Milwaukee's architectural heritage and lakeside living's enduring allure.

Inside the door of this home, visitors enter history through this grand foyer, where the original limestone arch frames a dramatic space. Black-and-gold ombré wall finishes by Carrie Chimenti create depth, complemented by Visual Comfort lighting and family heirloom artwork hanging above a waterfall console table.

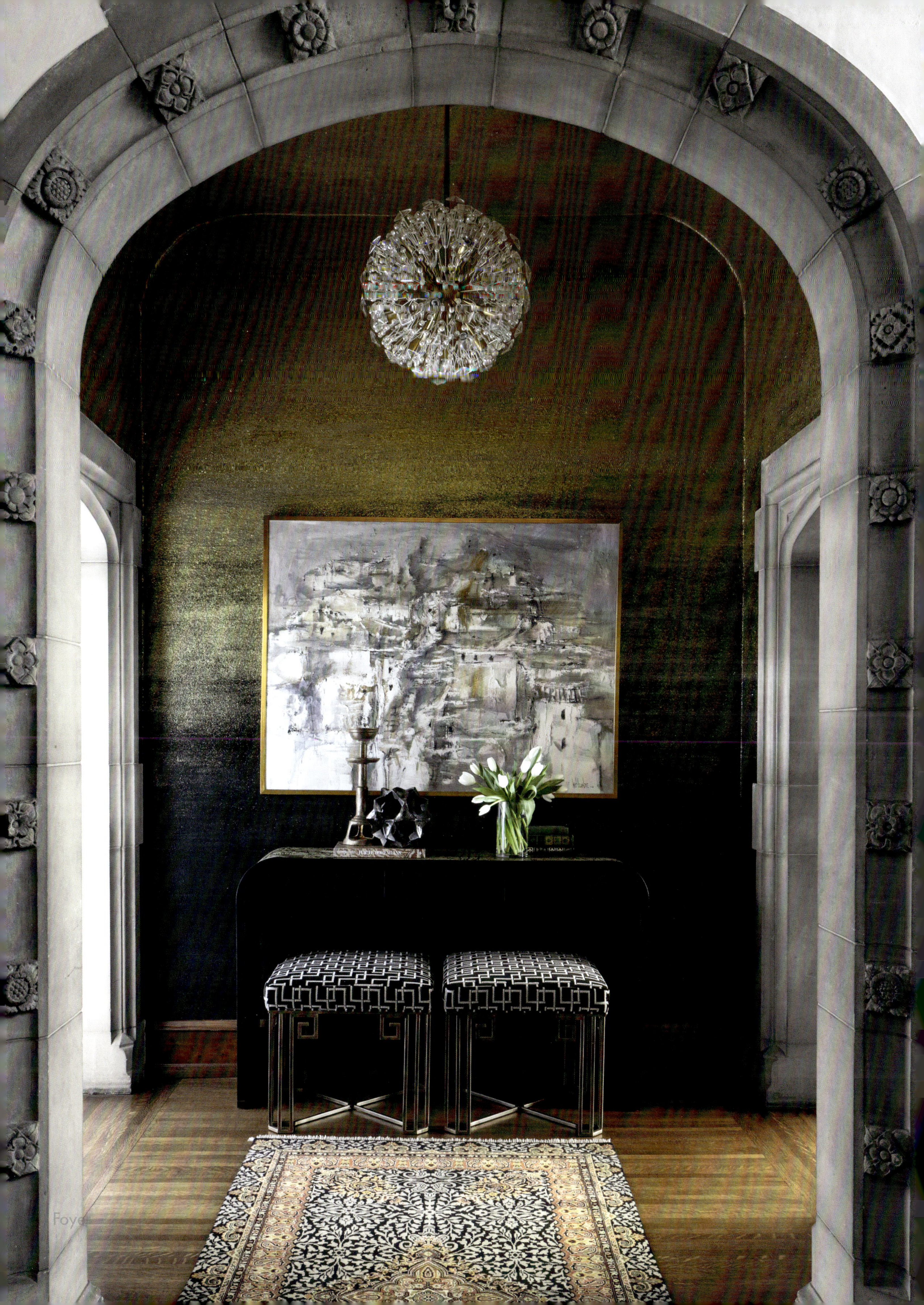

Foye

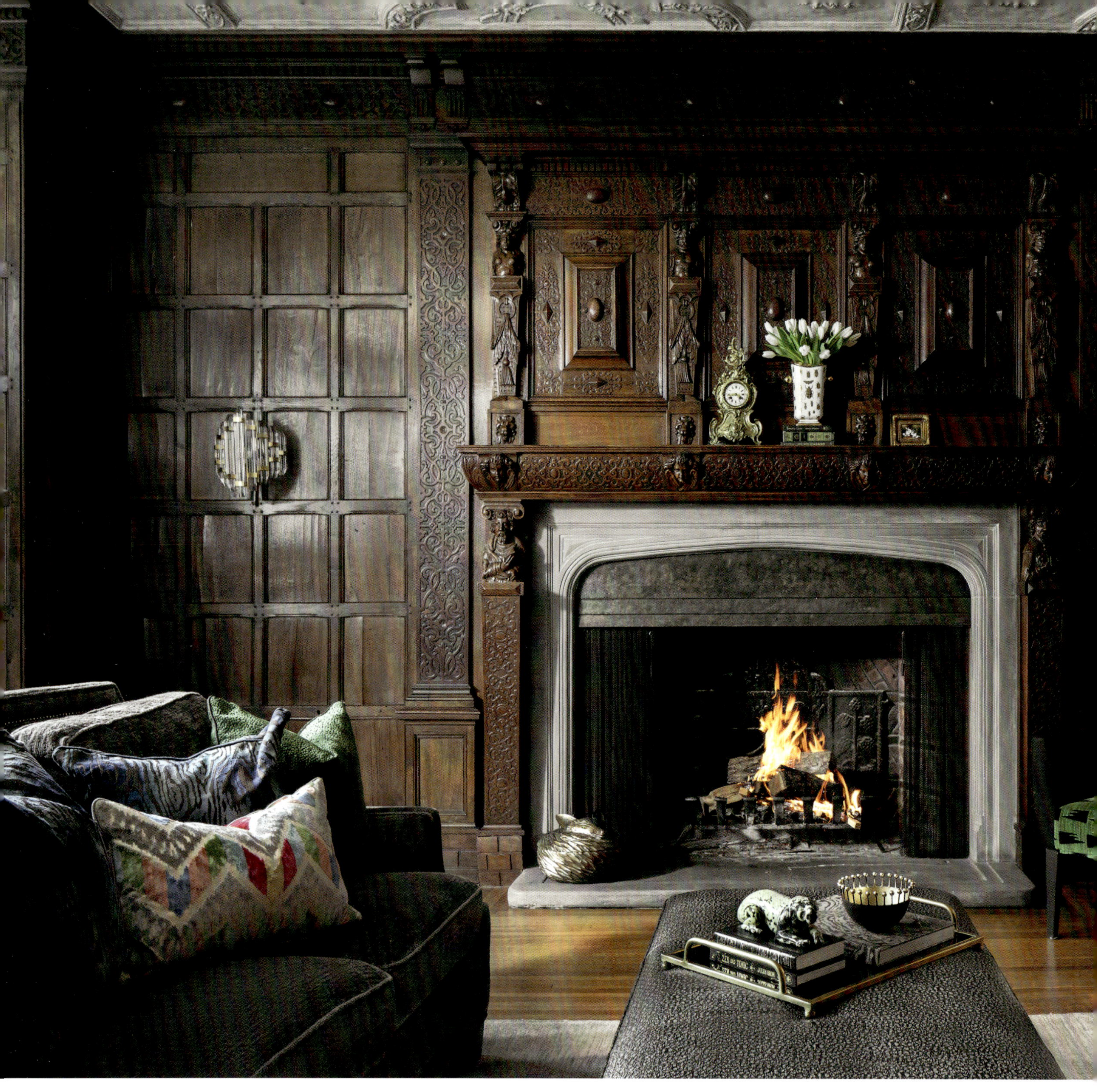

Left: Original paneling and plaster create timeless elegance in this living room. Visual Comfort sconces replace non-original brass fixtures, while the green wing chair deliberately introduces a contemporary element, subtly pushing beyond strictly period-appropriate design. *Right:* Historic linenfold paneling majestically frames the powder room entrance. Inside, a swirling floral wall covering delivers a bold, moody pattern that commands attention without compromising the home's character.

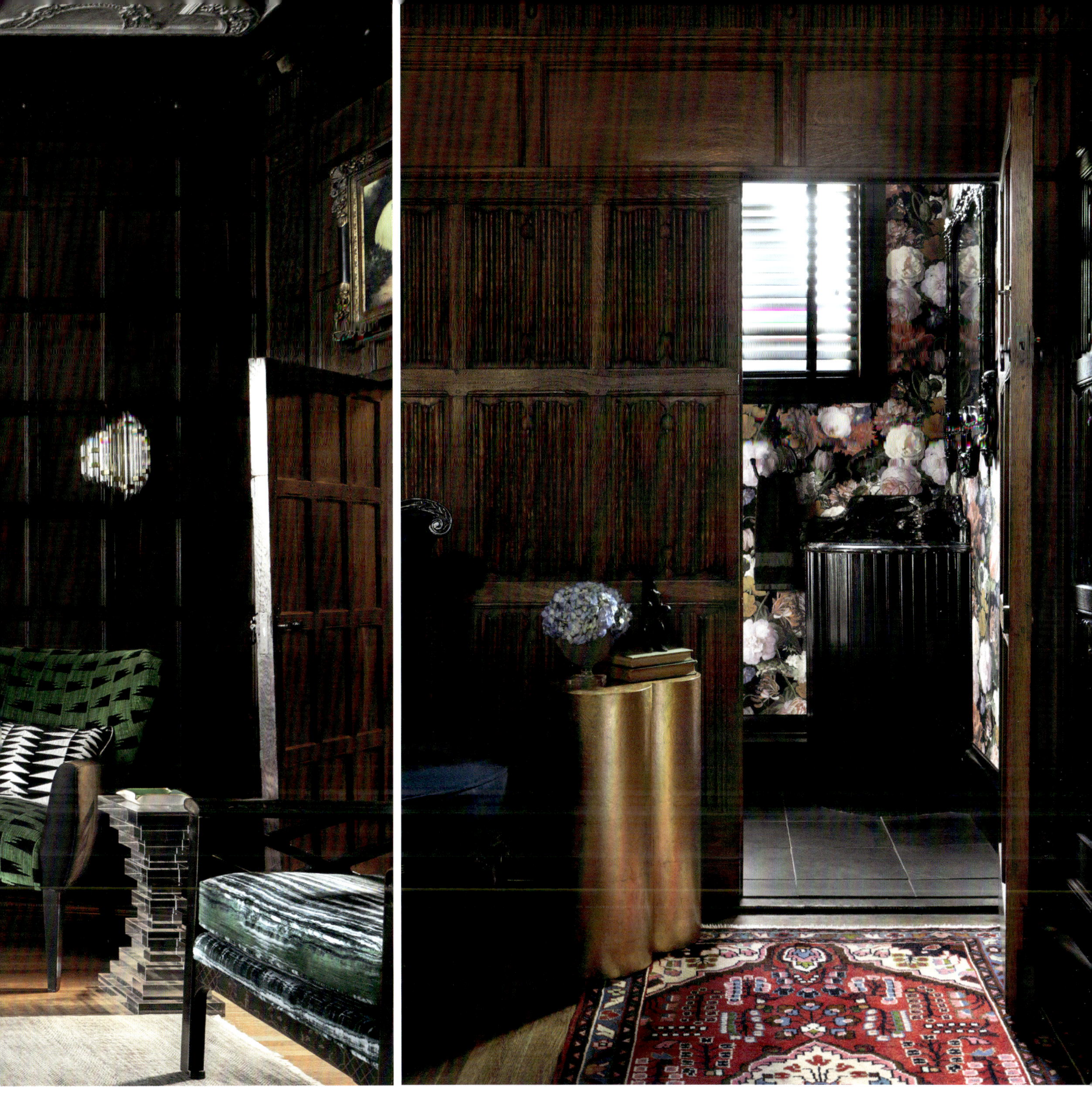

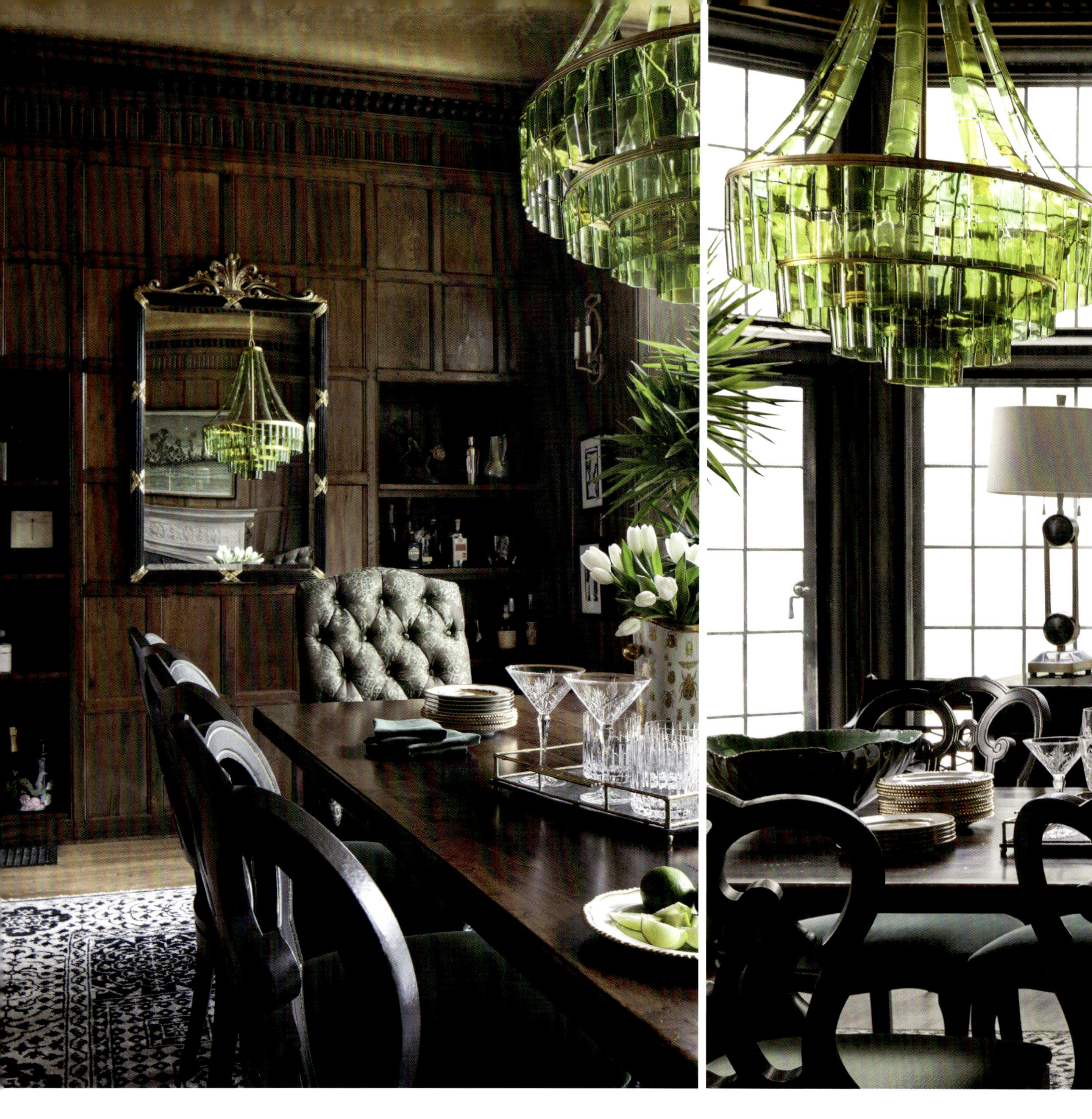

The dining room, layered in verdant hues, showcases a green-on-green palette anchored by a classic contrasting mirror. Antique side chairs upholstered in Schumacher velvet surround the table beneath Currey & Company's green glass chandelier, which is dramatically highlighted by glorious natural light.

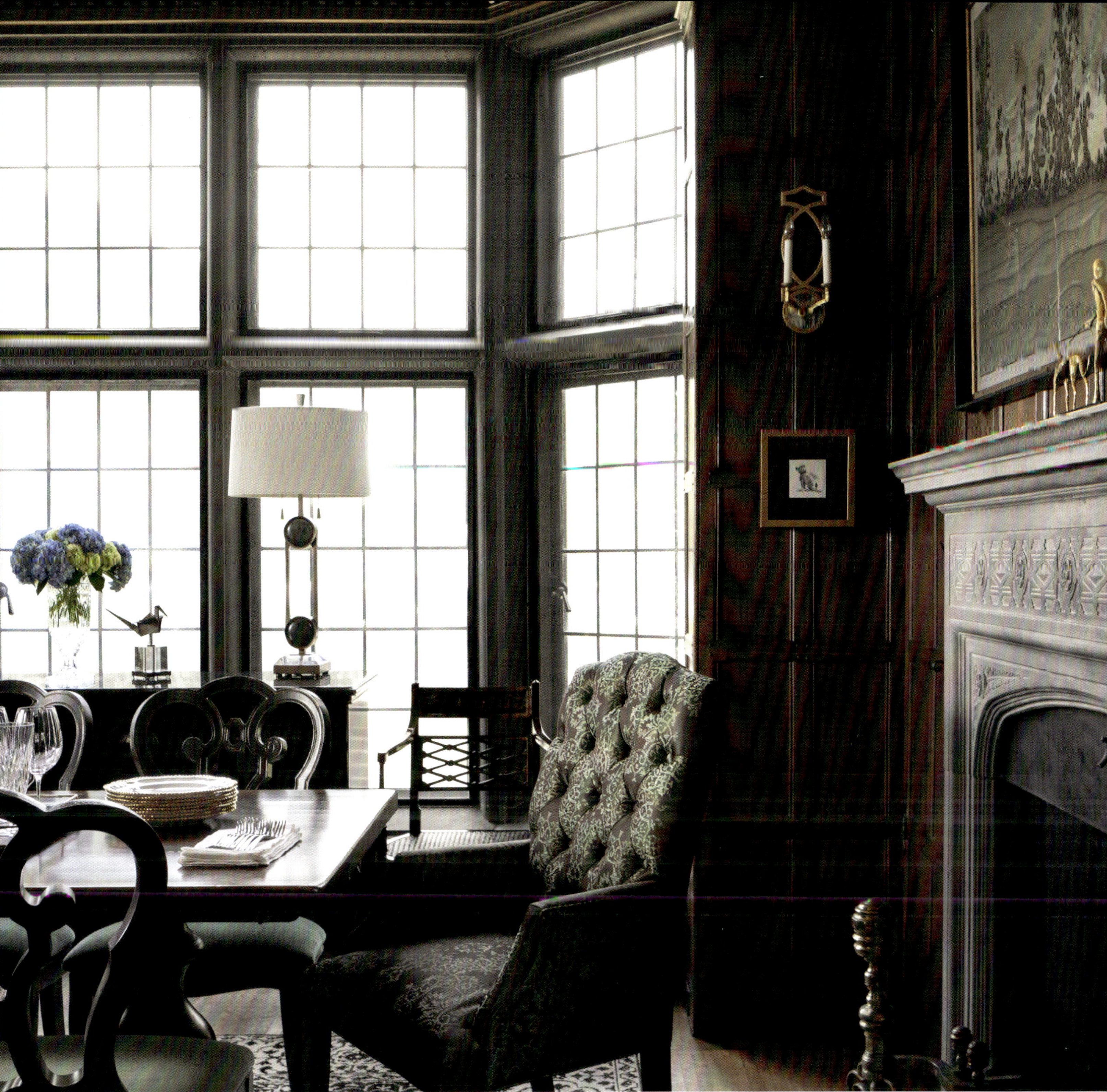

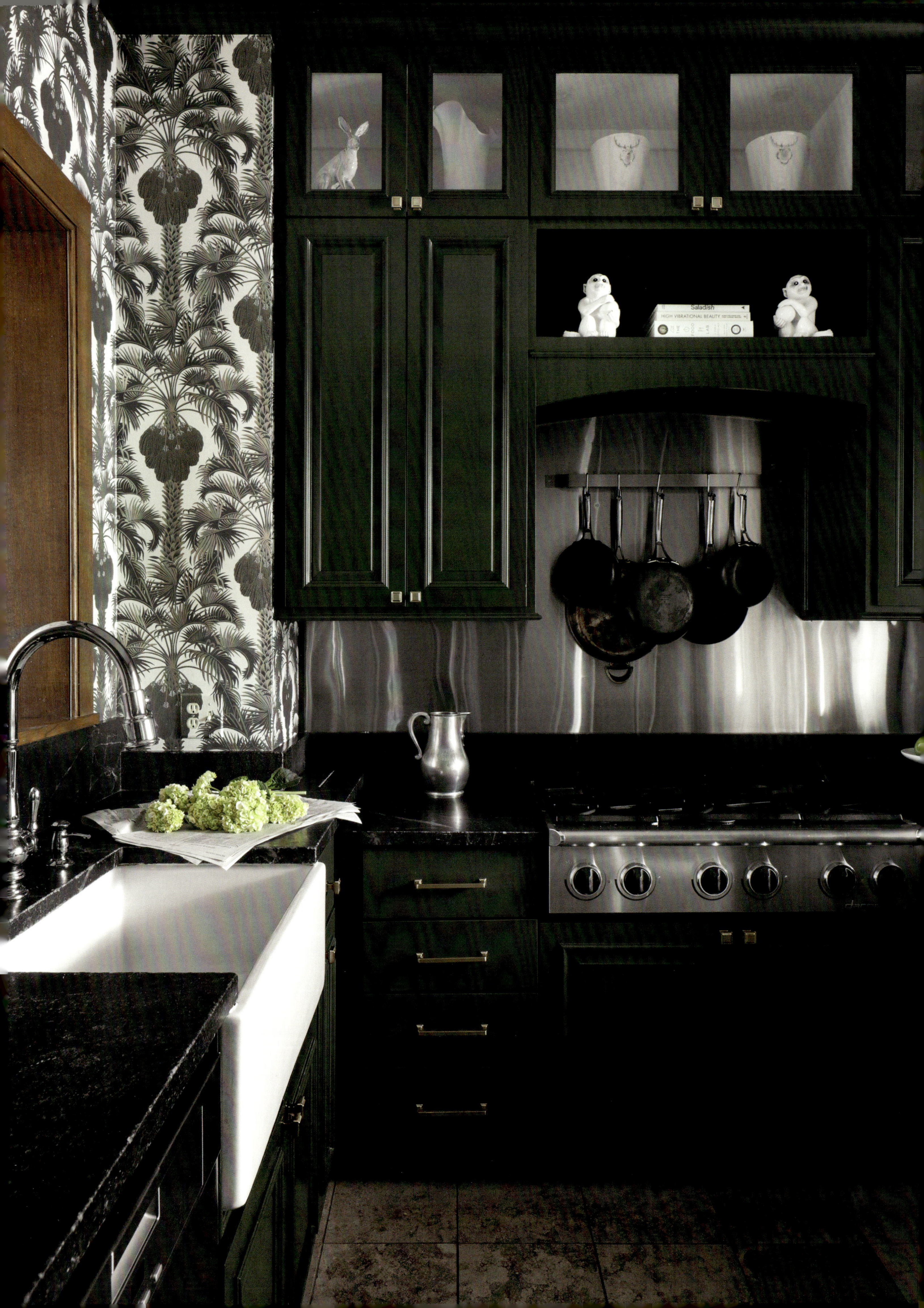
Saladish
HIGH VIBRATIONAL BEAUTY

The intimate kitchen showcases elegant Sherwin-Williams green cabinetry paired with Cole & Son's "Hollywood Palm" wall covering by Martyn Lawrence Bullard, where subtle gold accents in the paper and hardware create referential harmony.

One side of the thoughtful living room transforms a corner into a functional workspace featuring an oversized antique console as a desk, paired with chairs upholstered in Designers Guild fabric—positioned to capture breathtaking Lake Michigan garden views during daily use.

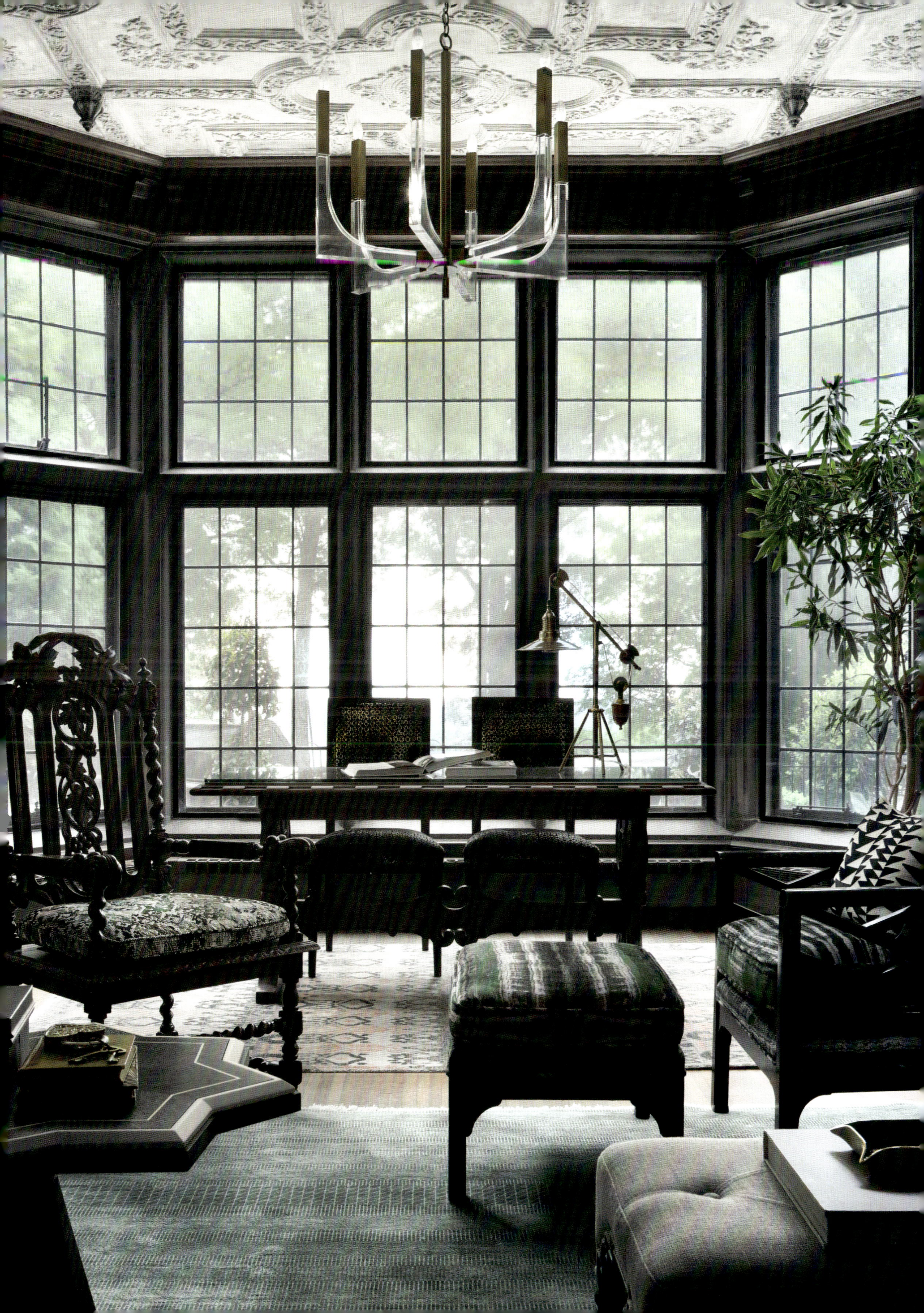

HEARTLAND'S EUROPEAN VILLA

Sarah Dippold Design

Tucked into the rural countryside of Culver, Indiana, a contemporary jewel box glistens with tranquil style. The home lends an effortless elegance to indoor-outdoor living, surrendering to the natural landscape with clean lines, earthy tones, and thoughtful design.

The first impression is one with lasting, timeless impact. Architect Jeffry Harting of GTH Architects envisioned an authentic, modern-day European villa in the heartland. To bring this vision to life, he arranged the main house, the satellite lodges, and the garage around a central pool to evoke Old World charm.

Stepping inside, interior designer Sarah Dippold's vision becomes apparent. The homeowners sought a "tailored but casual and comfortable space" to create a transitional aesthetic that would remain current for years to come.

To that end, Dippold chose a predominantly neutral color palette throughout the home, drawing inspiration from the earth tones evident just beyond the home's windows. This choice creates a calm atmosphere and allows the stunning countryside views to be the focal point. For contrast, warm woods, dark hardware finishes, and natural stone elements were added to prevent the bright, white spaces from feeling sterile.

Sleek and lightweight, custom-designed furniture pieces with subtly curved details carry a bright and sensuous airiness. Durable yet elegant fabrics ensure enduring hold without sacrificing style.

The pool house is a triumph of indoor-outdoor living. Two low-to-the-ground, oversized sectionals provide ample seating, without feeling heavy or overwhelming. A wood ceiling crowns the space with warmth and character while visually lowering the room's height to create an enveloping intimacy.

The kitchen shines with a specially designed hood as its focal piece. Dark and textured woven materials create a dramatic contrast with the surrounding lighter tones. This element and rich bronze hardware throughout the space anchor the room and add depth to the overall design.

The designer's commitment to creating a "warm and inviting but calm and 'quiet'" space is evident throughout the project. By carefully balancing modern elements with timeless design principles, this country retreat achieves a rare feat: It feels both luxurious and deeply comfortable, a true home away from home.

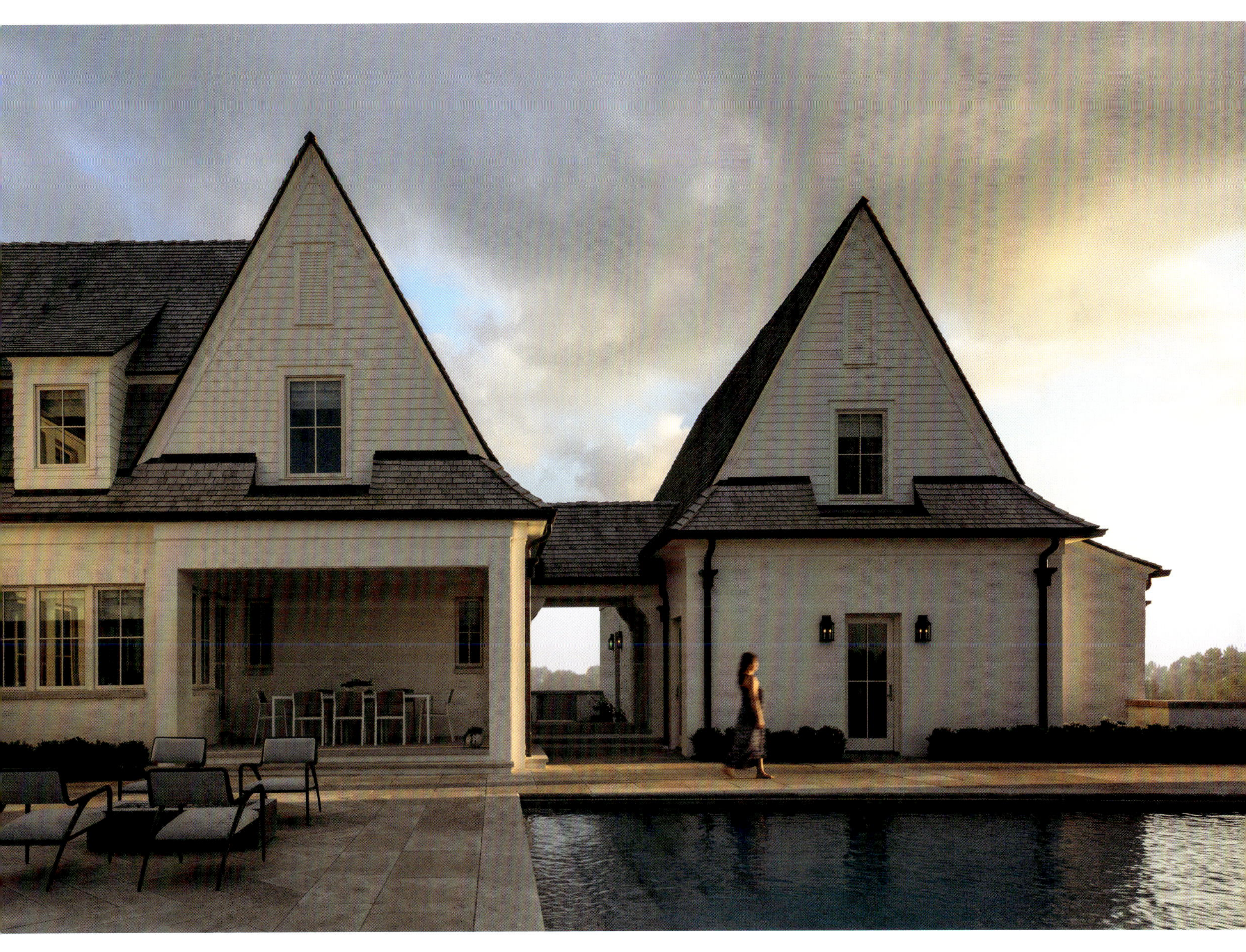

Viewed from behind, Jeffry Harting's European-inspired villa arranges the main house and satellite structures around a central pool, creating timeless Old World charm in a modern heartland setting.

The pool house features custom sectional pieces with low backs designed by Sarah Dippold. They are strategically arranged to maintain sight lines to the fireplace and pool area. Minimal outdoor furniture was selected for comfort and sculptural appeal. The modernist outdoor fire feature adds charm after dusk.

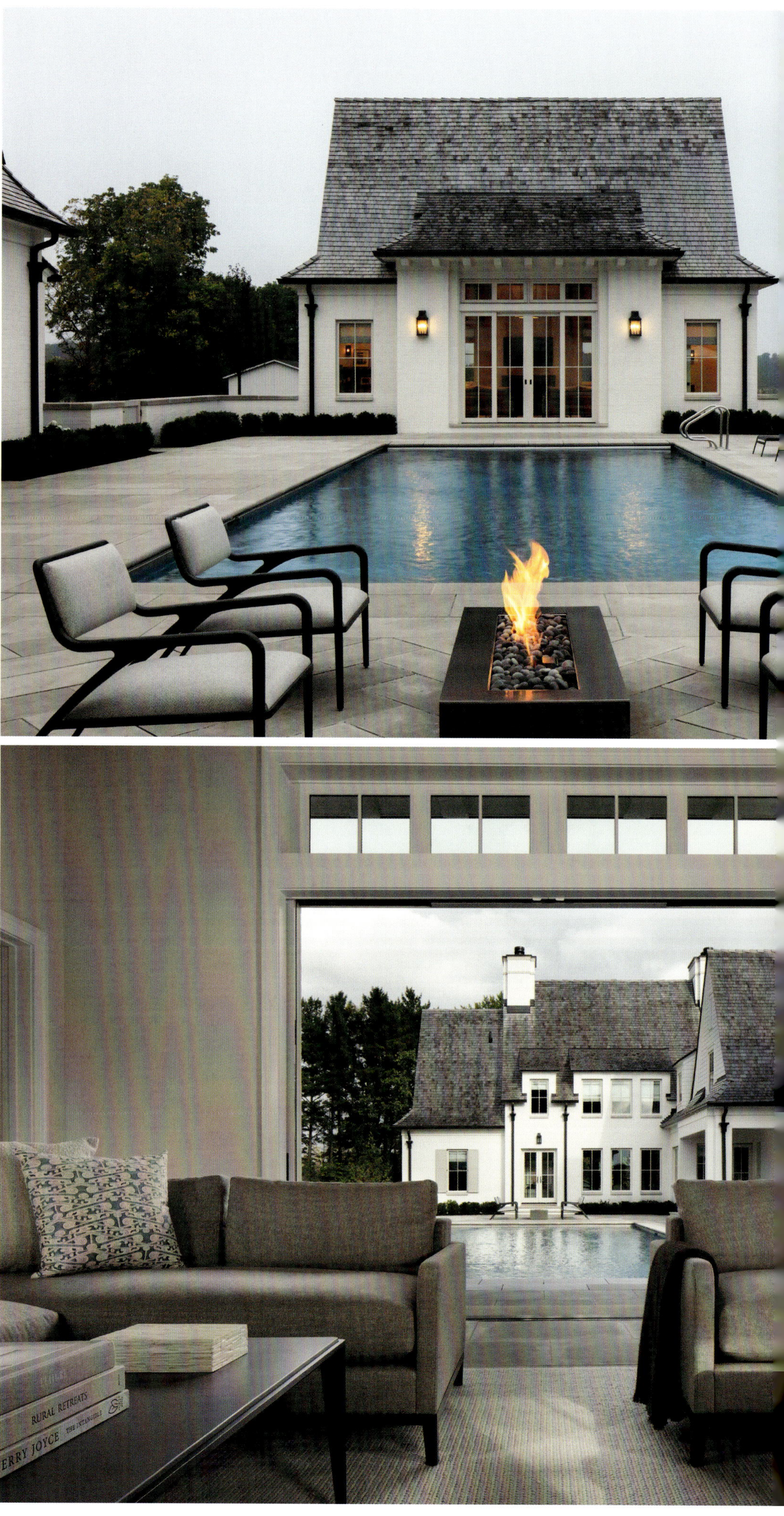

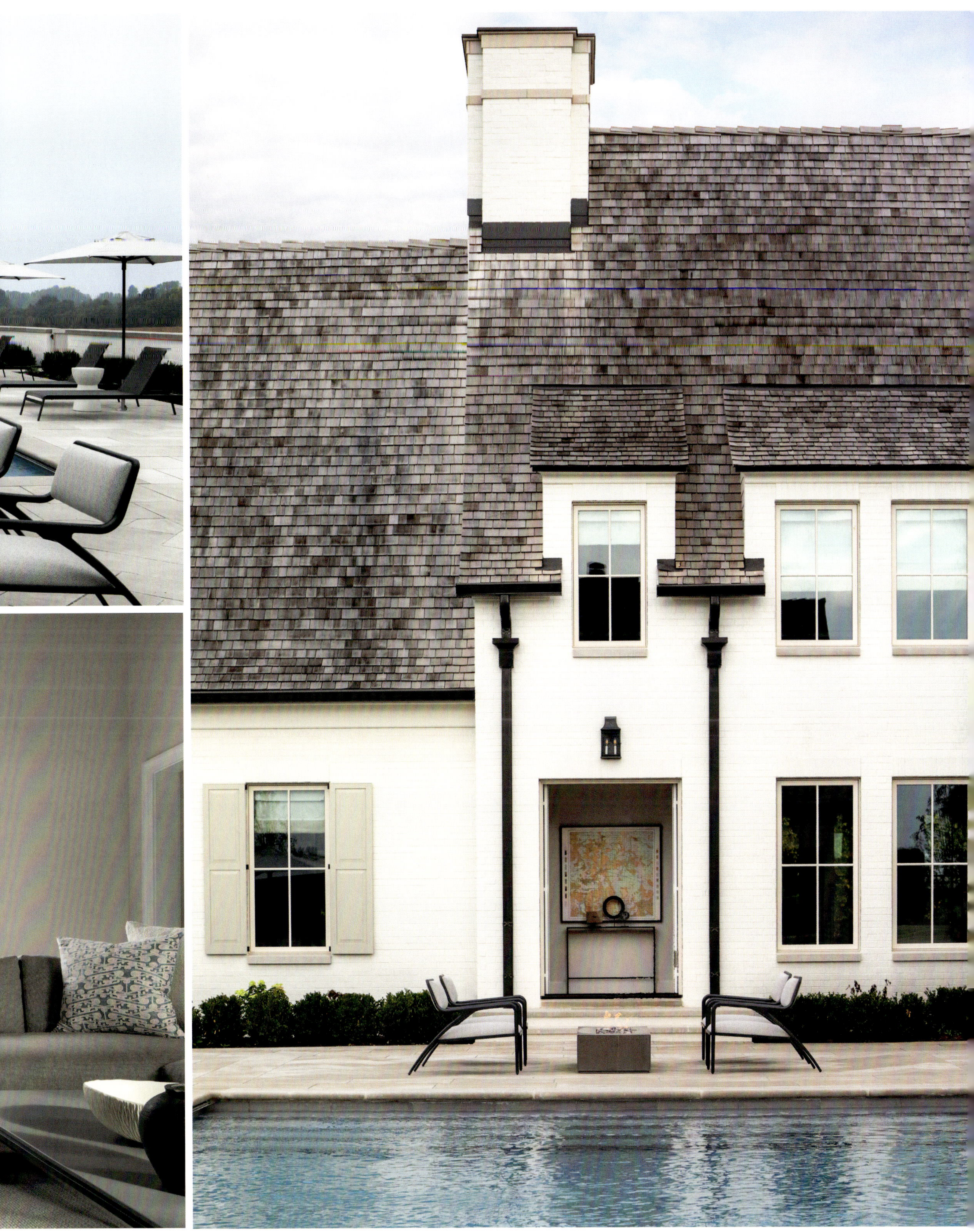

This crisp-lined living room features walls sheathed in Benjamin Moore's White Dove paint, complemented by a custom-carved Indiana limestone fireplace. Thoughtfully designed swivel chairs and a bespoke coffee table allow versatile enjoyment of both interior and pool views.

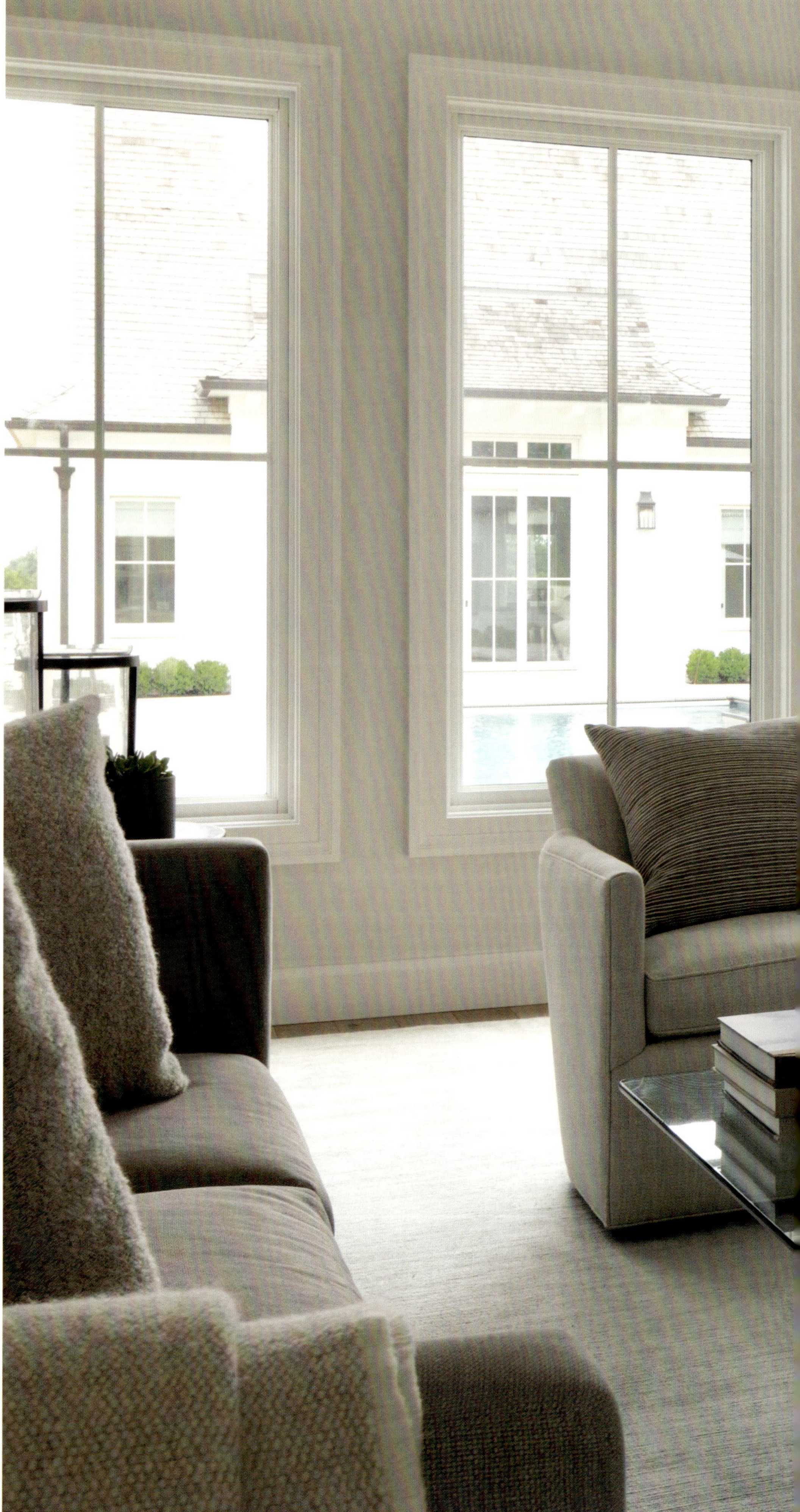

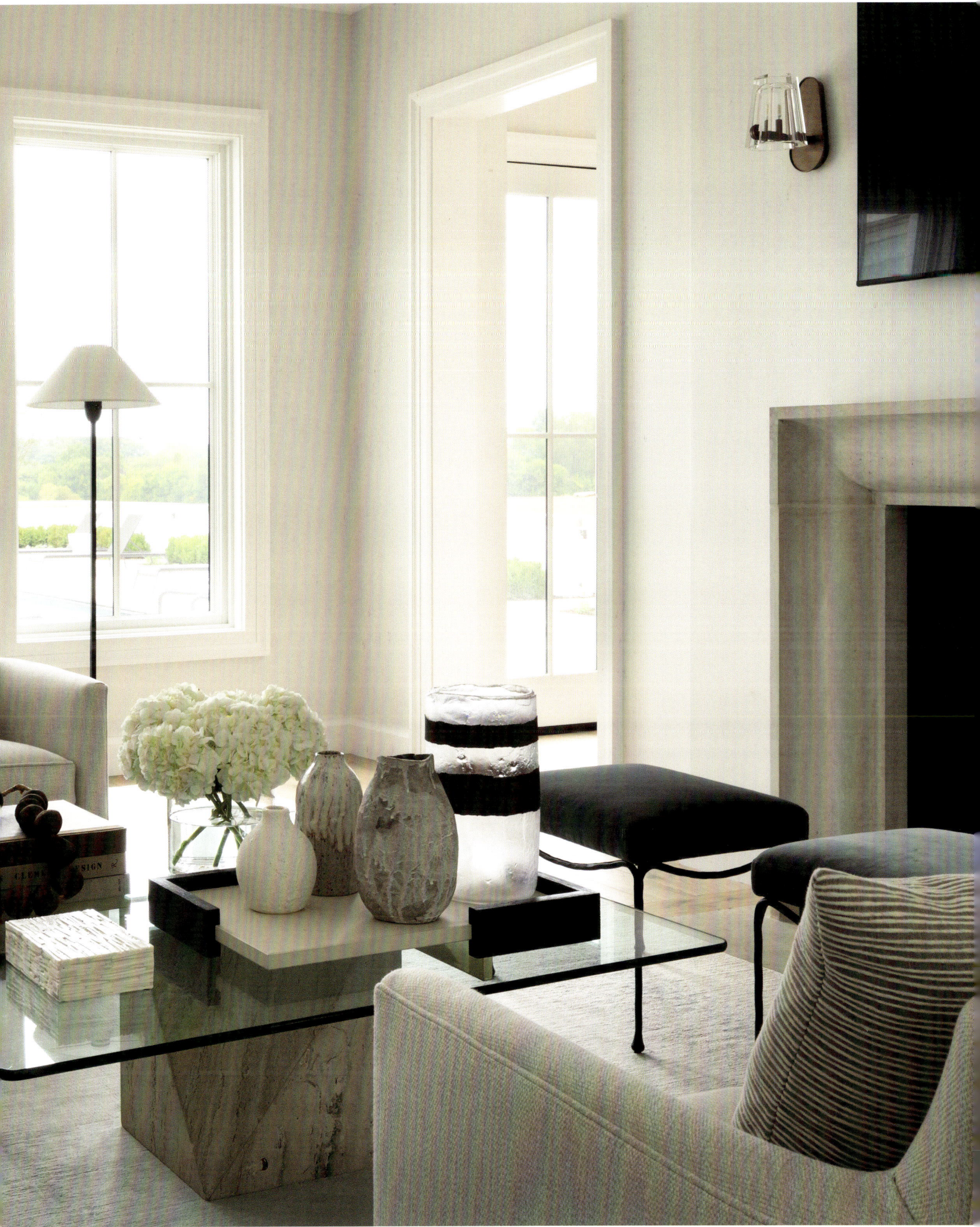

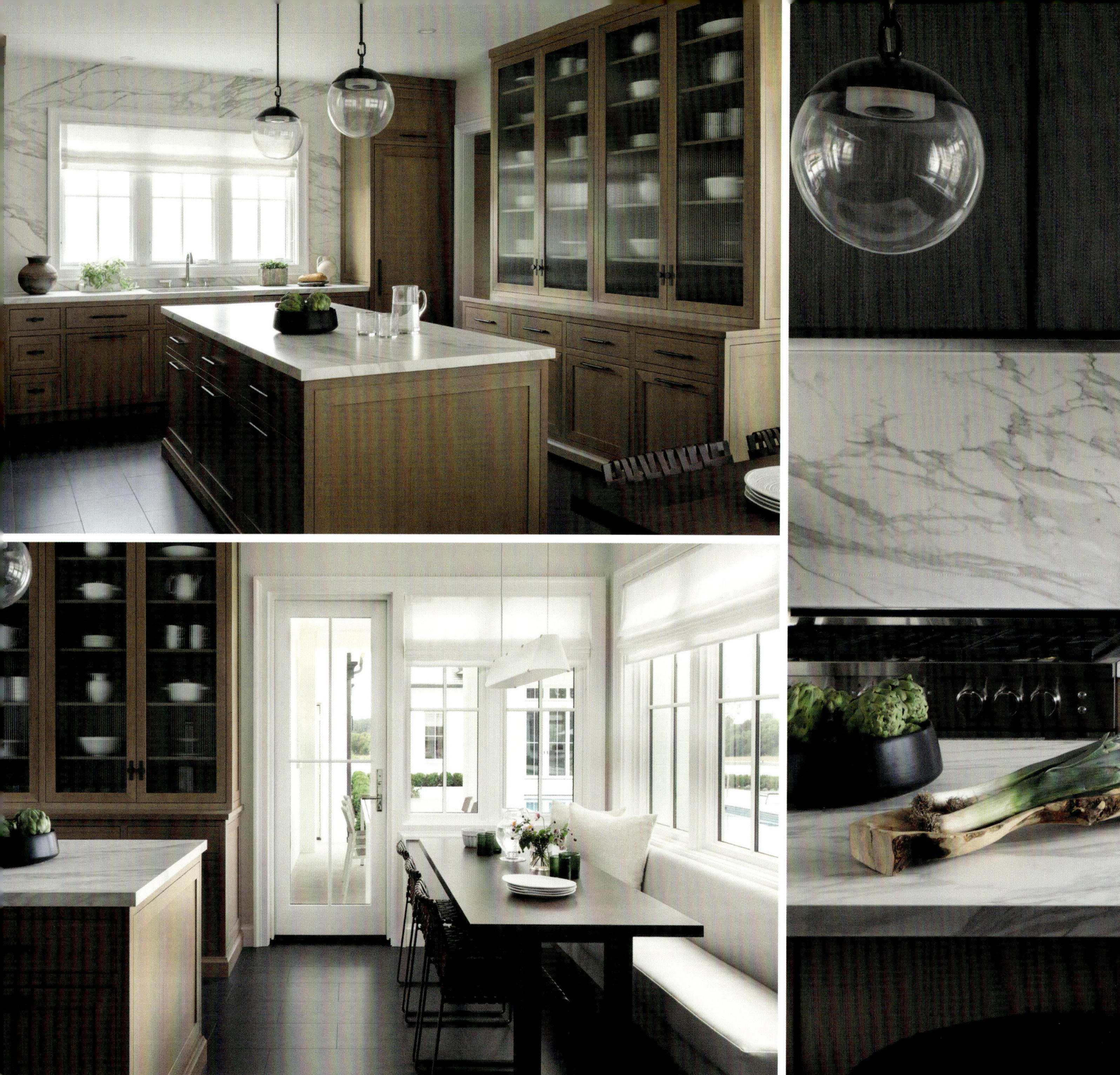

This well-appointed kitchen features white oak cabinetry complemented by porcelain countertops and backsplash chosen for their marble-like aesthetics without maintenance concerns. The custom-designed range hood incorporates commercial-grade linen-look paper in a steel frame, while reeded glass panels in the hutch add visual lightness.

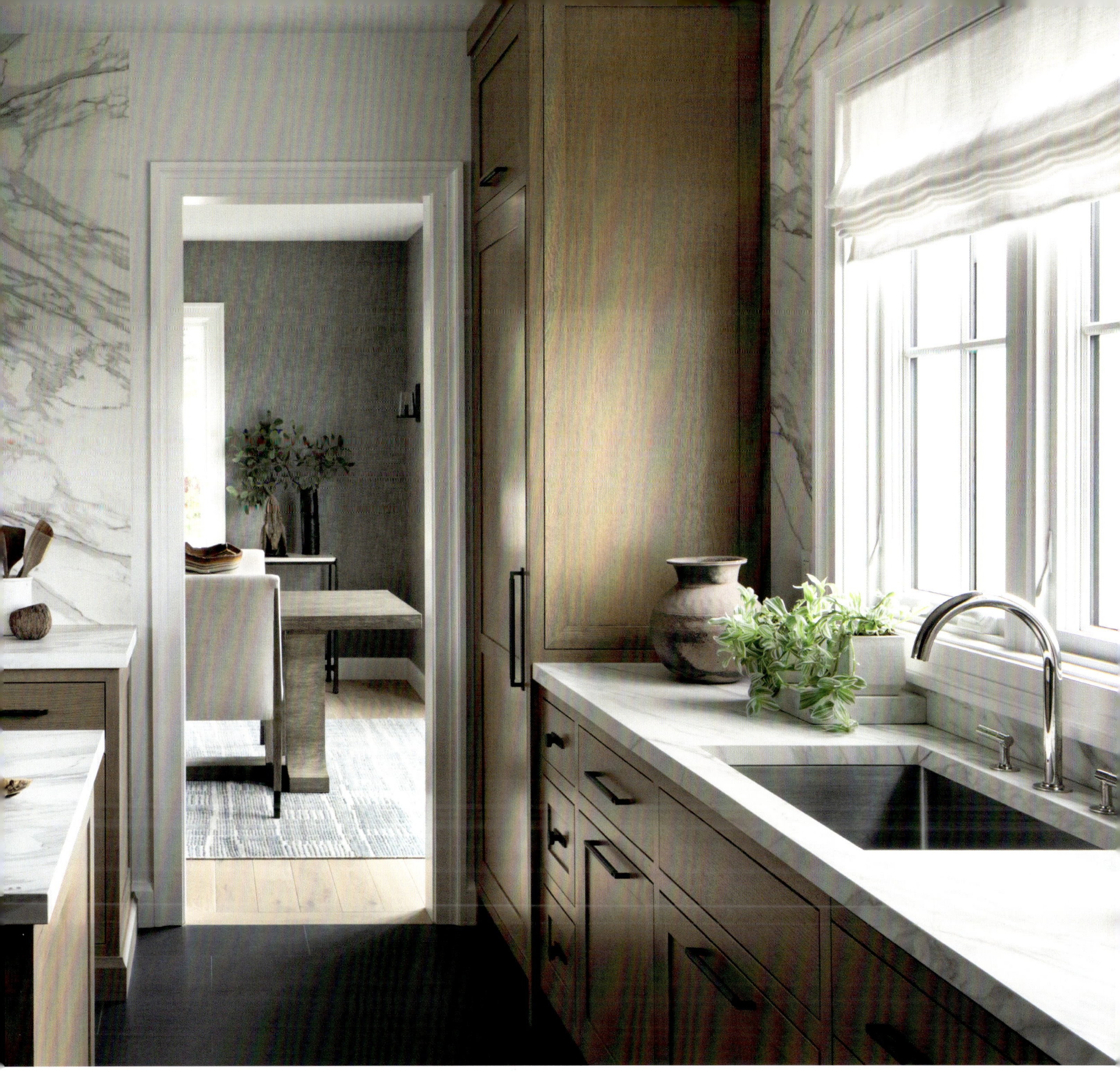

The interiors in this home balance a mix of warm and cool neutrals, exemplifying the home's "tailored but casual" aesthetic. Natural textures, custom limestone fireplace elements, and carefully curated furnishings create a space that feels both minimal and inviting—embodying the designers' vision of a modern yet timeless retreat.

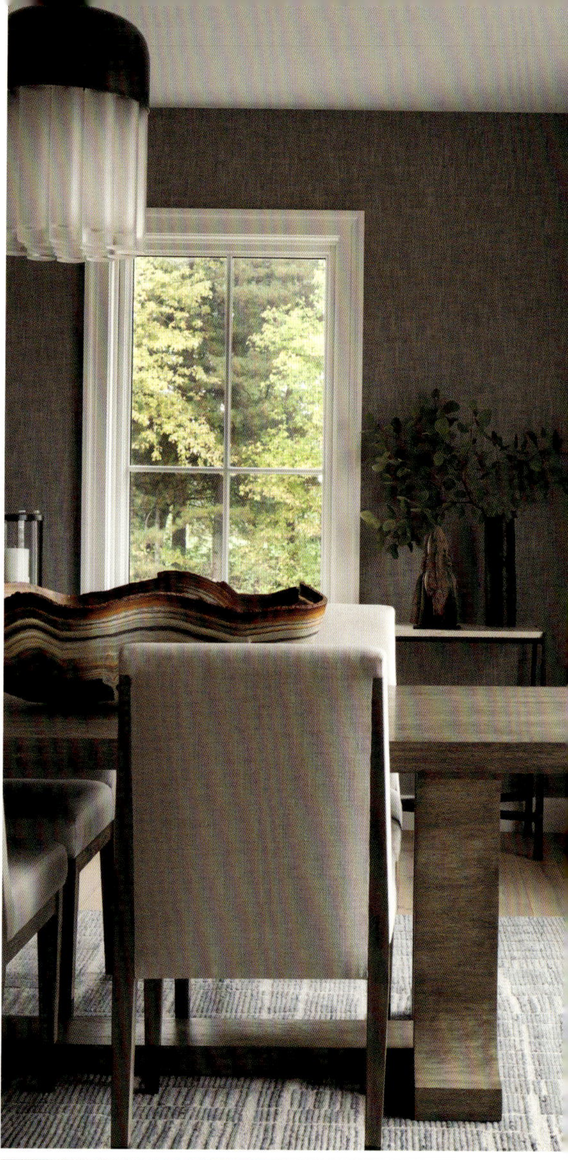

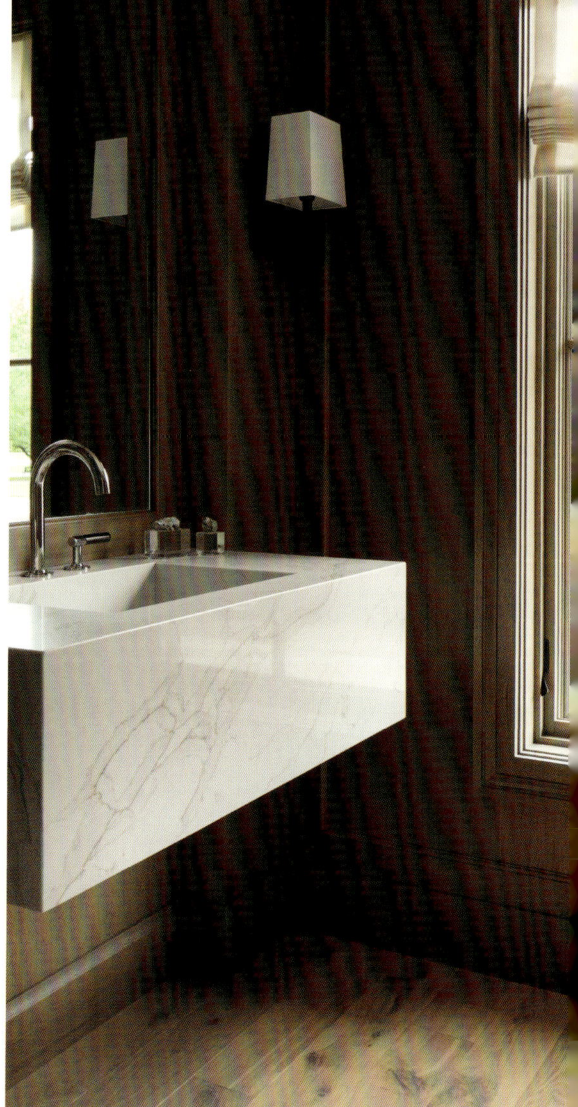

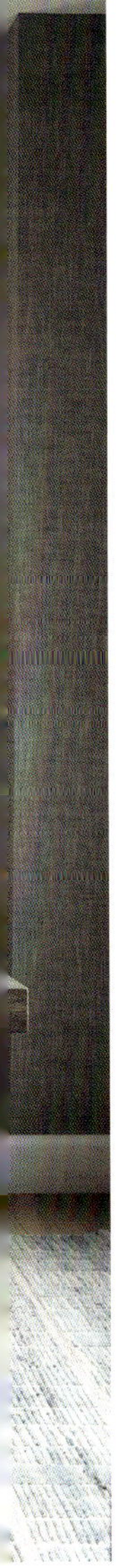

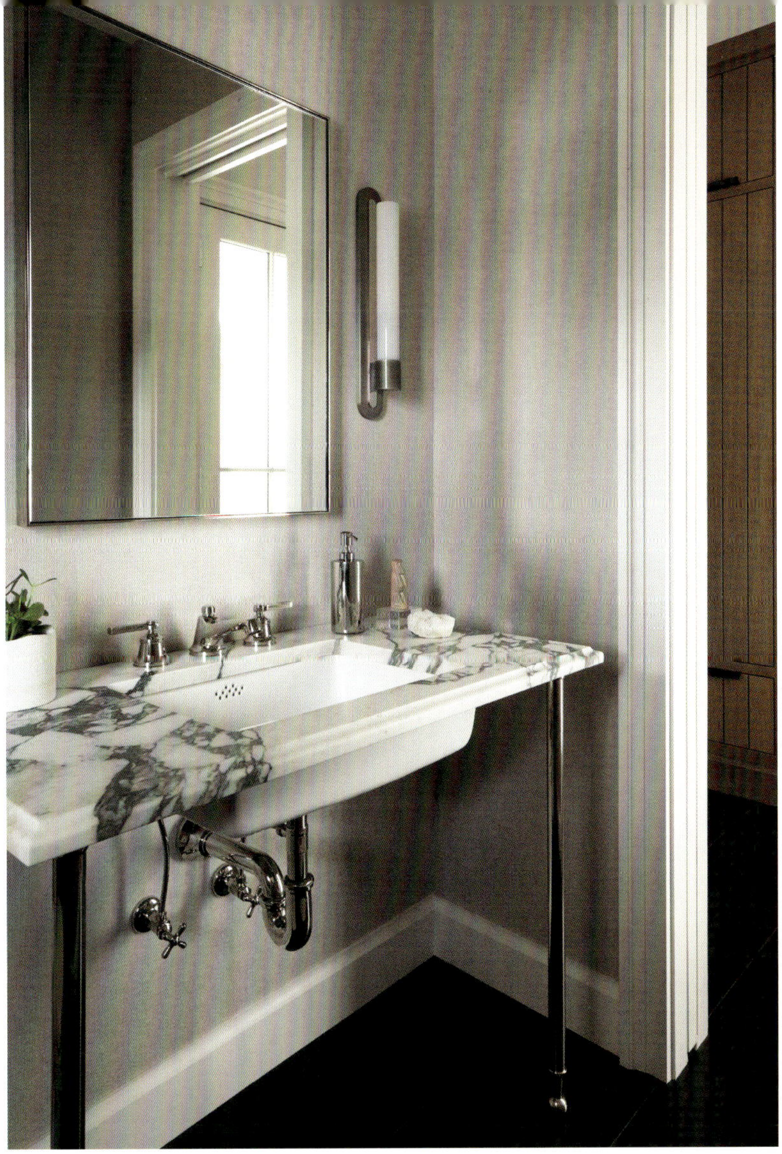

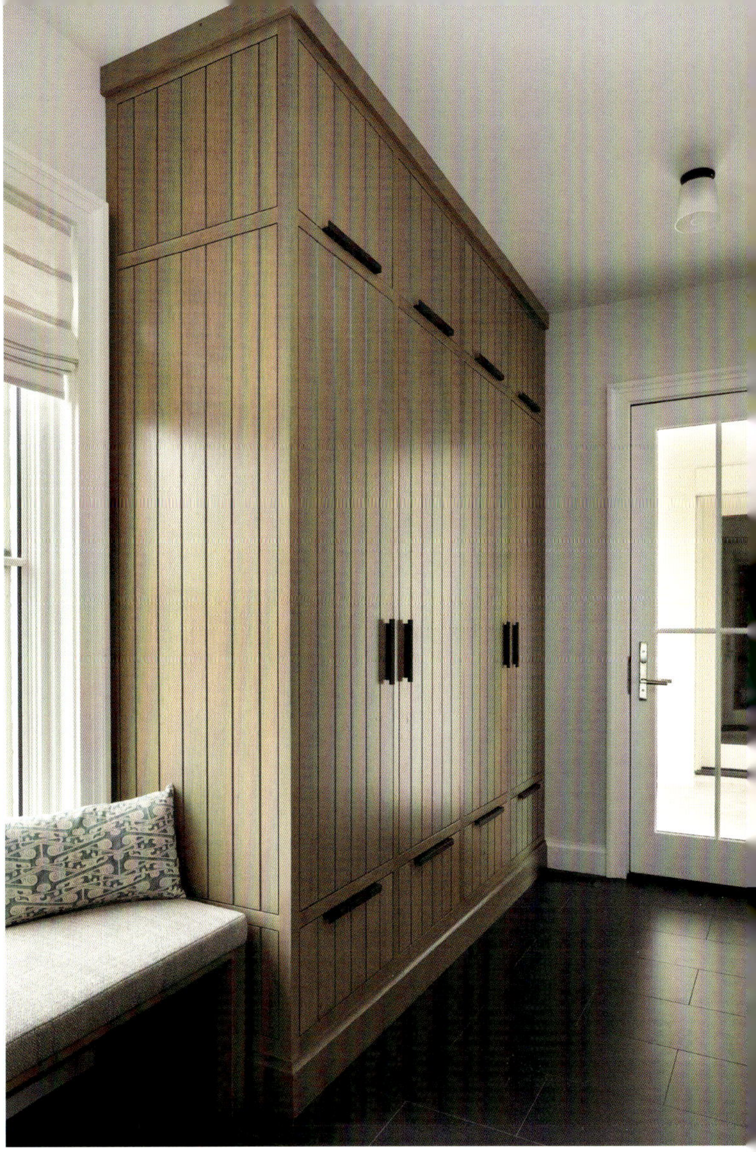

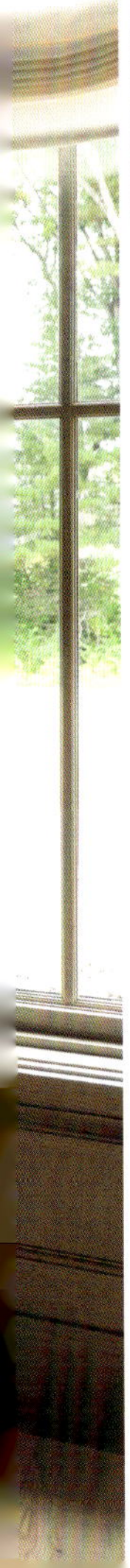

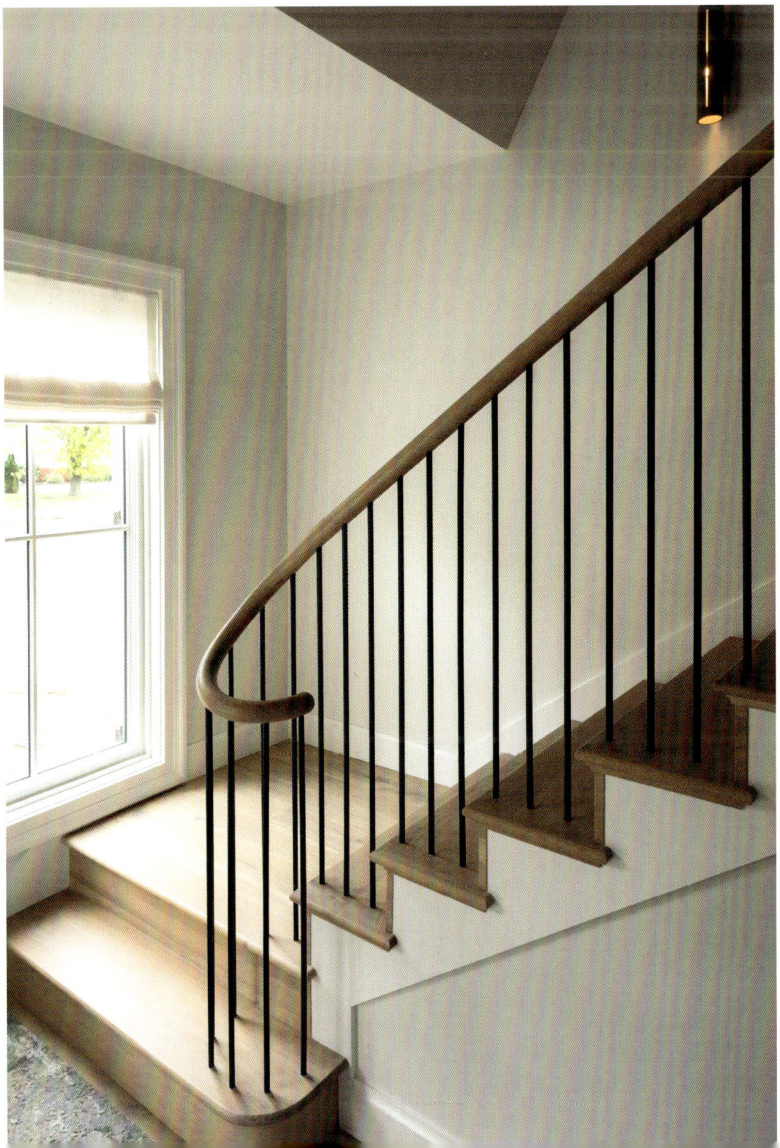

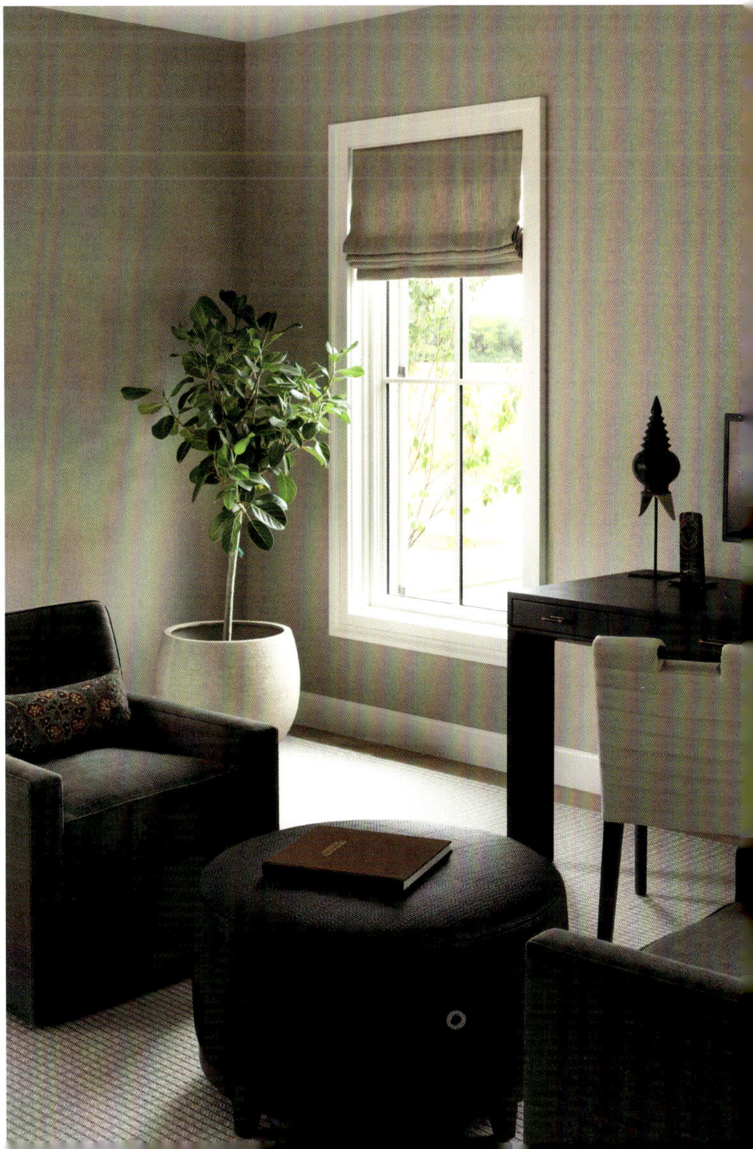

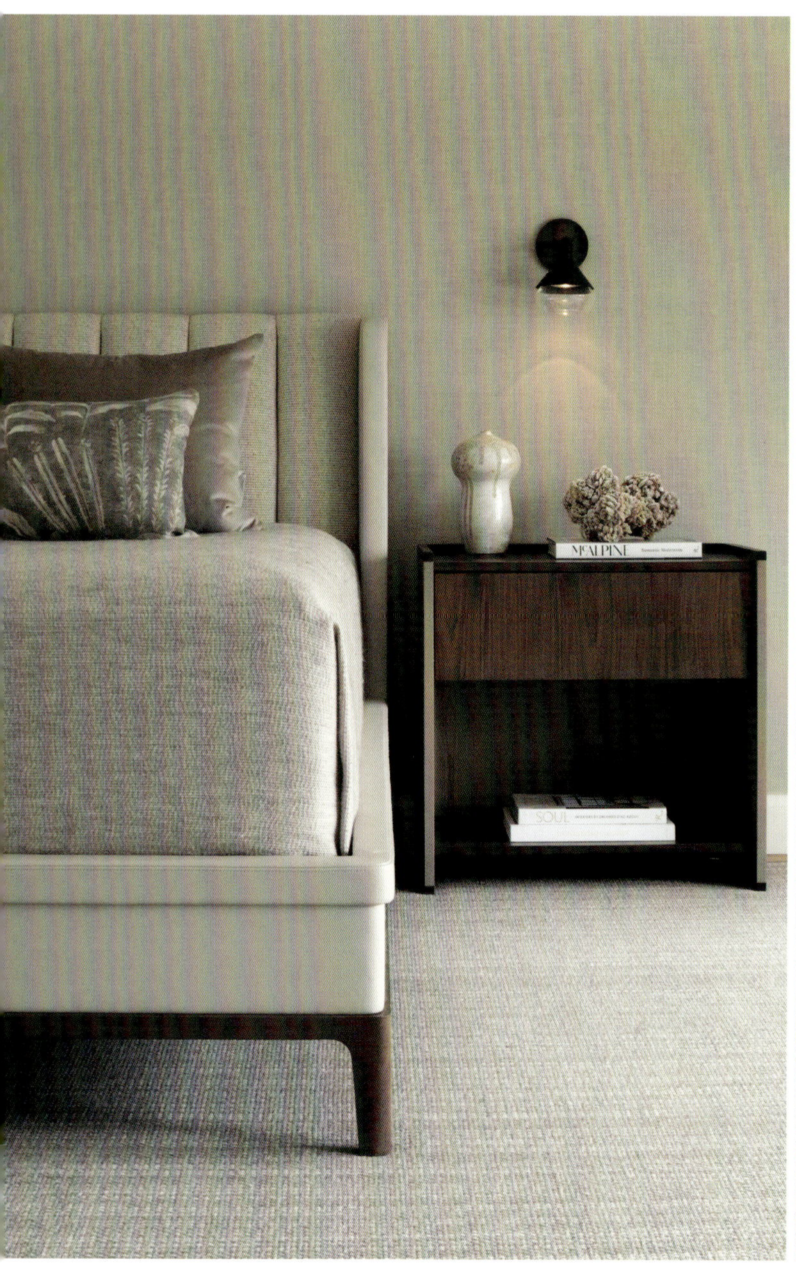

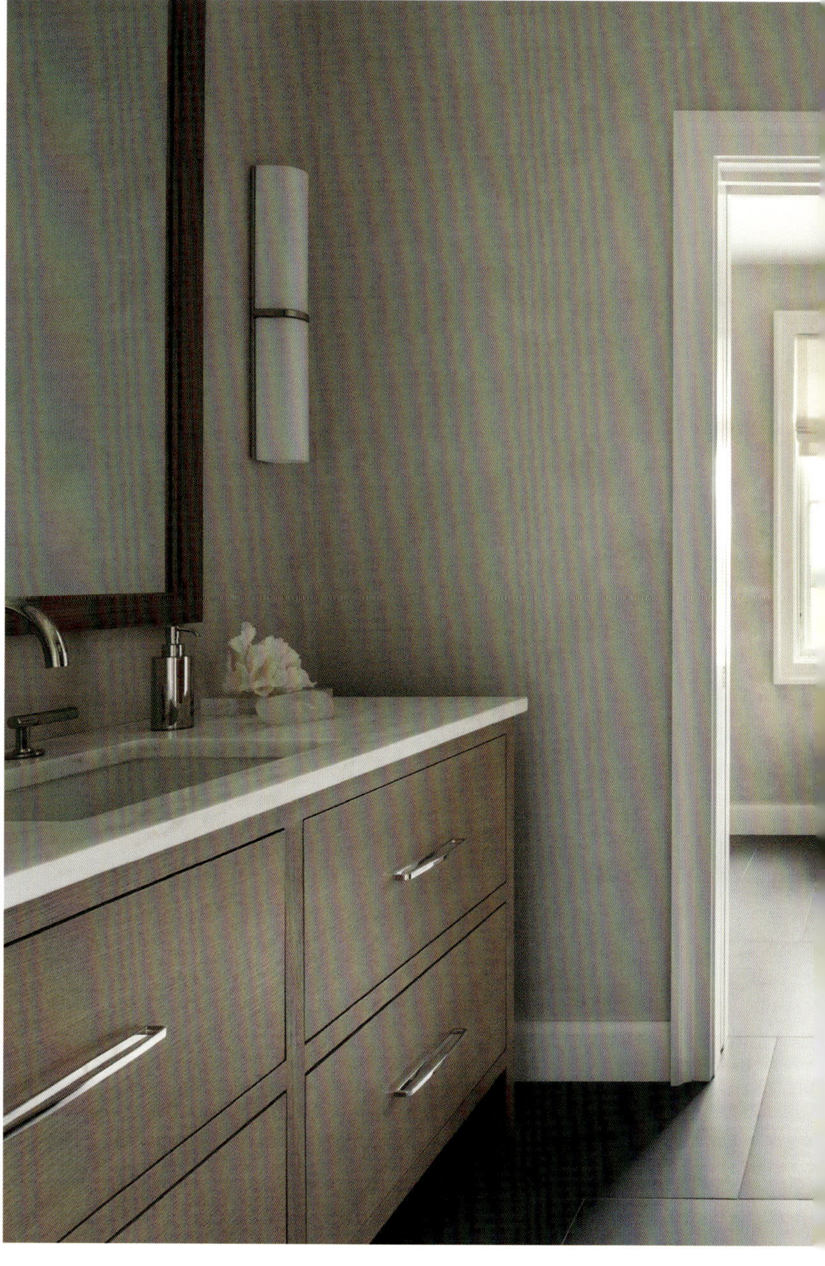

The serene primary suite features a luxurious Merida carpet and Aesthetics wallcovering. The adjoining bathroom showcases hand-applied plaster walls, white oak cabinetry, elegant Articolo sconces, and limestone flooring—a perfect balance of warmth and refinement.

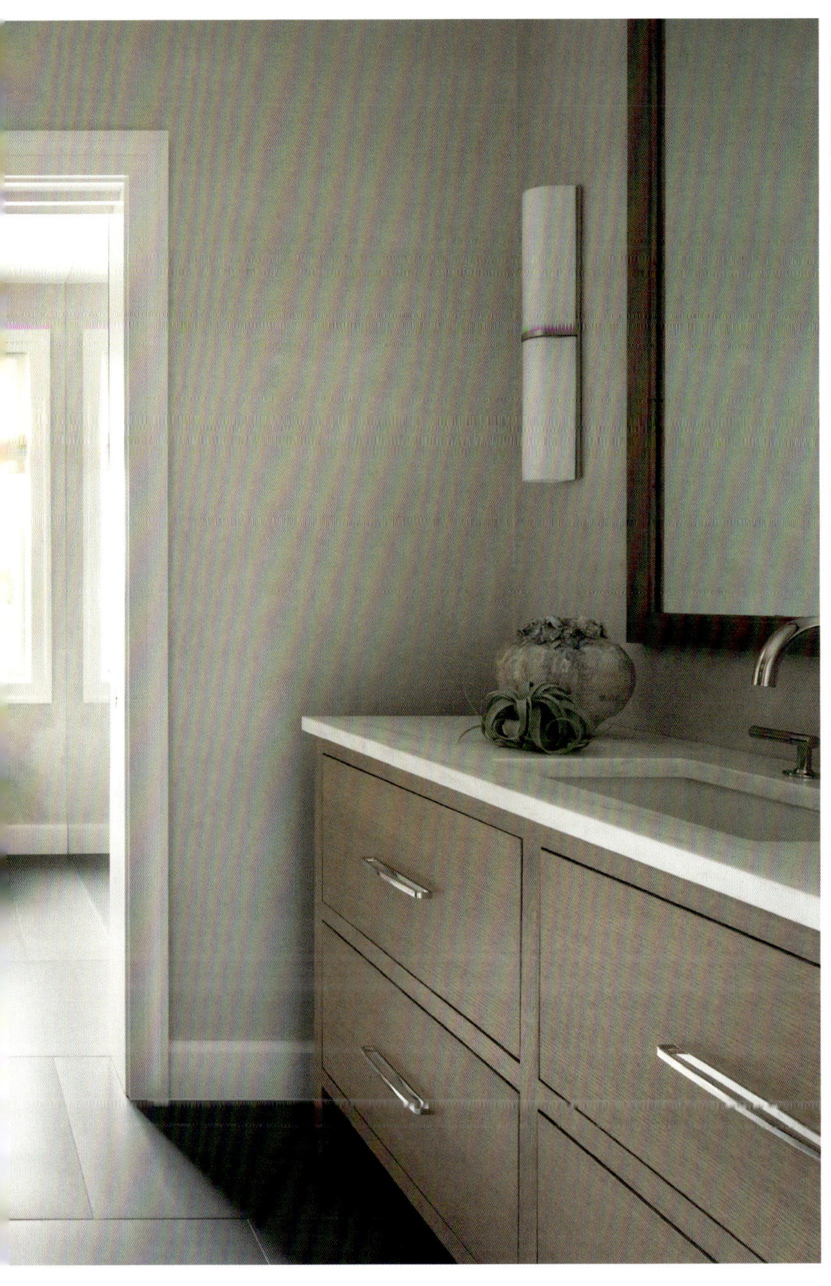
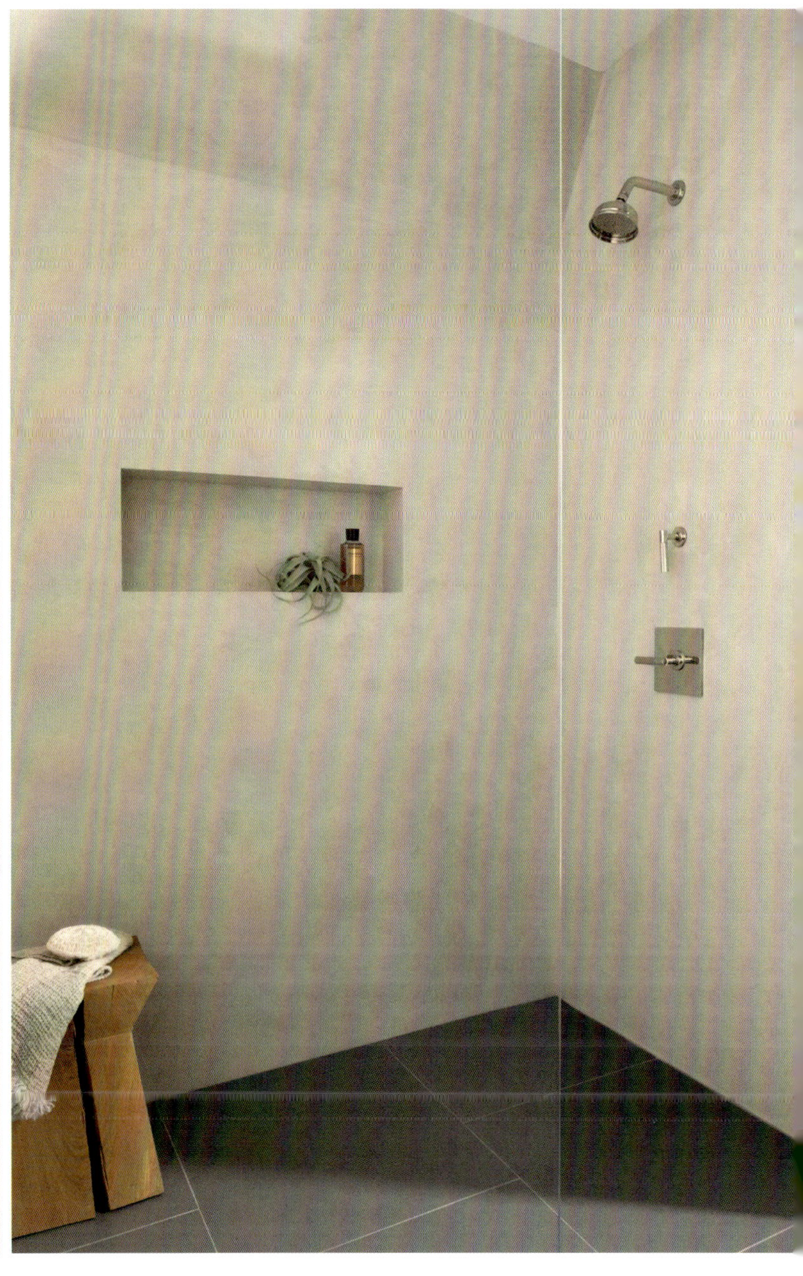

LADDER COMPANY #5

Mary Best Designs

Ladder Company #5, built in 1886 by Sebastian Brand in the heart of Milwaukee's East Side, served as a firehouse until 1914, when it was unceremoniously converted to a storage facility.

It remained that way until a pair of local entrepreneurs with a vested interest in historical preservation succeeded in their two-decade quest to acquire this architectural gem. Working with the architect James Stearns of Iron Jenny Design, their efforts culminated in a reimagined building that balances historical integrity and airy, modern comfort with sustainability, waste reduction, and a softened carbon imprint top of mind.

Turning their sights to the home's interiors, the homeowners sought Mary Best of Mary Best Designs, who is known for her innate ability to approach each project with strategic acumen and creative flair.

The original Cream City brick, a hallmark of Milwaukee's architectural heritage, inspired the home's color palette. Hints of mottled gold and pale pink—colors that conjure the Wisconsin sunrise—appear throughout the home's interior, most notably in a mohair sofa that seems to have absorbed the brick's warm glow. Richer, more saturated versions extend the reference, appearing in area rugs and patterned textiles. Soaring ceilings and large windows provide abundant natural light.

"My job was to contrast the hard surfaces of the interior architecture with soft, comfortable, inviting furnishings," Best explained. She succeeded in her task by choosing relatively streamlined silhouettes, interspersed with traditional accents. The industrial bones of the building—concrete floors, open glass staircases, steel beams—now coexist harmoniously with carefully considered furnishings that invite family and friends to relax in the space. "The juxtaposition of industrial and residential finishes creates a unique sensory experience that charms at every turn," she notes.

At its core, this is more than just a house; it's a community staple that beats with the rhythm of family life. With two college age children and a feline friend in residence, the space has been carefully curated to be "bright, cheerful, interesting, not fussy, everyday livable," exactly as the owners requested.

In this intimate corner, a bespoke Paul Downs dining set meets a vintage sideboard for stylish dining. Host chairs upholstered in Zak + Fox Tulu Sumac complement mohair side chairs illuminated by a Visual Comfort Viaggio chandelier. The artworks include two Madeline von Foerster paintings.

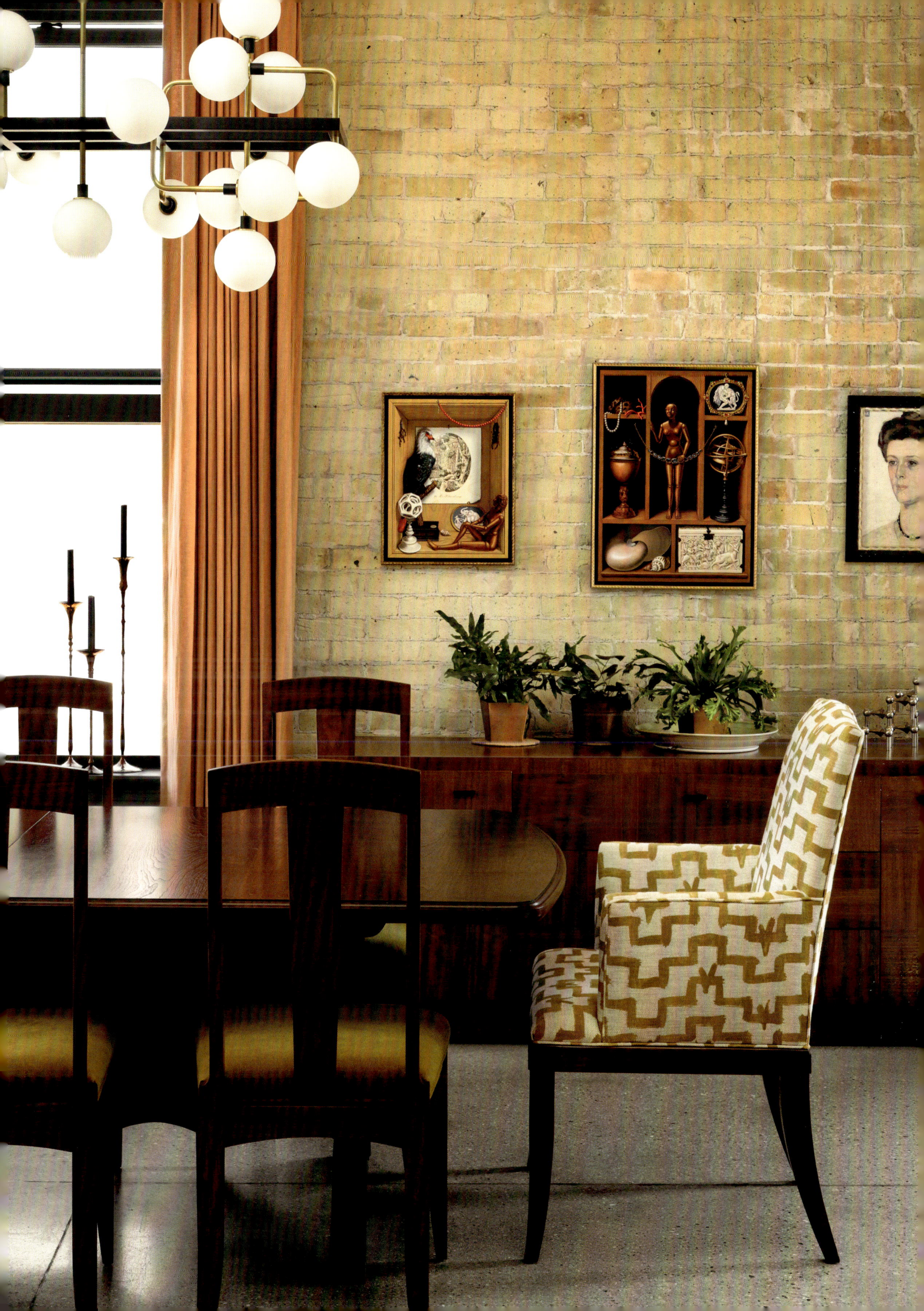

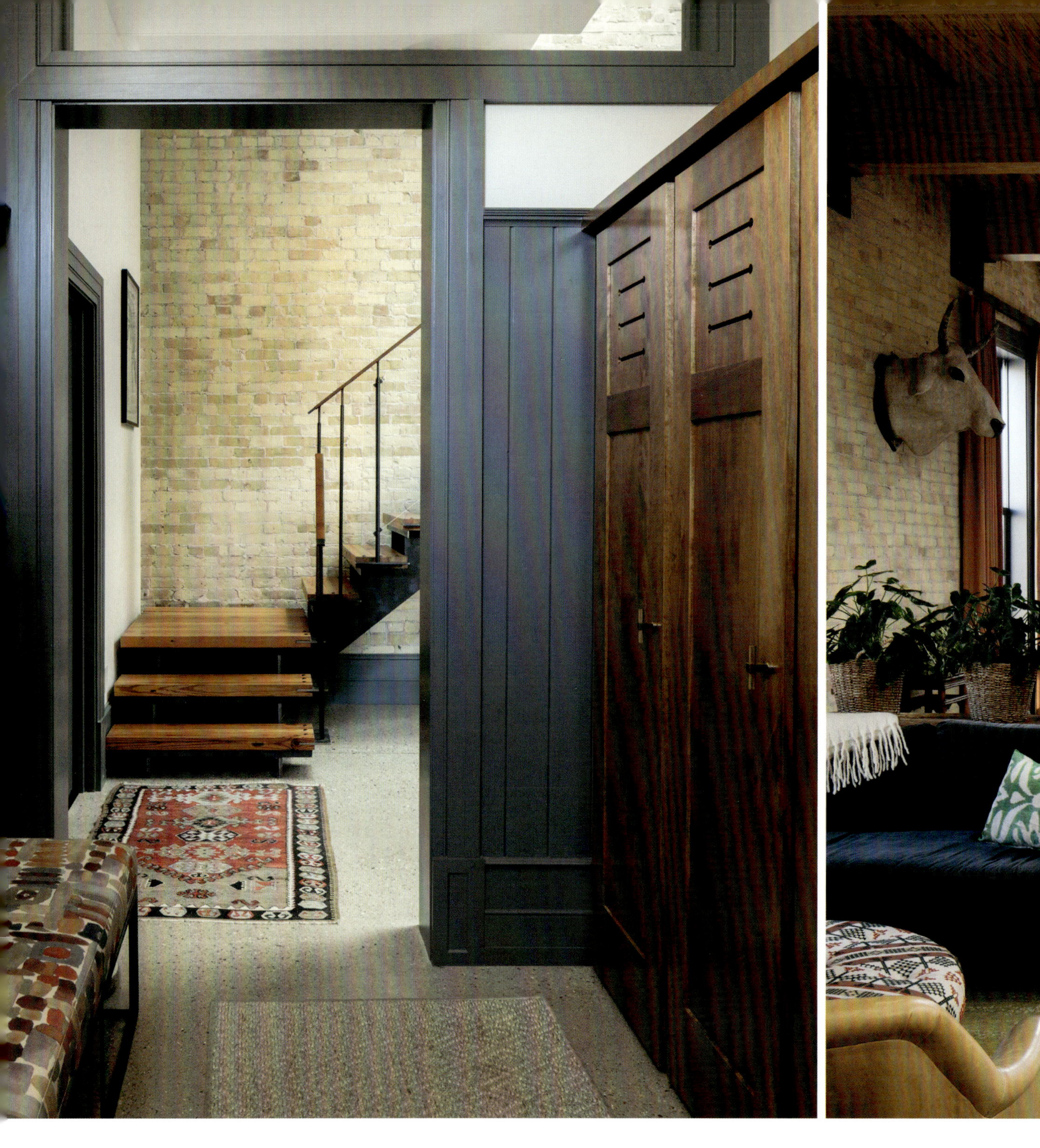

Historic Cream City brick is seen throughout this home, where old meets new through thoughtful material selection. Original Douglas fir—some reclaimed from 150-year-old first-floor lumber with growth rings predating the American Revolution—creates warmth in the timber ceiling beams and staircase treads.

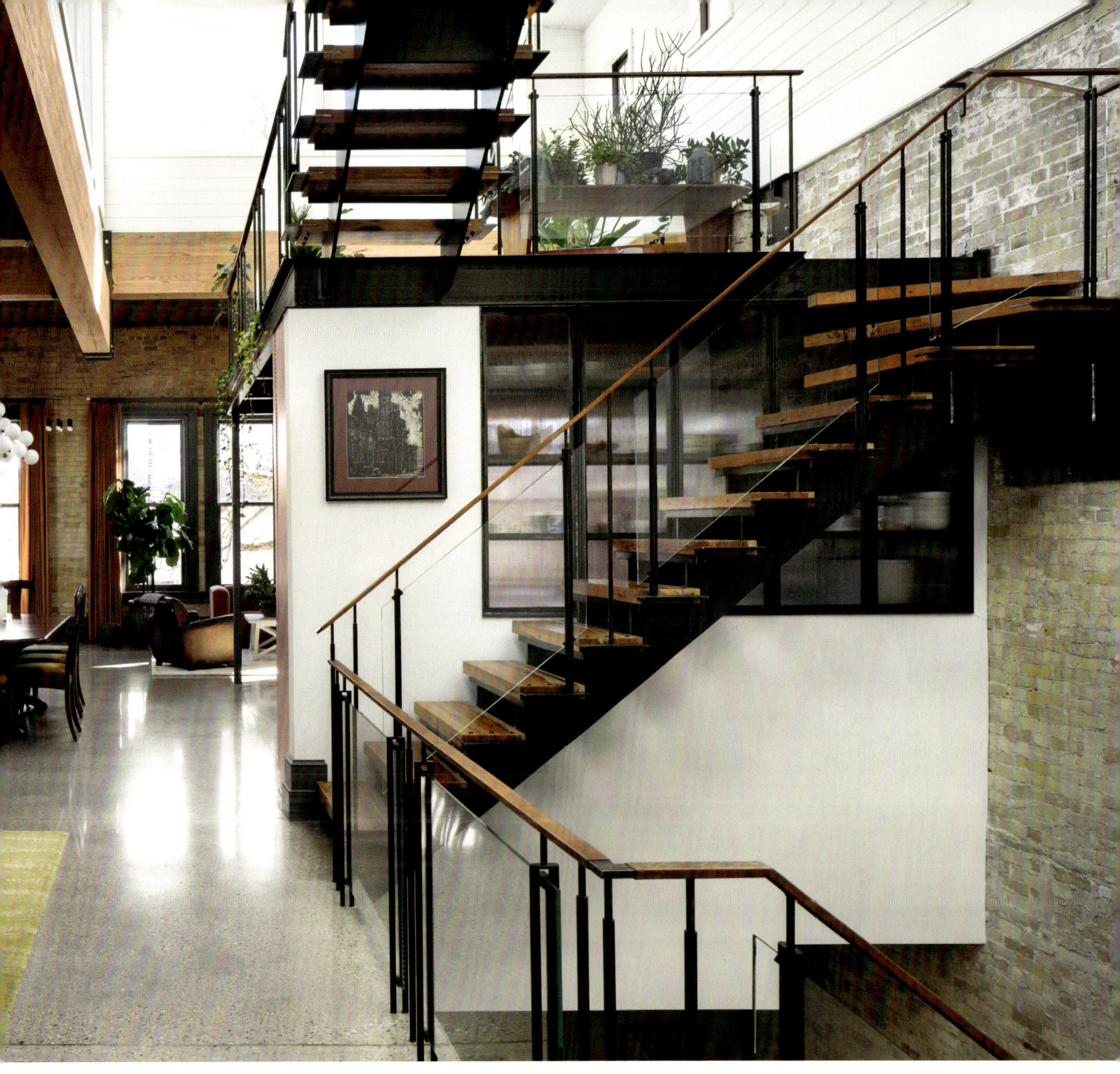

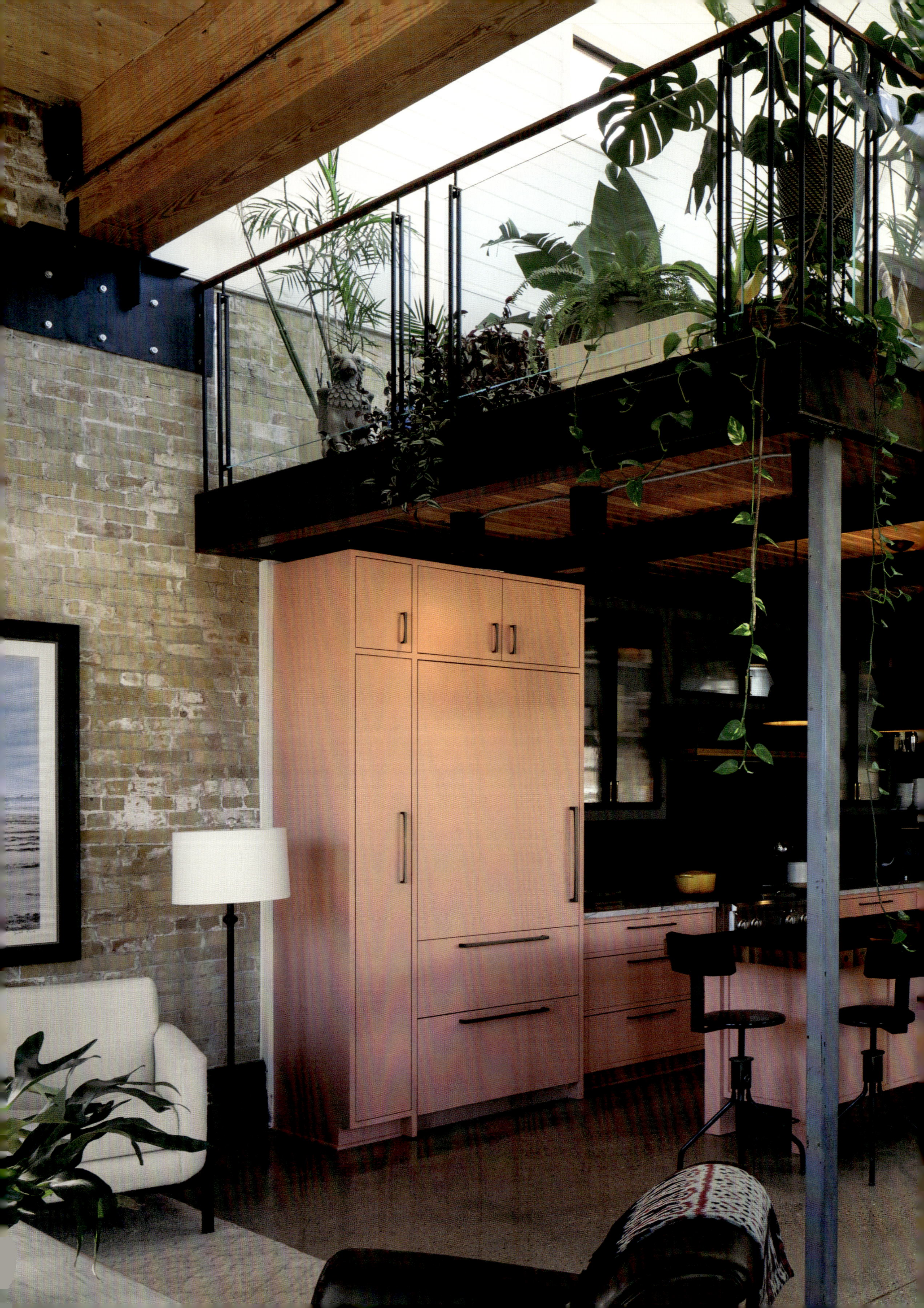

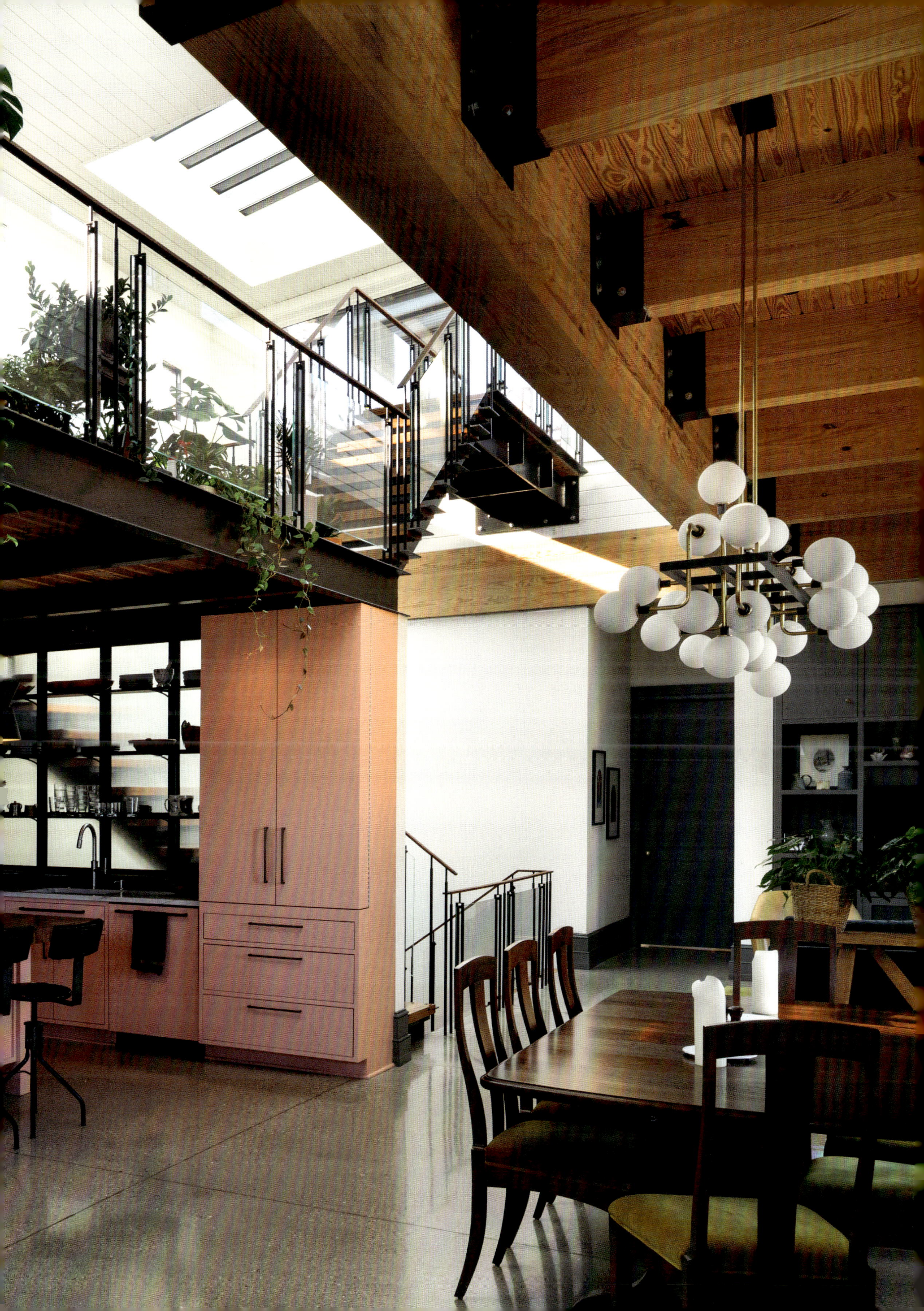

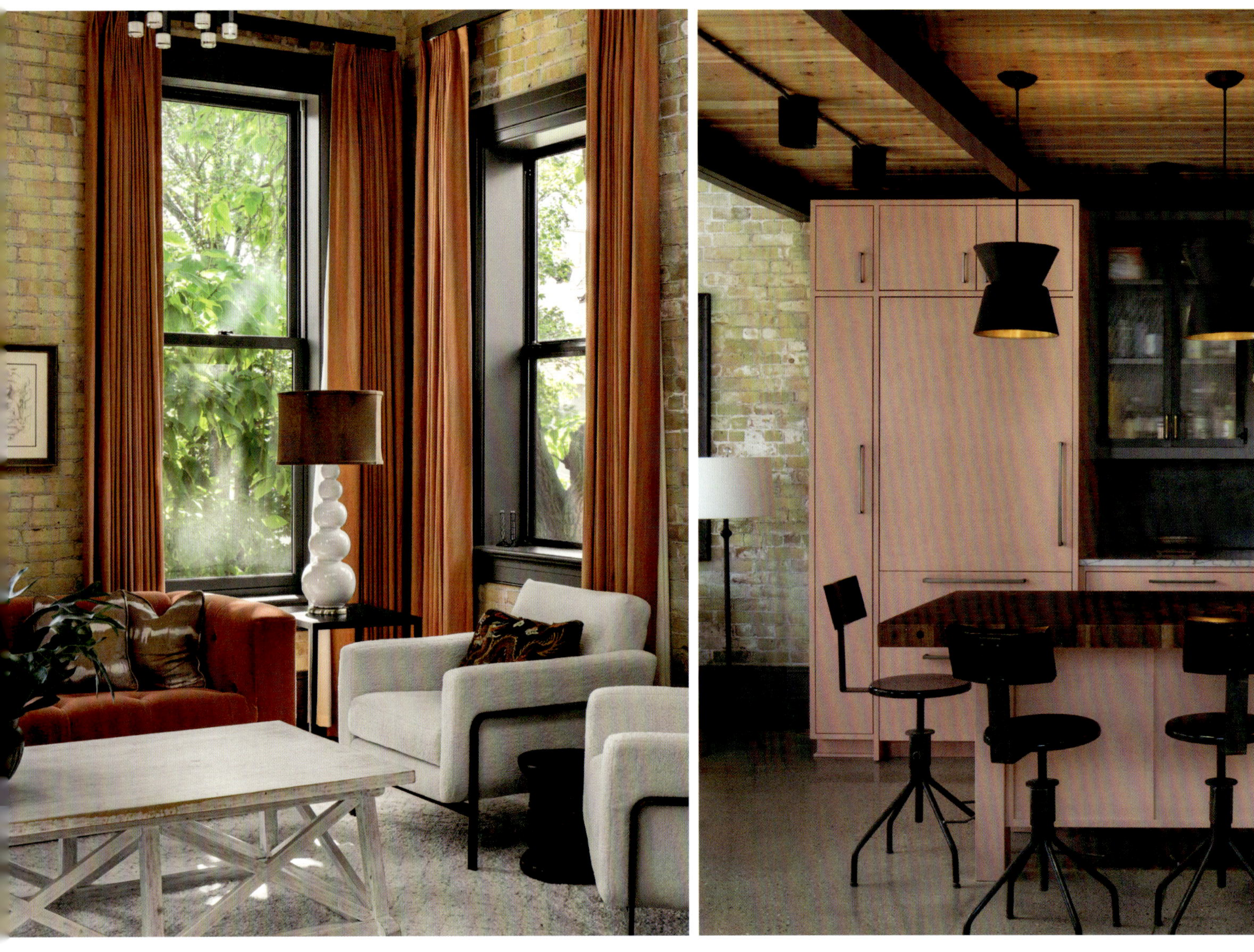

PREVIOUS: Hovering above a blush-pink kitchen with a welcoming breakfast bar, a versatile plant loft doubles as a sanctuary with comfortable seating, a compact desk, and space for indoor yoga sessions during colder months.

ABOVE: A thoughtful palette connects three distinct spaces: the living room on the left, the central kitchen, and the right seating area. Benjamin Moore's Kendall Charcoal unifies window surrounds, the kitchen backsplash, and bookshelves, while mixed steel elements and stained wood in the kitchen provide a collected-over-time contrast to the consistent gray-painted woodwork.

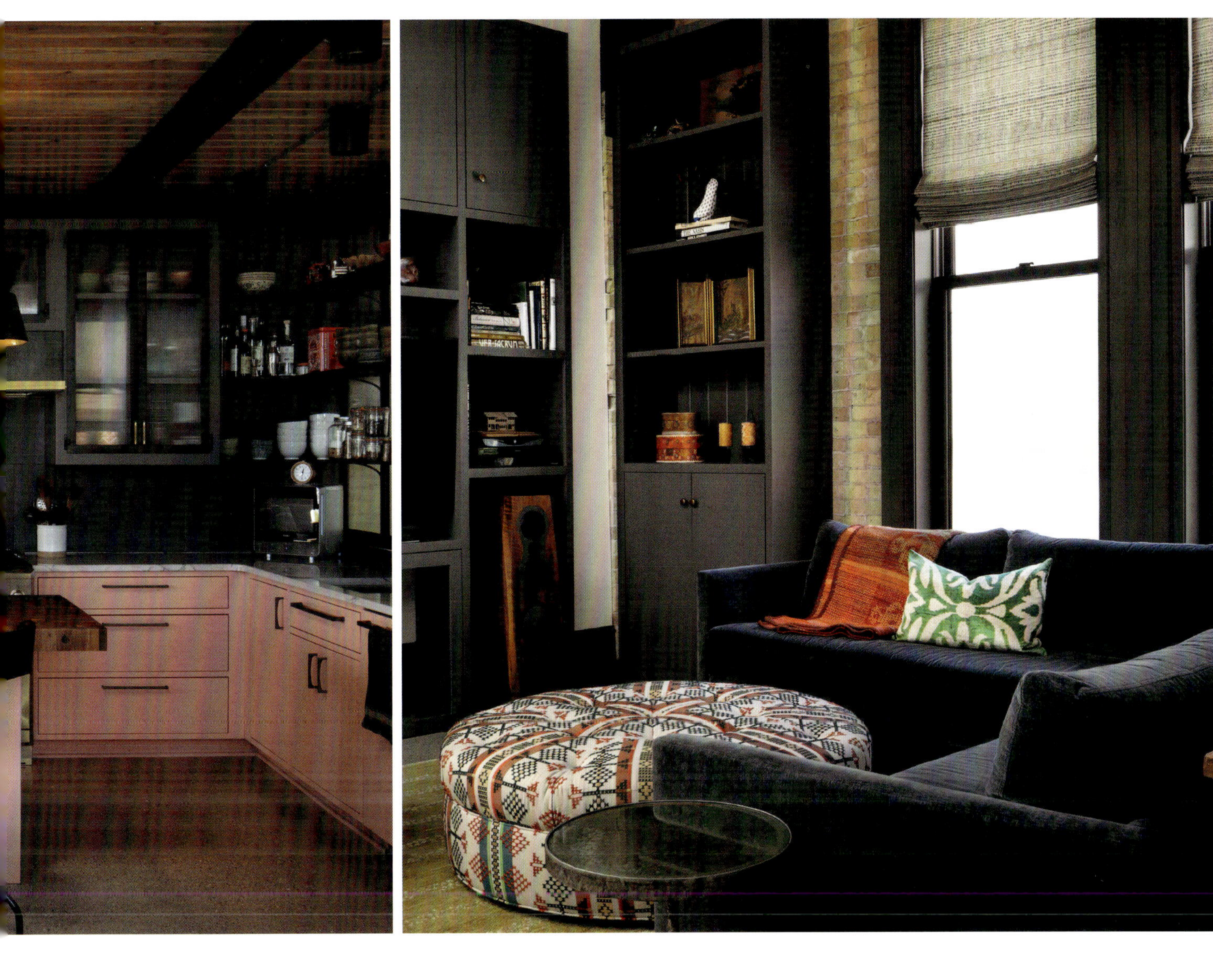

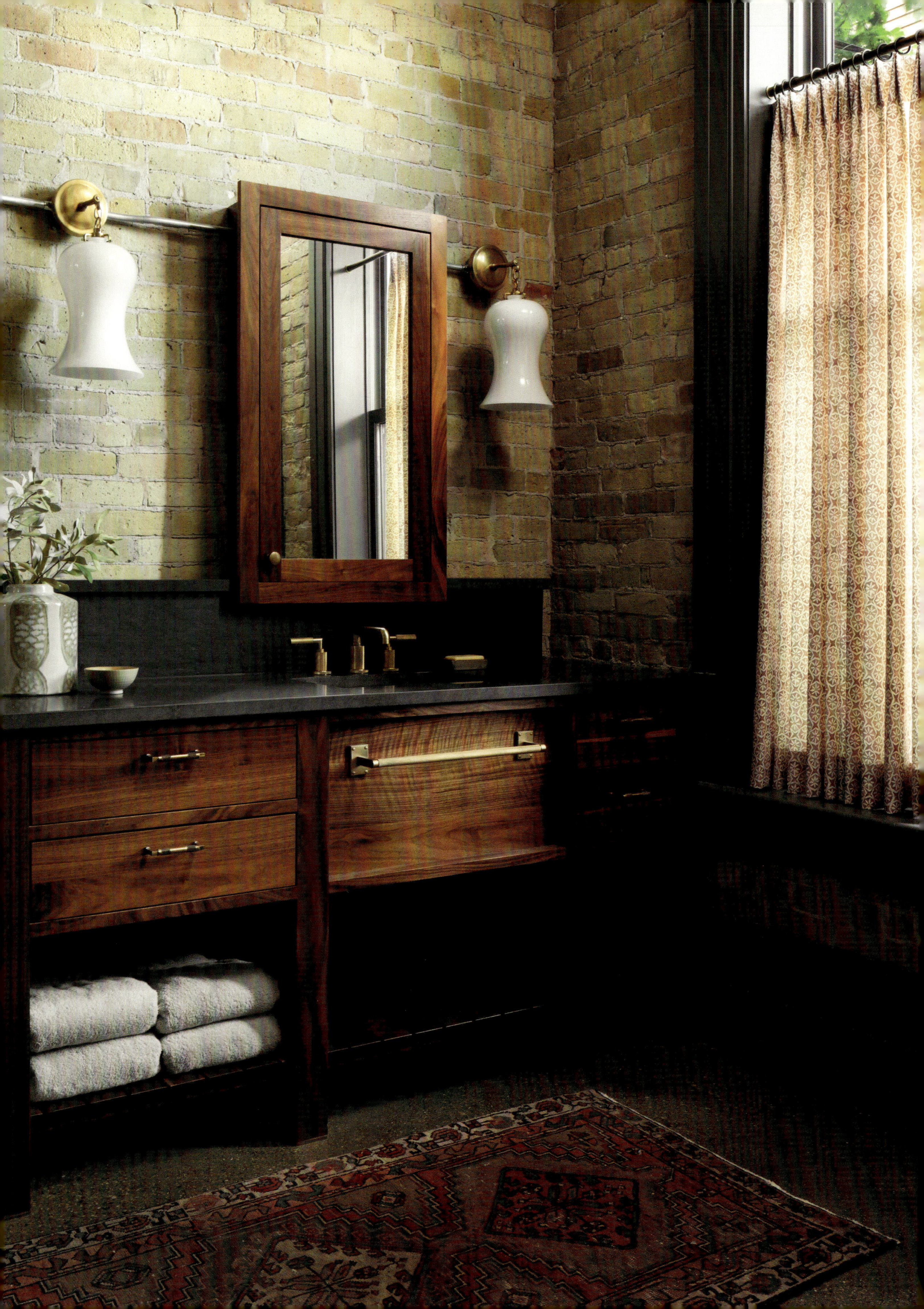

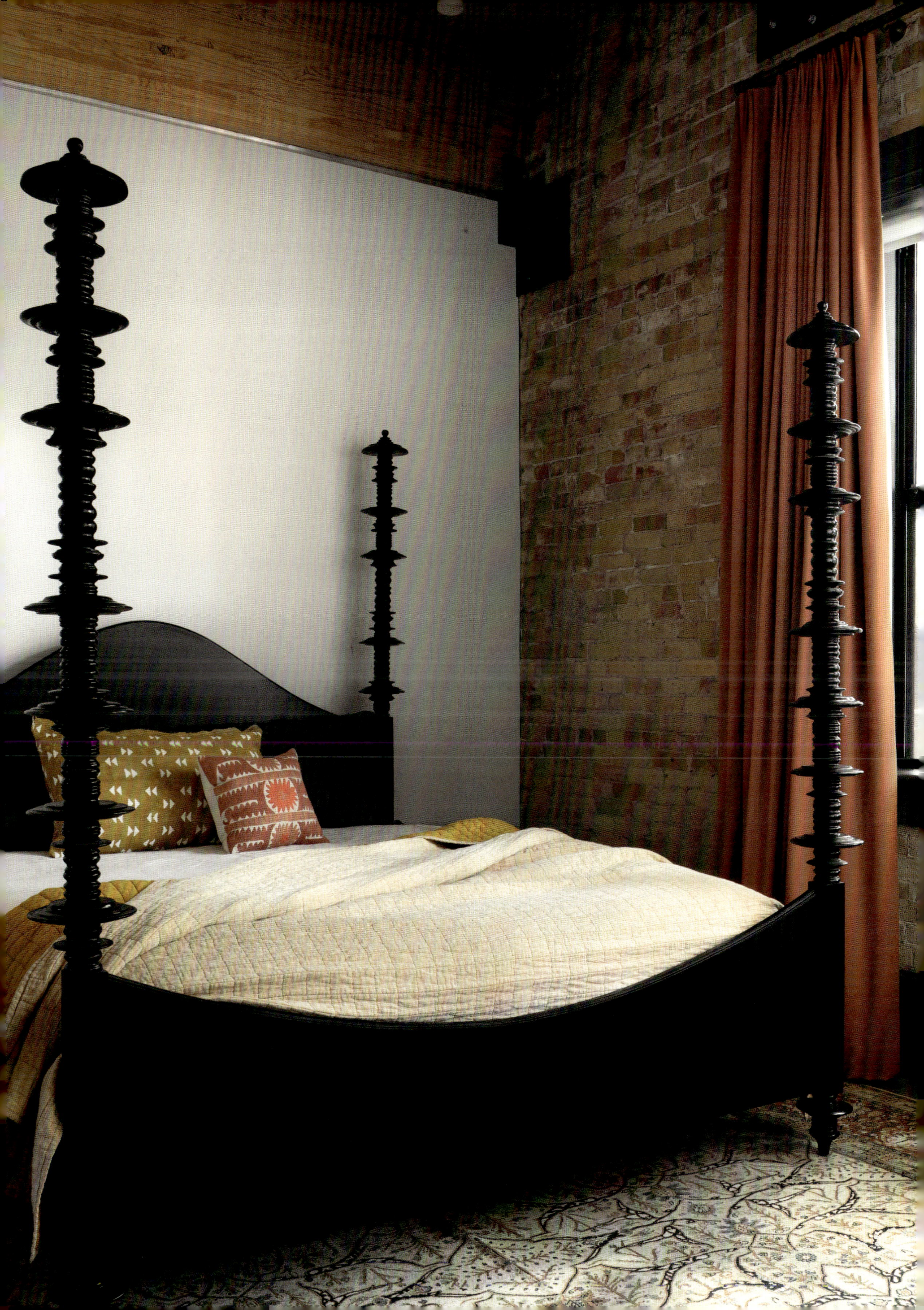

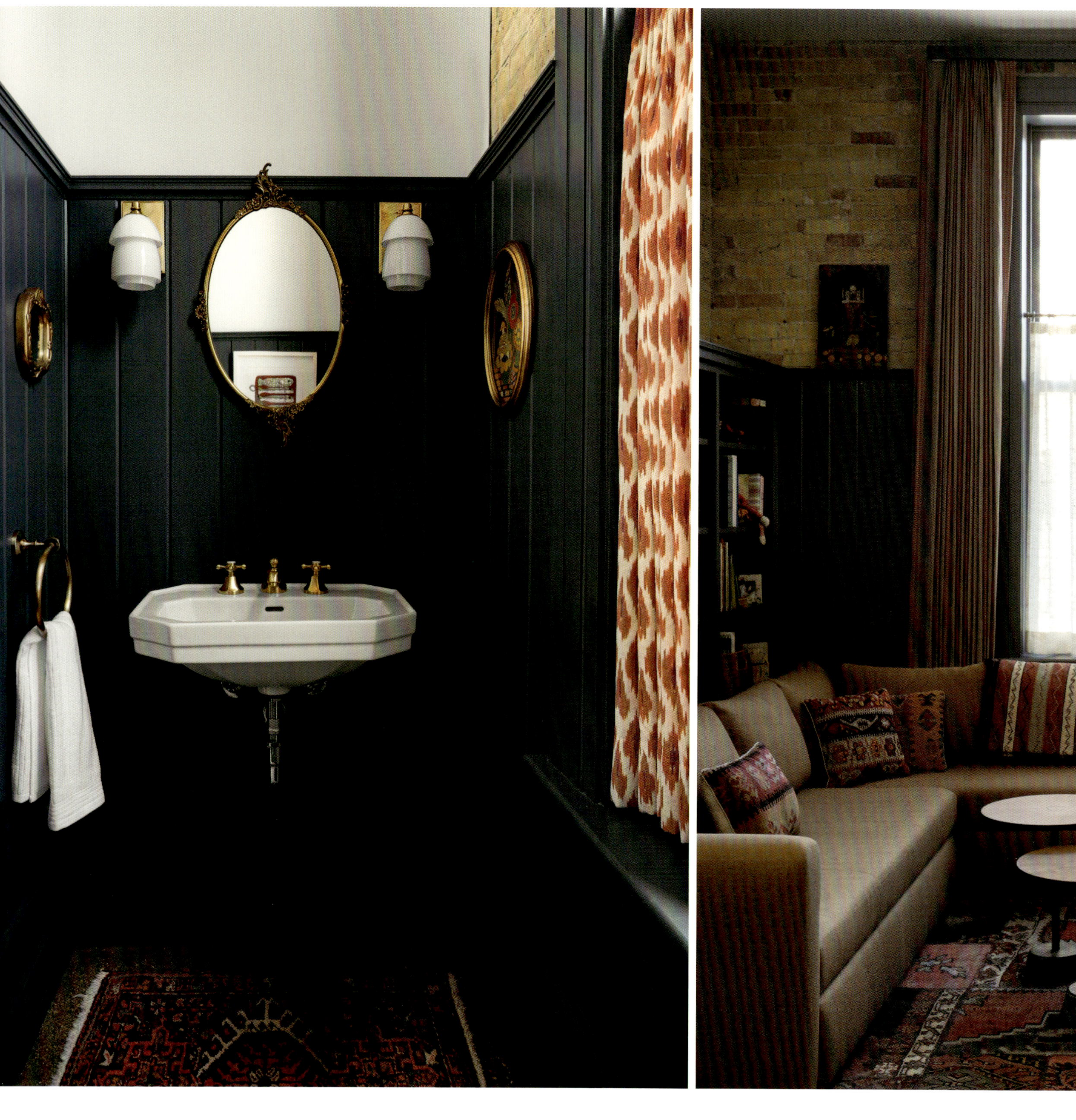

PREVIOUS: The primary suite showcases refined material choices with a walnut vanity and matching mirror in the bathroom, enhanced by brass fixtures and elegant soapstone countertops. Adjacent, the bedroom features a statement-making hand-carved mahogany bed from Noir Furniture that centers the space.

ABOVE: A harmonious trio of youth spaces includes a powder room painted in Farrow & Ball's Inchyra Blue, a "teen lounge" with a Room & Board sofa, and an ingenious bedroom featuring a suspended loft bed accessible via bookshelf stairs, finished in Farrow & Ball's Calke Green with Radish Moon draperies.

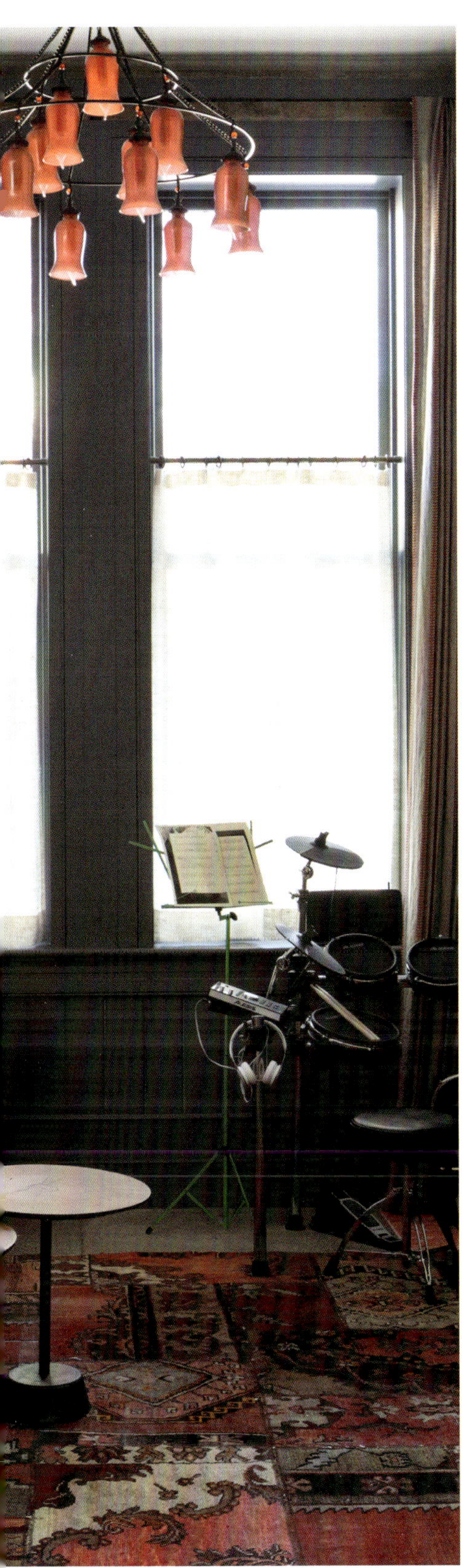

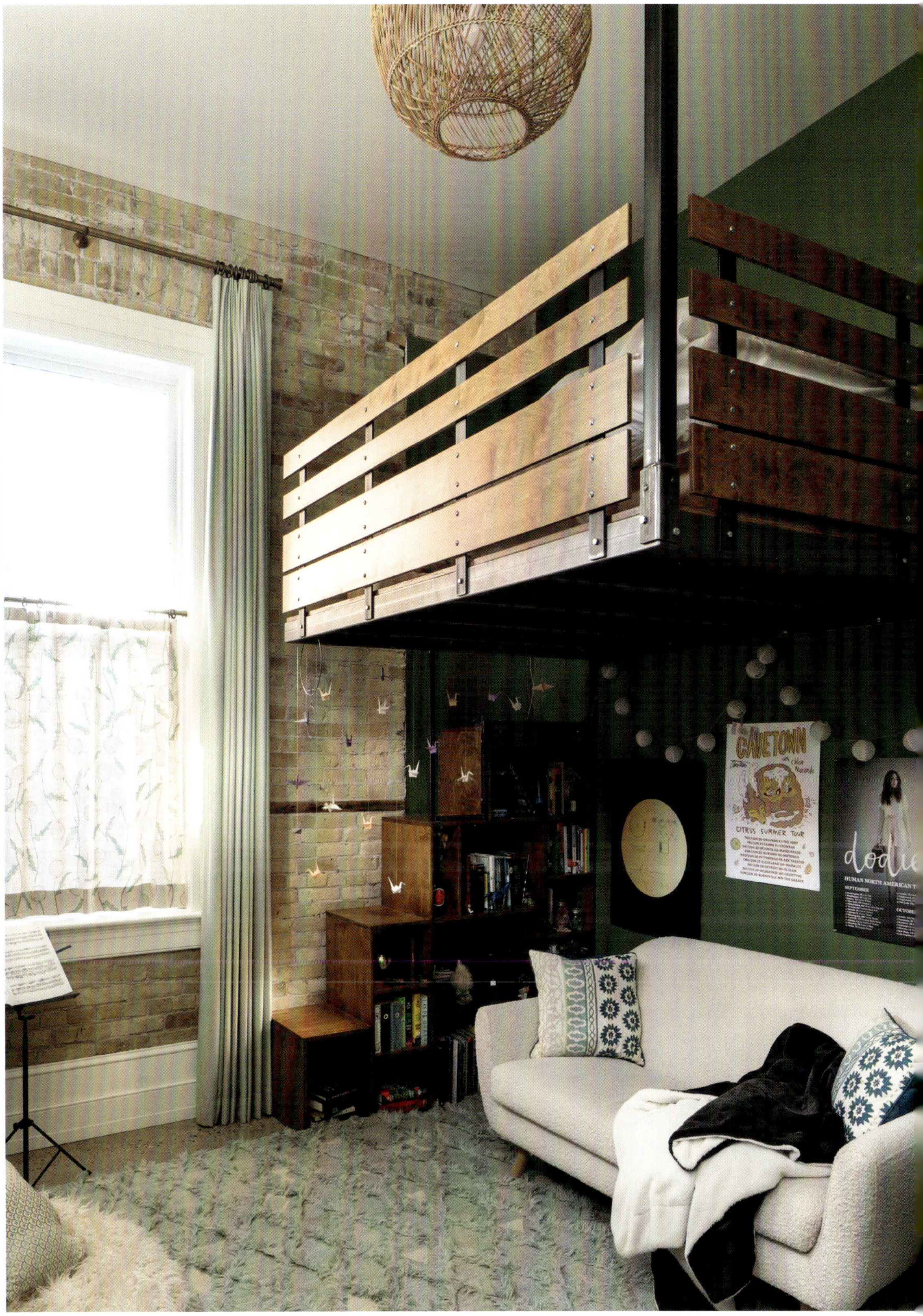

CHICAGO NOIR HIDEAWAY

Kelly Marie Brainerd / KMB Design | Consulting

What began as a standard builder's condominium in the heart of Kinzie Park just steps from the Chicago River was artfully reimagined by designer Kelly Brainerd for a returning client for whom she had previously designed a residence in Milwaukee. Their new collaboration resulted in a profoundly personal home that reflects the homeowner's personality.

The evolution of this home, completed in a six-month window, began with a bold stroke: Every surface—walls, ceilings, trim, and doors—was painted in Sherwin-Williams Black Magic. The resulting rooms create a private sanctuary where the inky surfaces absorb the frenetic tempo of urban living. They are captivating, dramatic, and moodily intimate.

The first-floor exercise room transformed into a cozy home theater. Movie nights now unfold in what was once a space for dumbbells and yoga mats. Sink-in seating and thick crimson drapes lend the space an old-school charm, complete with a nostalgic popcorn machine.

Upstairs, a fireplace replete with tufted seating serves as an inviting gathering spot. The bathroom evokes a nineteenth-century English flower shop with garden-print paper, salvaged hardware, and vintage subway tile. Completing the floor plan is a chef's kitchen anchored by an expansive granite cooking island and ringed in ample black cabinetry.

The third floor is a primary bedroom suite, with an open shelving system showcasing an impressive shoe collection. An adjacent master closet was outfitted with integrated laundry facilities. The fourth-floor guest suite crowns the home and gives visitors their private domain, with a spacious bedroom, a comfortable living room, and a full, beautifully appointed bath.

With this project, Brainerd challenged preconceived notions about Midwestern design by reconsidering that homes in this region must always reflect open prairies and changing seasons. From room to room, it reads more like a boutique hotel suite than a typical Chicago home, but it still maintains the warmth of a private residence for its multifaceted owner, a single professional who shares the space with a canine companion and frequently hosts visiting friends and family.

The existing staircase was transformed with a rich, warm brown stain applied to floors, banister, treads, and risers, while a plush runner provides comfort underfoot and noise reduction between floors. The landing showcases a cherished vintage rug that traveled with the homeowner from Milwaukee to Chicago, surrounded by the client's personally collected photography—featuring Tupac, Prince, and Muhammad Ali—newly unified through consistent matting and framing.

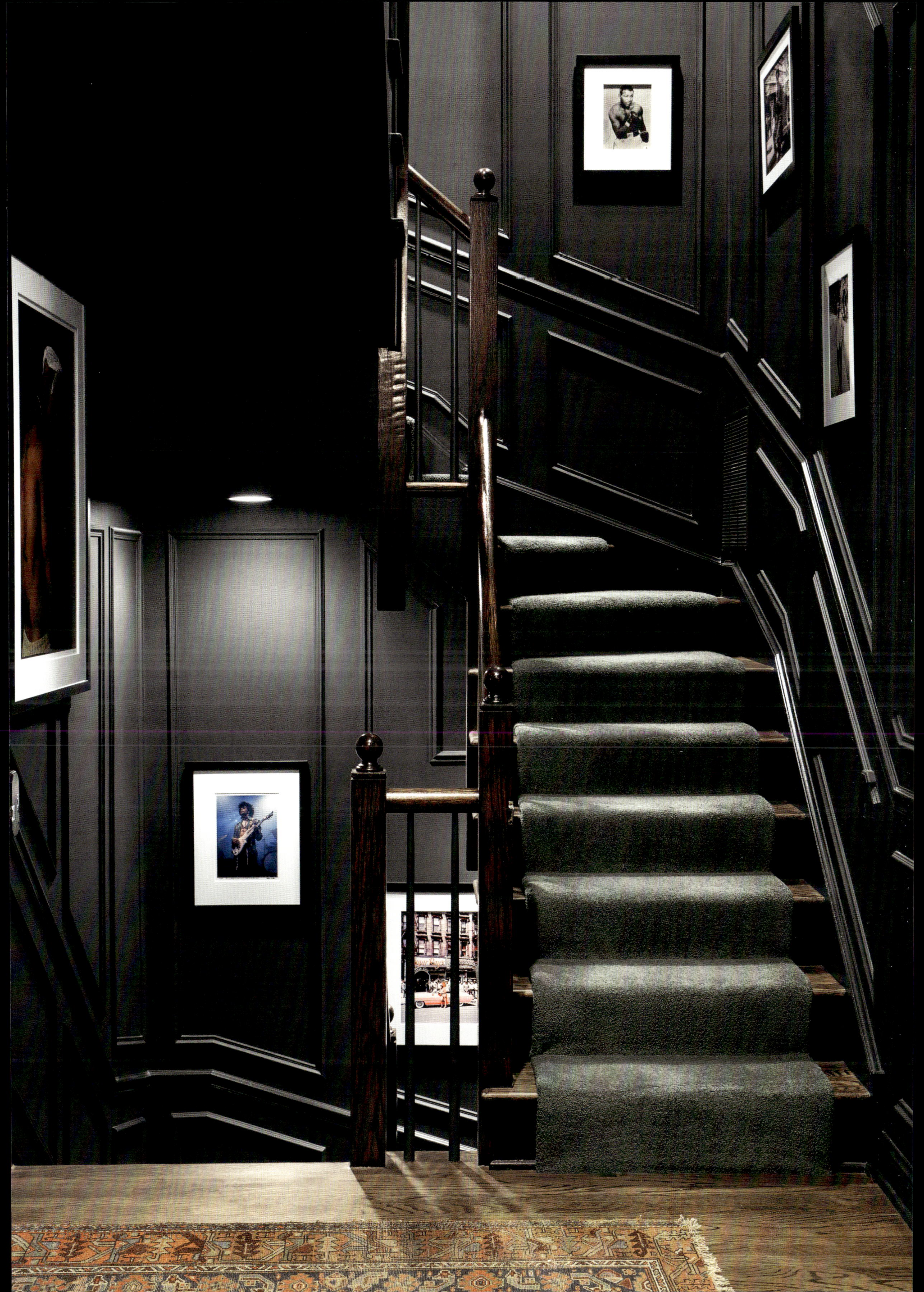

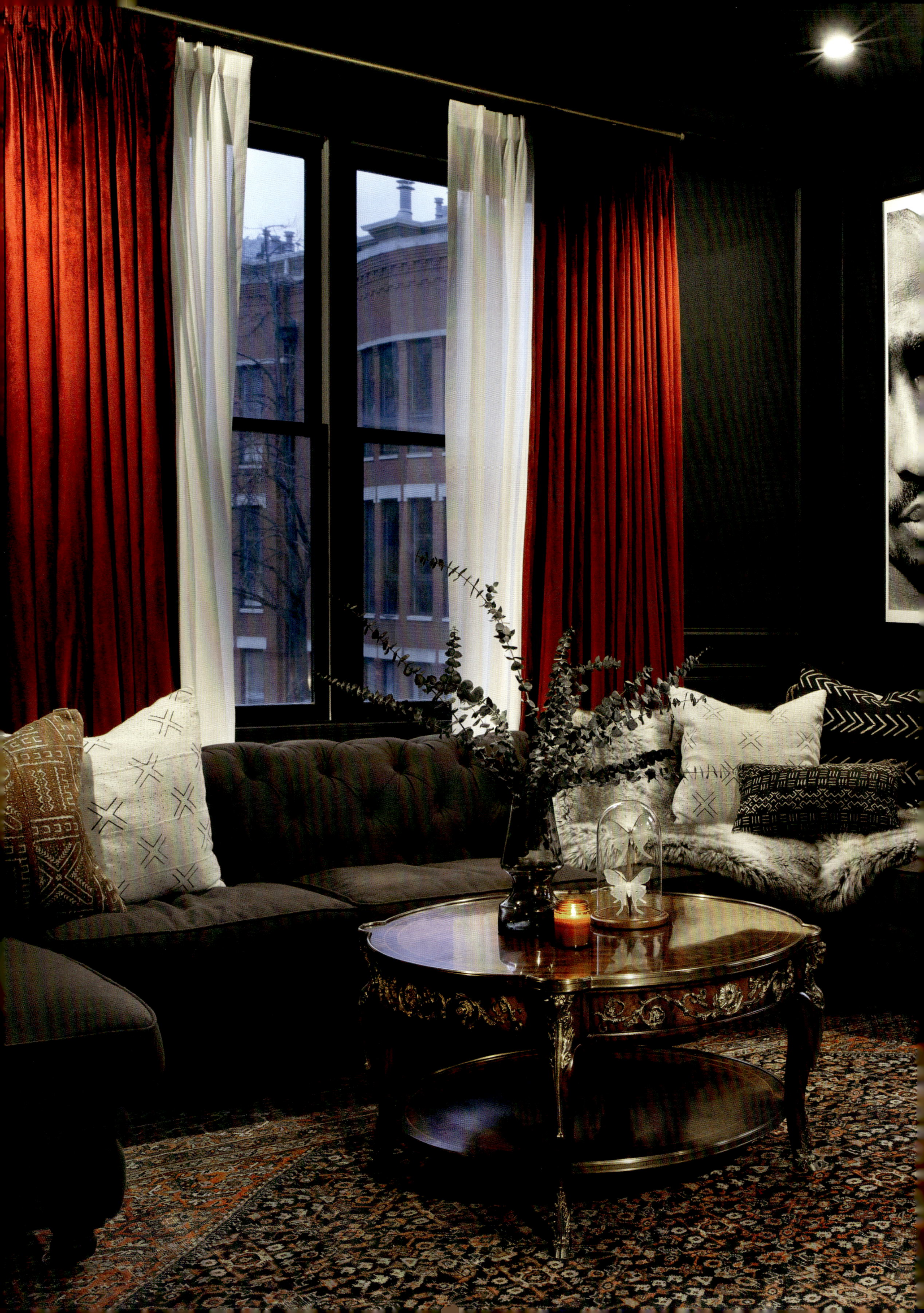

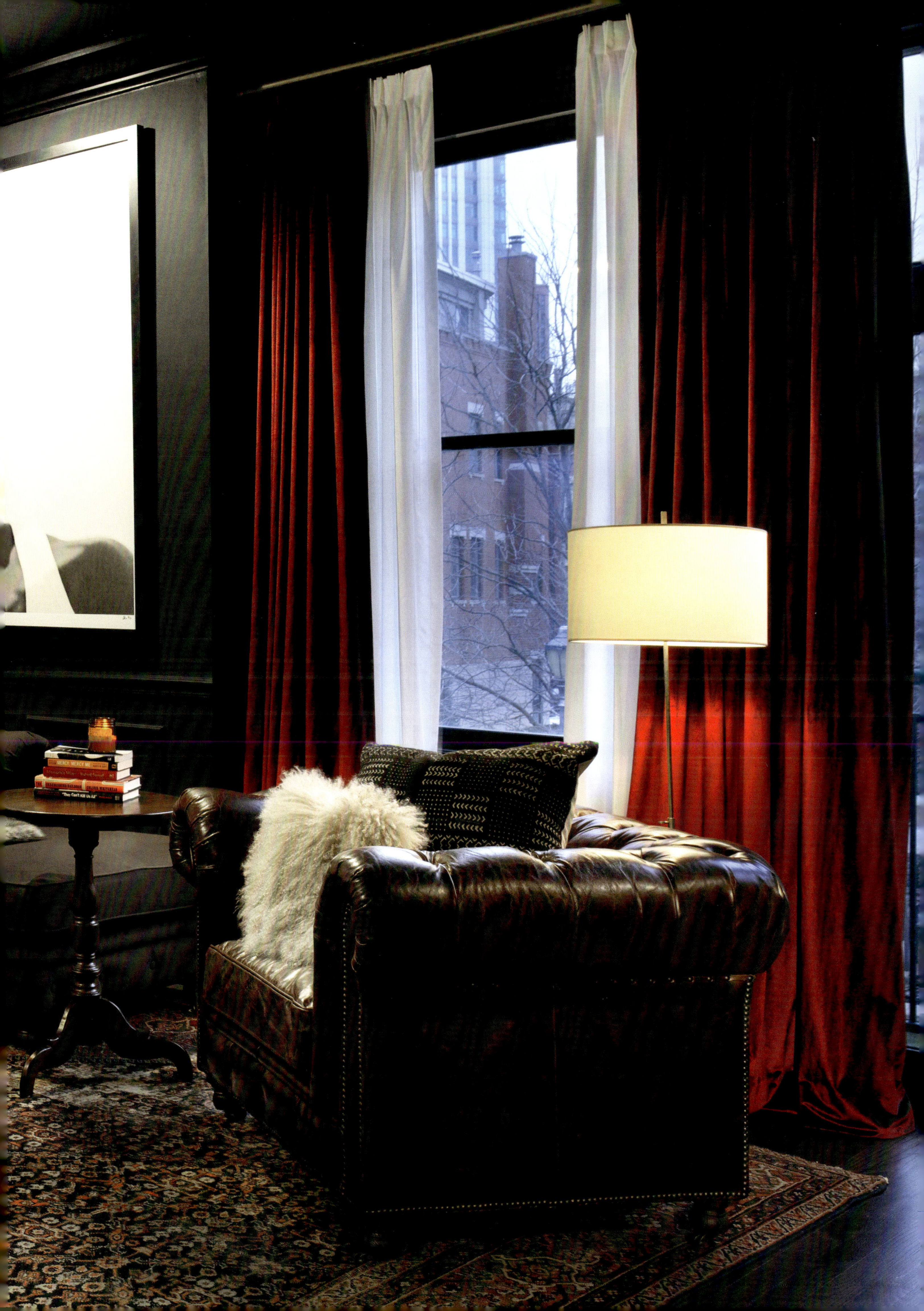
MERCY, MERCY ME
"They Can't Kill Us All"

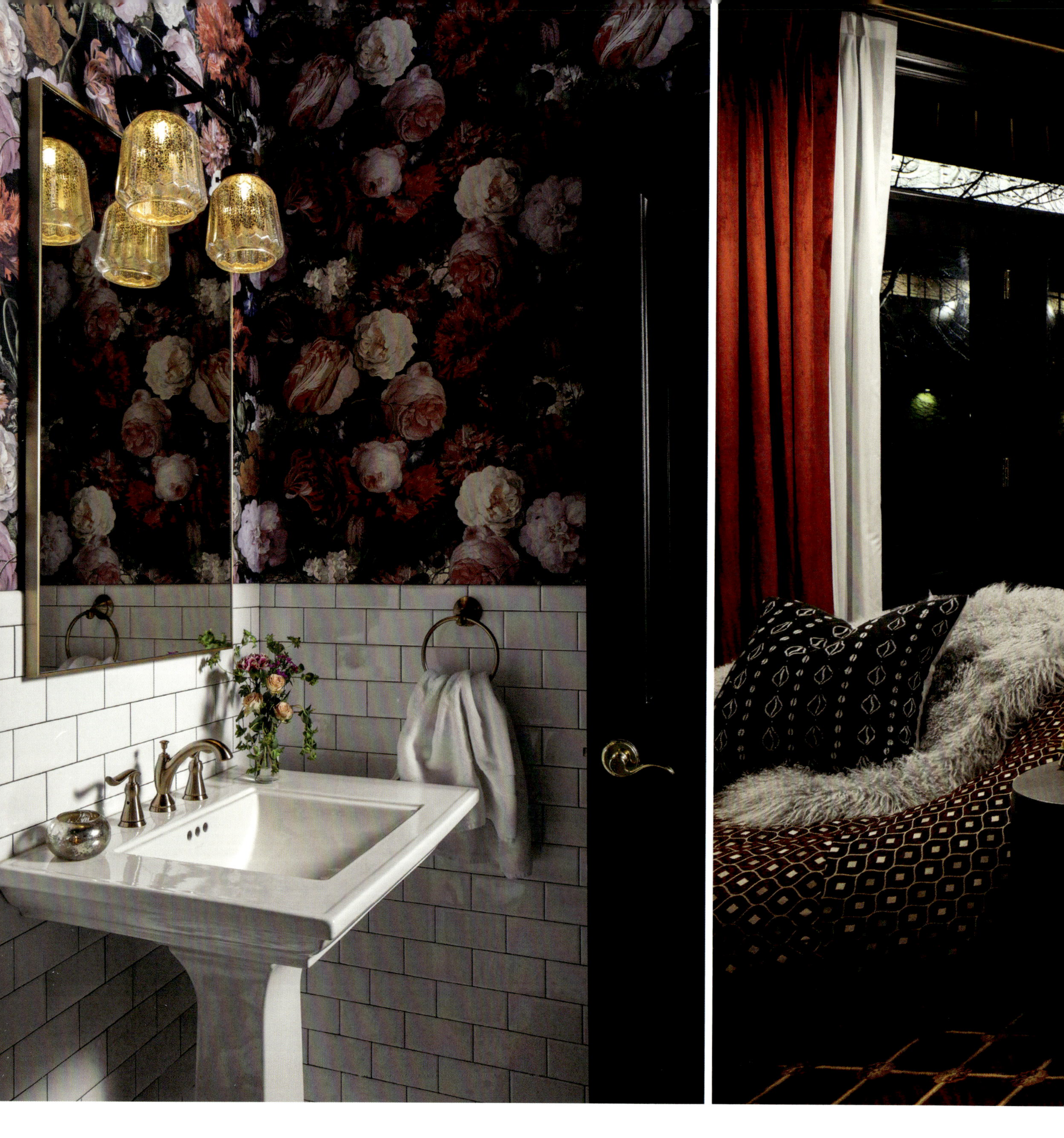

PREVIOUS: This inviting living room features a bespoke sofa designed specifically for ample seating. A handsome leather lounge chair creates balance, while the vintage coffee table—thoughtfully sourced from a local antique store—adds character. Wall art includes a powerful photograph by renowned artist Chi Modu of the late Tupac Shakur.

ABOVE: A thoughtfully designed full bathroom serves dual purposes—daily use and private accommodations for overflow guests who might utilize the comfortable media room as a sleeping space when the house reaches capacity. The media room features a generously sized button-tufted double chaise positioned for optimal viewing of the large television mounted on the opposite wall. A decorative bison head adds character to the cozy entertainment space.

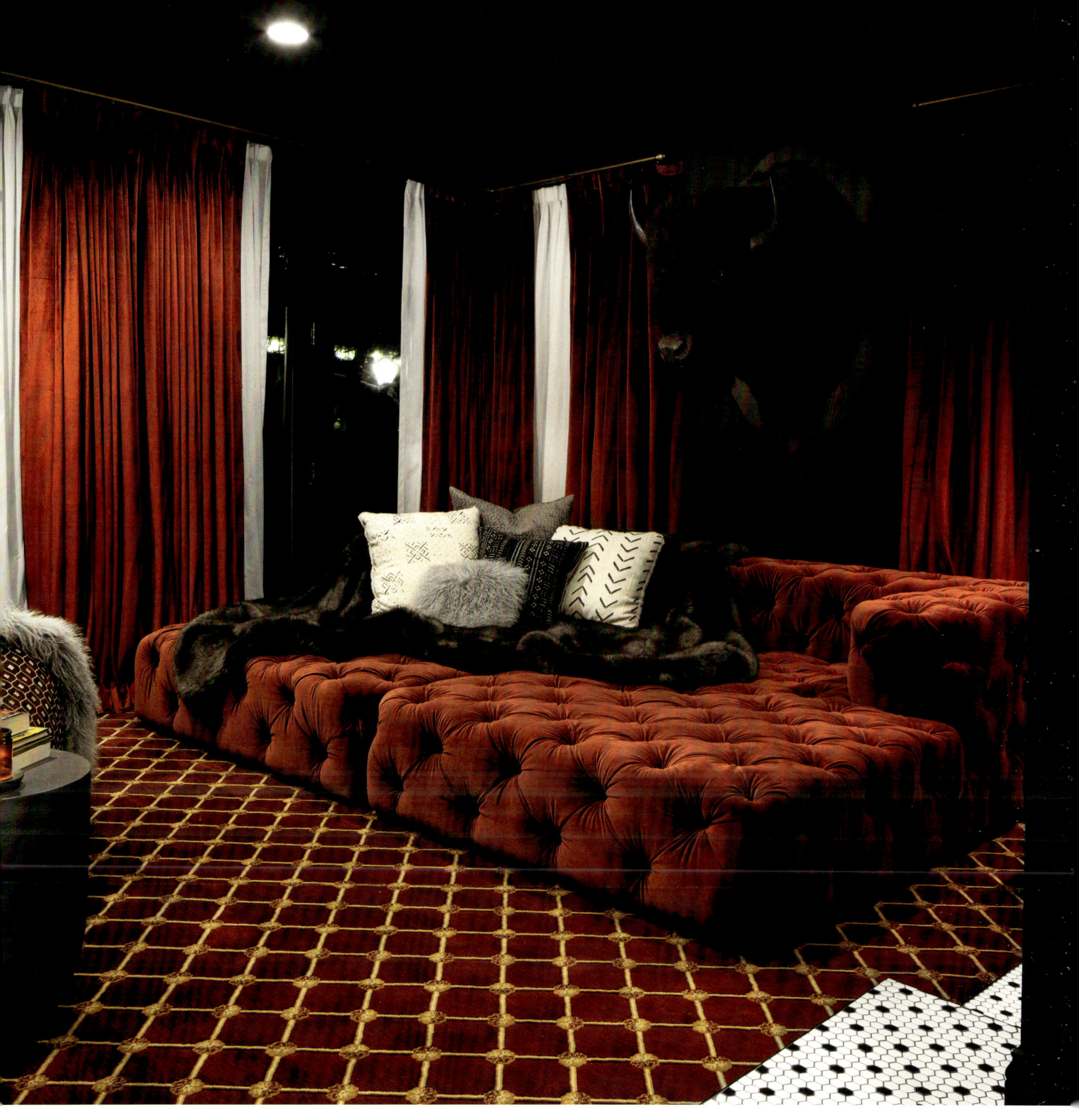

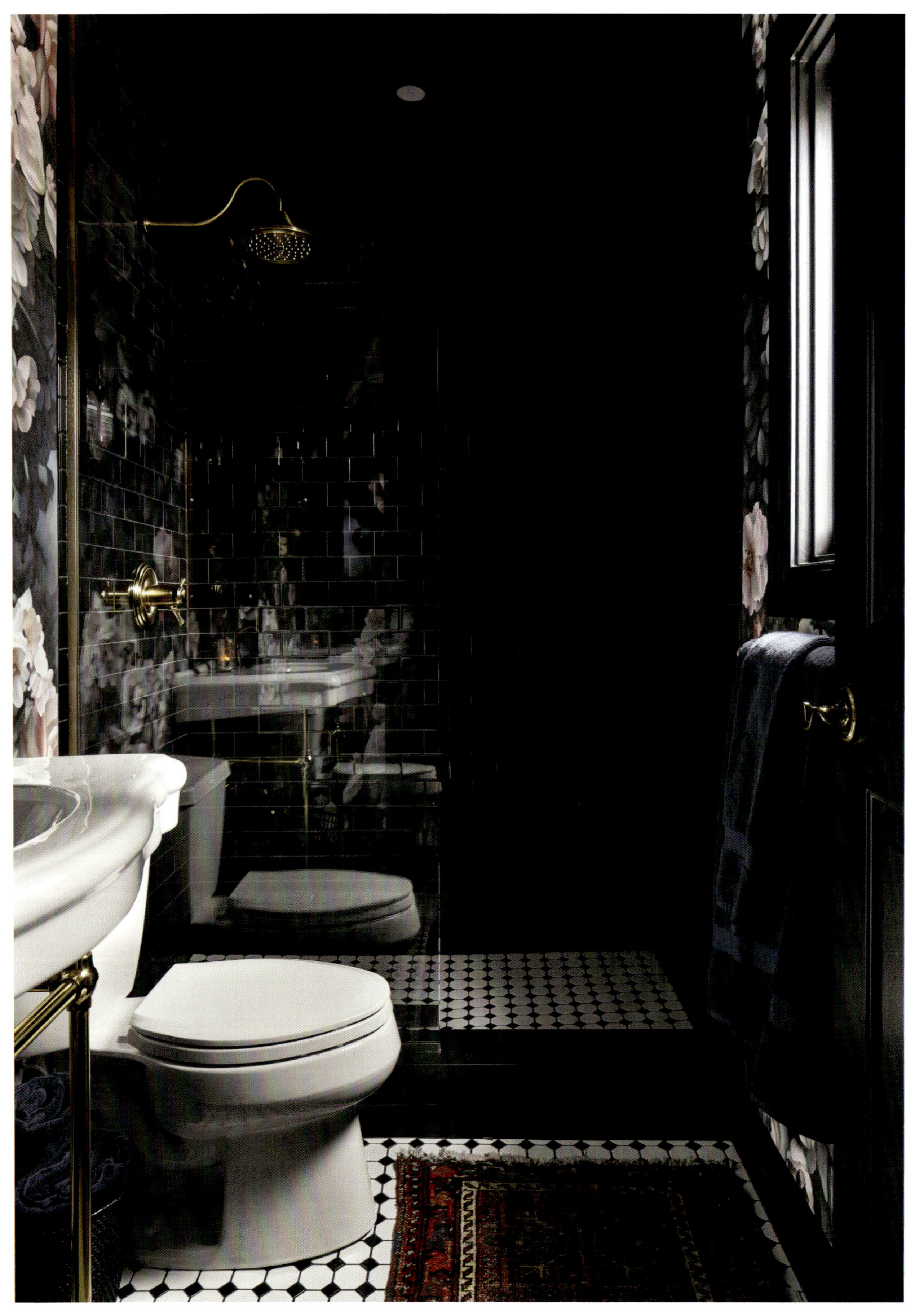

An exuberant, large-scale, pale pink rose pattern on a dramatic black background animates this showstopping bathroom. The shower features sleek black subway tile, while the floor draws inspiration from a cherished Chicago restaurant. Brass fittings add sophisticated metallic accents throughout.

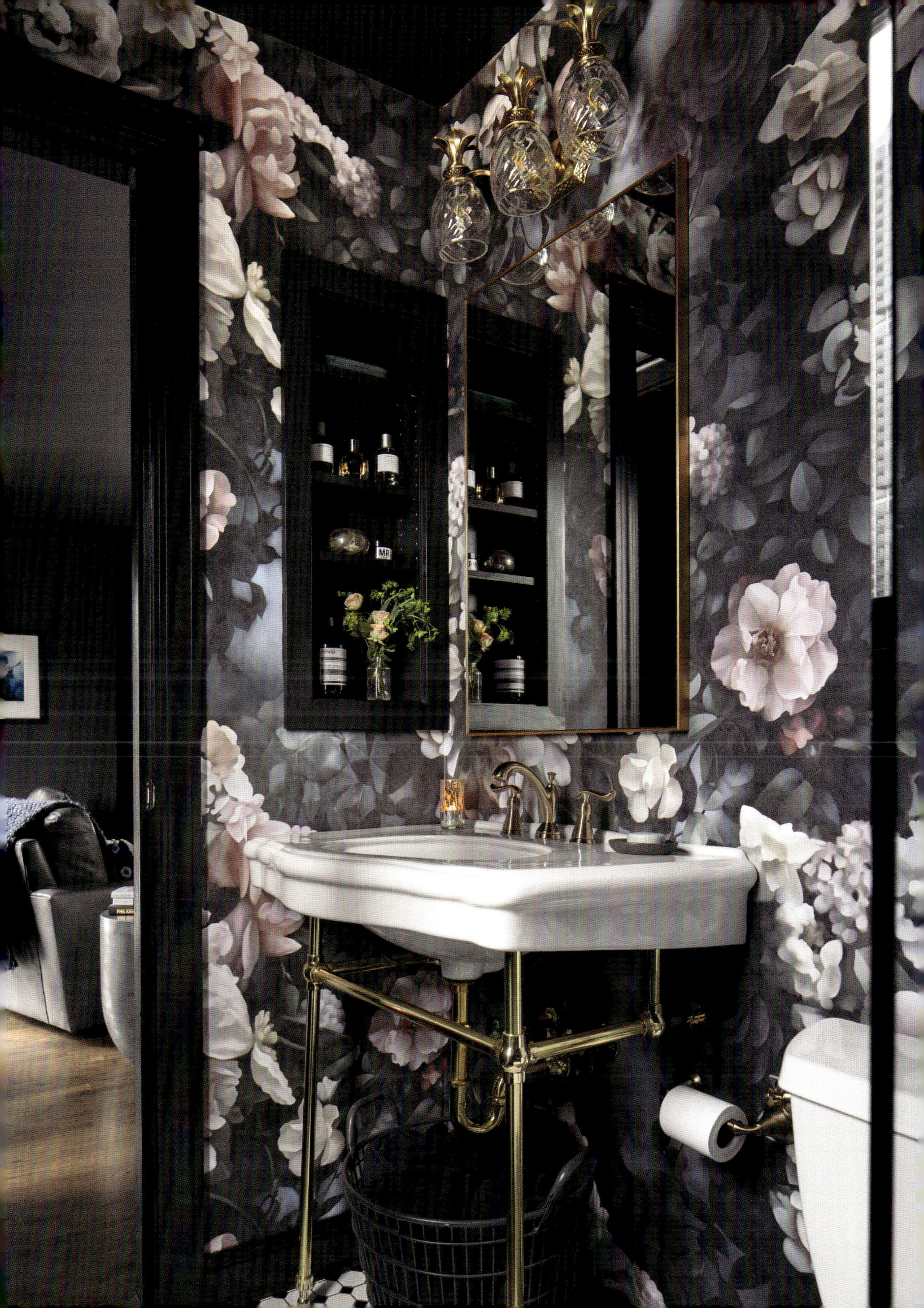
MR

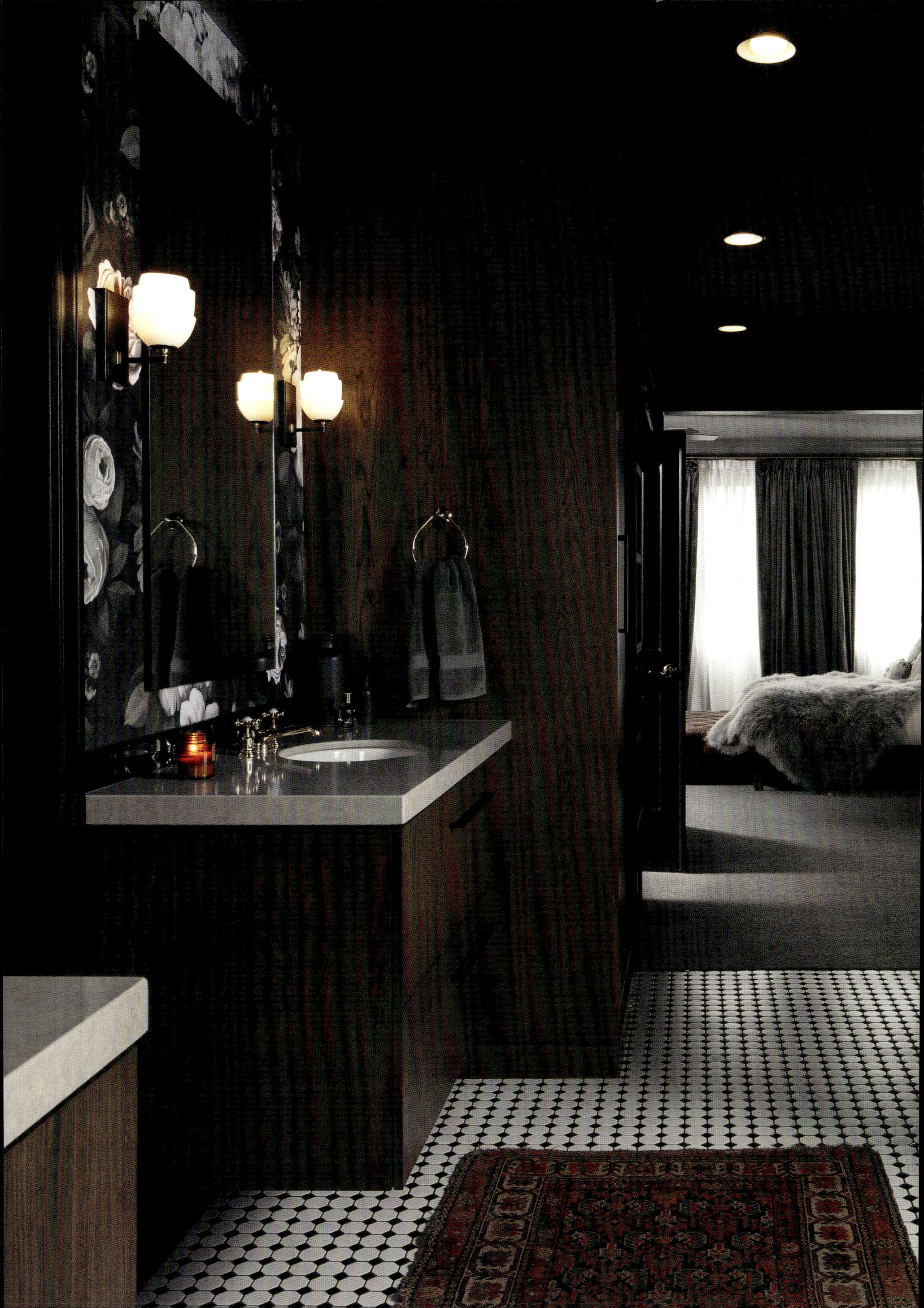

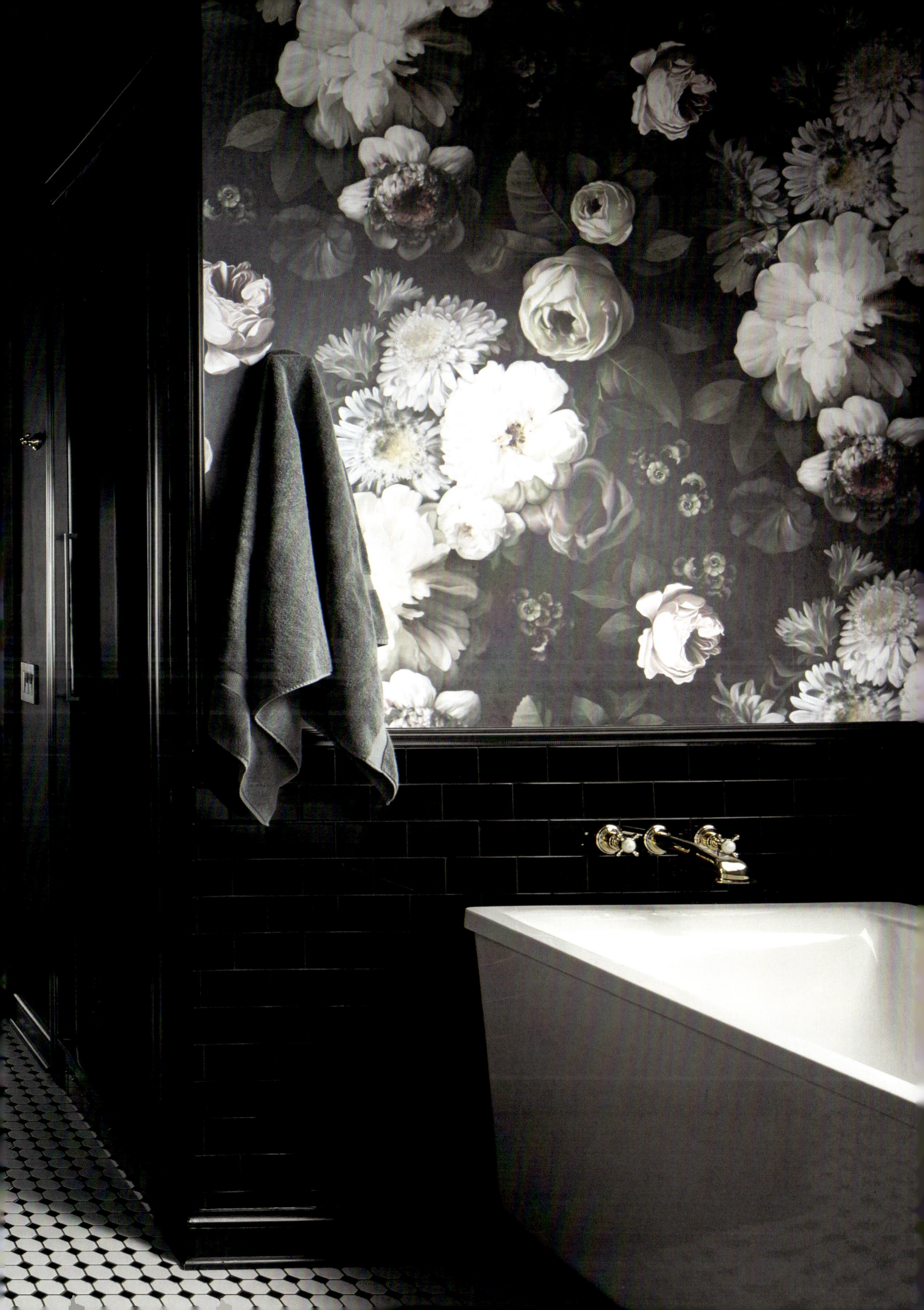

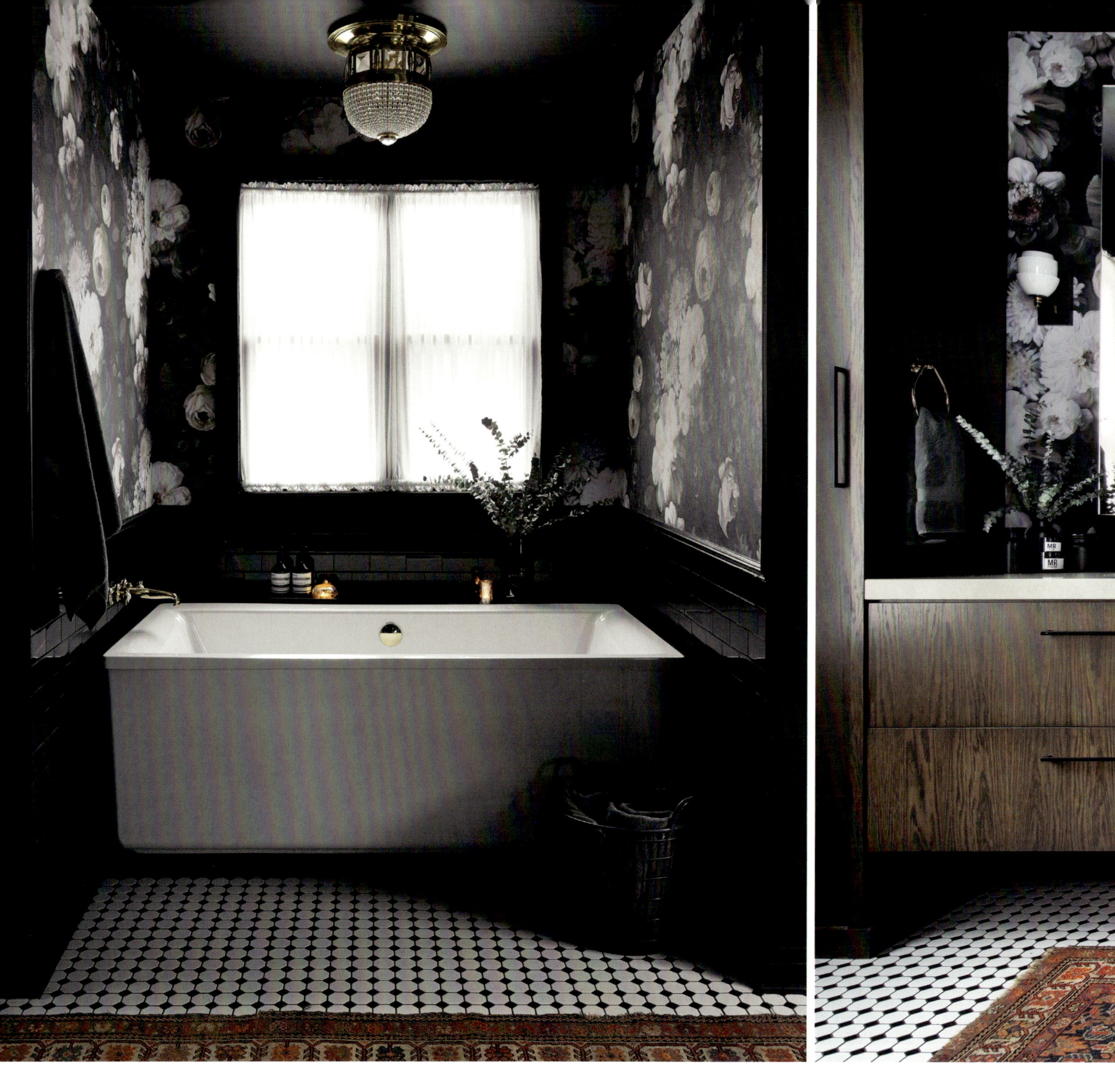

PREVIOUS: Ellie Cashman's dramatic floral wallpaper creates a bold backdrop in this classically appointed bathroom. Rich oak woodwork adds warmth throughout, while classic black-and-white octagon floor tiles lend a timeless sensibility. A deep soaking tub provides the perfect sanctuary for melting away daily stress.

ABOVE: This home's primary bath seamlessly connects to a luxurious dressing closet, ingeniously repurposed from a former bedroom. The homeowner's vision to create a comprehensive private suite prompted clever architectural modifications, including drywalling the original stair entrance and creating a new opening between the vanities. The well-appointed closet offers exceptional convenience with integrated laundry facilities—a washer and dryer discreetly incorporated for ultimate functionality.

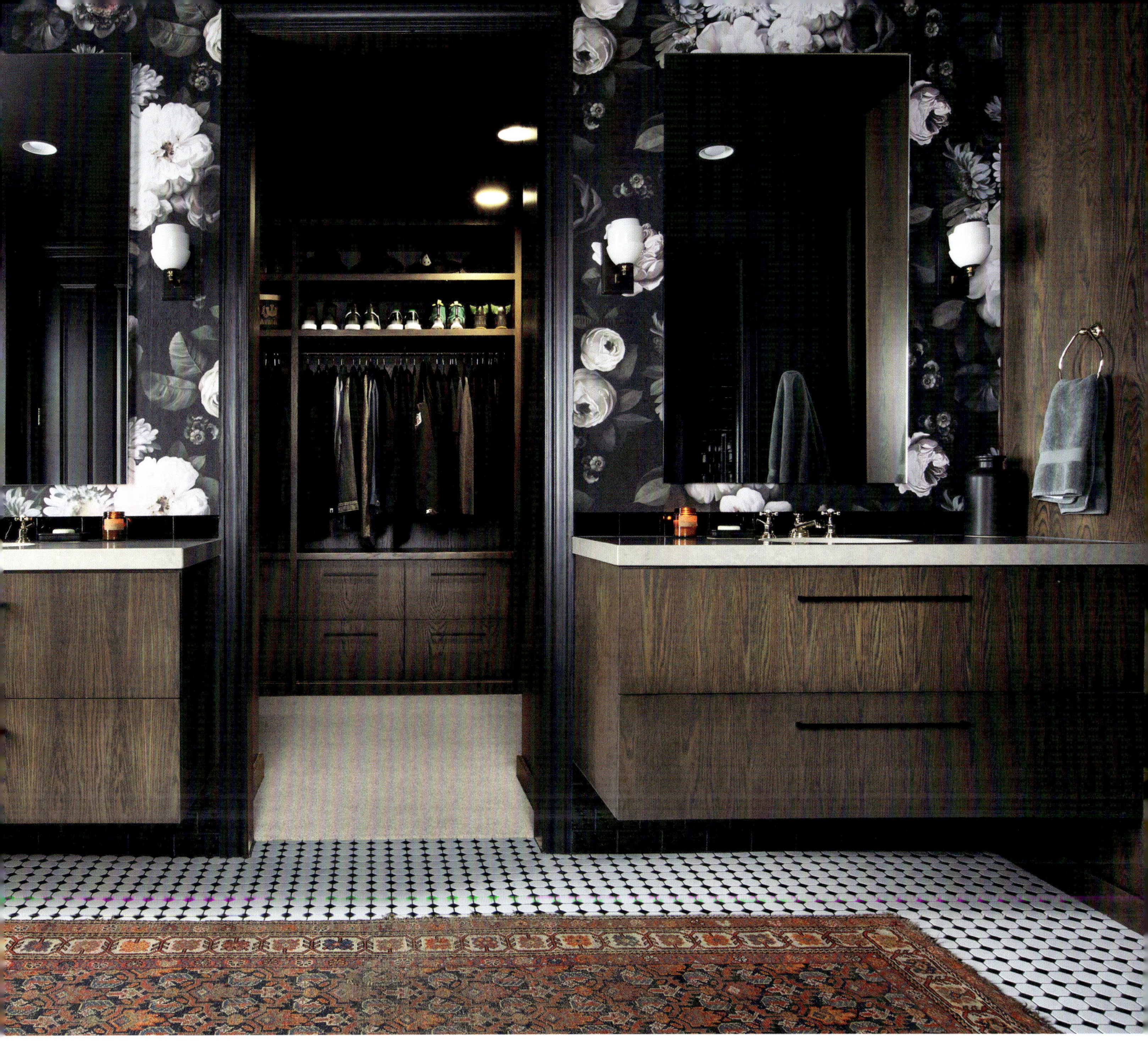

GOLD COAST REVIVAL

Aimee Wertepny / Project Interiors

"Vintage modern" is how designer Aimee Wertepny of Project Interiors describes this Lake Shore Drive residence, which merges neo-Gothic architecture with crisp, timely appointments. Working with her clients for the third time, Wertepny brought her signature touch to the 1929 apartment, preserving its historical character while infusing contemporary comfort.

The renovation speaks to both owners' creative backgrounds—one heads a marketing and design agency, while the other helms a film talent management firm. Their artistic sensibilities shine through nuances such as curved doorways and streamlined furniture silhouettes. All the while, smart-home technology systems integrate invisibly with period details, never upstaging or distracting from the charm of a bygone era.

Previous owners had already gutted the space, which allowed the design team to reimagine the interiors and still honor the building's heritage. Through detailed research, they delved into the original architectural elements and unlocked design secrets hidden in plain sight. The formal living room takes its cues from a hotel lobby design, with distinct seating areas that maintain intimacy within the larger space. A separate bar and lounge area, finished in rich materials, provides a more casual setting for evening relaxation. The primary suite, with premium lake views, connects to a luxurious bathroom, while a second bedroom welcomes the owners' daughter during her visits home.

In the bathrooms, marble vanities and designer fixtures create an air of sophisticated luxury. The powder rooms are infused with a dramatic flair and statement-making finishes, showcasing the home's refined custom ironwork. Throughout the residence, contrast—deep, saturated hues in compact rooms juxtaposed with bright, open spaces—brings fresh energy to the building's storied architecture.

Sweeping walls of glass capture Lake Michigan in all its moods while washing the rooms in natural light—a constant reminder of the home's prime position along Chicago's waterfront. Even with the bustle of the Gold Coast outside, soundproofing affords a peaceful retreat above city streets.

The result respects the building's origins and today's lifestyle needs—a balance that is "vintage modern." It aptly describes a home that honors its architectural heritage while providing a contemporary living experience.

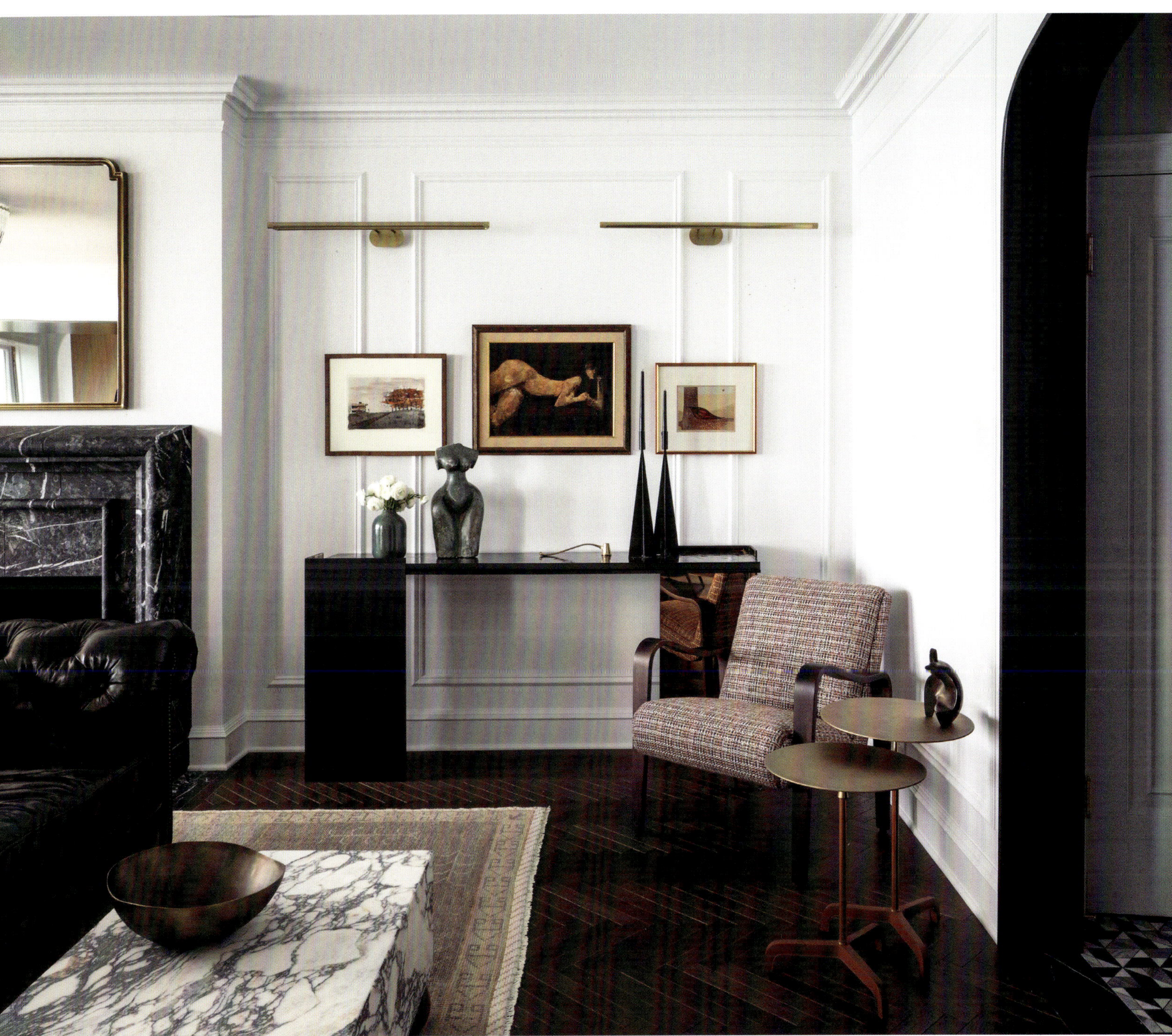

A commanding Breccia Nera marble hearth establishes the bold black-and-white palette that defines this sophisticated Chicago duplex. The scheme advances with inky leather Chesterfield sofas, which anchor the space alongside a sleek white marble coffee table and an angular steel-and-mirror console. Underfoot, dark walnut-stained herringbone wooden floors add rich, textural warmth.

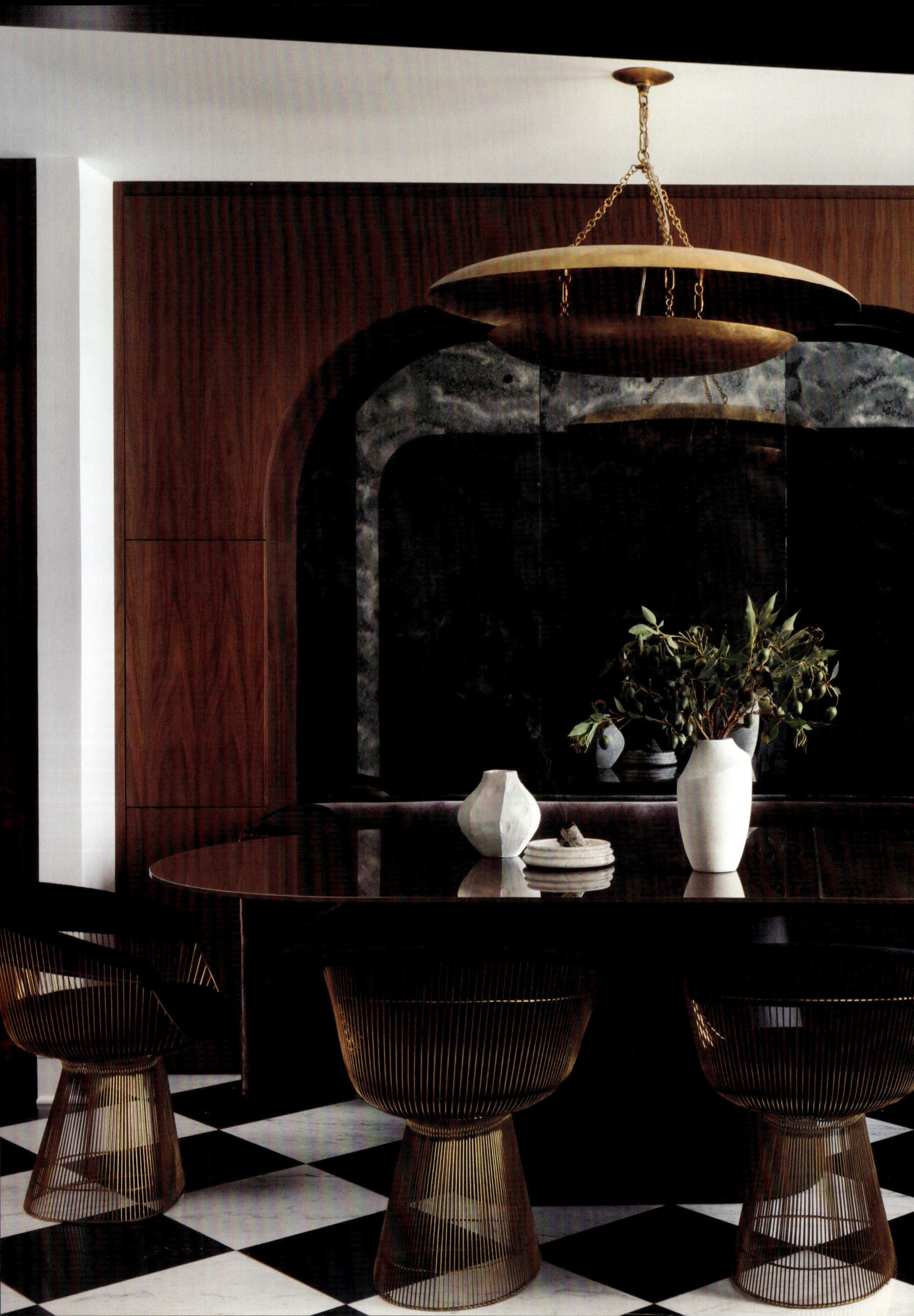

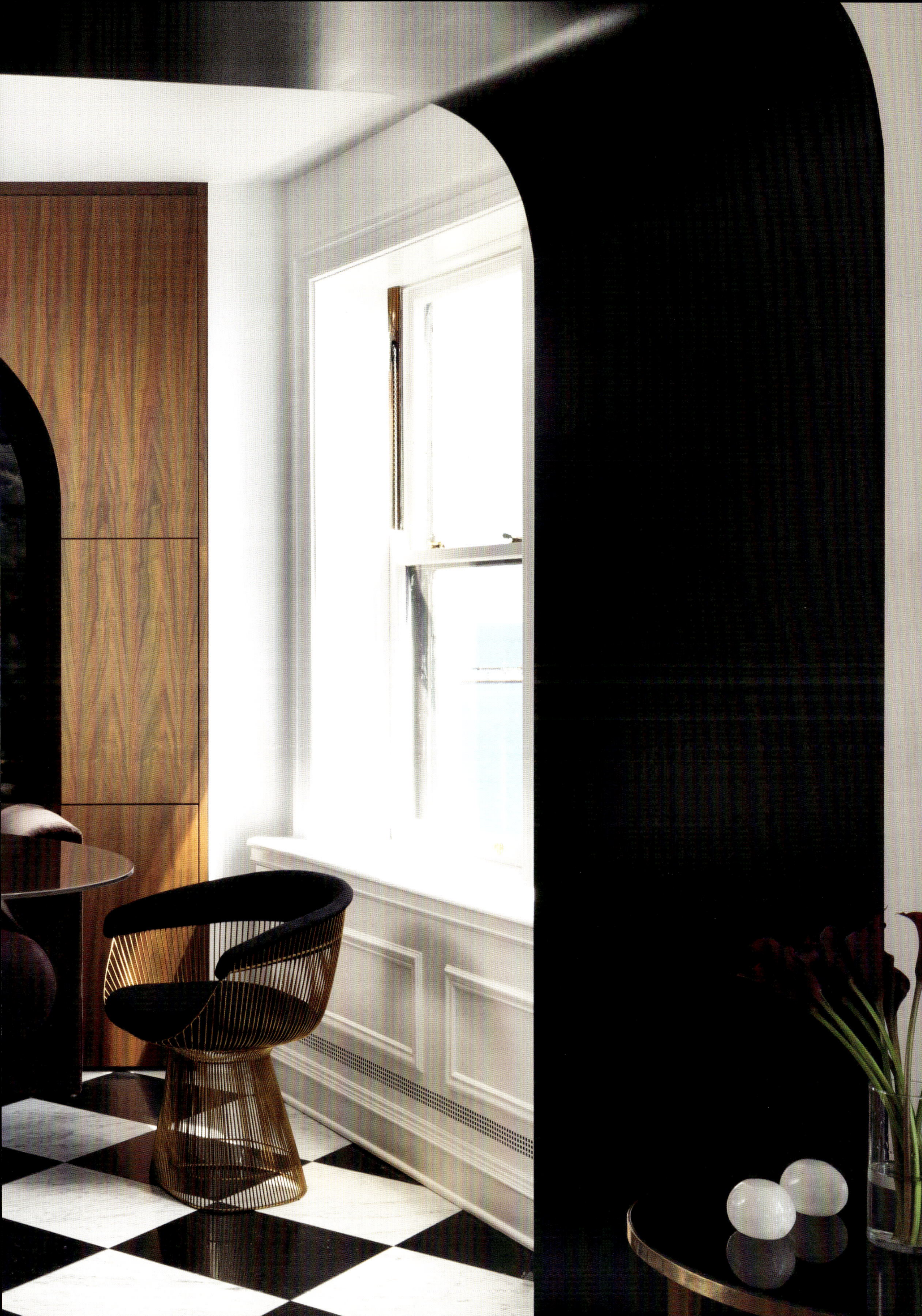

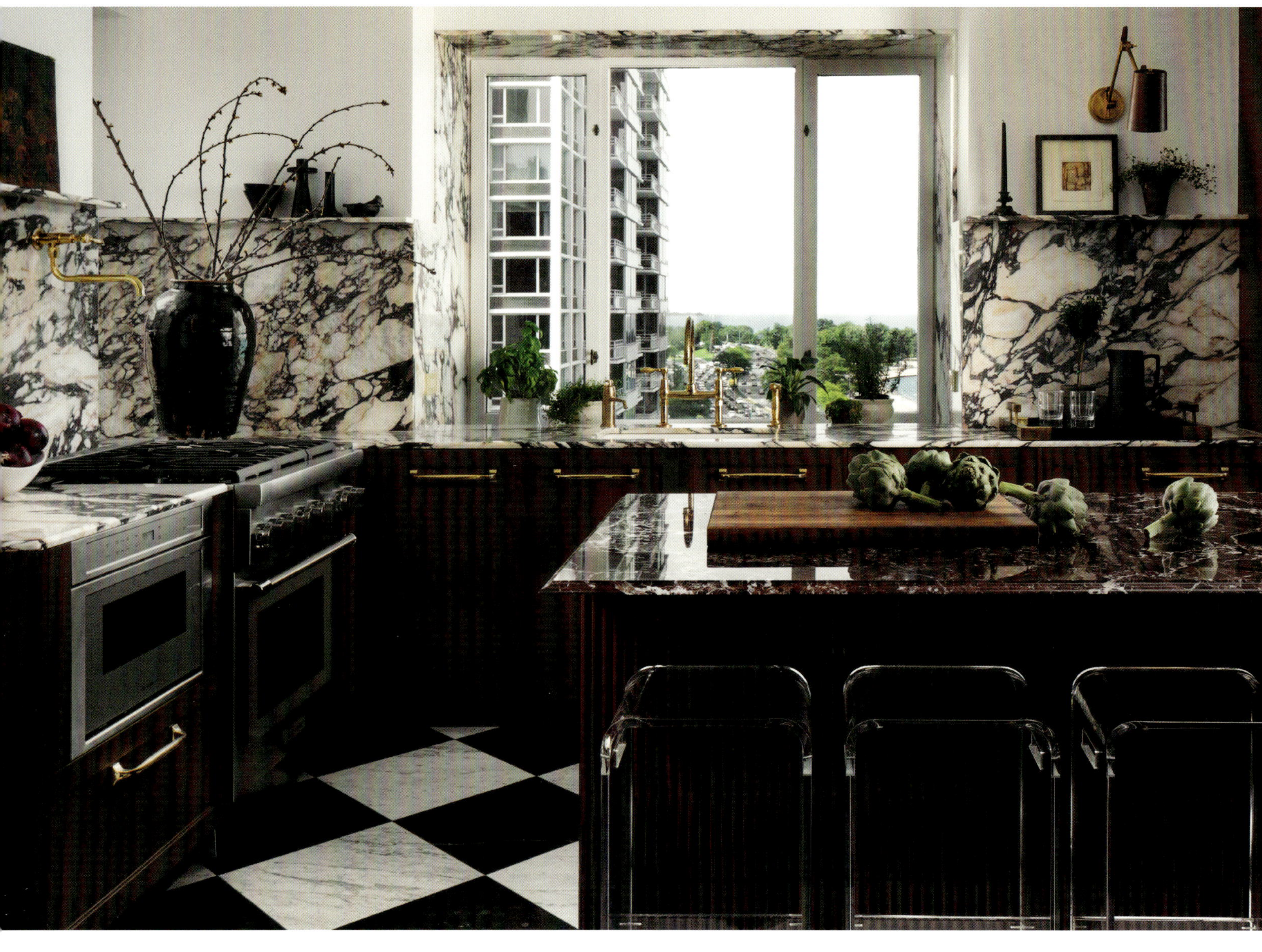

PREVIOUS: A sleek Modloft pedestal table surrounded by iconic Warren Platner armchairs with lustrous gold-toned bases creates an austere focal point in the dining room. The custom-crafted archway dramatically frames a built-in banquette, complemented by antique mirror panels. The eye-catching light fixture is from Arteriors.

ABOVE: Custom walnut cabinetry with reeded island detailing creates a stunning backdrop for the kitchen's marble elements, including checkered tile flooring and contrasting marble surfaces. The brass fixtures and fittings are from Waterworks, the sconces are from Visual Comfort, and sleek Thermador appliances complete this art deco–inspired culinary space.

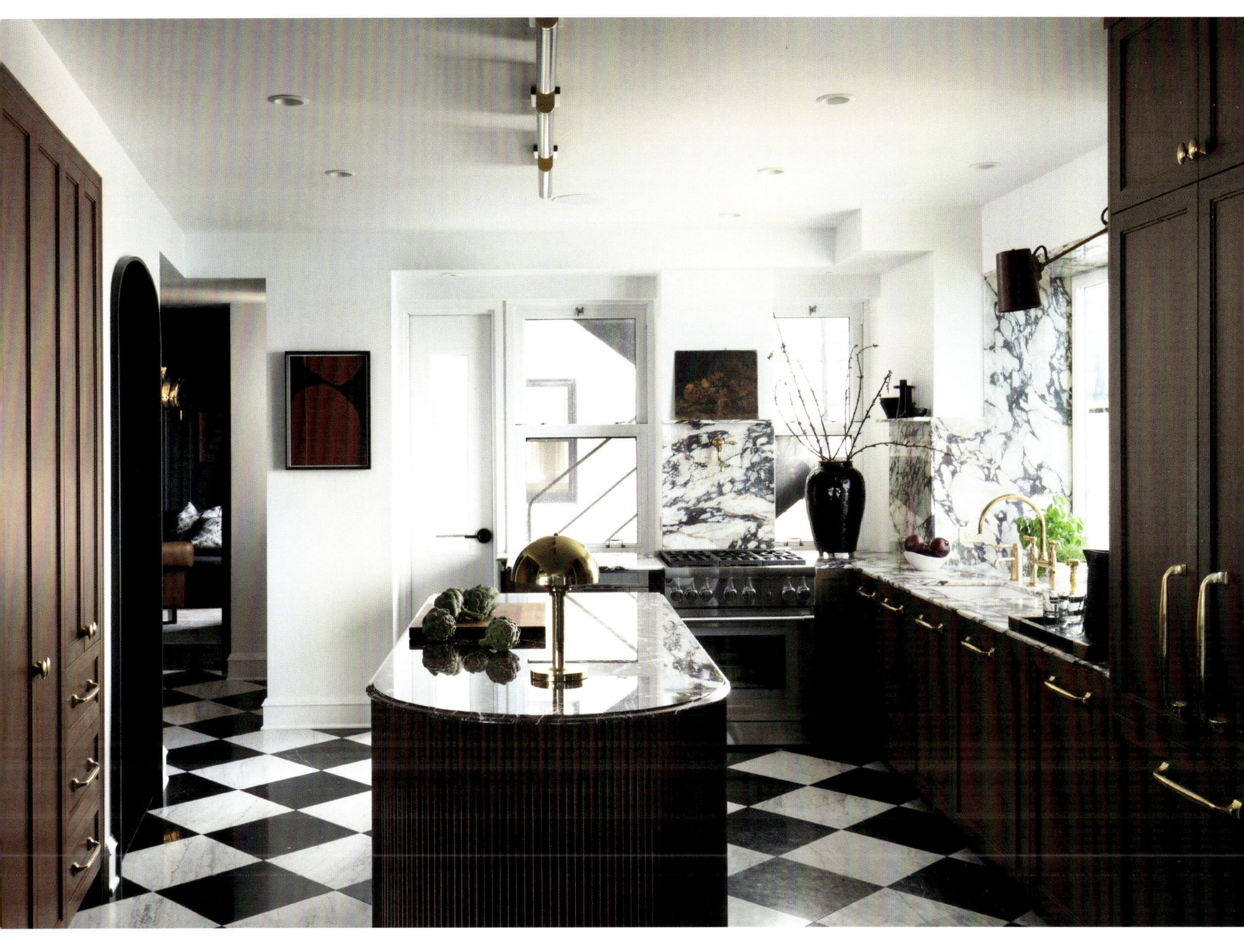

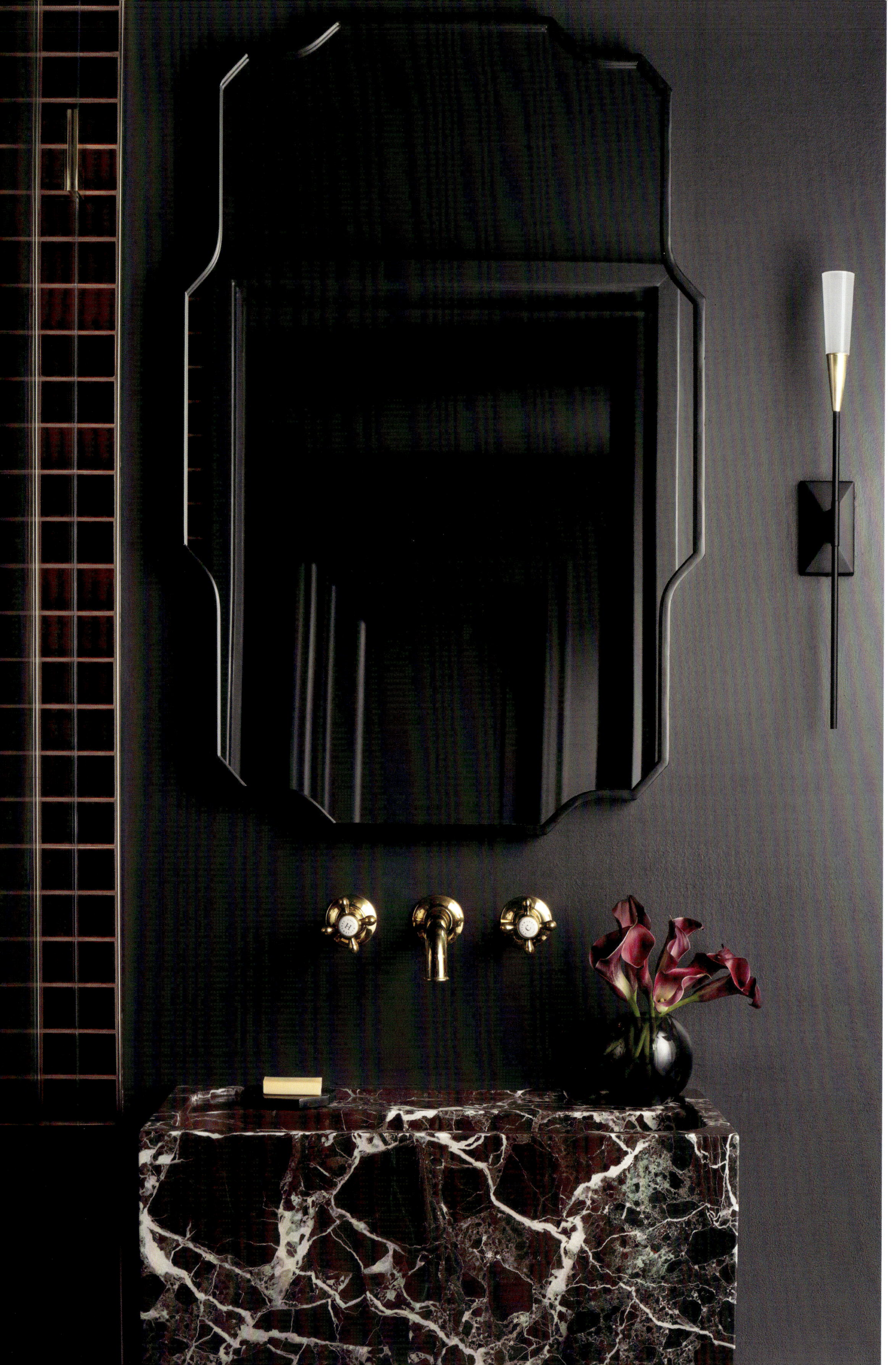

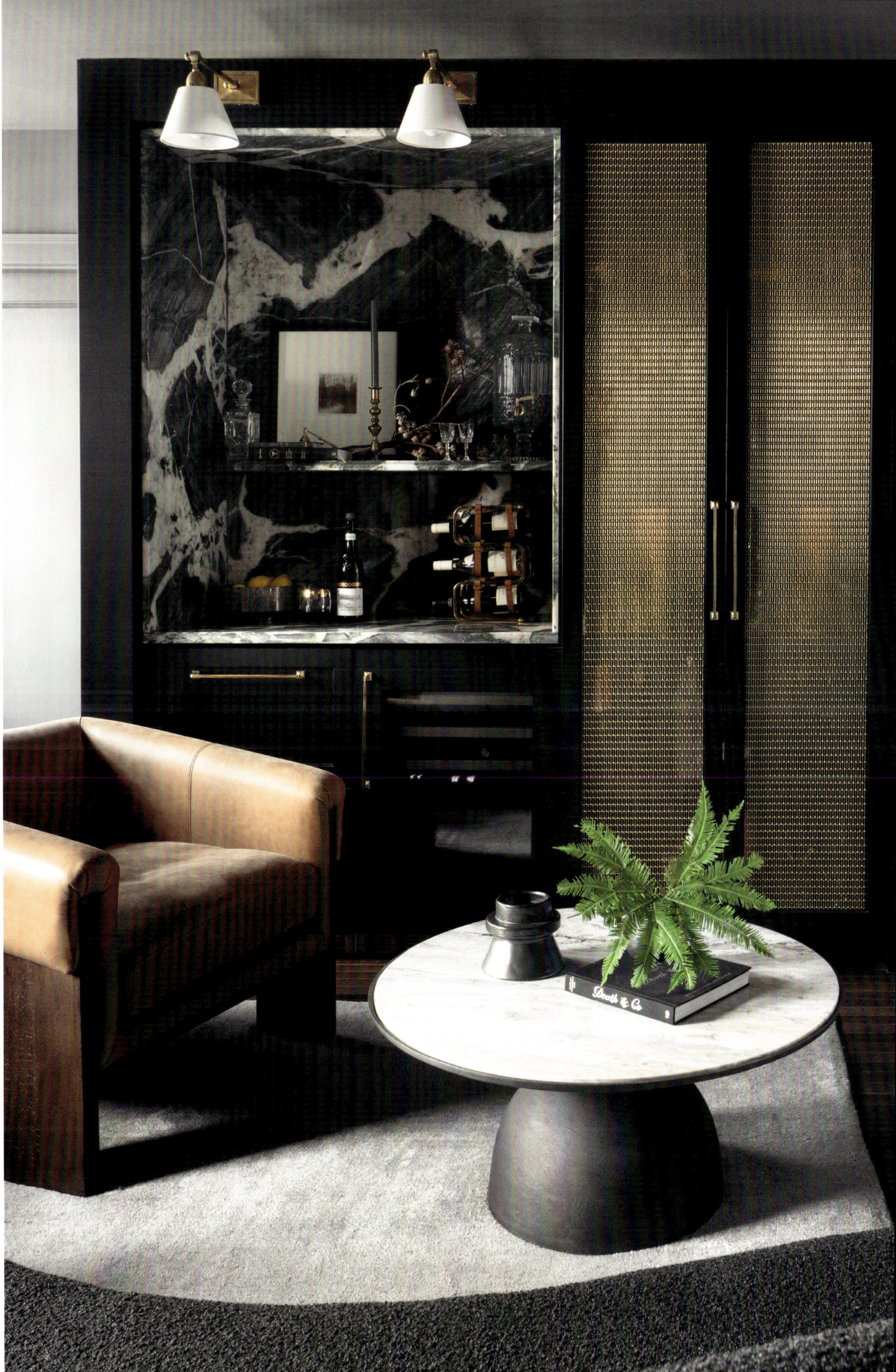
Death & Co

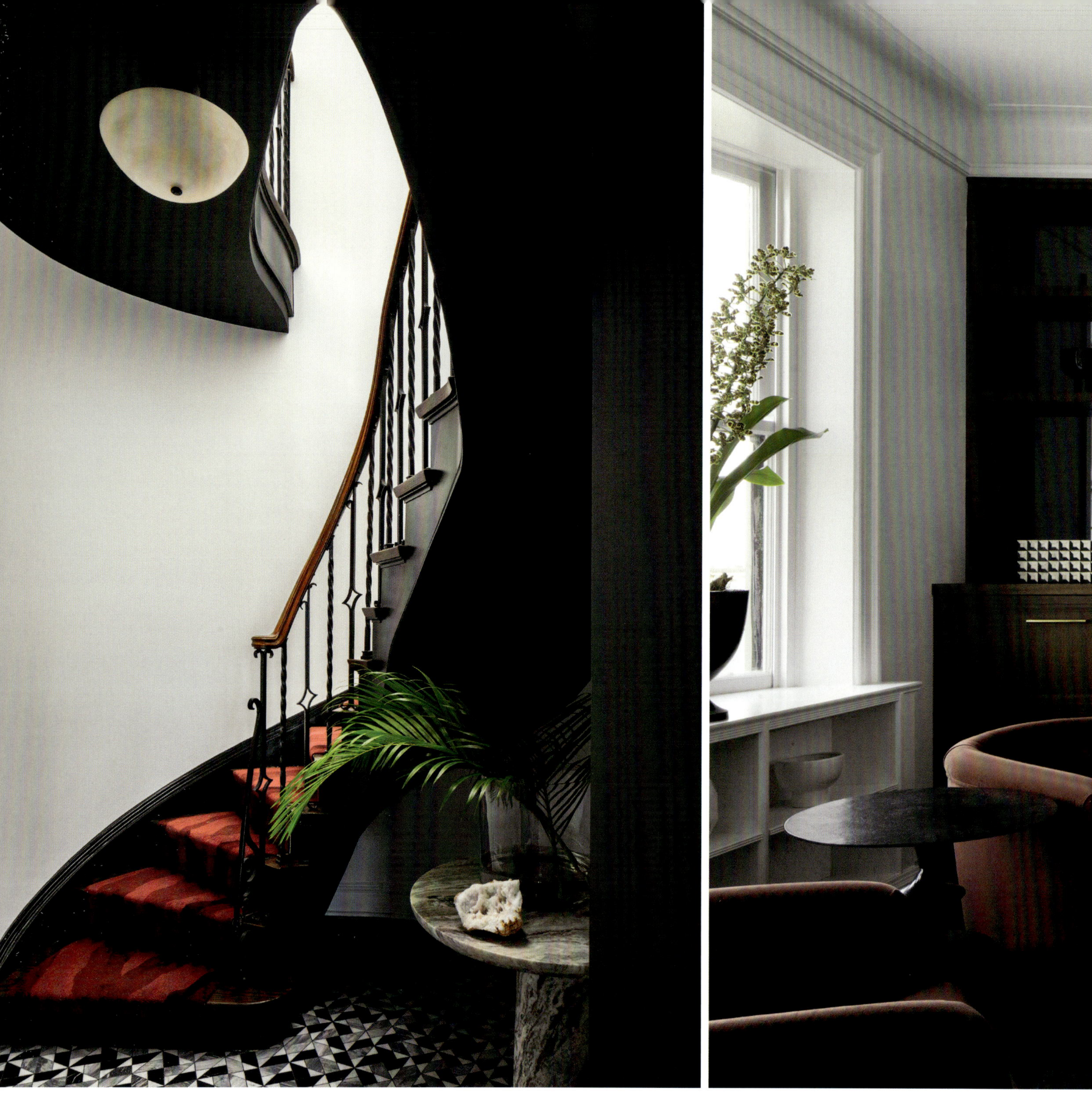

PREVIOUS: *Left:* Enveloped in deep black paint, a striking Rosso Levanto marble sink transforms this powder room; its swirling patterns introduce a kinetic, naturalistic element to the intimate space. *Right:* A custom built-in bar complements a rich leather modernist club chair, creating an inviting corner at cocktail hour.

ABOVE: Vibrant crimson accents strategically enliven the home's design. The staircase runner cascades like flowing lava, while matching velvet club chairs (*at right*) add rich color to the home office. Custom built-ins flank an art deco–inspired fireplace, complemented by an elegant bronze-finished desk that anchors the workspace.

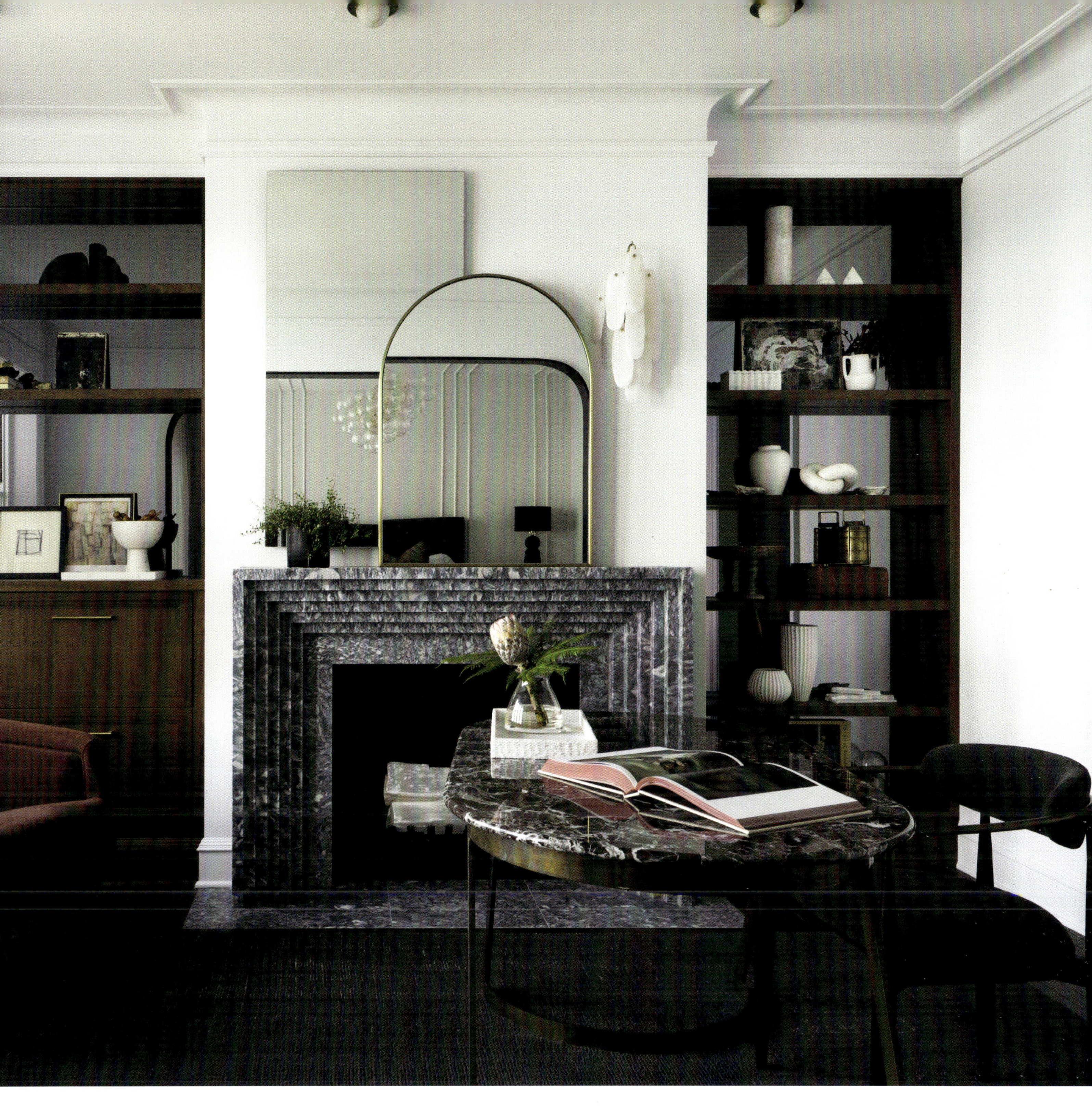

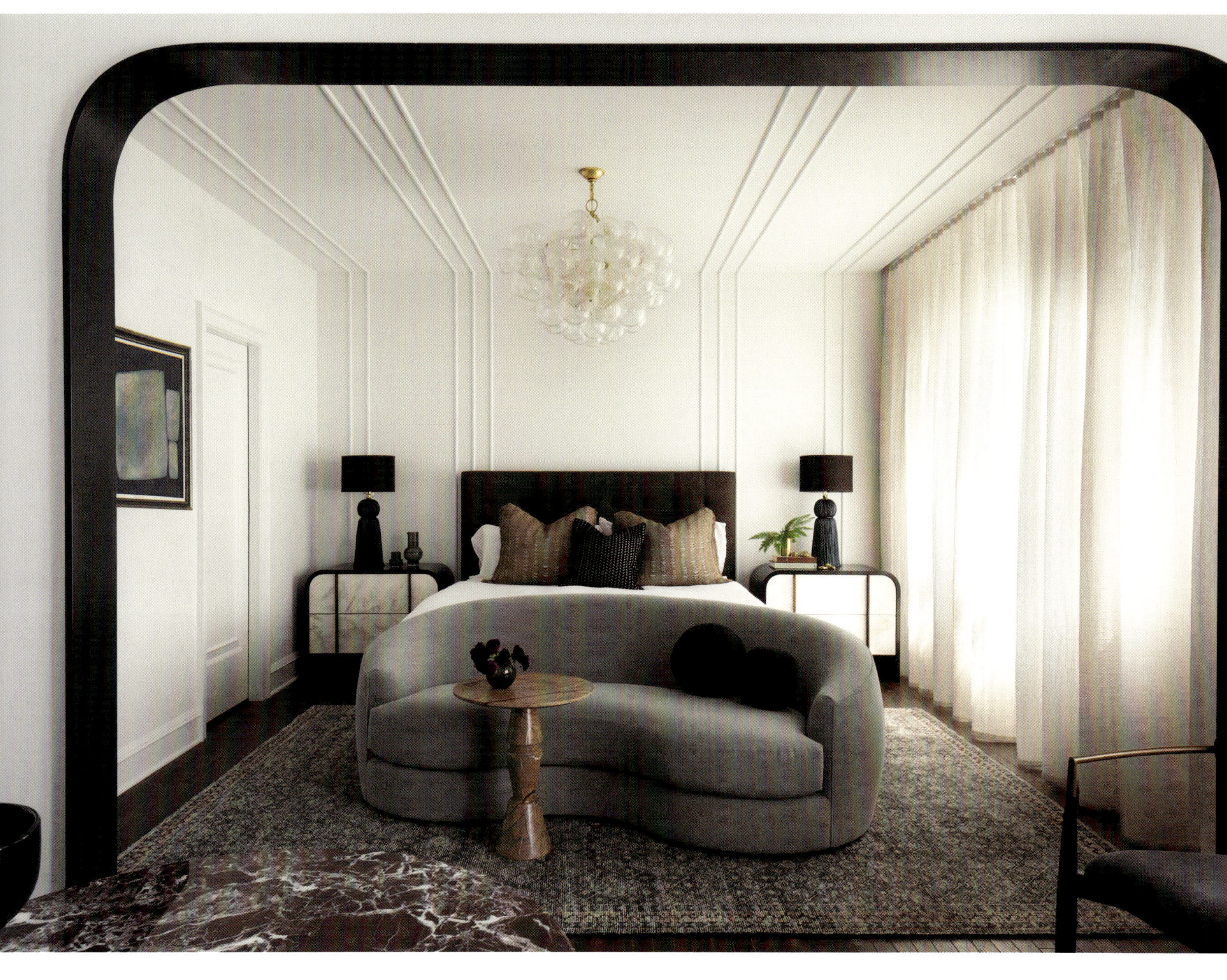

The primary bedroom features graceful curves that soften the architectural lines throughout the space. This flowing aesthetic appears in the arched opening (previously dividing two smaller combined bedrooms), the rounded bedside tables, and the feminine silhouette of the bed-end sofa. The gentle color scheme continues into the primary bathroom, where a subtle Roman shade offers privacy while bathing.

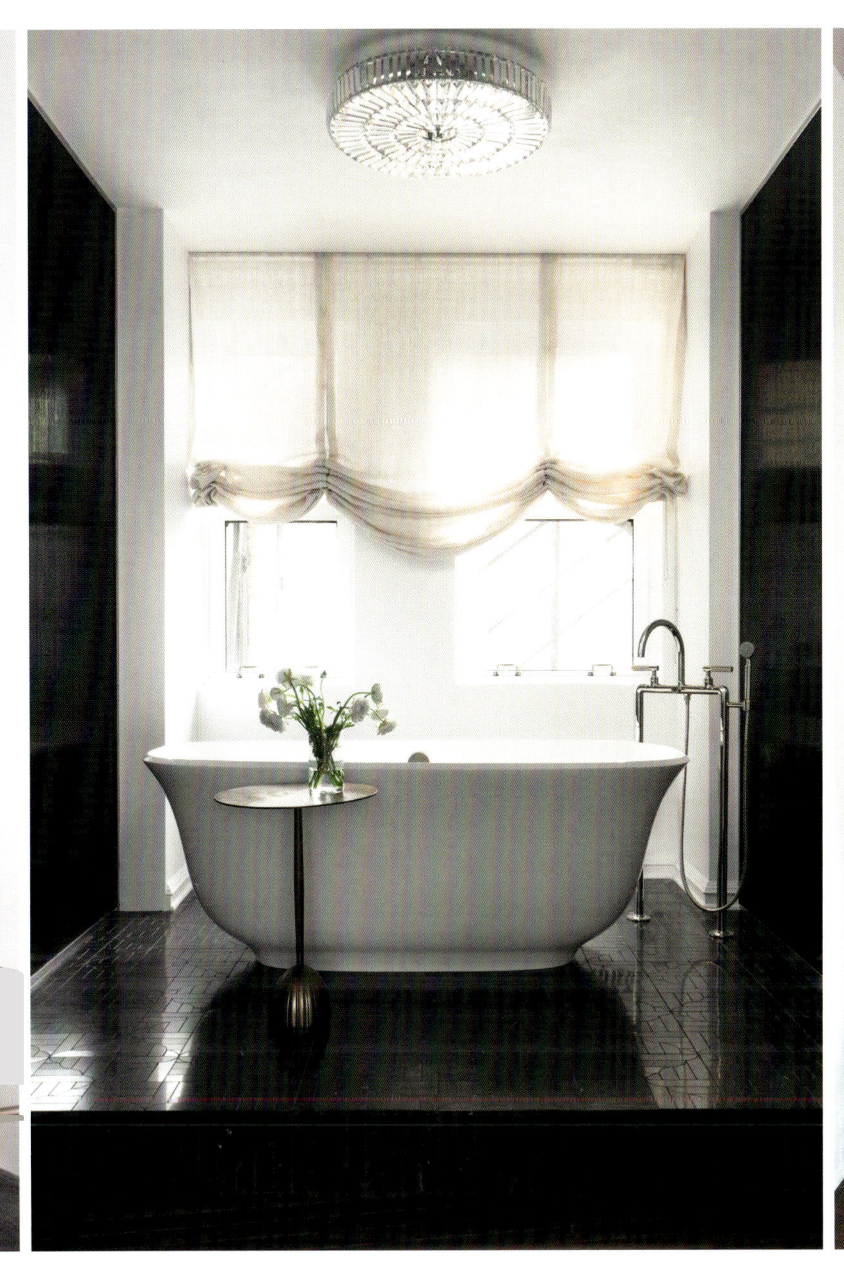
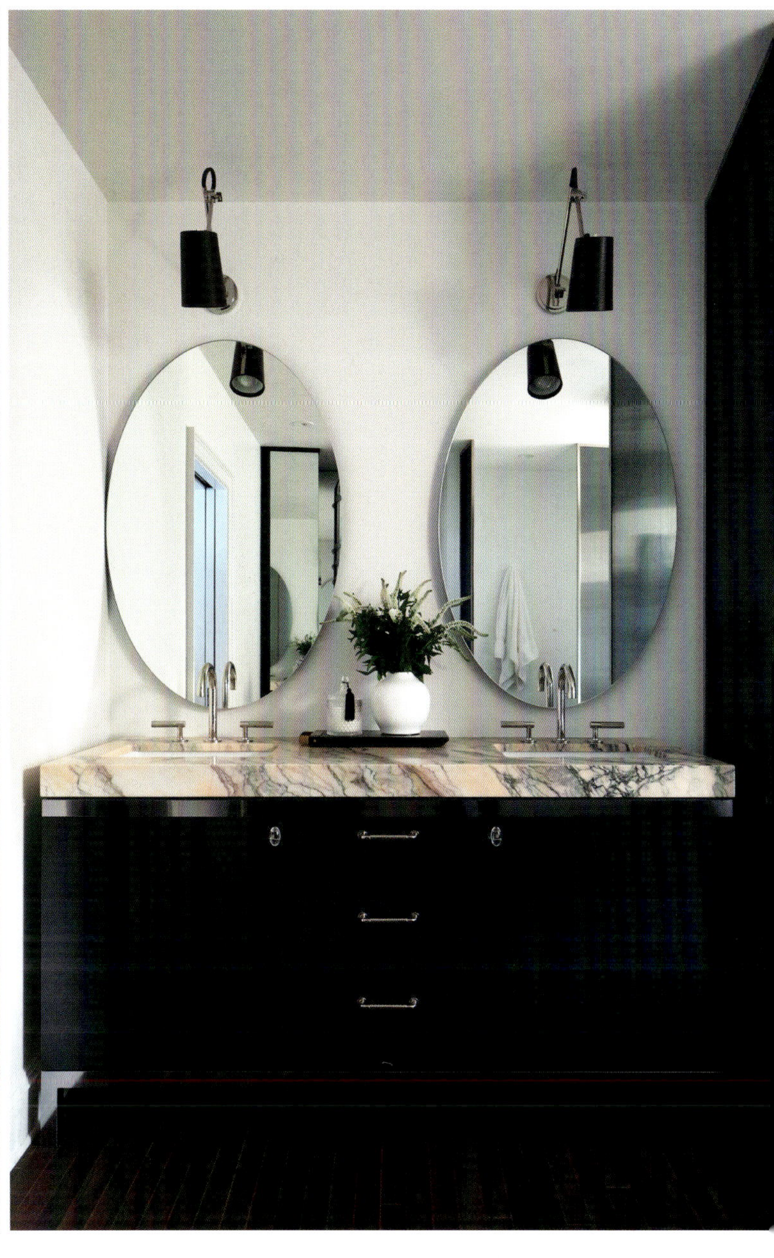

EXPANDING THE FAMILY TREE

Lauren Warnock / NavyBlack

This unique compound near Lake Michigan's shores demonstrates how creative vision can transform separate properties into a cohesive entertainment haven. The owner, who runs Revel Global Events, needed a space that would mirror the adaptability of her professional work in arts and entertainment. Working with designer Laurent Warnock of NavyBlack Studio, they created a property that seamlessly transitions between intimate family gatherings and large-scale entertaining.

The estate began with the main house, affectionately dubbed "the castle," a historic-style property continually evolving through regular updates. During the COVID-19 pandemic, opportunity knocked when an adjacent property became available. The owner seized the chance to expand, converting the neighboring house into a guest retreat and unifying the backyards. The connected outdoor space now features a pickleball court and serves as a bridge between the two structures.

Perhaps the most striking feature is the treehouse that pierces the property's heart. This fully electrified retreat, built around a living tree, transforms what could have been merely functional guest quarters into something magical. The tree grows through the building, creating a stunning marriage of natural and built environments that captivate visitors.

The compound's design carefully balances the owner's "more is more" entertainment background and practical functionality. Warnock, who had previously worked with the client on her Logan Square property, played a crucial role as editor, finding the sweet spot between bold expression and livable spaces. The result accommodates the quiet moments of family life—the owner shares the home with her spouse and two adopted children—and the vibrant energy of hosting up to seventy-five dinner guests.

Each space maintains its distinct character while contributing to the whole. The compound functions as a unified entity while preserving each structure's charm. It's a testament to how thoughtful design can create spaces that adapt to life's varying demands while maintaining their connection to nature and family living.

Castle Abri, a stately 1920s fieldstone residence in Long Beach, Indiana, welcomes visitors with its distinctive ivy-covered turret and stone walkway. Set on an acre of manicured gardens with two ponds, this architecturally significant yet sunny family home features vaulted ceilings and abundant natural light.

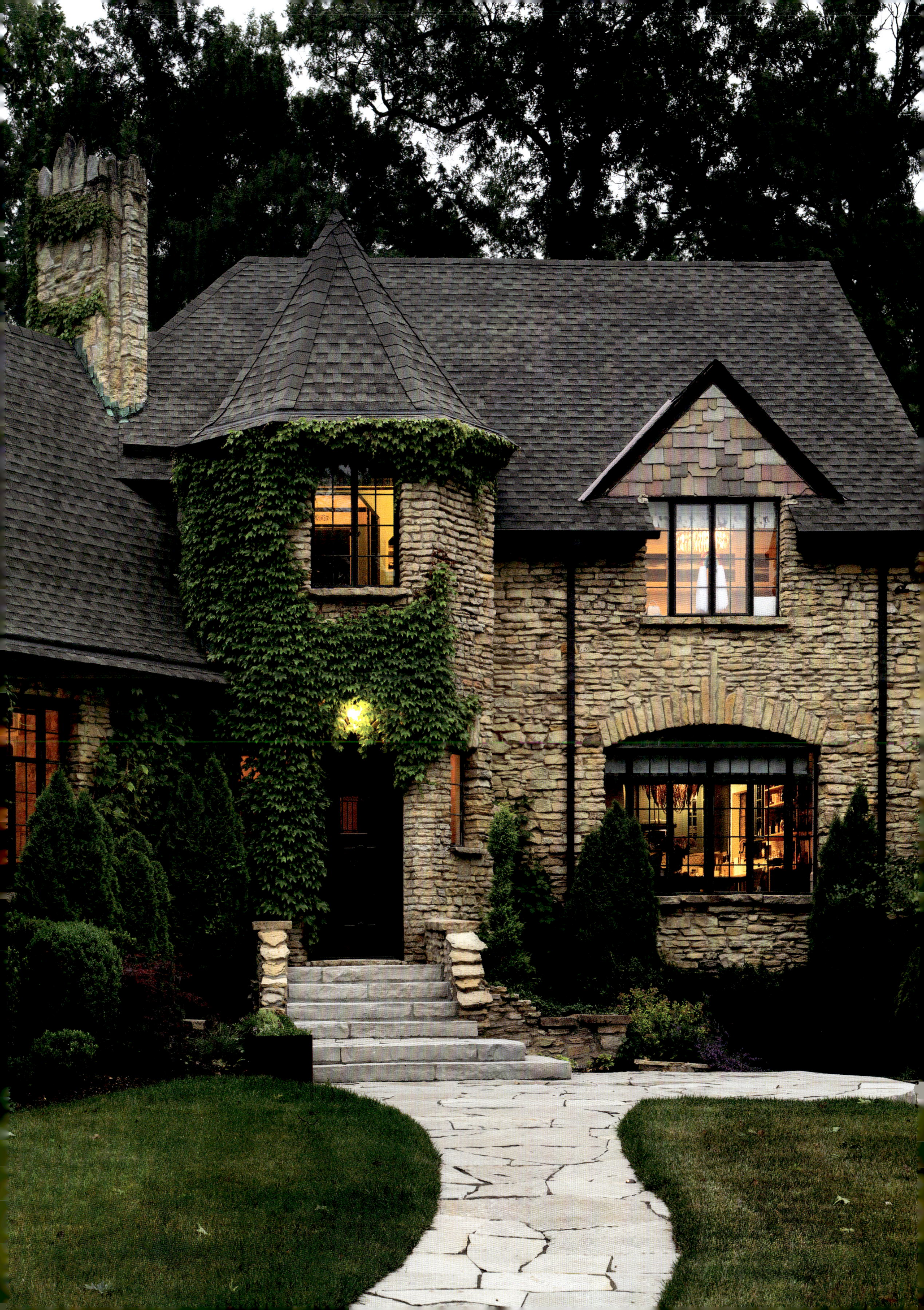

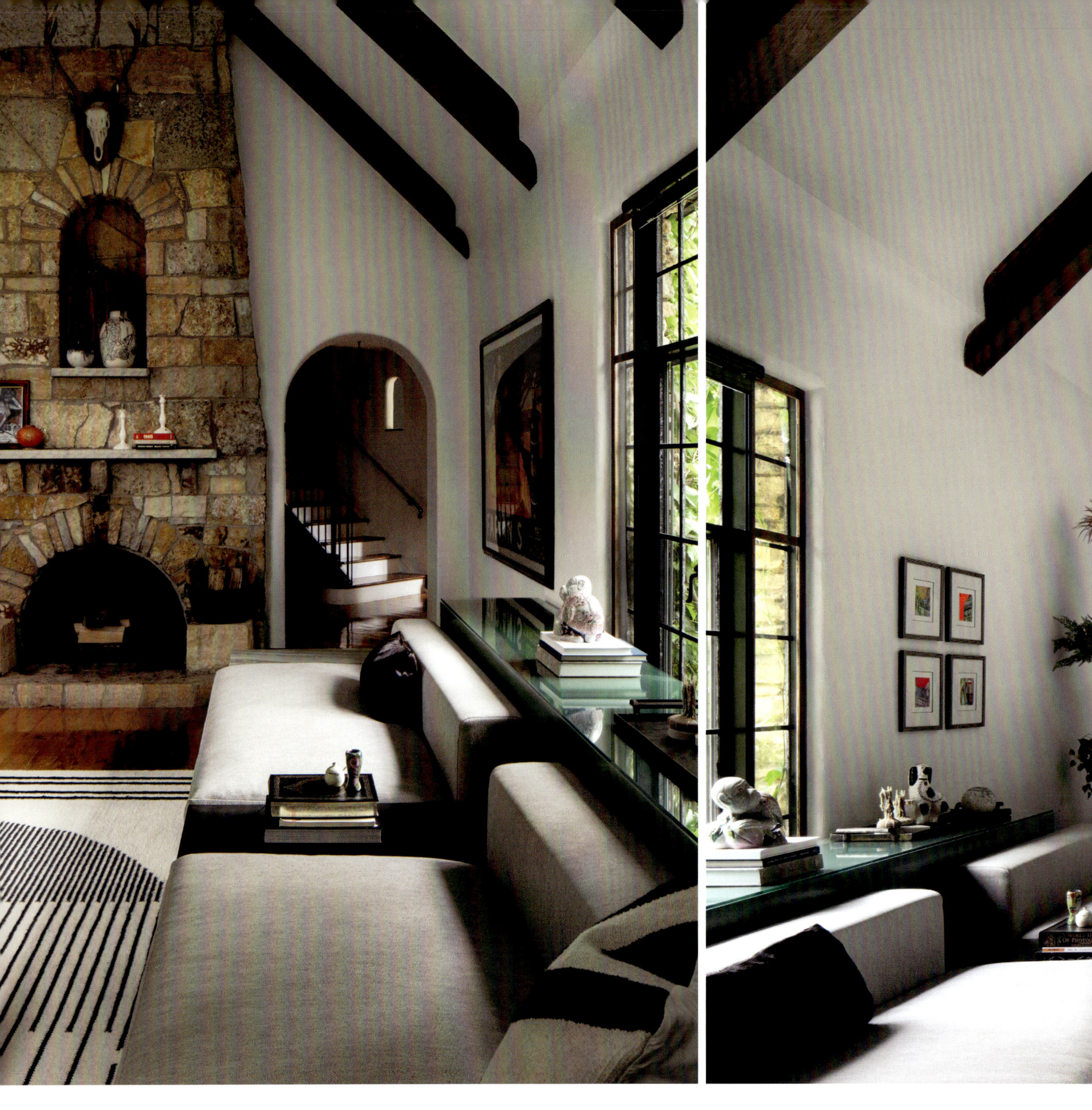

The spacious living room features an original stone fireplace and custom-made wraparound banquette in durable Xorel fabric that withstands beach life. The homeowners' art collection includes striking black-and-white animal prints that playfully contrast with the coastal setting.

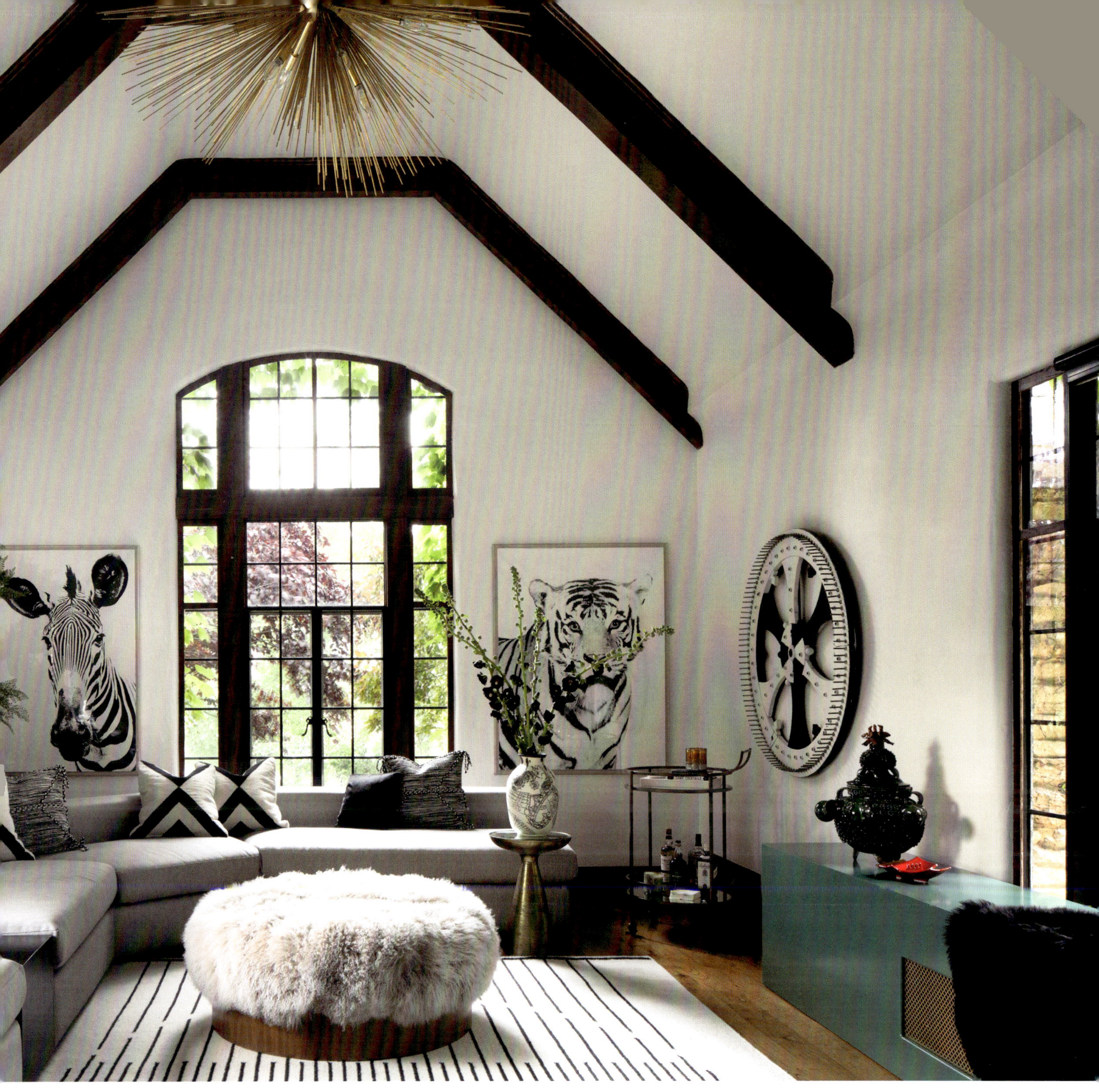

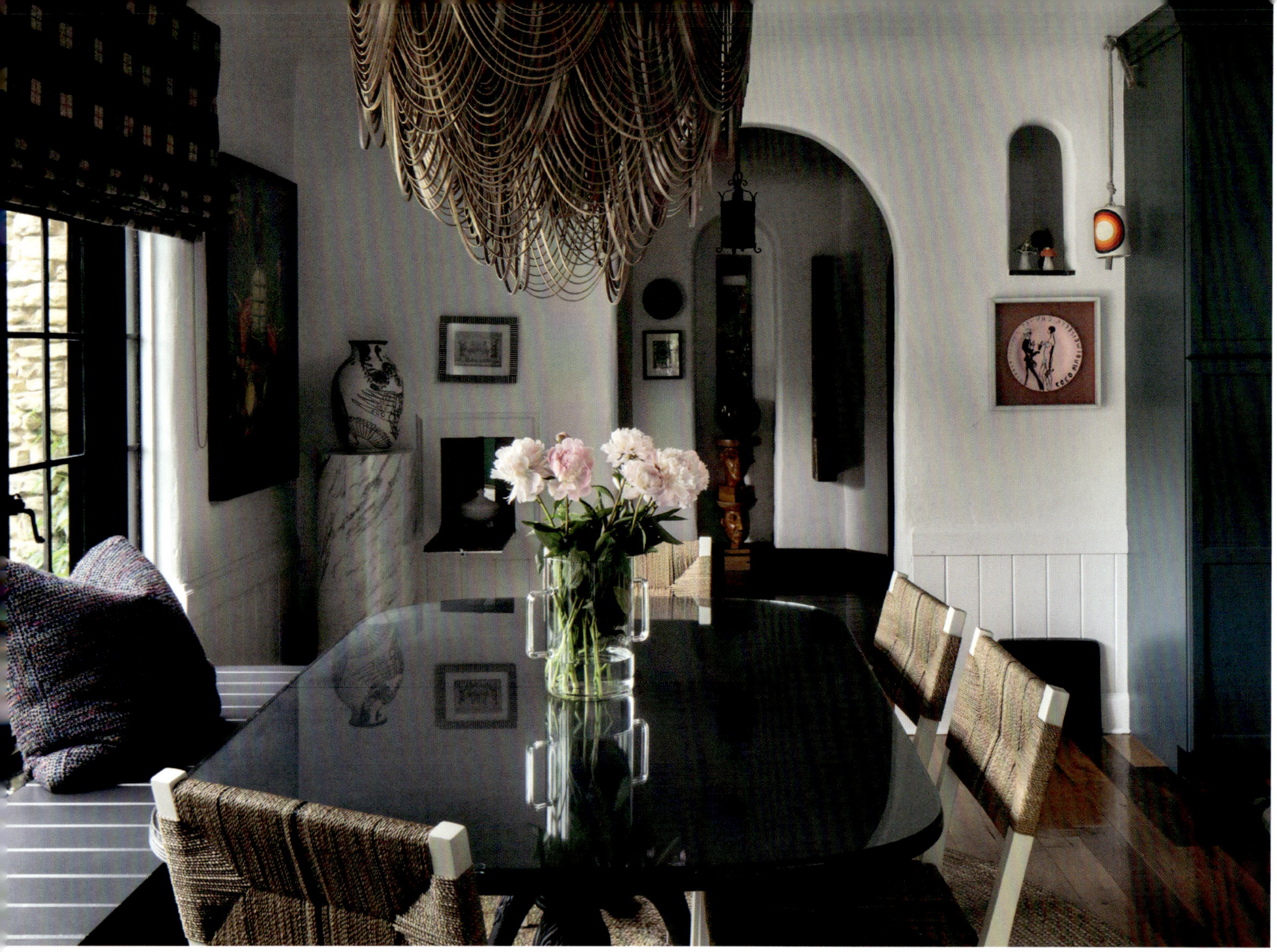

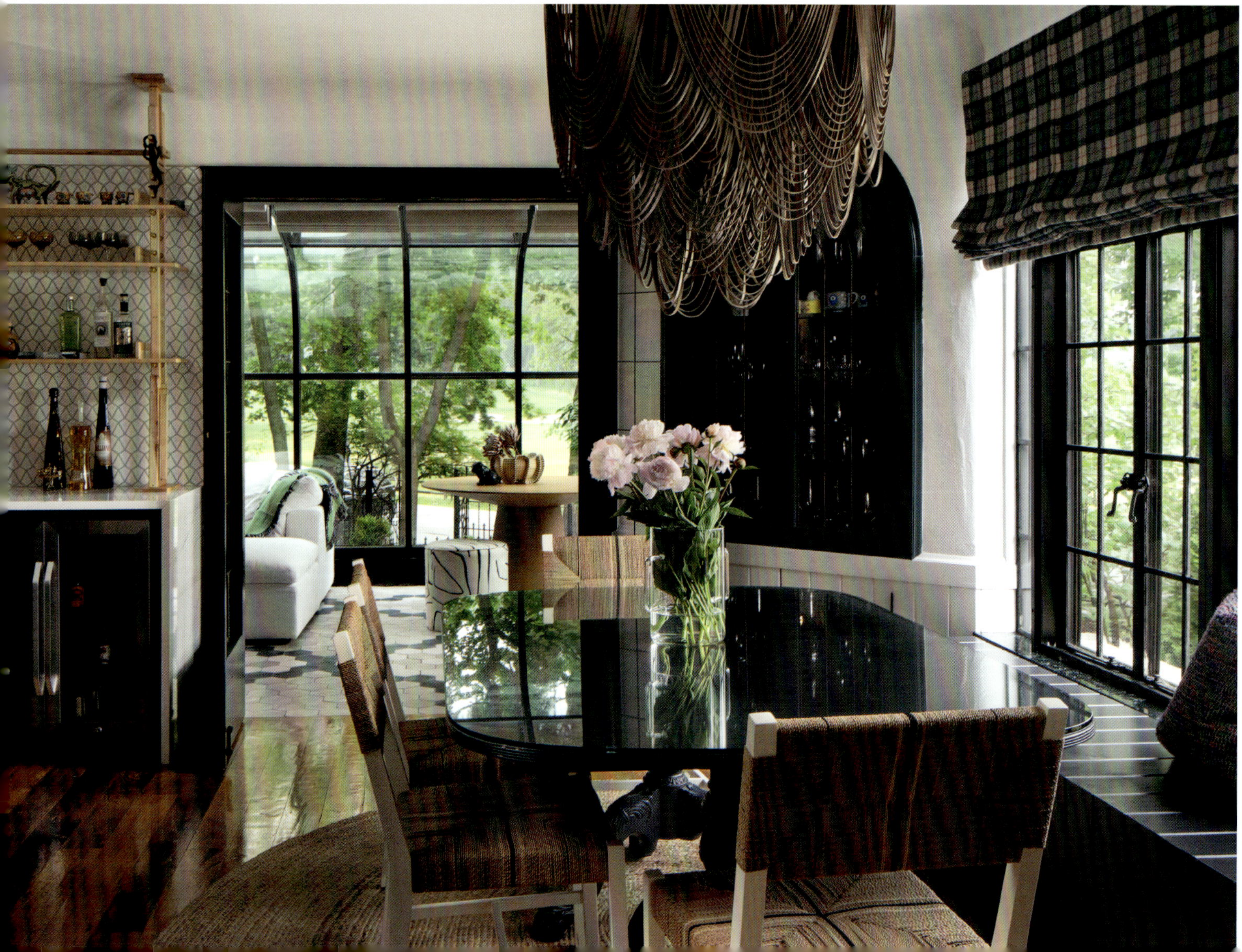

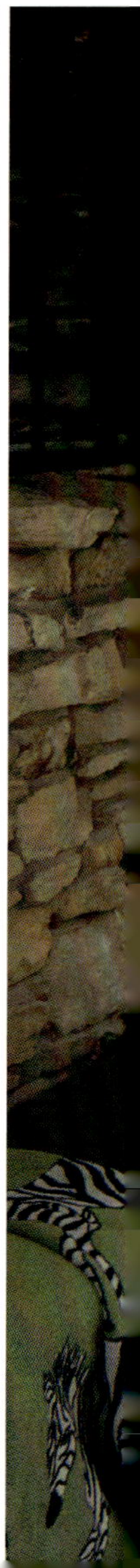

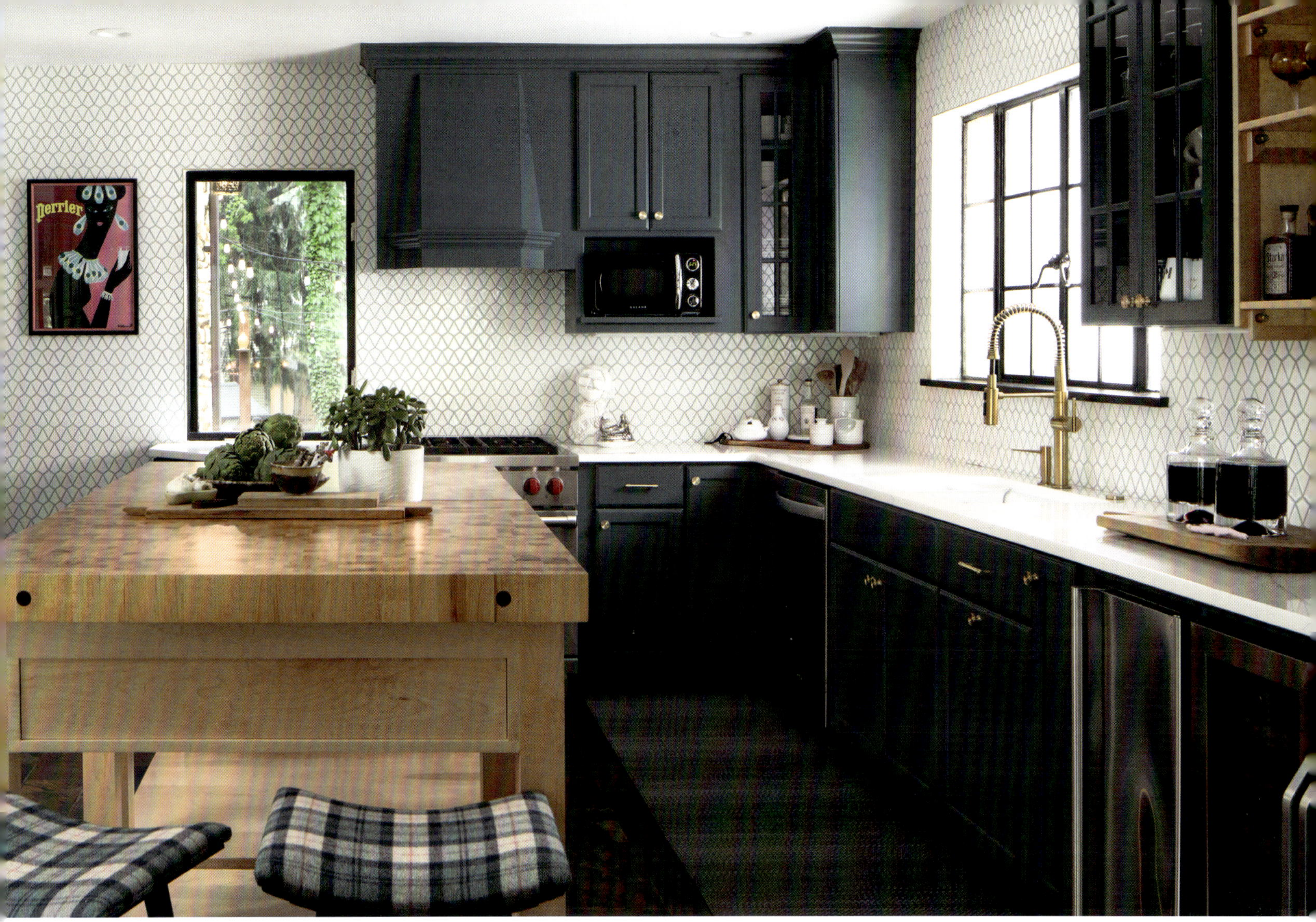

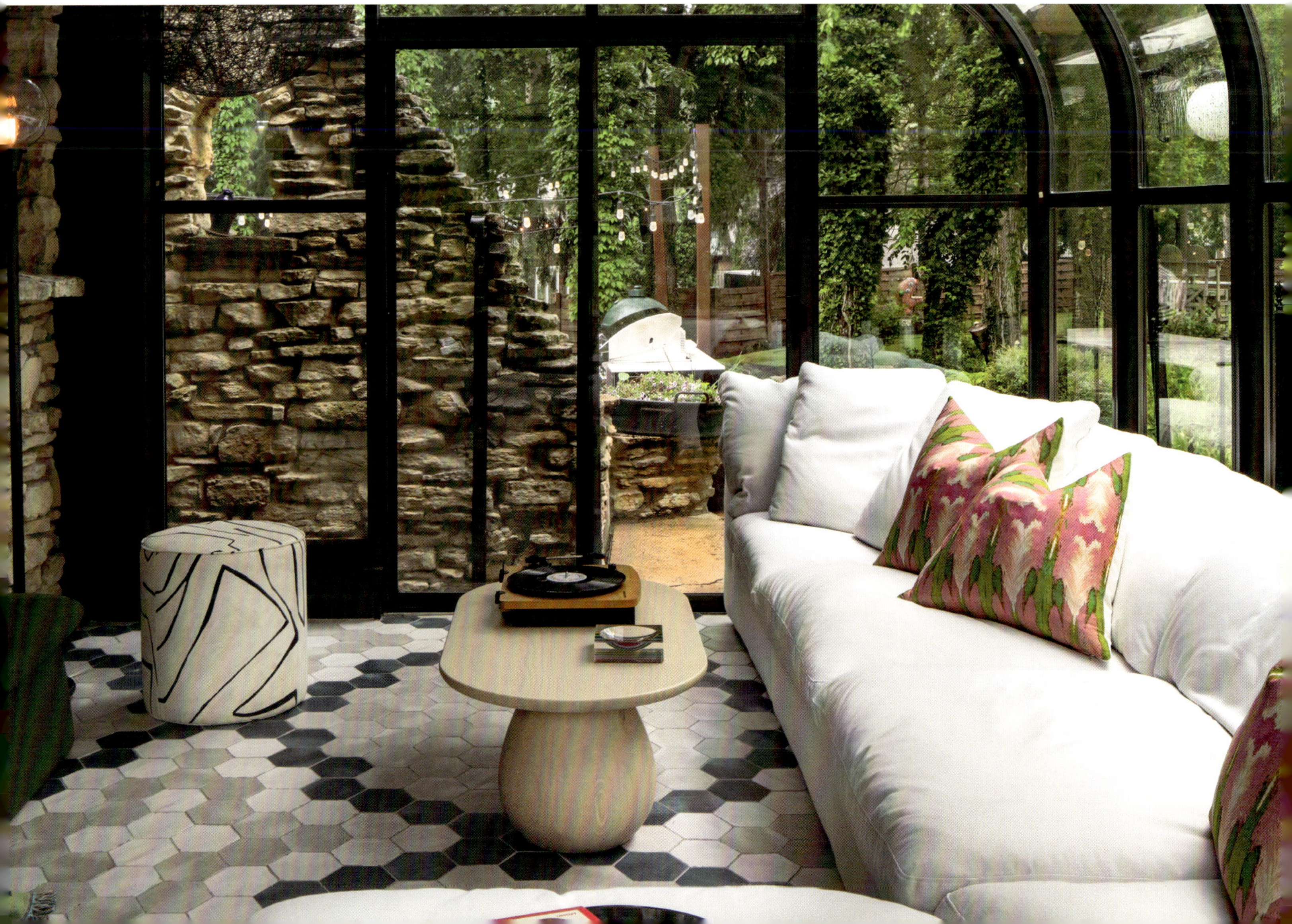

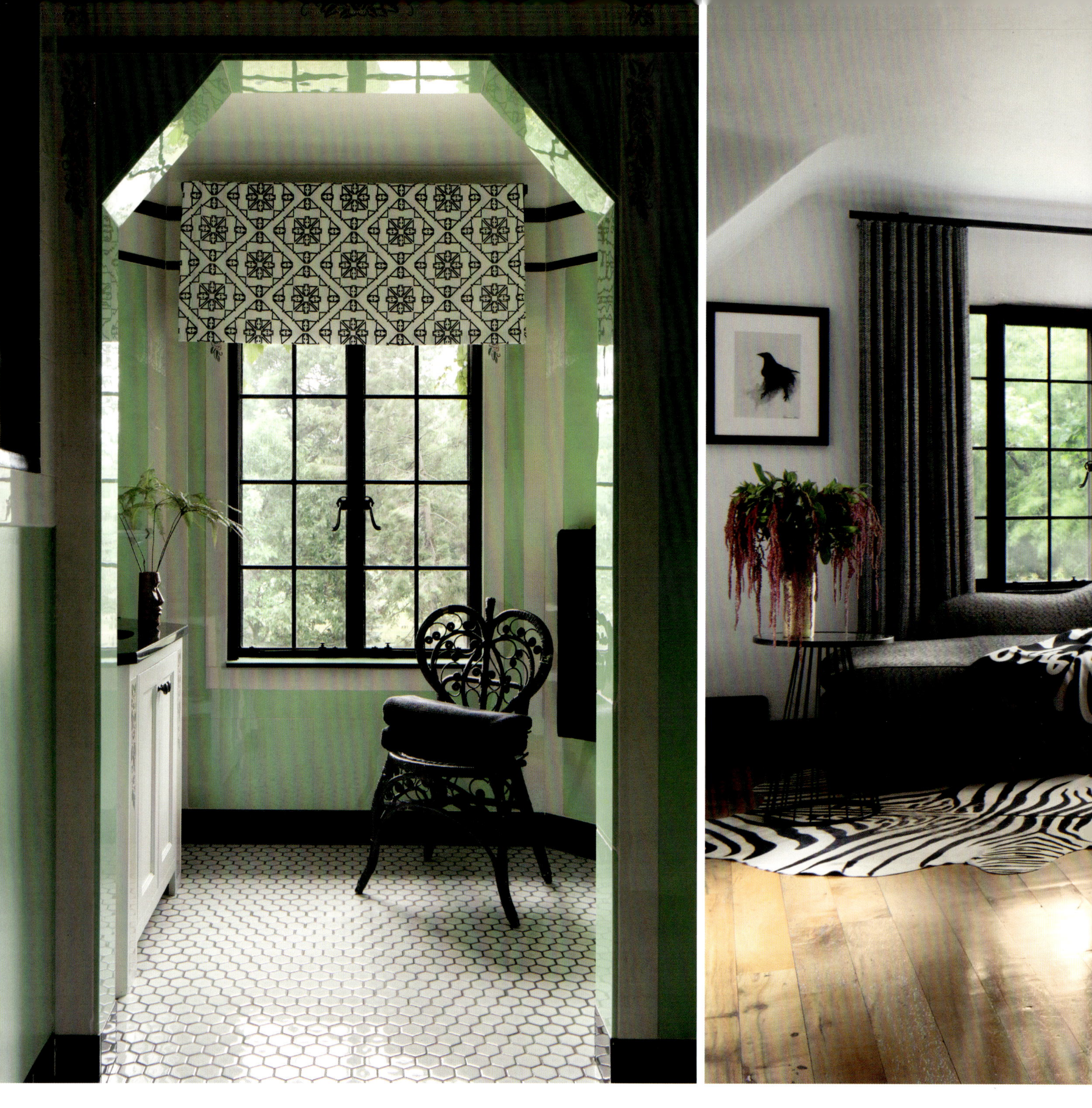

PREVIOUS: The eat-in kitchen flows into a sunroom featuring a modernized vintage tile pattern in teal, pink, and mint green hues that inspired the kitchen's design. An African chandelier from Ngala illuminates the space, complemented by plaid fabrics and colorful cabinetry.

ABOVE: *Left:* The bathroom showcases original green tiles that add vintage character. *Right:* A serene bedroom features an exquisite custom bed by Lagomorph Design crafted from exotic woods, complemented by artwork by Francine Turk. The window treatments echo the home's black-and-white theme.

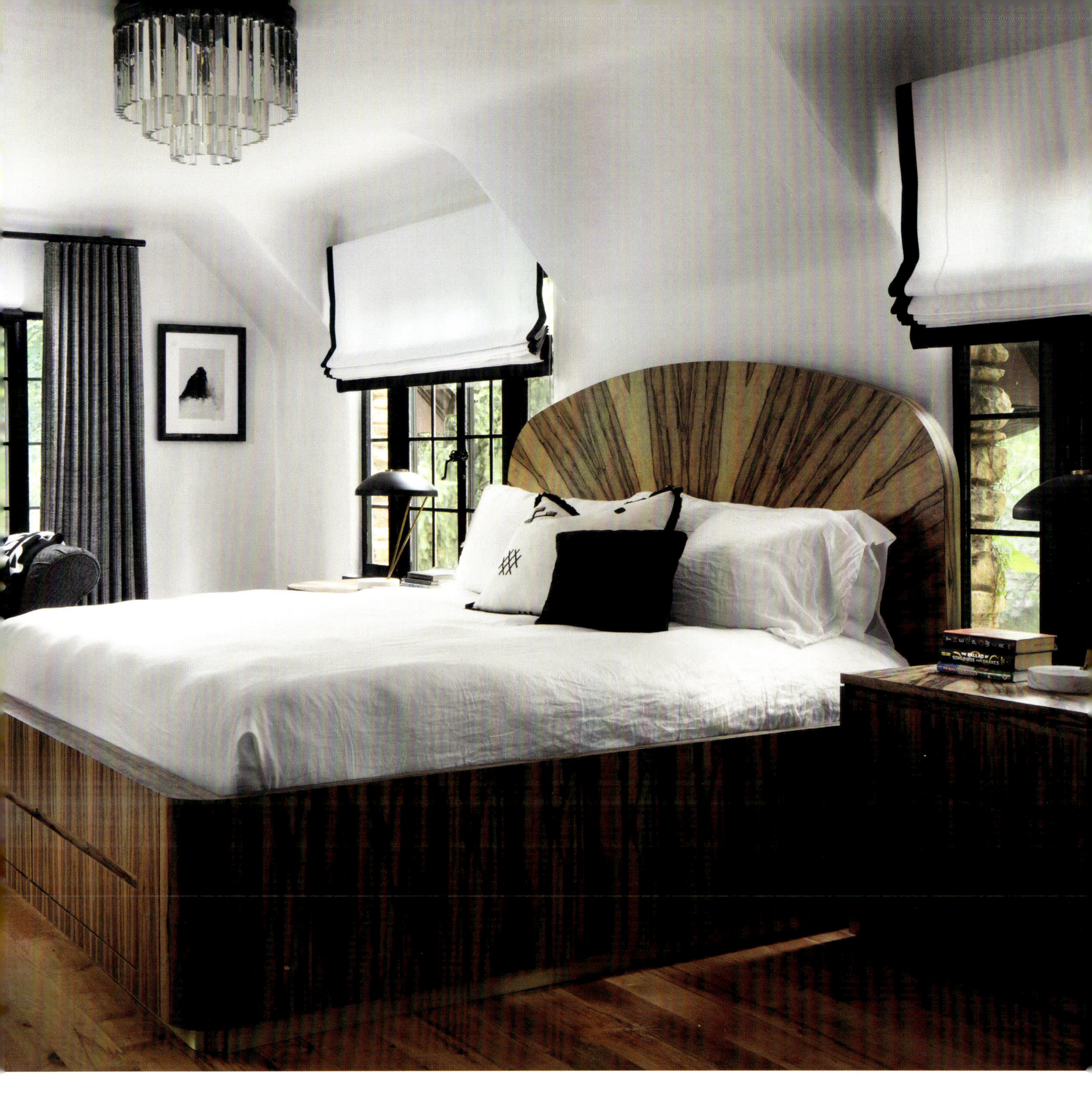

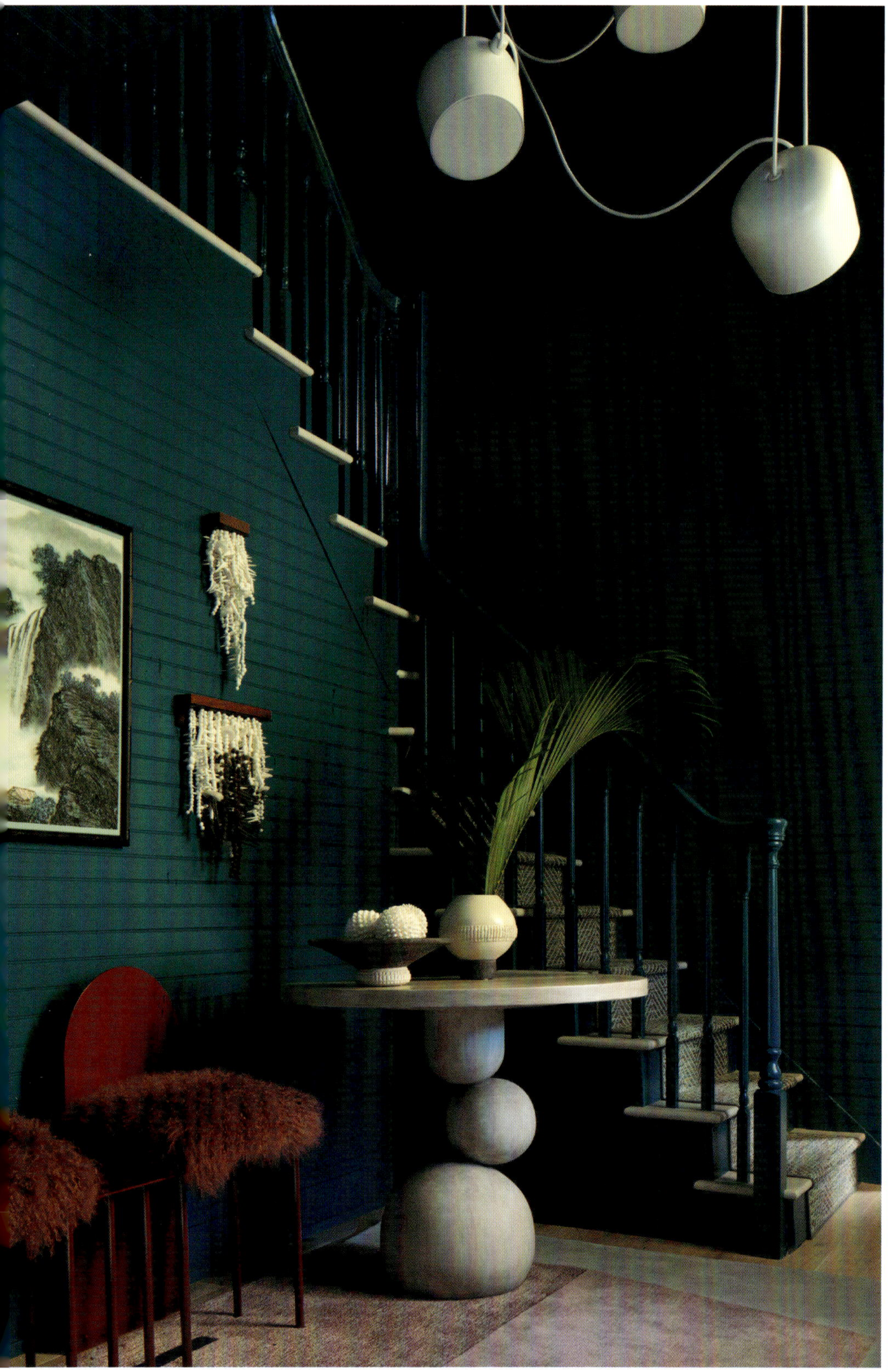

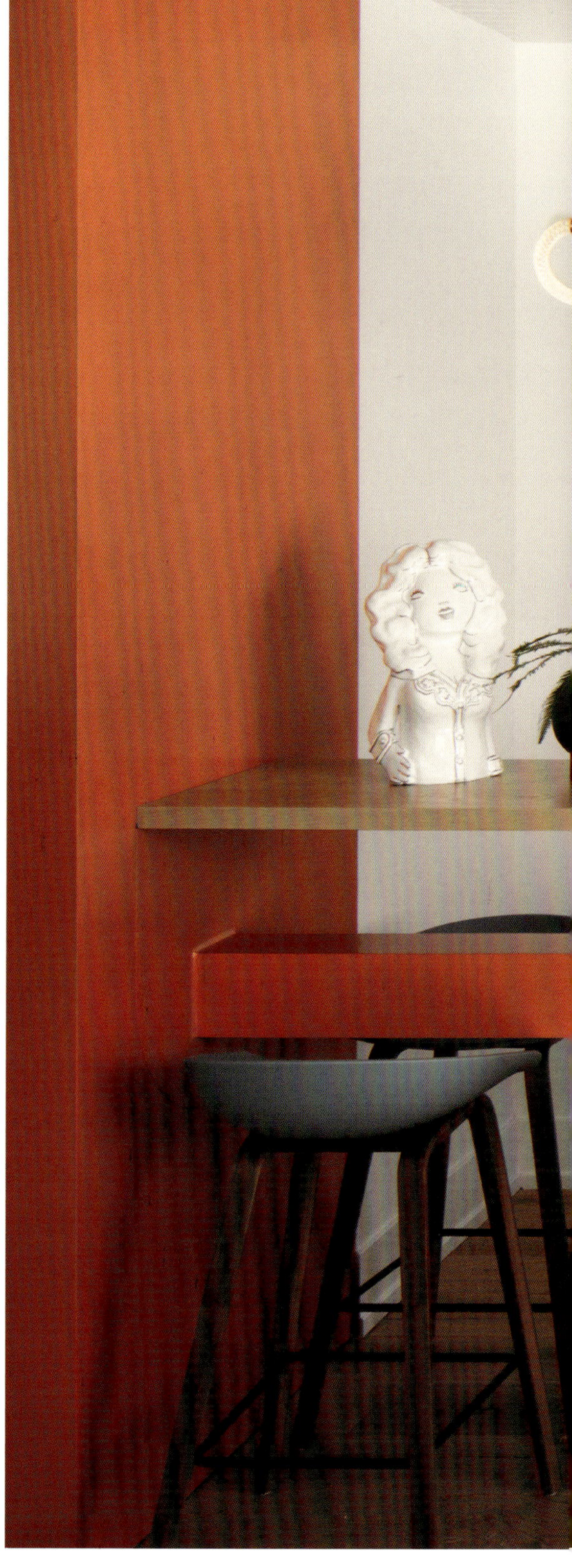

Left: The foyer welcomes visitors with its deep teal walls inspired by Lake Michigan, leading upstairs to the second floor. *Right:* A surfboard-inspired cantilever breakfast bar from Artemest features a vibrant orange seat that beautifully complements the teal, both colors inspired by lakeside sunsets.

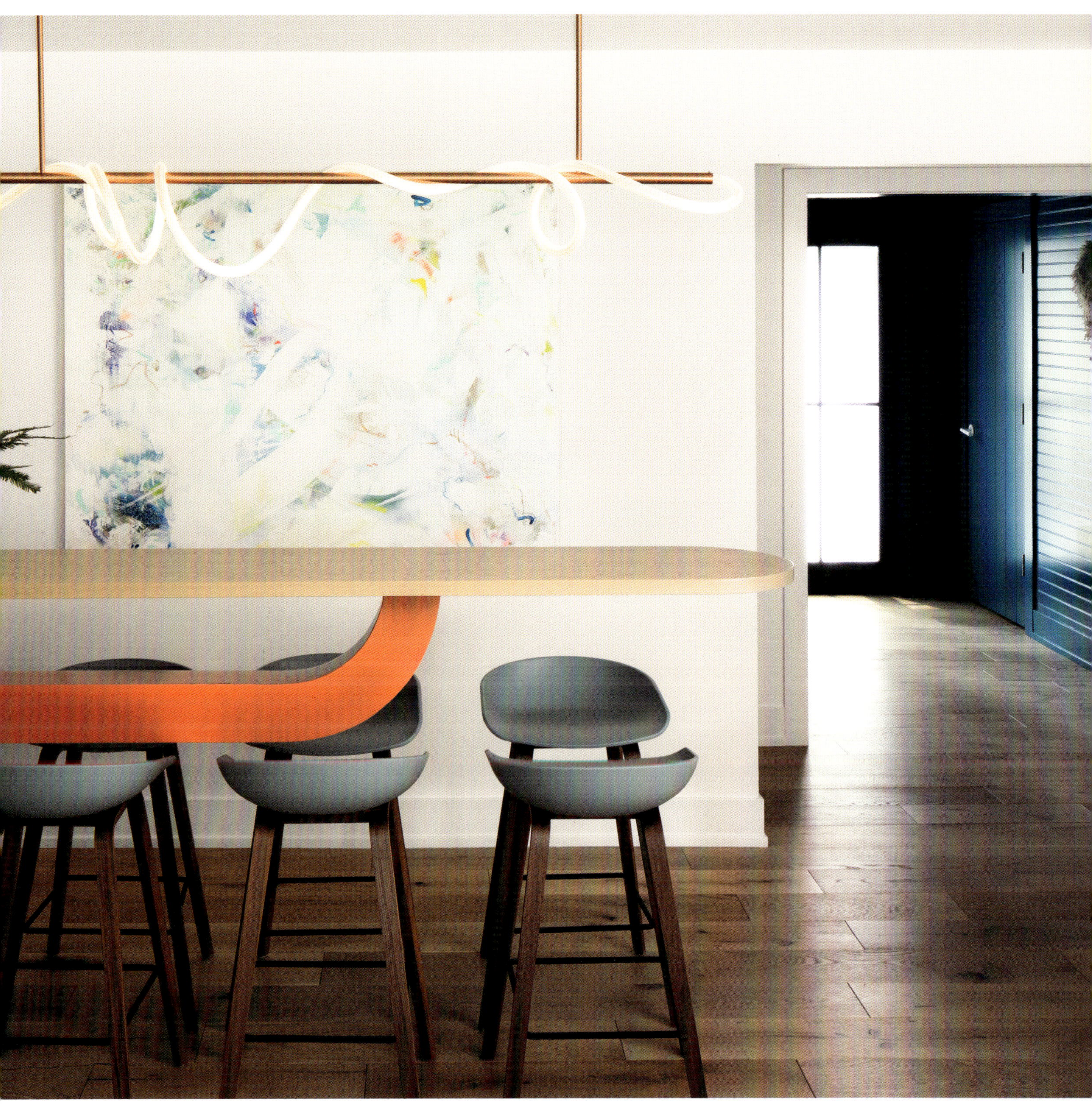

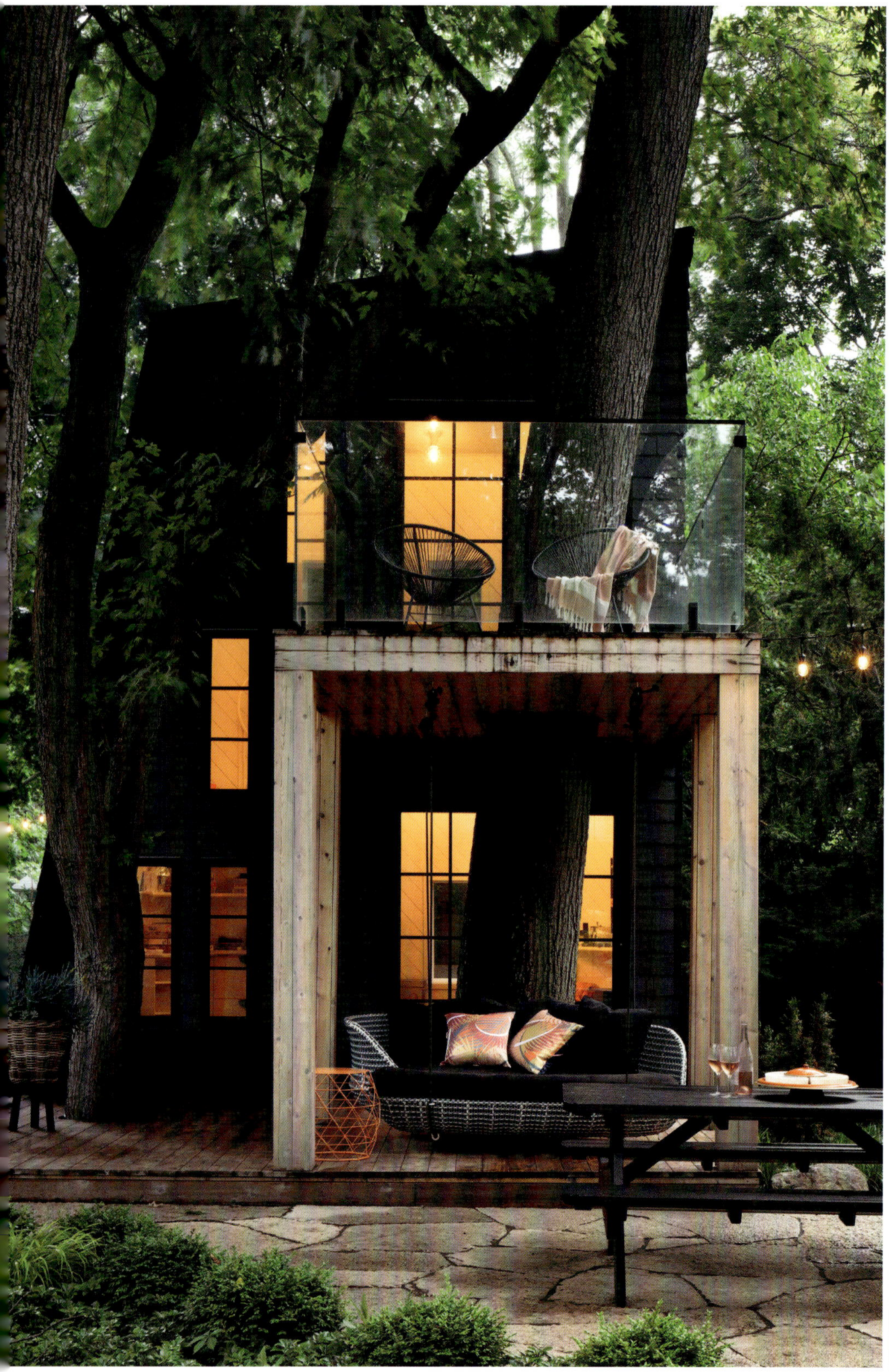

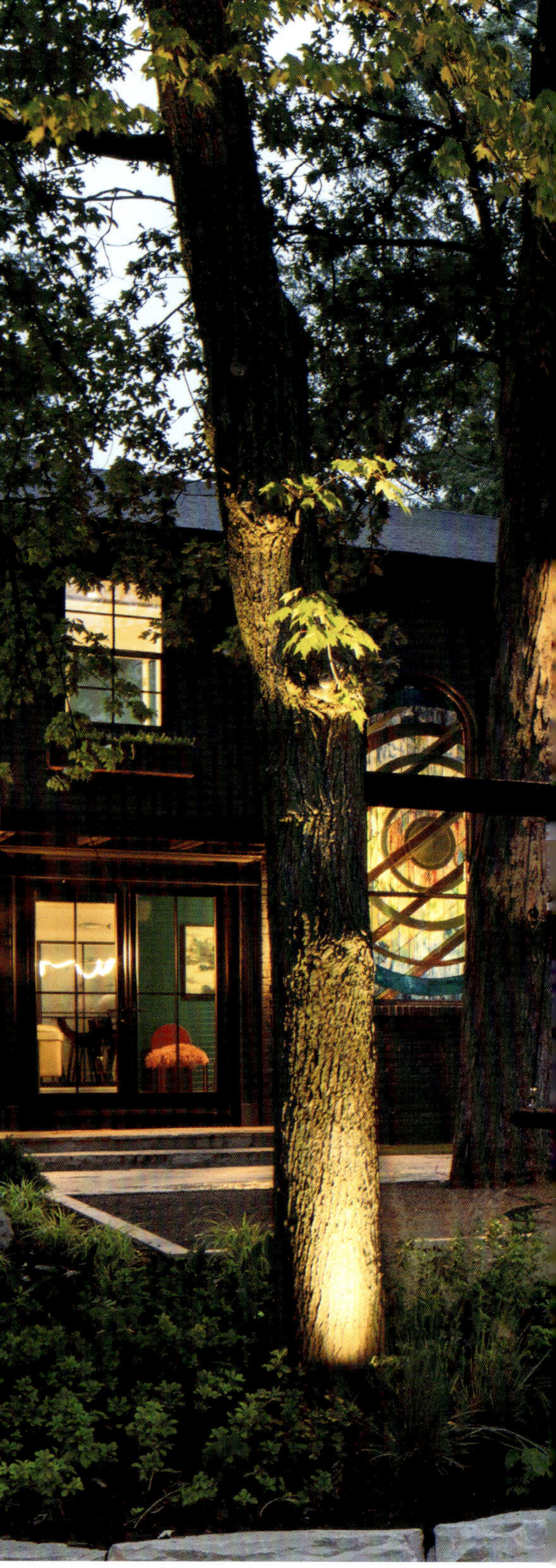

Left: The custom-designed treehouse by Filoramo Talsma architects features a swing suspended beneath its second-floor balcony. *Right:* The black-painted guesthouse, acquired just before the COVID-19 pandemic, showcases a striking stained glass window and whimsical sculptures, including a surfboard-riding frog.

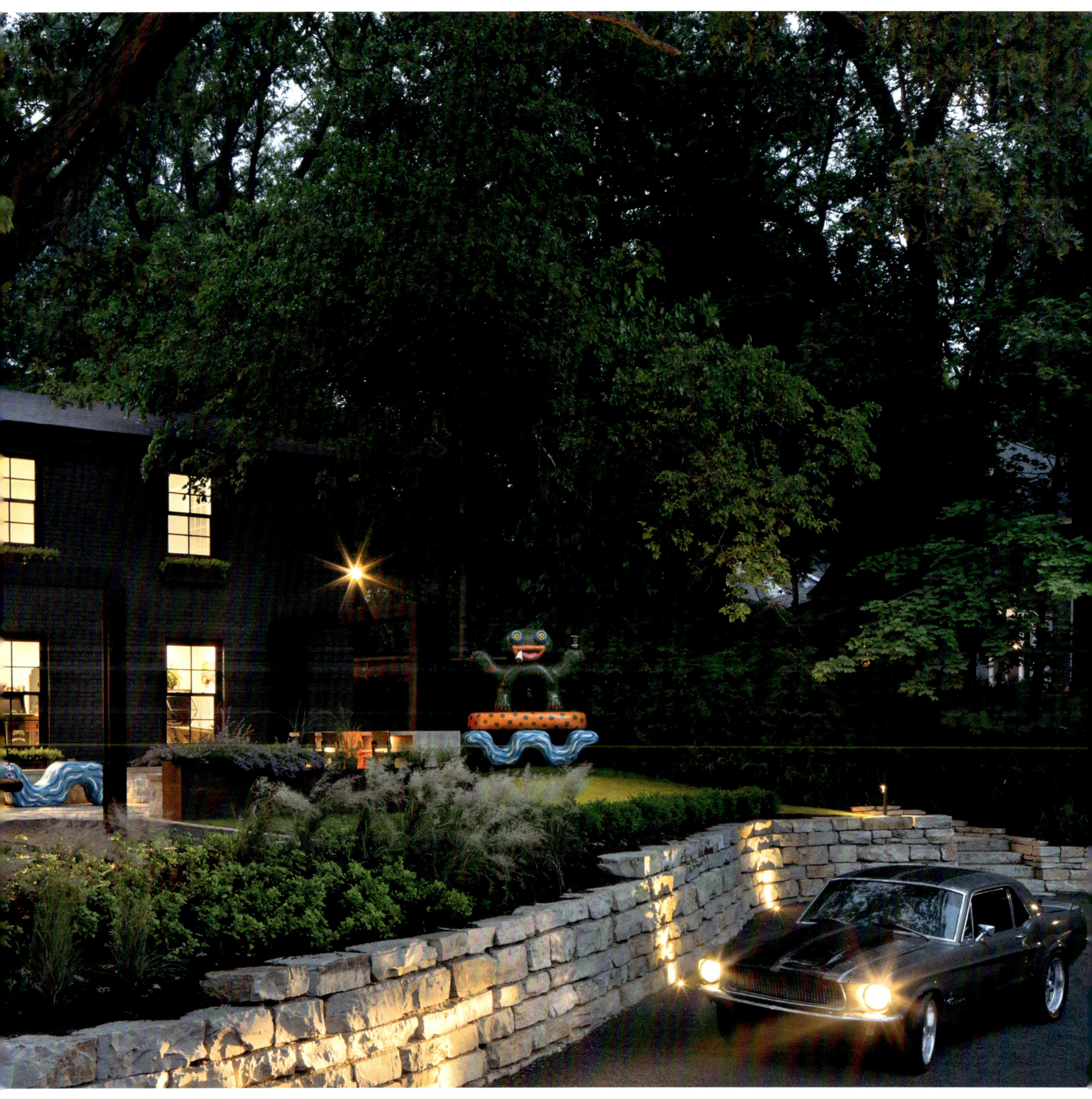

MODERN LODGE

Lucas Goldbach / En Masse

Set on 40 woodland acres overlooking the Wisconsin River, this contemporary lodge reimagines the structural vocabulary of traditional Midwestern cabins for modern family life. Designed and built by En Masse Architecture as a second home for a busy Madison-based family, the residence creates a rural sanctuary for relaxation and entertaining.

Rustic-refined architecture employs heavy timber construction throughout the main living spaces—while avoiding the conventional log cabin aesthetic. Local Fond du Lac stone grounds the structure in its natural surroundings, with many of the boulders sourced directly from the site or nearby locations. The wood and stone contrast with modern cabinetry and fixtures for a sophisticated yet durable environment.

At its heart, the home is designed for gathering. With seven bedrooms, including a multilevel bunk room sleeping ten and hotel-style guest rooms with queen beds, the lodge can comfortably host up to twenty-four people. The spaces flow from intimate areas perfect for the inner circle, to generous communal zones that accommodate extended family and friends.

The home's relationship with the surrounding topography is expressed through thoughtful architectural features. For example, a convertible dining room transitions seamlessly from indoor to outdoor space via sliding doors, while a covered "grill porch" enables nearly year-round outdoor cooking. Expansive windows are framed by structural timber elements, carefully directing views toward the river and surrounding forest.

Comfort and sustainability underpin the home's design. Radiant heating for efficient climate control in the larger spaces, high-performance windows, and reclaimed wood for floors and ceilings complement the timber framework.

With recreation in mind, a massive "toy garage" accommodates the family's vehicles, including space for a full-size RV with pull-through capability. Additional amenities include a thirty-seat theater room in the basement.

As one of En Masse Architecture's first major commissions, this lodge exemplifies its ability to create architecturally significant and deeply personal spaces. The result is a modern retreat that honors its Midwestern context while providing homeowners with a durable, beautiful setting for the business of life.

This intimate turret space functions as a four-season room where the family gathers for games and conversation over drinks. Featuring reclaimed oak from local barns and Wisconsin stone, it can transform into a screen porch with cascading woven lanterns in warmer months.

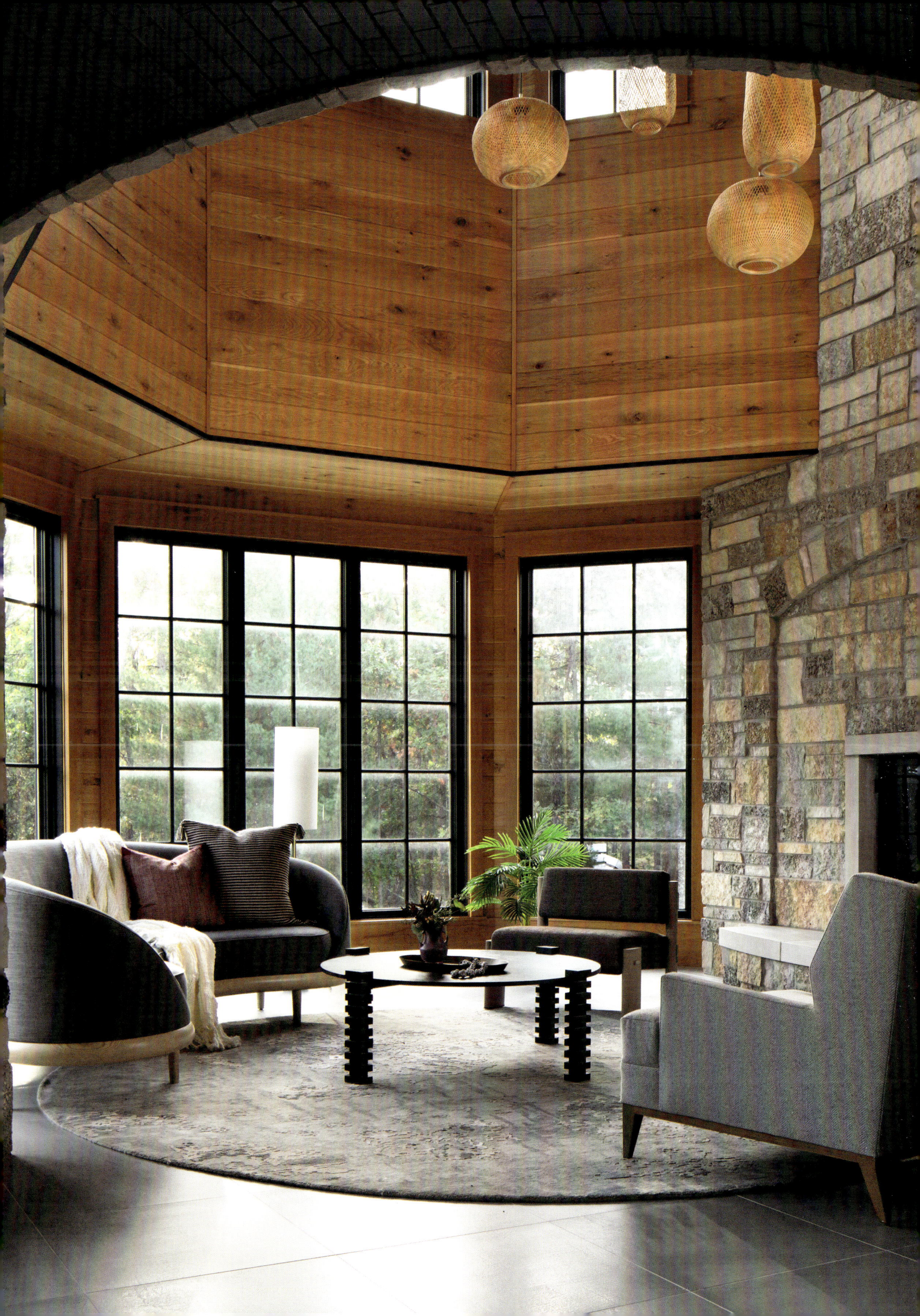

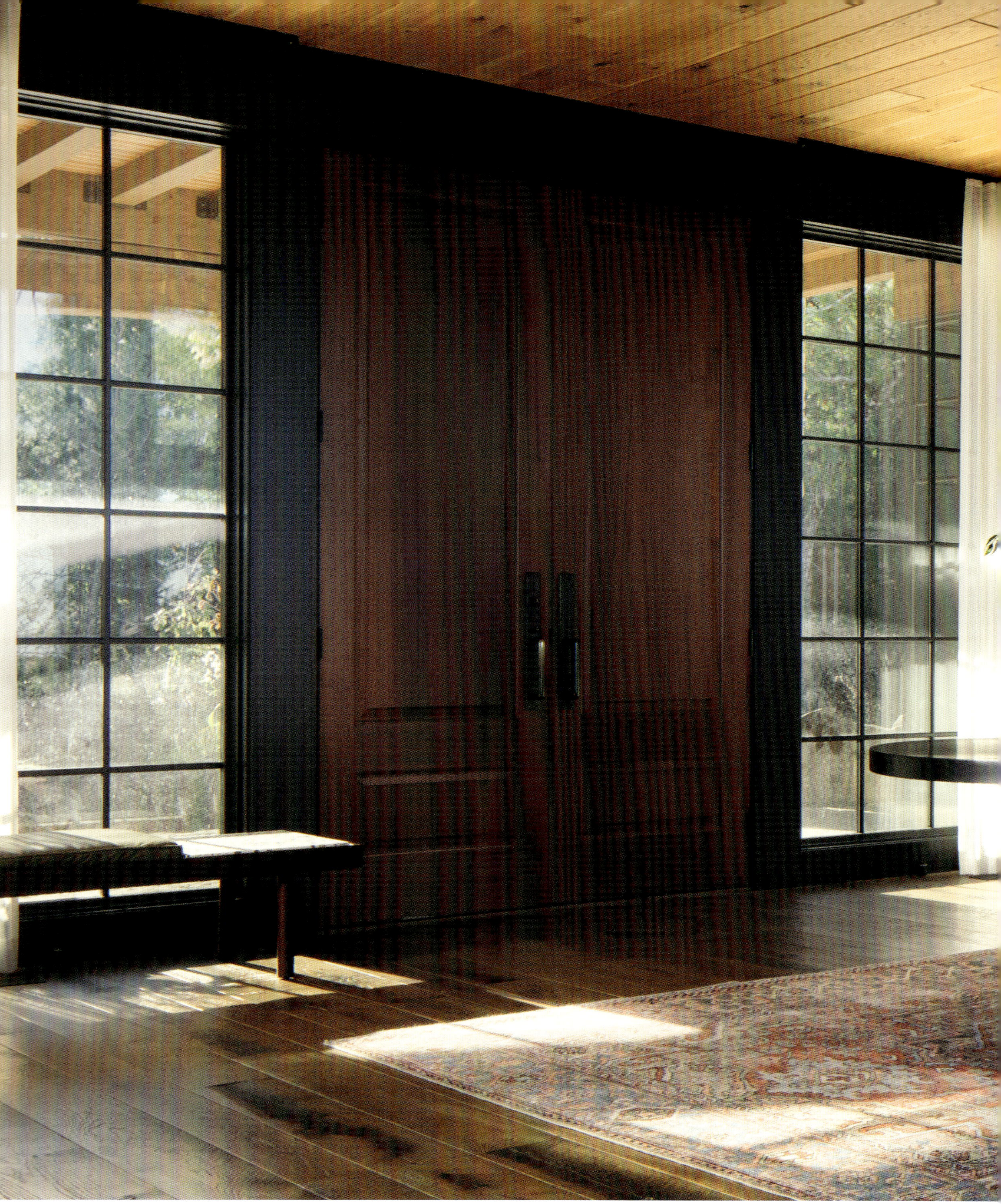

The impressive entryway spans 35 feet wide by 20 feet deep, connecting the kitchen and staircase while showcasing structural heavy timber beams that support a two-level catwalk above. Both ceiling and floors feature oak from the same source—dressed overhead, and rougher-hewn reclaimed barnwood underfoot.

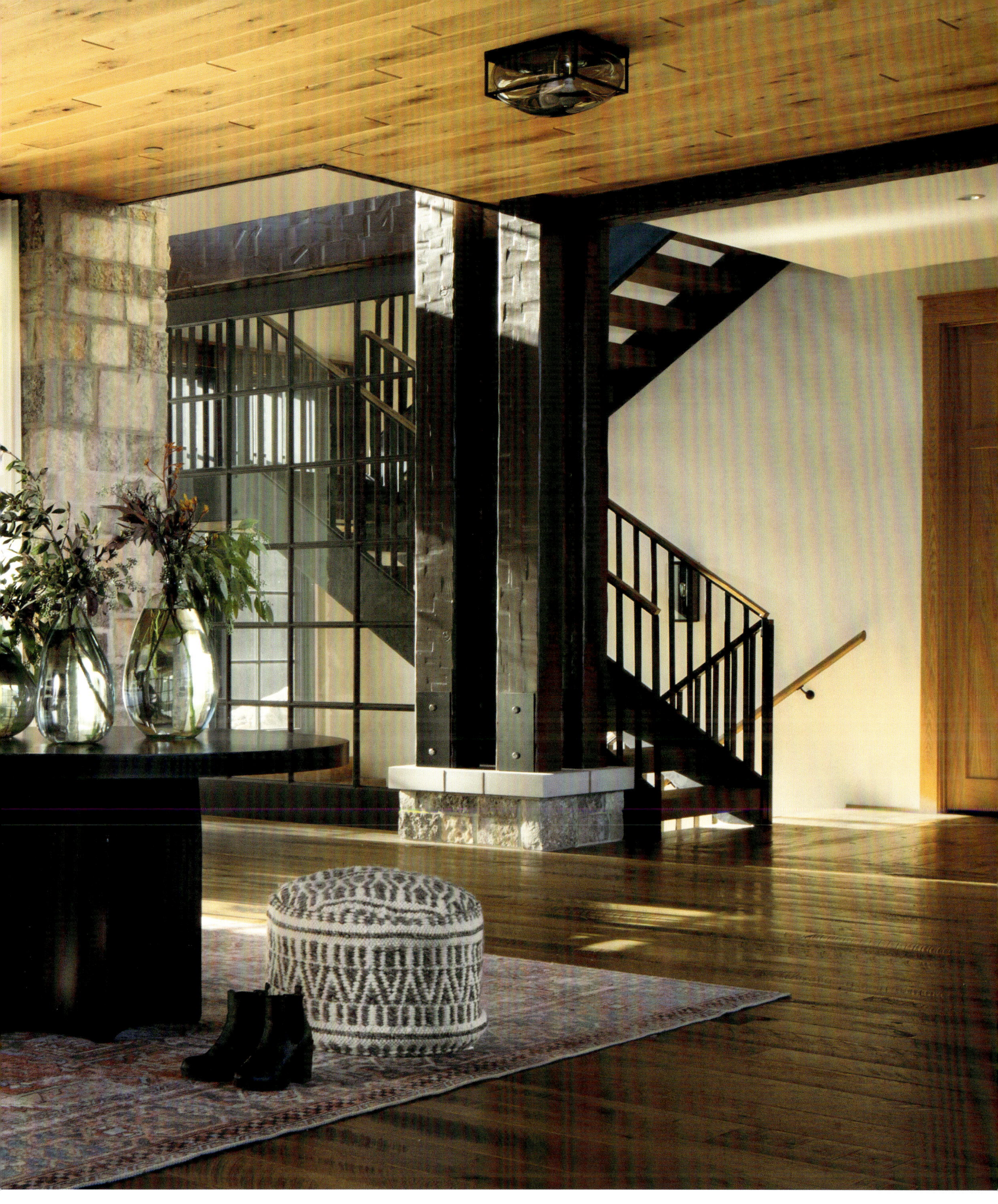

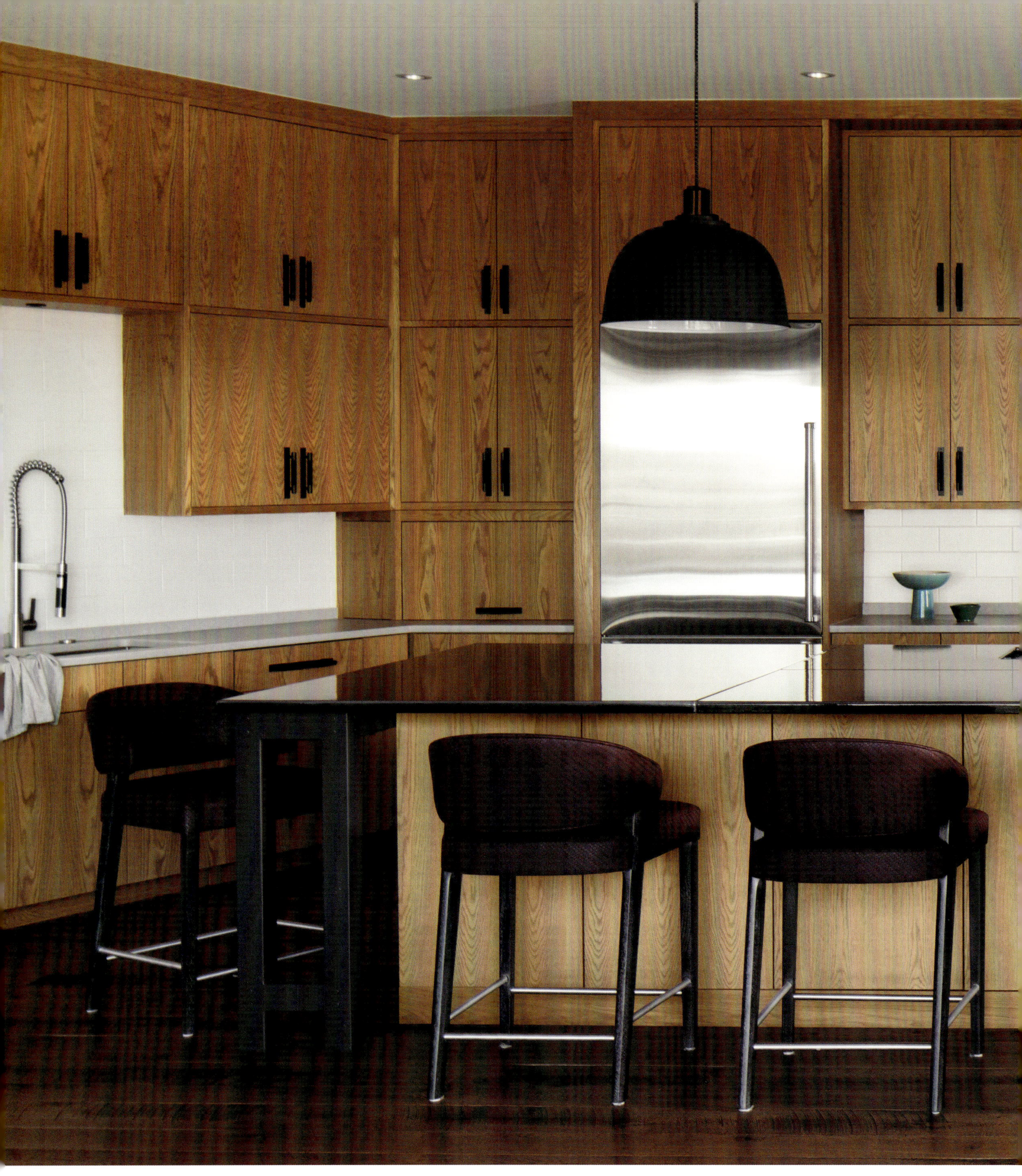

This central kitchen anchors the home, connecting the great hall, study, mudroom, and grill porch. Custom white oak cabinetry with metal accents pairs with quartz perimeter countertops, while the striking island features glazed volcanic Pyrolave stone with ceramic accents.

NEXT: This versatile dining room features a rear wall of stackable windows that open completely to create a covered outdoor space in warm months. Fireclay glazed brick ceilings complement Waterworks porcelain tile flooring in warm gray tones that echo the local exterior stonework.

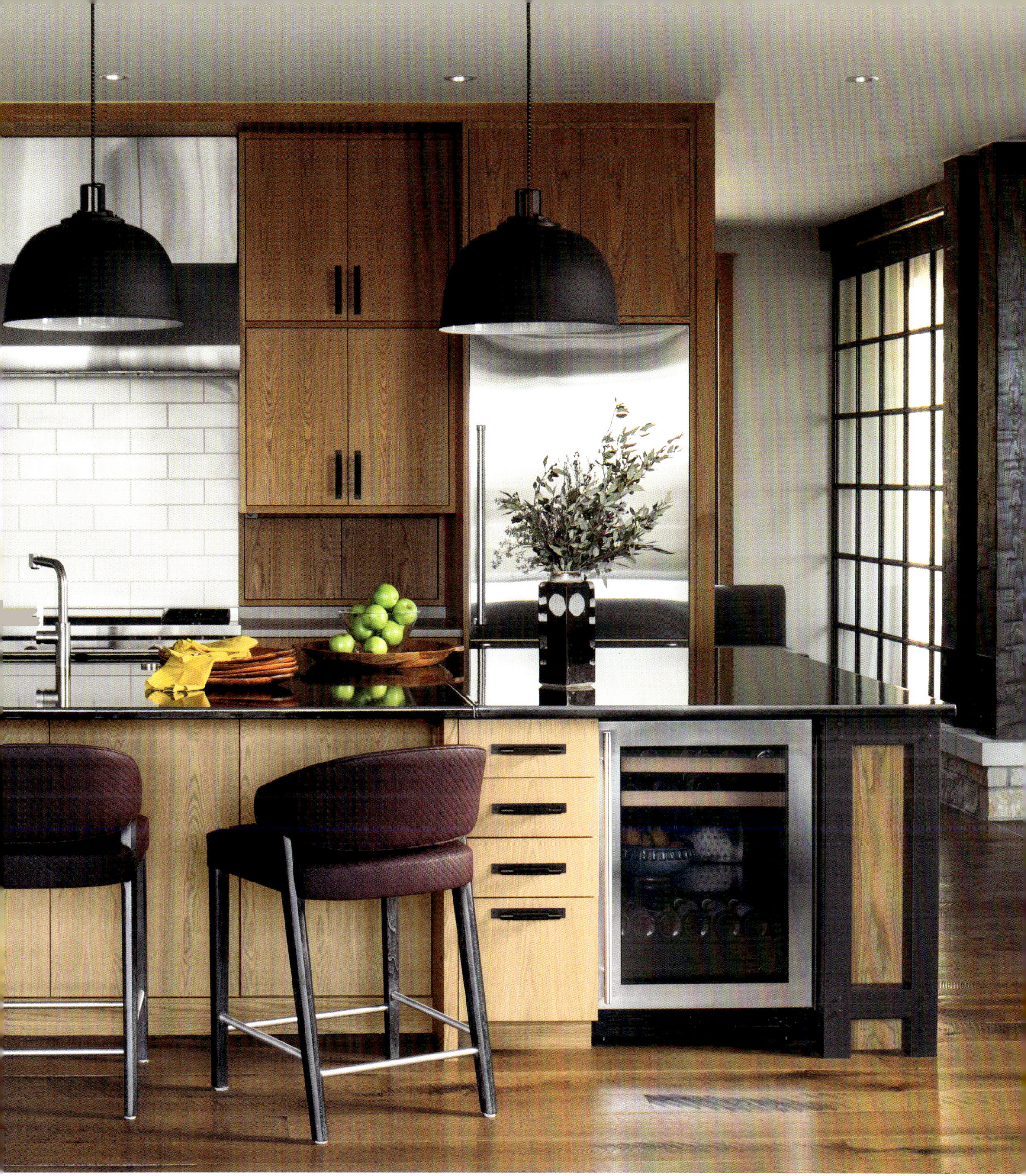

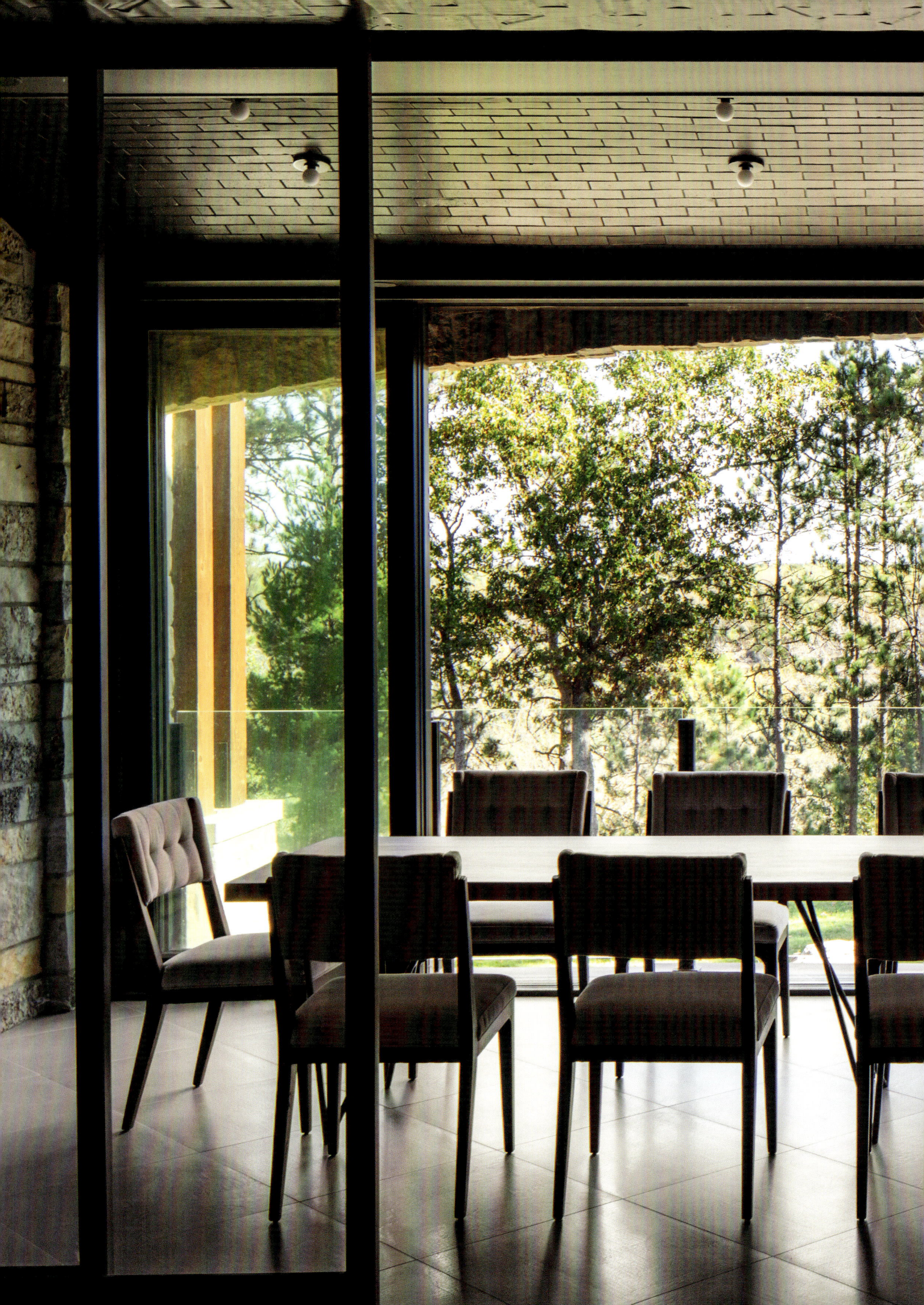

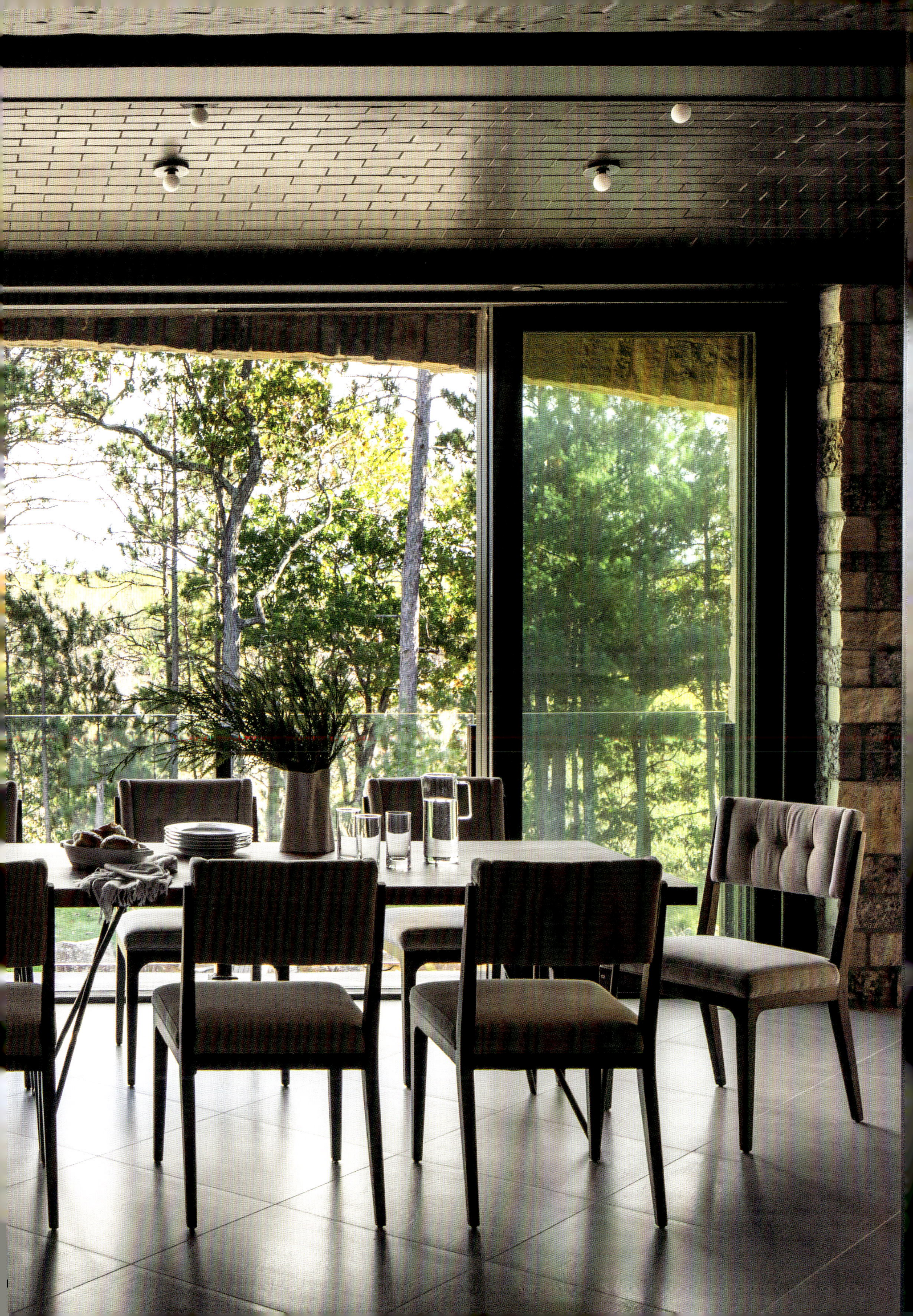

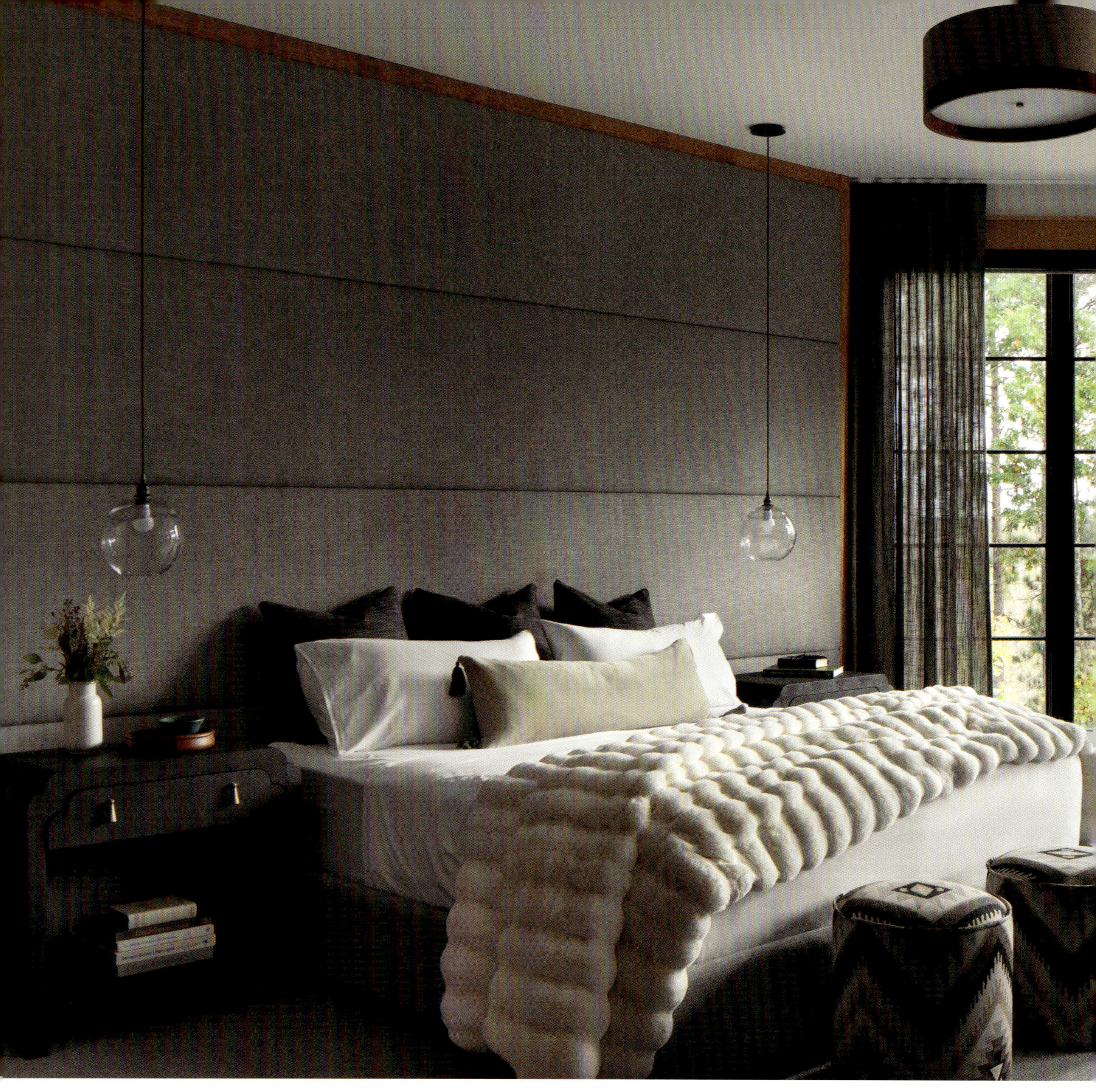

ABOVE: *Left:* This main-level primary bedroom offers a soft respite from the home's more robust architecture. It features an acoustically enhanced upholstered wall, black-framed windows with coordinating sheers, and an emerald leather daybed that reflects the verdant surroundings beyond the windows. *Right:* A luxurious soaking tub anchors the primary bath, positioned to be visible along the home's central axis when doors open.

NEXT: This rear elevation showcases the home's engagement with its wooded Wisconsin River setting through nearly one hundred windows and multiple sliding doors. The glass-walled great hall, arched dining room, and Tourette-style four-season room create seamless indoor-outdoor connections, while private balconies grace guest suites above.

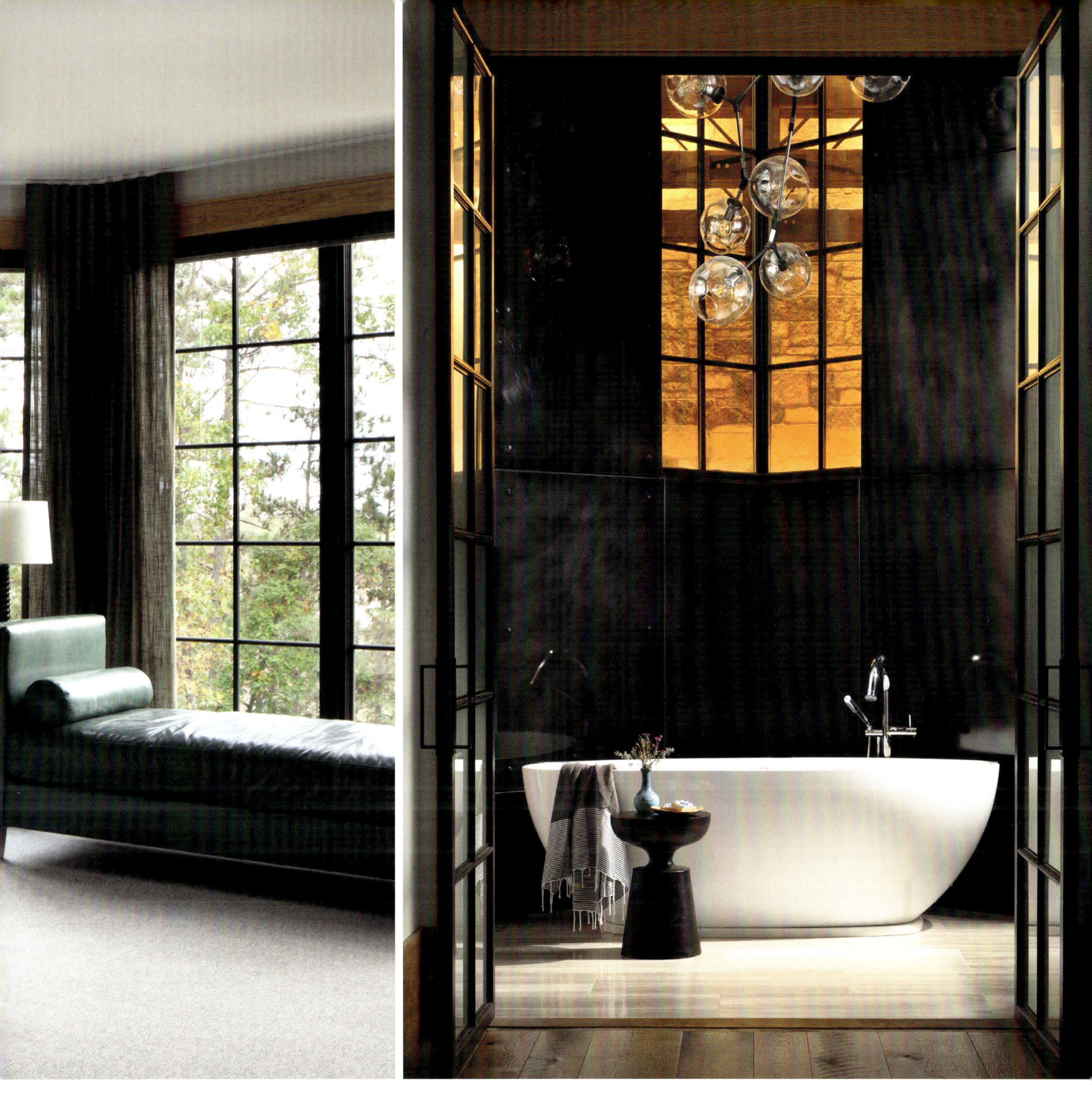

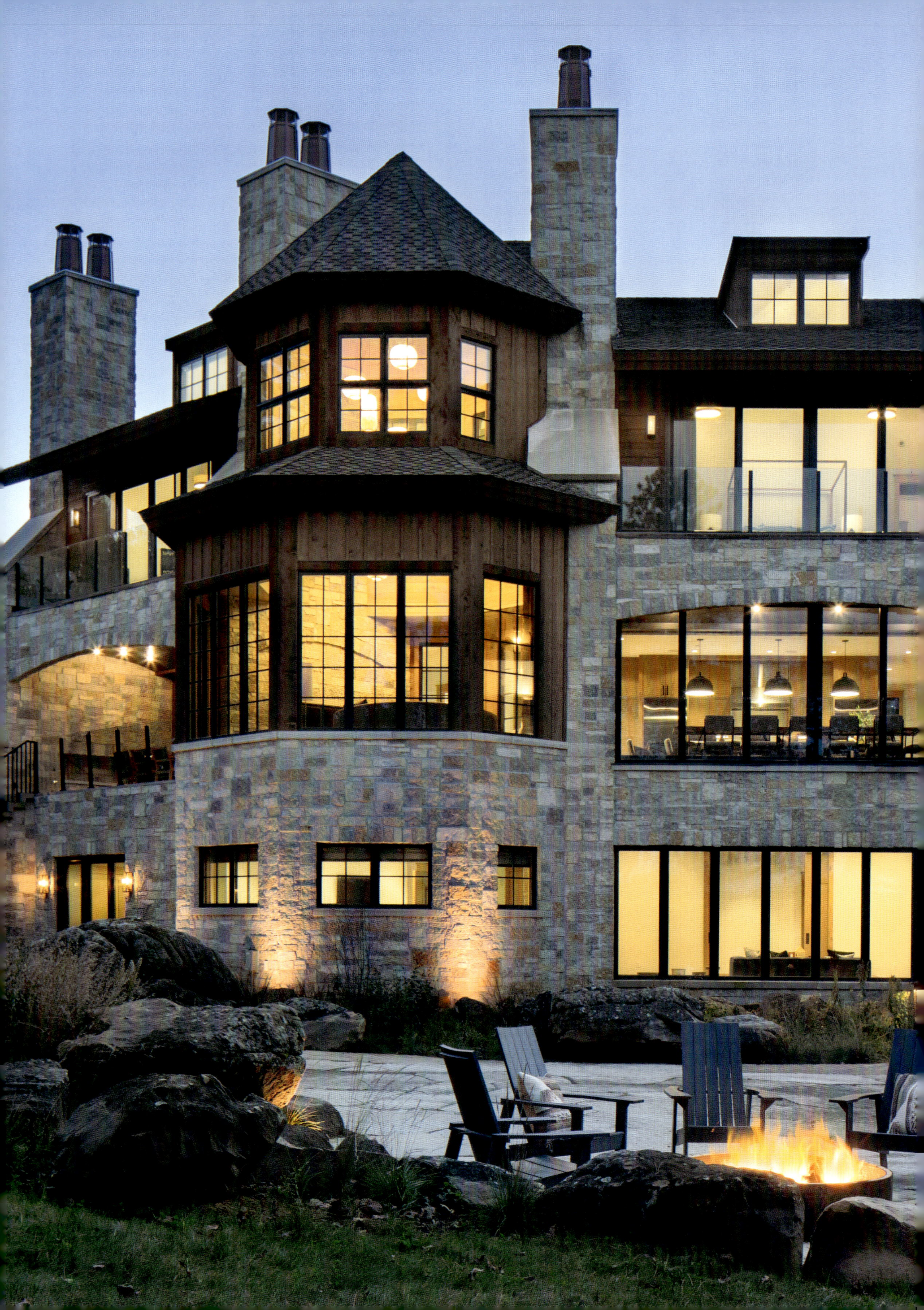

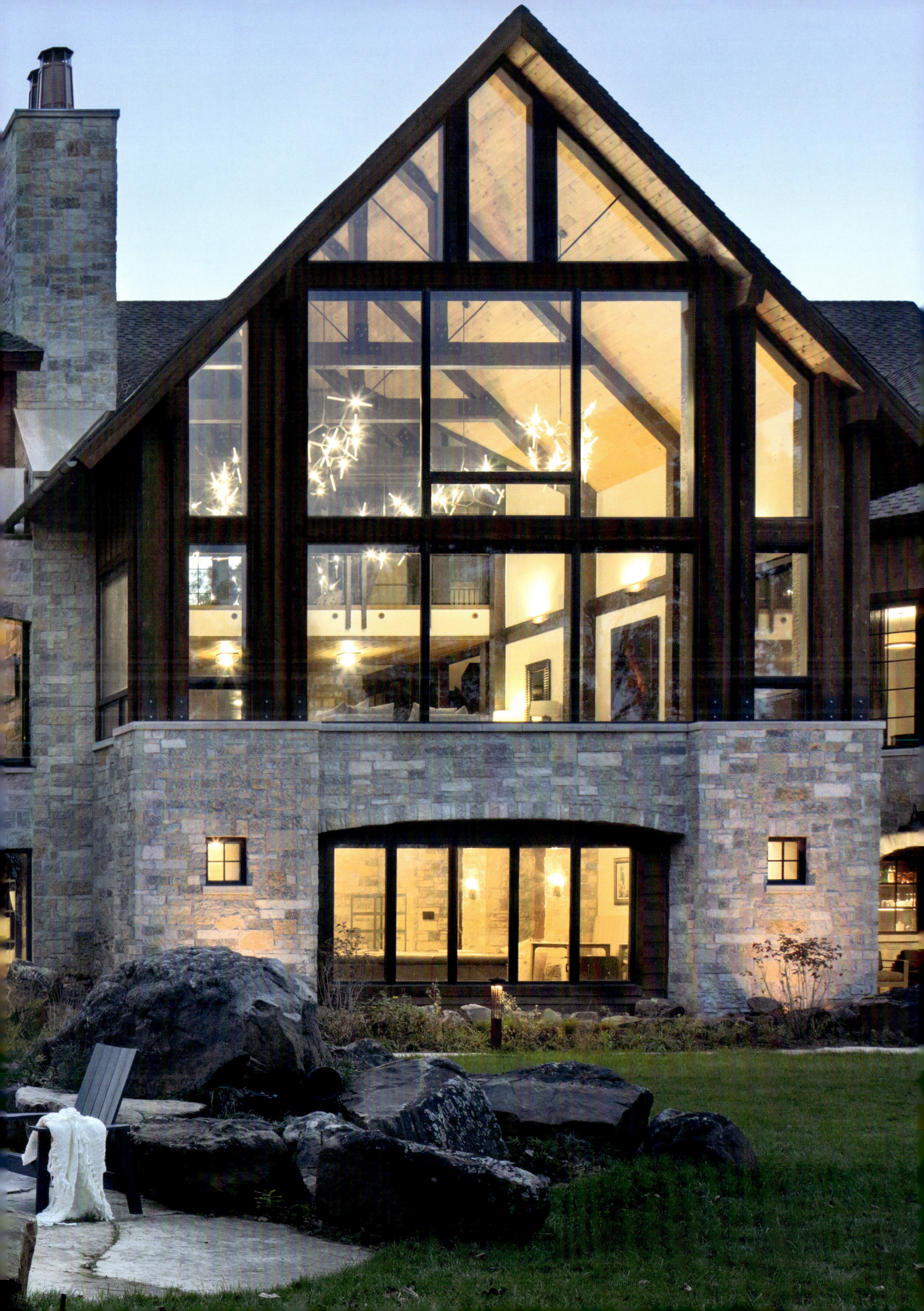

HIDDEN BACHELOR HAVEN

Kelly Marie Brainerd / KMB Design | Consulting

Designer Kelly Brainerd transformed this former commercial building in the heart of downtown Milwaukee into a unique residence that is both a private sanctuary and a social hub for its globe-trotting owner.

The home's unassuming exterior, hardly recognizable as a residence, belies the architectural innovations within. A deft juxtaposition of aged and contemporary finishes is revealed inside the front door. For example, the original glazed and Cream City brick walls, unique to the area, nod to the building's history while framing the modern interventions with an air of timelessness.

The ground floor was designed with stylish living in mind. Expansive and light-filled, the main space coexists with a four-car garage that houses a collection of vintage automobiles. Just next door, a truncated basketball court with a soaring ceiling adds an unexpected, athletic grandeur. A billiard table completes the recreation tableau.

Ascending to the upper level, one discovers the owner's private domain. The primary bedroom suite, TV area, and access to a rooftop patio create a self-contained apartment within the larger structure, drawing a domestic distinction from the communal regions below.

Milwaukee's Midwest climate is quartered in distinct seasons, and Brainerd's design fully embraces these variations, from snow to sun. Above the structure is a communal outdoor patio outfitted with streamlined furniture and a fire pit perfect for al fresco entertaining. A second patio space is accessible through the primary bedroom.

For the long winter months, multiple skylights bathe the interior architecture with natural light, creating a bright, airy atmosphere regardless of the weather outside. Their addition transforms the massive space into something paradoxically cozy and intimate.

Personal touches, from a vintage Cadillac sign to custom wallpaper featuring murals from the owner's hometown, meld seamlessly with the building's industrial bones in a classic-cool refinement reflective of the proprietor's personality.

As American cities focus on sustainability, this Milwaukee residence shows how a subdued commercial space can transform into a fresh haven through conscious creativity and skill.

This striking building facade conceals a unique dual-purpose design. The large opening on the left provides access to an indoor half-court basketball court with a second-floor viewing area, occupying the front third of this 28-by-90-foot structure. The remaining space houses equal-footprint living areas across two floors, creating a harmonious balance between recreational and residential functions.

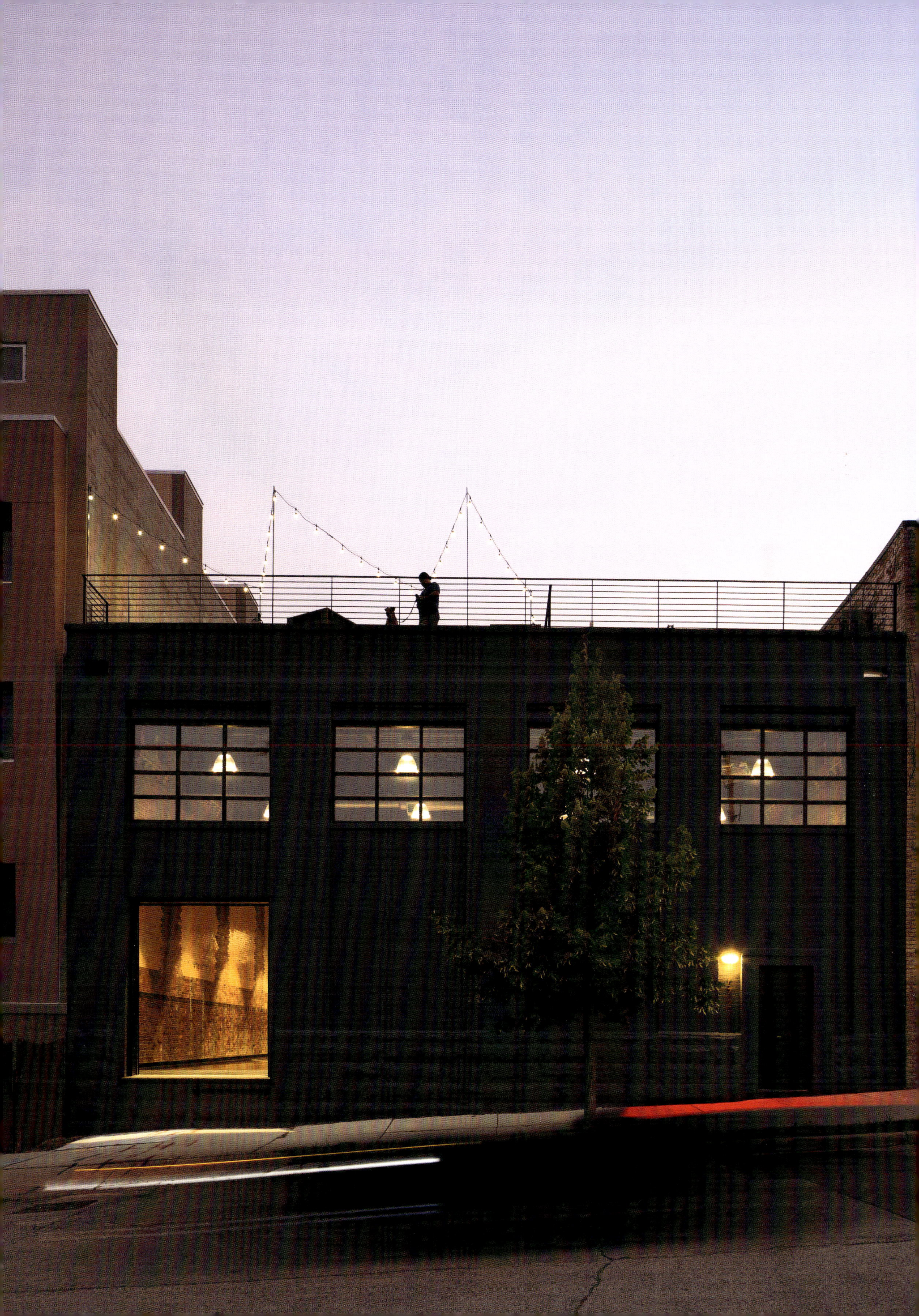

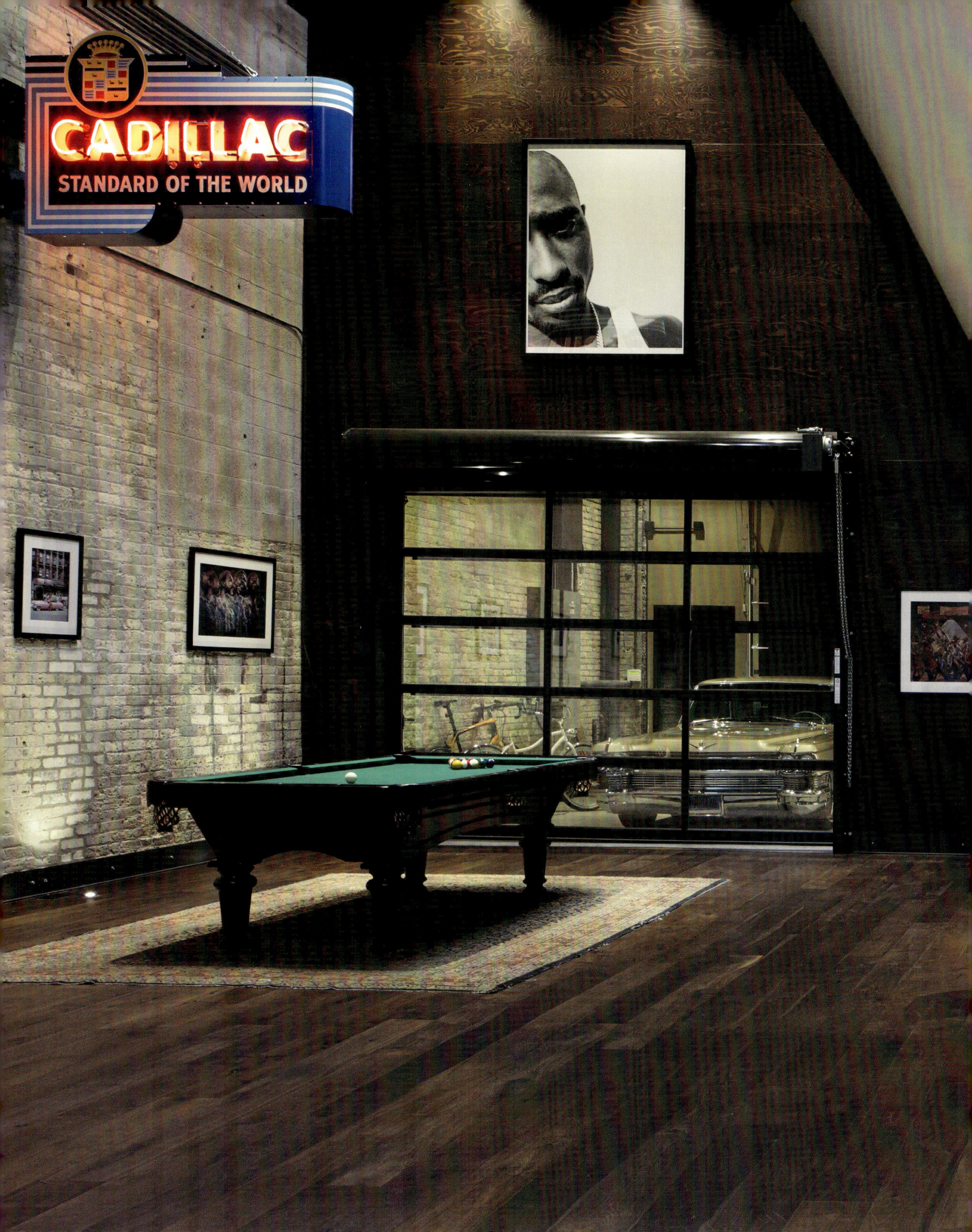
CADILLAC
STANDARD OF THE WORLD

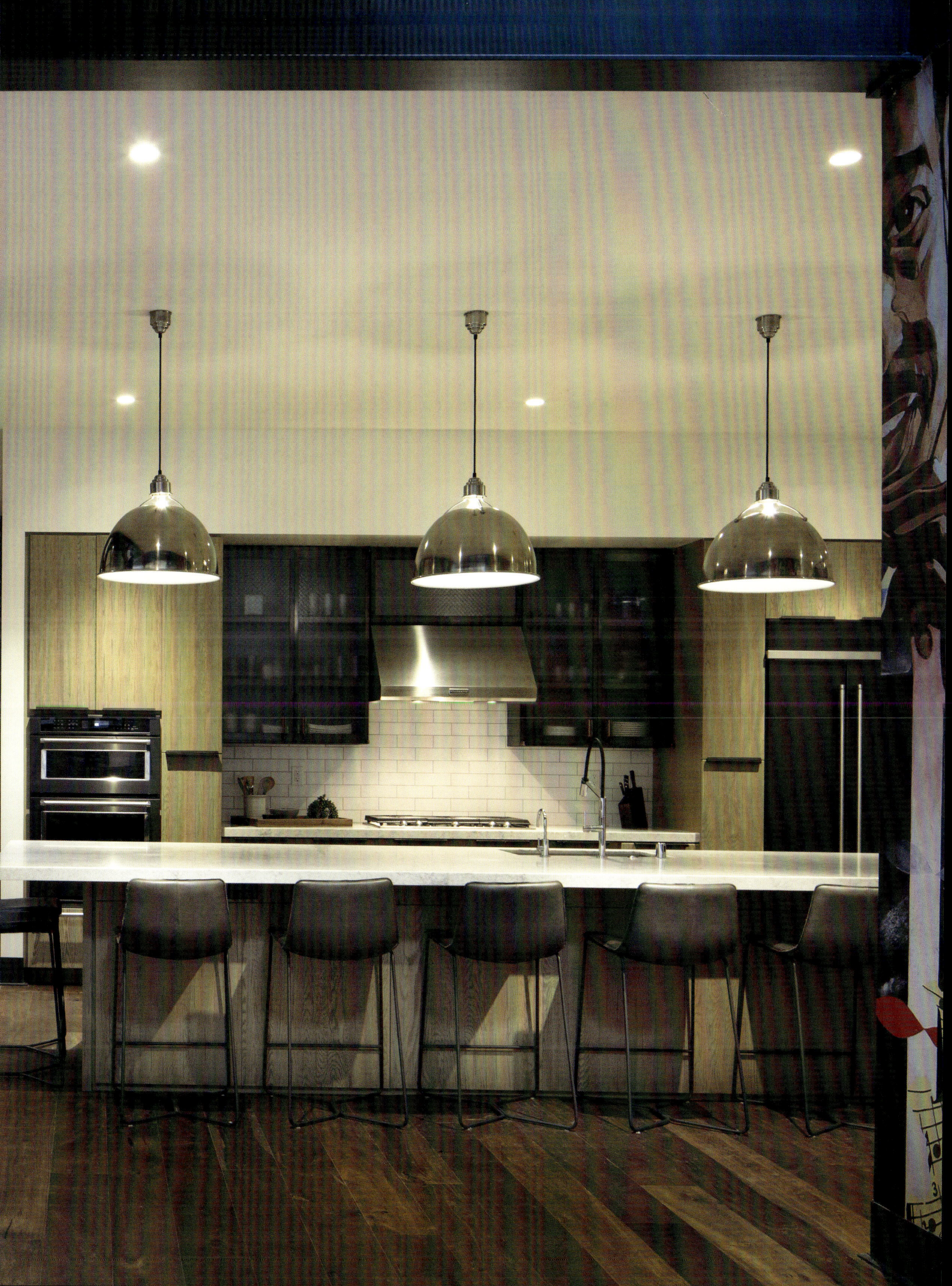

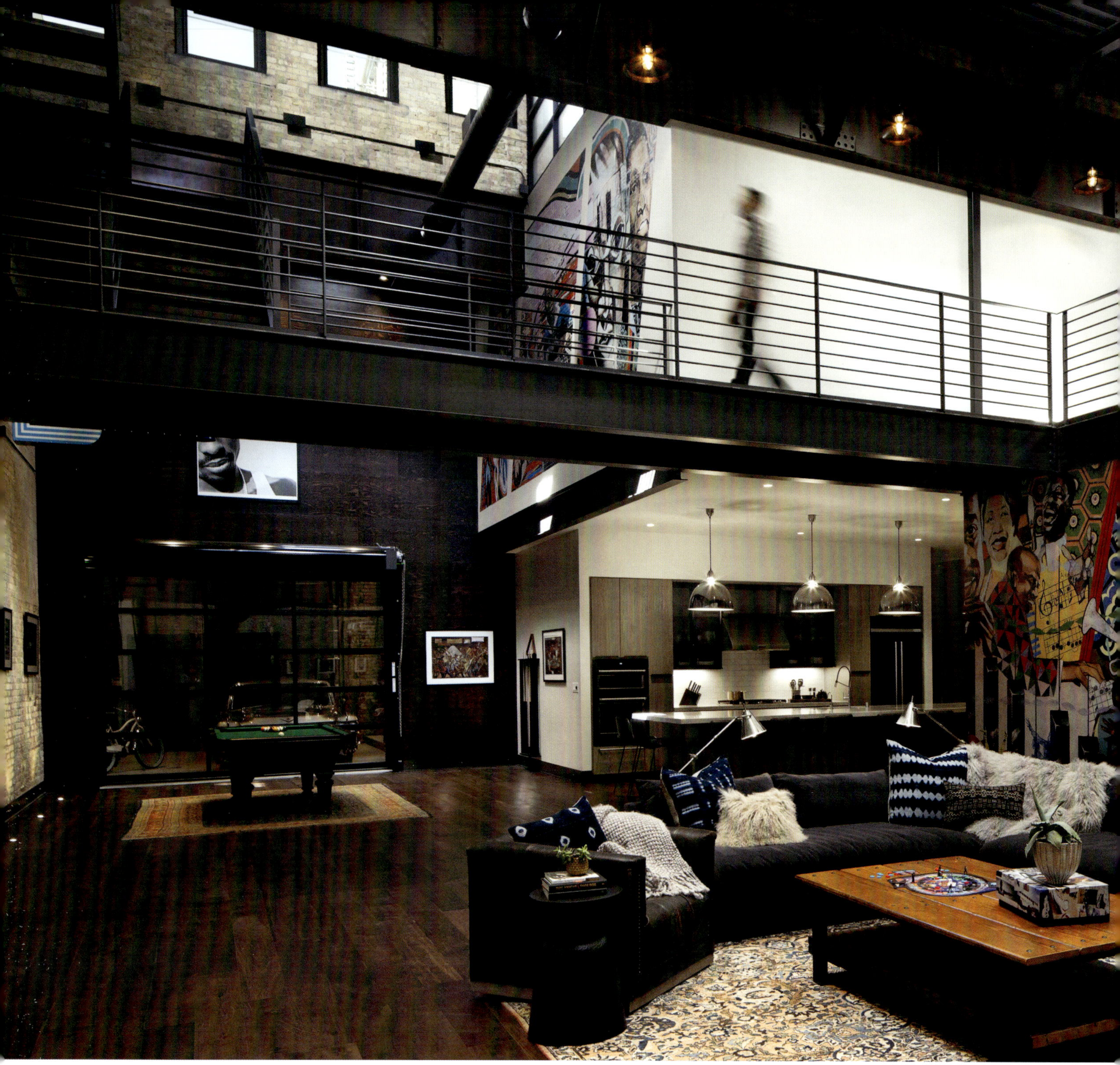

PREVIOUS: This innovative open living area blends automotive passion with modern living. The striking illuminated Cadillac sign—custom-made to replicate a vintage original and specially installed by an art-hanging crew—serves as a captivating focal point. Glass doors strategically frame rotating displays from the owner's extensive vintage car collection housed in the adjacent four-car garage, creating a dynamic visual connection that transforms prized automobiles into living art.

ABOVE: This expansive open living area features custom-sized murals re-created from significant Chicago street art that the homeowner passed daily on childhood walks to school. Photographed and printed on wall covering, these meaningful pieces—a larger installation on the lower level and a complementary smaller work above—establish a personal connection to the city's cultural landscape.

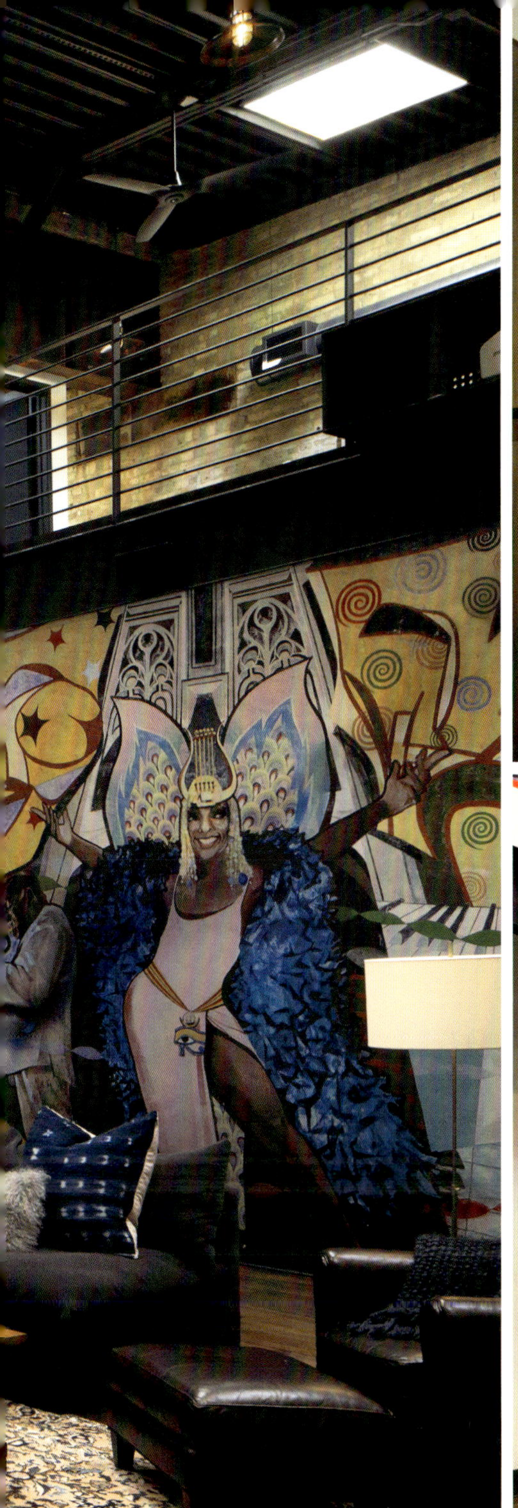

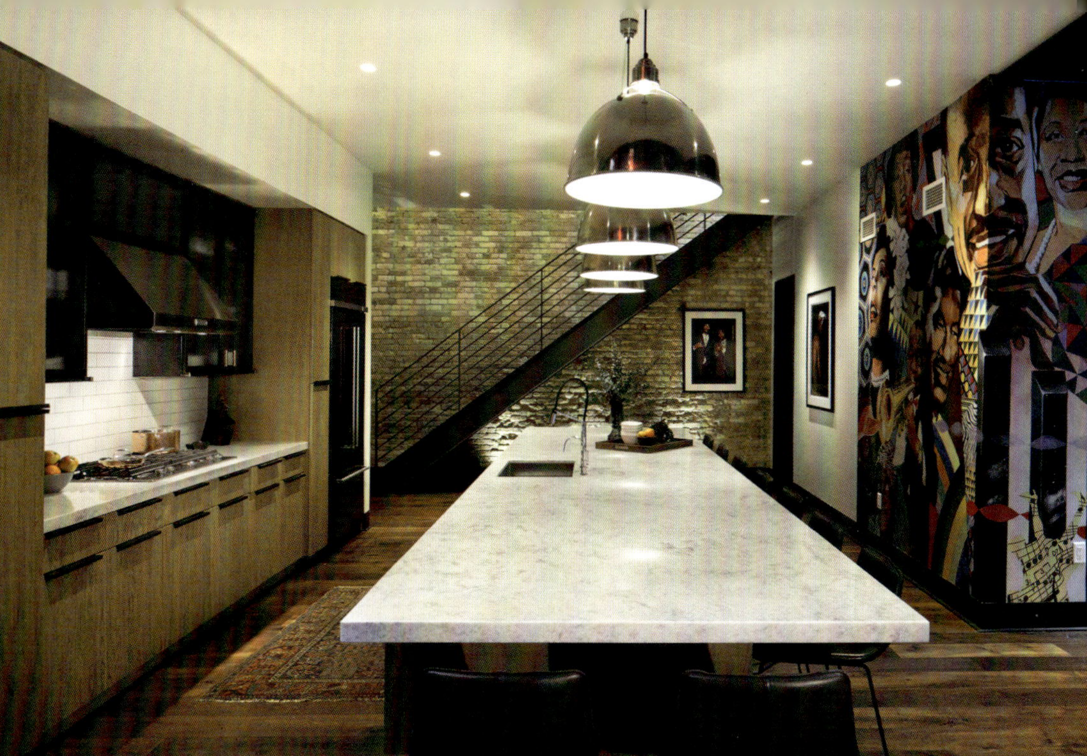

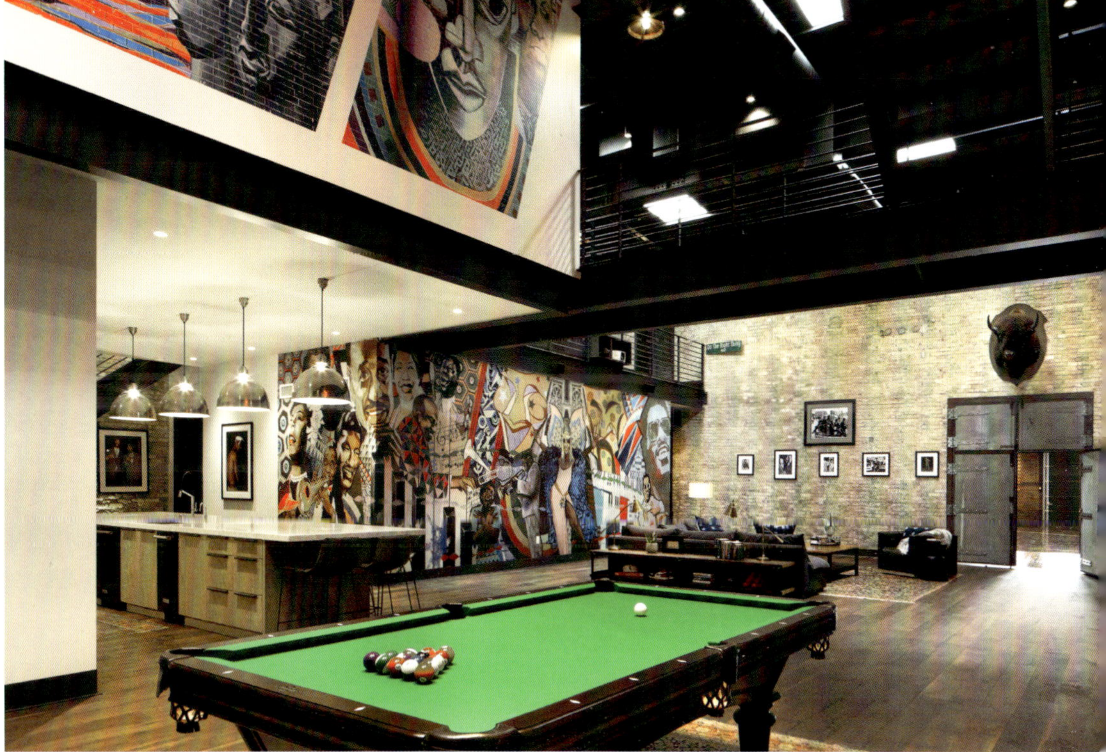

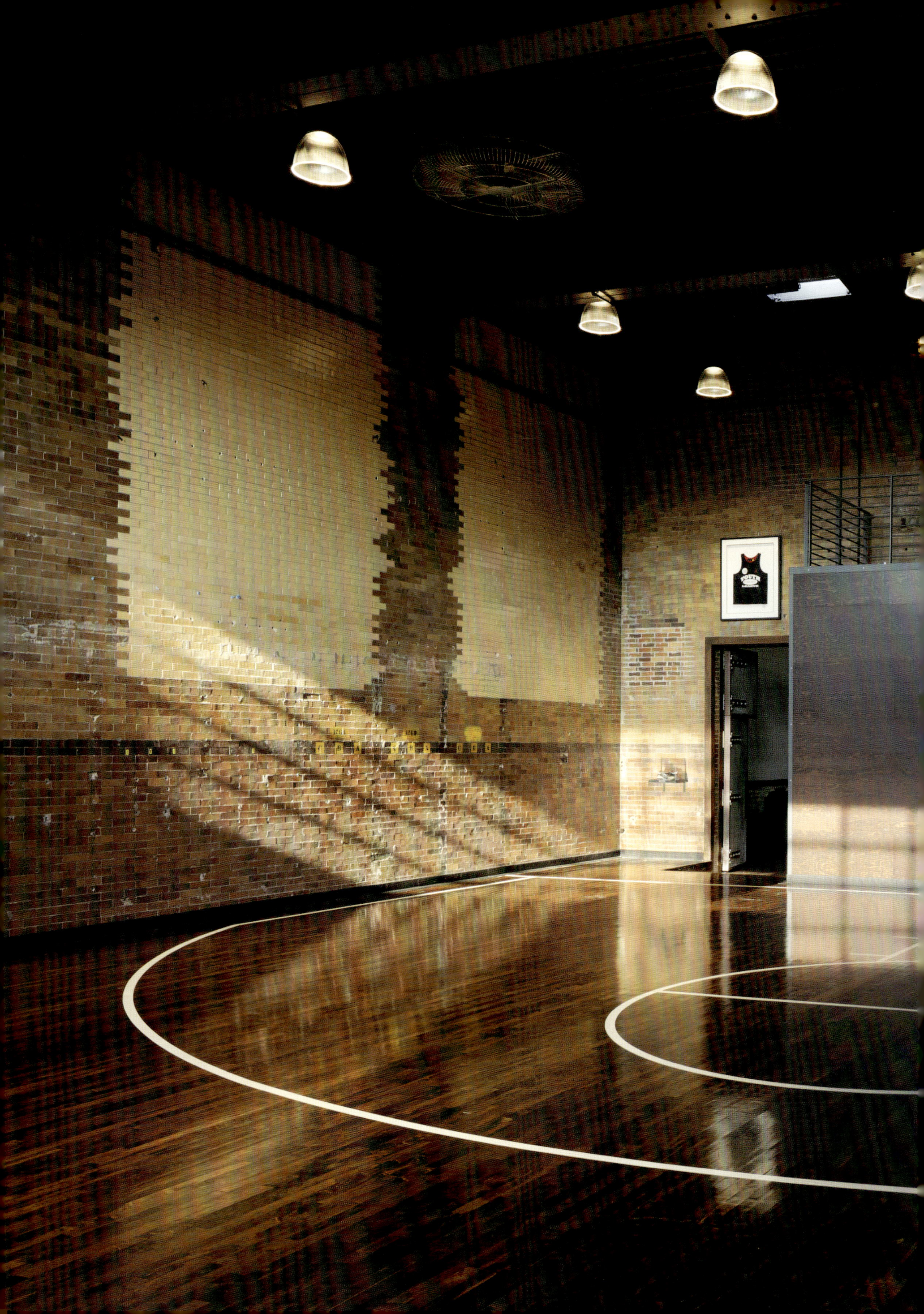

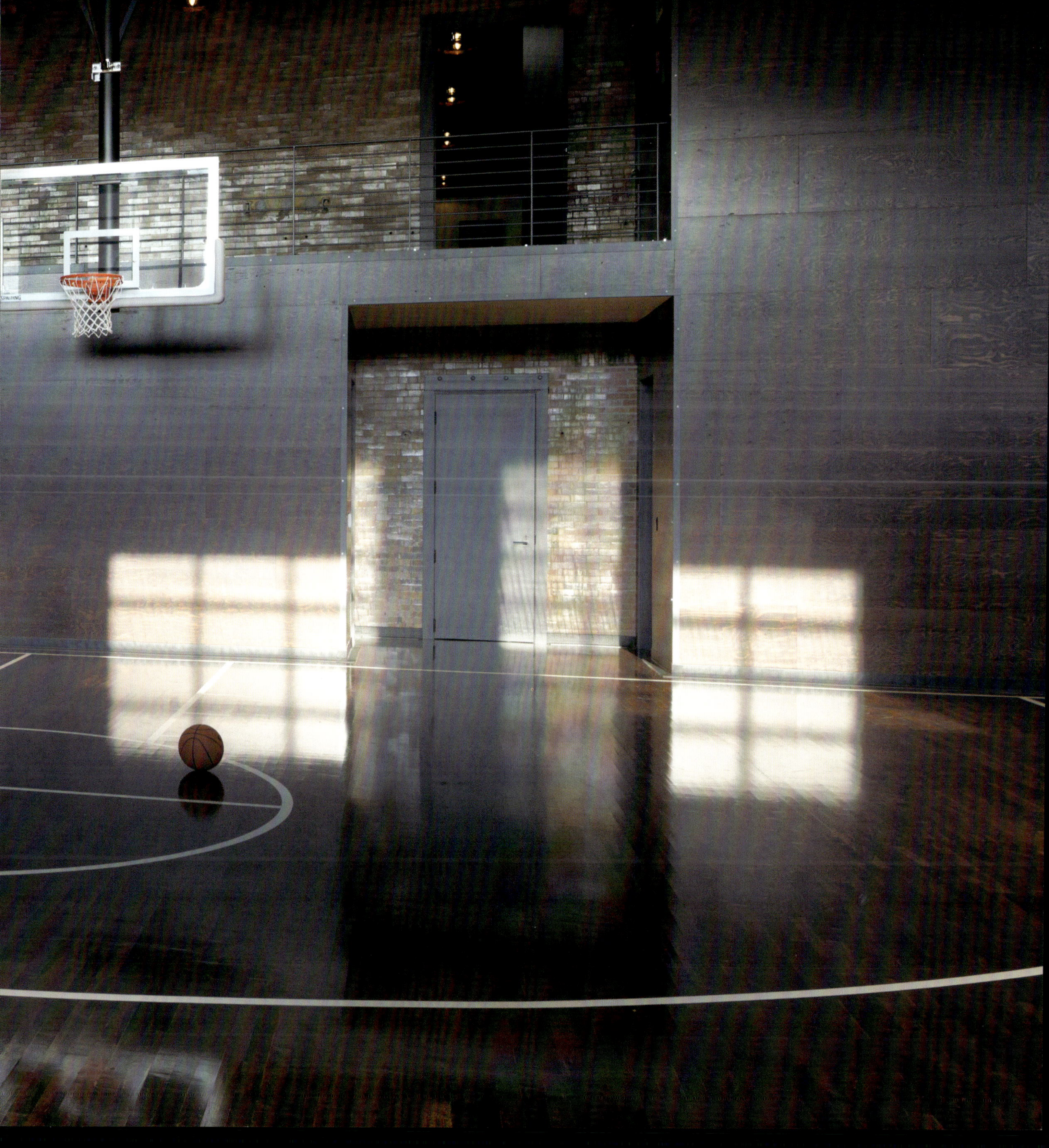

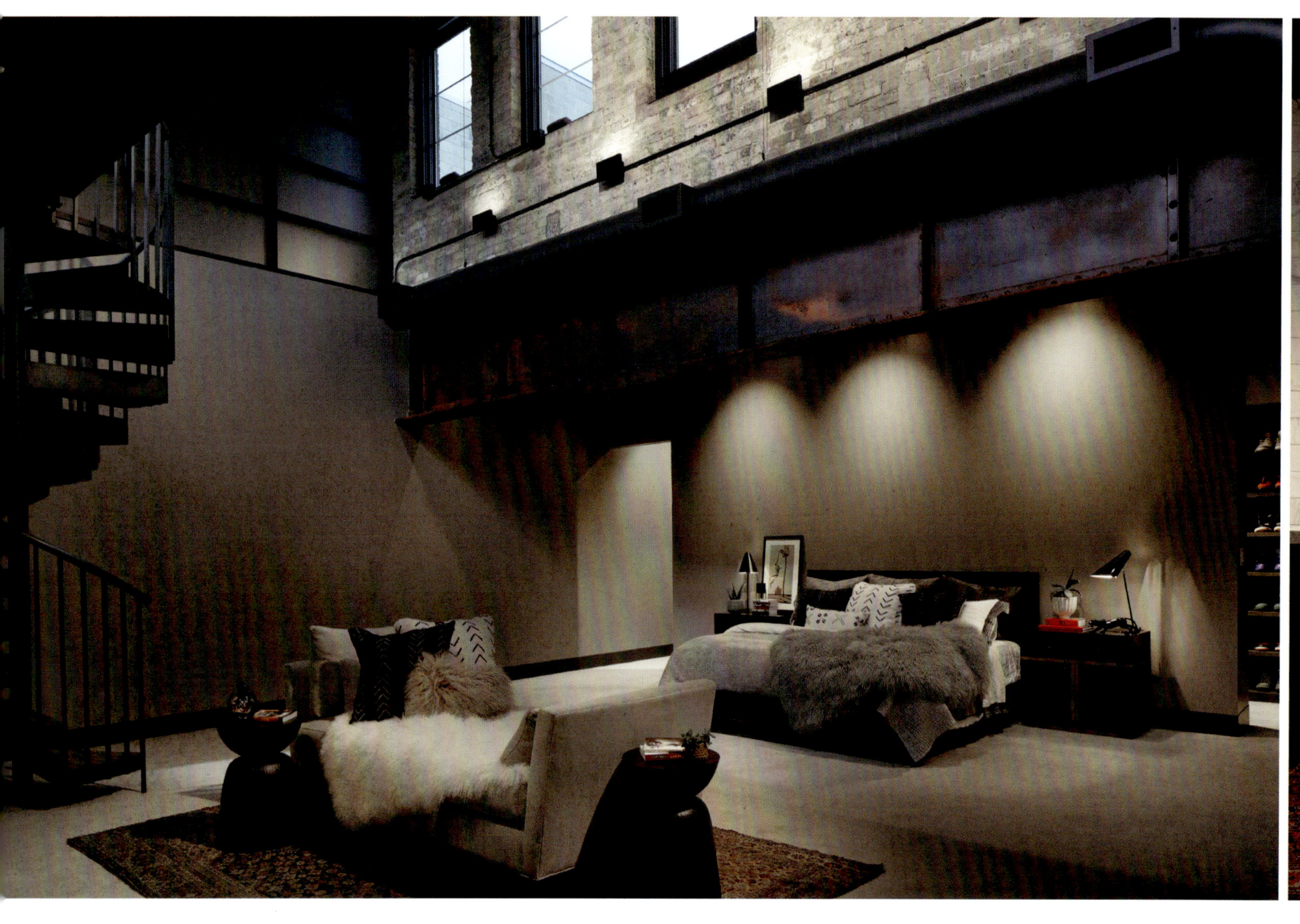

PREVIOUS: This front-facing half-court basketball court, accessible through the large opening visible on the building's facade, retains elements of its original character. Beautiful glazed brick walls—preserved from the space's previous iteration—bounce light throughout the area, while filled-in windows on the south side reveal hints of the structure's architectural evolution.

ABOVE: The second-floor primary bedroom and bath create a private sanctuary adjacent to the media room. This thoughtful arrangement balances private relaxation with entertainment, featuring a vintage record player and curated vinyl collection. Elegant marble tile walls elevate the bathroom, while a nearby spiral staircase leads to an elevated walkway connecting to a private west-facing patio.

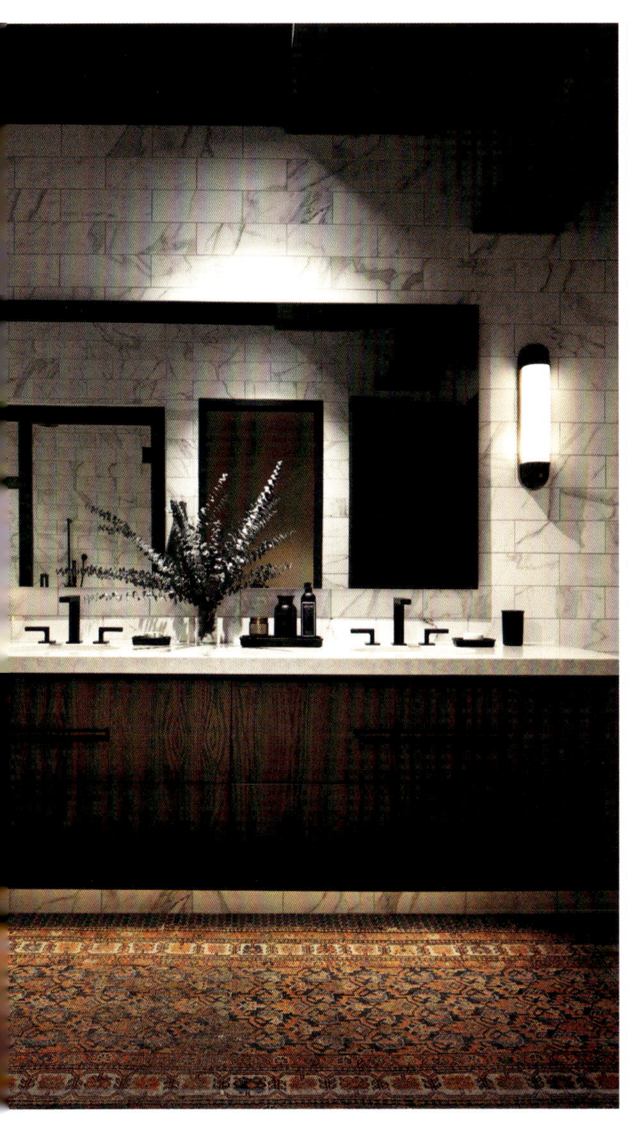

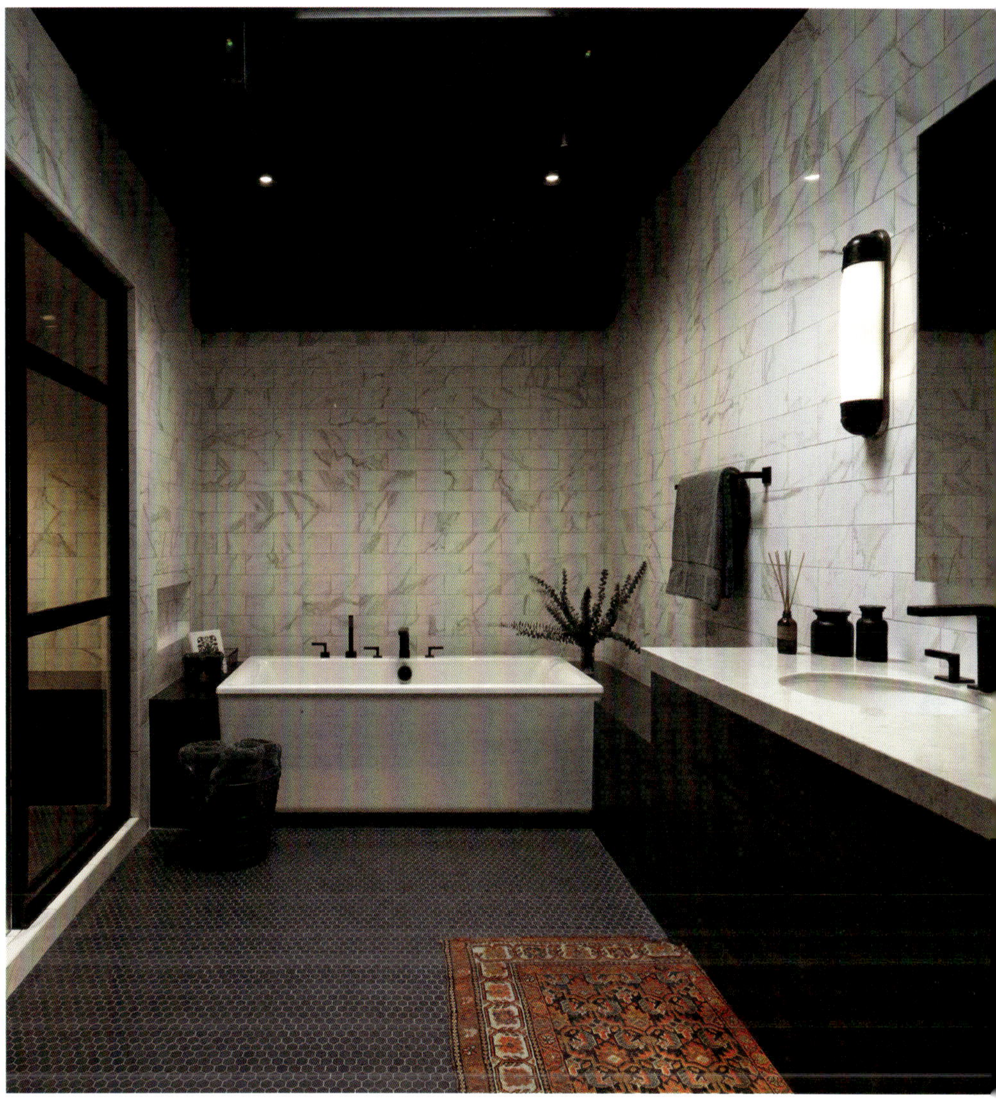

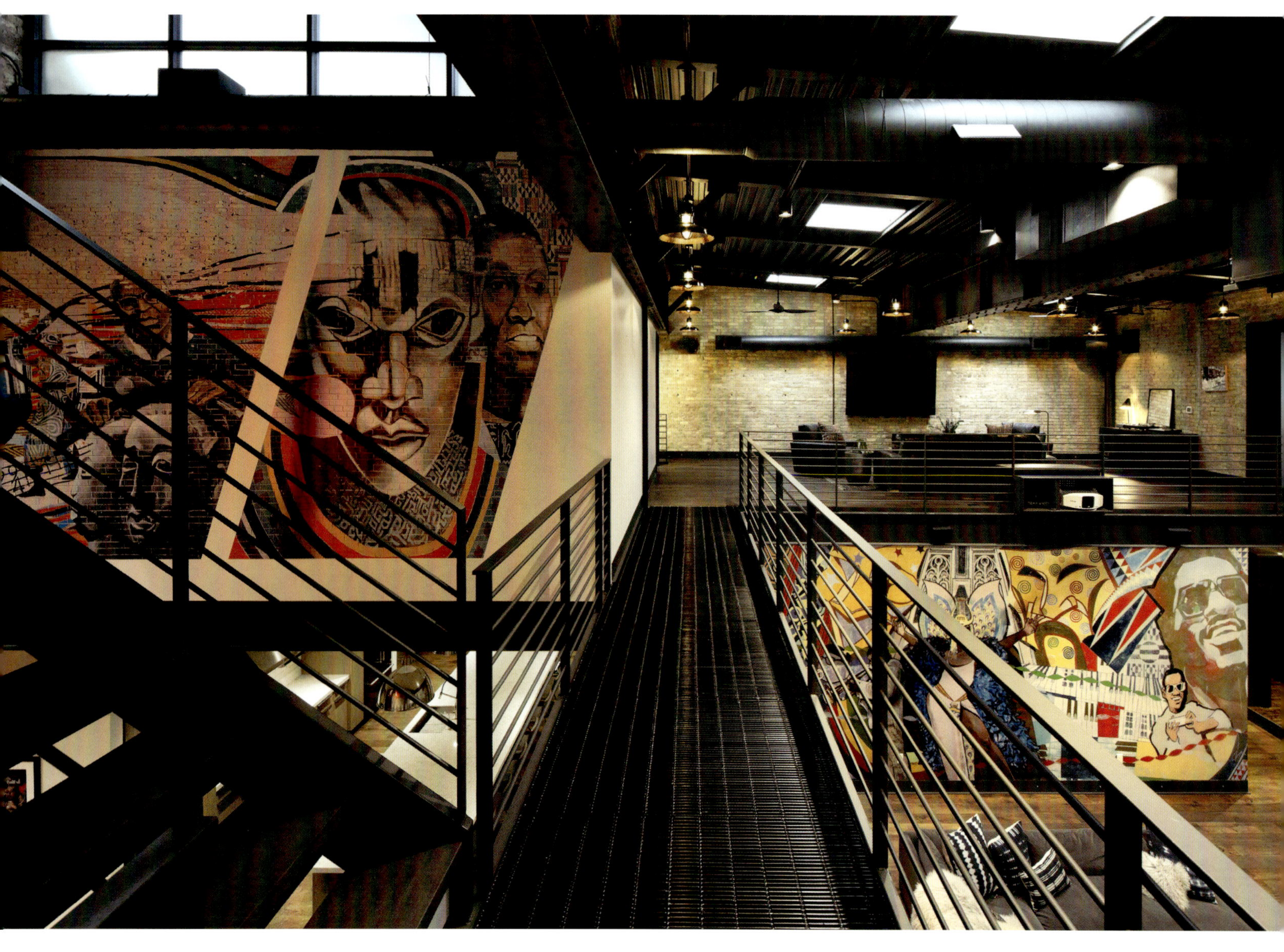

This airy hallway creates a gallery-like transition, leading to a media room adjoining the master bedroom. Note the centrally mounted projector, which displays onto a dramatic two-story screen in the living room below. Outside, a thoughtfully positioned sofa faces east toward Lake Michigan, providing a serene vantage point for glorious sunrise views from this elevated outdoor retreat.

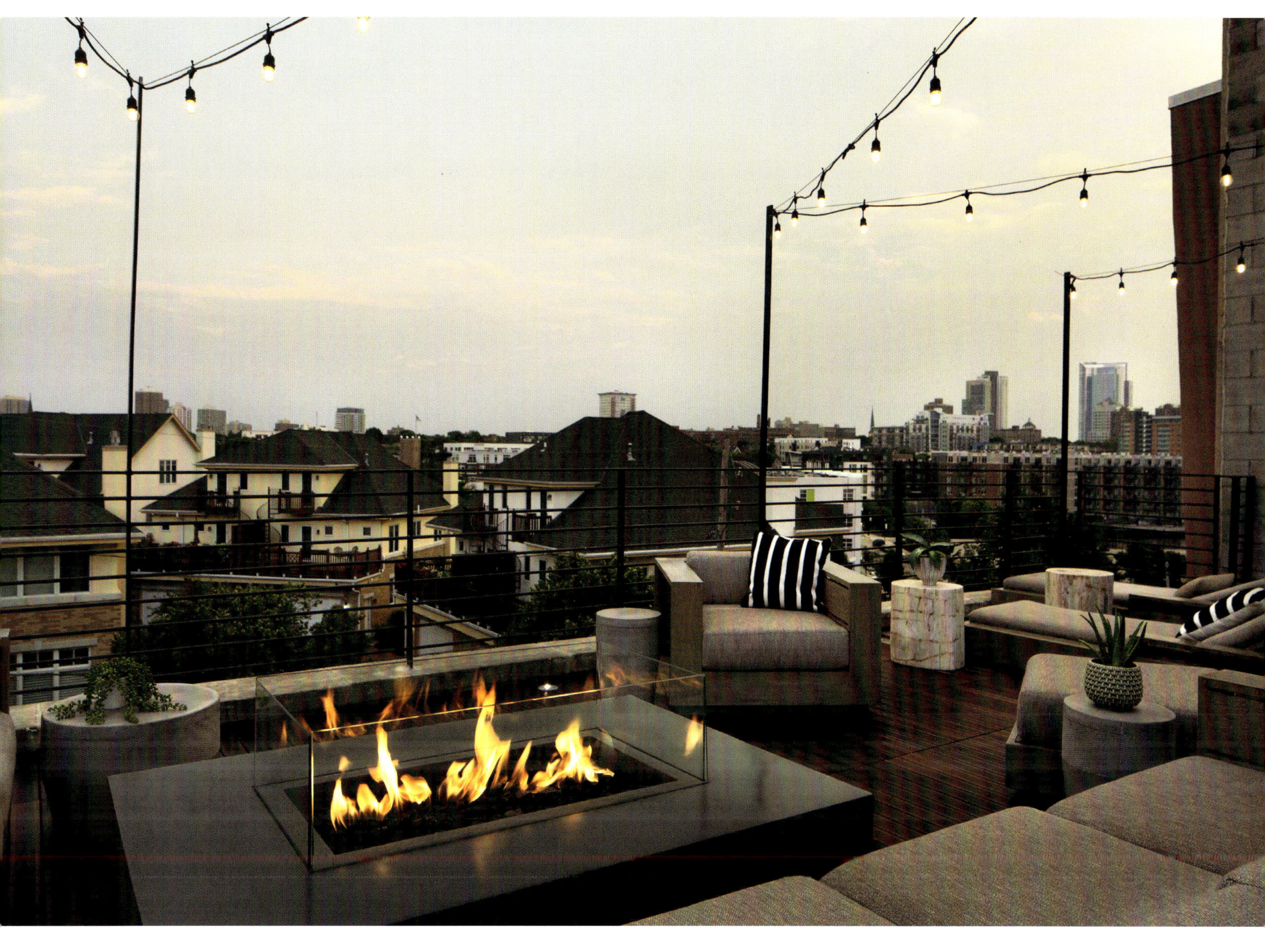

RARIFIED FLAIR

Hayley Kauffmann / Hayley Maureen Interior Design

Few contemporary urban dwellings capture the essence of Midwestern domesticity quite like this remarkable Chicago penthouse. It challenges our preconceptions of high-rise living. The home, perched twenty-seven stories above Streeterville's discreet streets, manages to reconcile the seemingly opposing forces of metropolitan sophistication and familial warmth.

The residence—expanded through the lucky acquisition of an adjacent unit—speaks to what architectural historian Vincent Scully might have termed the "poetry of domestic space." Initially conceived as a developer's sanctuary, the penthouse was transformed by Hayley Kauffmann of Hayley Maureen Interior Design, who deeply understood the relationship between architecture and social ritual. The resulting combined space features additional bedrooms, a private screening room accommodating seven, and a paneled private library. Each of those spaces features a stone fireplace, adding to the home's charm on Chicago's notoriously blustery days.

With their rich materiality and considered details, the interiors recall the traditional detailing of more historical structures while advancing a thoroughly contemporary narrative. The decision to outfit an interior room as a cinema—a winter refuge from Chicago's notorious climate—speaks to the thoughtful programming of the finest residential design.

Perhaps most notable is the penthouse's relationship to the exterior world—a dialogue between contained space and urban context. The terrace, one of Chicago's finest, commands spectacular views of both Lake Michigan and the Chicago River, while providing an outdoor living space that rivals those found in suburban estates. Adding a powder room adorned with cloud and crane wall covering—a whimsical reminder of one's elevation—and a convenient kitchenette transforms this aerial garden into the perfect entertainment venue.

Considering the evolution of urban residential design, this penthouse is a testament to the possibility of creating genuine homes within the vertical realm. It demonstrates that with thoughtful design and careful attention to materiality and space, the warmth and hospitality characteristic of Midwestern domestic architecture can indeed flourish at the pinnacle of a high-rise. This truth adds another chapter to our understanding of contemporary living.

This elegantly refined home office features floor-to-ceiling cerused gray hickory millwork, which seamlessly unifies walls, shelving, and the elevated coffered ceiling. Custom cabinetry cleverly conceals building systems and powered shades while adding a foot of height to the space.

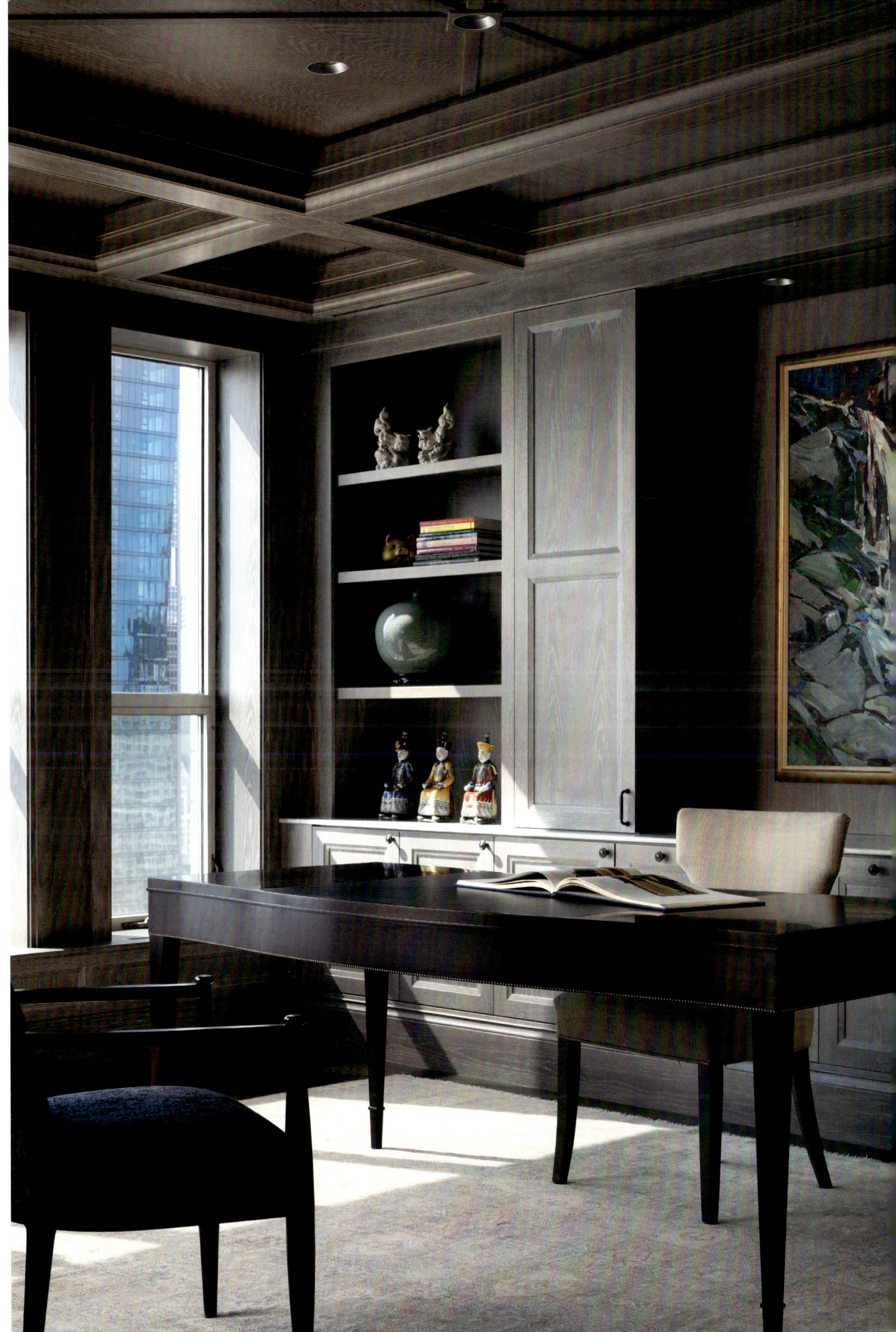

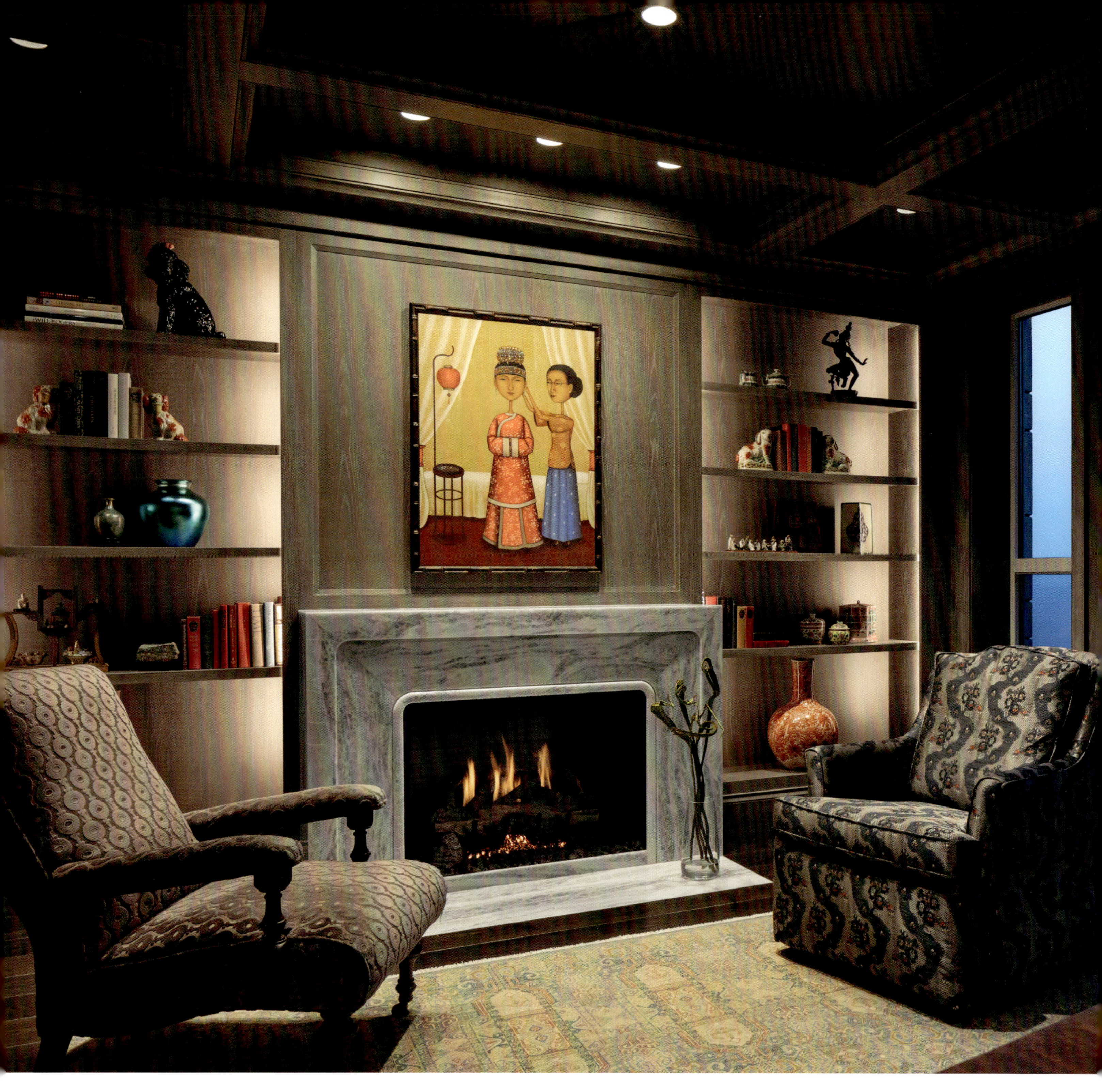

Left: This eclectic library corner features a Calcite Azul marble fireplace anchoring a thoughtfully curated space. The Dedar "Delicious Manners" chair with distinctive floral stripes complements Asian travel treasures and layered textiles, creating an artfully collected atmosphere rather than an overly coordinated design. *Right:* From the entry, a custom glass-and-metal door etched with an organic pattern offers a glimpse into the richly appointed office, where lake views and layered textures invite a closer look.

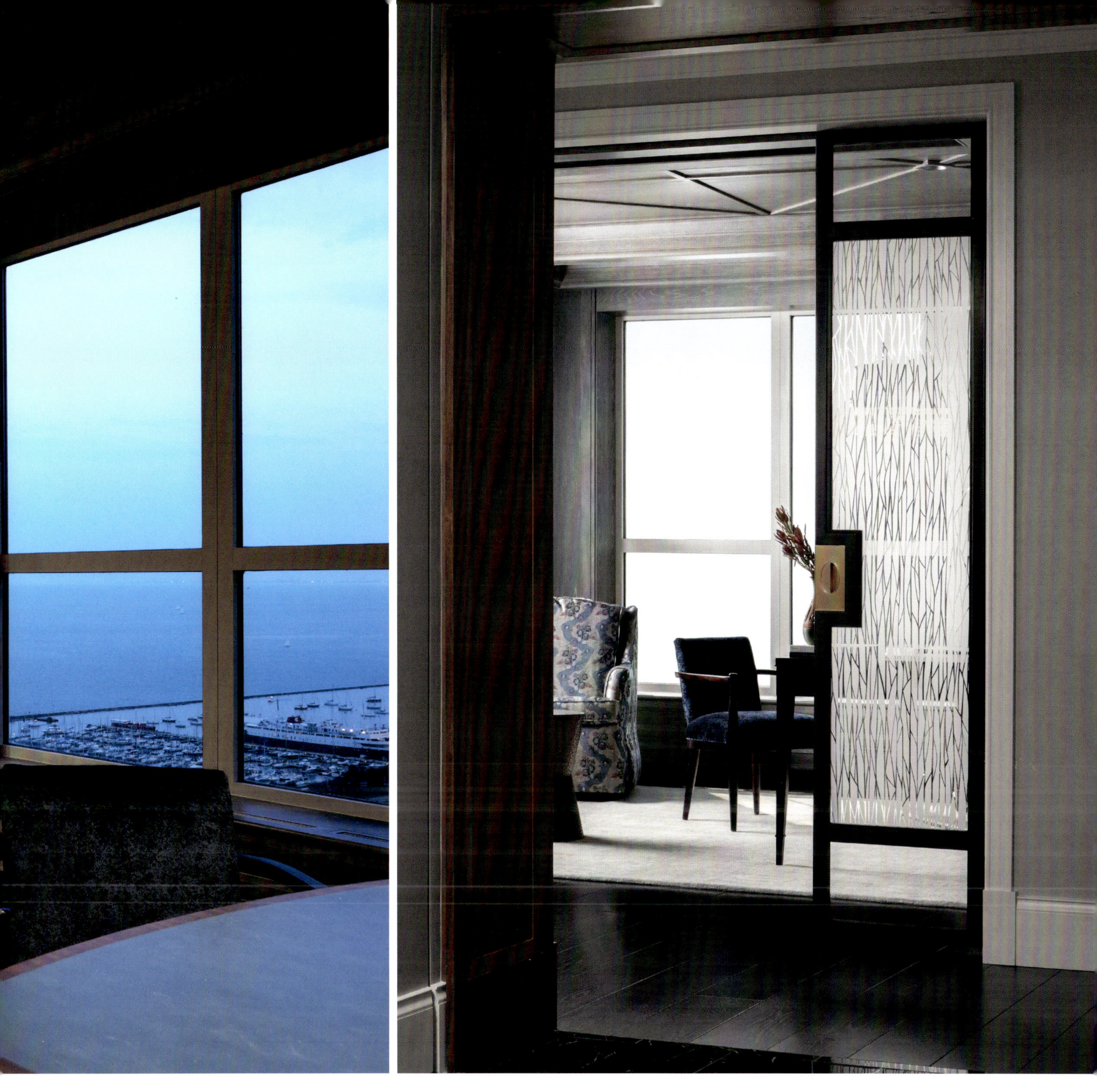

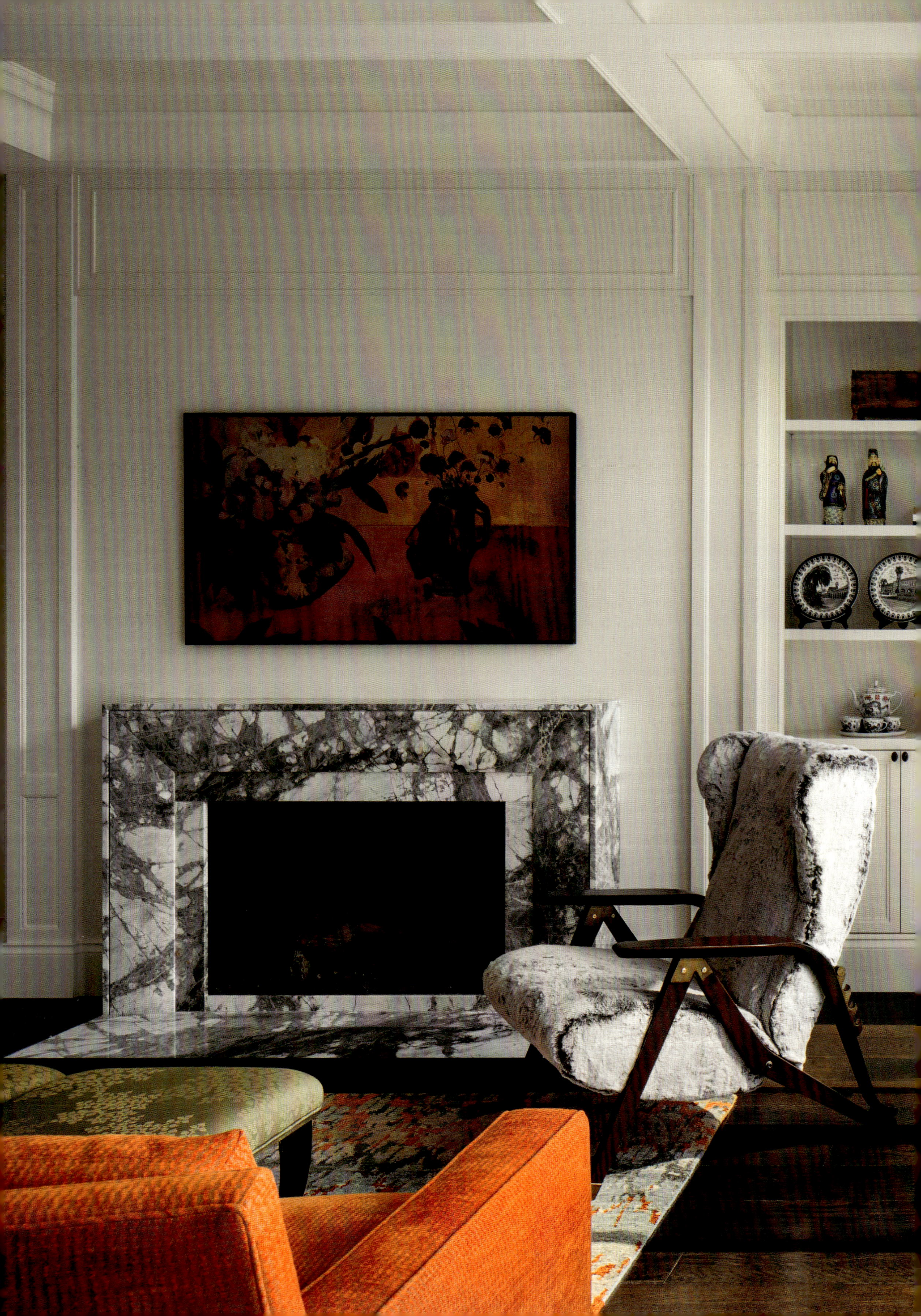

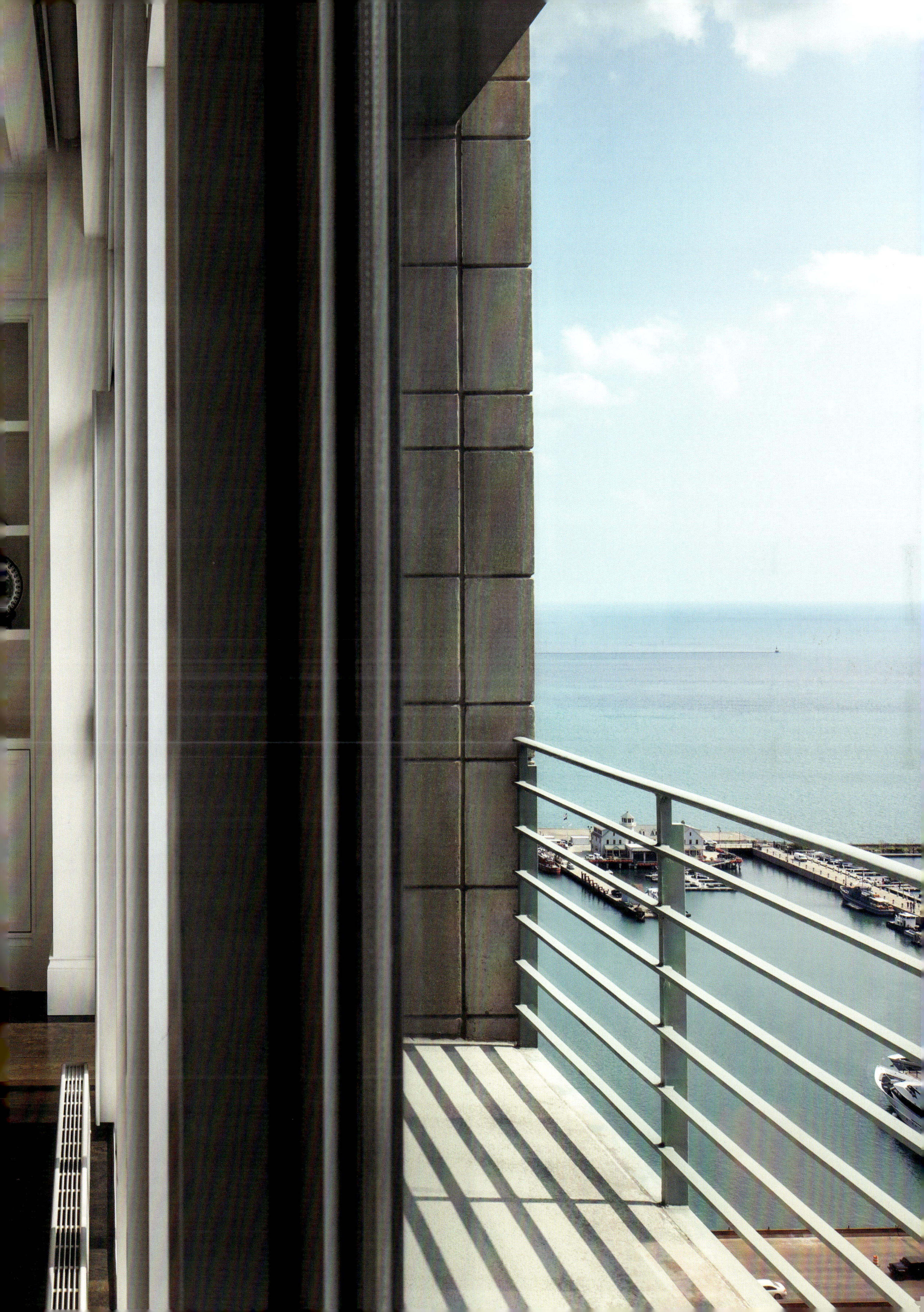

PREVIOUS: The airy living room is bathed in Benjamin Moore's Linen White and opens to one of three main-level terraces overlooking Chicago Harbor. A custom Invisible Blue marble fireplace echoes Lake Michigan's hues, while cleverly designed ceiling details add an impressive 18 inches of height to the space.

OPPOSITE: A handmade white oak wet bar, stained blue, features Invisible Blue marble countertops with a matching backsplash, a hammered polished nickel sink, Sub-Zero refrigeration drawers, and stemware storage—all complemented by espresso-toned, wide-plank oak flooring. A wine bar is opposite this composition.

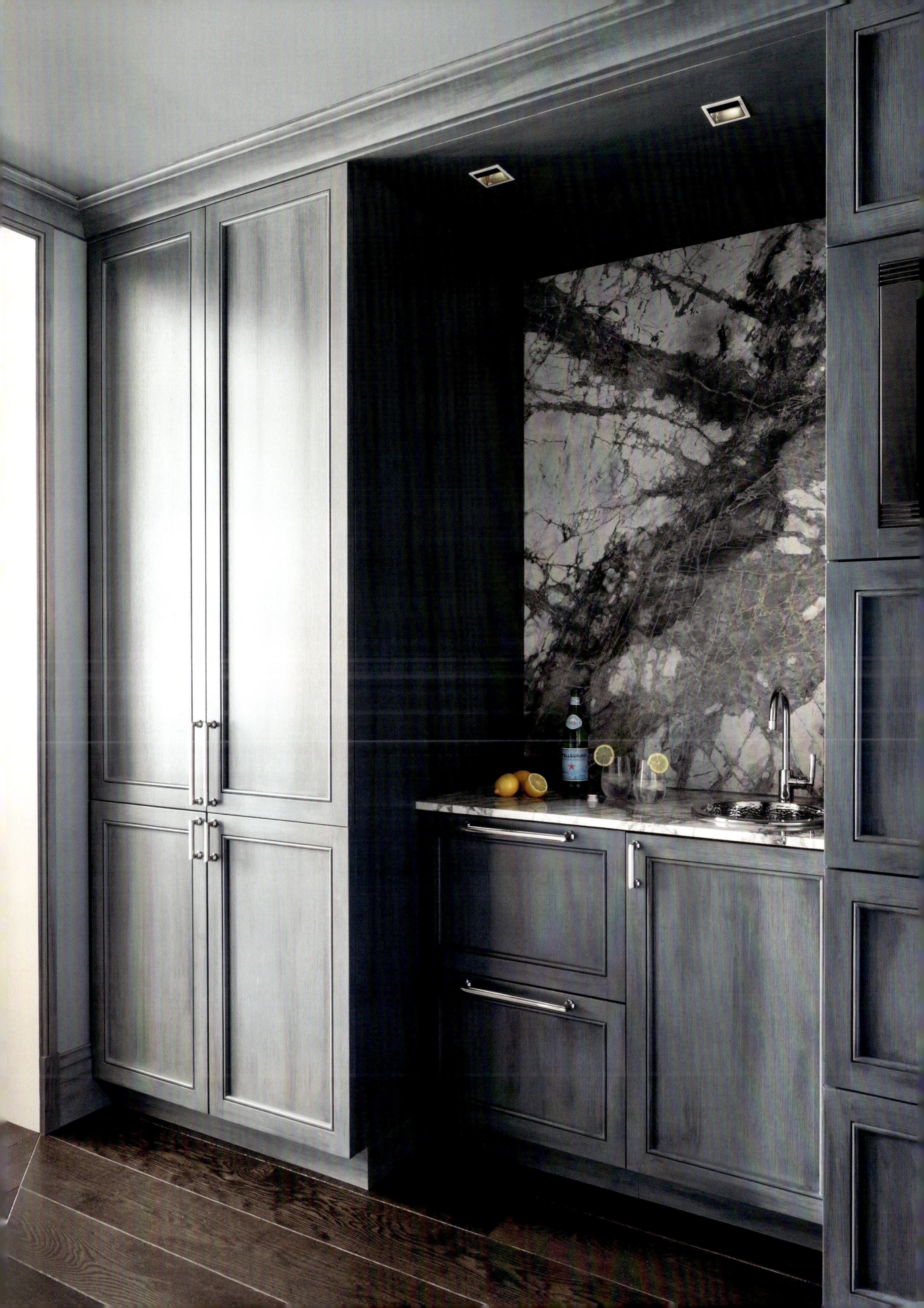

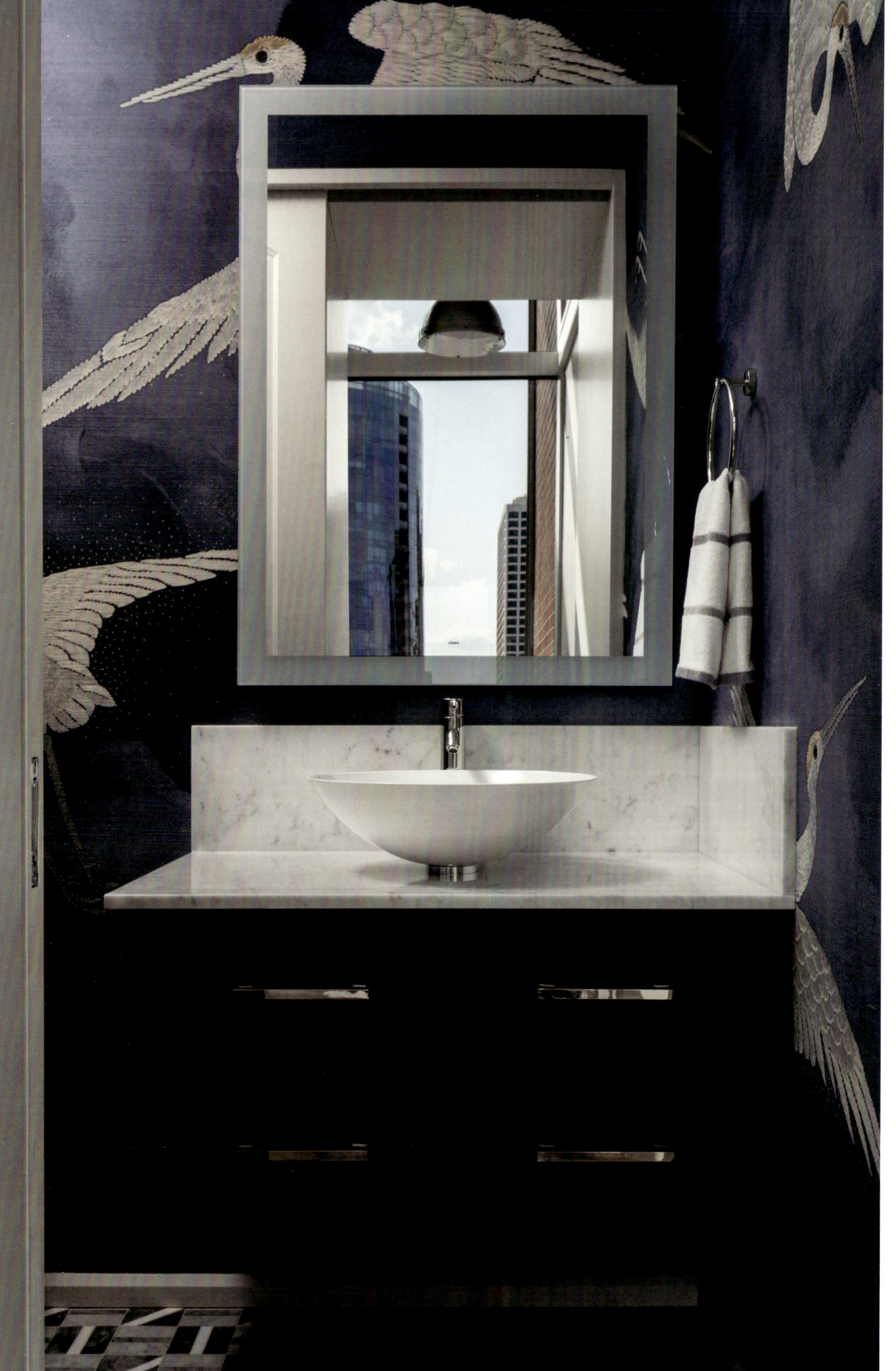

Discreetly tucked within the home's upper terrace kitchenette, this sophisticated powder room features Phillip Jeffries "Flight" wall covering in Blue Heron, Ann Sacks Liaison Elm stone mosaic flooring with nautical flag motifs, and mirrors reflecting Chicago River views.

The space-efficient upper terrace kitchenette packs remarkable functionality into just 35 square feet, with custom cabinetry housing a wine refrigerator, a full-size refrigerator, a dishwasher, a Wolf burner, a microwave, and warming drawers—all anchored by elegant Blue De Savoie marble surfaces. A Takashi Murakami painting adds a note of colorful whimsy.

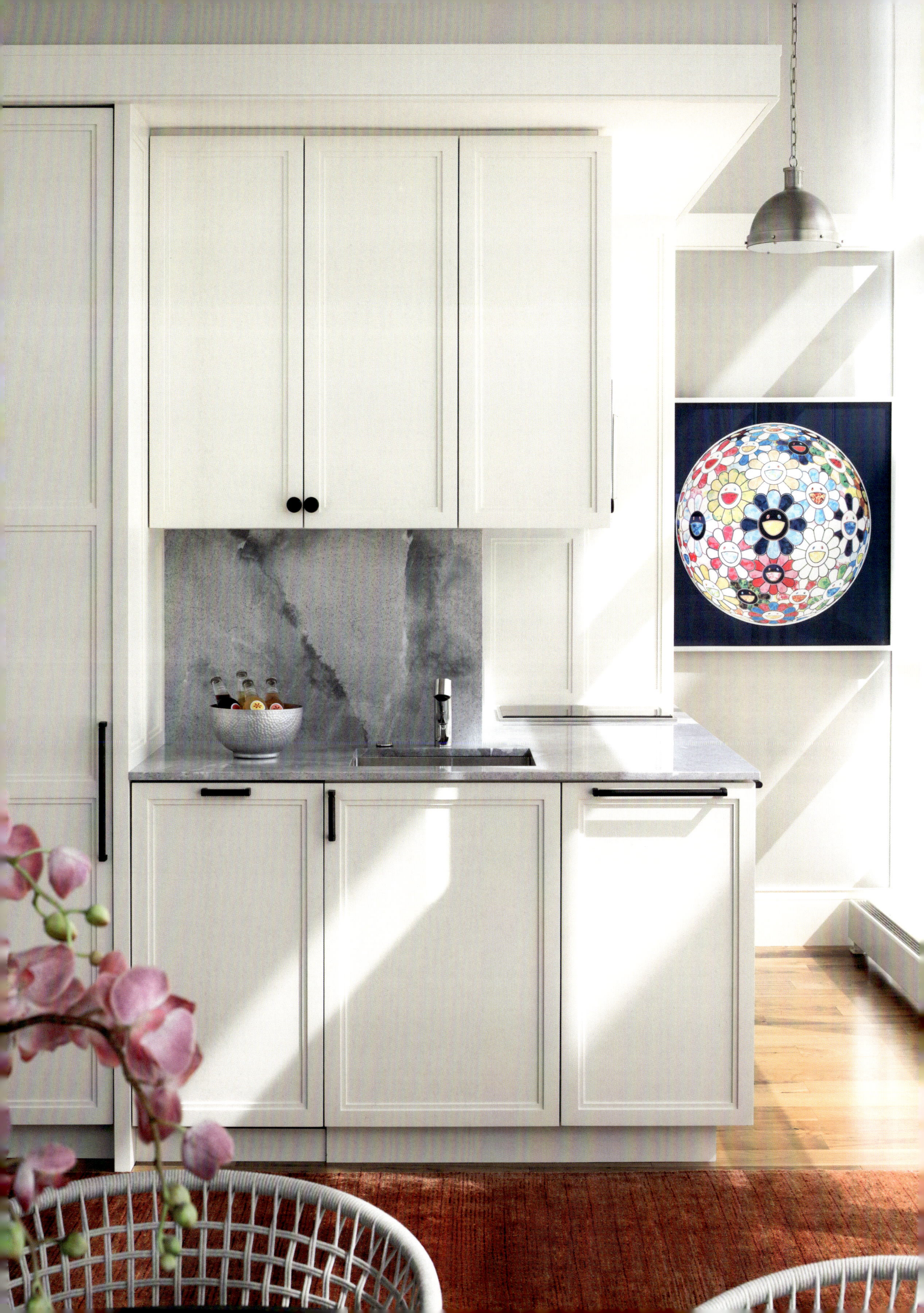

TUDOR TREASURE

Amy Carman Design

Where stately homes crown Milwaukee's River Hills district, a 1920s Tudor mansion has undergone a metamorphosis that bridges past and present with remarkable grace. This architectural journey transformed a maze of compartmentalized spaces into a harmonious dwelling that honors its historical roots and modern family life. To award-winning designer Amy Carman, blending the then with the now is a familiar task, one that she consistently invigorates with sparkling style and élan thanks to her extensive knowledge of historical design.

The elements of a 1920s Tudor interior fall into place like the pieces of a complex puzzle, from formal living areas to servants' quarters. The new stewards, a culinary-passionate physician and a mechanical engineer, brought refreshing vision to the home's aged walls.

The heart of the transformation centered on the kitchen, which had previously been sequestered behind a warren of formal rooms, its potential locked away like a hidden garden. The renovation orchestrated a bold spatial revolution, dissolving barriers to craft a generous culinary sanctuary from two former rooms. Adjacent to this new hub, an architectural afterthought—a storage space riddled with doorways—blossomed into an elegant wine room, where the butler's pantry meets contemporary entertaining space.

Light streams through with luminous zeal. Tall, expansive windows modeled after the home's original leaded glass portals reach down to the counter height to foster a warm and enchanting dialogue between the kitchen and the garden backdrop. On the opposite end of the kitchen, a generous opening flows to an airy living space that was previously the dining room.

Despite the entertaining-friendly updates, the home's storied charm is sealed through a respectful balance of old and new. Like a master composer working with historical themes, the design team preserved the Tudor's architectural integrity while orchestrating spaces for contemporary living. Period details converse easily with modern interventions, creating an authentic and fresh environment. The result is more than mere renovation: It's a renaissance, proving that historic homes can embrace the present while keeping their soul intact.

Pierre Jeanneret–inspired cane chairs surround an ebony-stained table that doubles as a homework space in the home's dining room. The original fireplace, updated with Calacatta Viola marble, anchors the Benjamin Moore Classic Gray walls, where the client's modern screen prints create a collected feel.

NEXT: In this view, a vintage-inspired Noir Furniture chandelier hangs from the original plaster ceiling medallion, complementing the preserved crown molding that frames the dining space. An Audubon print adds a subliminal natural note.

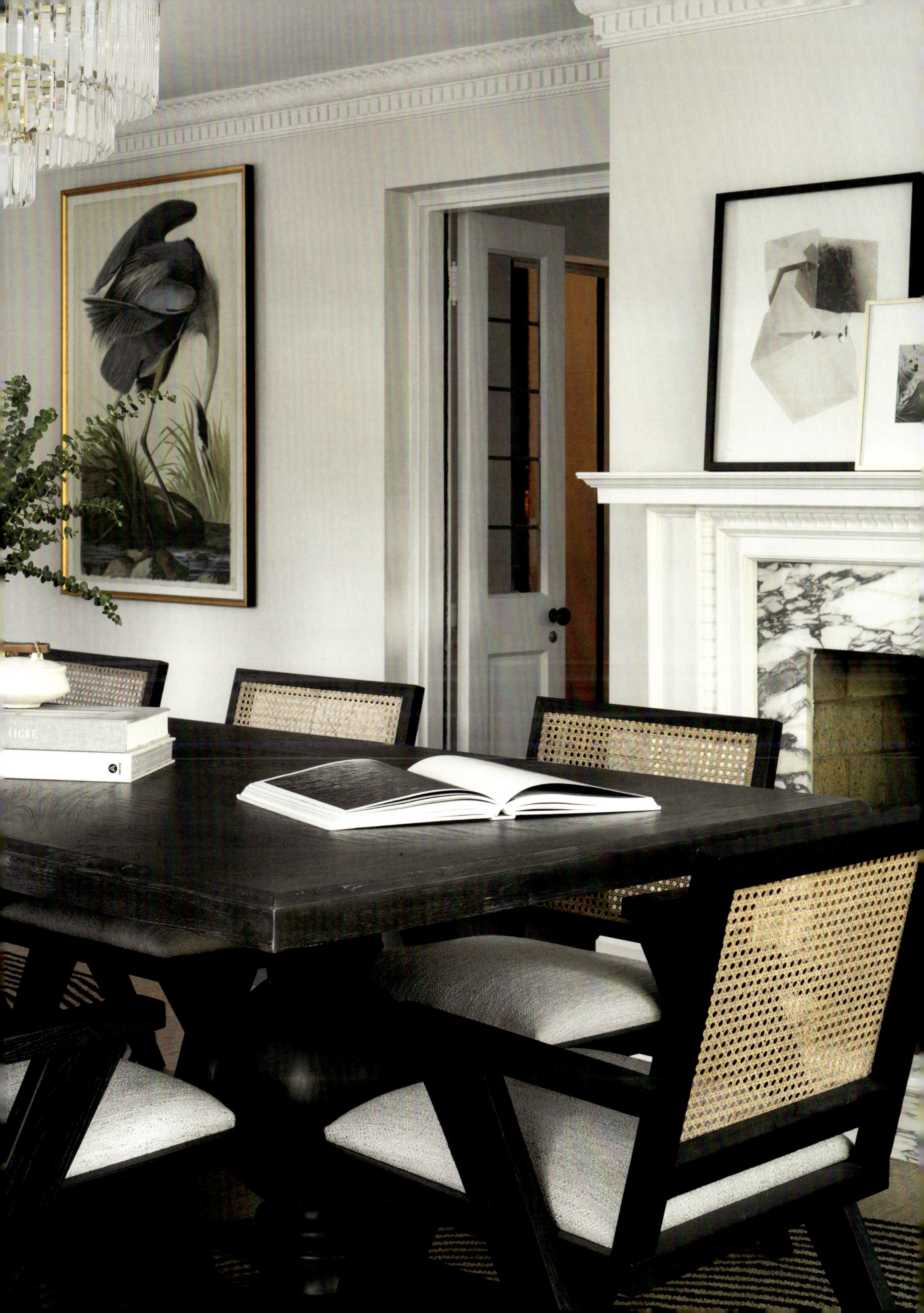

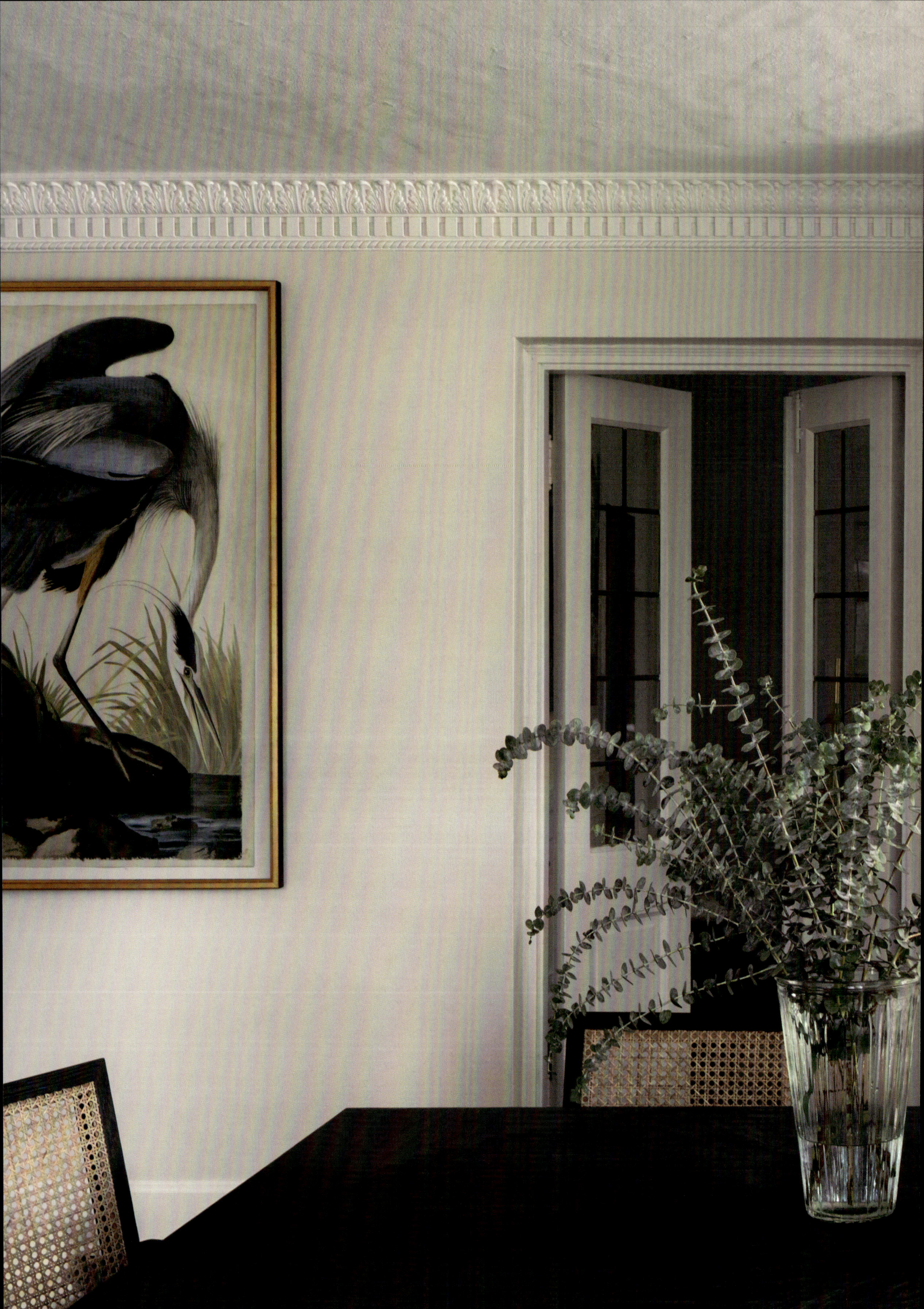

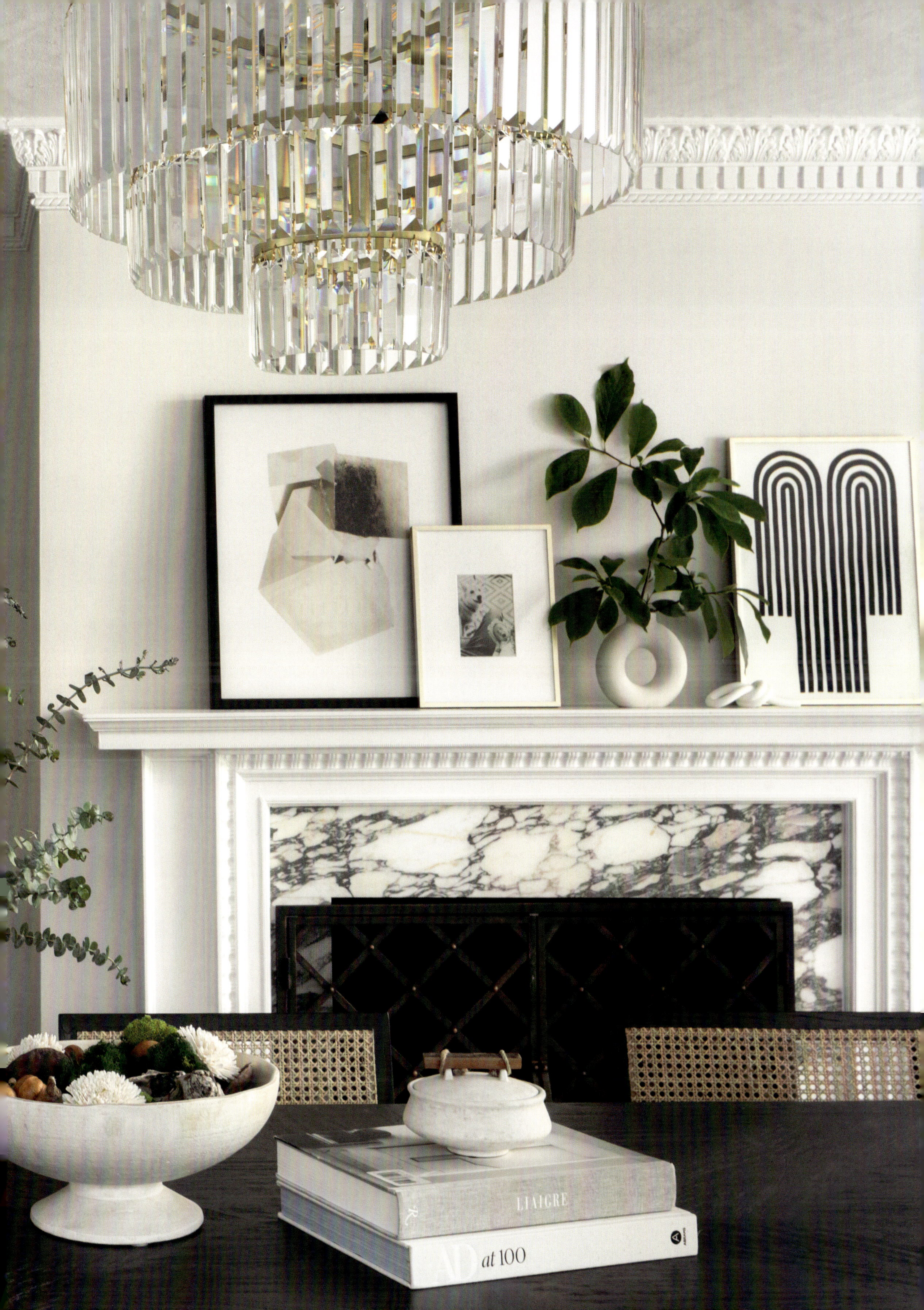
LIAIGRE
AD at 100

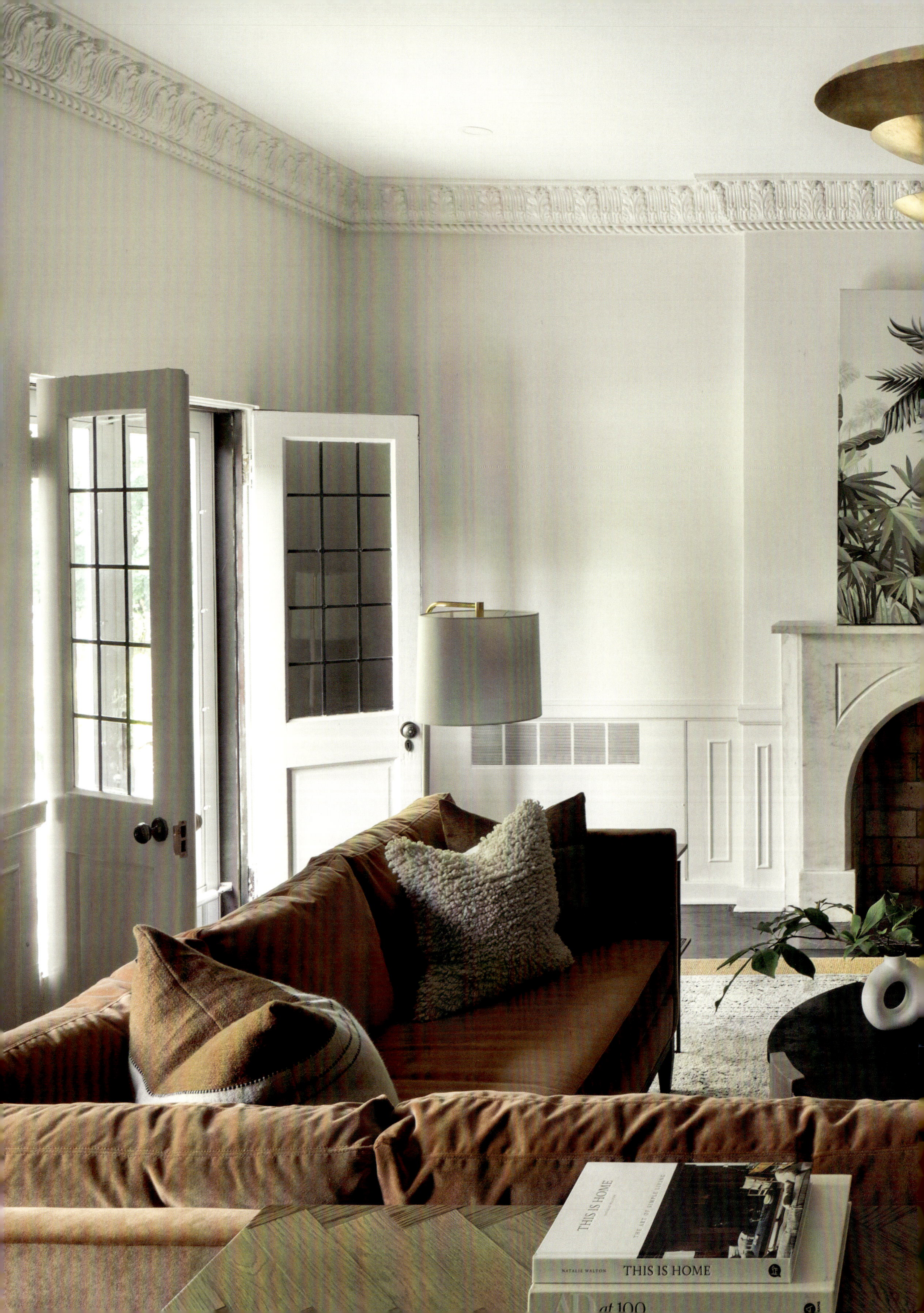
THIS IS HOME
THE ART OF SIMPLE LIVING
NATALIE WALTON
THIS IS HOME

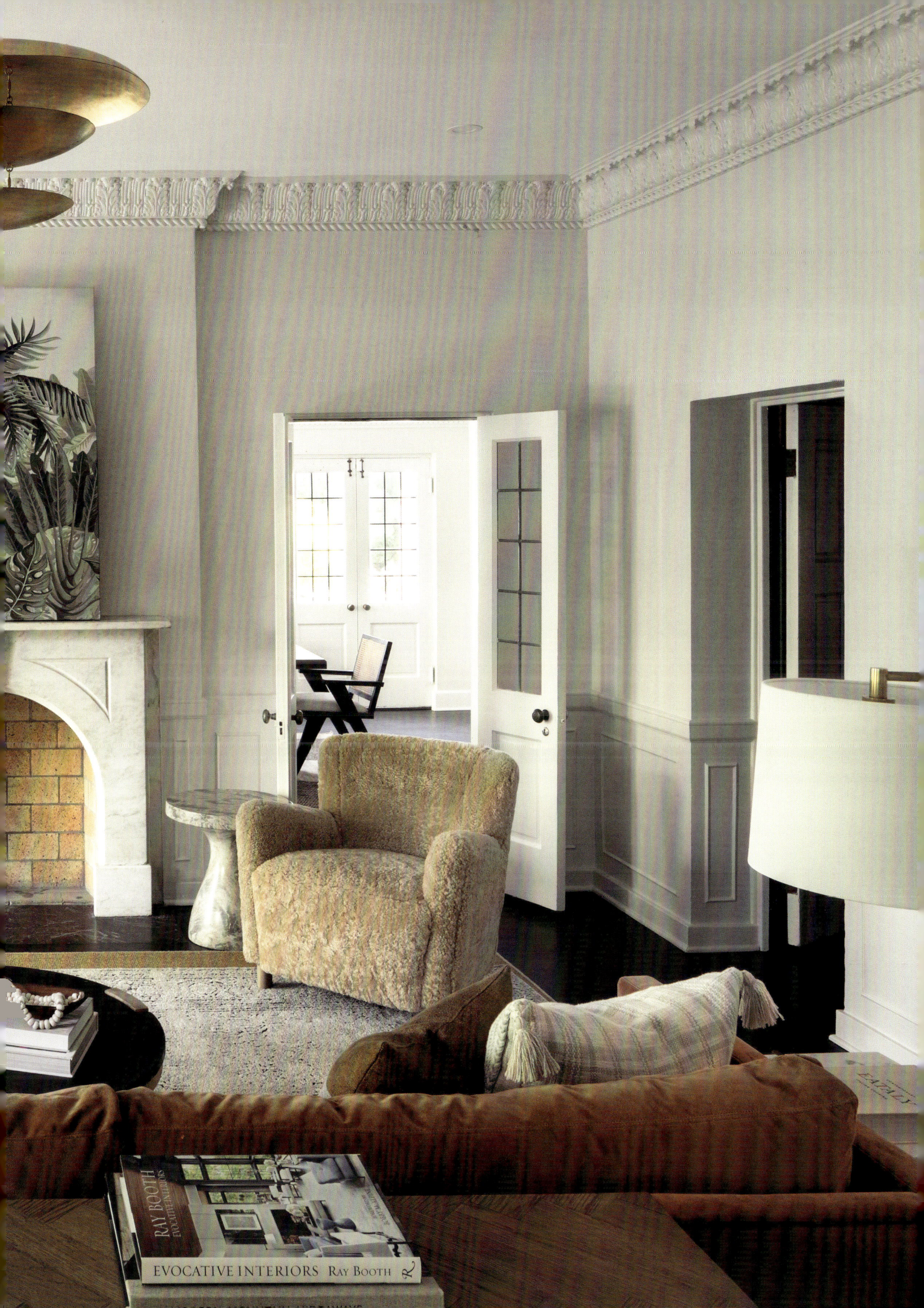
RAY BOOTH
EVOCATIVE INTERIORS
EVOCATIVE INTERIORS Ray Booth

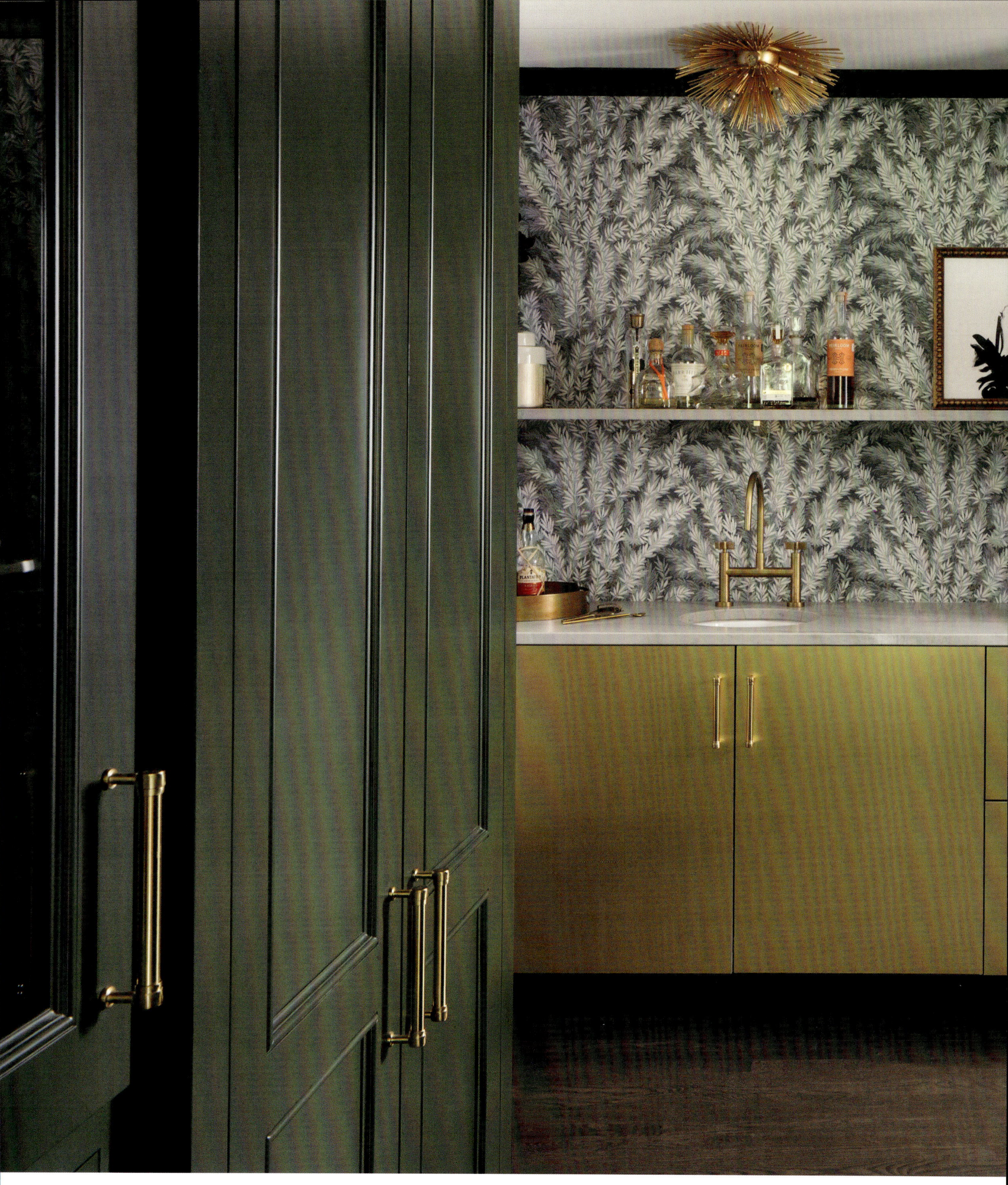

PREVIOUS: Once the formal dining room, this warm living space preserves the original marble fireplace and leaded glass doors. New openings connect to the wine room and butler's pantry, while French doors lead to the private patio. The palette draws inspiration from the clients' daughter's beautiful red curls.

ABOVE: The elegant butler's pantry transformed an underutilized storage room by removing awkward closets. Cole & Son's densely patterned Florencecourt wallpaper in gray green gives the room a jewel box feel, complemented by brass-clad cabinetry and a gold sea-urchin-inspired light fixture.

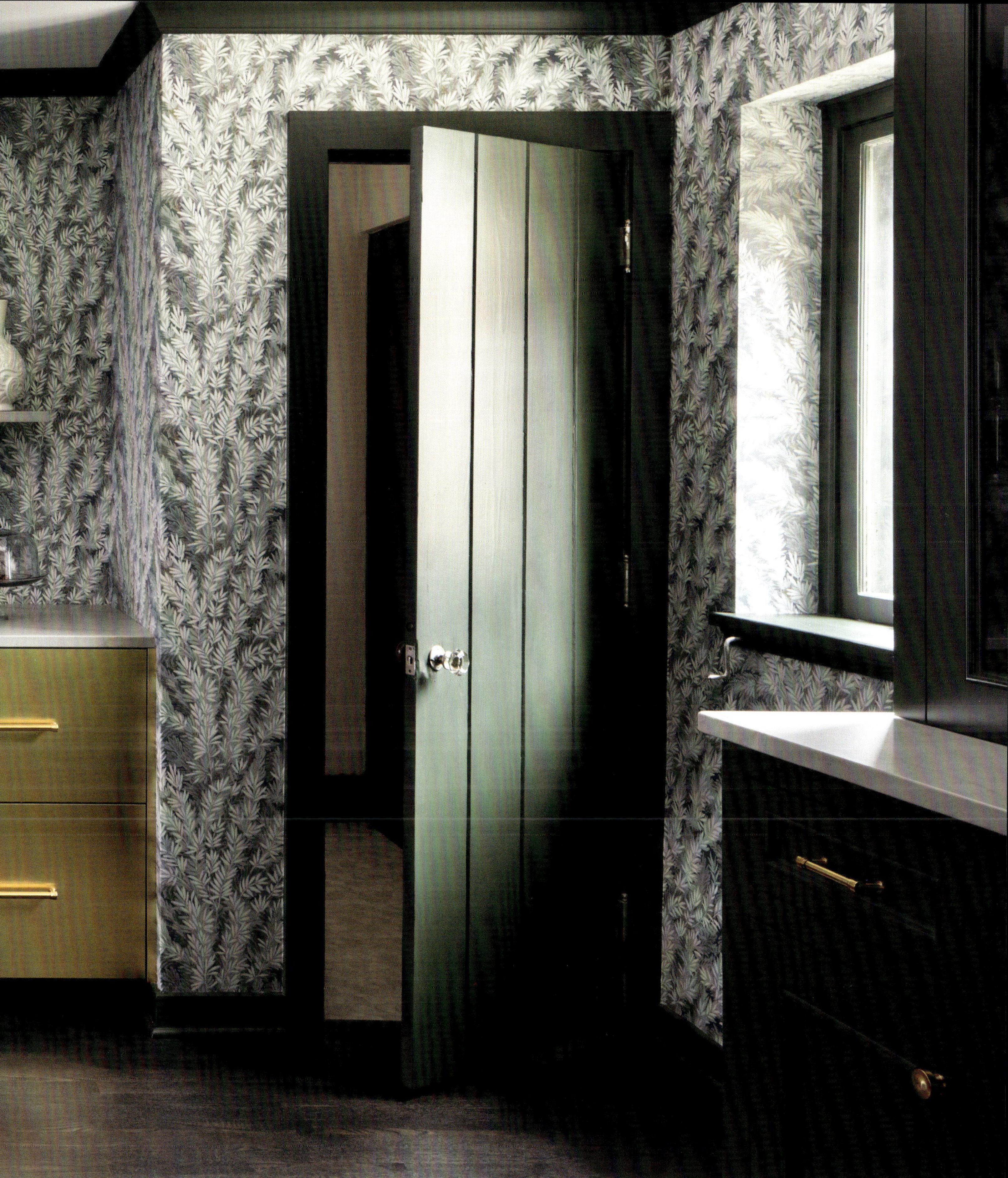

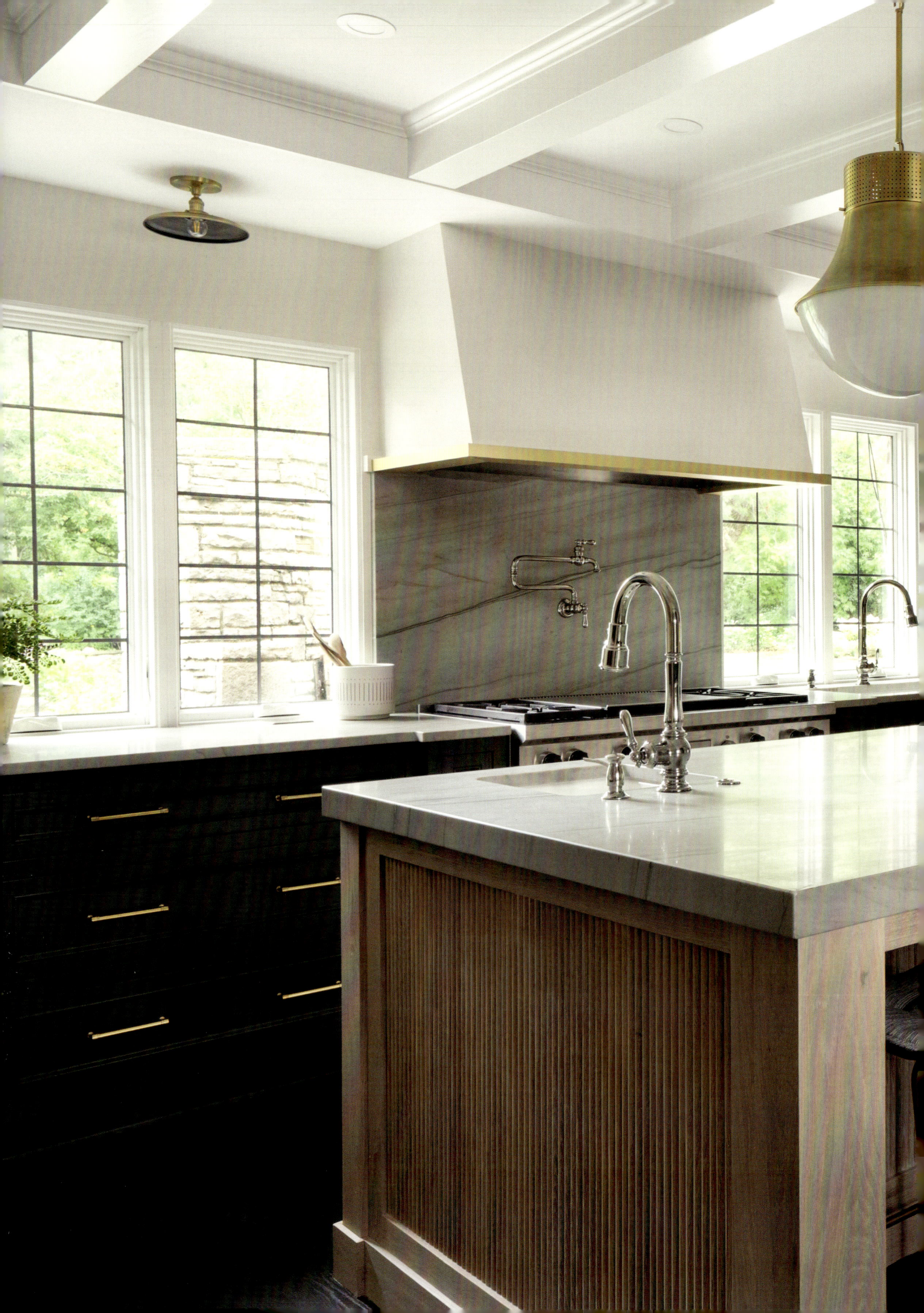

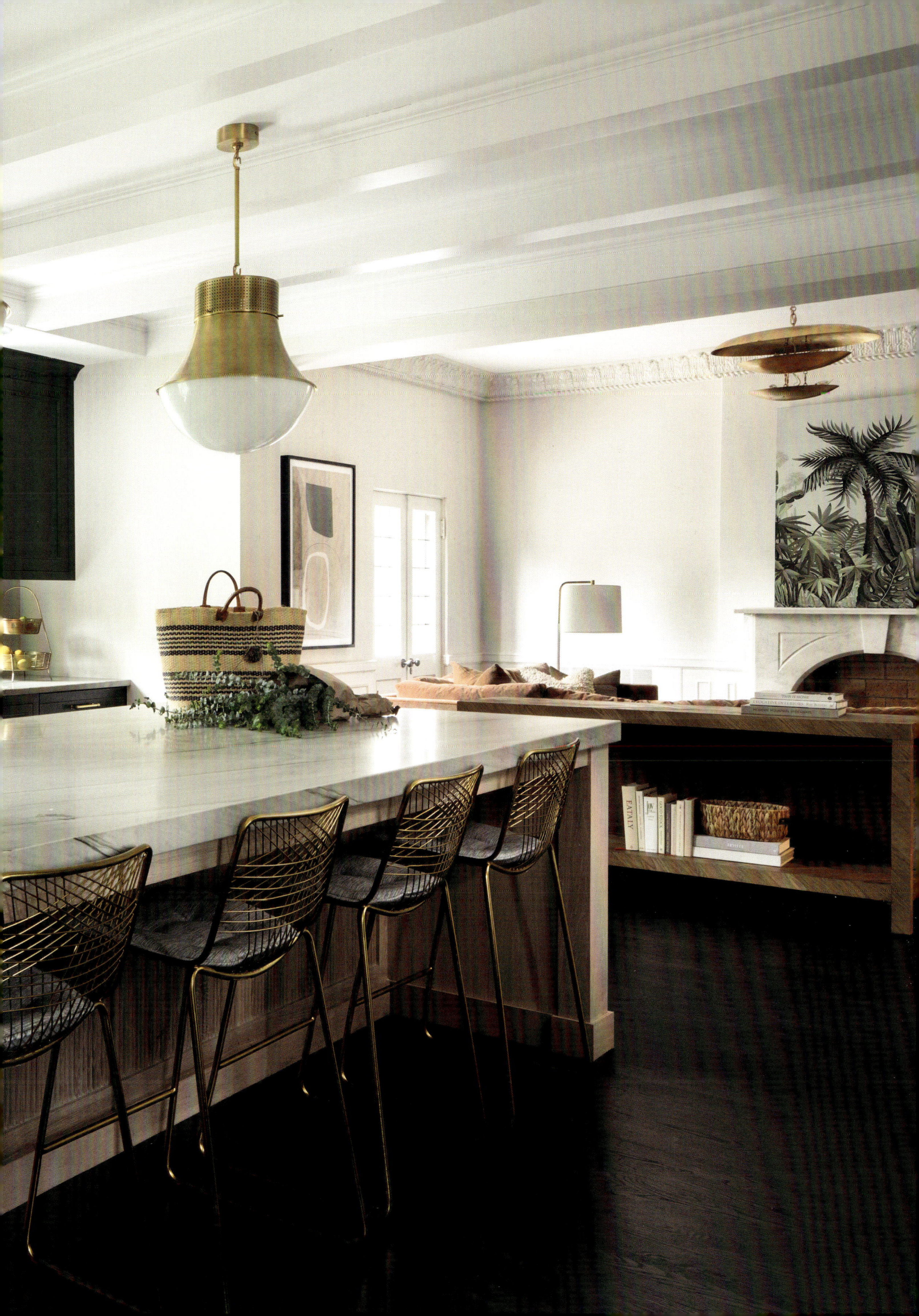

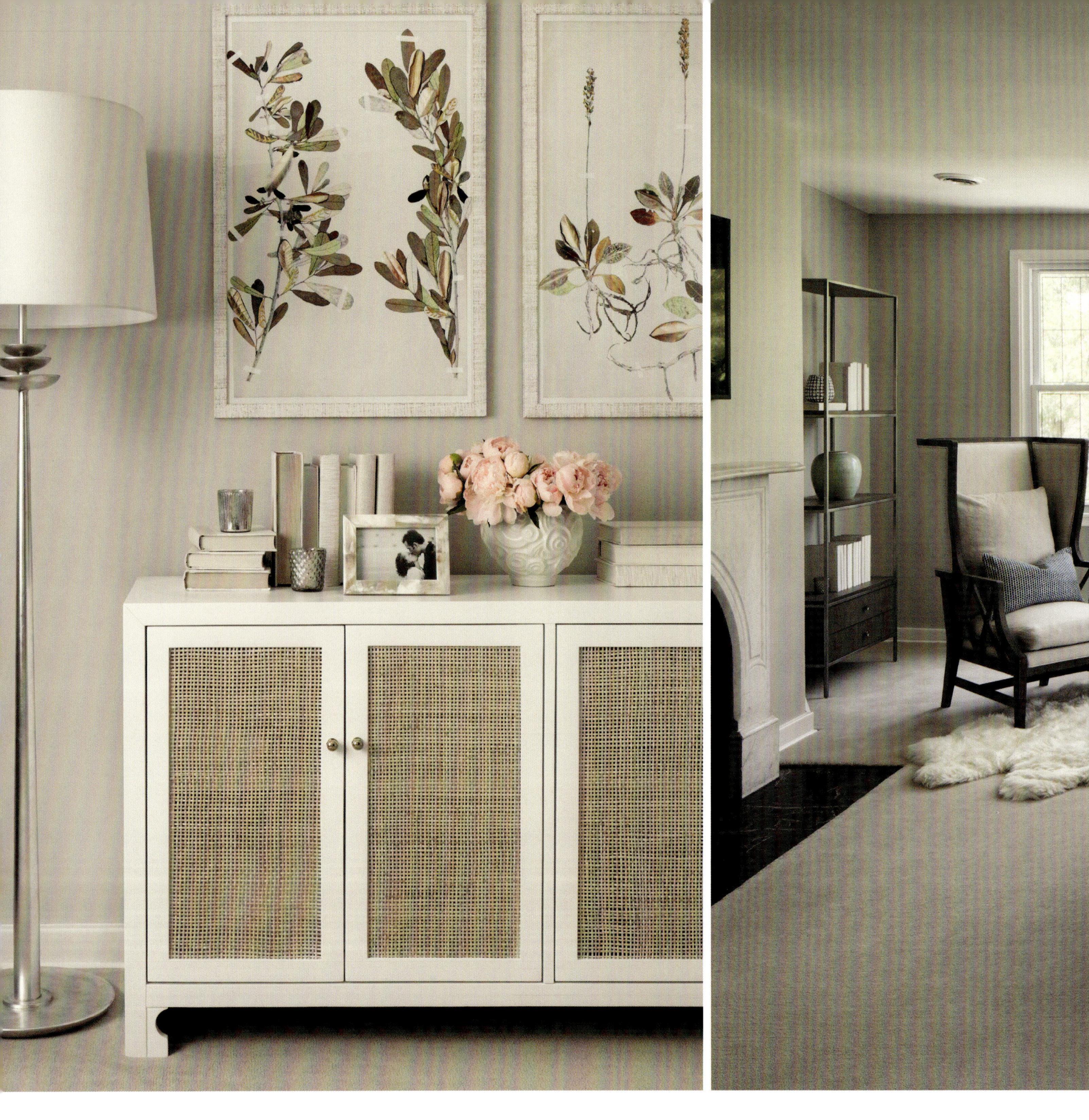

PREVIOUS: This enlarged kitchen was designed for two passionate home cooks, replacing their modest previous space. The expansive island features practical quartzite countertops and a prep sink, creating the perfect spot for ambitious baking projects and entertaining family and friends.

ABOVE: The rest-inducing primary bedroom captures stunning south- and east-facing views of the home's expansive gardens. Window treatments were deliberately omitted to maintain the open, airy atmosphere and make the surrounding trees a natural focal point.

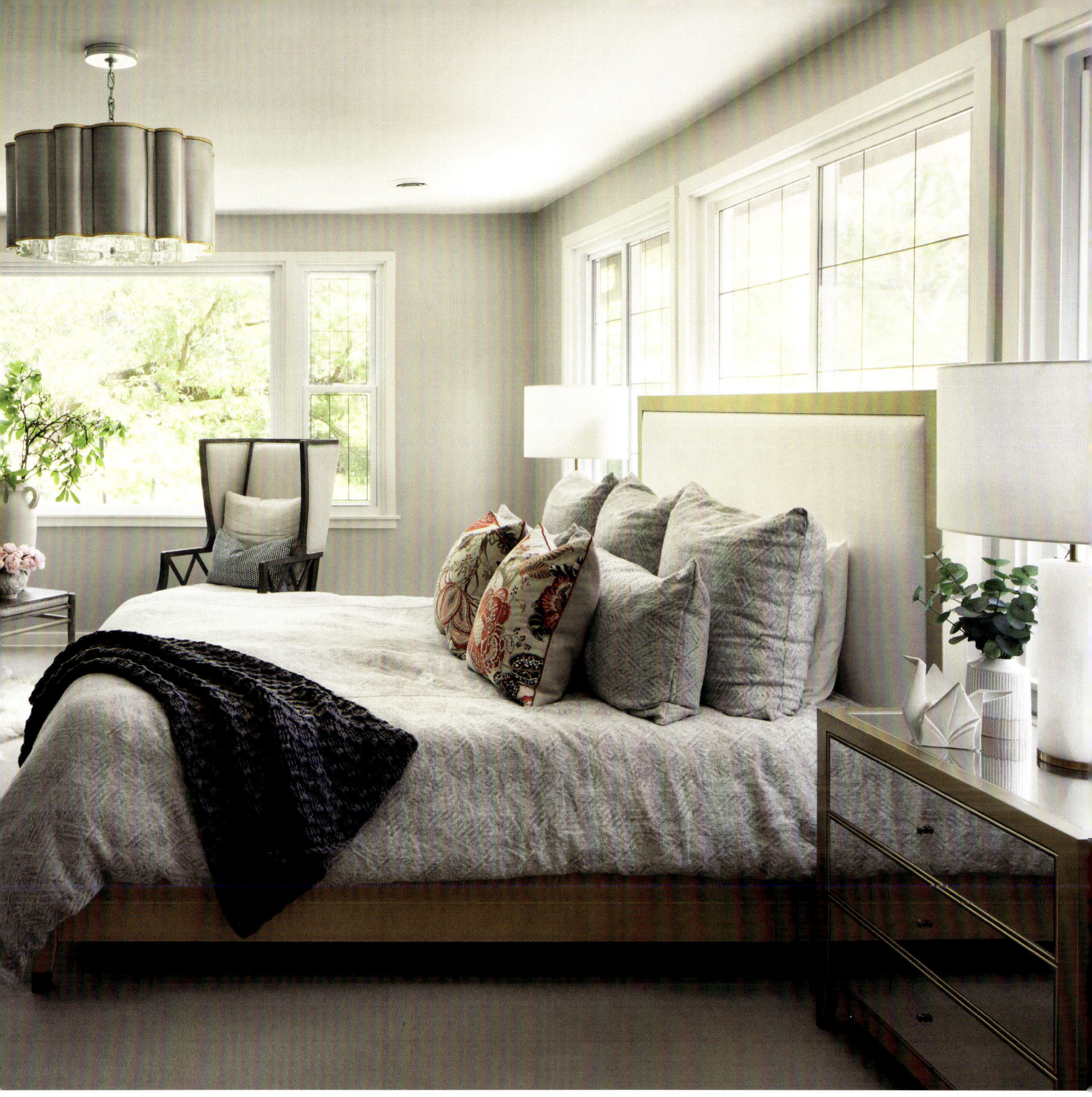

1912 FARMHOUSE

Kelsie Lally / Ameena

When Kelsie Lally of Ameena Design first saw this 1912 farmhouse in Van Dyne, Wisconsin, its true character was hidden beneath asphalt shingles. The property represented more than just a renovation project—it was the continuation of a hospitality legacy that had remained in one family for over a century before being sold to new owners in 2019. "We had no idea what it would look like," recalls Lally, "but we knew there was history worth preserving."

That history came alive when Lally met a woman who had lived in the farmhouse in the late 1940s. Her stories of weekly Sunday baths from fresh rainwater siphoned from second-floor windows in an era before indoor plumbing inspired Lally to incorporate the property's rural roots into the modern design.

A pristine palette of black, white, and red runs throughout the home. Original maple floors are preserved on the first level. Second-floor pine planking showcases thoughtful treatments—some rooms feature painted white floors, others maintain the natural wood finish, and the vestibule is grounded in a crisp checkerboard pattern.

The renovation required creative problem-solving. In order to connect the newly added second-floor bathrooms, modern plumbing infrastructure was hidden in what appear to be decorative wooden beam columns. Lally also transformed the attic space into bedrooms. Her background in architectural design allowed her to strategically remove collar ties while maintaining structural integrity and allowing the perfect amount of natural light to illuminate the quarters.

Among the details rewarding observant guests are collected antiques, rewired vintage light fixtures, and subtle red accents—as seen in the red cable suspending a pendant lamp against Cole & Son's iconic tree wallpaper.

Set on sprawling acreage, the farmhouse is a hospitality venue surrounded by pastoral beauty. Inside, the Highland cow wallpaper nods to the actual Highland cattle grazing on the property. In addition to the cattle, mammoth donkeys and beefalo roam the grounds, and peacocks, chickens, ducks, and turkeys complete this working hobby farm experience.

Now, a timeless homestead is suited for modern living while respectfully preserving the stories embedded in its walls—heritage and hospitality delicately unfold with each passing season.

This charming 1912 farmhouse welcomes visitors with its Benjamin Moore Heritage Red front door, setting the tone for the subtle red accents that echo throughout the historic and inviting rural residence.

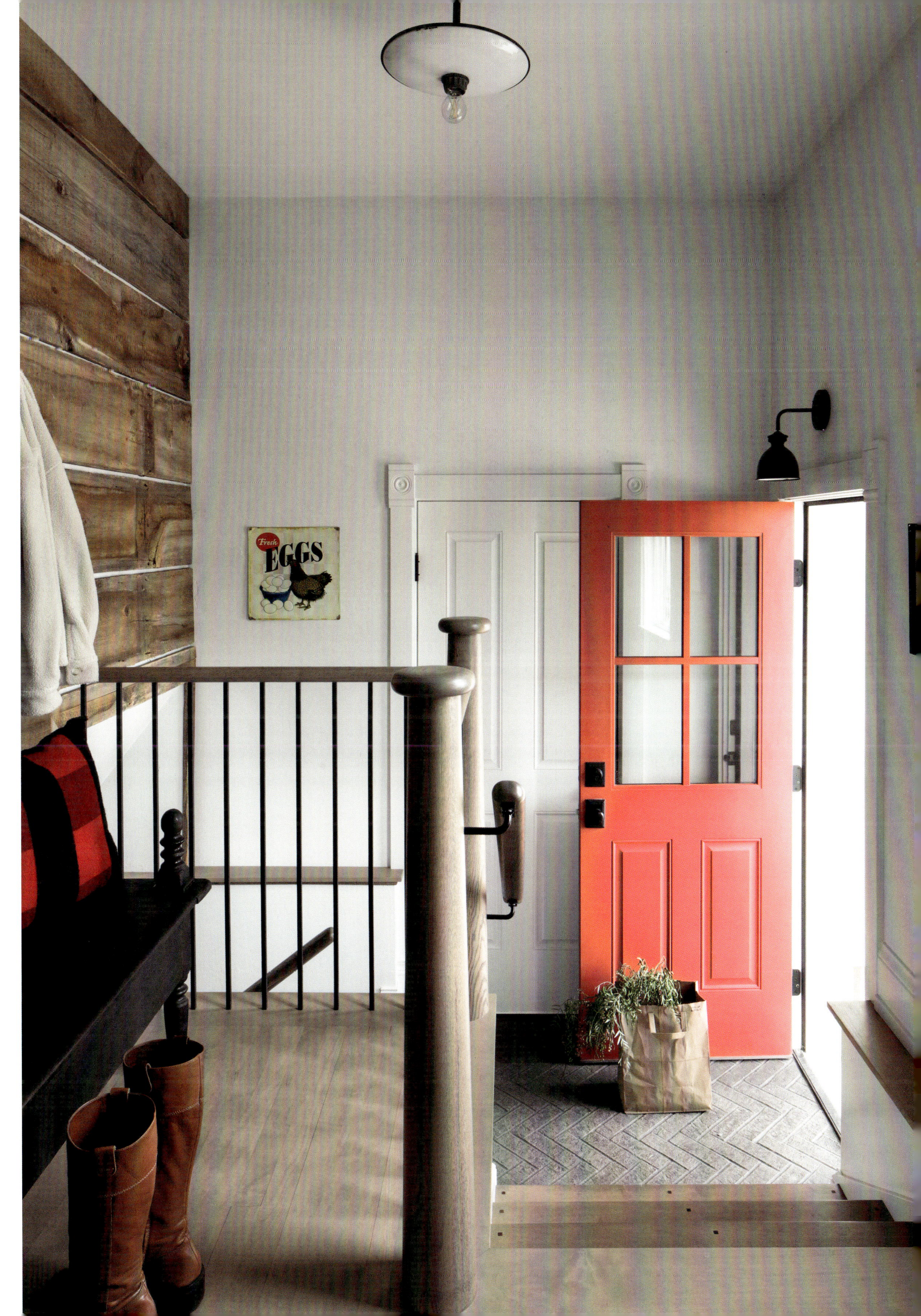
Fresh
EGGS

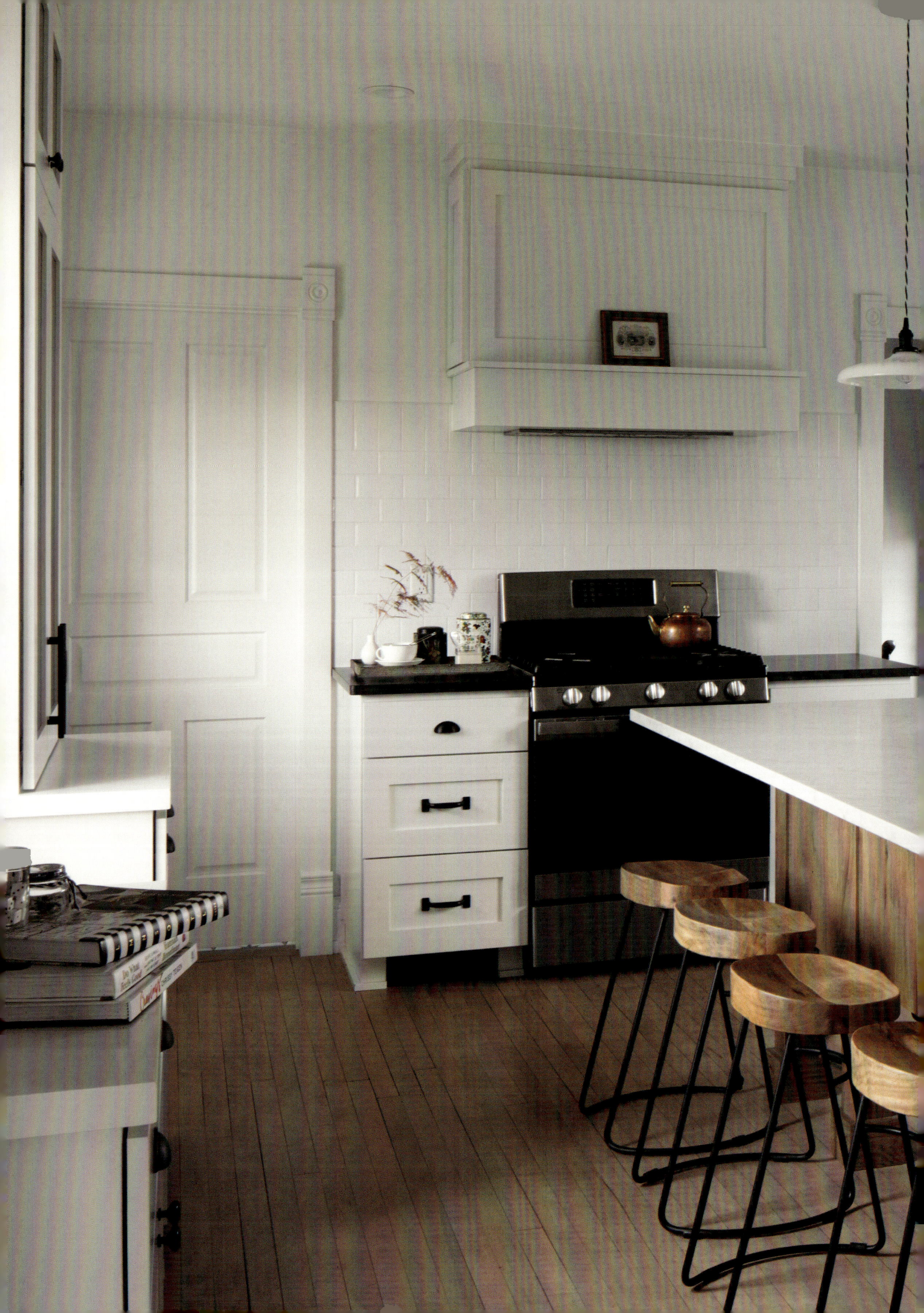

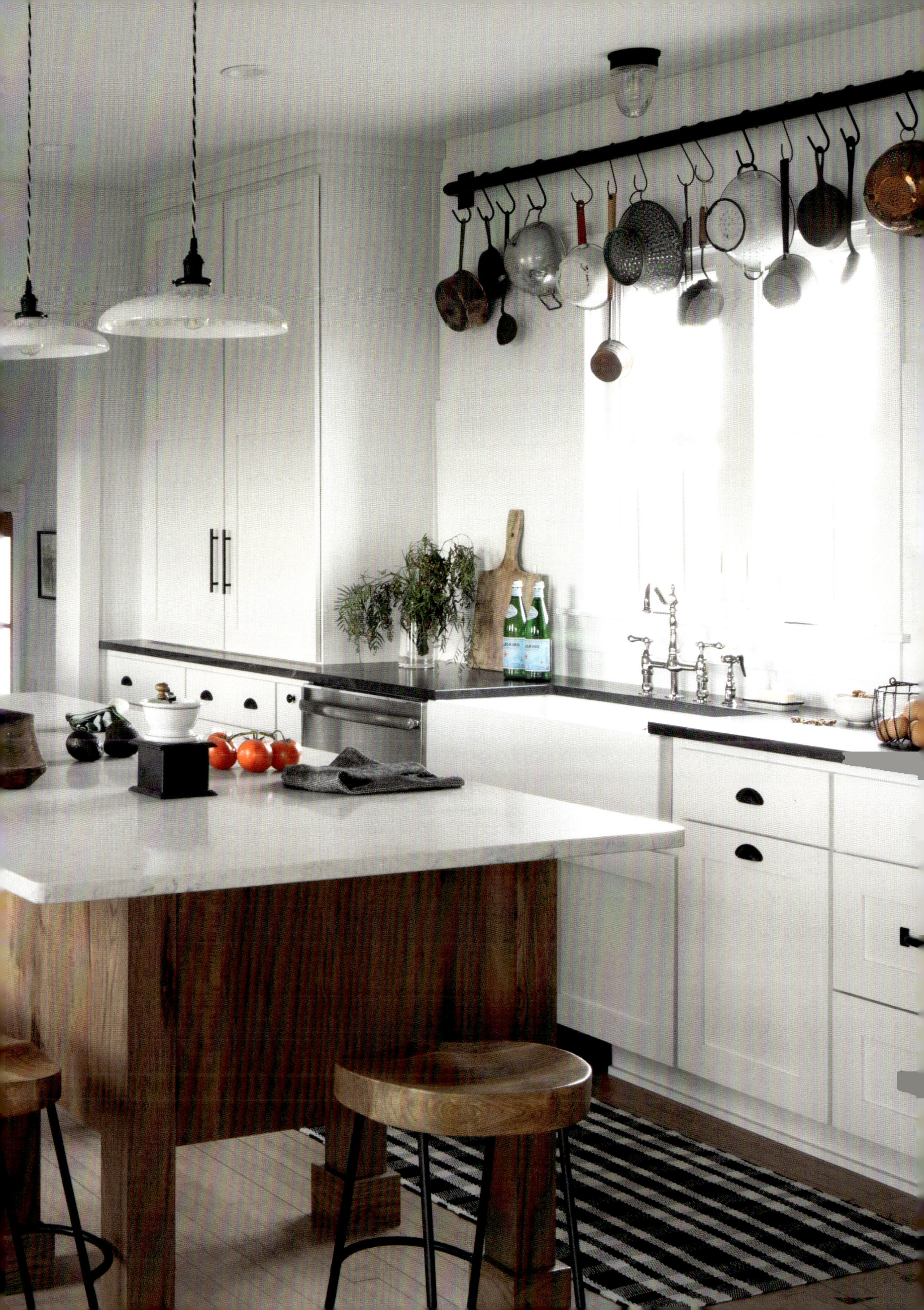

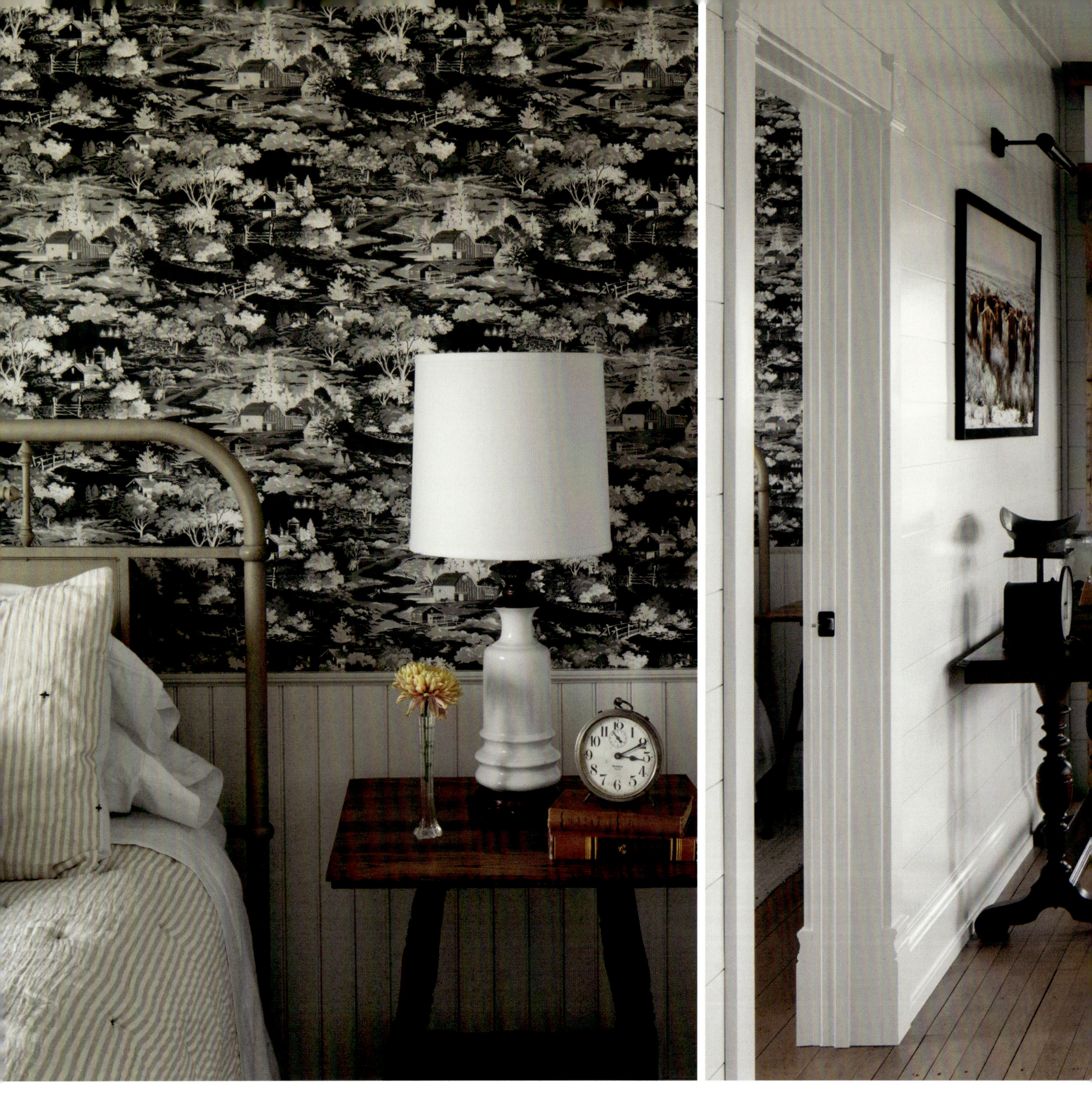

PREVIOUS: A thoughtfully restored 1912 farmhouse kitchen features Sherwin-Williams Pure White walls, locally sourced antique treasures hanging above the window, and Heritage Lighting milk glass pendants with black-and-white braided cords illuminating the welcoming island.

ABOVE: *Left:* Vintage charm defines this bedroom, featuring York "Homestead" wall covering, white-and-khaki antique ticking on the bed, and a primitive 1920s pine bedside table acquired from a local antique store. *Right:* This carefully preserved dining room showcases the home's 1912 heritage with antique furnishings, including reupholstered black chairs and a custom copper light fixture with patinated fittings. The white door, originally the home's main entrance, now conceals a closet after renovations in the 1960s.

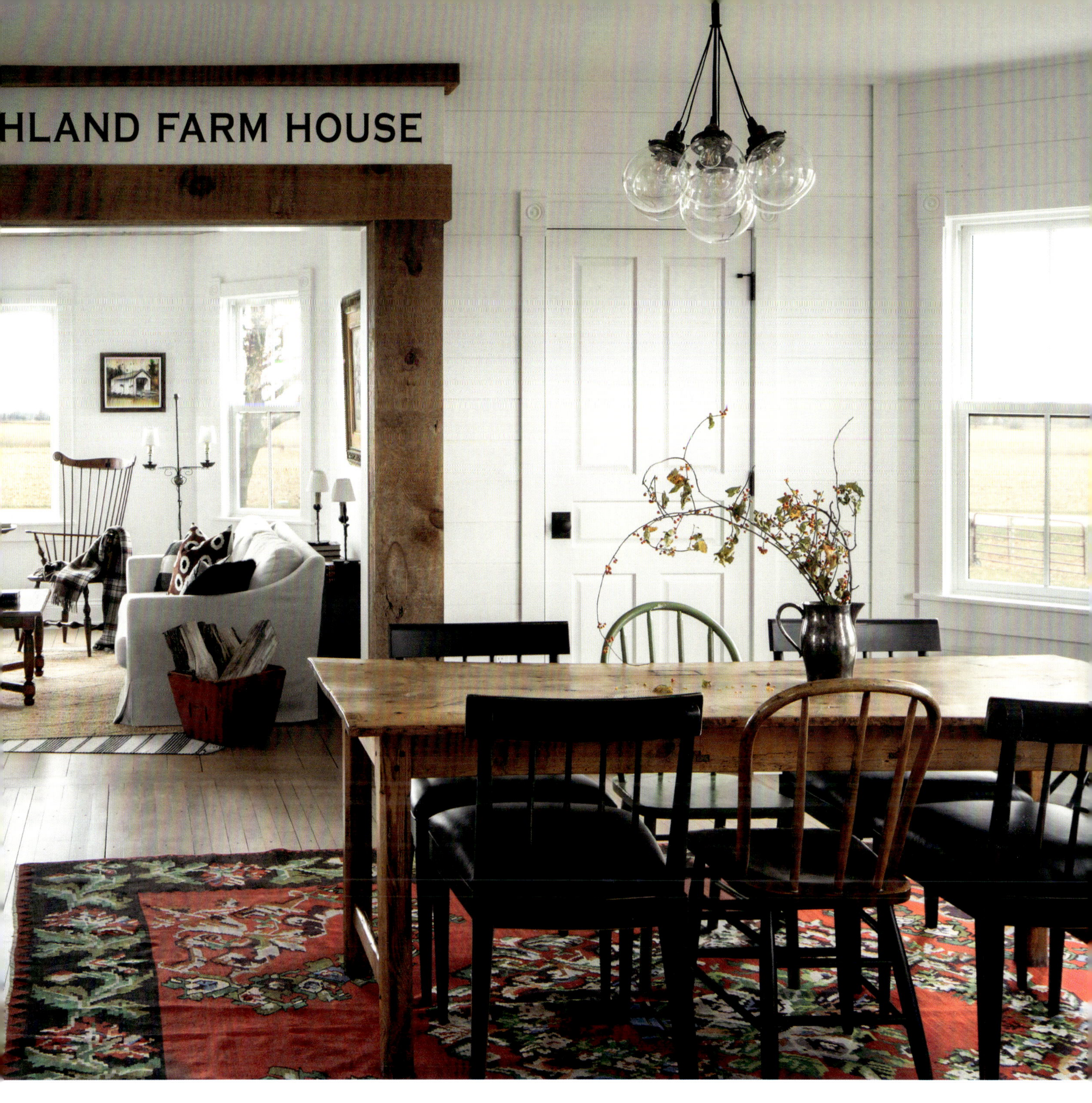
HLAND FARM HOUSE

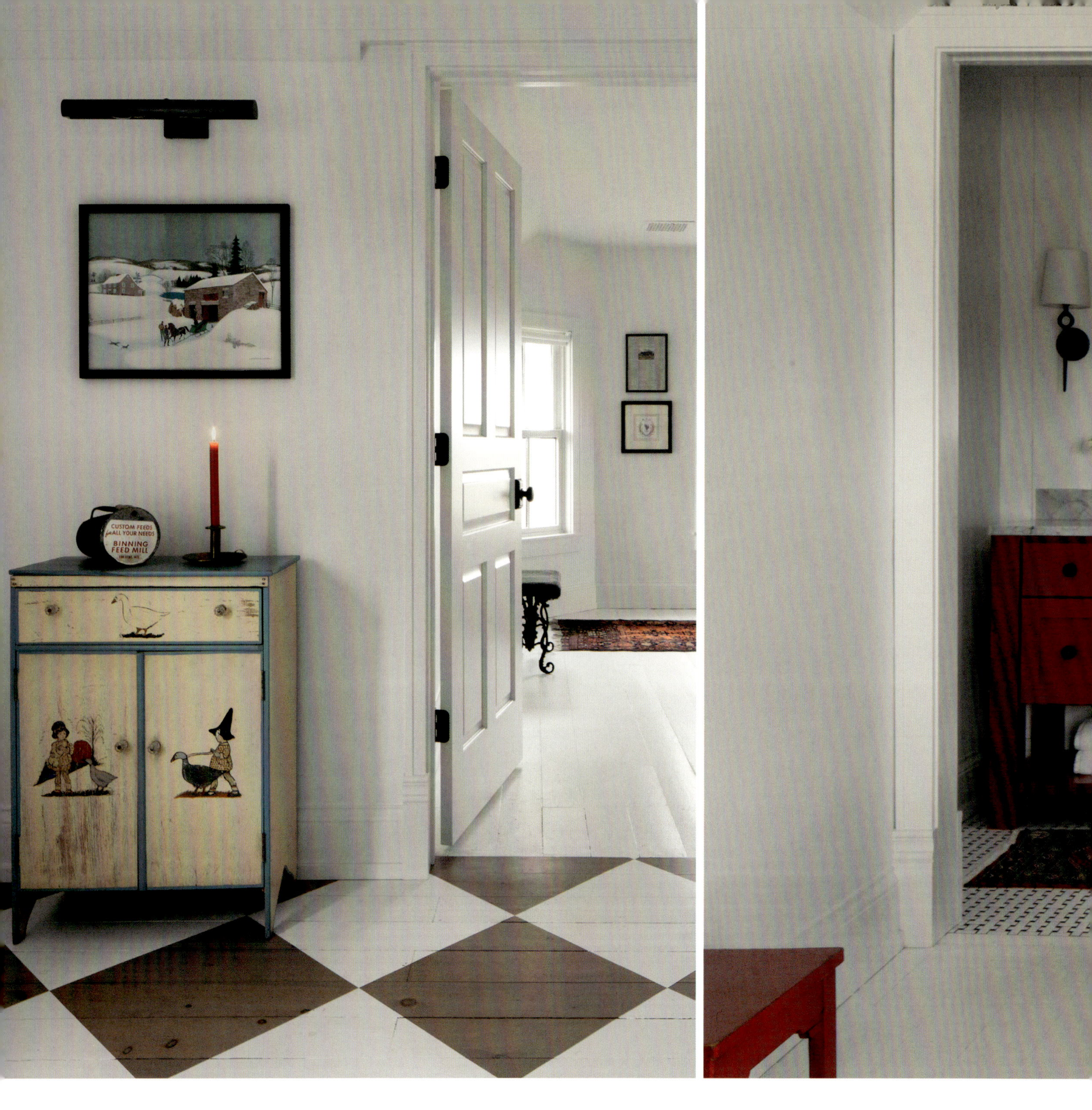

Left: A clever painted checkerboard pattern defines the oddly shaped second-floor hallway, functioning as a permanent "rug." ***Right:*** The primary bedroom continues the home's black, white, and red theme with Cole & Son's "Woods" wall covering in onyx/white. Millwork and floors are kept white to showcase carefully chosen accents.

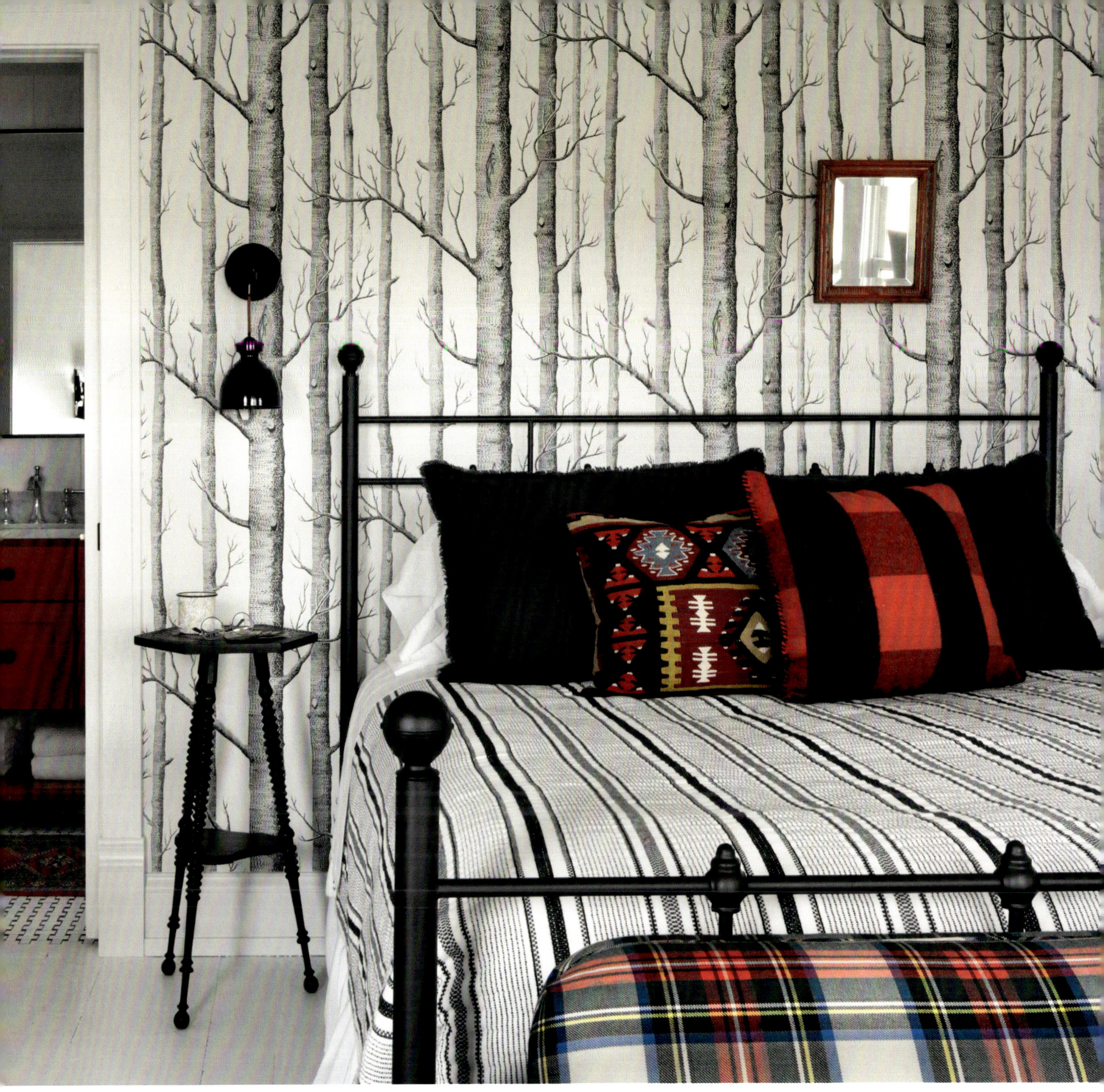

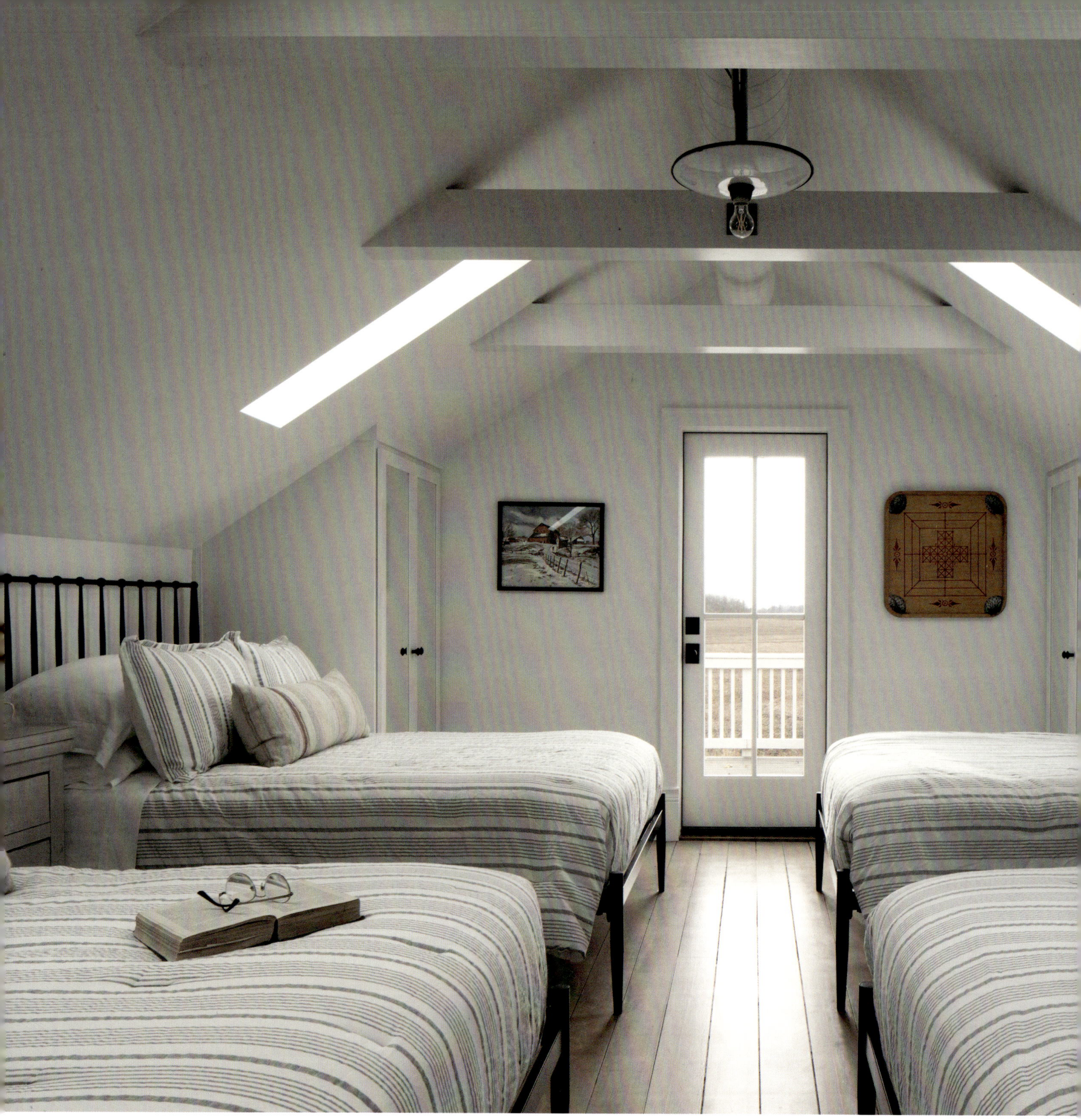

ABOVE: This ingenious bunk room transformation reclaimed attic space by strategically excluding closets and low-ceiling areas from square footage calculations. Structural collar ties were wrapped in wood, with skylights installed between retained beams to achieve the required natural light for comfortable guest accommodations.

NEXT: A transformed space that once housed two separate bedrooms, this whimsical children's bunk room features Juliet Travers's "Highland Fling" wallpaper showcasing Highland cows. Other highlights of the room are custom-designed ladders and vintage star lights salvaged from a 1920s New York theater.

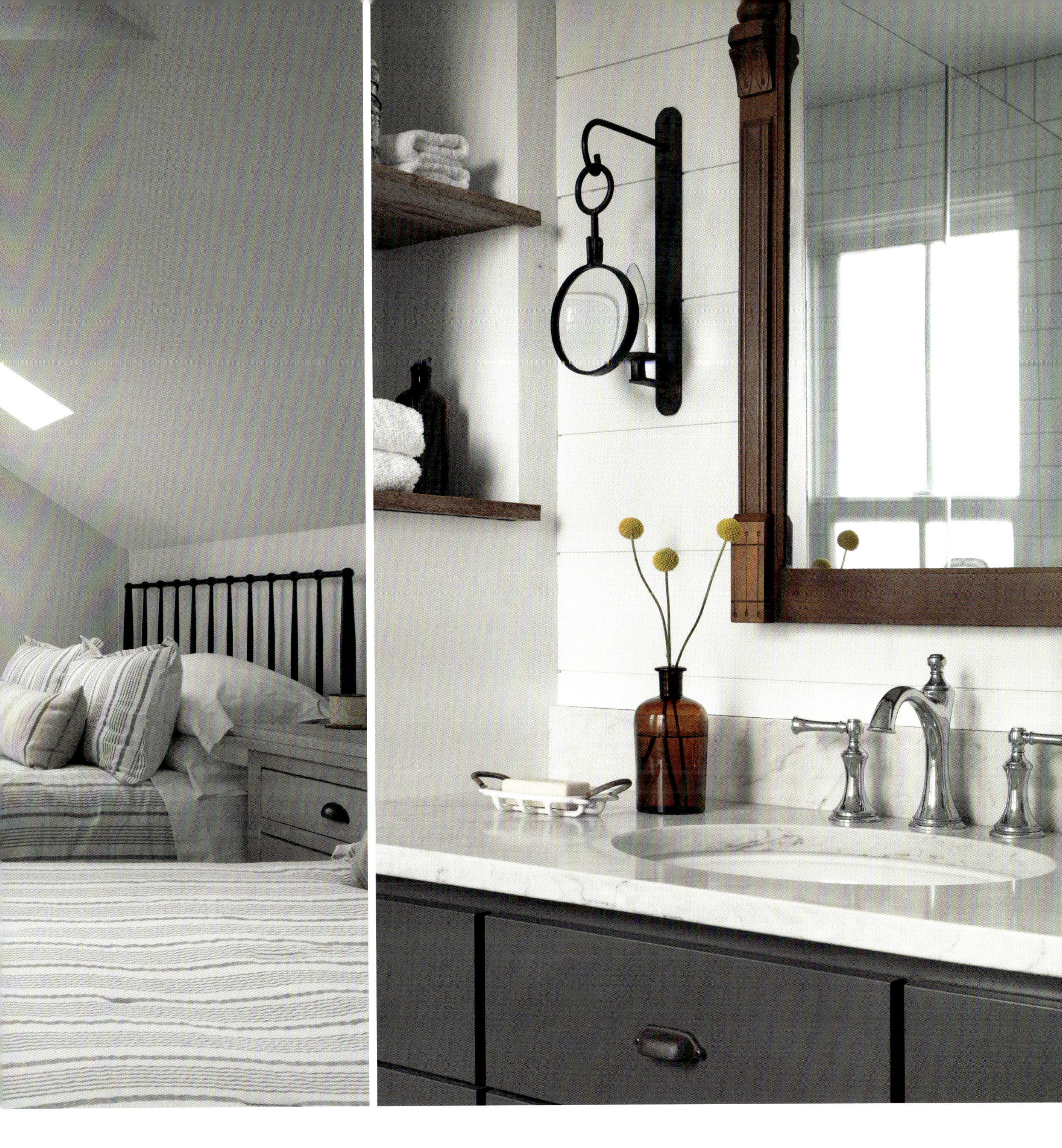

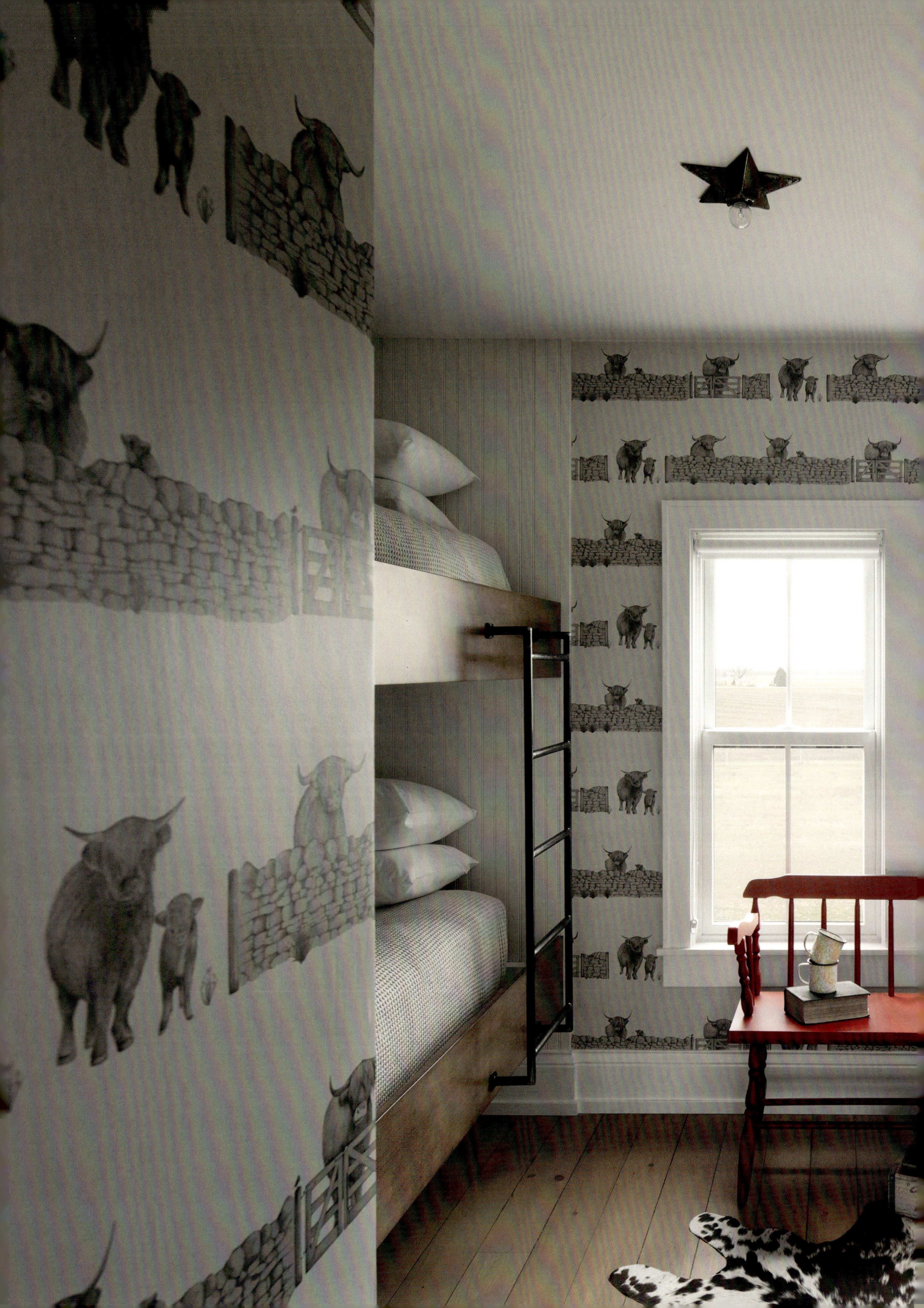

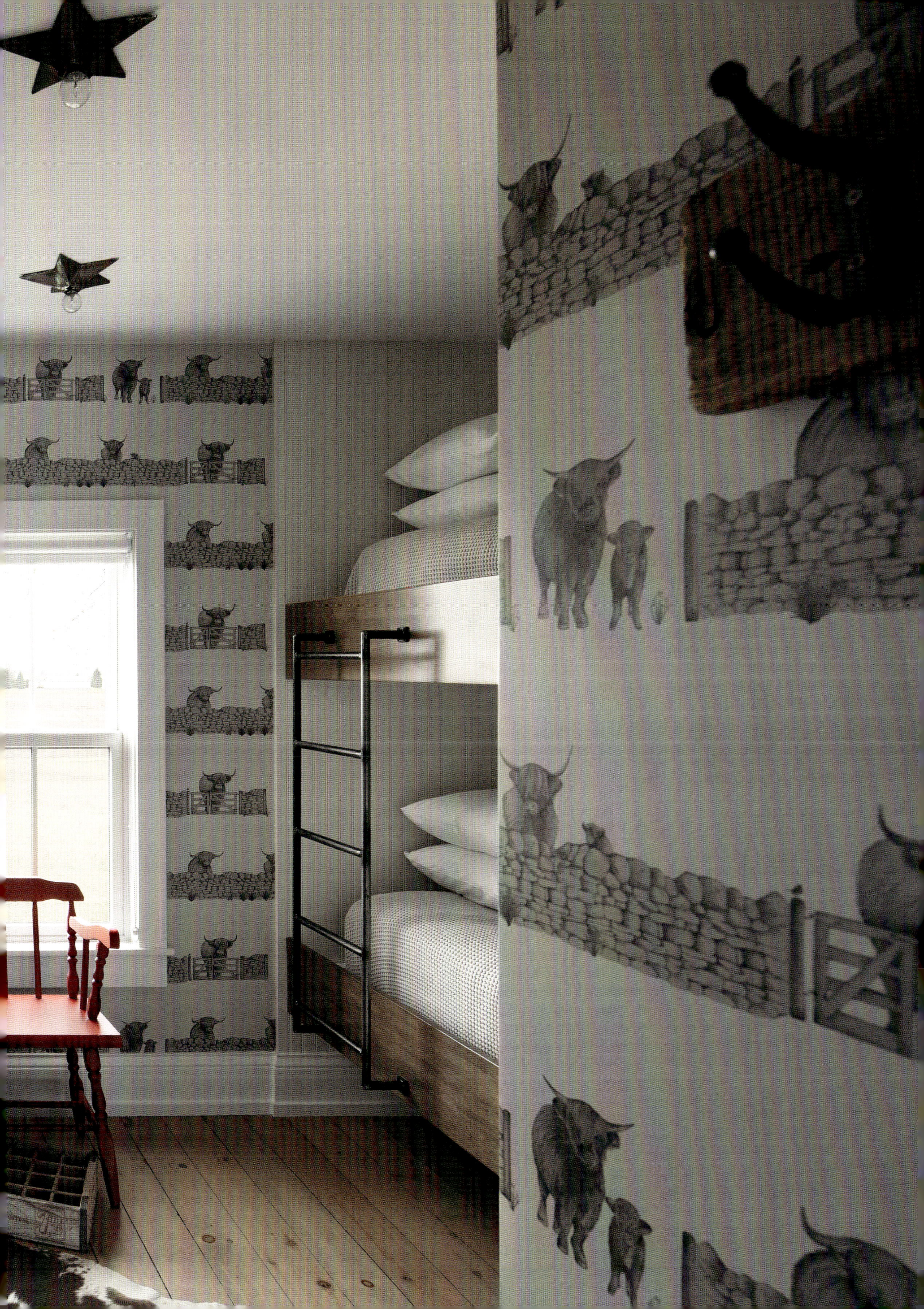

ELKHART LAKE RENOVATION

Amy Carman Design

Elkhart Lake, Wisconsin, is home to the legendary Road America raceway. The historic 4-mile circuit draws in motorsport enthusiasts from across the Midwest. Here, families, racing purists, and weekenders who camp along its rolling hills create a vibrant community bonded by speed and tradition. Nearby, Amy Carman transformed a nondescript side-by-side condo into a sophisticated retreat that celebrates family togetherness and automotive passion.

The homeowners, an insurance company executive and his family, are multigenerational visitors to Elkhart Lake's racing scene who had long searched for the perfect vacation home near this storied raceway. This condo boasted a prime location just blocks from the beach, but the property's early 2000s interior—characterized by beige carpets, beige walls, and compartmentalized rooms—required a complete reimagining.

"We gutted it down to the studs," Carman explains, "and re-created a high-quality, authentic interior space utterly designed for family, for getting away, for relaxing and conversation."

The owners' Porsche collection influenced design choices throughout the home, particularly in what Carman calls the "library bar" on the lower level. This space deliberately counters the stereotype of the "depressing Wisconsin tavern basement," instead functioning as a multifaceted gathering area where family members socialize, play, and craft together.

Automotive references appear throughout the home. A window seat is upholstered in authentic Porsche material. The German automaker's leather-trimmed floor mat even serves as an area rug. A long ribbon of bookcases display car memorabilia alongside wine, spirits, board games, and craft supplies.

"Any way we could get a nod to their love of cars, we would work it in," Carman notes.

For the family that owns the property, this reimagined condo represents more than just a vacation home—it's a space that harmoniously blends their passion for automotive heritage with their desire for authentic family connection. Through careful design choices, Carman has created a residence that honors both the racing culture of Elkhart Lake and the personal relationships that flourish within the home's walls.

What was once a confined galley kitchen was transformed into an expansive gathering space. The renovated kitchen now flows seamlessly from the living room. Removing walls and entry closets created room for a gracious island and completely transformed this home's heart.

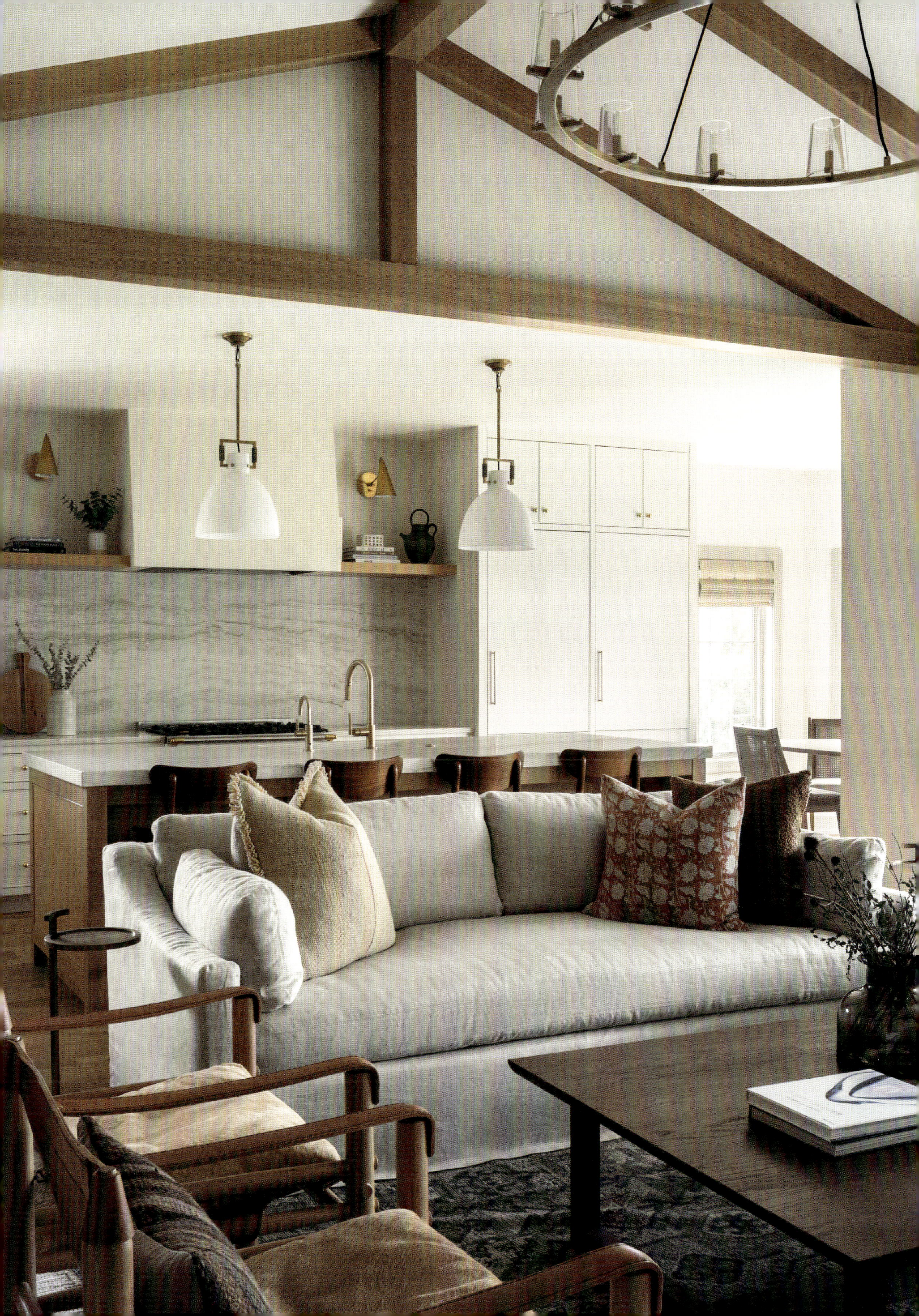

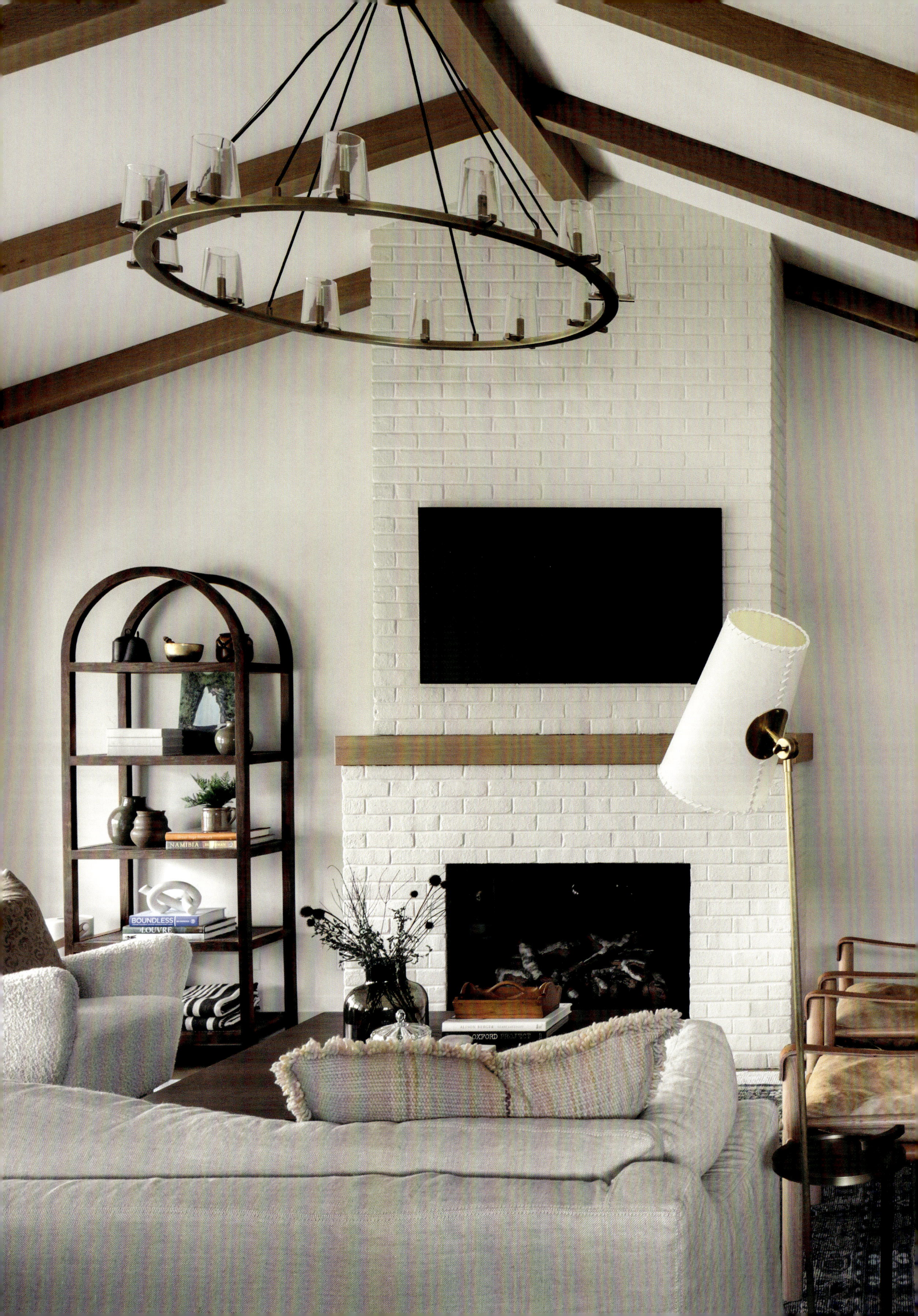
NAMIBIA
BOUNDLESS
LOUVRE
OXFORD PROJECT

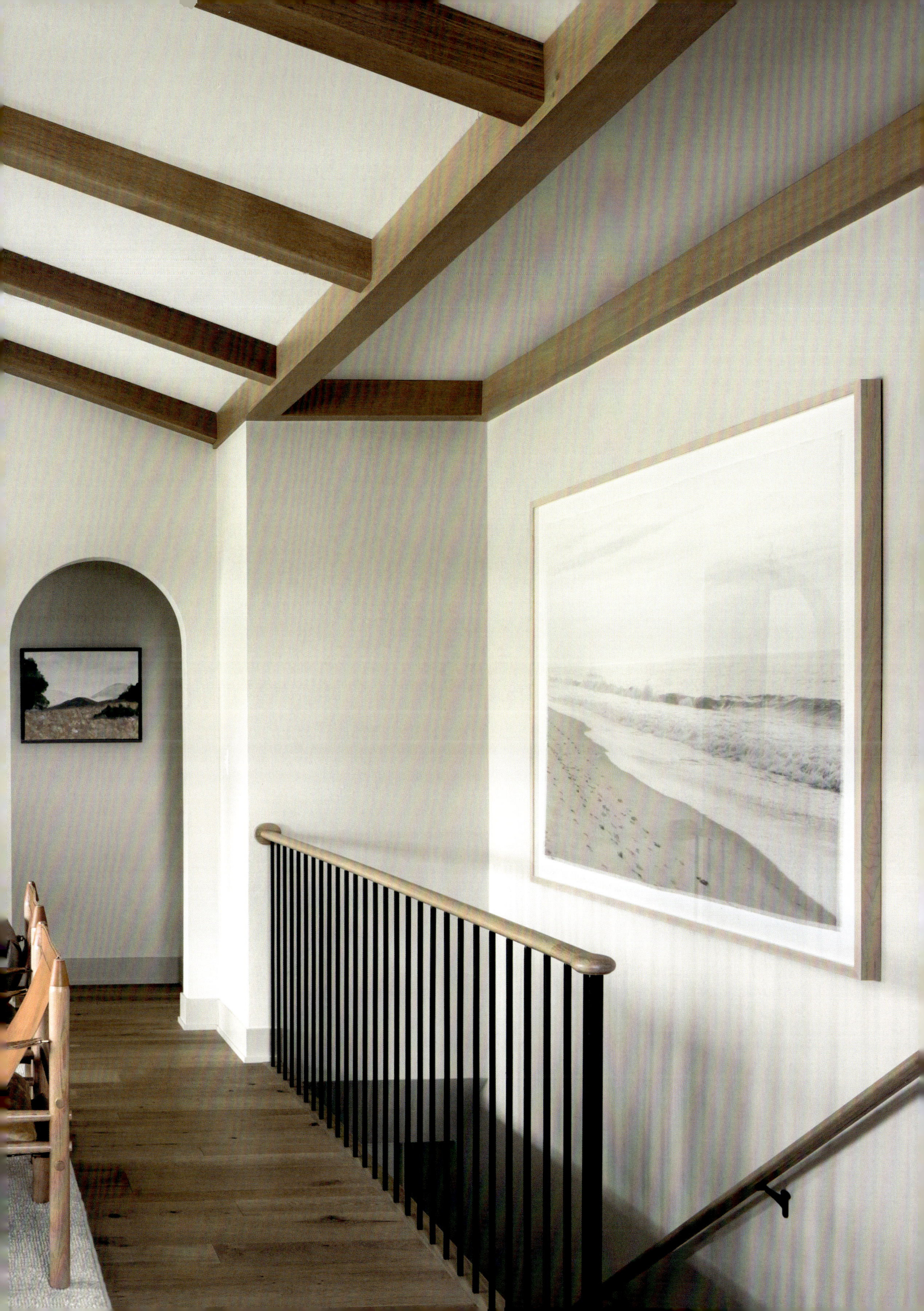

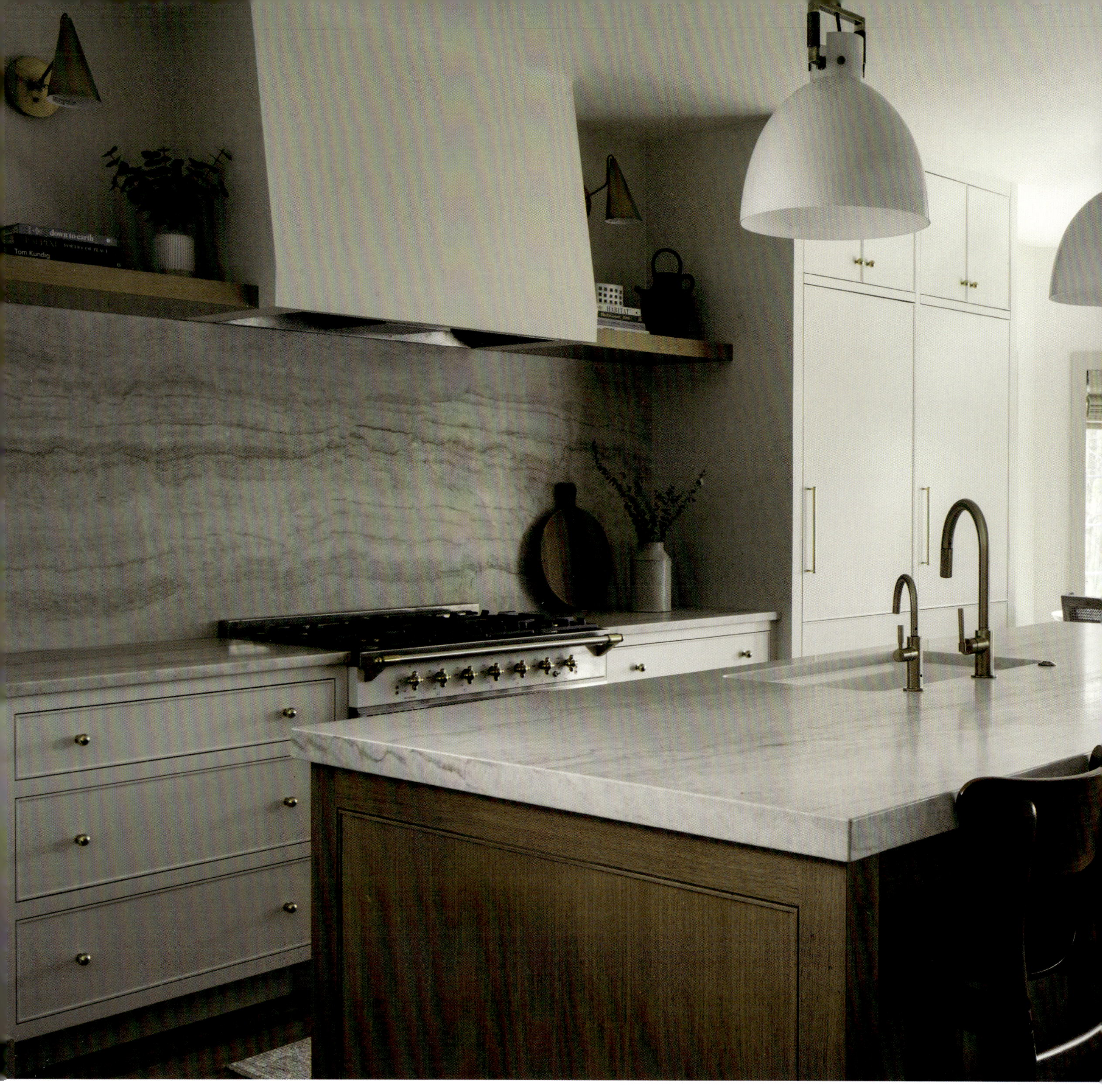

PREVIOUS: The reimagined living space centers on a relocated fireplace, now framed by elegant wooden beams against the vaulted ceiling. A new drywall archway creates a private approach to the primary bedroom while providing the perfect wall for artwork display.

ABOVE: The striking island features Bianca Perla quartzite with a thick mitered edge and leathered finish. A round white oak table in the adjacent breakfast room pairs beautifully with elegant cane-backed dining chairs.

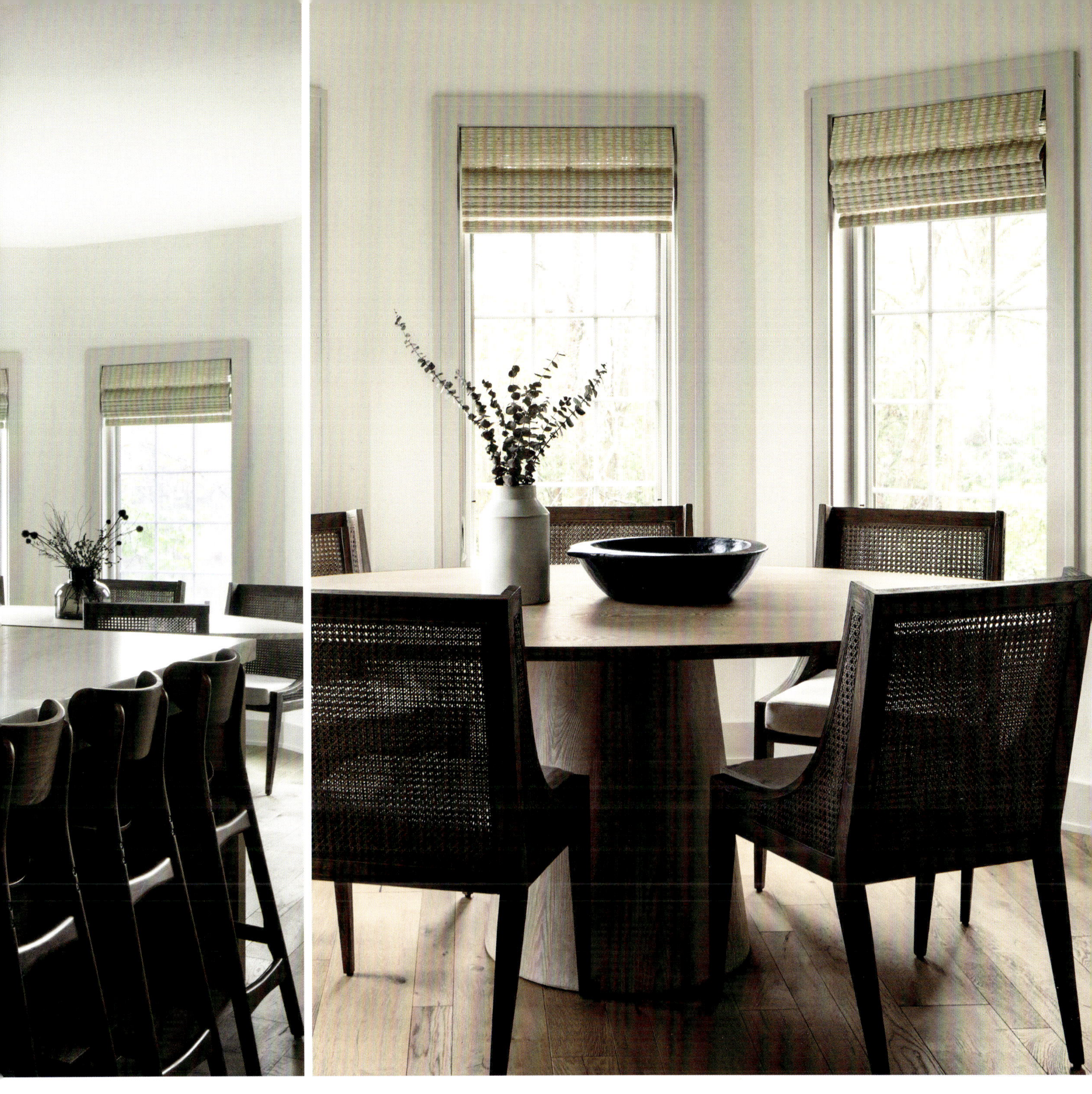

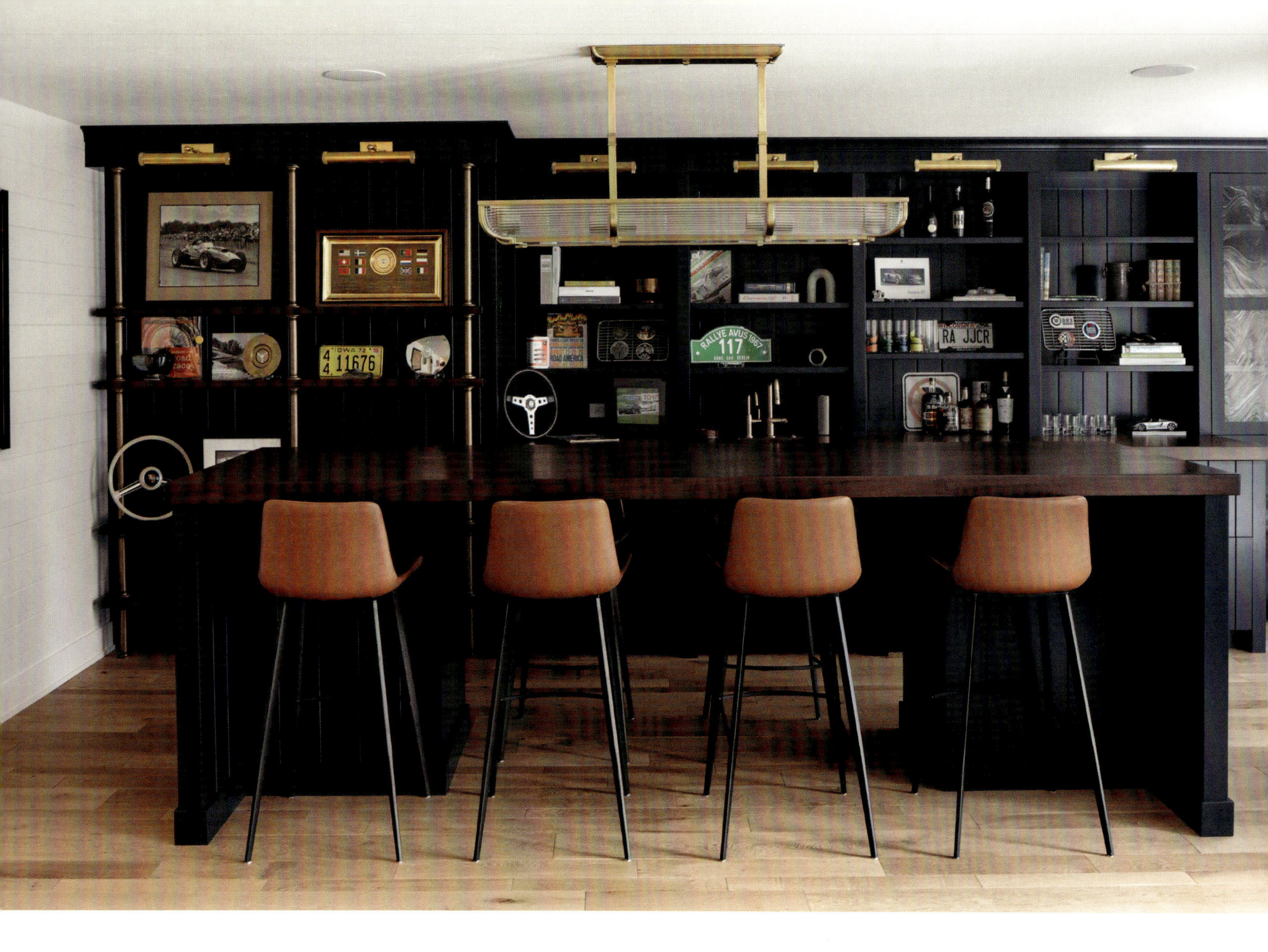

This family- and guest-friendly library bar accommodates six guests with seating on both sides, which is perfect for game nights and family gatherings. Painted in Portola Newton's Indigo, the space extends to a cozy nook featuring a plaid window seat and two leather club chairs.

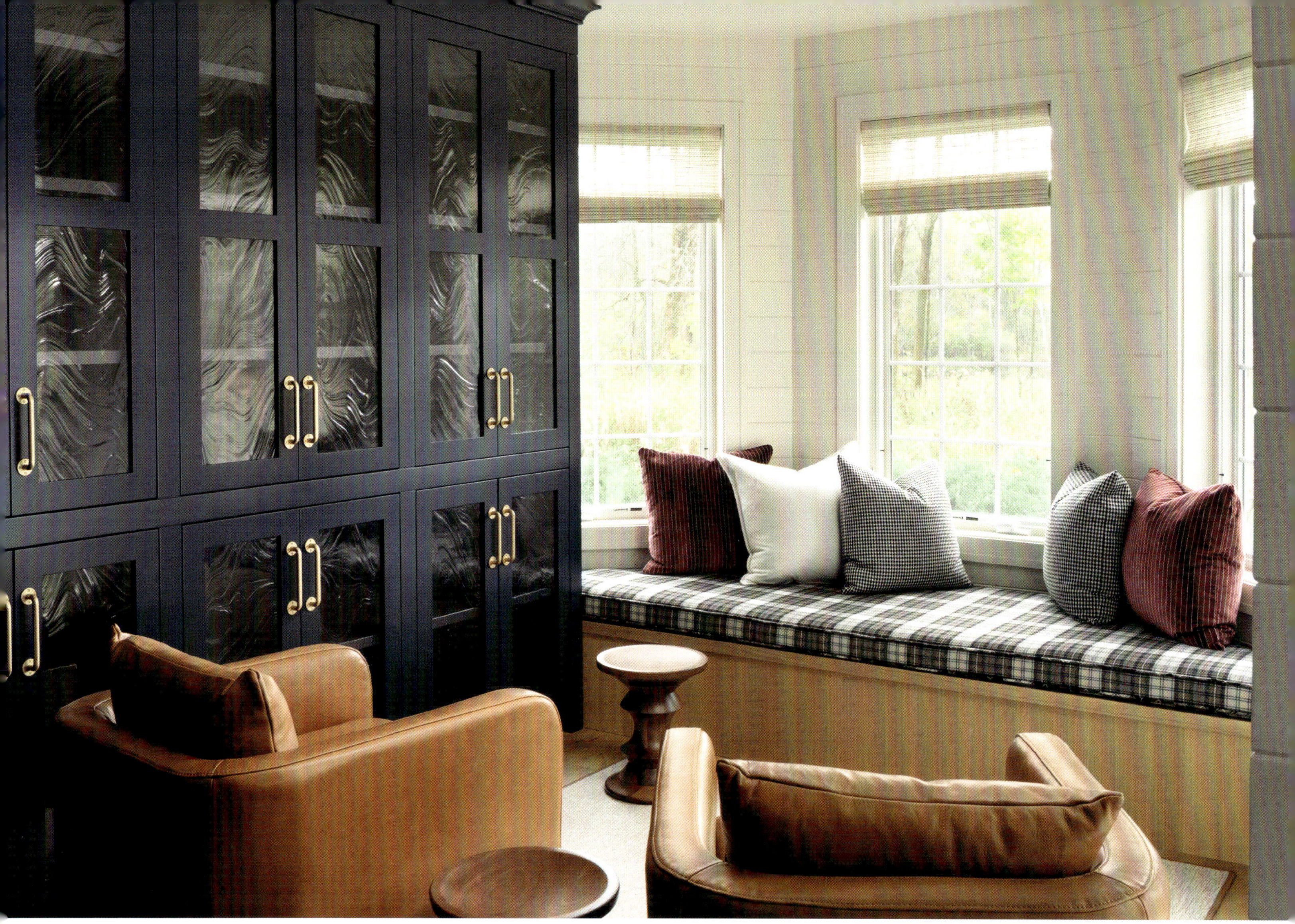

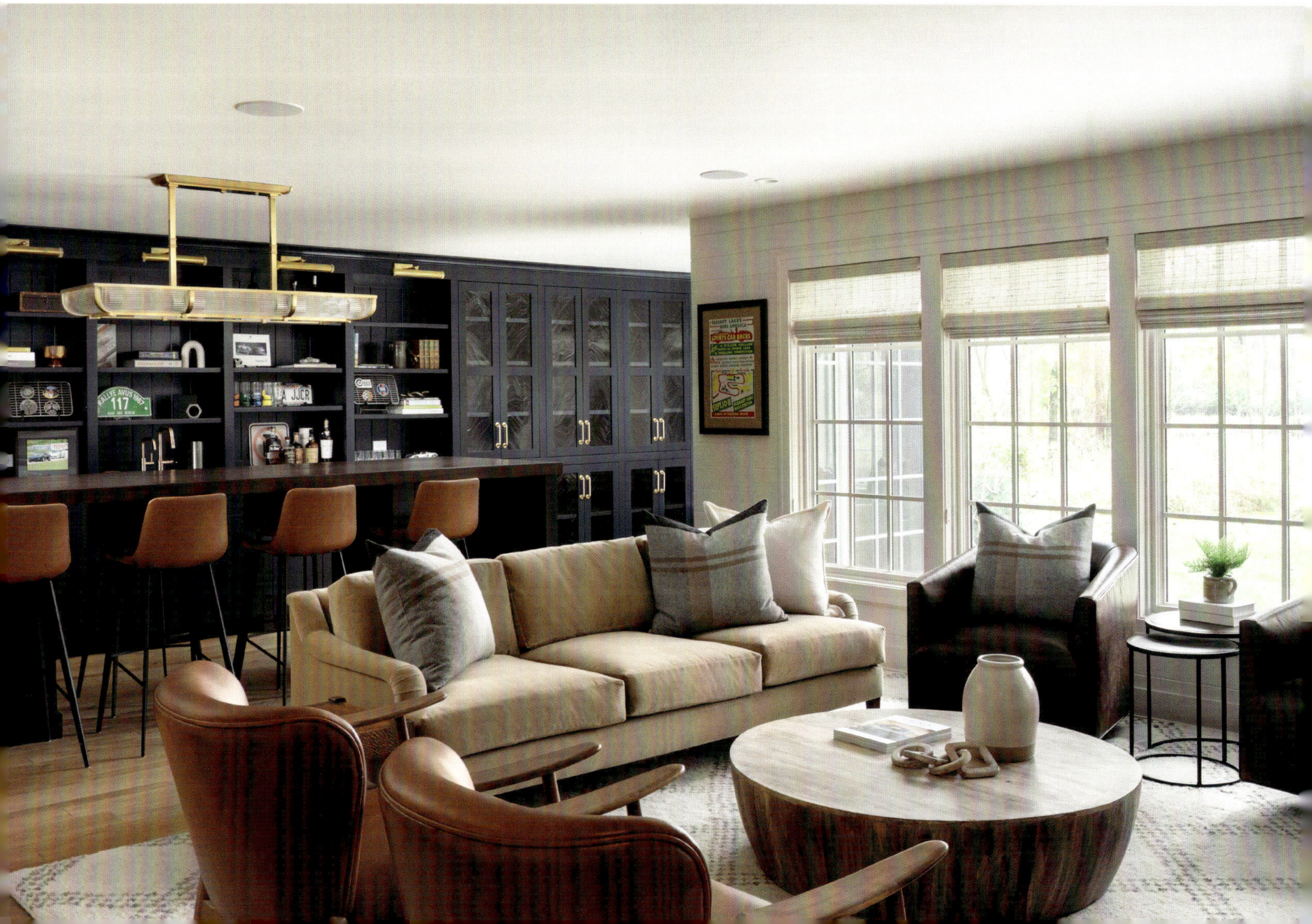

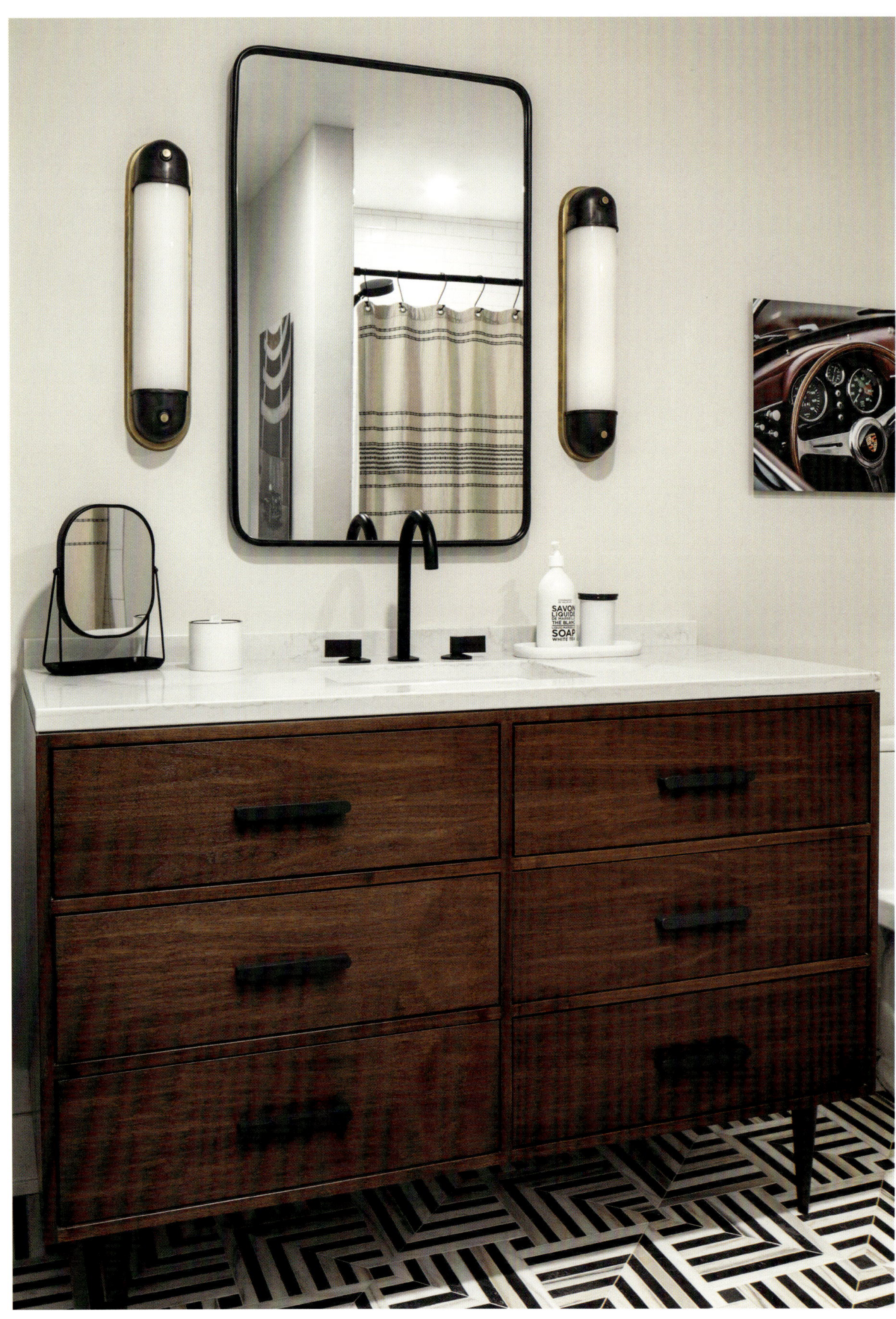

Left: The lower-level guest bath showcases an art deco–inspired green-and-white marble mosaic floor by Ann Sacks. *Right:* Located on the first floor, the primary bedroom features a custom boucle-upholstered headboard complemented by a hand-knotted wool area rug in warm, inviting tones.

NEXT: Though the space is small, the family's daughters chose to share this room with queen-sized beds. Unifying the space is a custom tambour headboard made of white oak and featuring hidden storage and charging stations. The vintage van photograph is a nod to the family's passion for classic cars.

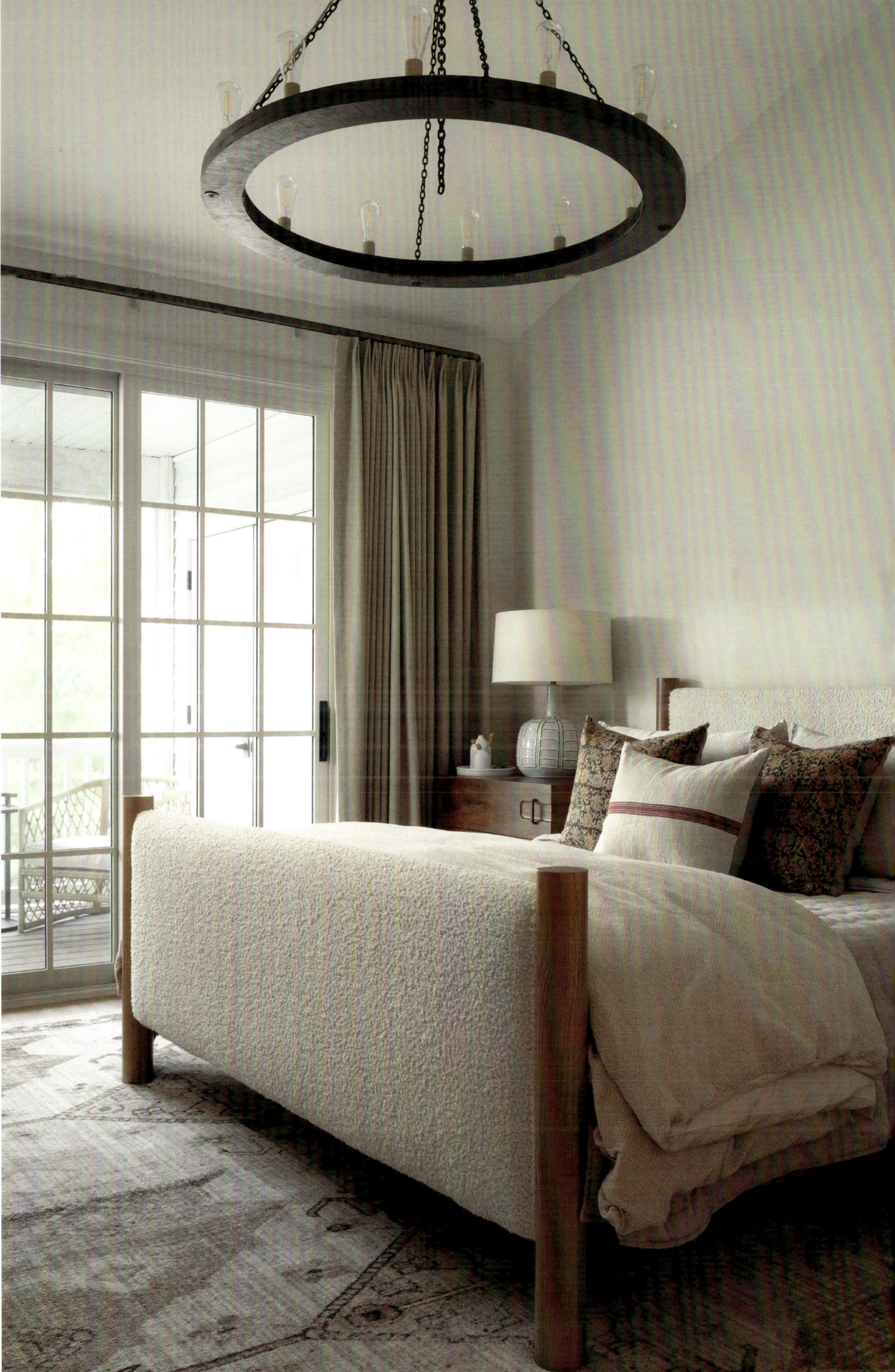

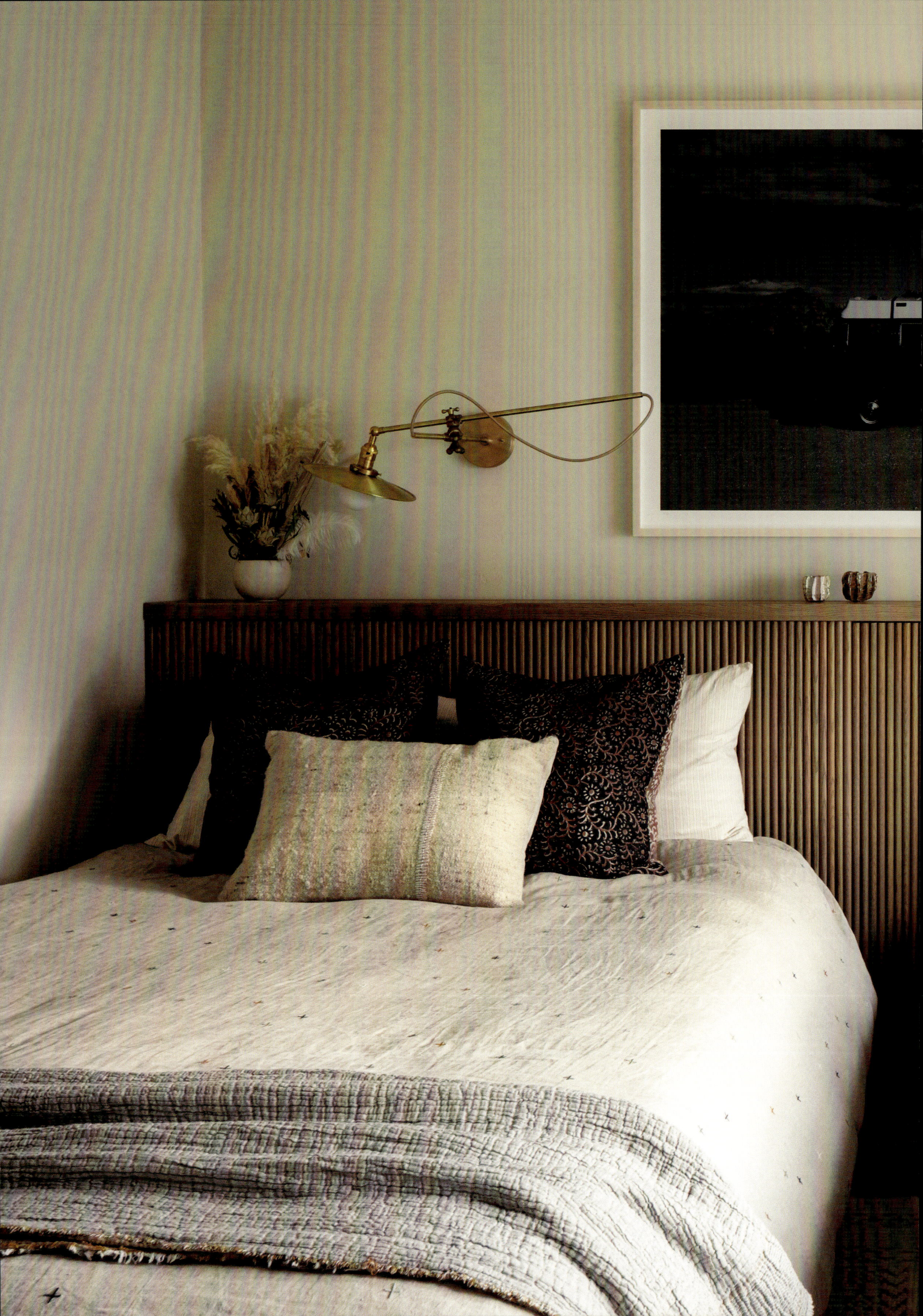

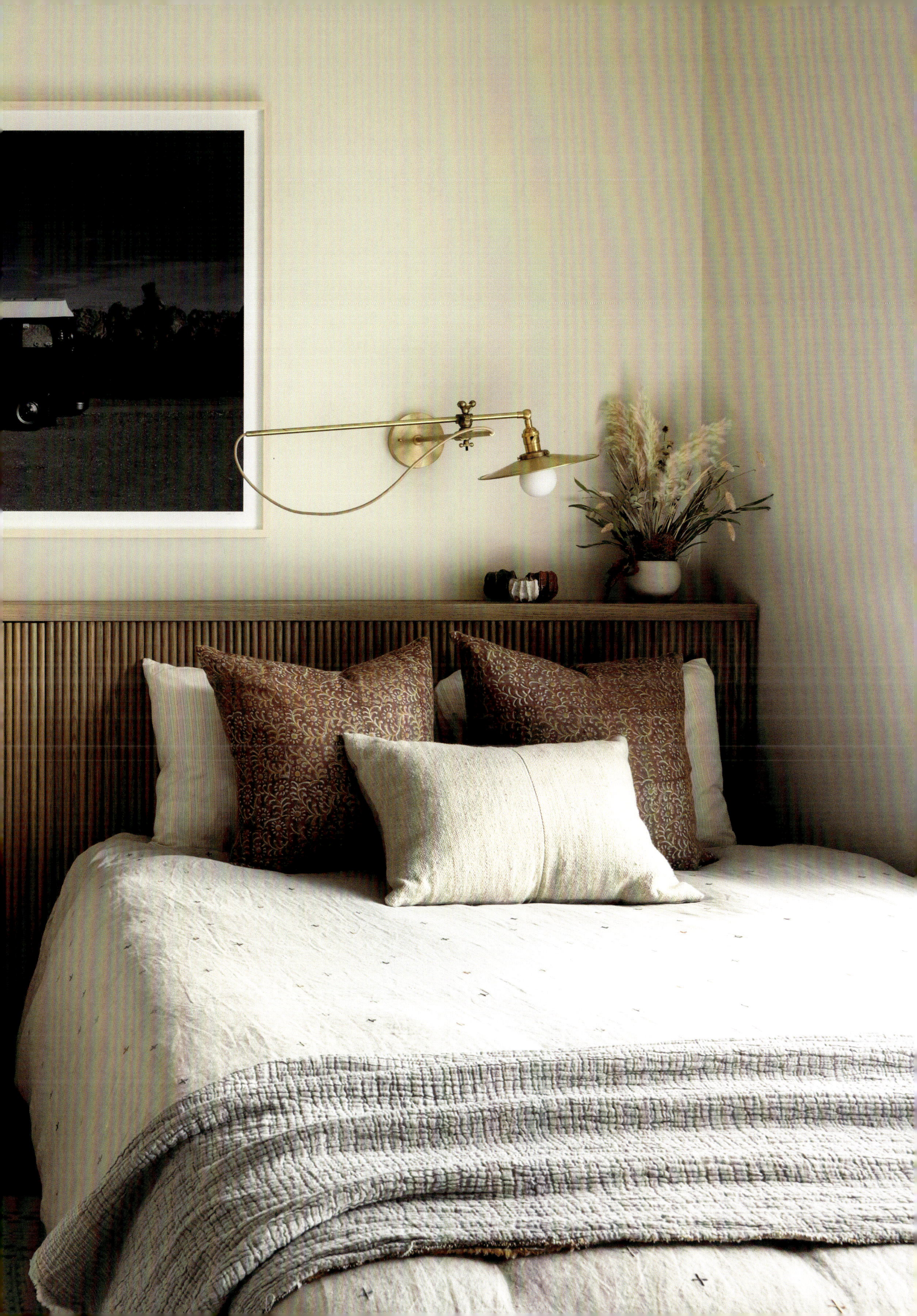

CREATIVE SANCTUARY

Elissa Scrafano / Scrafano Architects

In Chicago's historic Printer's Row neighborhood, Elissa Scrafano and Carol Barrett of Scrafano Architects renovated a 2,700-square-foot loft for their client as a testament to urban revival and personal transformation. What was once part of the fabled "Adventurers Club" now serves as a sophisticated residence for a couple who consider themselves adventurers in their own right. Their home is filled with unique collectibles and artifacts from their world travels.

Constructed in the 1890s as part of the printing industry, the building retains its industrial character with exposed brick, original flooring, and generous natural light. The architectural and interior design team holistically approached the space, creating what Scrafano described as a "woven mix of intimate tucked-away living spaces within the expansive open areas typical to a loft."

The designers took advantage of the wall-to-wall windows along both east and west edges, placing the expansive kitchen and main living spaces along one side and bedrooms along the other. Between these anchor points, they crafted smaller cozy nooks—an office, a library, and a small art studio—that "stitch the fabric of the two sides of the environment together," allowing natural light to flood the main spaces while filtered light trickles into the interior areas.

After raising their family in the nearby suburbs, the owners wanted to enjoy city life again. Their loft now provides space for creative pursuits and gracious entertaining. Scrafano explained that the designers created a sunroom atrium "filled with foliage, between a wall of exterior windows and a wall of glass," bringing the outdoors in.

Personal touches tailor the home to its owners, who bring complementary creative sensibilities to their space. Quirky details abound, including a small painting studio and a wall-to-wall bookcase that "playfully displays artwork and historical objects alongside books." The result is a beautiful, eclectic mix of old and new. In this three-bedroom, three-bathroom home with a sunroom, these empty nesters can pursue their creative interests while maintaining a welcoming space for family and friends in a historic Chicago neighborhood.

This thoughtfully designed corner bar integrates seamlessly with the kitchen millwork. Repurposed radiator grilles from Etsy add distinctive character to the custom shelving, while the creative seating solution features open suitcases transformed into charming, conversation-starting slipper chairs.

NEXT: The east-facing living room features custom walnut cabinetry and bookshelves complemented by unique collected treasures. A pull-down map conceals the TV—a nod to the owners' teacher parents—while the bottlecap "taxidermy" head commemorates their global adventures.

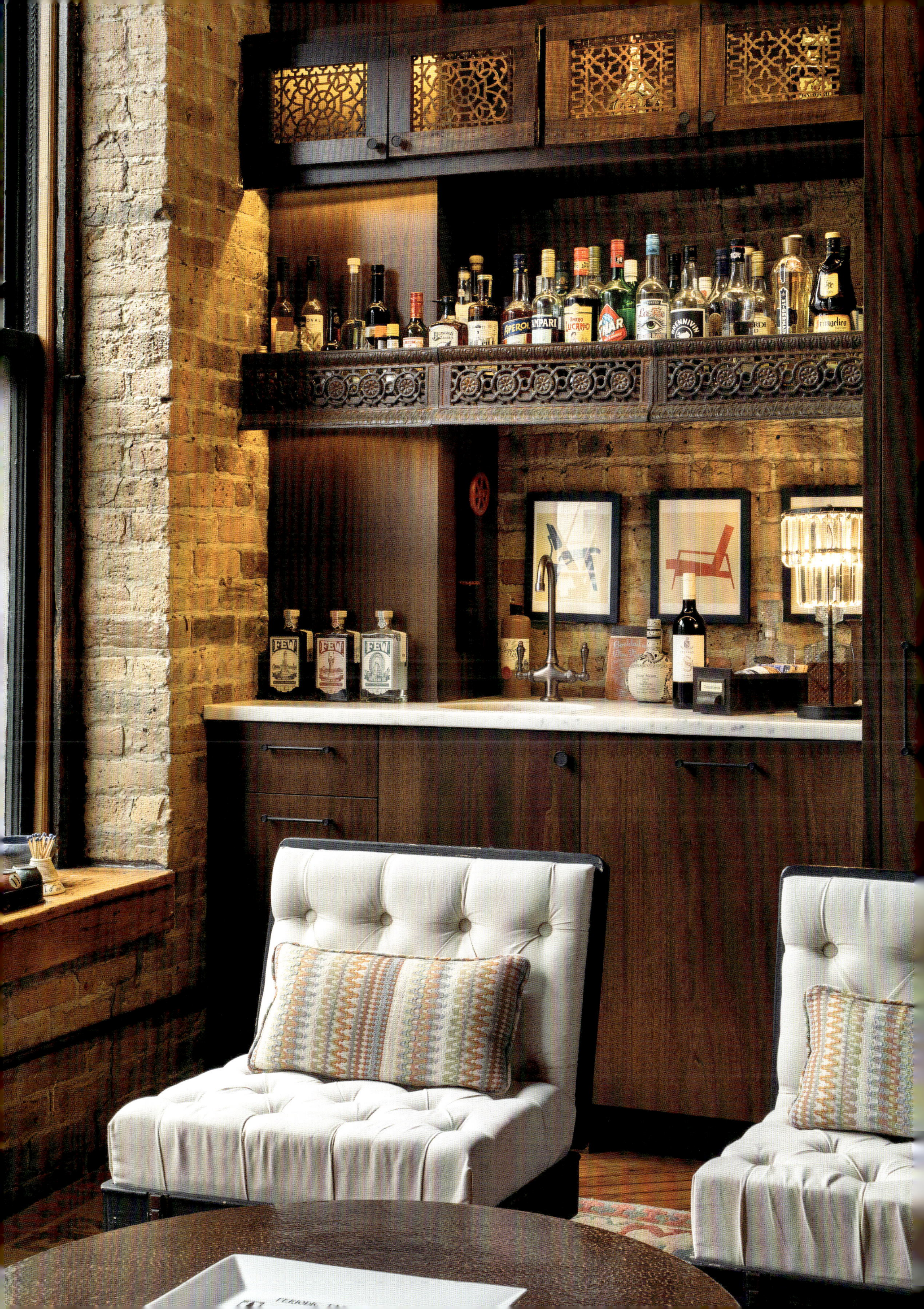
APEROL
Frangelico
FEW
FEW
FEW

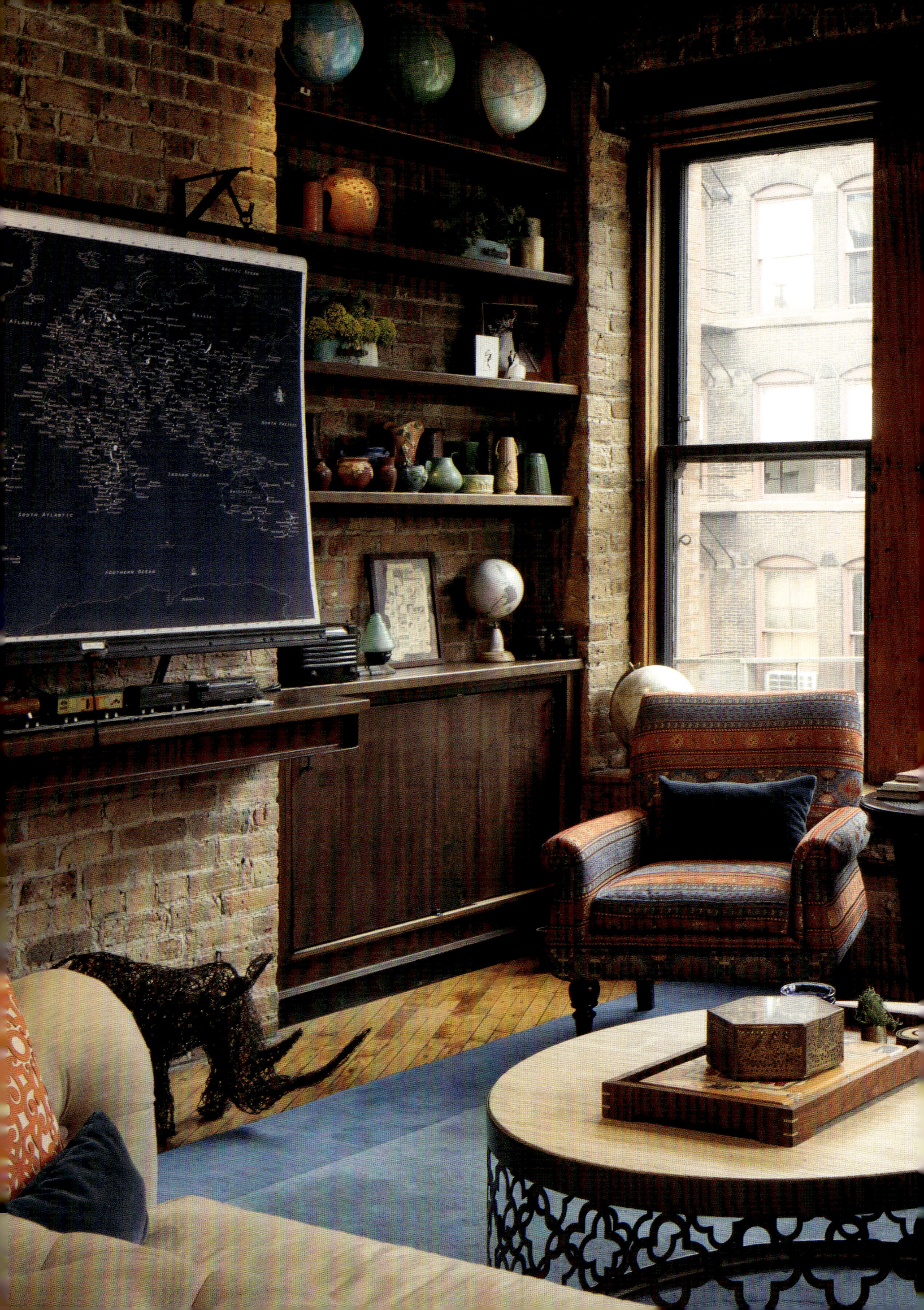
ARCTIC OCEAN
Russia
ATLANTIC
NORTH PACIFIC
INDIAN OCEAN
Australia
SOUTH ATLANTIC
SOUTHERN OCEAN
Antarctica

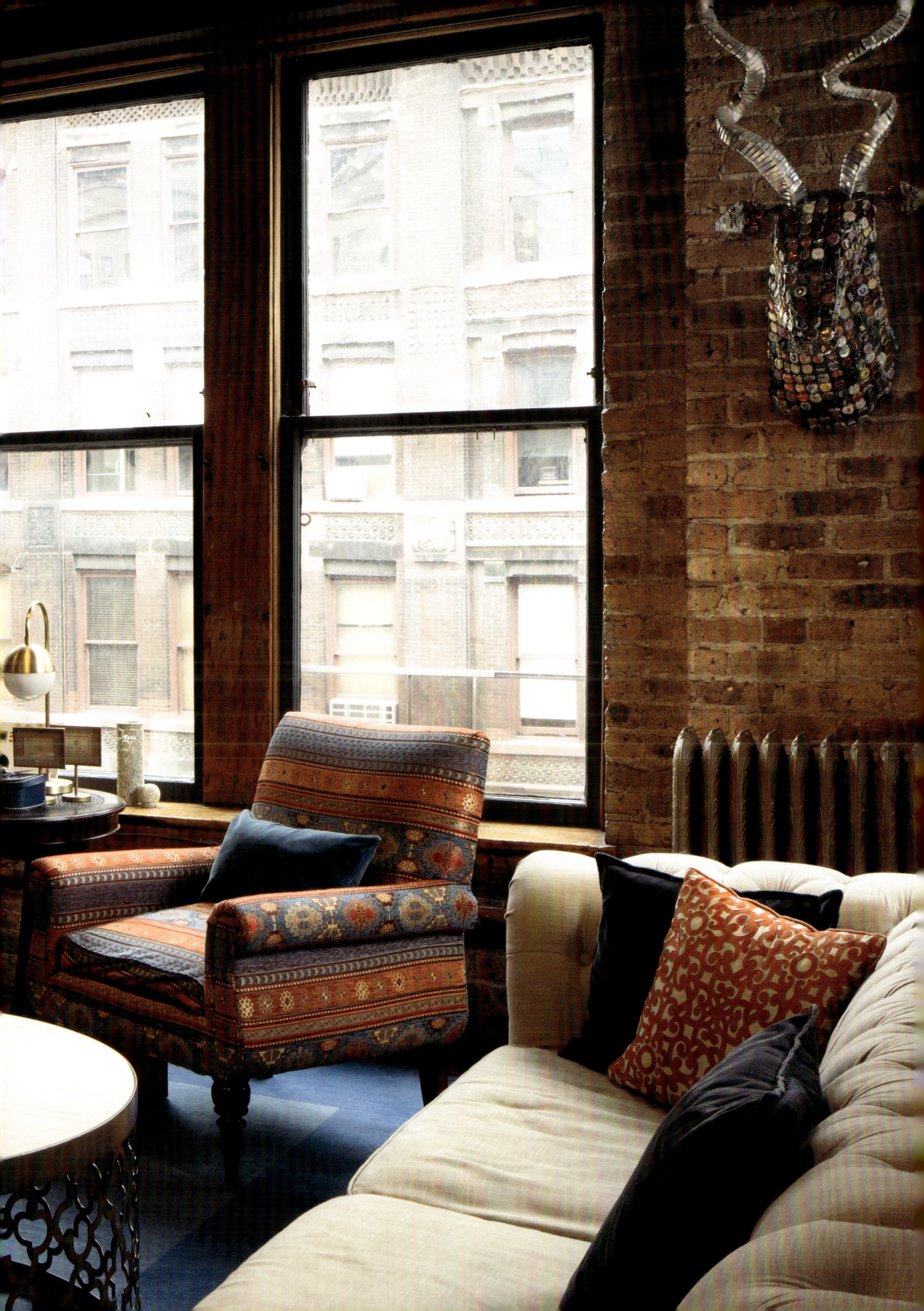

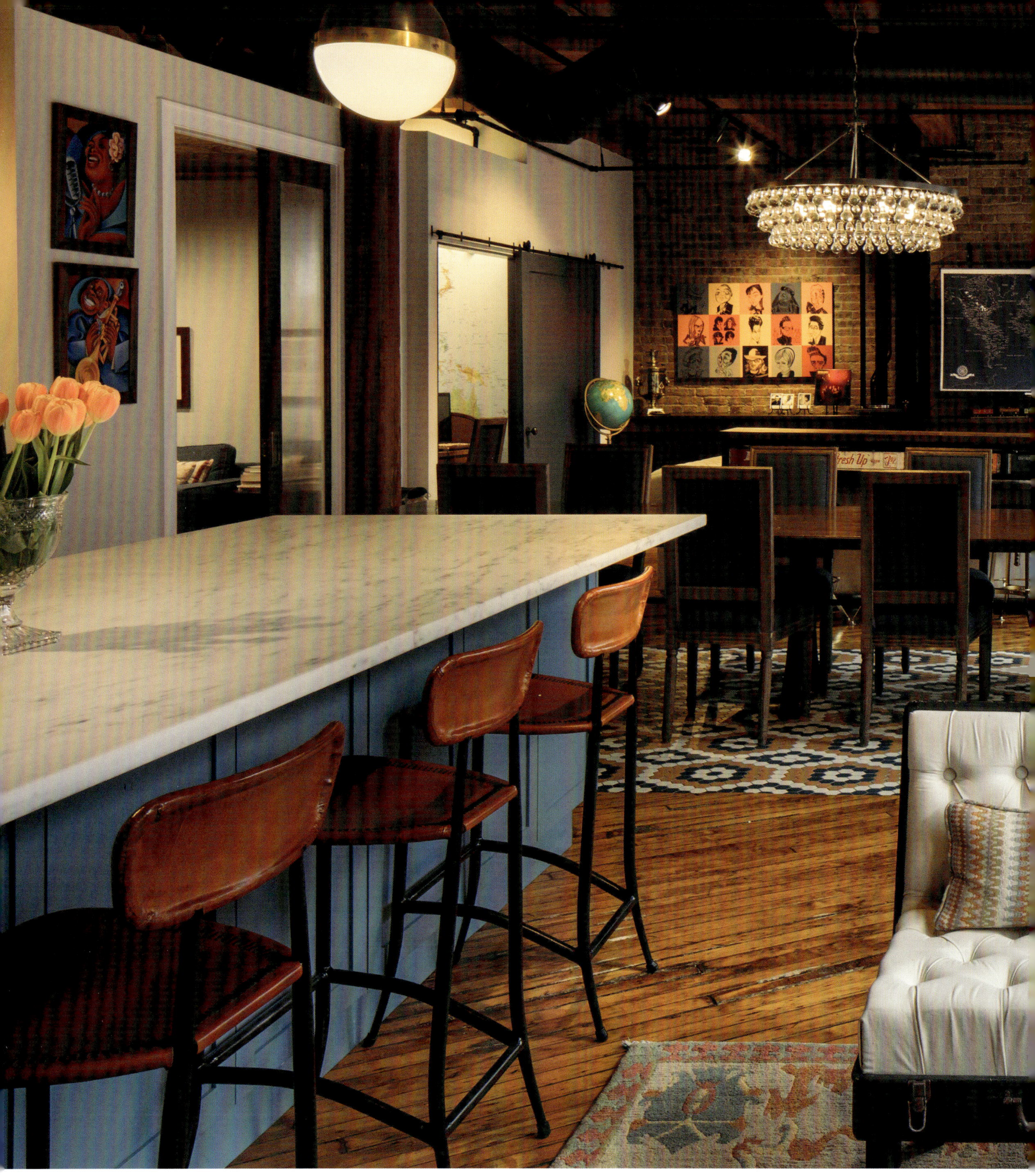

ABOVE: The thoughtfully restored loft maintains its original character through preserved brick walls, ceiling beams, and wood floors. Modern interventions include a custom inset tile "rug" beneath the dining table, an exposed electrical conduit, black-painted HVAC ductwork, and refurbished vintage radiators.

NEXT: An intentional interplay of complementary blue and orange creates visual energy throughout this working kitchen designed for serious entertainers. This chef-worthy space transitions to refined walnut in the bar areas, reflecting one owner's painterly sensibility.

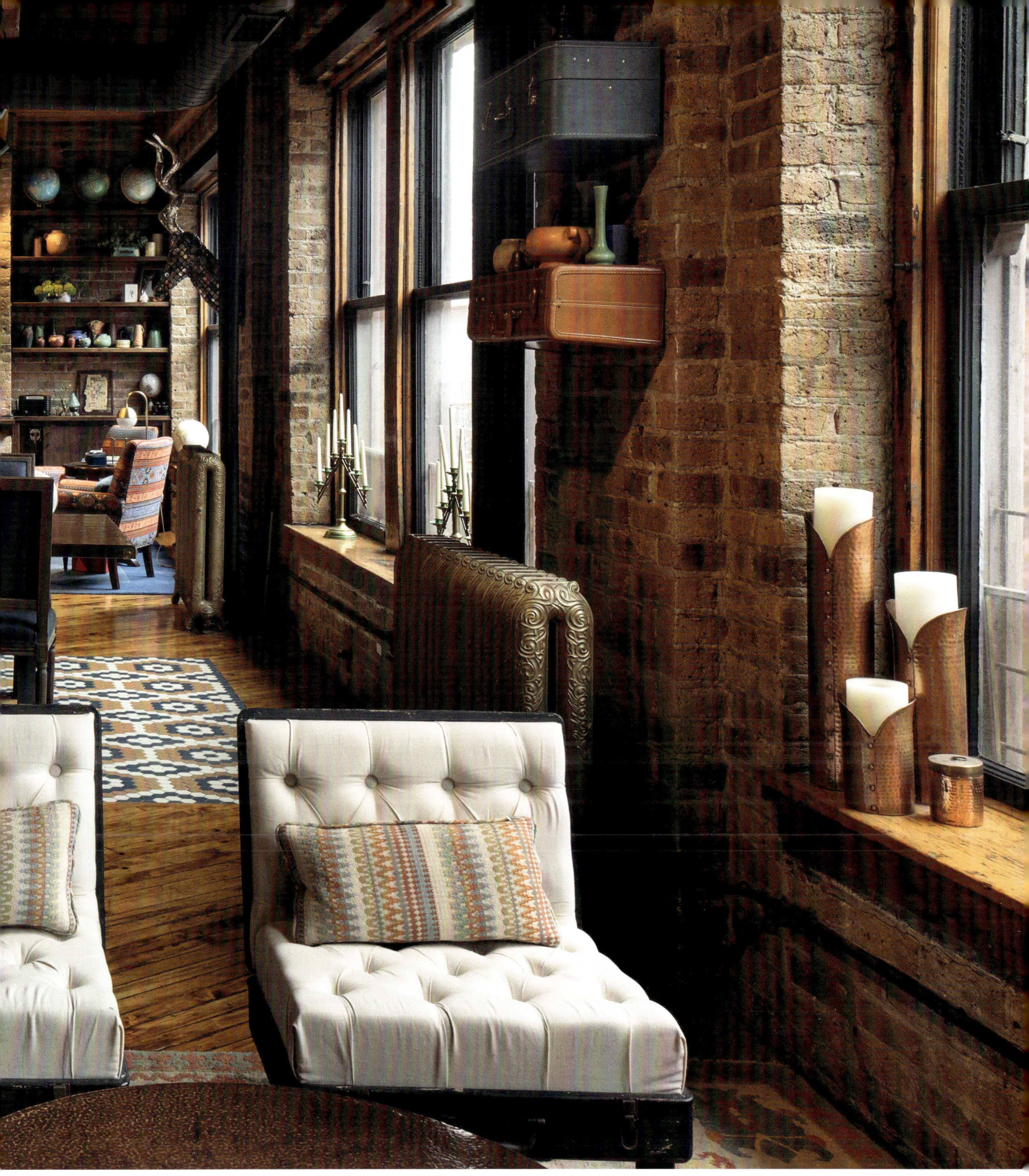

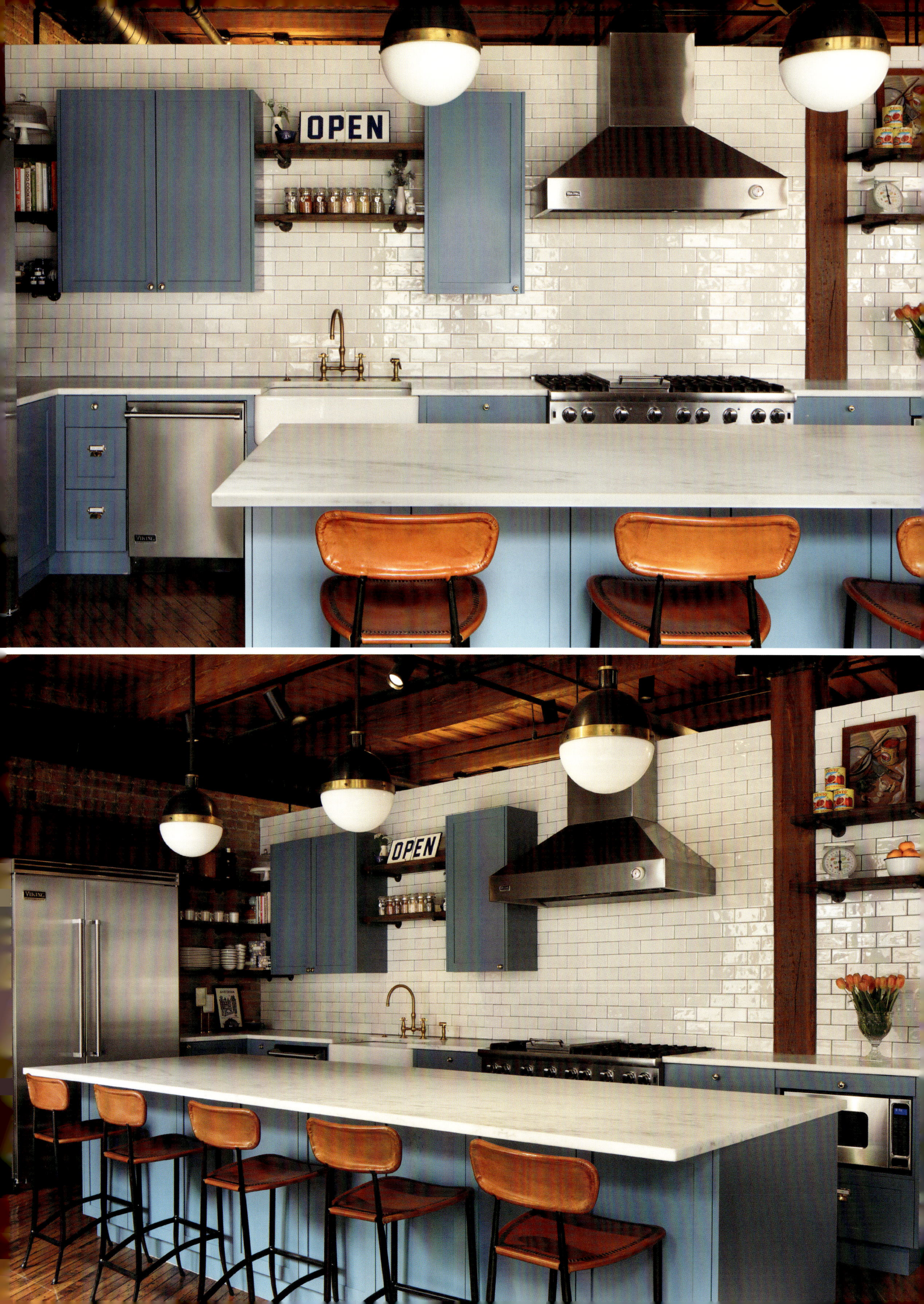
OPEN

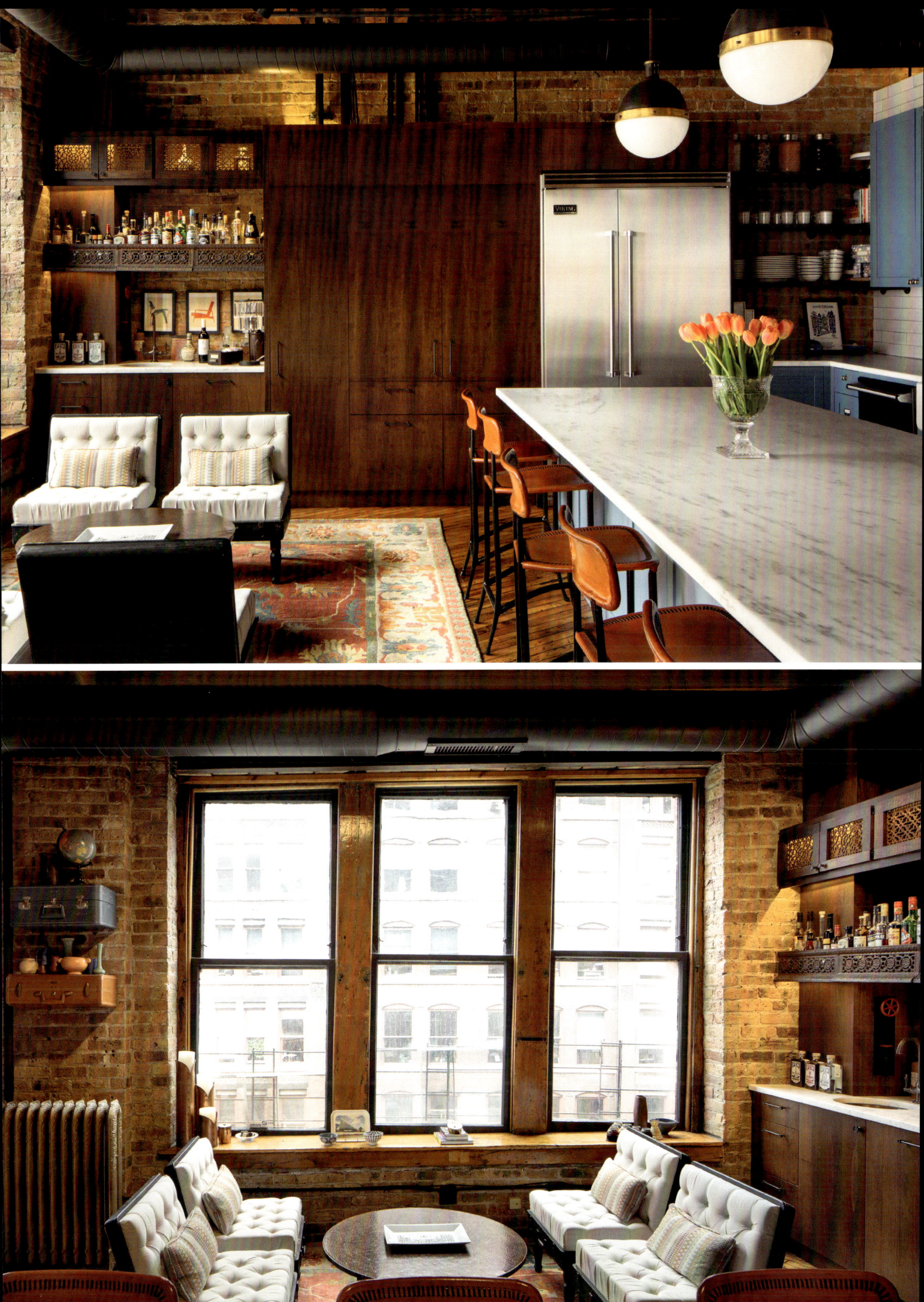
VIKING

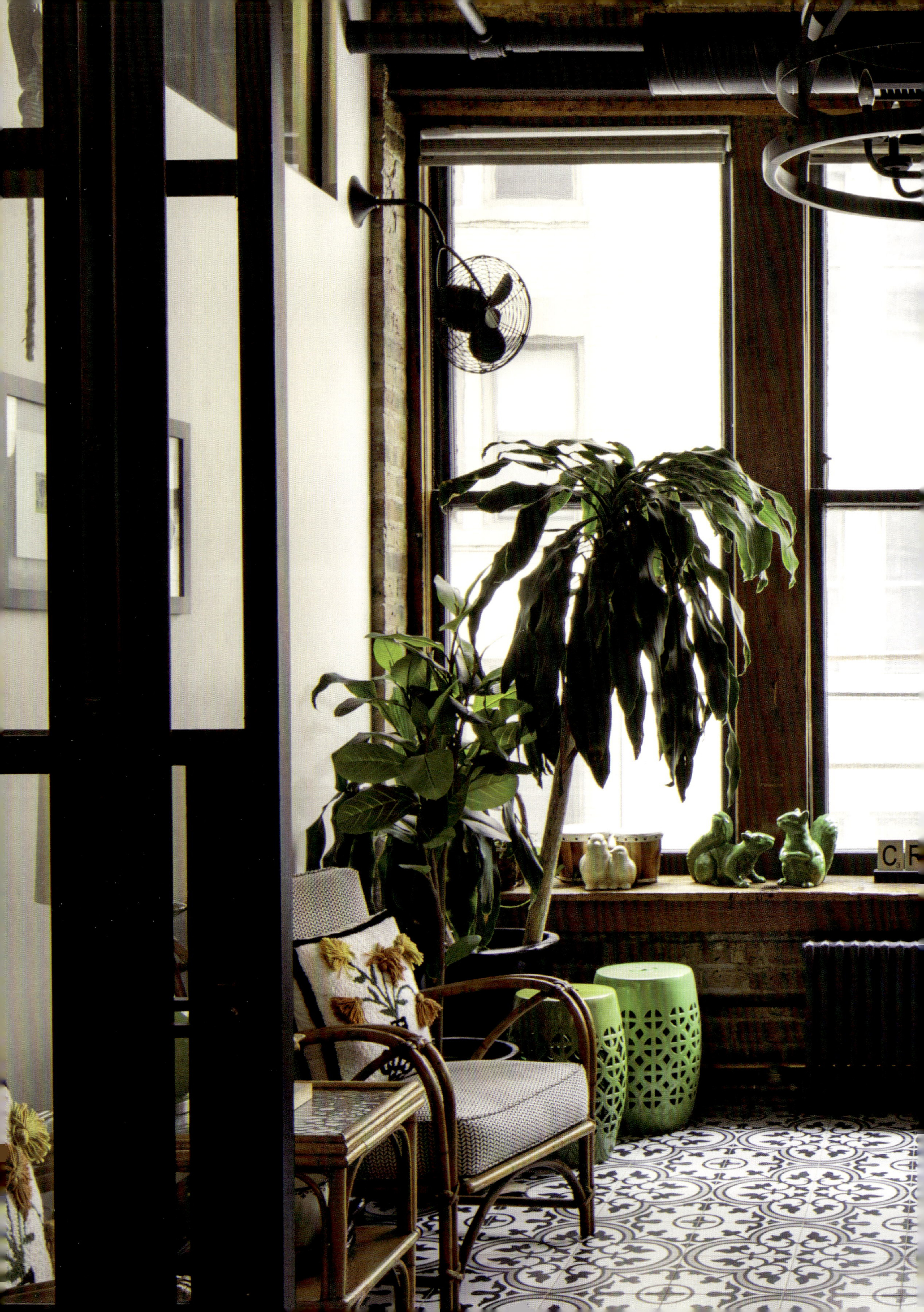

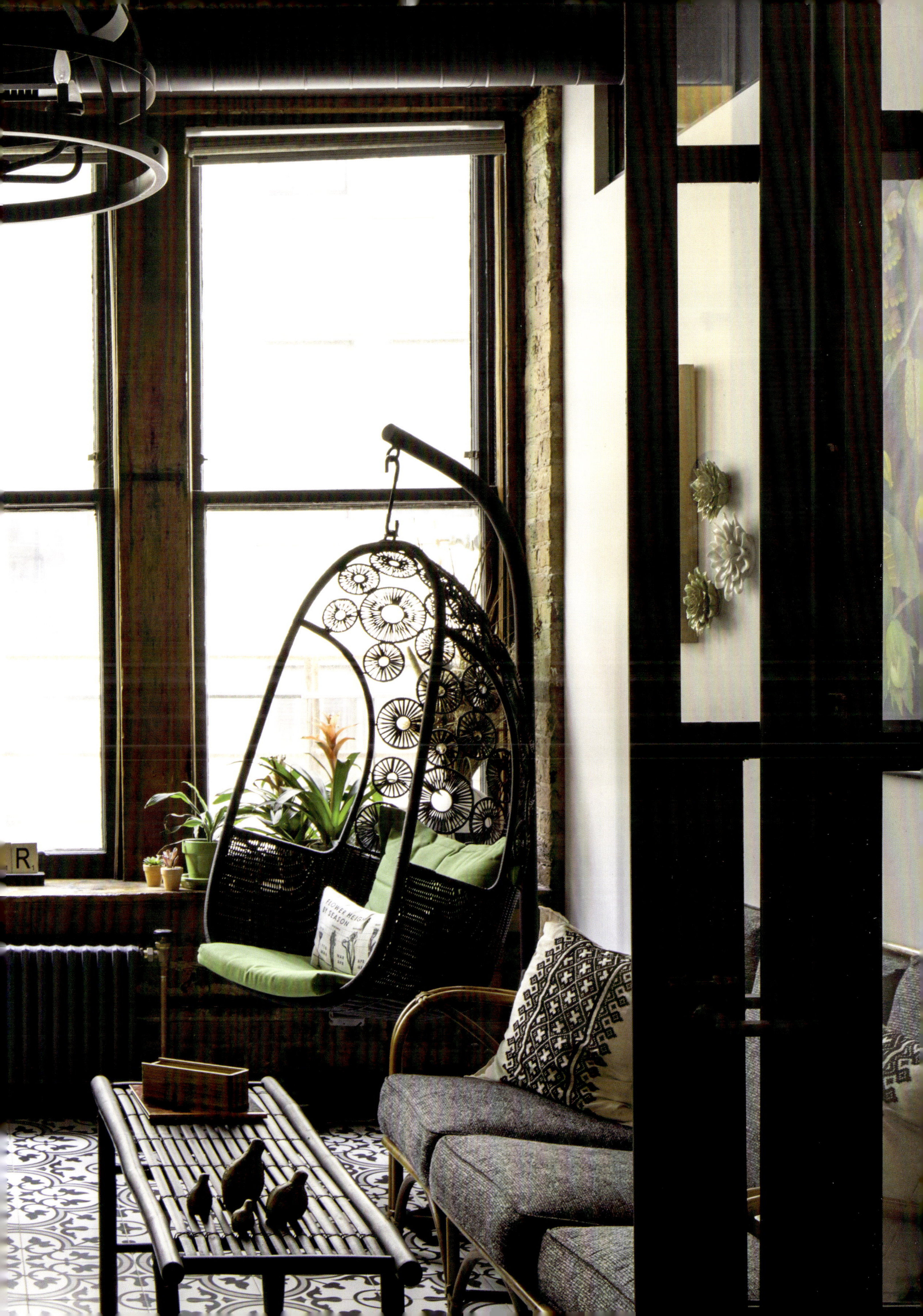
R

PREVIOUS: An inventive sunroom transforms a central space into a year-round Moroccan-inspired courtyard retreat. Added glass doors, tile flooring, and outdoor furnishings surrounded by lush plants create a cherished "indoor yard" where residents gather for reading and conversation throughout all seasons.

OPPOSITE: The primary bedroom introduces a distinctive black-and-white palette that sets it apart from other spaces in the home. This deliberate design choice maintains the residence's strong graphic elements while creating a more serene atmosphere through strategic touches of yellow and living greenery.

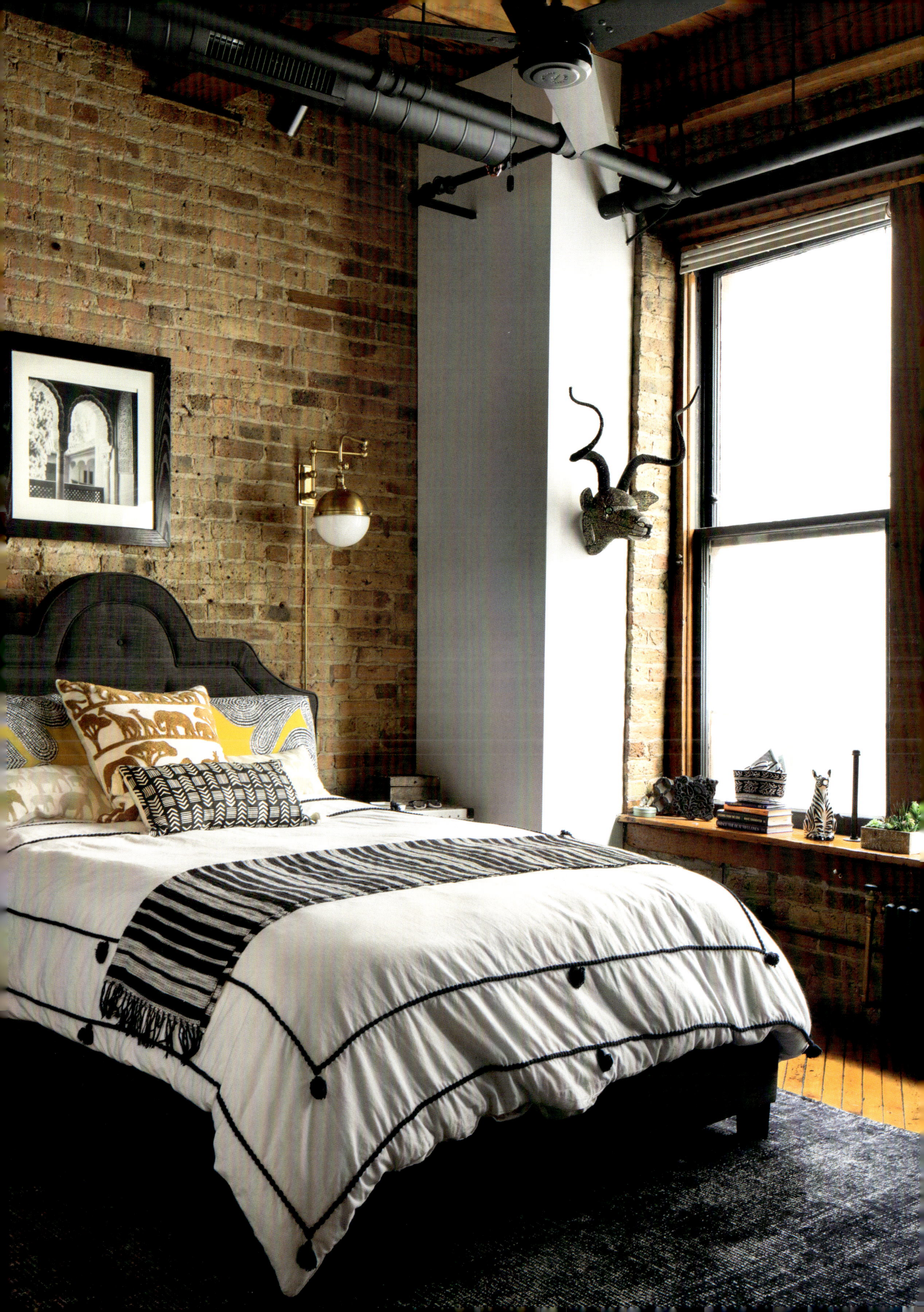

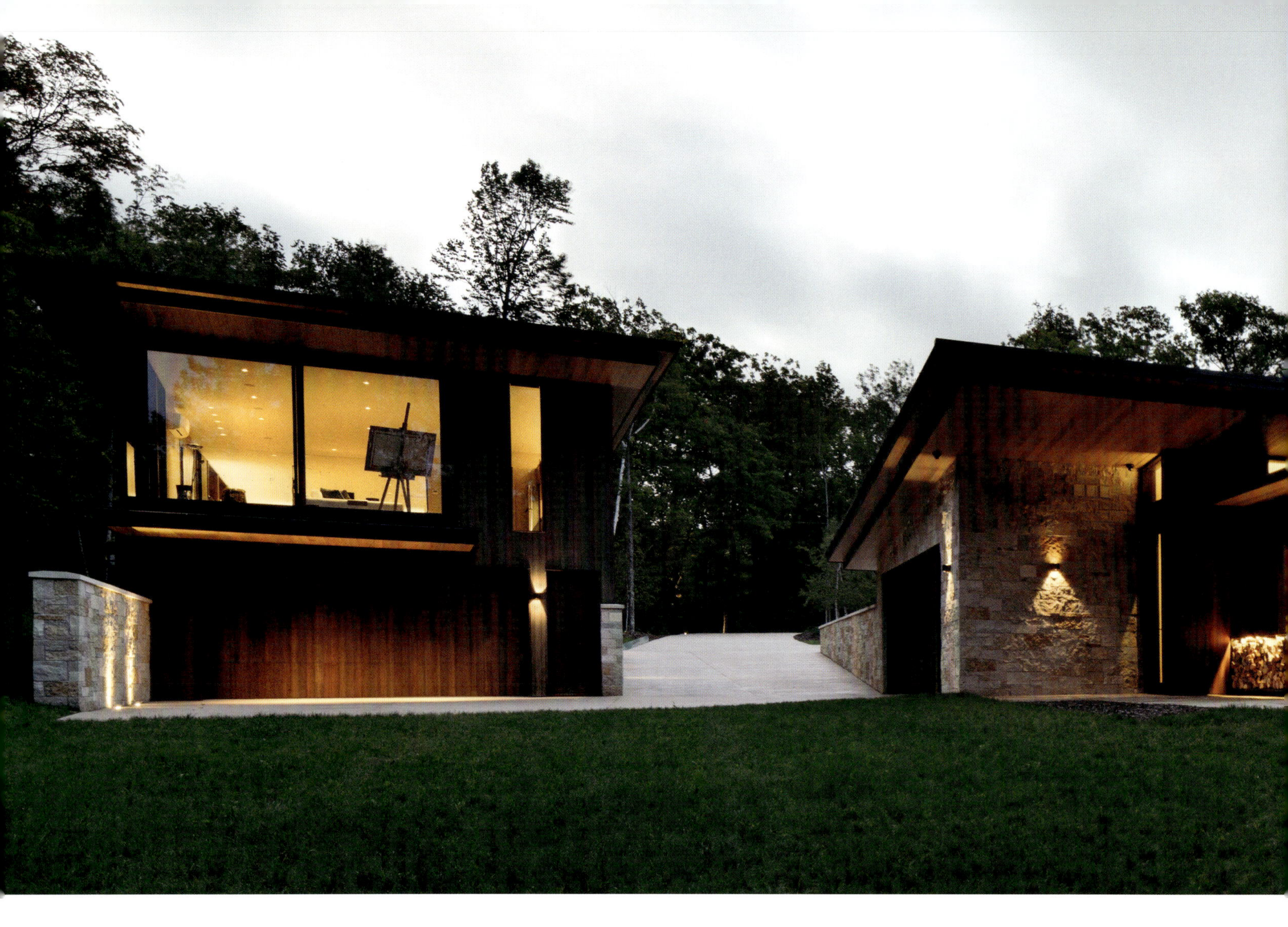

STONE HEARTH

John Vetter / Vetter Architects

Door County, Wisconsin, is colloquially referred to as the "Nantucket of the Midwest." And this remarkable waterside residence there embodies what architect John Vetter calls "a sense of discovery and journey" regarding its unique topography and the owners' multifaceted aesthetic preferences.

Atop a limestone outcropping, the property looks toward Green Bay, where spectacular sunsets unfold nightly. Vetter's holistic design approach encompassed architecture, interiors, furnishings, and the landscape as a "total work of art" that feels intrinsically connected to its surroundings.

Approaching from the driveway, visitors encounter the home's most humble facade—a deliberate contrast to conventional residential design. The structure is organized as four distinct "pavilions": the main living area, the primary bedroom wing, a guest wing, and a separate outbuilding housing an art studio and music space. This arrangement provides the retired owners with intimate spaces for when it's just the two of them and with expanded living areas for guests.

Local limestone is prominently featured throughout. In a remarkable display of resourcefulness, massive slabs unearthed during excavation were repurposed both in the landscape and as dramatic architectural elements—most notably as the monumental hearthstone in the main living area.

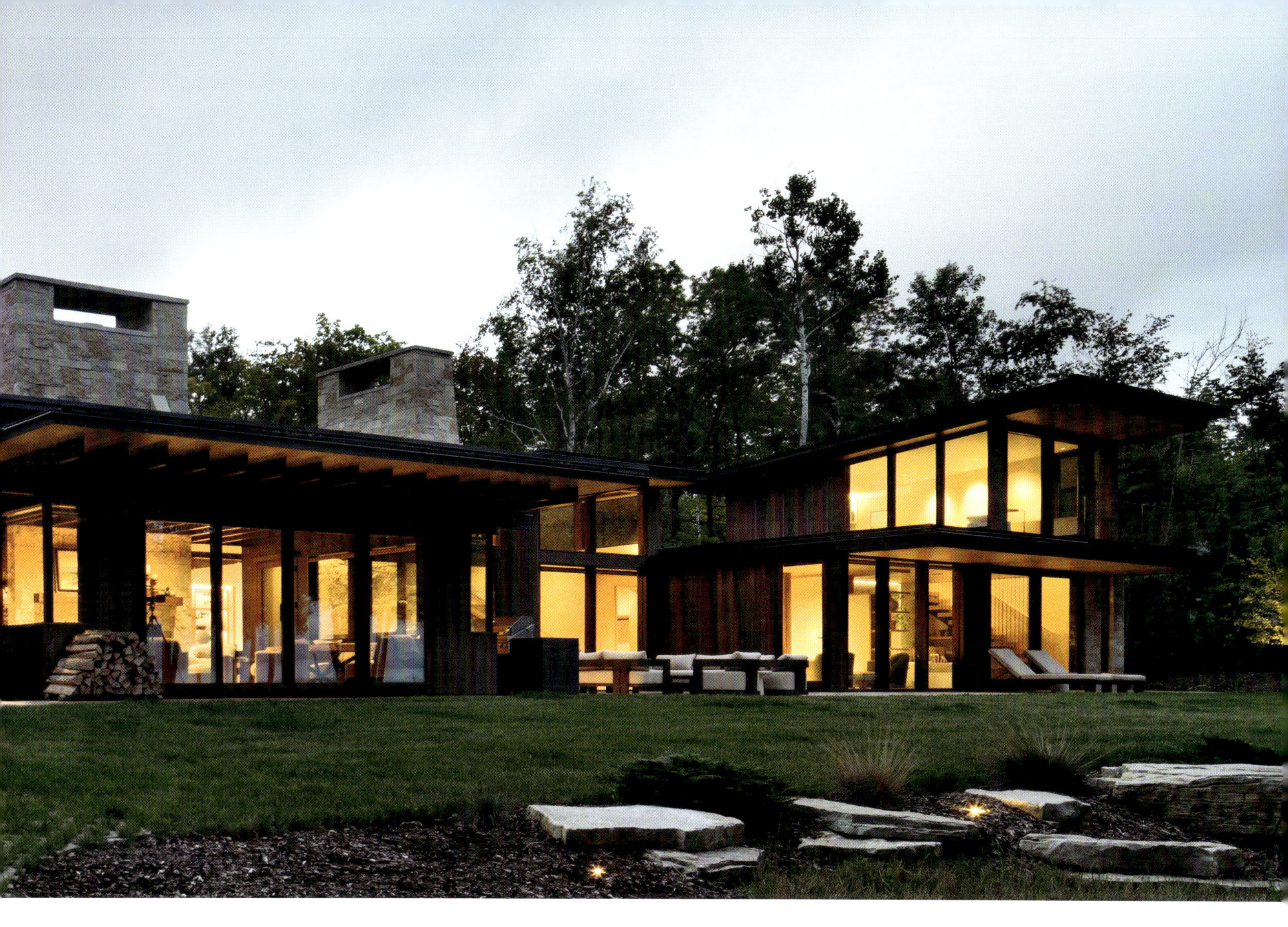

Floor-to-ceiling lift-slide doors dissolve boundaries between inside and out, particularly in the primary bedroom suite, which includes a spa-like bathroom and a private writing studio for one of the owners. This connection to nature is a recurring theme, with carefully framed views and layered outdoor spaces creating a progression from the main house down to the waterfront.

The design balances the owners' differing aesthetic preferences—traditional and contemporary elements mingle seamlessly through Vetter's sleight of hand. The result is a sculptural, somewhat organic form that draws inspiration from architectural masters while establishing its distinctive presence in Door County's dramatic landscape.

Low-slung on the horizon, the home's water-facing facade showcases local limestone and expansive glass. Its humble expression belies the four-pavilion structure, harmonizing with the recently landscaped terrain as it cascades down Door County's rocky peninsula to Green Bay's edge.

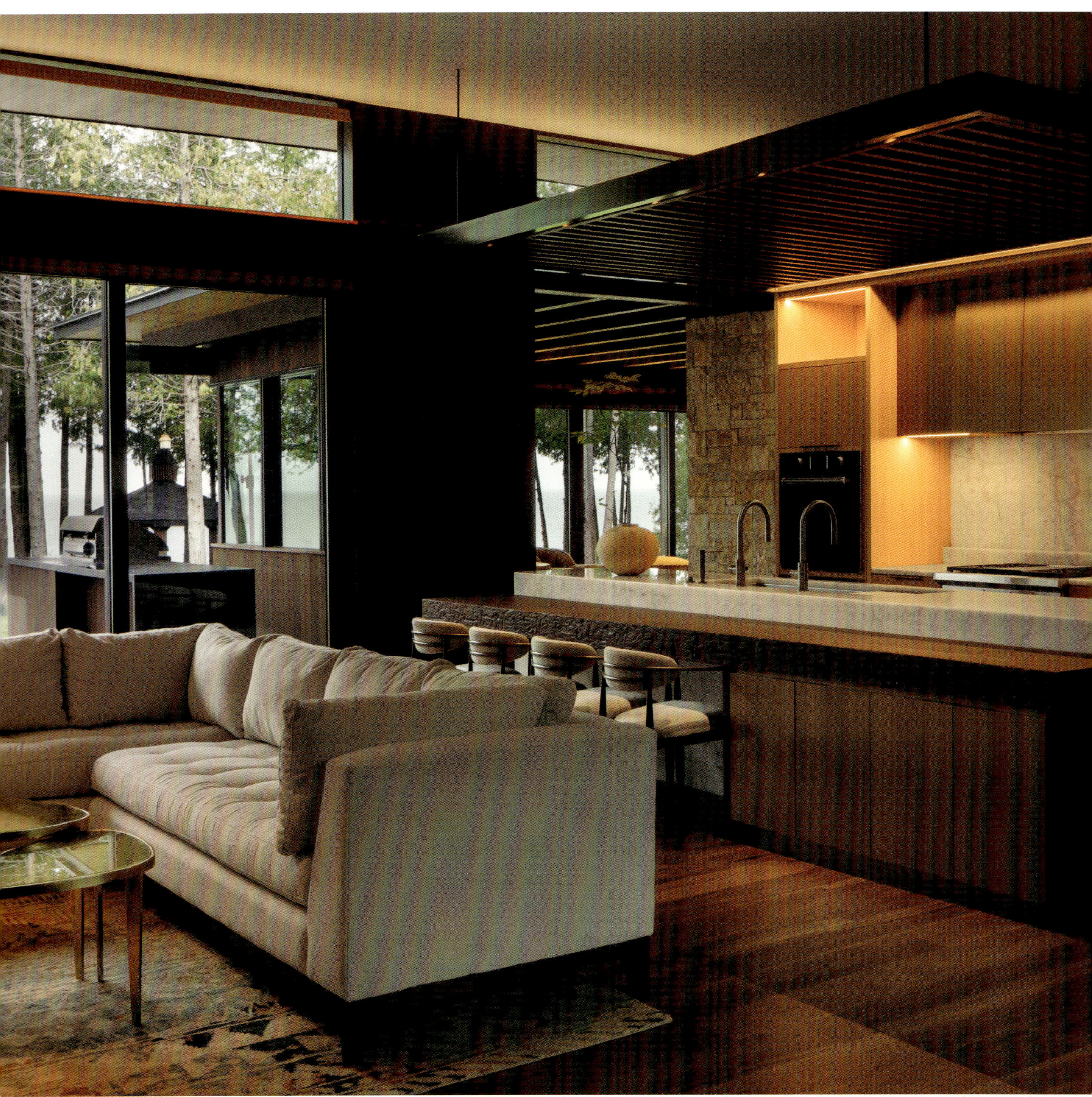

Warm hickory floors flow from the gourmet kitchen with rift-sawn white oak cabinetry and striking iceberg quartzite countertops to the inviting breakfast area, which can be seen on the right. The mahogany-topped island with metal-faced cabinets echoes the distinctive hood, creating seamless sophistication between spaces.

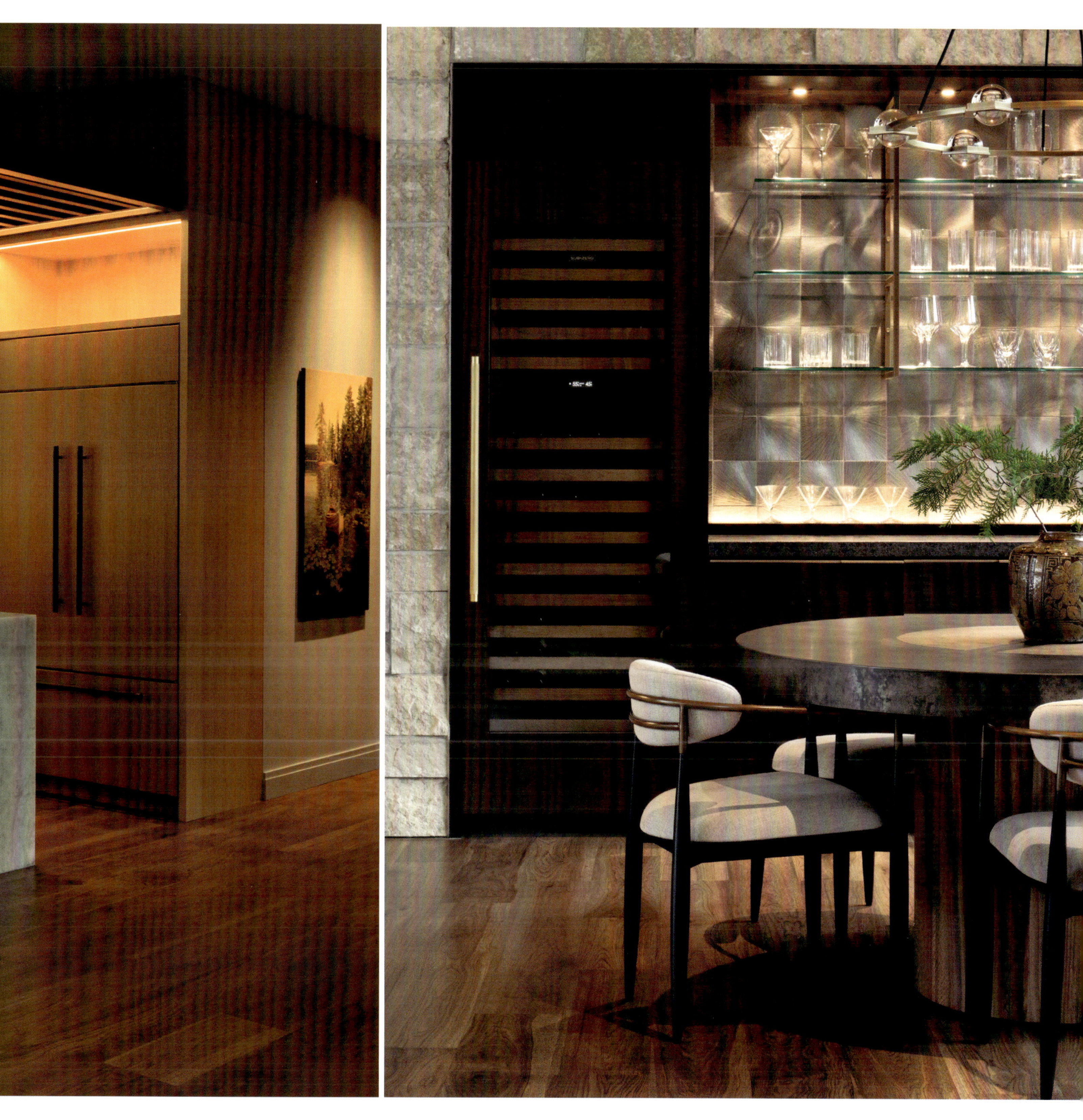

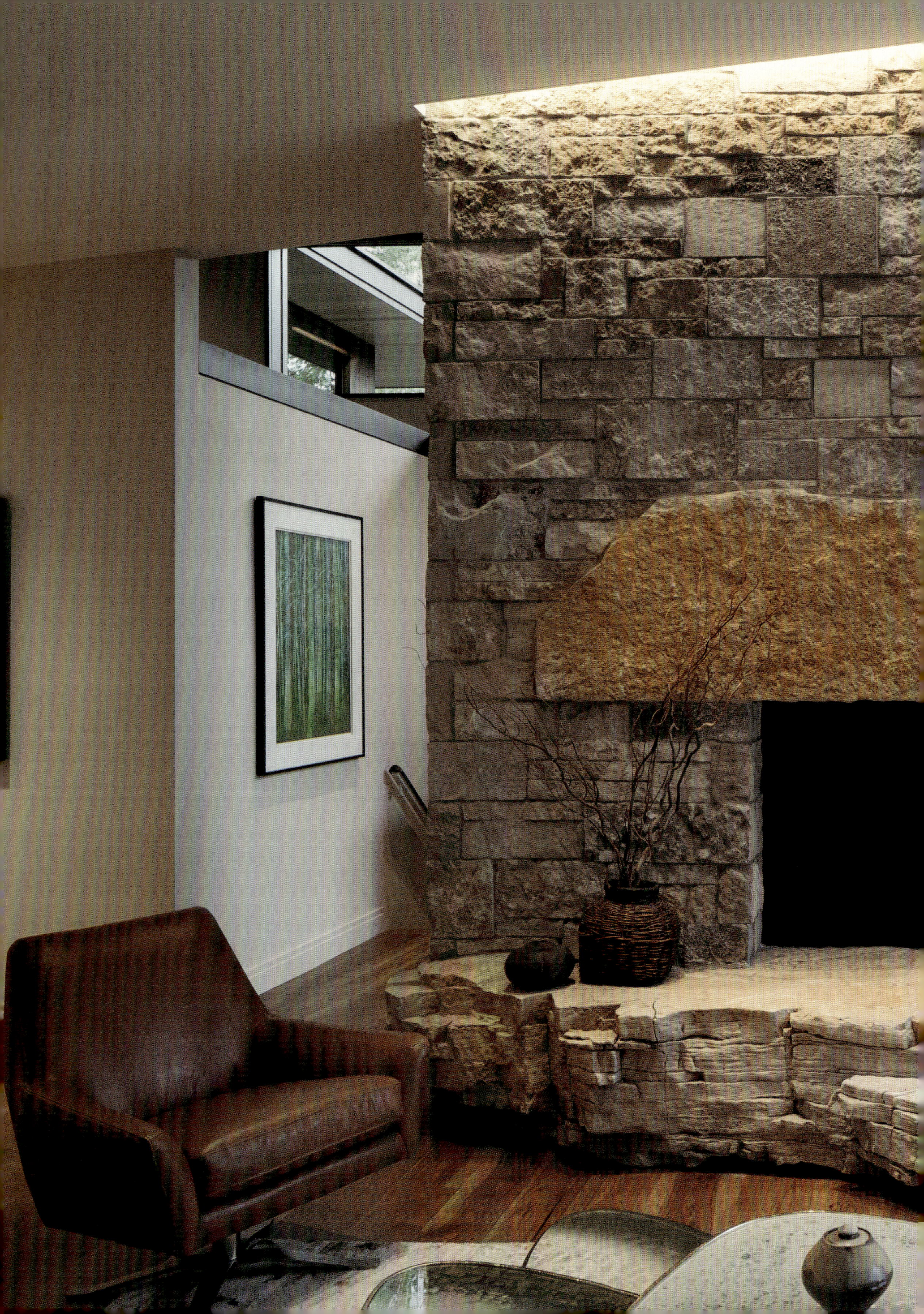

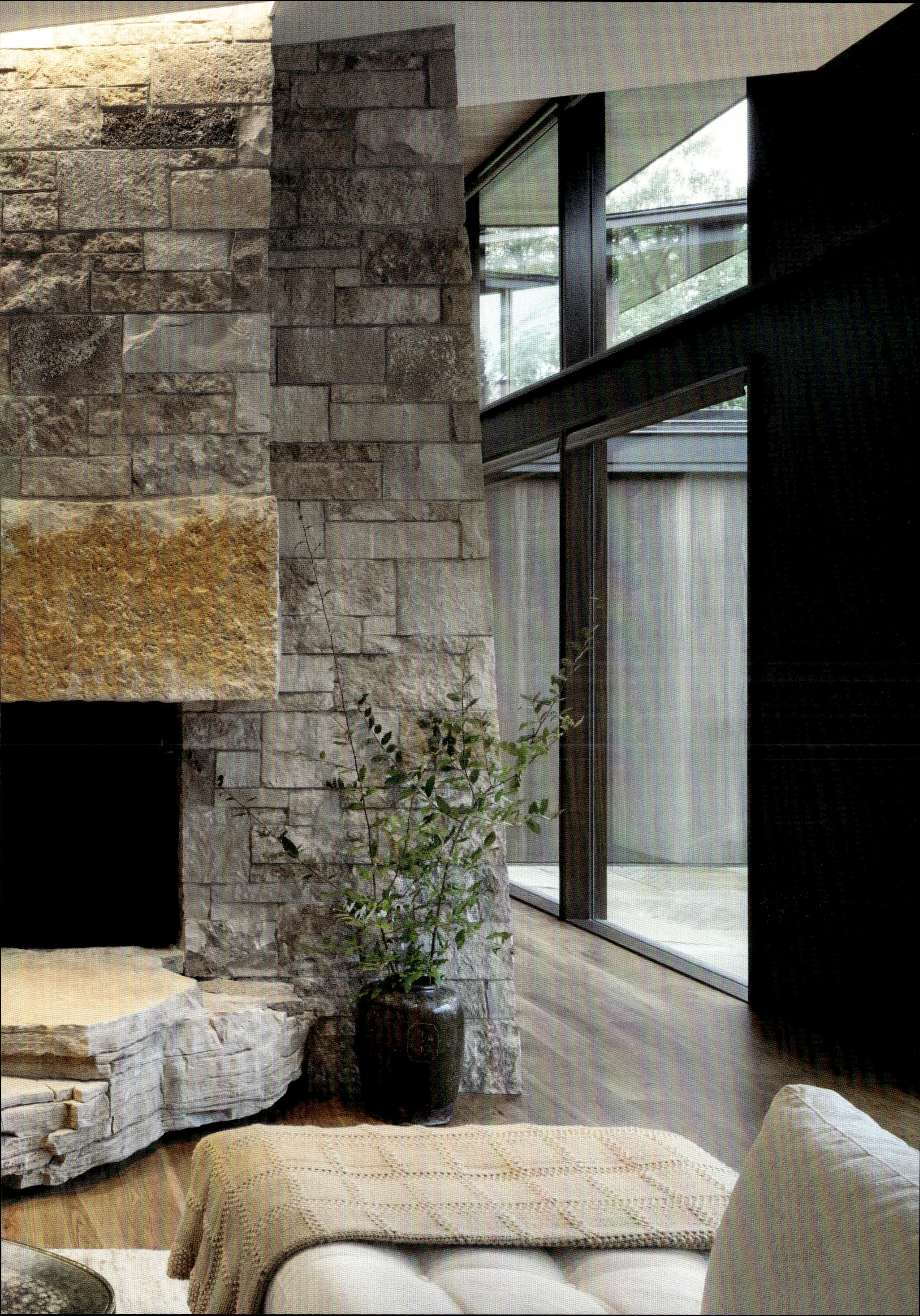

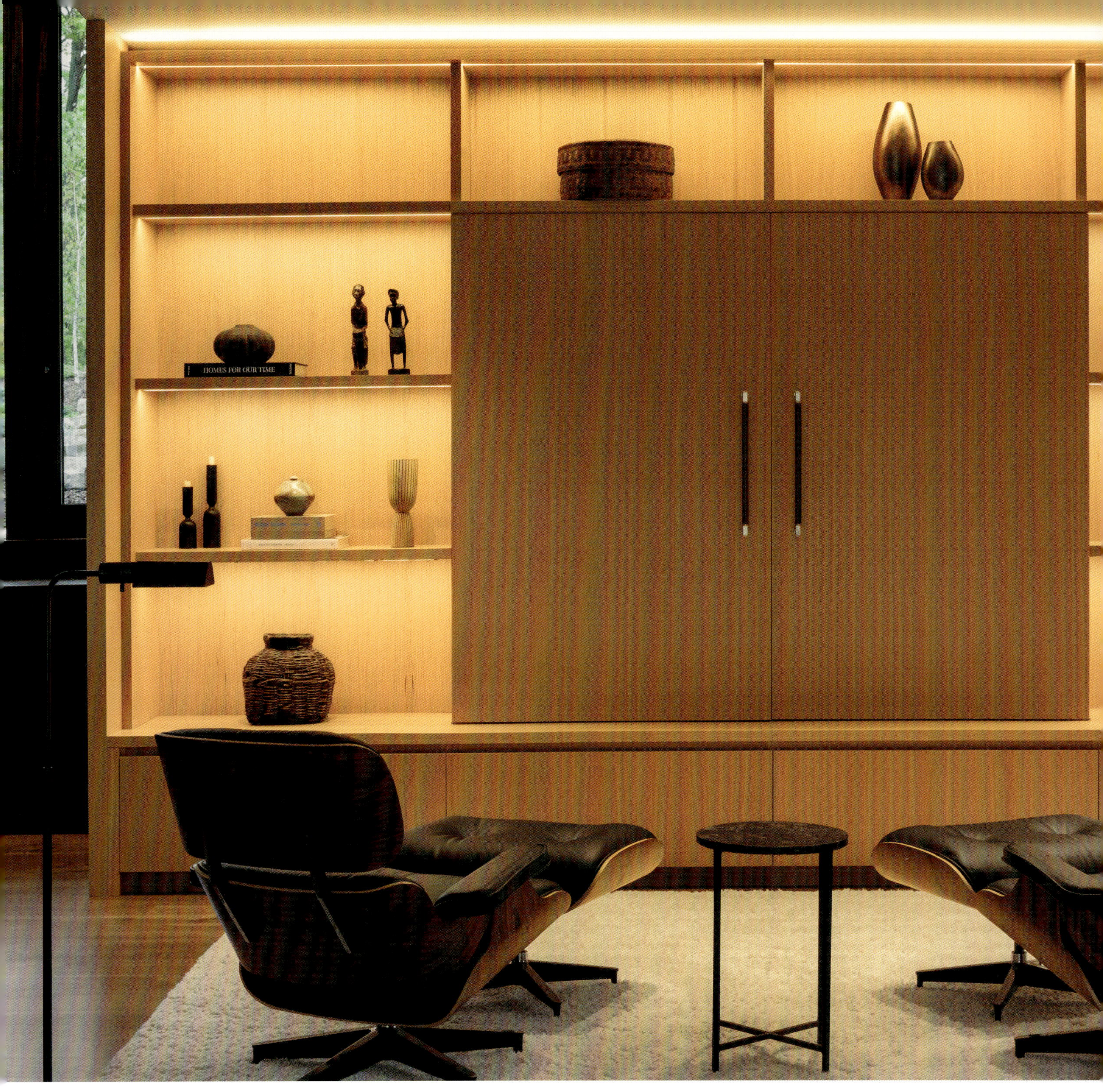

PREVIOUS: A massive limestone slab excavated from the property during the construction stage is featured in this monumental stone hearth. This dramatic architectural centerpiece exemplifies the home's intimate connection to Door County's rocky peninsula landscape.

ABOVE: *Left:* A polished media alcove invites relaxation with iconic Eames lounge chairs and concealed entertainment behind sliding doors. *Right:* The powder room showcases raw authenticity through its live-edge walnut countertop, carved stone sink, unlacquered brass fixtures, and striking metal tile accent wall.

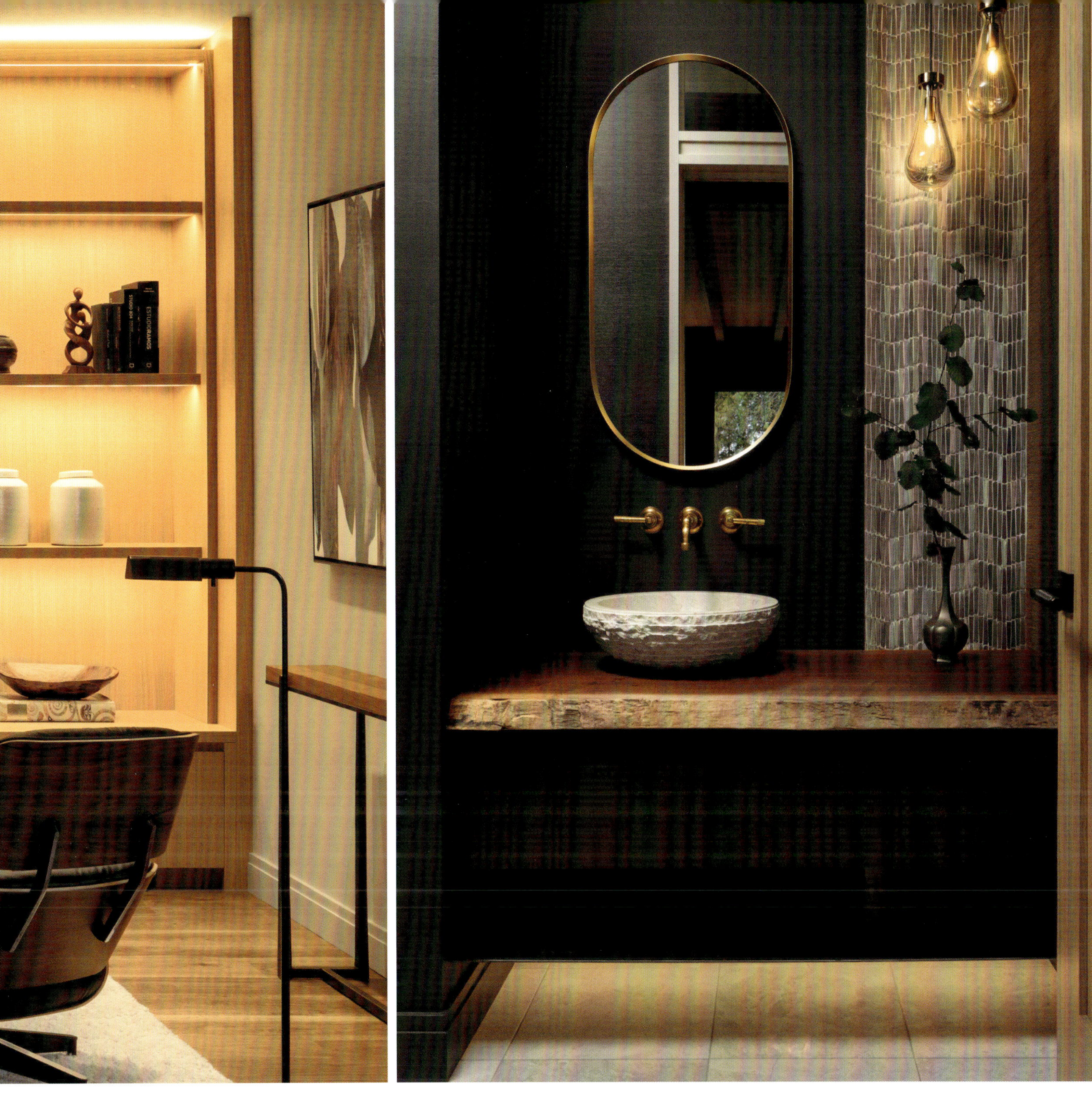

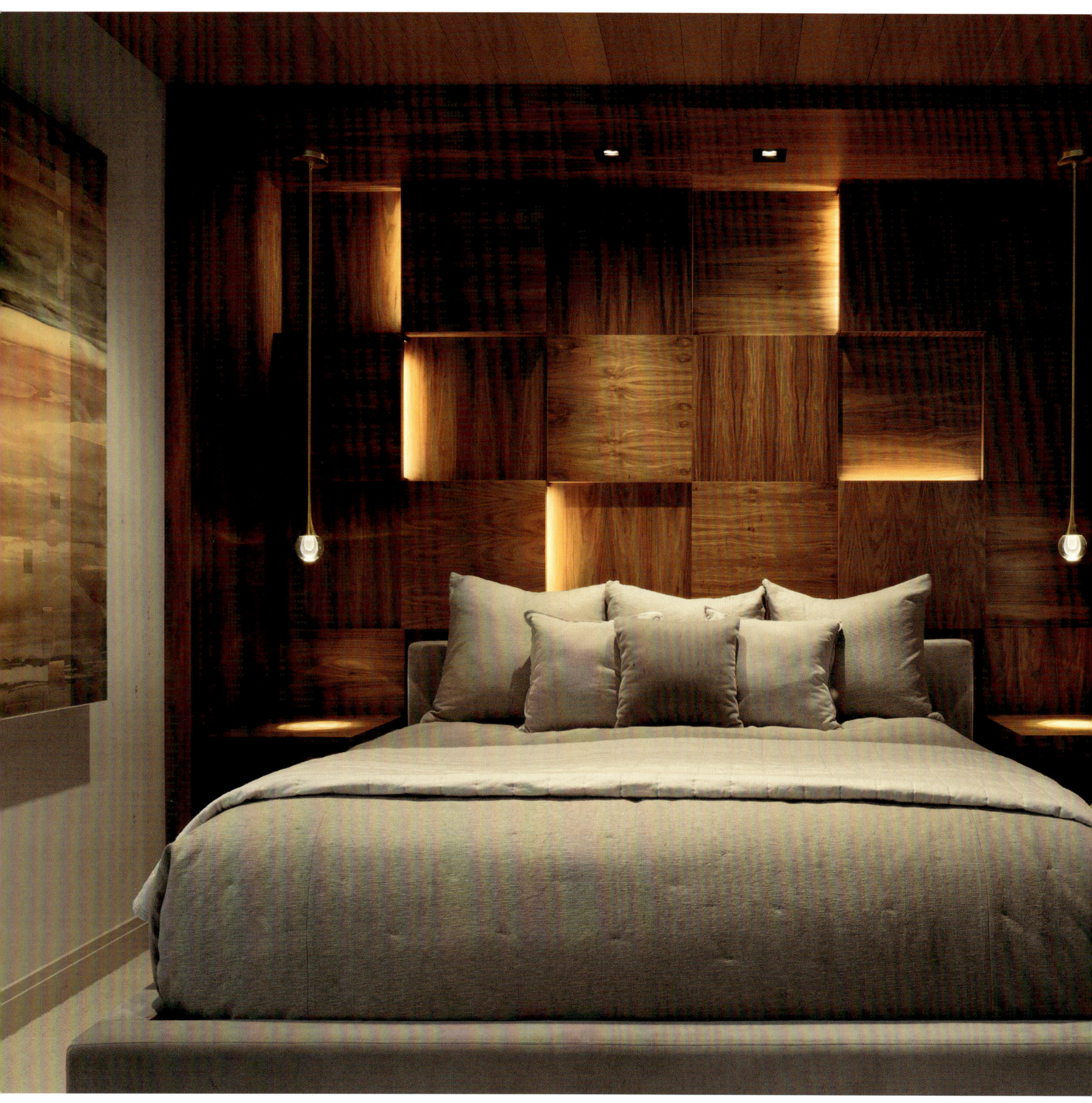

Left: Serene and sculptural, the primary bedroom's striking integrated headboard wall draws inspiration from Door County's limestone strata. Thoughtfully placed lighting accentuates the varying wood planes, creating a contemplative sanctuary. *Right:* The stairs go to the owner's private writing and meditation studio above.

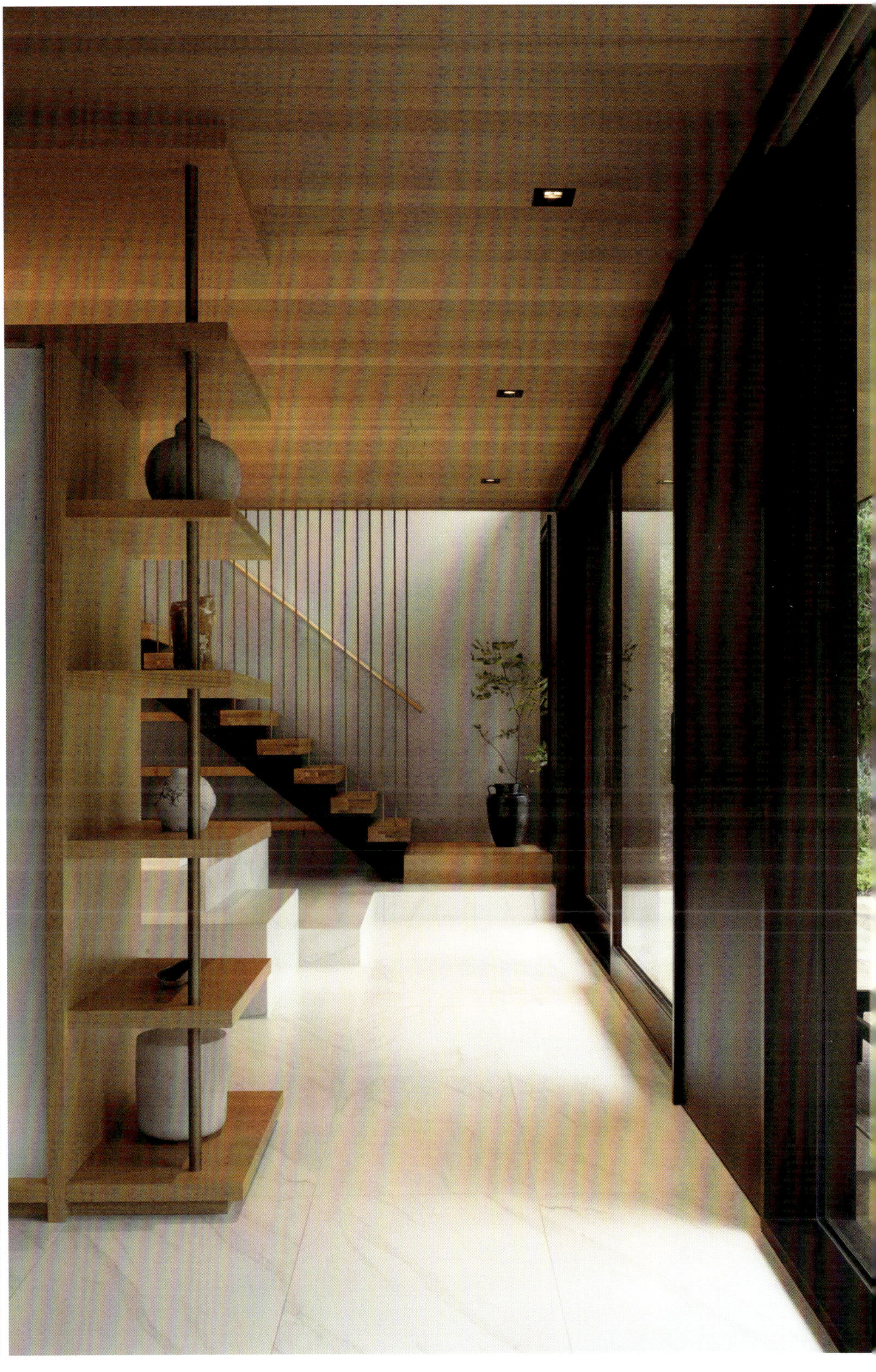

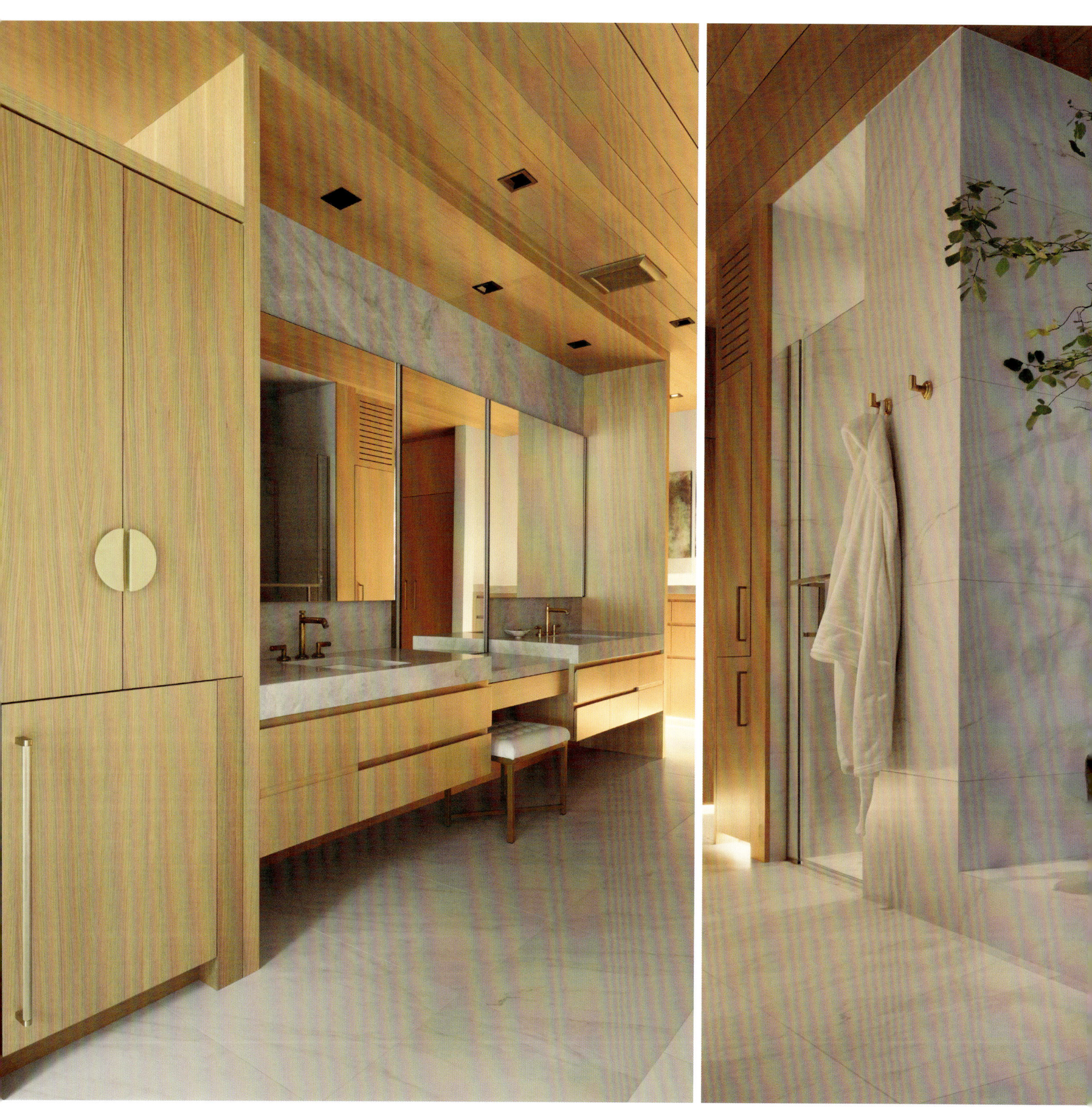

Left: Bespoke cabinetry and an integrated bench seat define the dressing area. *Right:* Elevated on a natural pedestal, the sculptural bathtub emerges organically from the same homogeneous material as the surrounding floors and walls—a deliberate architectural homage to the stone outcroppings visible through the panoramic windows.

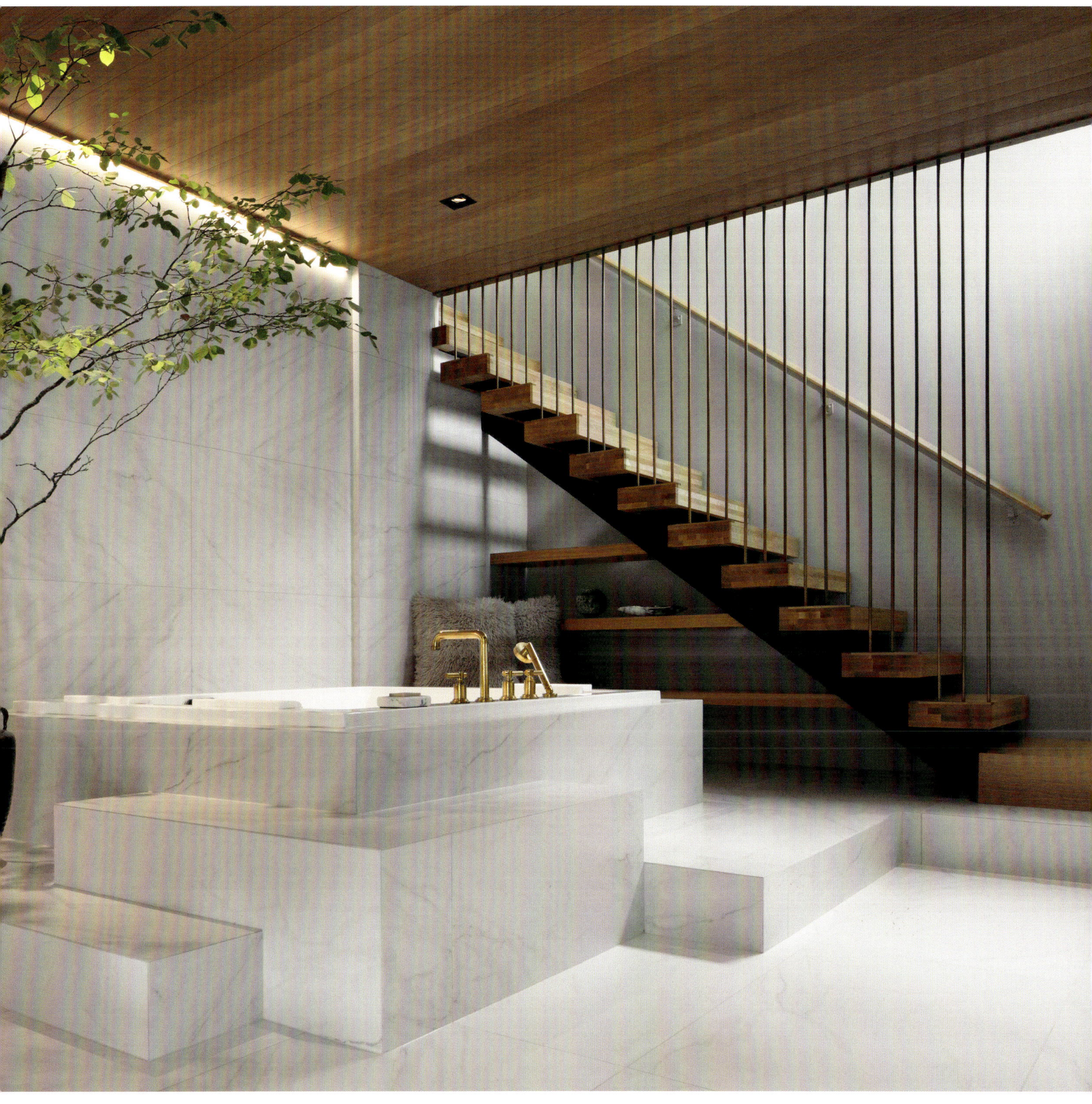

HOMEWARD BOUND

Anna Franklin / Stone House Collective

Nestled on the shores of Big Silver Lake in Wautoma, Wisconsin, this lakeside retreat represents more than just a seasonal home—it's a profound connection to family history and cherished memories. The residence is designed by Anna Franklin of Stone House Collective and balances sophisticated comfort with personal significance.

One of the homeowners grew up spending summers on this lake, making this project especially meaningful. When the opportunity arose to build here, the couple envisioned a place that would serve as a private sanctuary and a welcoming space for entertaining guests—a true heart of family life where they could enjoy time with their adult children and grandchild.

Franklin's design philosophy centered on honoring the spectacular lakeside setting. Floor-to-ceiling windows throughout the home frame breathtaking views, deliberately minimizing window treatments in favor of integrated Lutron systems that maintain the visual connection between indoors and out. "The focal point was always the lake," explains Franklin. "We focused on bringing the outside in and the inside out through color palette and furniture choices."

The interior architecture features reclaimed wood headers and thoughtful woodwork that create an elevated cabin aesthetic—rustic yet refined. Anchored by a rich green, a soothing color palette grounds the space while visually connecting to the surrounding forest. Throughout the home, antique rugs add warmth and character.

The heart of the residence is its open-concept living area, where the kitchen, dining, and living spaces flow together while maintaining subtle delineation. This central hub was designed specifically for family gatherings and entertaining lake neighbors, accommodating both winter football-watching sessions and summer cocktail parties with equal ease.

The primary bedroom suite—situated on the first floor to ensure ease of access for the homeowners during any phase of life—continues the serene, muted palette. Antique pieces, including bedside tables, a bench, and the rug, infuse the space with worldly flair.

After a year of construction, the lakeside legacy estate stands as a testament to Anna Franklin's ability to translate family fortitude into a livable place of enduring beauty and comfort.

The light-filled open kitchen features deep green cabinetry set against walnut notes that echo the surrounding forest, complemented by open shelving and minimal cabinetry to maintain the airy flow connecting to the lake views beyond.

NEXT: In this broad view, the custom kitchen blends modern functionality with rustic charm through reclaimed Wisconsin barn timber headers, Visual Comfort pendant lights chosen for their vintage character, and a vibrant Door County art piece punctuating the earthy palette throughout. Millhouse Cabinetry created the fitted furniture.

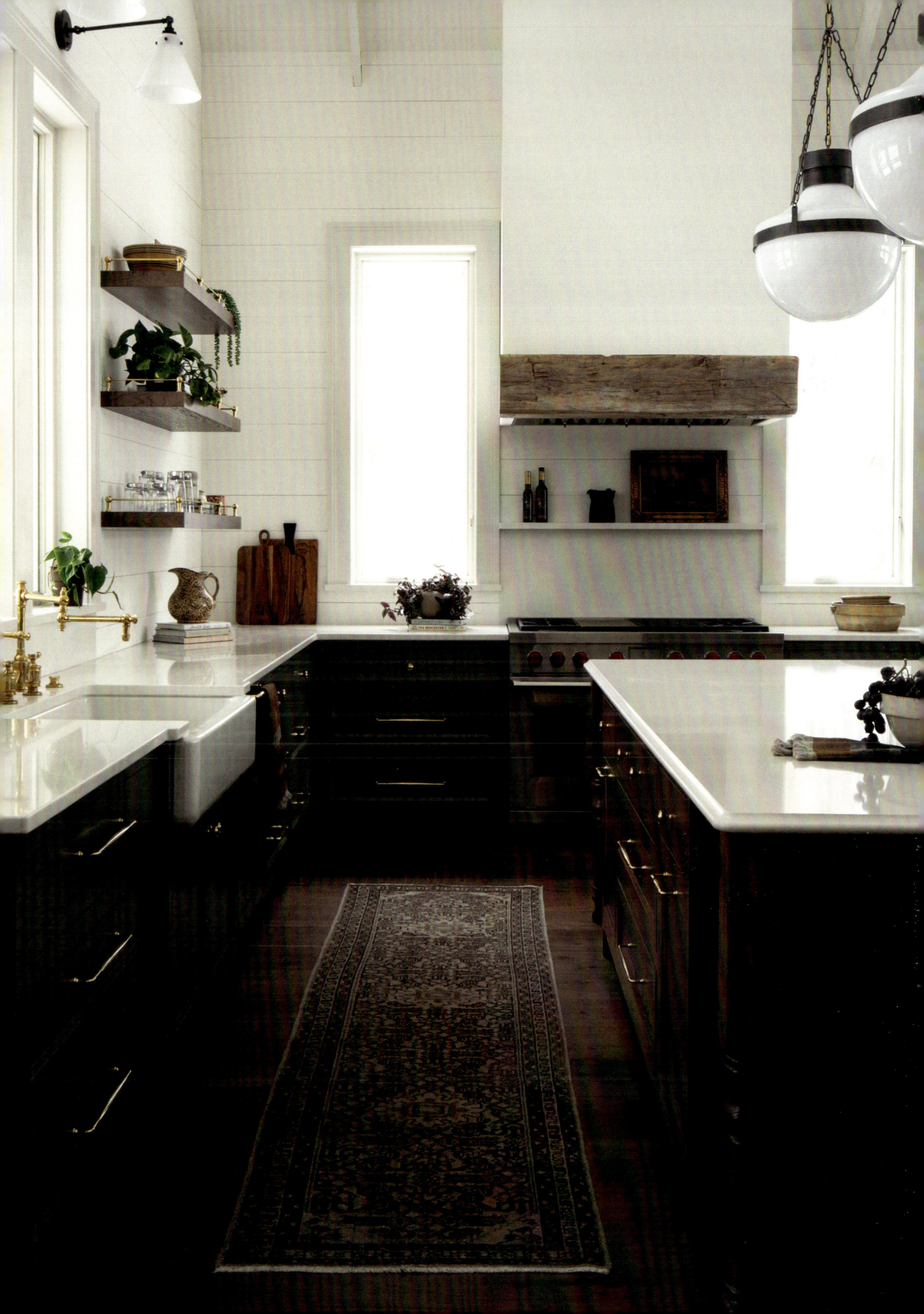

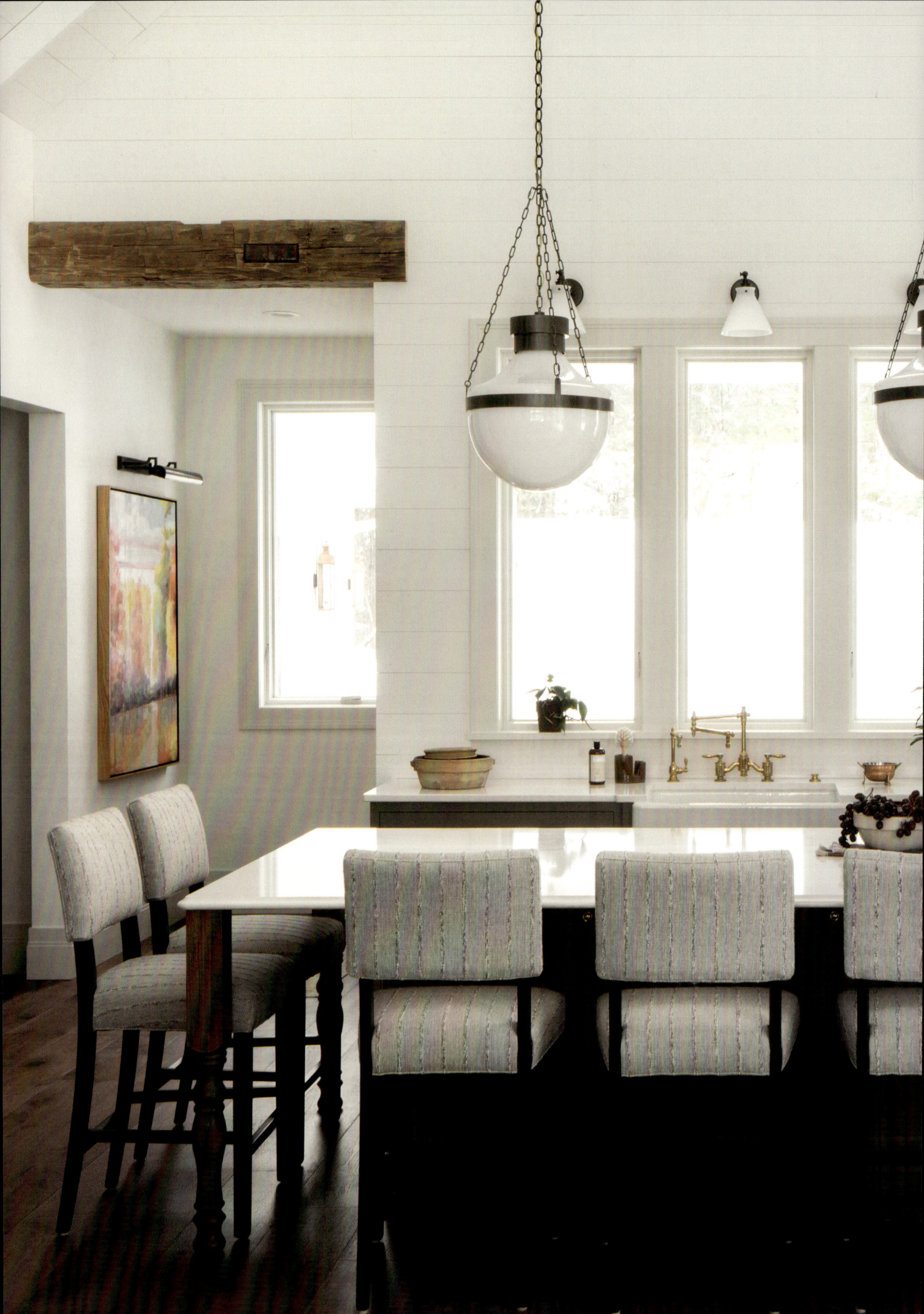

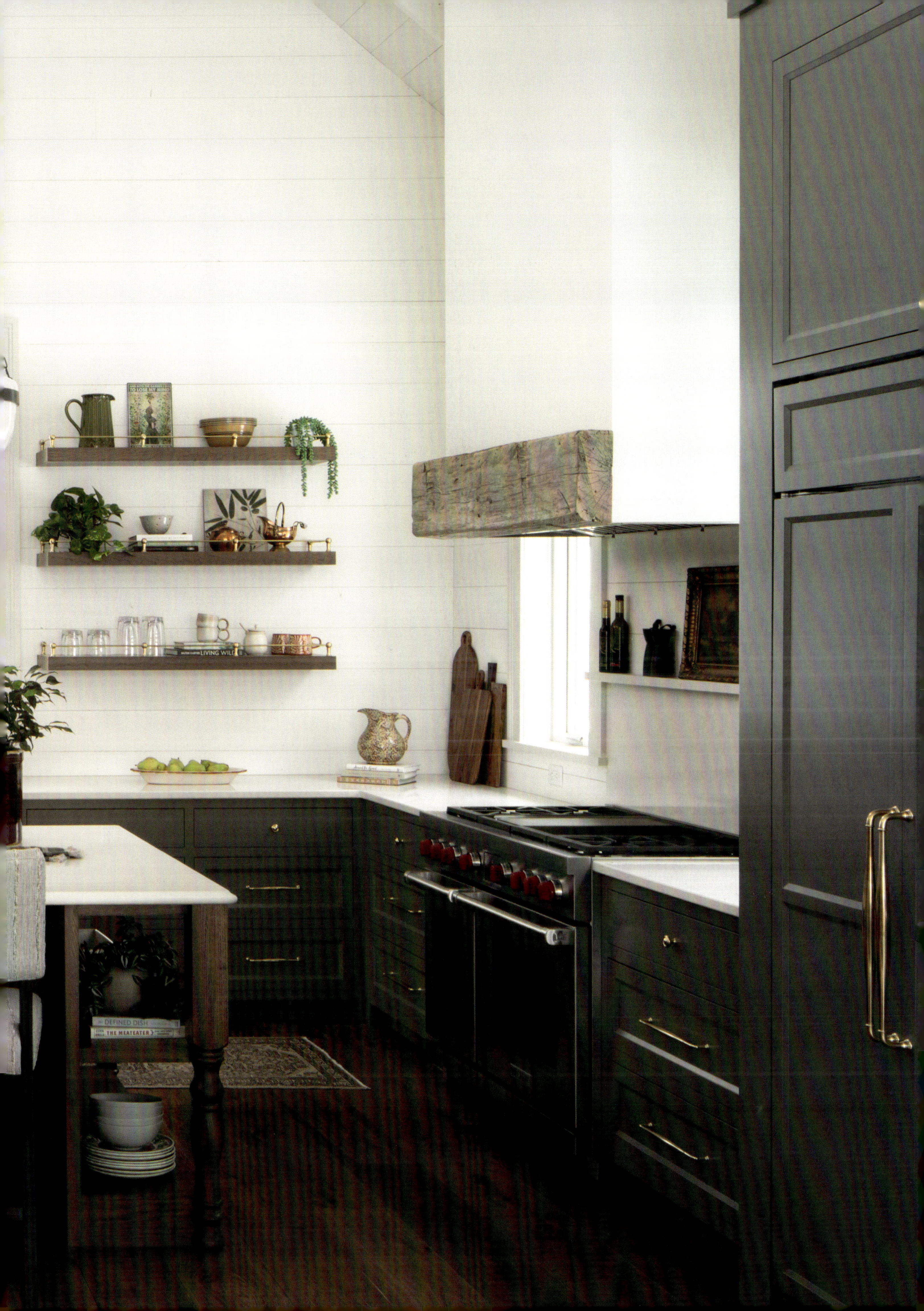
DEFINED DISH
THE MEATEATER

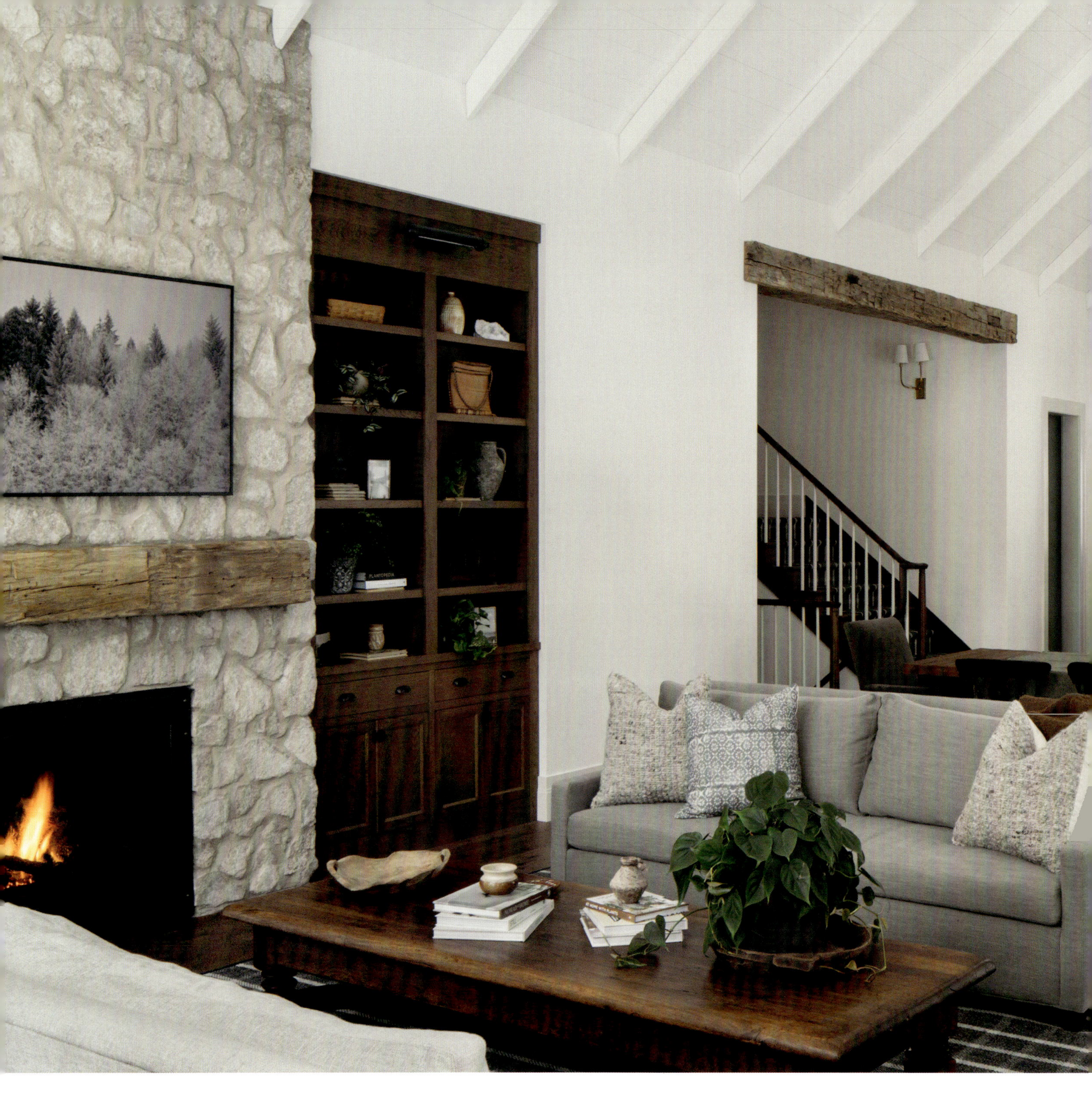

The home's welcoming great room features a custom-designed seating area with bespoke furniture, anchored by a full-height stacked stone fireplace. The statement staircase with reclaimed beams and a decorative runner leads to a guest level with two bedrooms.

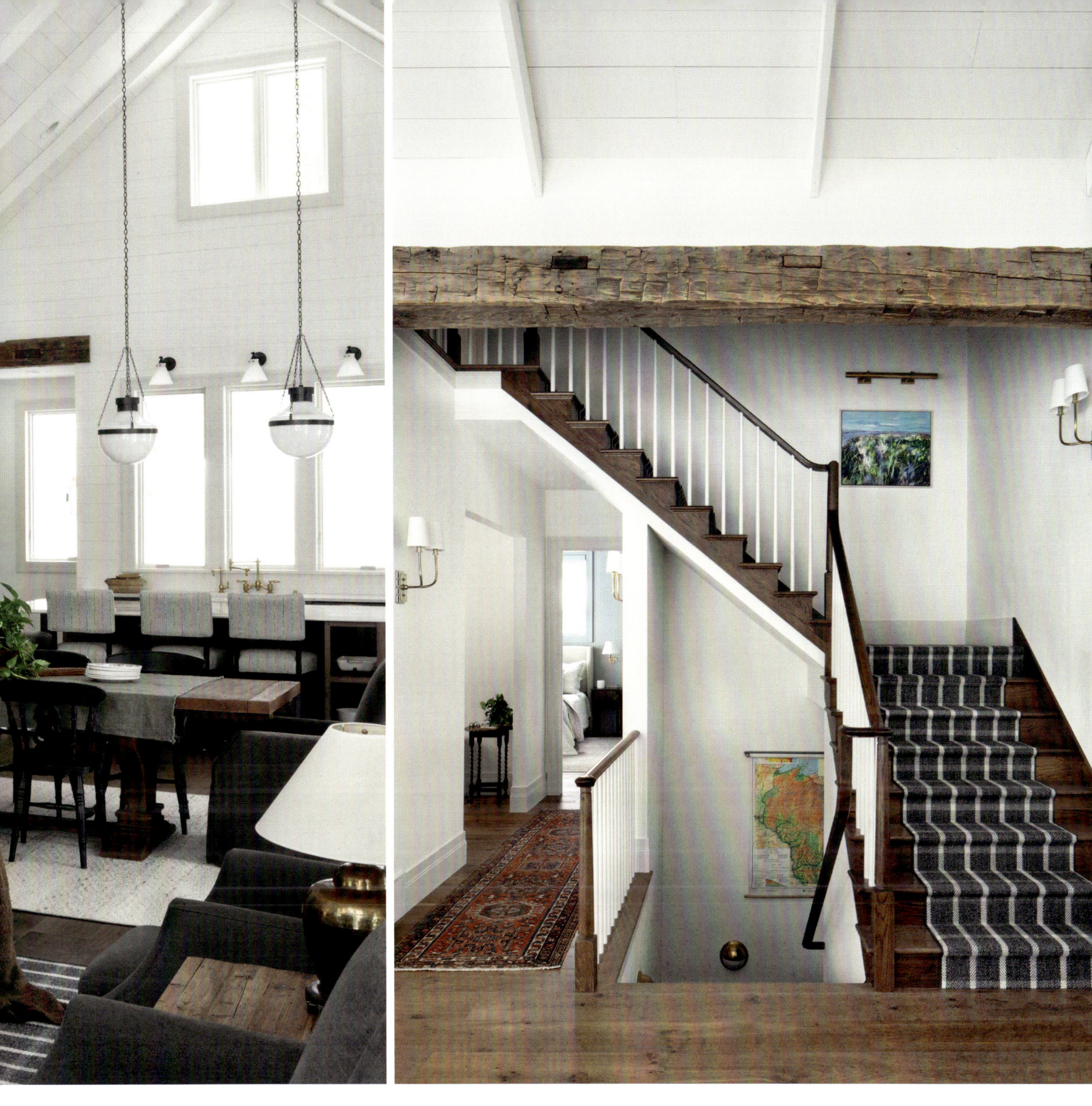

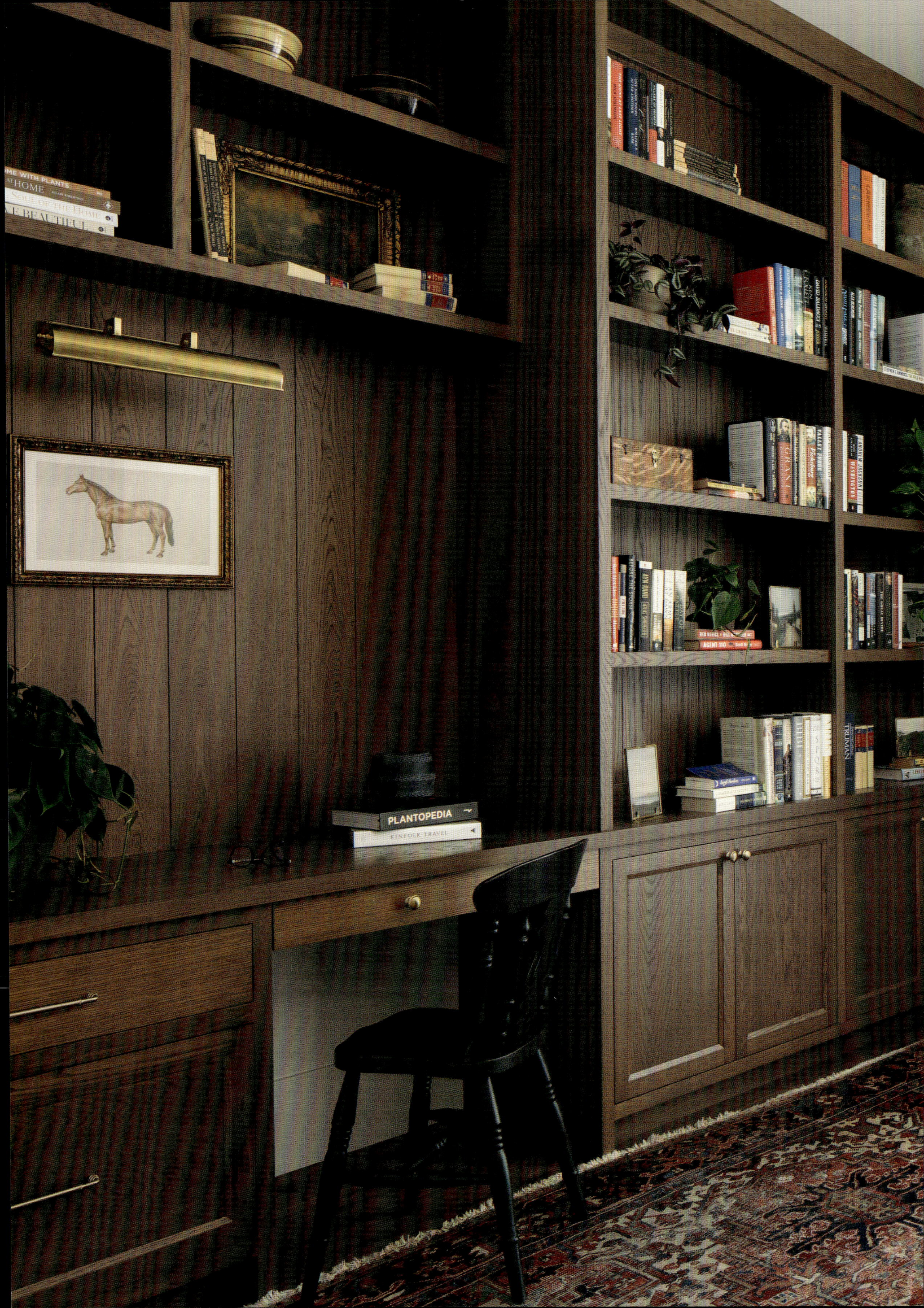
PLANTOPEDIA
KINFOLK TRAVEL
AYN RAND
AGENT 110
TRUMAN

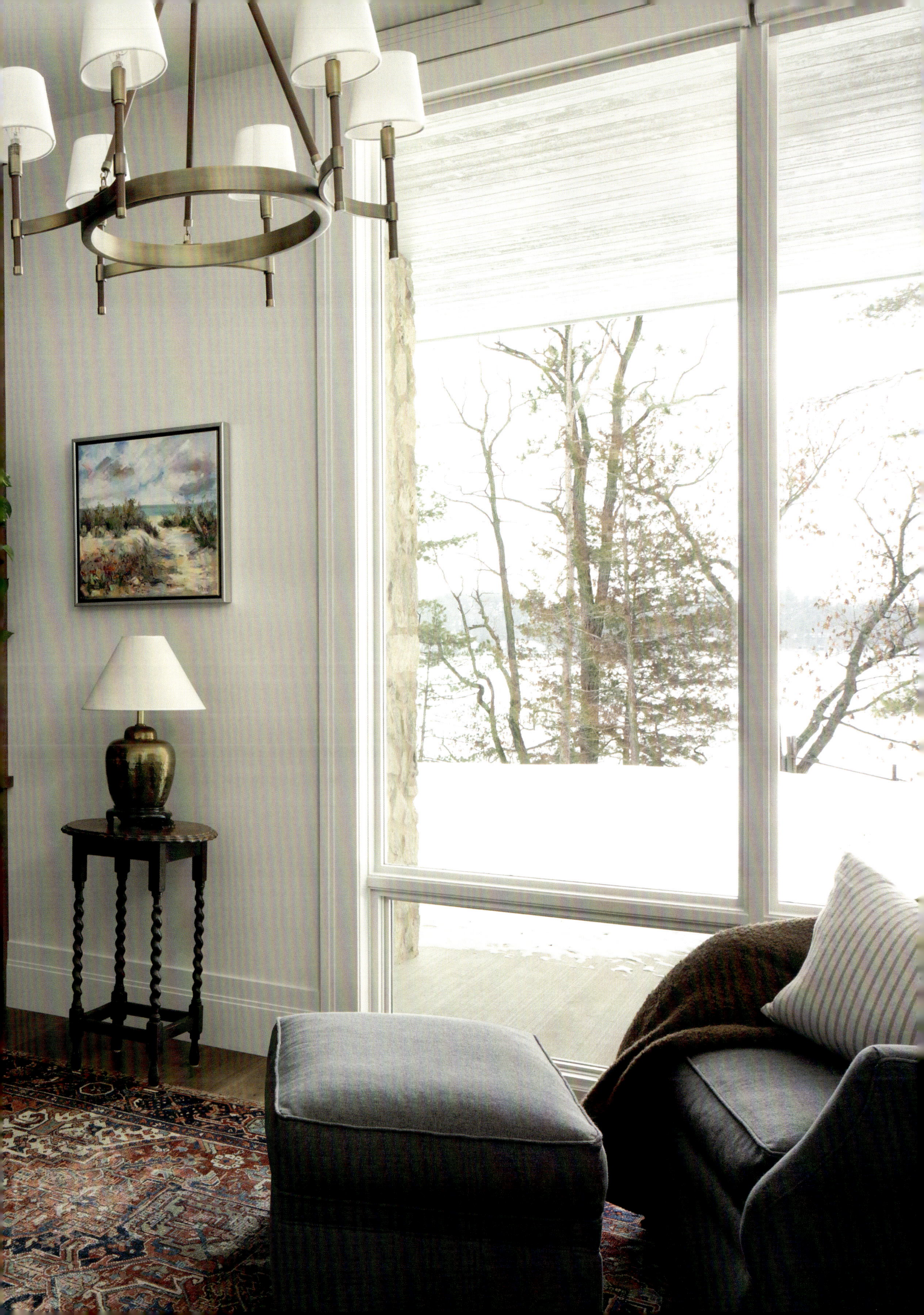

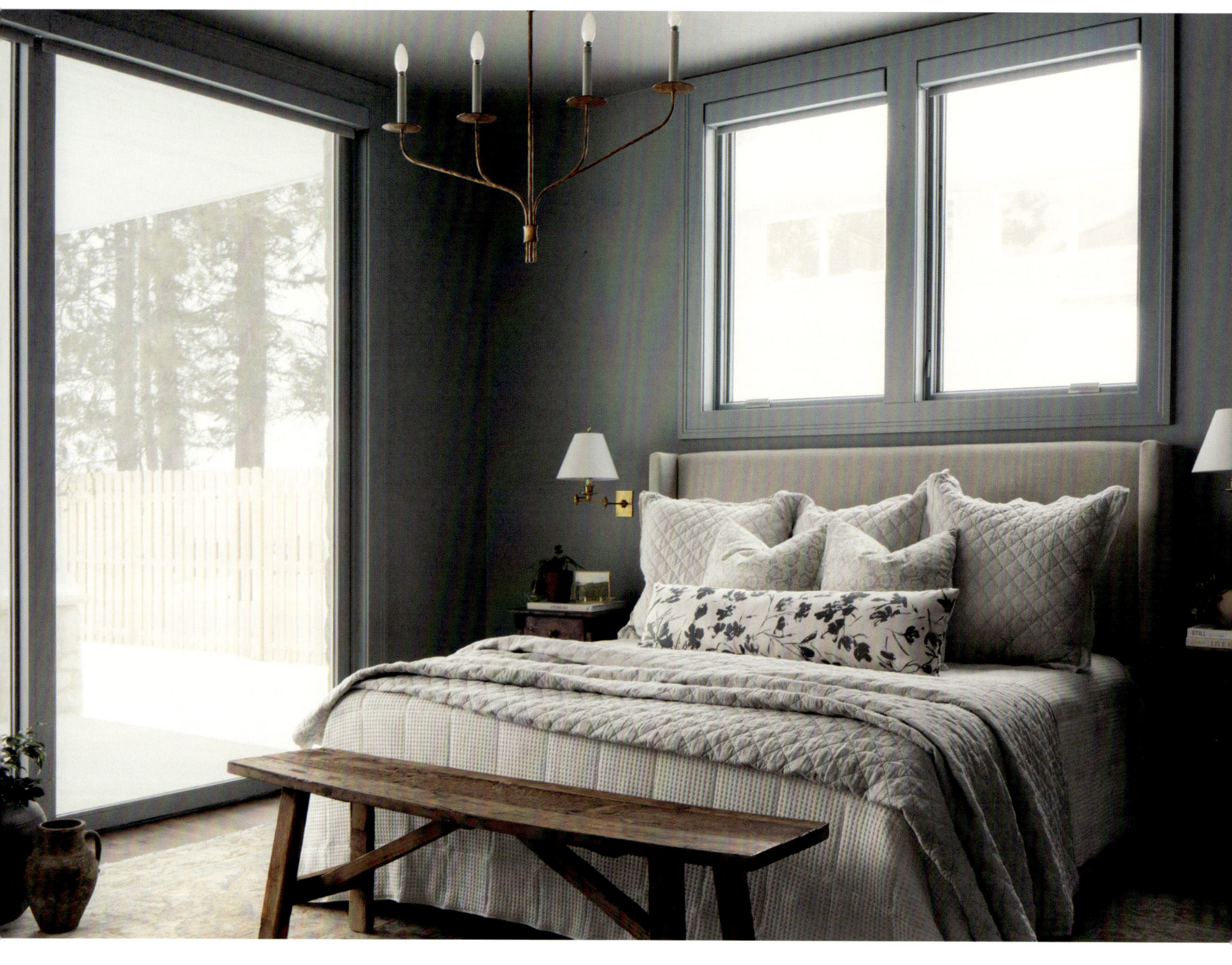

PREVIOUS: A dual-purpose library is both a workspace and a reading sanctuary, thoughtfully designed for the book-loving homeowner who cherishes building his literary collection. Positioned to showcase lake views, it balances functionality with the tranquil natural setting beyond.

ABOVE: This cocooning bedroom, color-drenched in Benjamin Moore's Puritan Gray with matching Lutron window treatments, flows into a sophisticated bath featuring Gala Grey marble surfaces, Cambria Malvern countertops, and a Milky Way White polished marble shower floor.

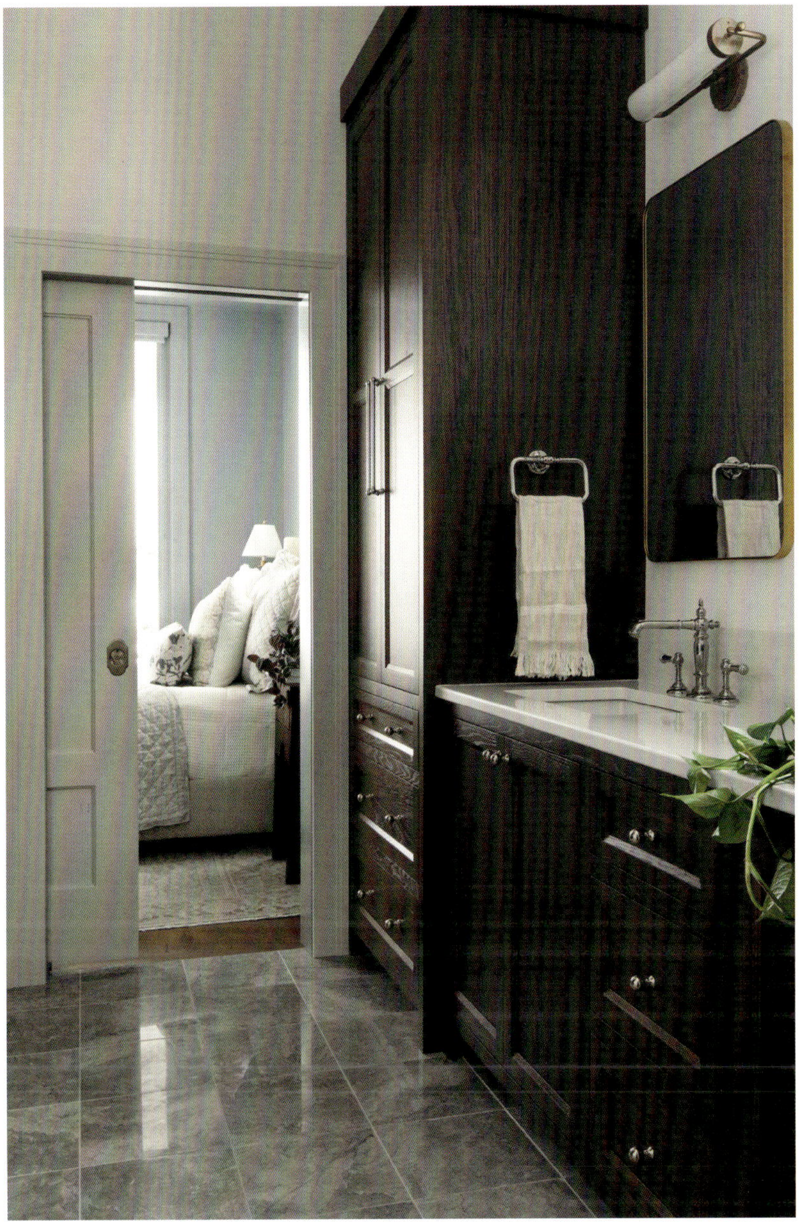

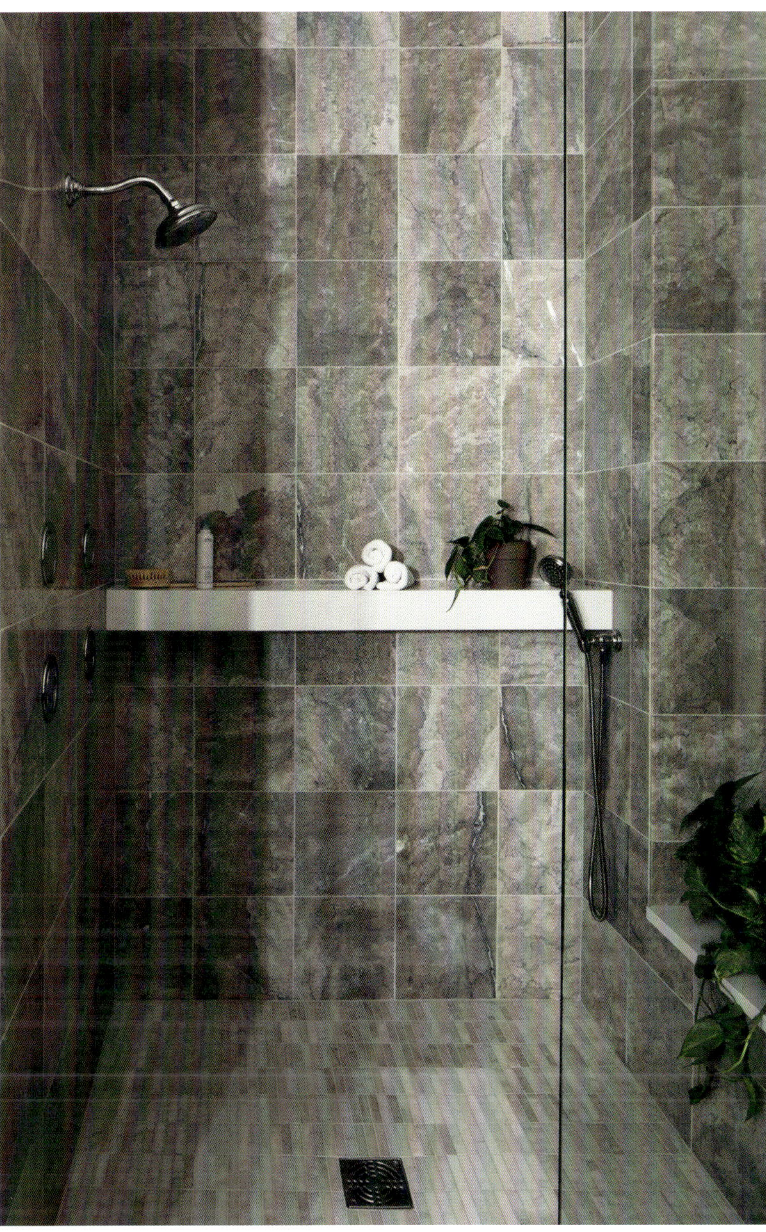

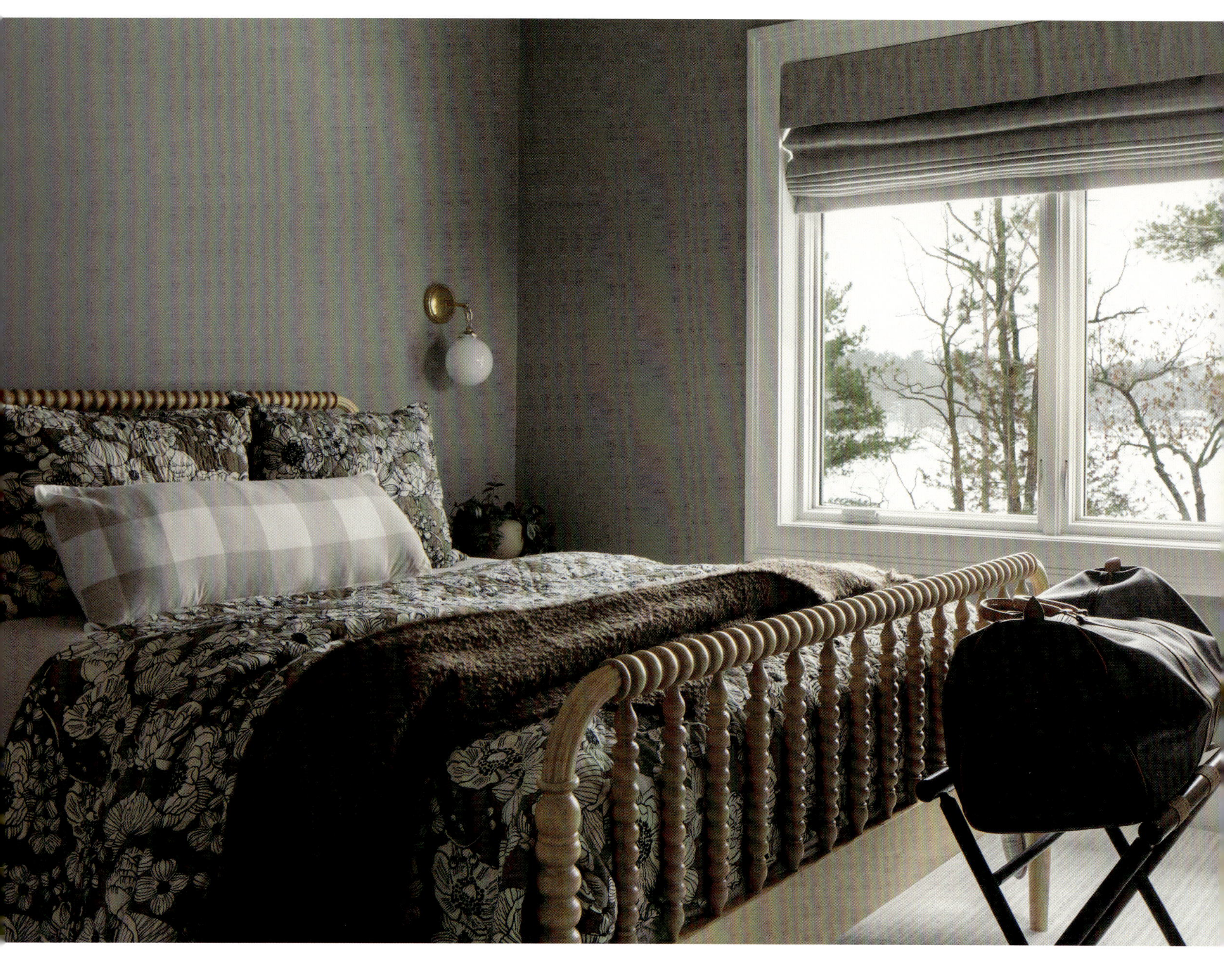

In this thoughtfully designed guest suite, natural-fiber bedding from Amity Home and Parachute creates an inviting retreat. The furniture-inspired vanity with Visual Comfort sconces complements the dramatic Midori Green tiled shower, balanced by a timeless marble checkerboard floor.

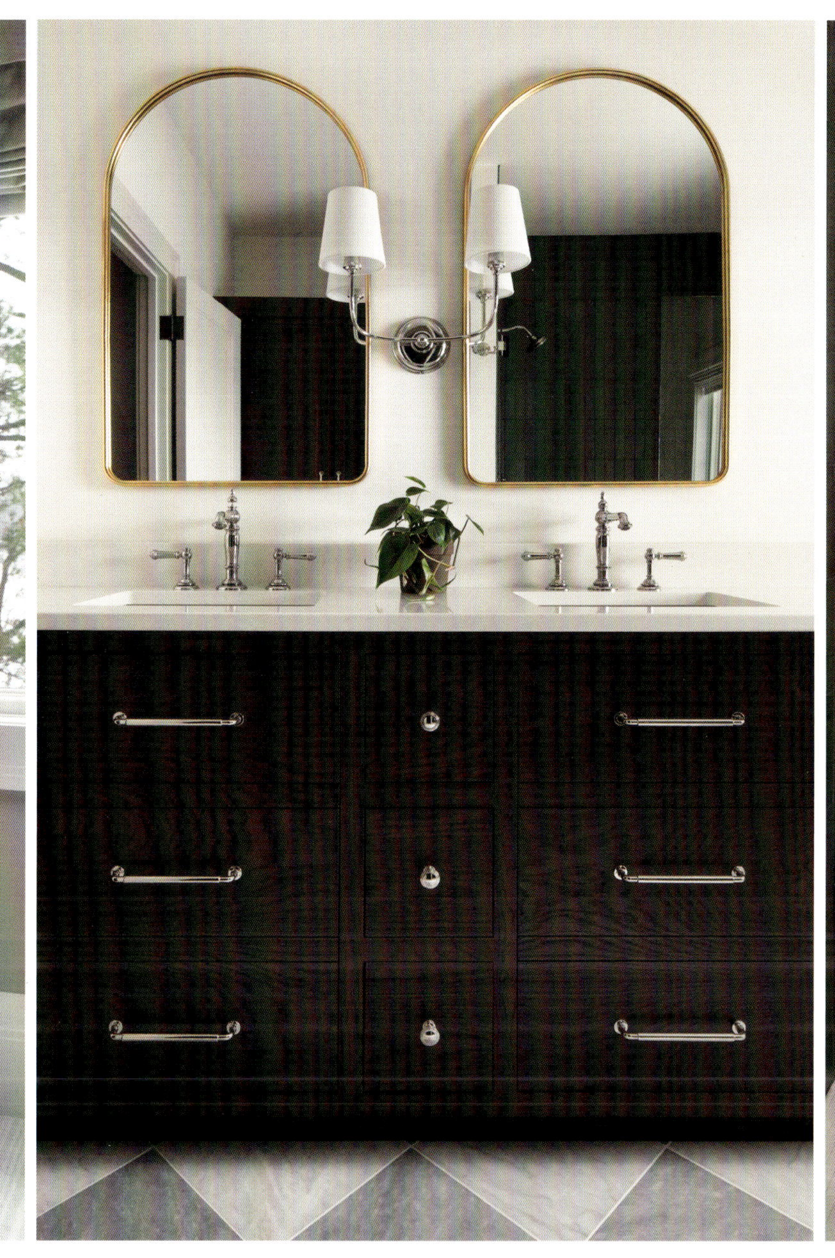

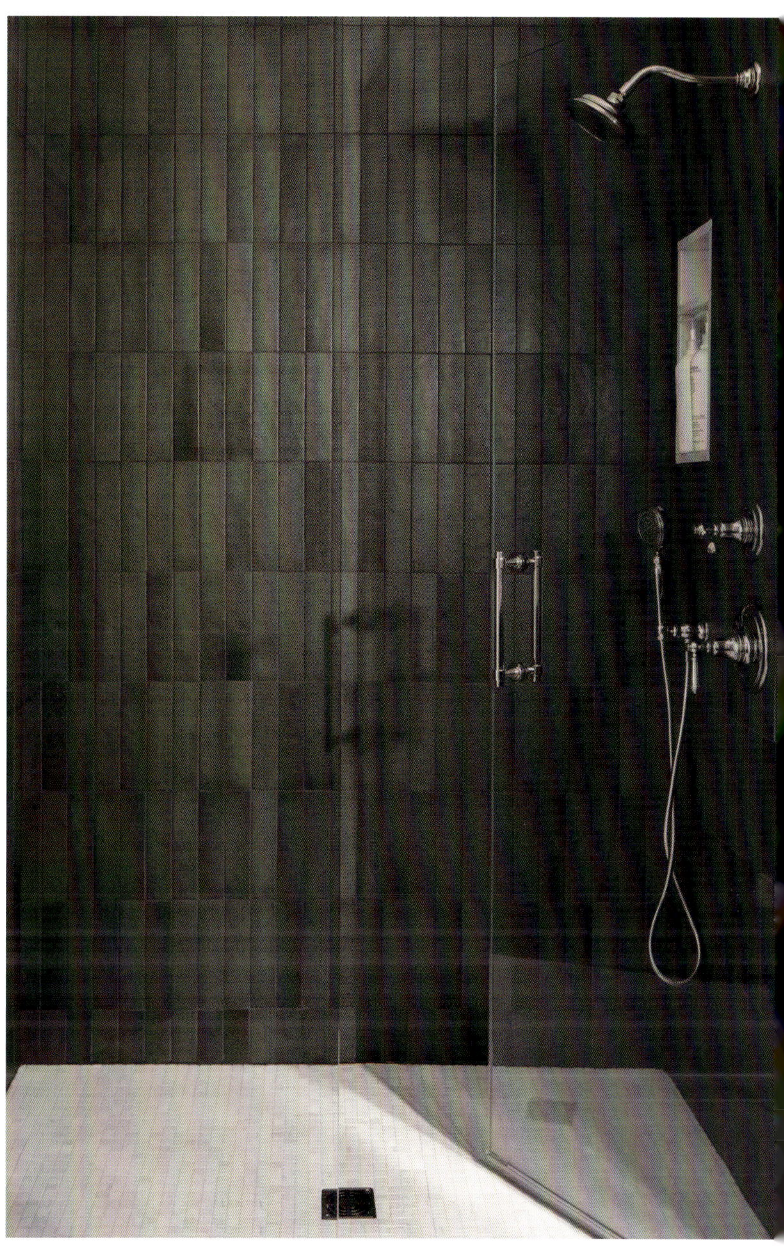

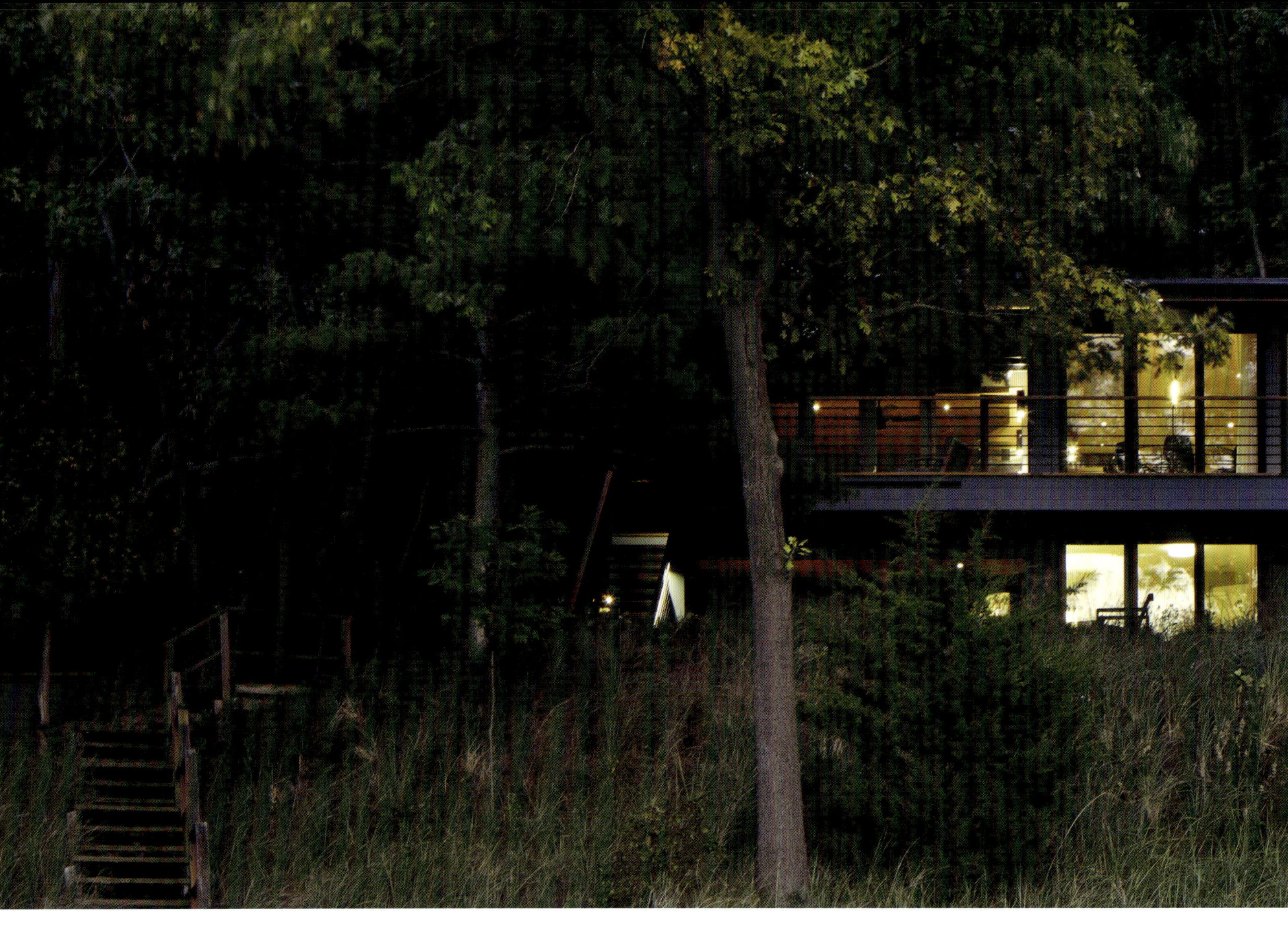

NATURAL PALETTE

Elissa Scrafano / Scrafano Architects

On the shores of Lake Michigan in Bridgman, Michigan, sits a remarkable transformation—a 1972 summer home reimagined as a sophisticated year-round retreat. Once described as "heating wood falling apart" but "in a great location," this property has undergone an extensive remodel to become a regular escape from Chicago life for its owners.

Elissa Scrafano and Carol Barrett of Scrafano Architects collaborated closely with the owners to create a home that balances modern style with lakeside charm. The plan included a new addition that houses the primary bedroom and bath suite and blends seamlessly with the renovated original.

One of the project's most ingenious interventions involved the basement level, previously enclosed by a concrete wall. Now, sliding doors connect to a walkway leading down to the beach. This transformation created a seamless indoor-outdoor flow capitalizing on the property's Lake Michigan frontage.

The continuous glass doors along the west facade introduce lake views and connect with multiple outdoor entertaining areas. The property now features a stone patio with a fire pit, lounge area, and spa overlooking the dunes and the beach. An outdoor shower beneath the stairs adds a playful yet practical element to the lakeside lifestyle.

A generously proportioned screened porch serves as an essential transitional space, allowing the owners to entertain and enjoy Michigan's beautiful summer, spring, and

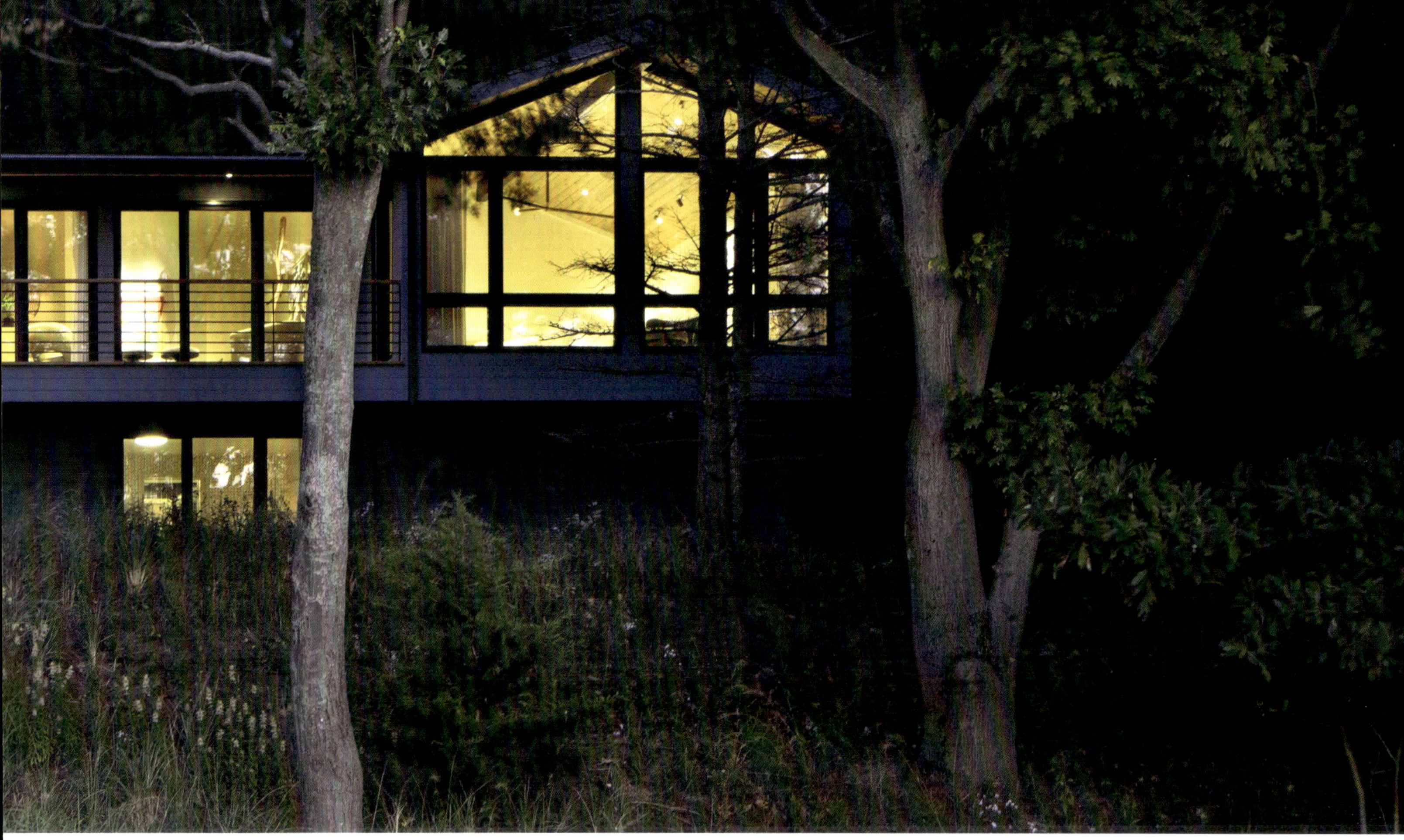

fall seasons while remaining protected from the region's "brutal" mosquitoes.

The collaborative approach between designer and client yielded a four-bedroom, three-and-a-half-bath modern home with finishes and furnishings that perfectly suit the owners' entertaining lifestyle.

The visual connection between interior spaces and the surrounding landscape creates what one designer describes as a strong architectural statement when "you just see nature" without visual interruptions. The renovation brought in abundant natural light and expanded views of the dunes, woods, and lake and created a more seamless connection to the outdoors.

This transformation turns a modest cabin into a refined lakeside retreat—one that embraces its surroundings while preserving the original home's scale and the character of the neighboring community.

Originally a modest three-season cottage, this expanded lakeside abode features thoughtful additions that preserve the wooded landscape. Floor-to-ceiling windows in the primary suite offer filtered lake views through preserved trees, while large sliding doors connect interior spaces to nature.

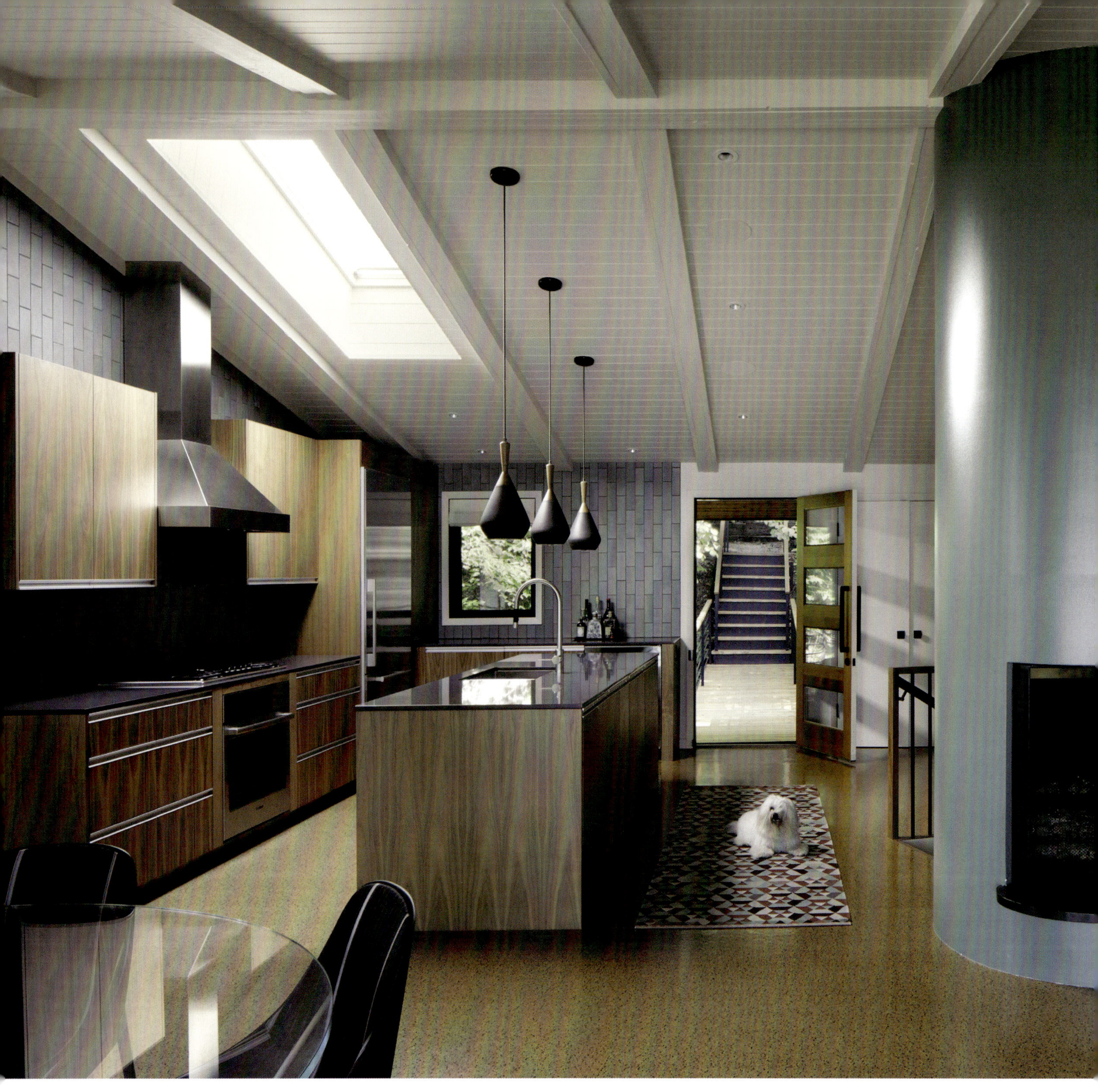

The reimagined kitchen features custom walnut cabinetry by Priebe, Heath ceramic tile in Chalk-Gunmetal 5, and Zandur cork flooring with polyurethane sealer. The original fireplace is sheathed in a new plaster finish, while Benjamin Moore Gray Mist paint completes the polished palette.

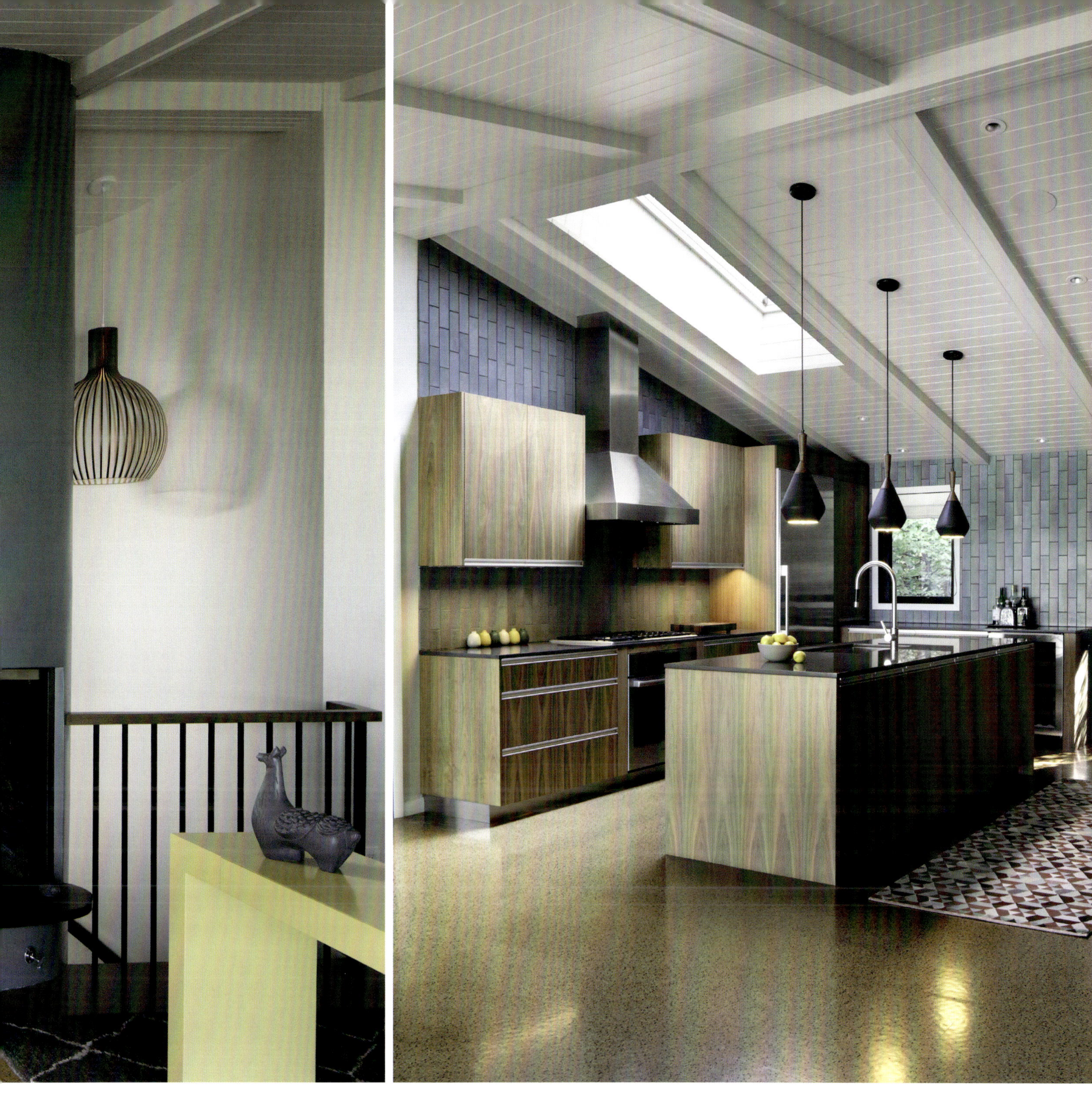

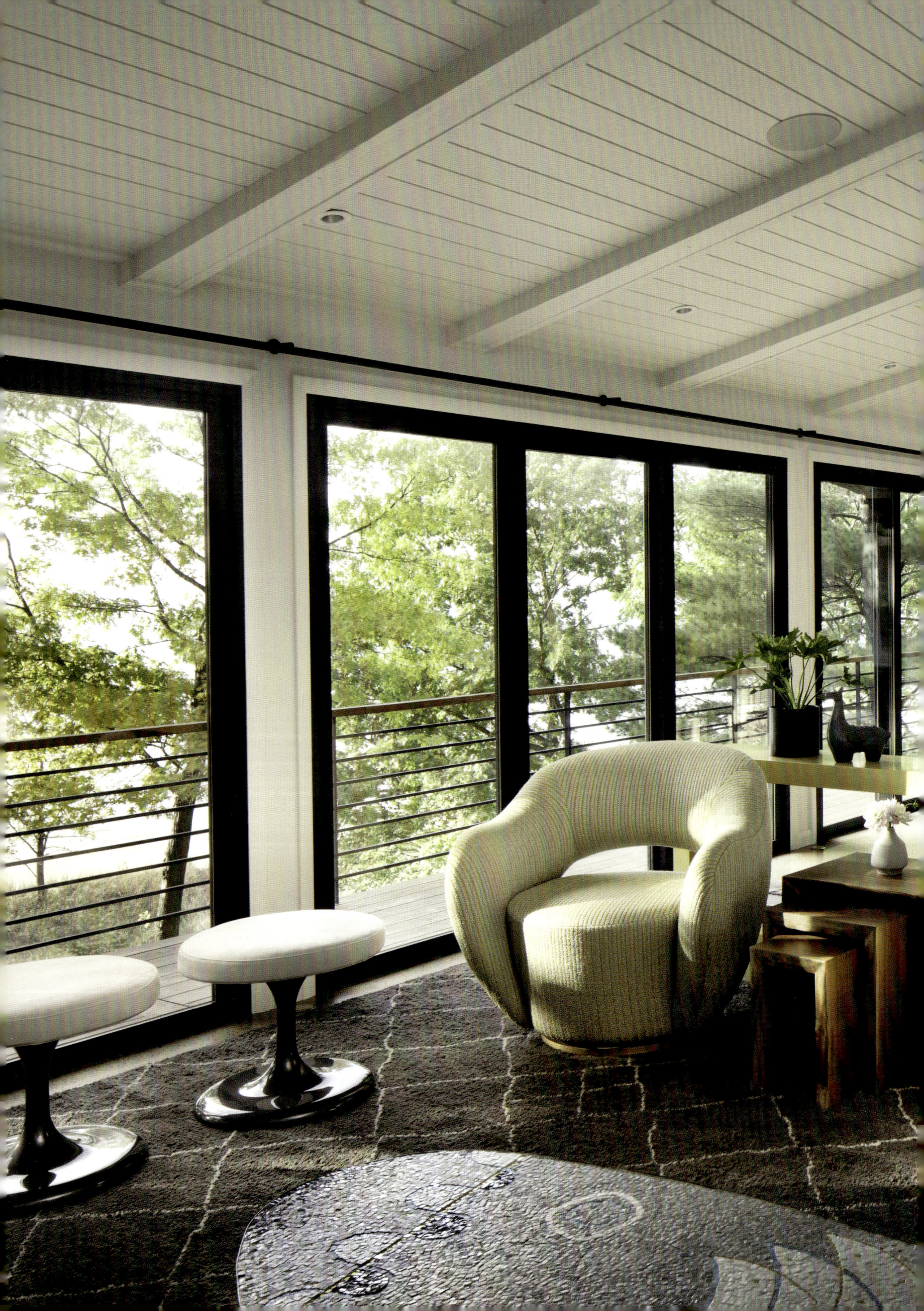

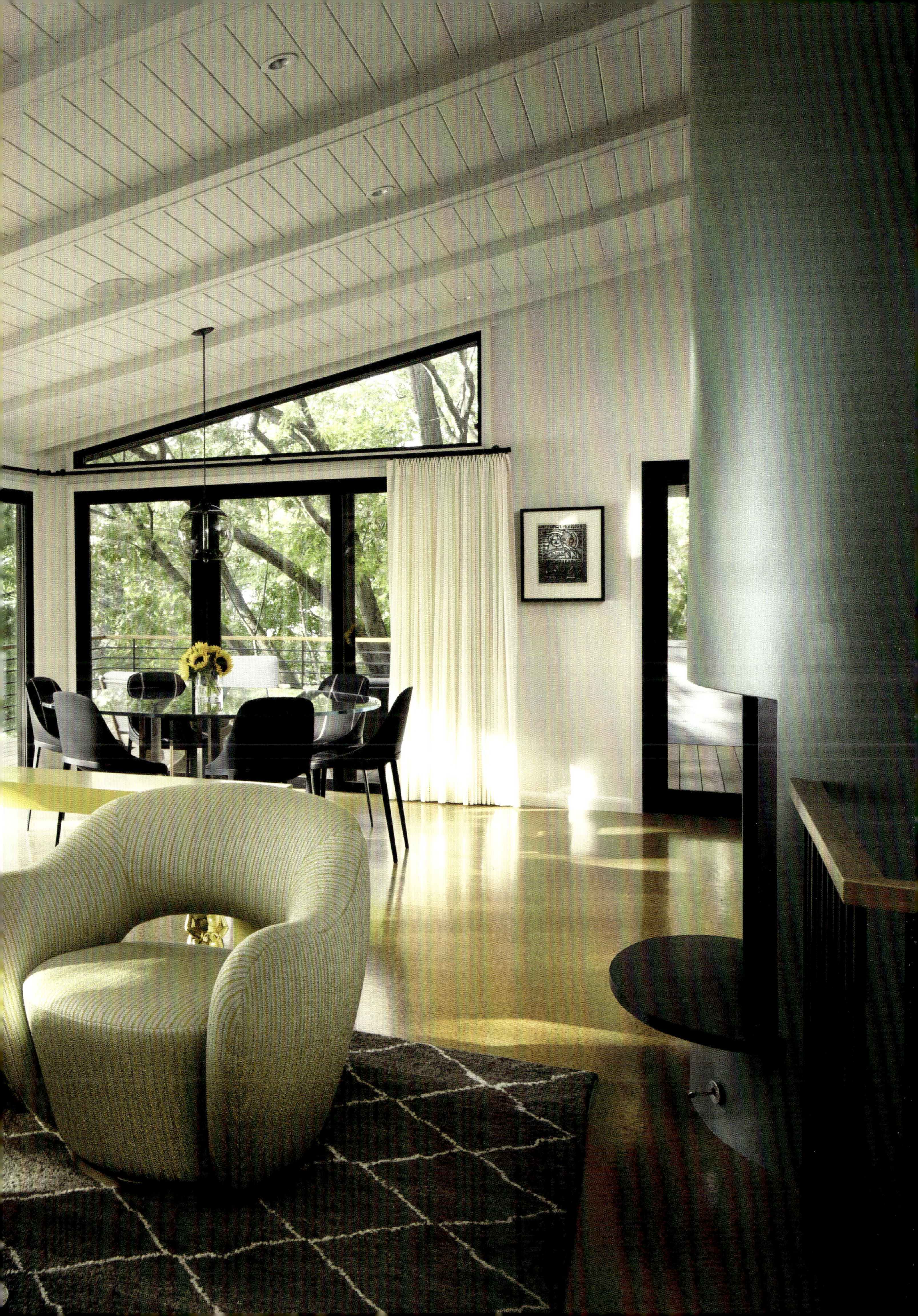

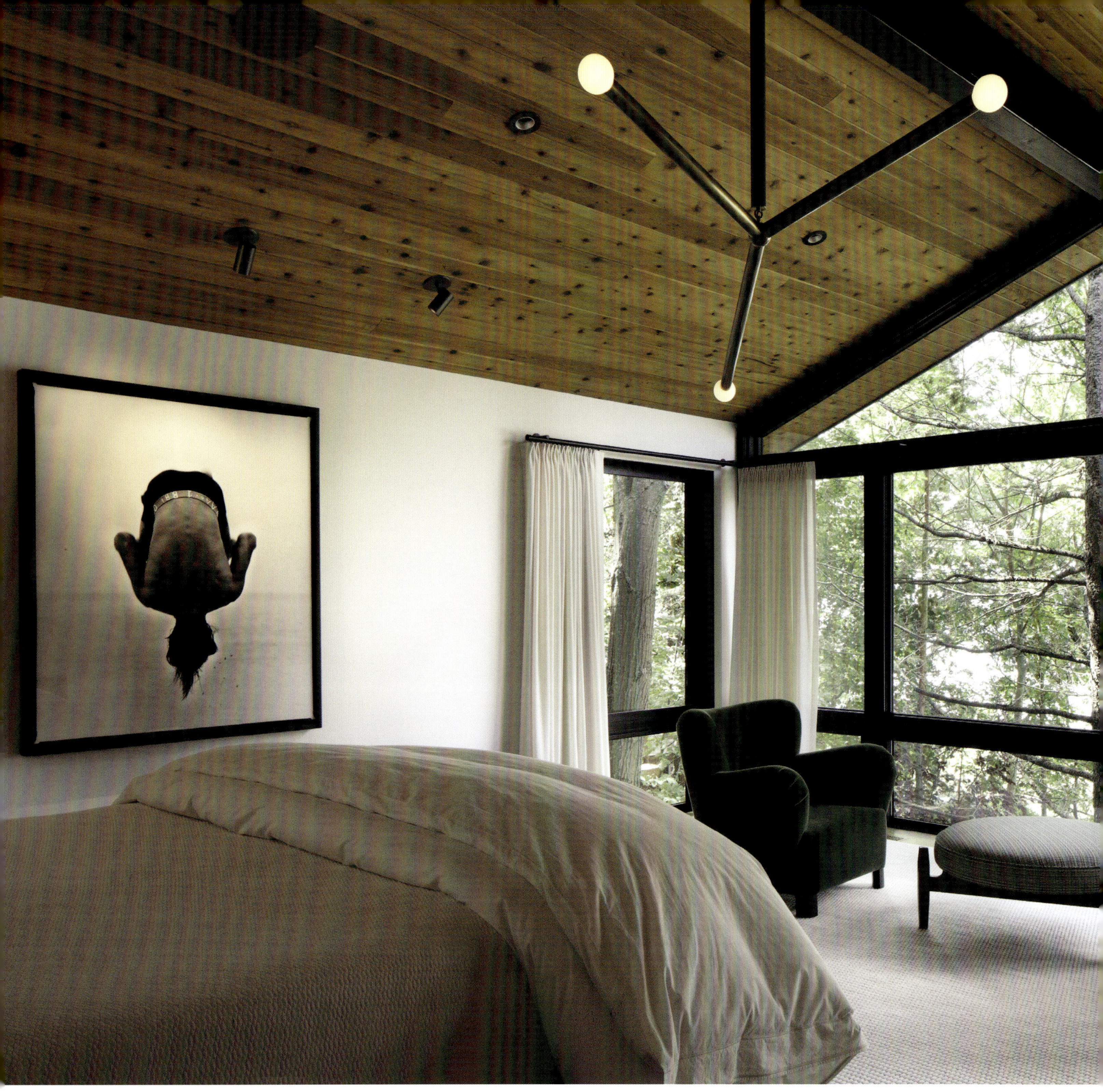

PREVIOUS: The transformed living room features exposed rafters and tongue-and-groove ceiling, with expanded west-facing lake views through generous new windows and doors. The thoughtfully curated interior showcases the owners' vintage furniture collection, creating an authentic, timeless atmosphere.

ABOVE: This new primary bedroom/bath wing embodies a Zen, spa-like aesthetic. Its west-facing windows capture filtered lake views through privacy-providing trees. The intentionally subdued furniture and finishes recede into the background, allowing nature's ever-changing canvas to command attention.

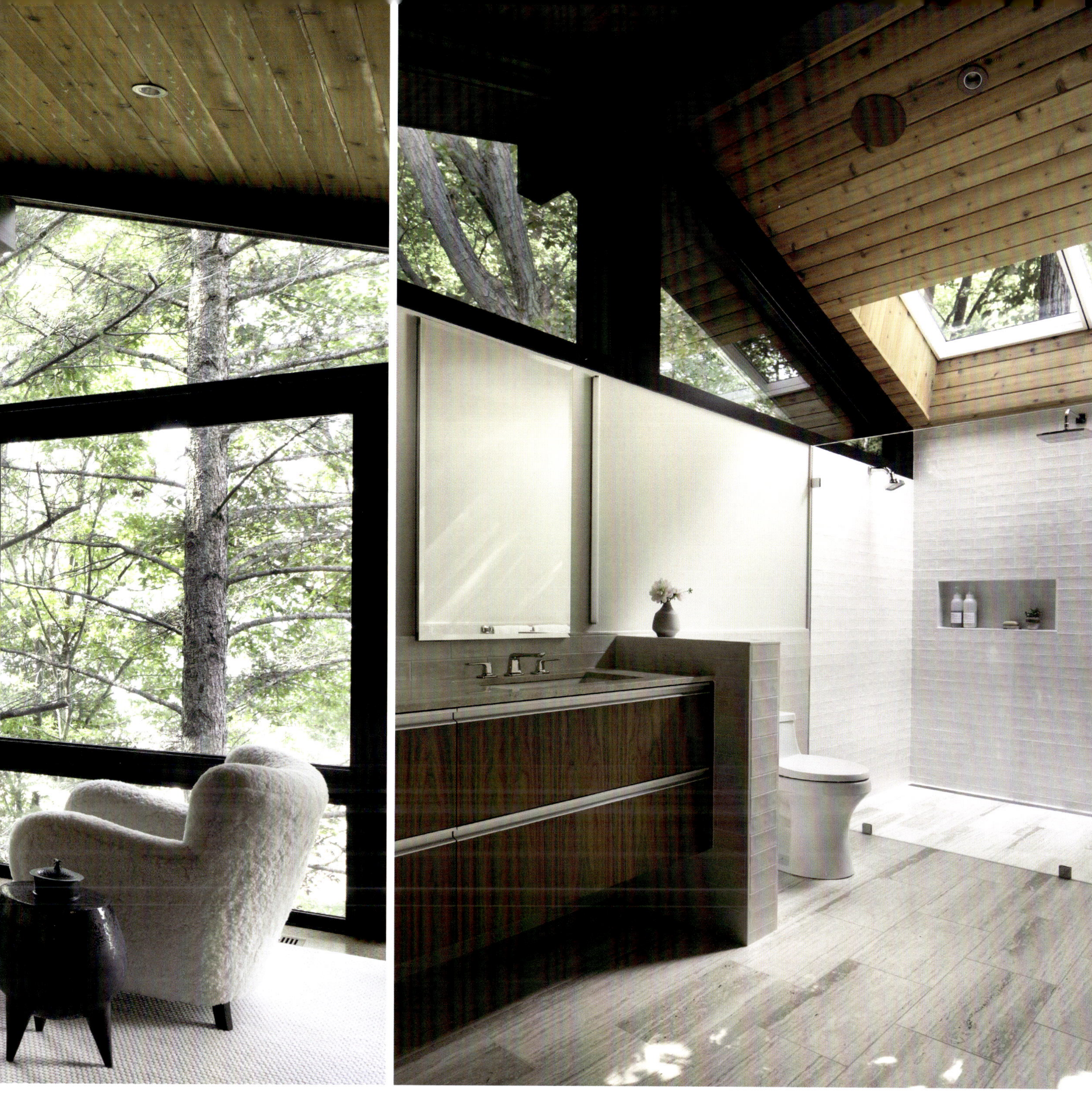

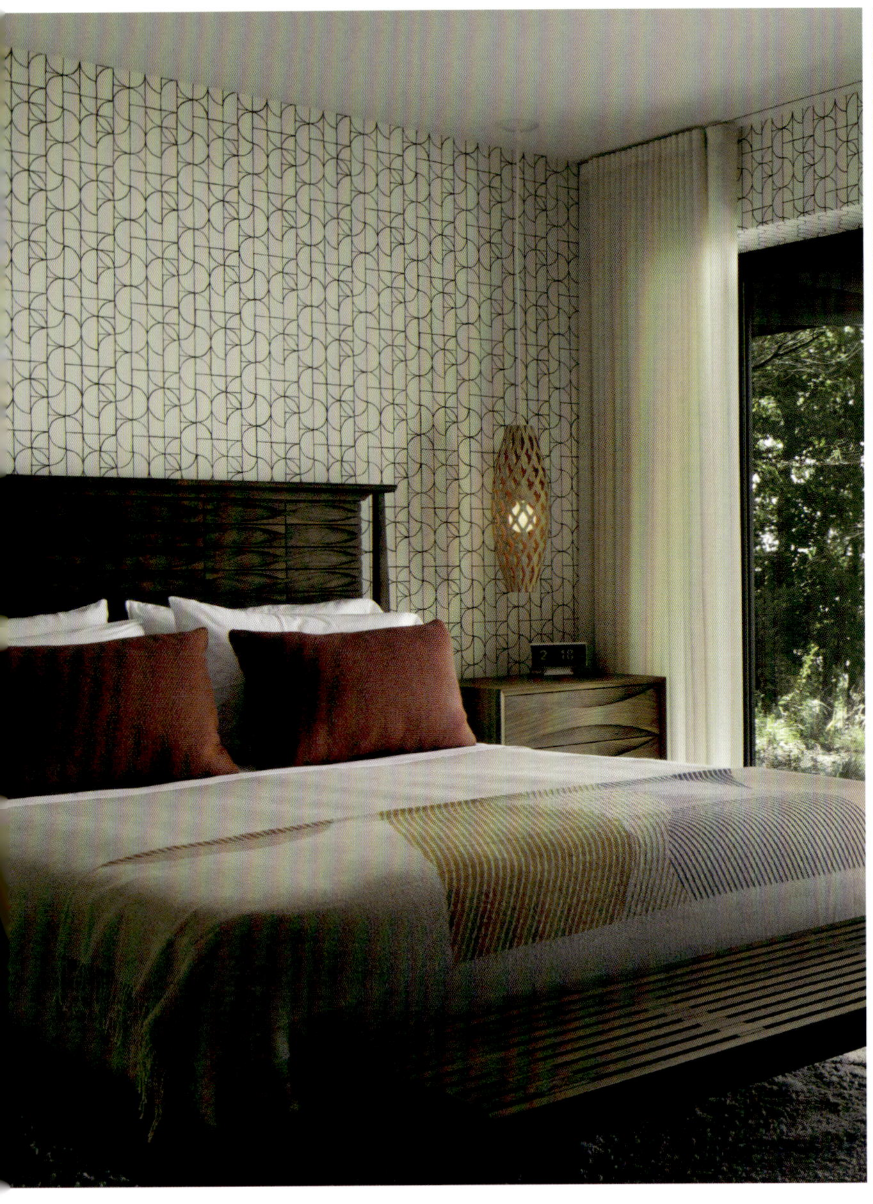

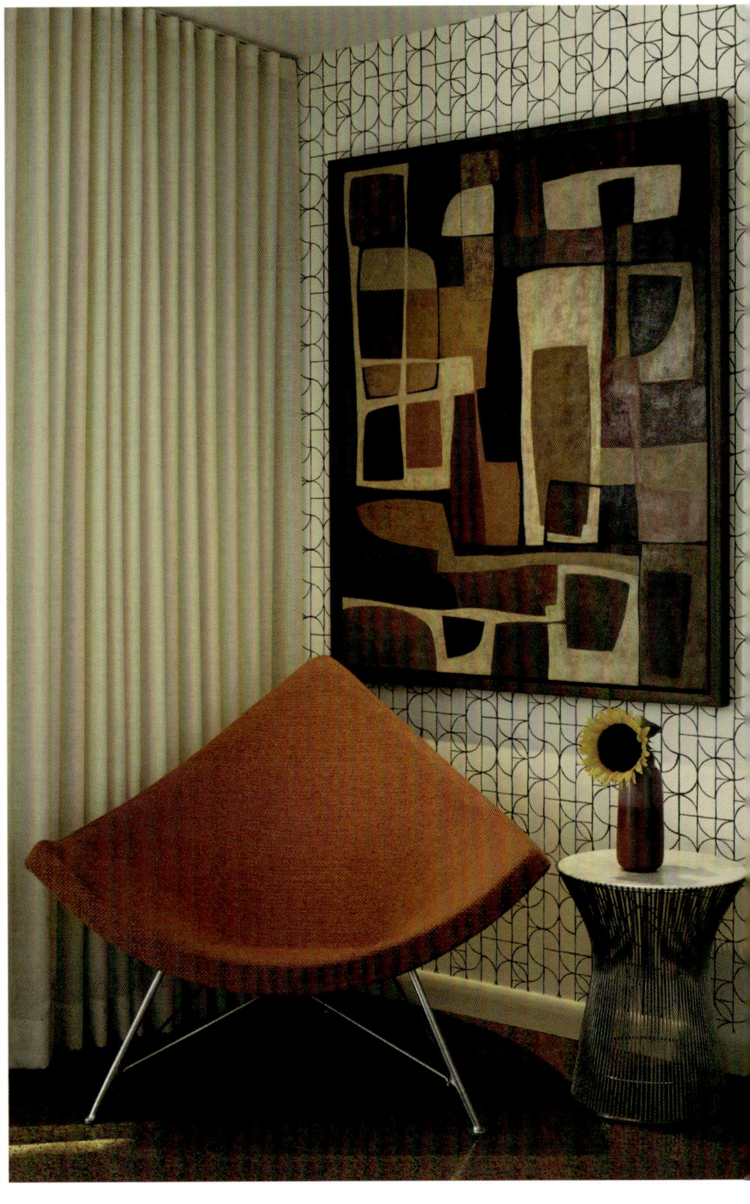

ABOVE: This guest suite is located on the transformed lower level and showcases the owners' impeccable midcentury modern aesthetic. Once a dingy basement, the space now features sliding glass doors providing direct access to the paved patio and lake, complemented by an oversized shower designed for comfortable accessibility.

NEXT: This strategically positioned west-facing deck of ipe wood, also known as Brazilian walnut, connects the dining room and screened porch, offering prime sunset vistas over the lake. Steel railings with ipe caps provide safety while maintaining views, and stairs lead to the lower patio, fire pit, and beach.

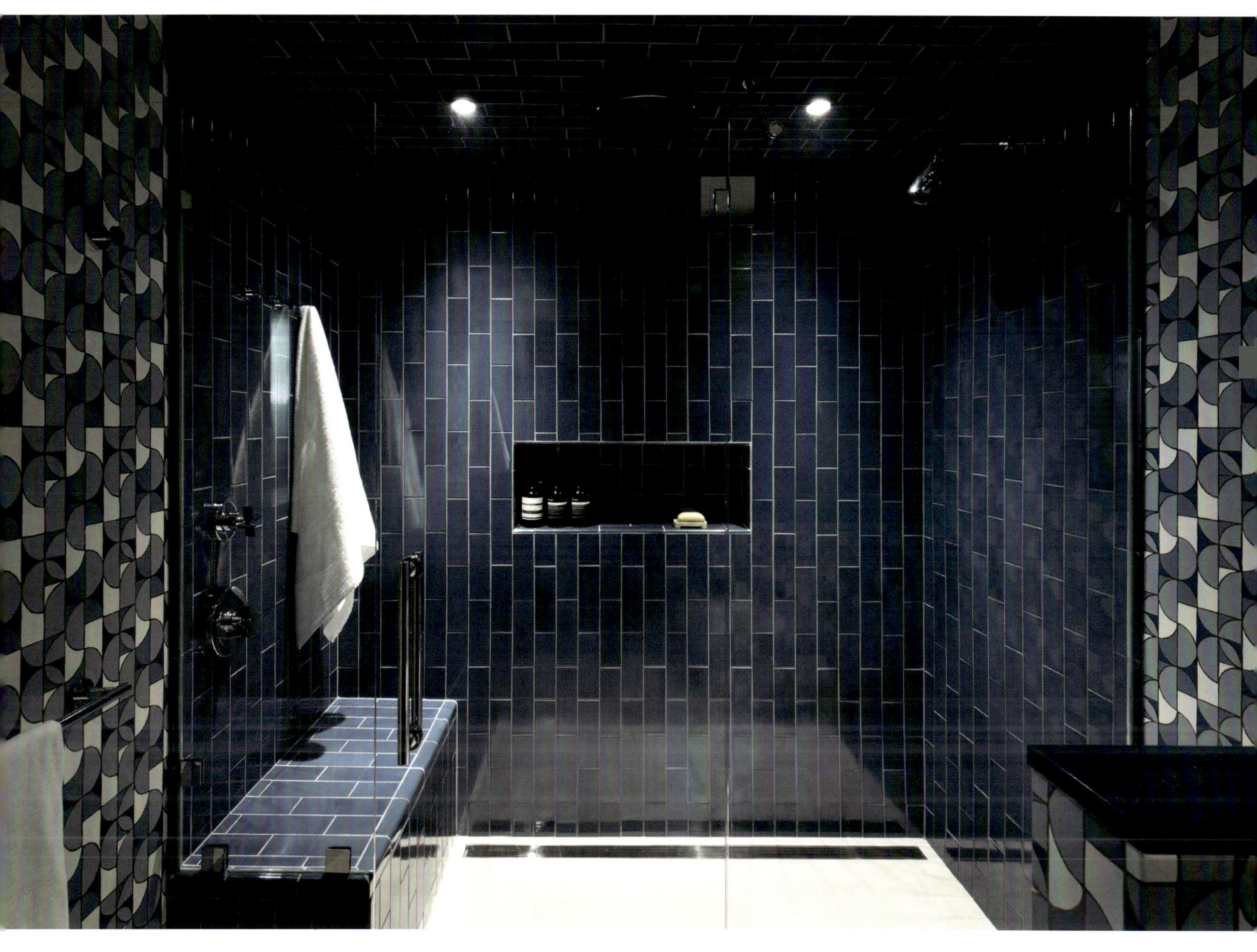

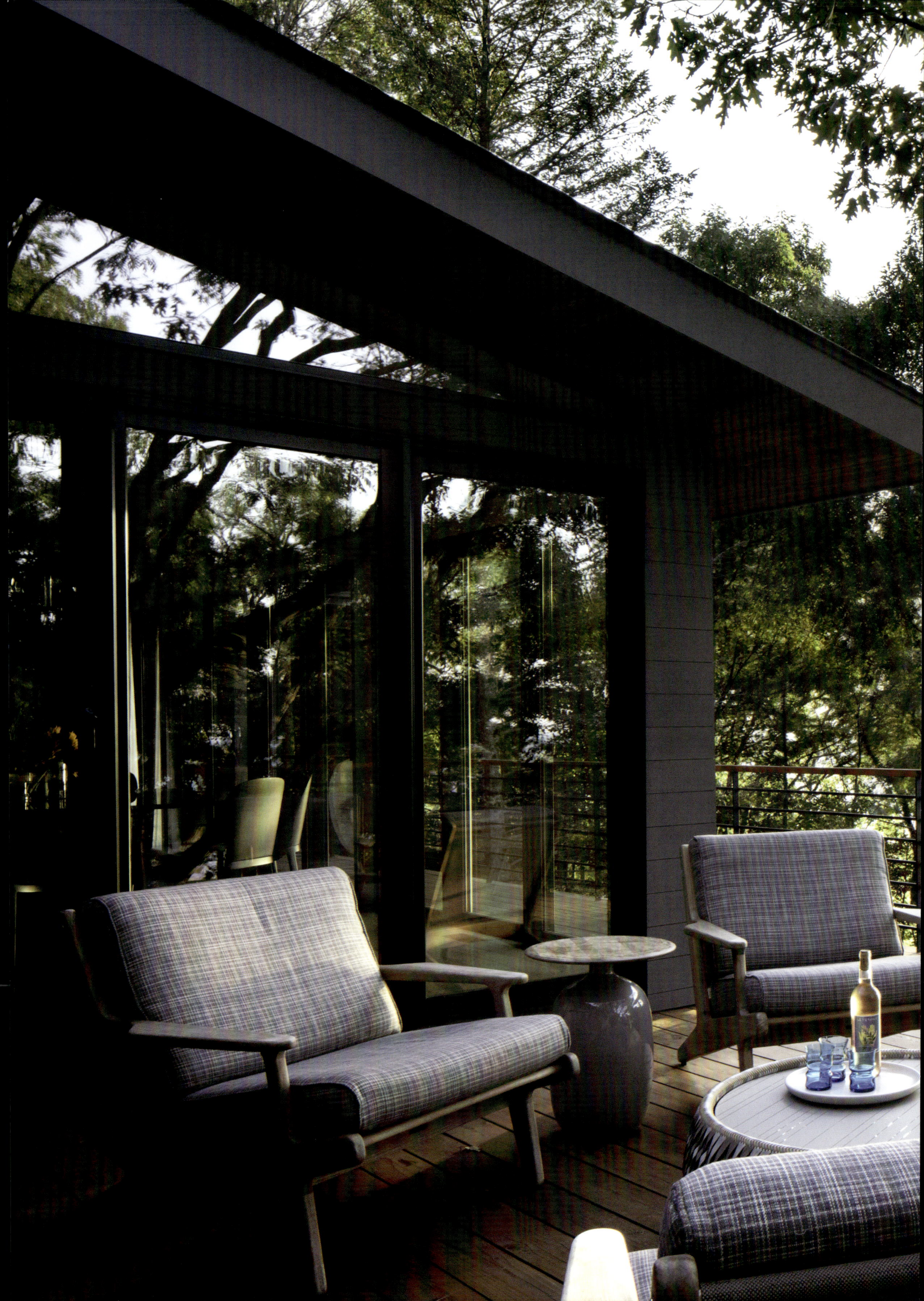

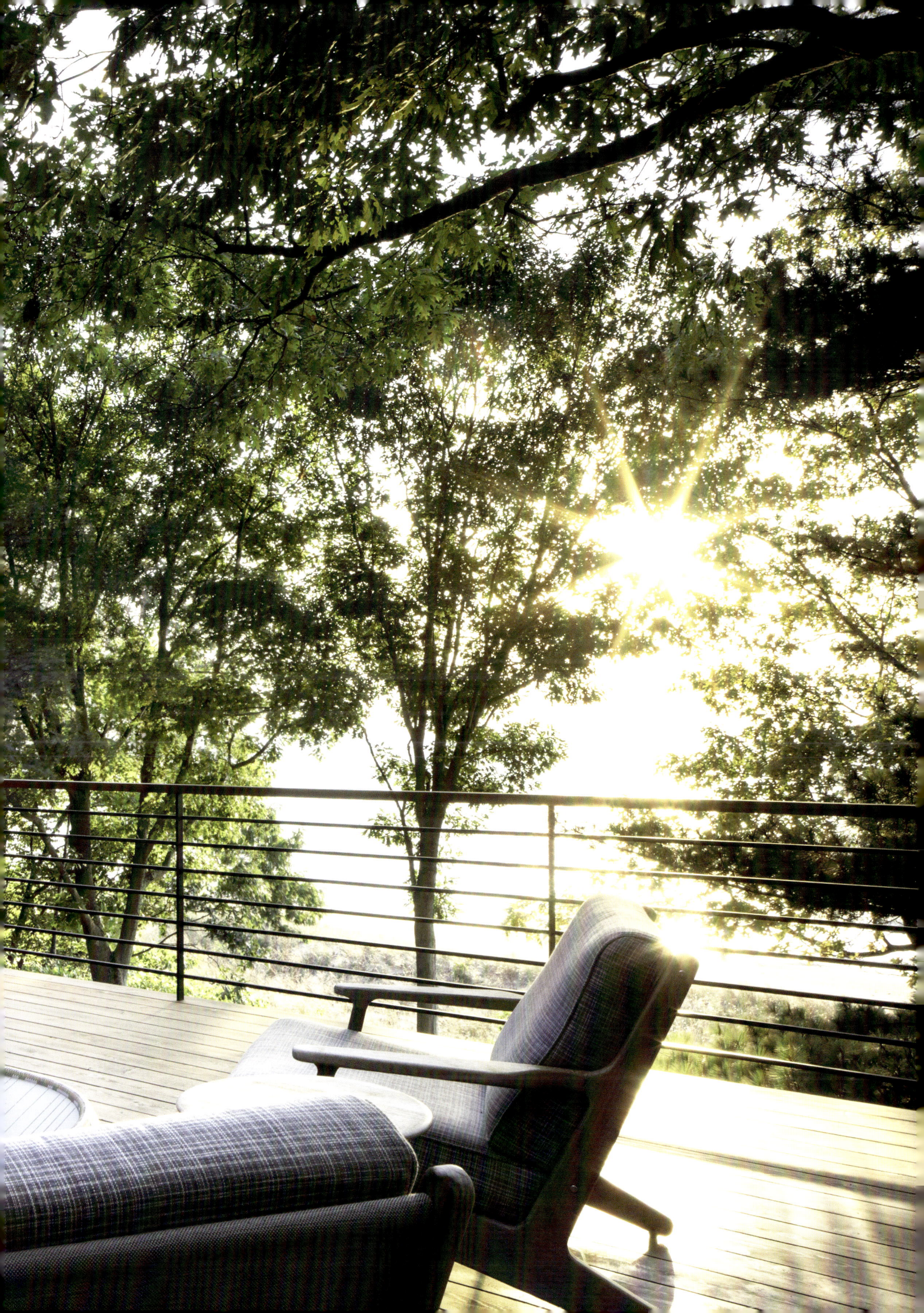

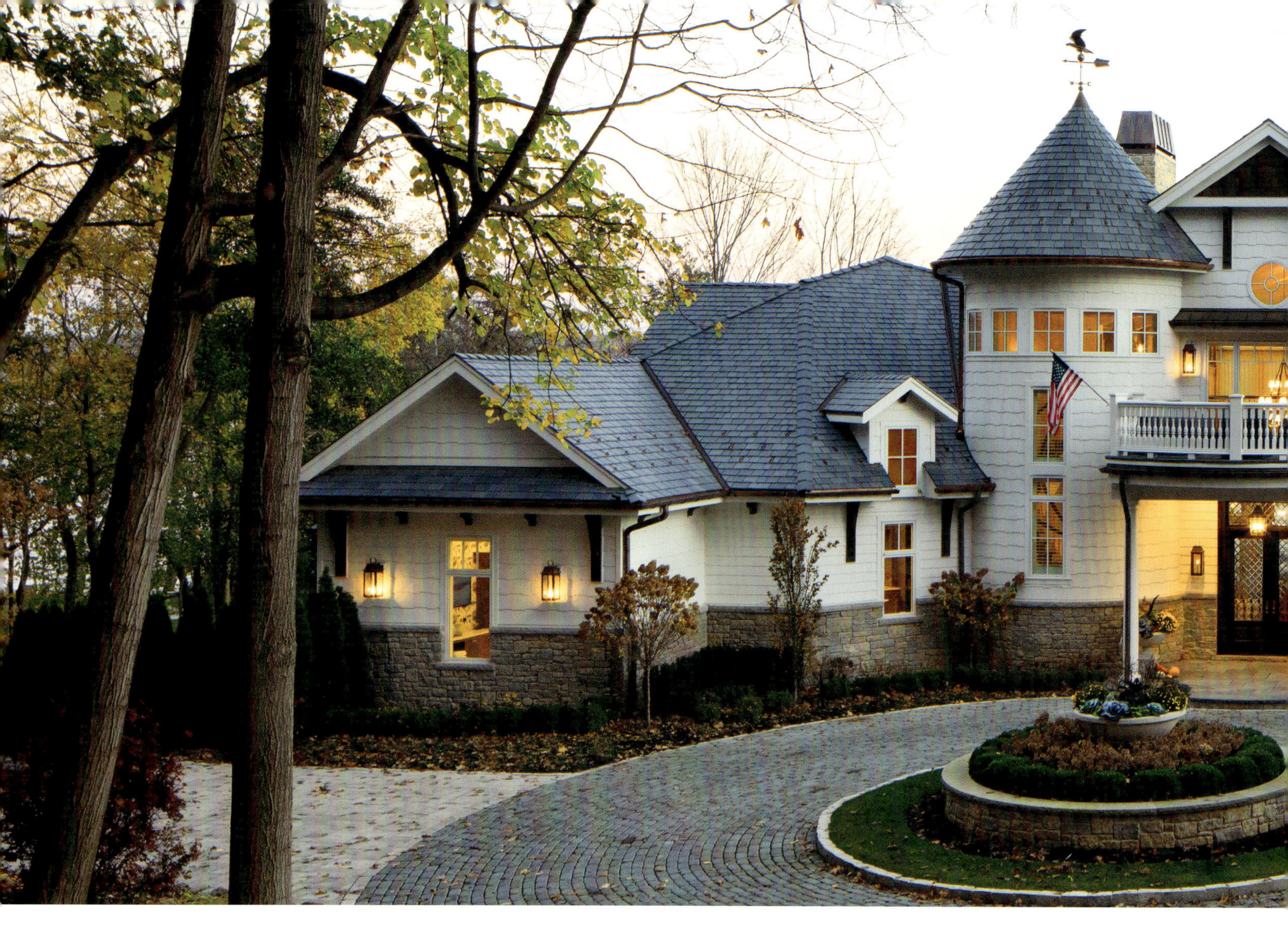

LAKESIDE REVERIE

Philip Sassano / The Design Coach

With its crystal-clear waters and historic legacy as a getaway for Chicago's elite, Lake Geneva provides a stunning backdrop for luxury homes that blend into the natural landscape. The area's unique character spotlights architecture that unites Midwestern warmth with resort sophistication and natural beauty.

On these coveted shores sits a remarkable 10,000-square-foot residence that embodies "Grand Cottage"—a design philosophy that scales inviting charm to opulent proportions. With its impressive 220 linear feet of shoreline, this lakeside retreat balances splendor with comfort.

The Design Coach designers, headed by Philip Sassano, asked the clients for specific moments they envisioned experiencing in the space—Sunday afternoons, Friday evening arrivals, extended stays—and reverse-engineered the design from these emotional touchpoints.

The home's lateral footprint allows each of the five bedrooms to enjoy lake views—a rarity in newer builds, which typically prioritize square footage by building upward. This parallel orientation to the shoreline creates a stately presence while preserving the intimate connection to the water.

The entryway features vertical woodwork rising 20 feet, complemented by carefully selected artwork that prevents the voluminous space from feeling empty. In the kitchen, marble tiles extend from countertop to ceiling, framing

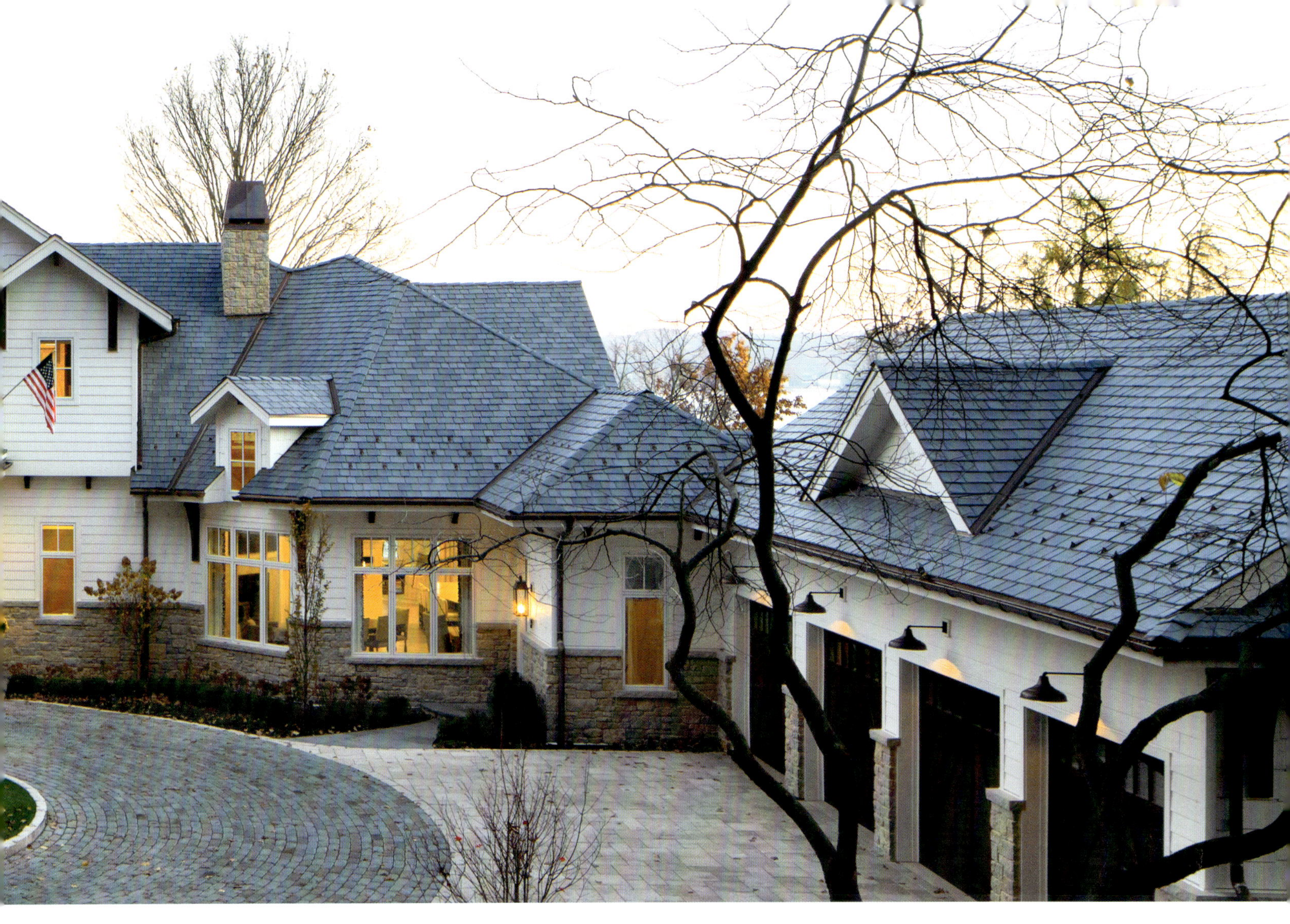

windows with minimal wood transitions, while a custom range hood is a focal point.

Reclaimed materials realize the client's desire for an established look. The mudroom floor features one-hundred-year-old reclaimed Chicago brick, thin-cut to maximize the historical material while providing durability—a subtle nod to the Midwestern mindset.

A whimsical "boat bar," crafted by Larry Lang and patterned after the historic vessels that tour Geneva Lake, is made from authentic boat materials, from mahogany detailing to marine hardware. This "Gilded Lady" adds nautical character to the entertainment space.

Though initially conceived as a weekend and summer retreat, the home has become a year-round escape from suburban life. Here, the owners can "lose a month" in comfort and style, surrounded by tailored elegance that never sacrifices livability.

Nestled on Lake Geneva's shore, this residence showcases DaVinci faux slate roofing, authentic copper gutters and chimney shrouds, elegant bluestone pavers, and a porch, with HB&G railings and Bevolo lighting accentuating its timeless lakeside charm.

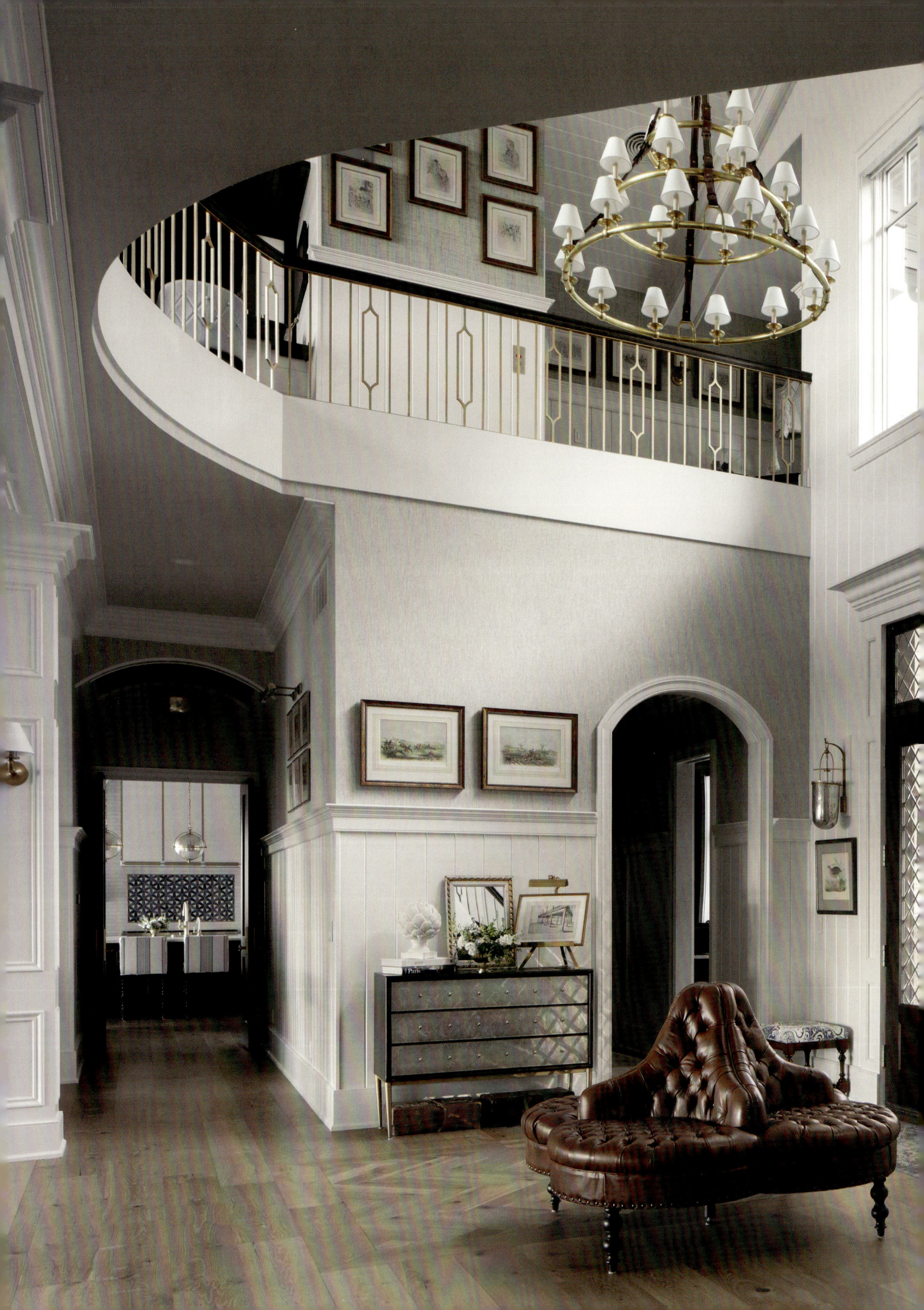

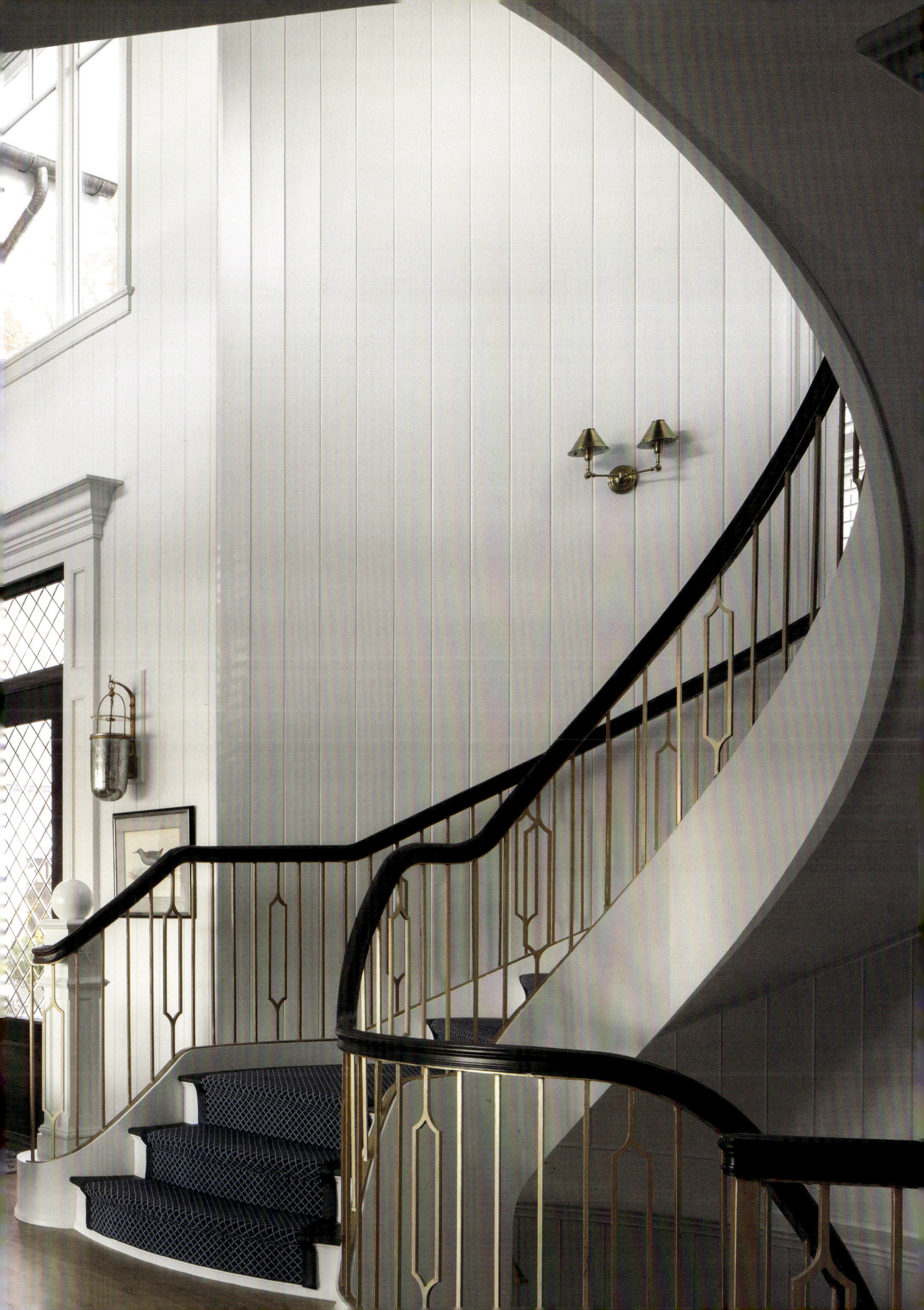

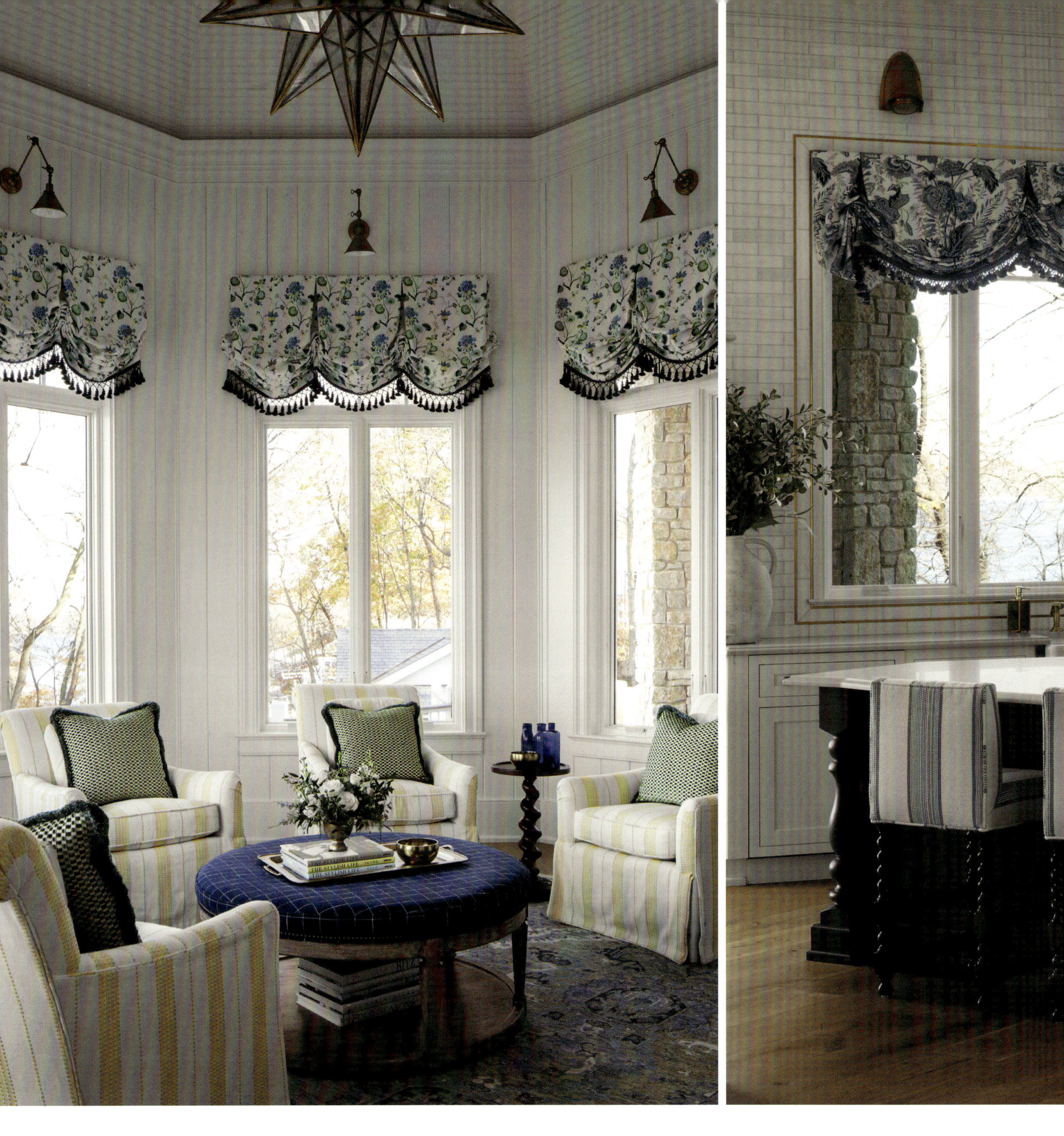

PREVIOUS: The soaring 20-foot entryway features floor-to-ceiling vertical woodwork and a staircase with elegant metal spindles. Carefully curated artwork prevents the grand space from feeling cavernous, while a round seating piece inspired by New Orleans hospitality furniture adds functional warmth.

ABOVE: The kitchen showcases floor-to-ceiling marble tile, custom framing around windows, and a statement range hood. Adjacent, the former dining space was reimagined as a sunny "morning room" with comfortable seating, transforming an occasionally used breakfast nook into an all-day gathering spot.

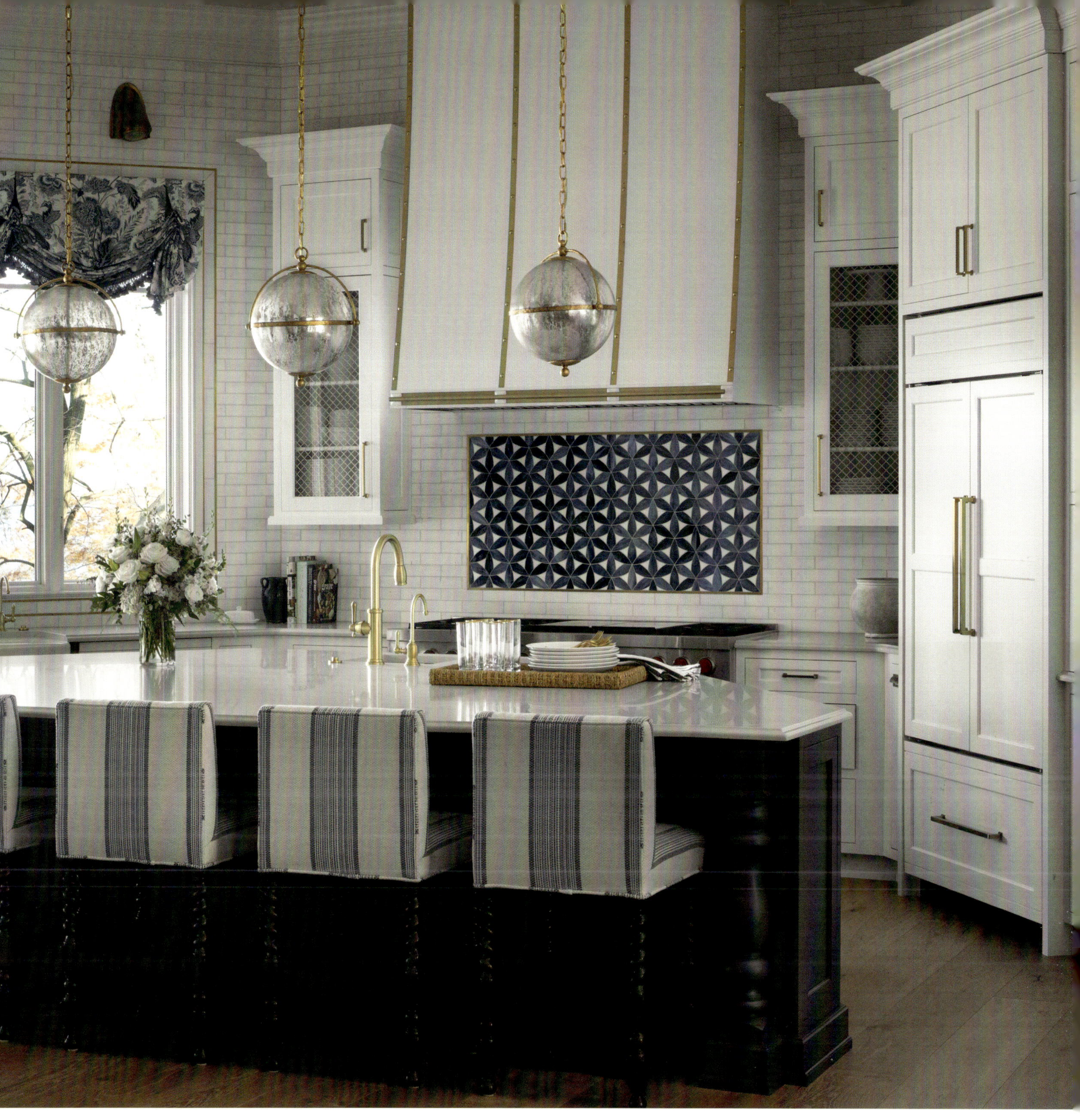

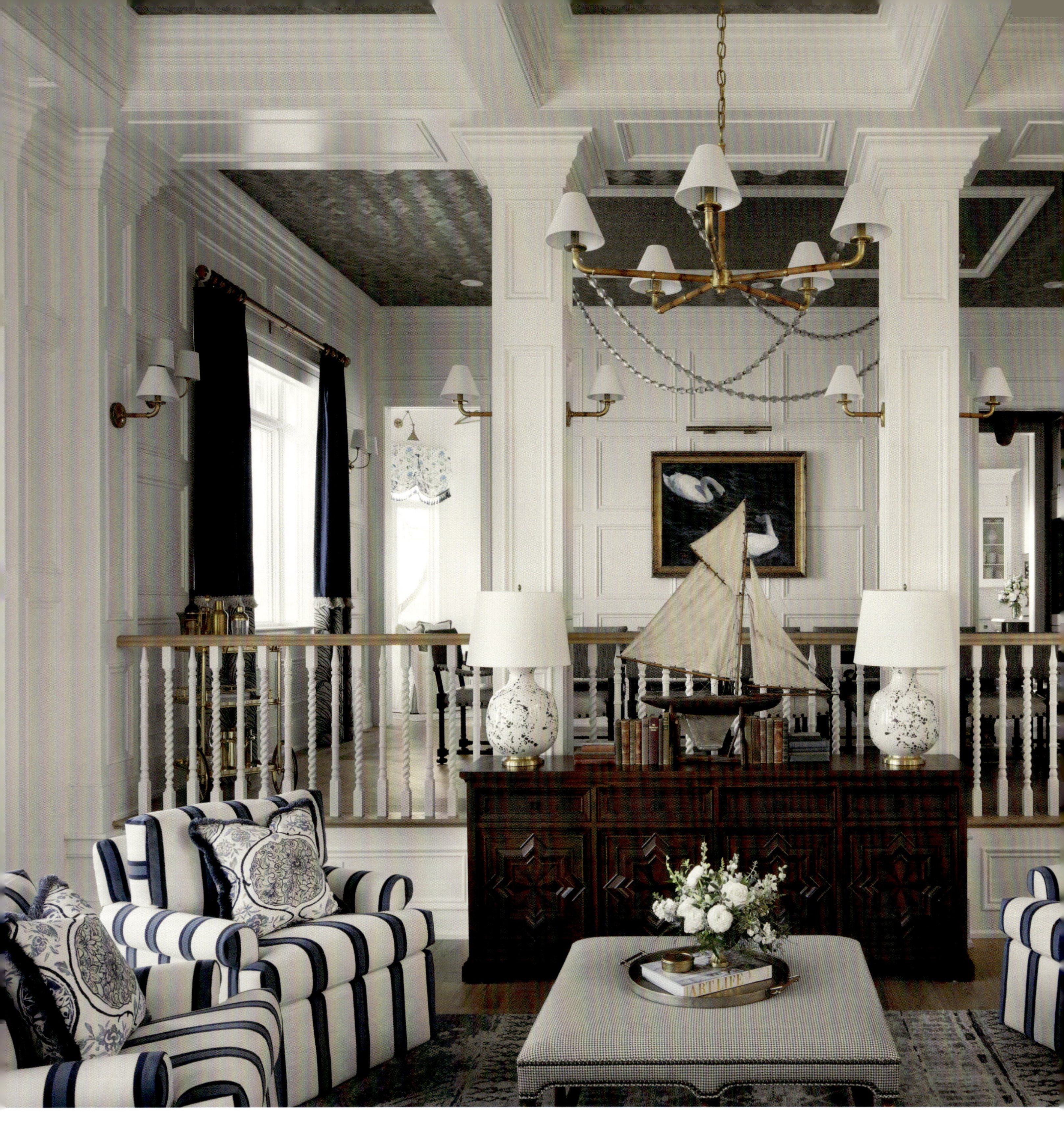

The millwork-rich dining room is elevated from the lake room and connected by columns with integrated lighting. Ralph Lauren fixtures crown the dining space, while Thibaut blue-and-white striped indoor/outdoor fabric and Schumacher accents create an elegant yet informal atmosphere where lakeside views dominate.

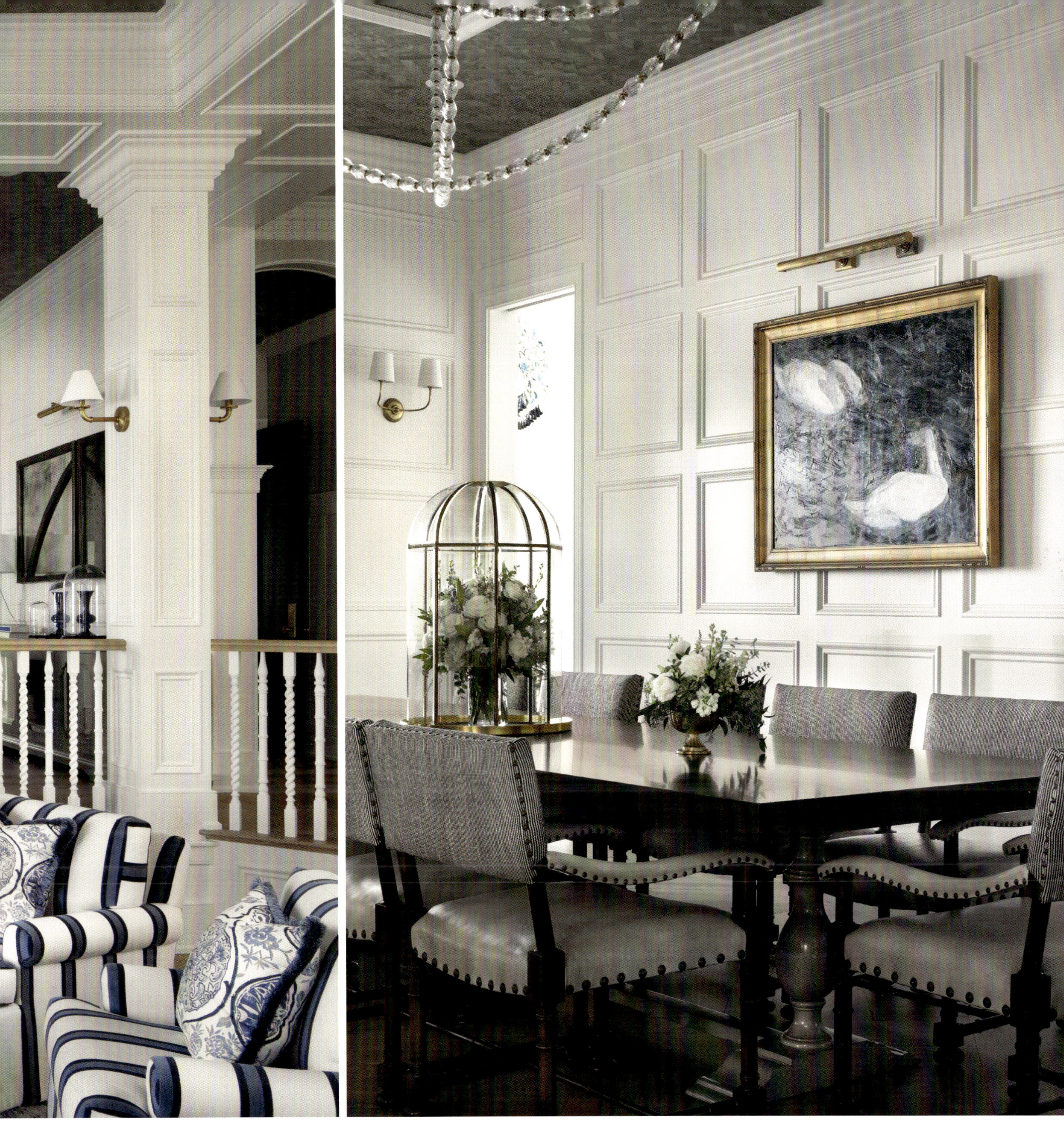

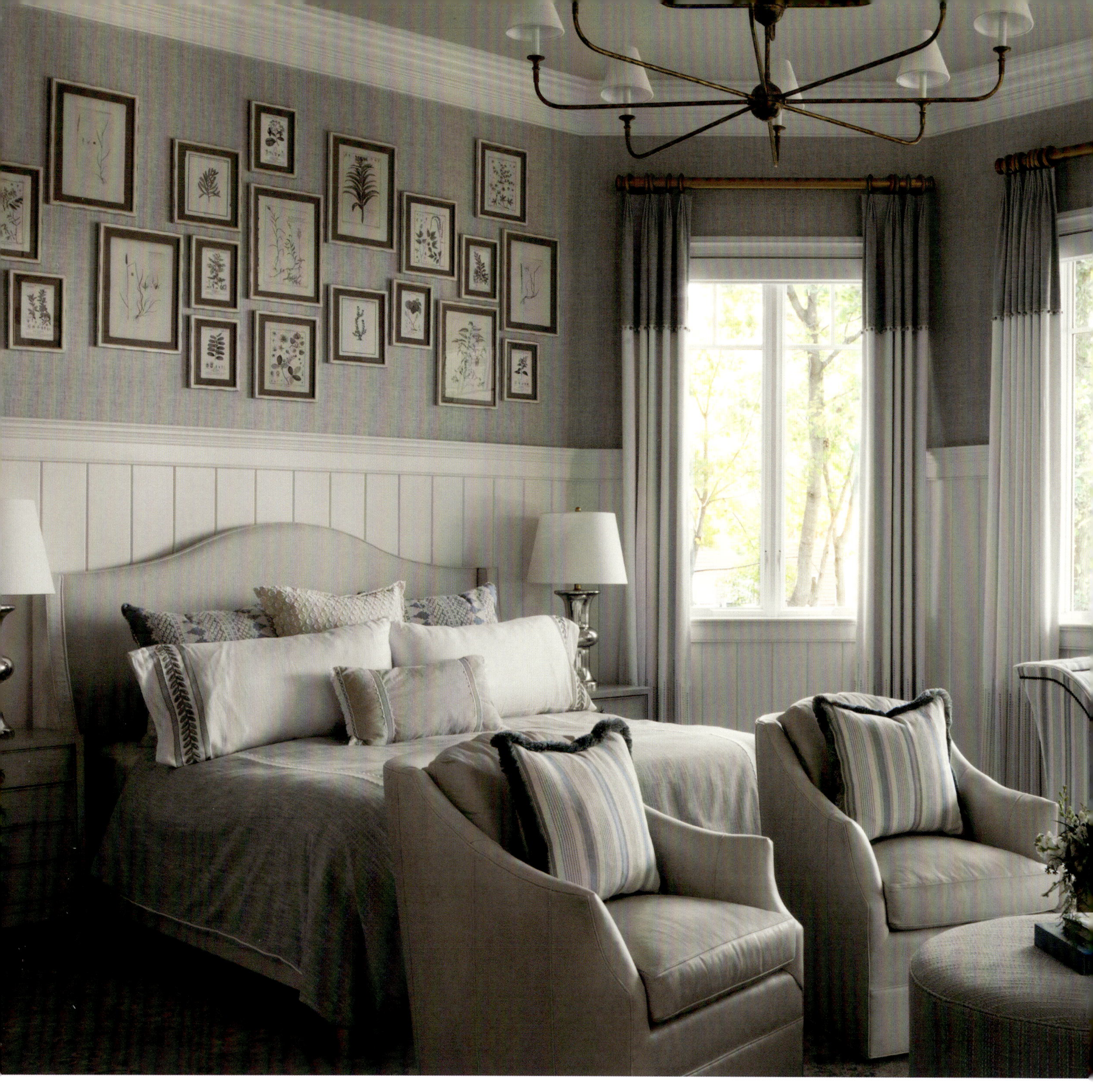

Left: Inspired by vintage French botanical prints from the 1850s, this spacious primary bedroom features a central seating area anchored by a fireplace opposite chairs fronting the bed. It is part of a more extensive suite that includes a gentleman's quarters. ***Right:*** The elegant powder room showcases Phillip Jeffries's gold-accented grass-cloth wall covering and a striking blue vanity.

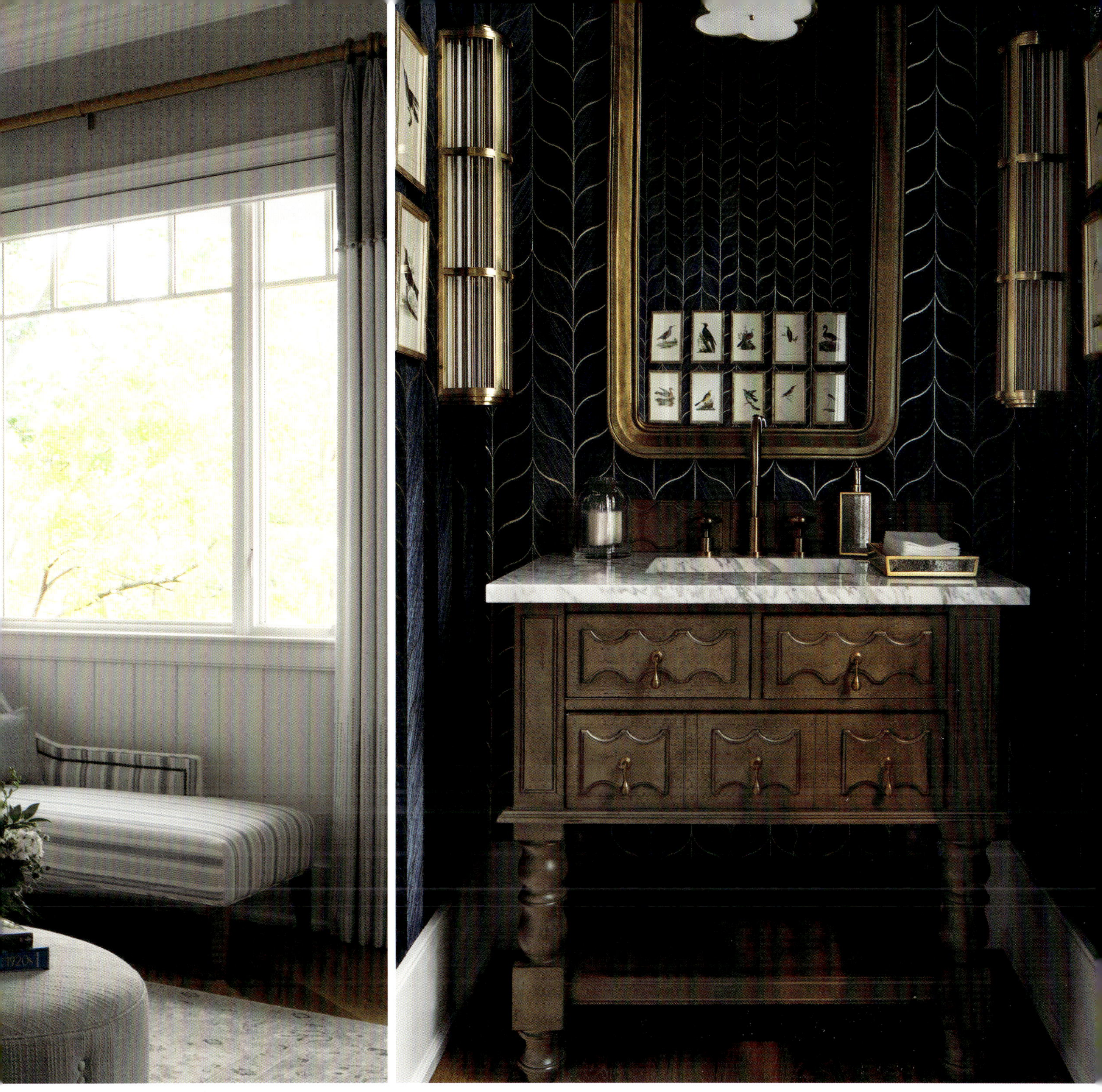

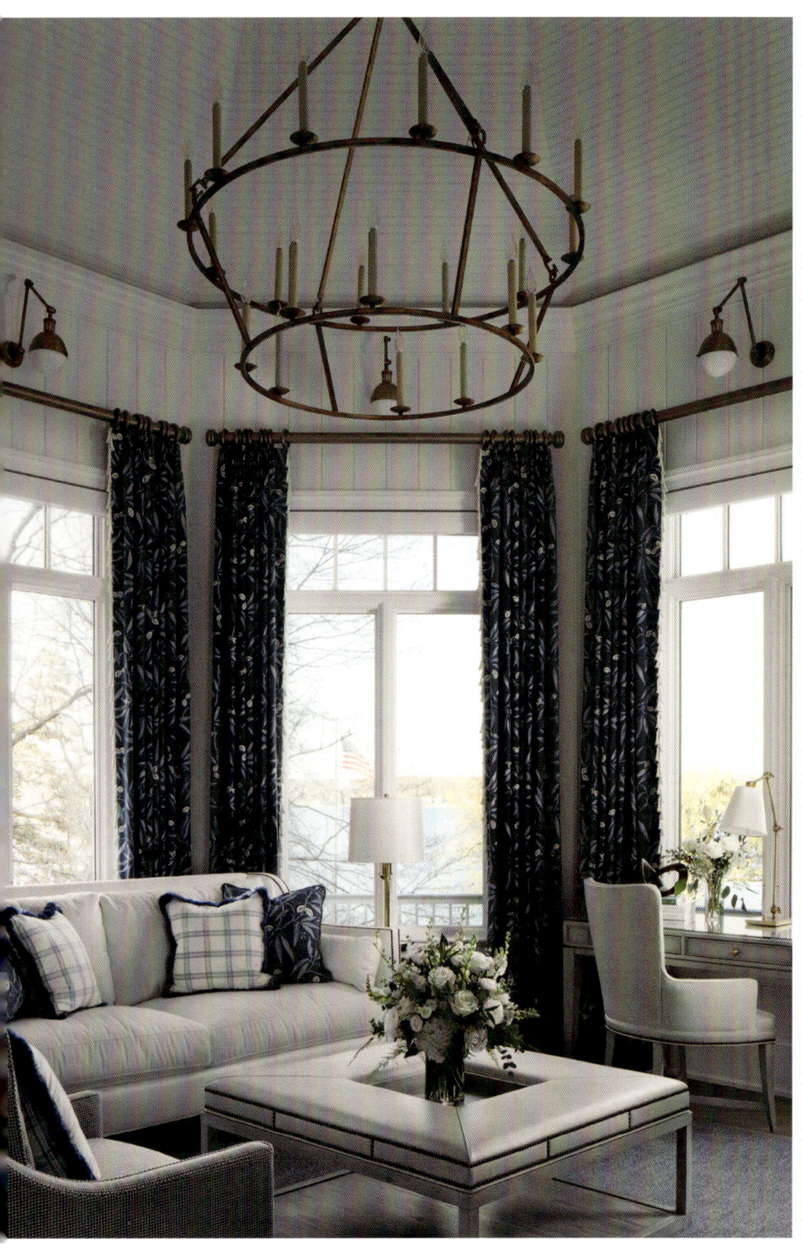

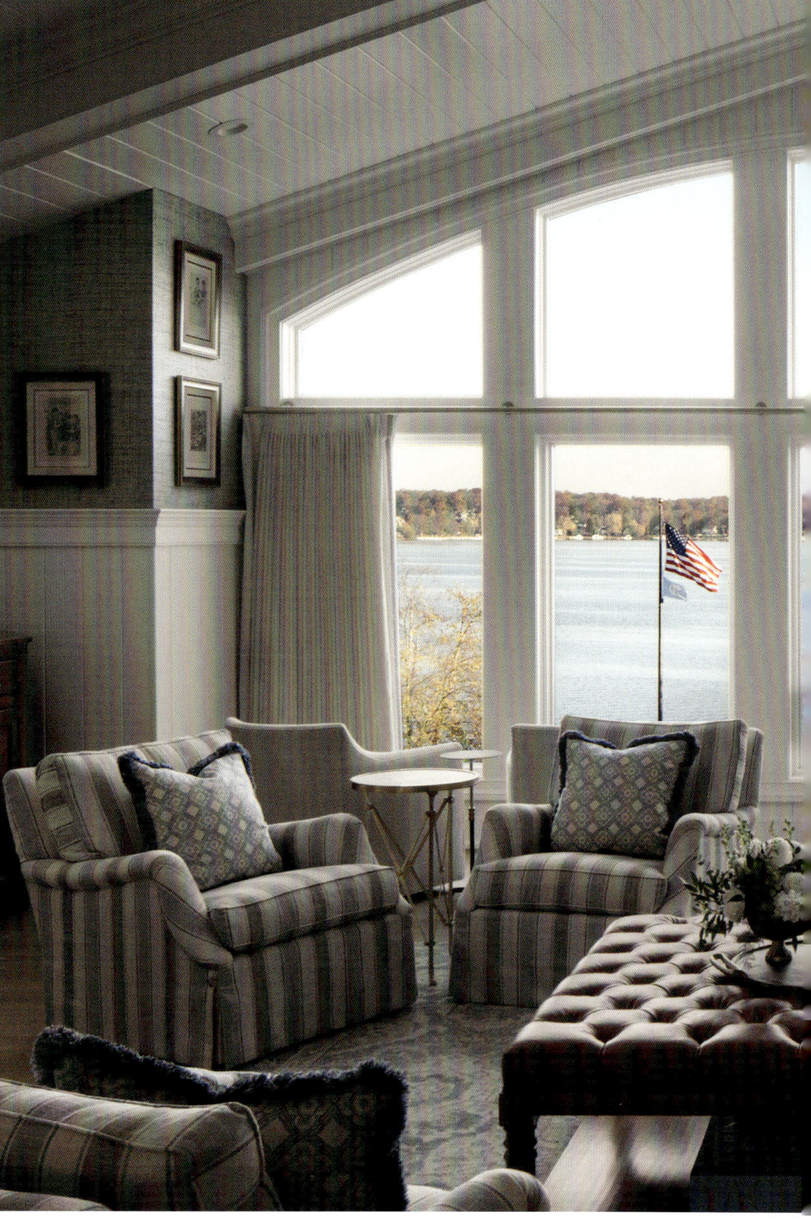

Left: The primary sitting room creates an elegant transition between the main bedroom and the gentleman's quarters. *Center:* The lofted living room showcases spectacular lake views and a classic wooden boat bar for gatherings large and small. *Right:* The mudroom features rare reclaimed century-old Chicago brick, discovered just 45 miles away in Rockford.

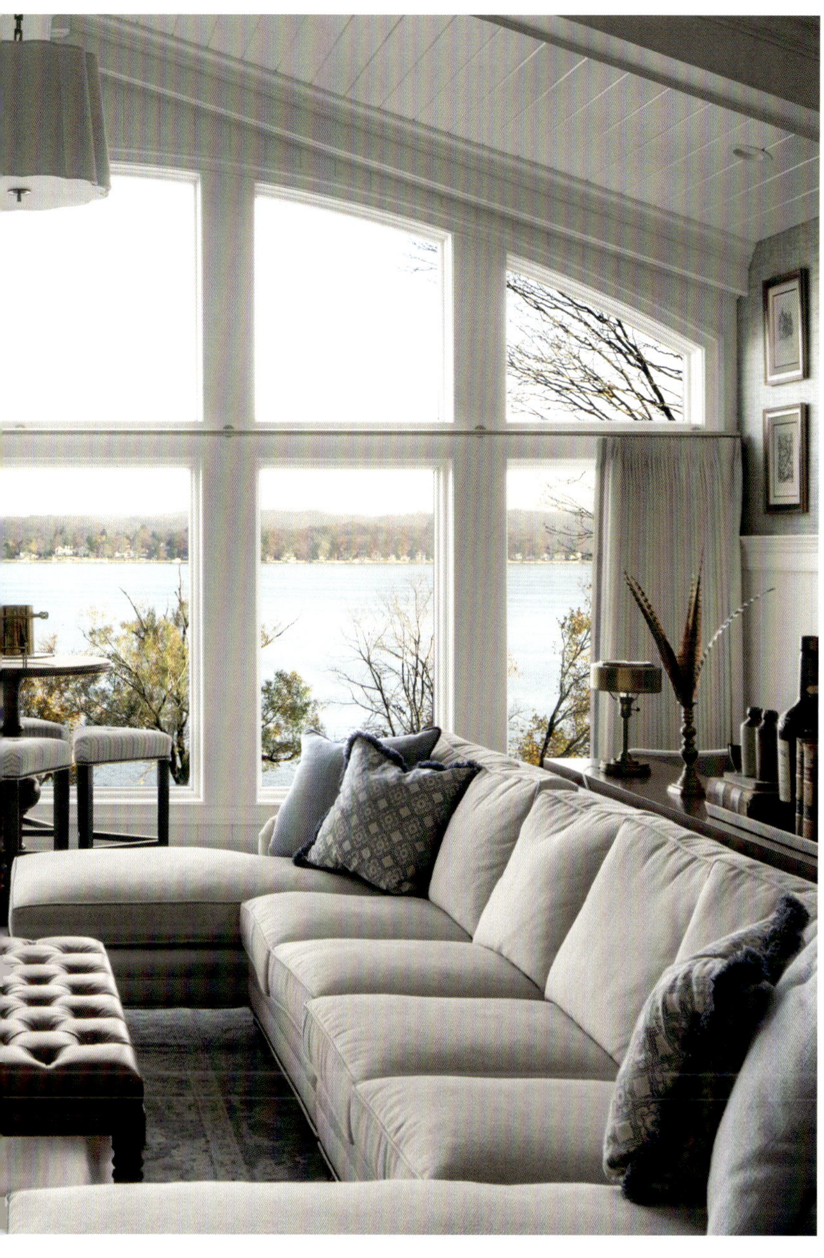

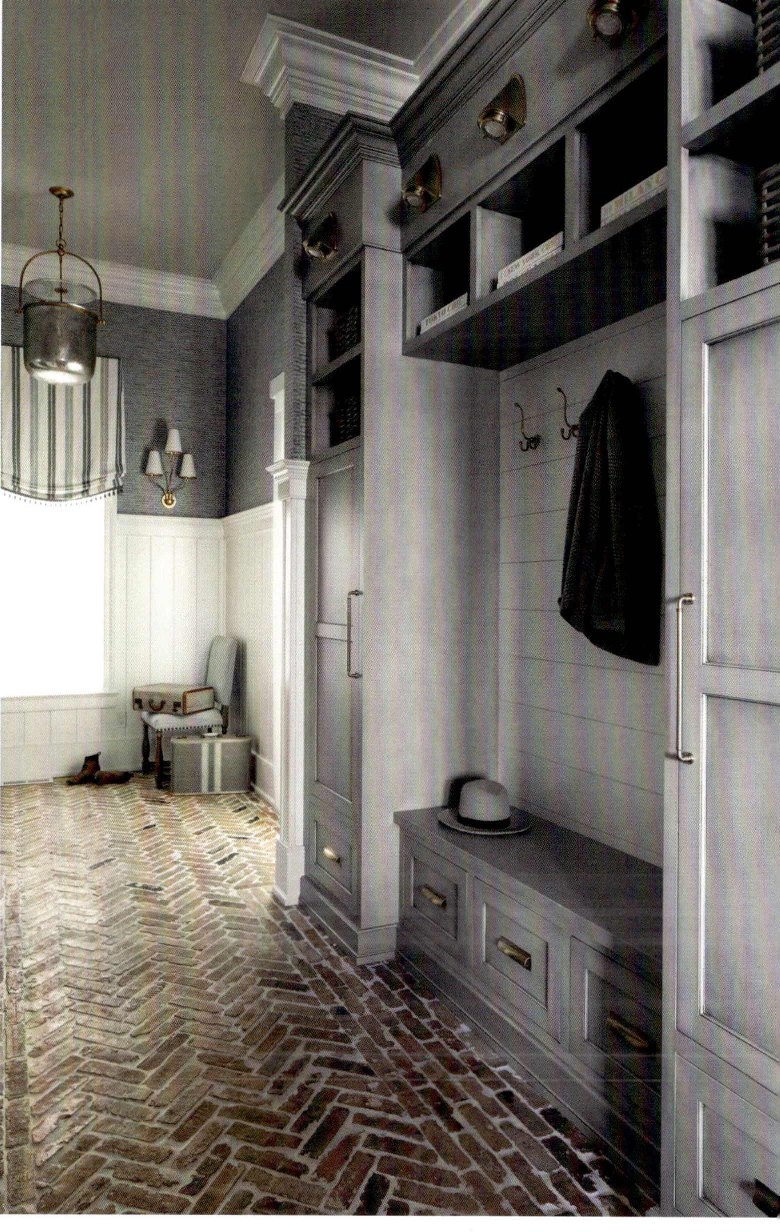

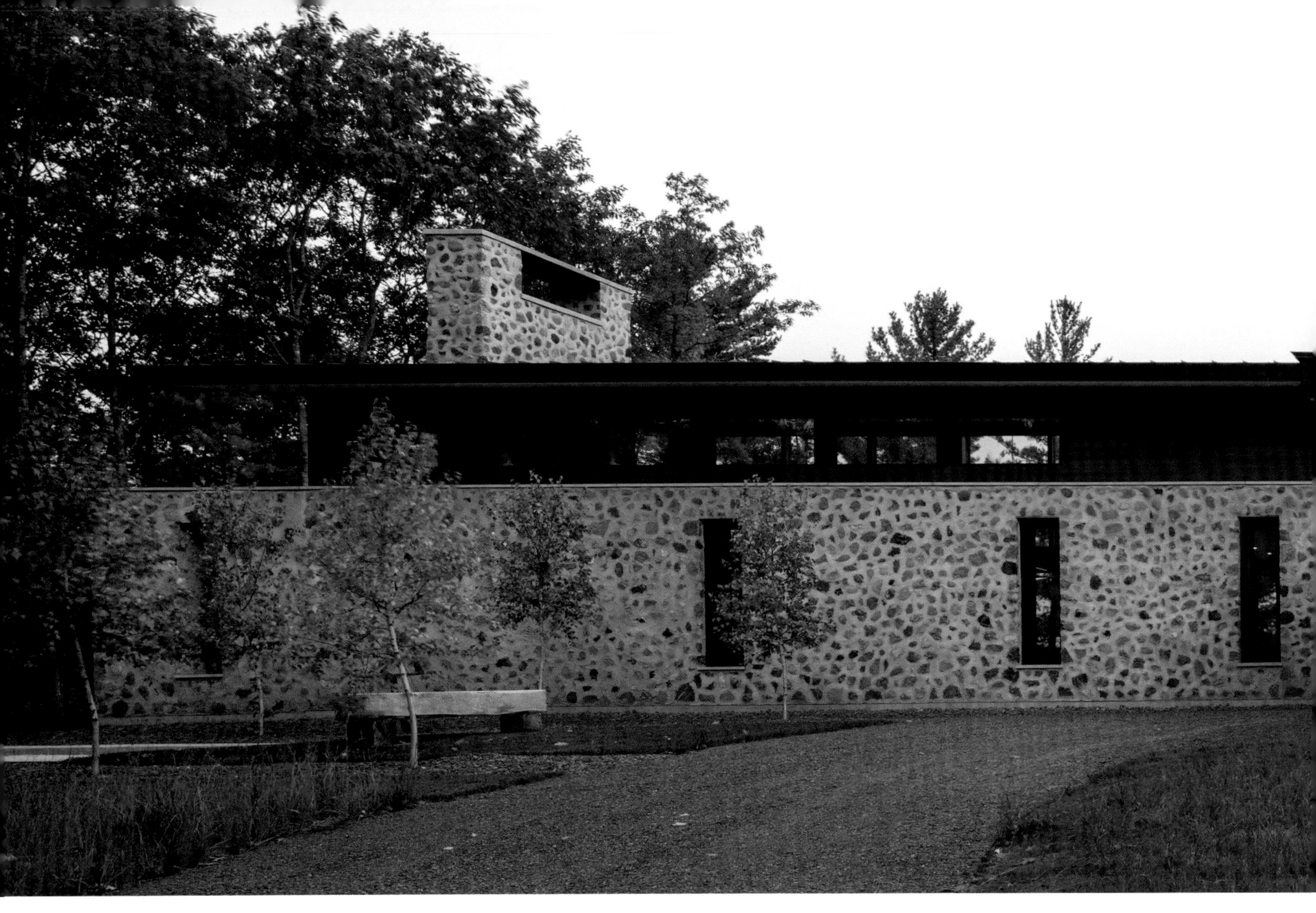

LEGACY ON THE LAKE

Amy Carman / John Vetter

Camp Spirit Lake represents the culmination of a decade-long relationship between architect John Vetter, interior designer Amy Carman, and their clients in Lac du Flambeau. What began as a comprehensive master plan evolved into a striking central gathering space that transformed from a secondary residence into the family's primary home following the pandemic.

The clients, who had previously worked with Vetter on neighboring property renovations, acquired this adjacent land to create a legacy home where the extended family could gather for generations. The owners affectionately referred to their vision as a "VFW post" or lodge—a modern interpretation of northern Wisconsin's rustic cabin tradition.

Architecturally, Vetter drew inspiration from Wisconsin's camp and farmhouse vernacular, reimagined through a minimalist modern lens. Flanking the central lodge are three identical cottage-like guest quarters, each carefully proportioned to maintain visual harmony. Indigenous materials ground the building in its location; locally sourced Wisconsin fieldstone forms a substantial base that anchors the structure, continuing inside to create the central fireplace, which serves as the gathering space's focal point. An extensive window system creates seamless indoor-outdoor connections, while a standing-seam metal roof nods to the region's agricultural buildings.

Interior designer Amy Carman faced the challenge of reimagining northern Wisconsin's cabin aesthetic without

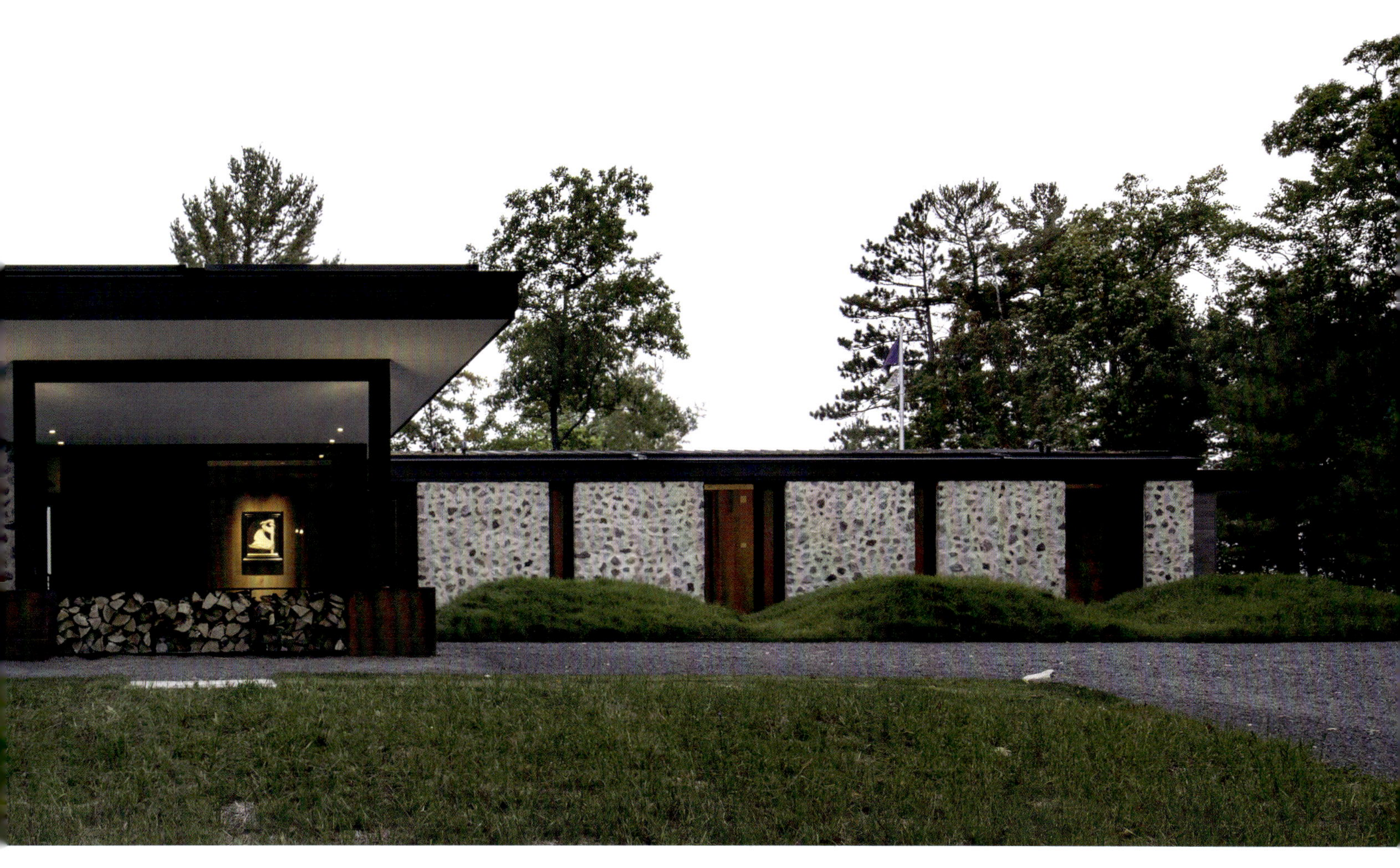

resorting to clichés. She opted for sophisticated rift-sawn white oak throughout rather than traditional knotty pine, respecting camp architecture while elevating it. The three guest suites feature built-in beds, en suite bathrooms, custom wardrobes, and private entrances to the backyard.

In the lower-level bowling alley, Carman offset the lack of natural light with a built-in movie screen that is connected to a lakefront camera. "Surveillance art," as the owner calls it, allows guests to watch lake activities while enjoying indoor recreation alongside the arcade, bar, and sauna.

Through their collaborative vision, Vetter and Carman achieved what the architect describes as a "holistic" experience—a thoughtful balance between architectural authenticity and interior innovation that makes Camp Spirit Lake not merely a home but a destination for memory making, perfectly fulfilling its owners' desire for a place where families can gather for generations.

The home's front elevation showcases locally sourced Wisconsin field stone, which weights the structure to the ground while creating a dialogue with the interior. The curving entry drive adds a juxtapositional geometric note.

NEXT: The spacious living area features an Italian Molteni&C wool sectional paired with a Rietveld-designed Cassina lounge chair. Beyond, Mike Dreeben's custom 12-foot solid walnut dining table sits beneath David Weeks's spear-like steel chandelier, while a striking woven tapestry of Mexican pesos adorns the wall.

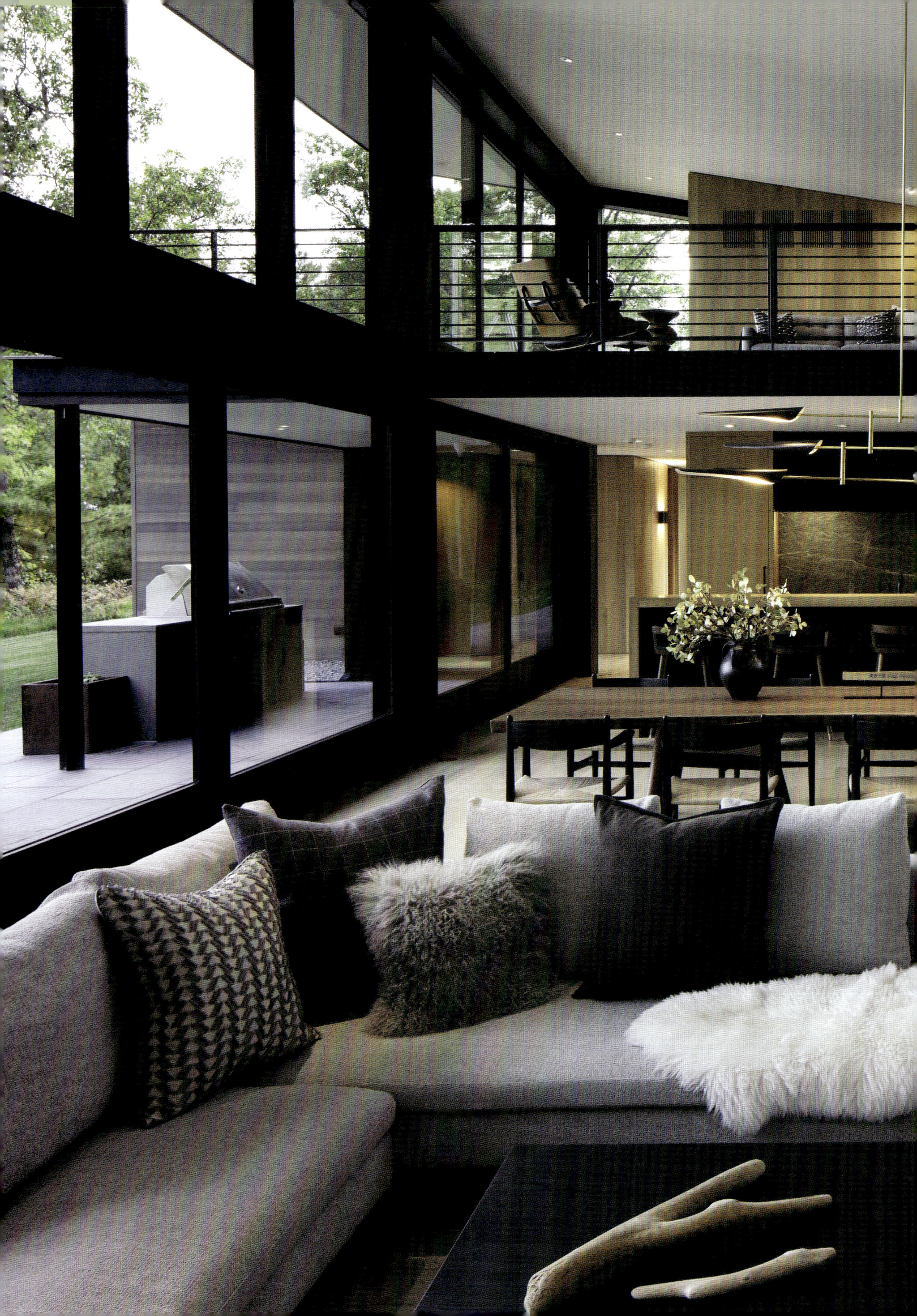

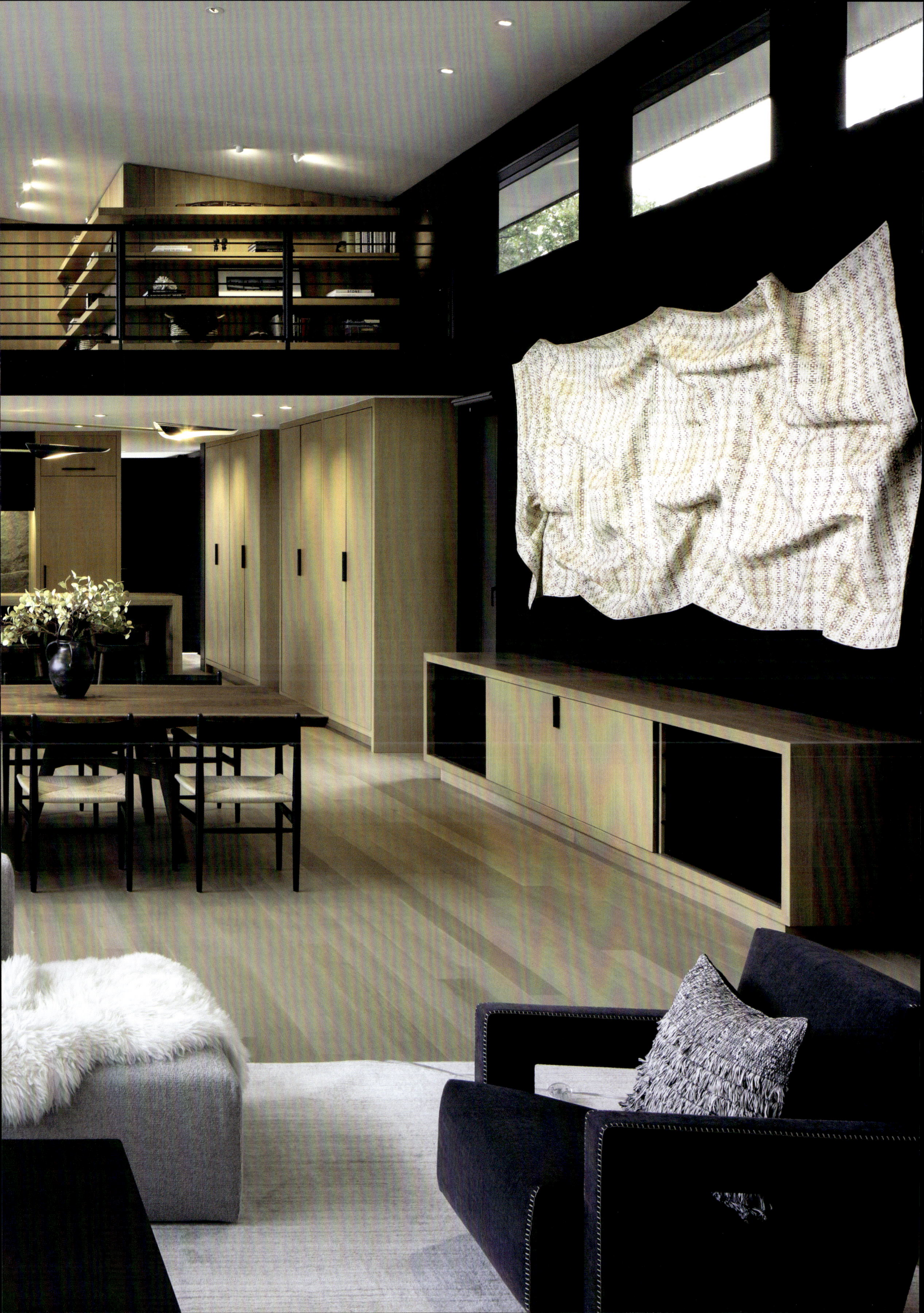

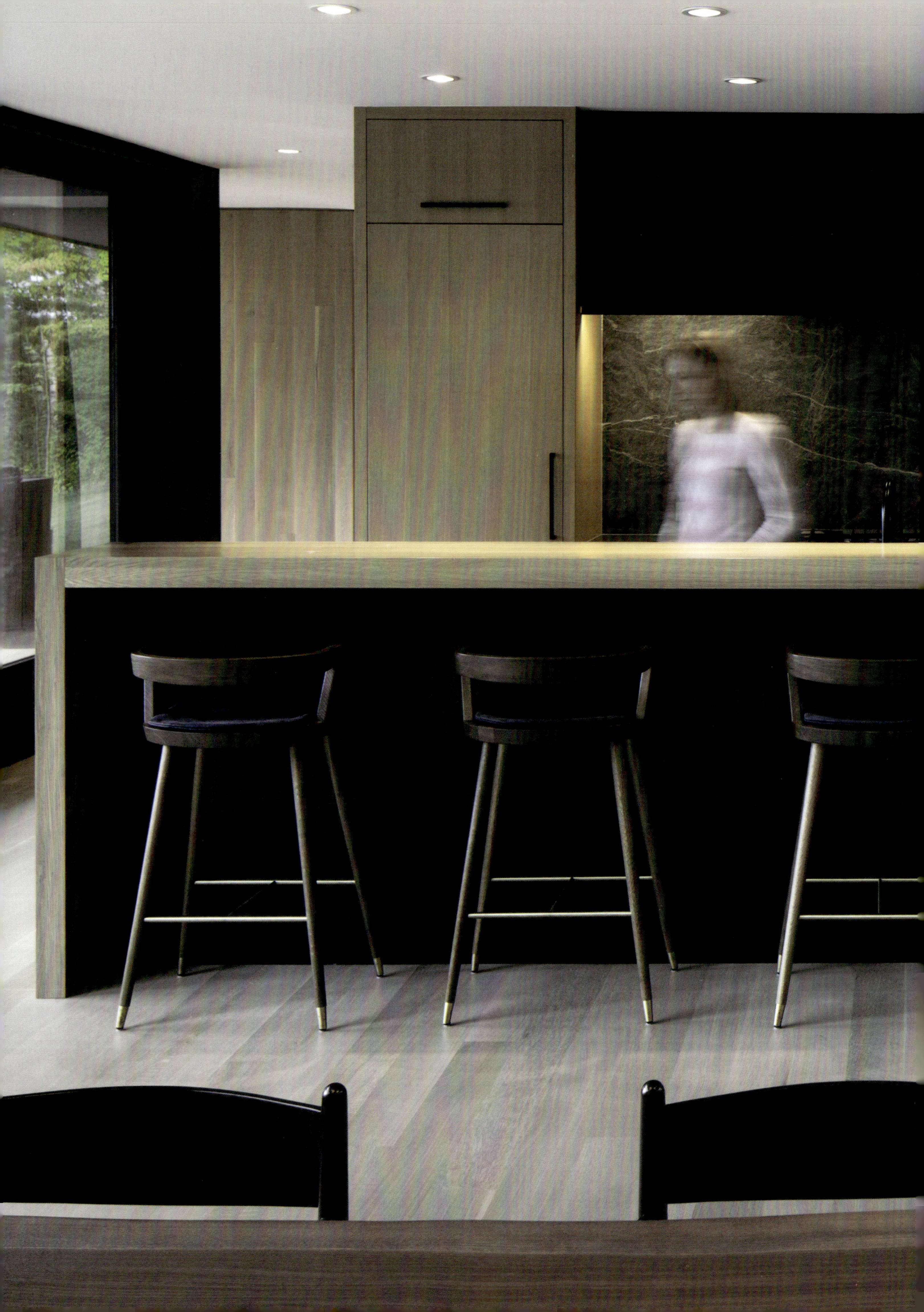

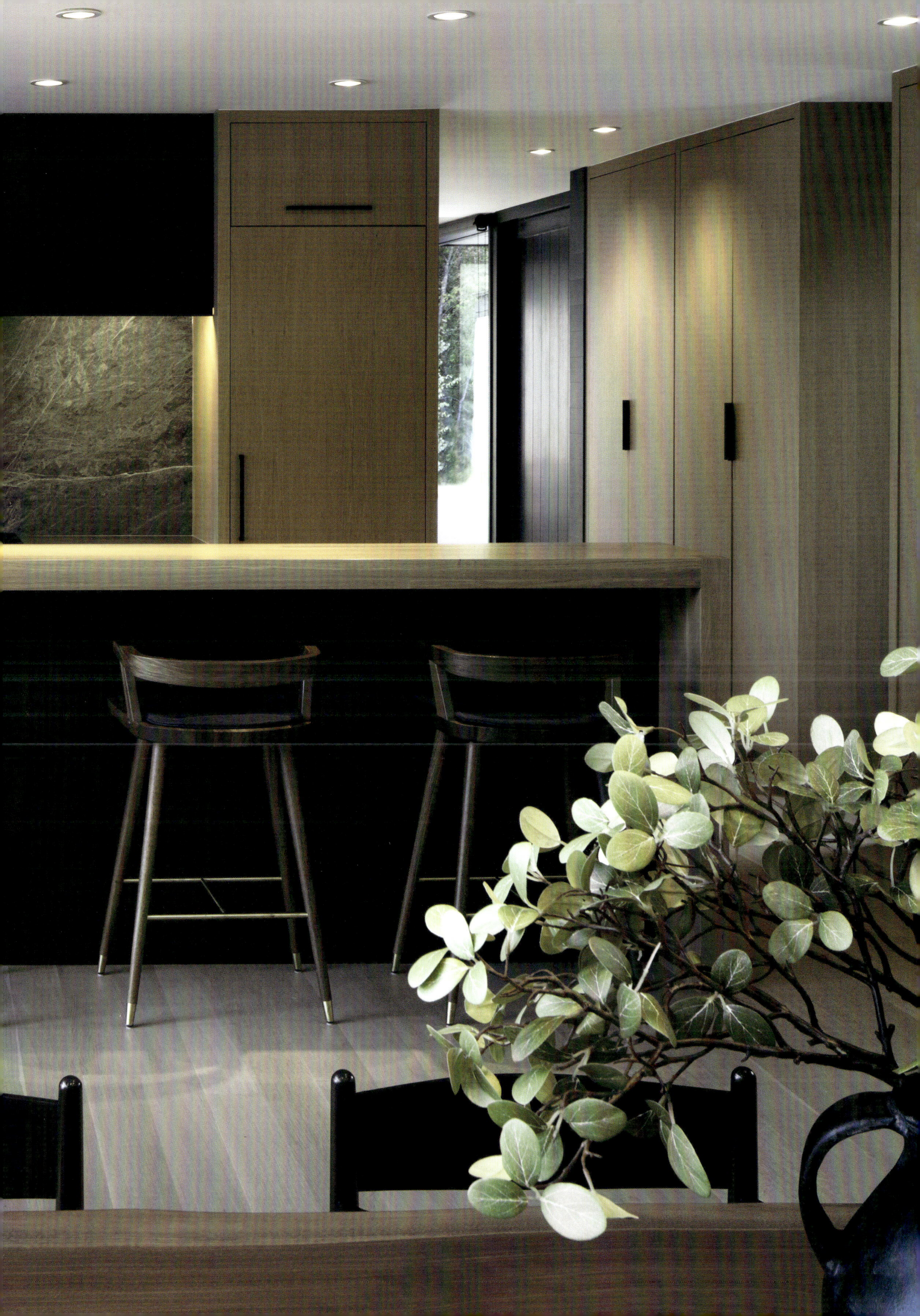

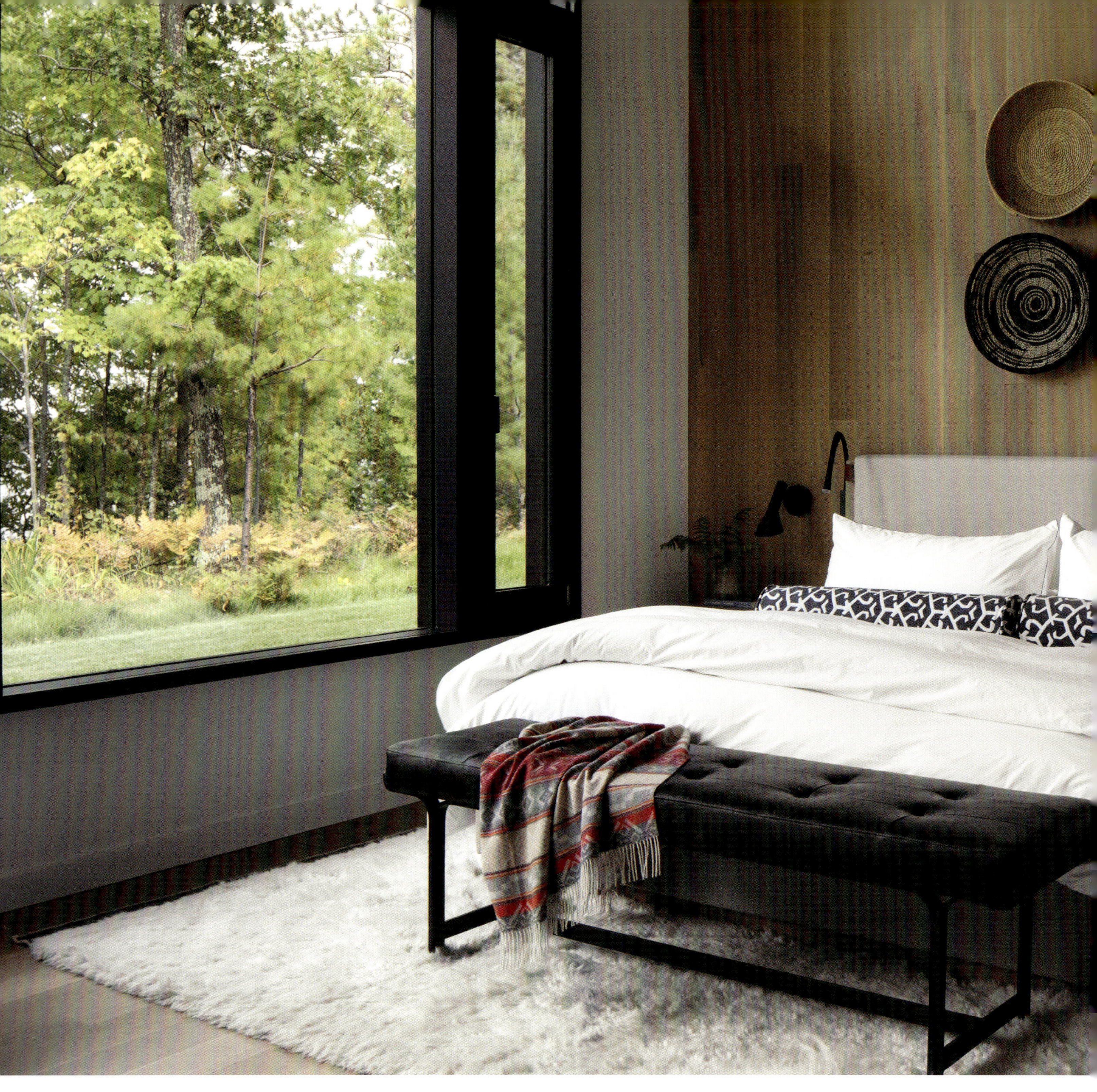

PREVIOUS: Designed in white oak, burnished steel, and Atlantic quartzite, this distinguished central kitchen features a raised counter of solid white oak with impressive interlocking dovetails at the corners. It comfortably accommodates five guests for casual dining.

ABOVE: Each of Camp Spirit Lake's three identical guest suites offers the refined comforts of a boutique hotel: custom-made beds with floating nightstands, built-in desks and wardrobes, fully appointed baths, cozy seating areas, and private lakeside walkouts.

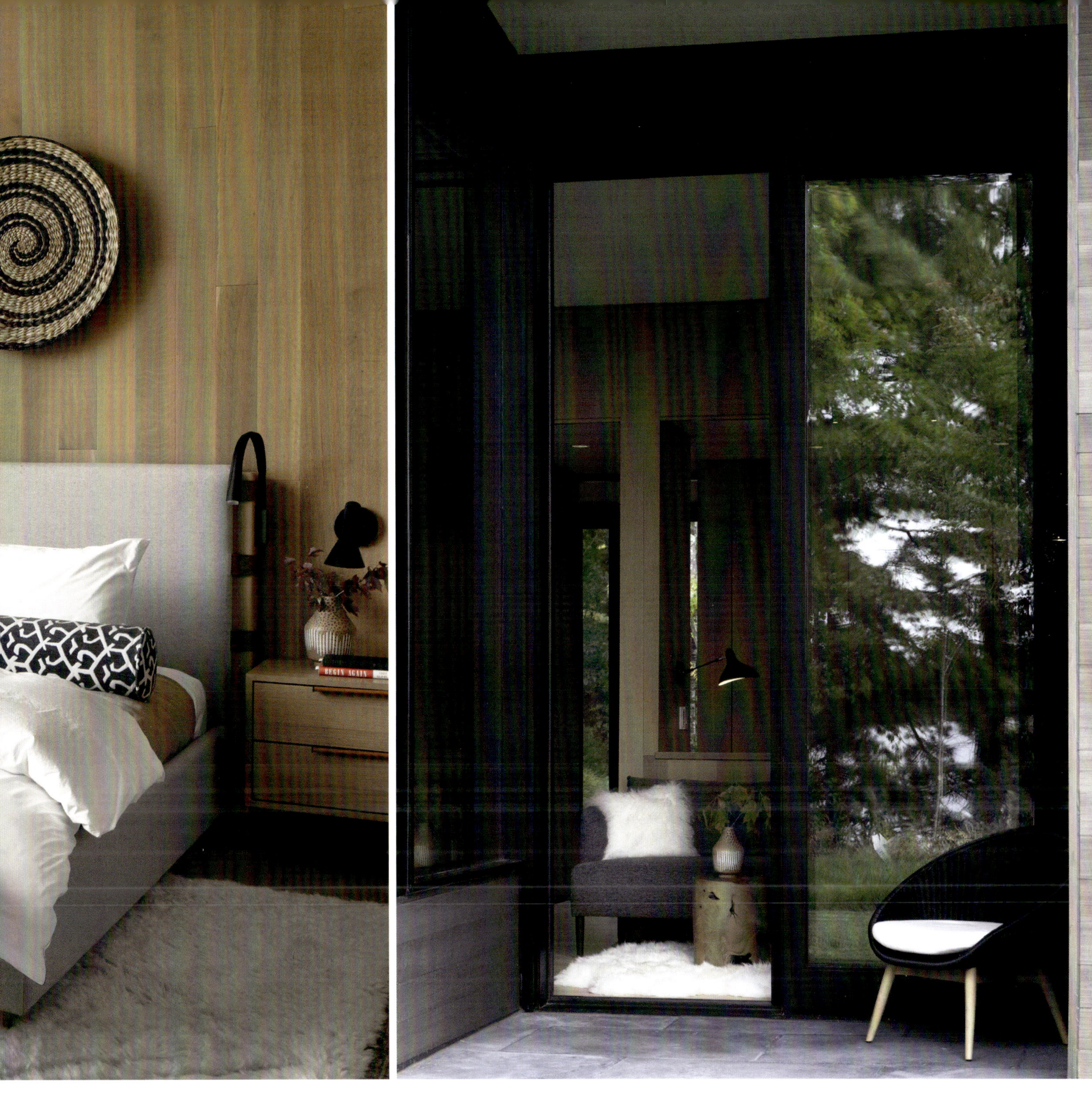
BEGIN AGAIN

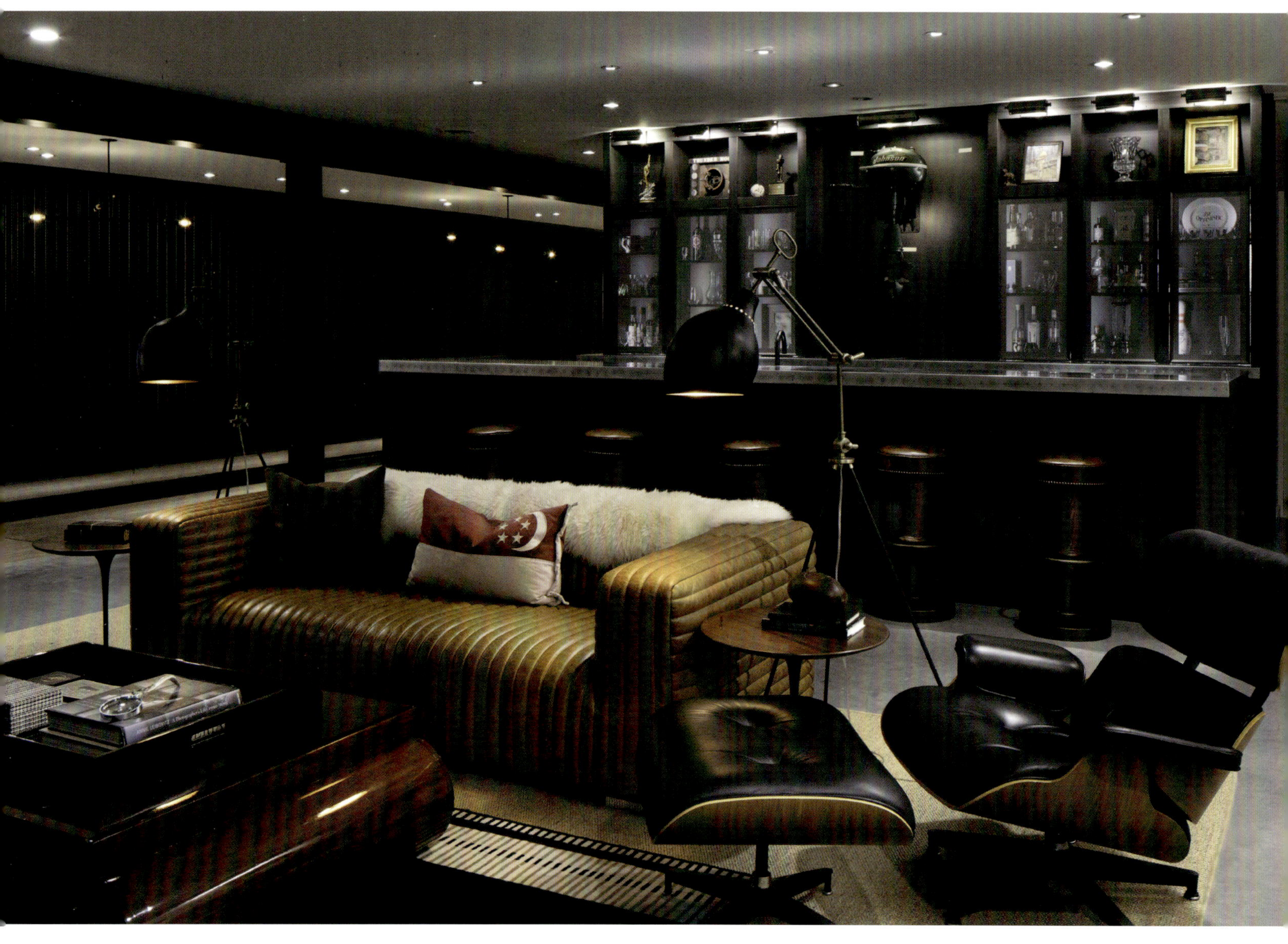

ABOVE: The lower-level entertainment zone features two full-length automated bowling lanes for family tournaments alongside vintage pinball machines. A zinc-topped bar anchors the space, complemented by perforated metal cabinetry displaying family artifacts and a leather sofa with channel stitching echoing the maple bowling lanes.

NEXT: The lakeside home nestles harmoniously among surrounding trees. Expansive glass blurs indoor-outdoor boundaries while a standing-seam metal roof completes this modern interpretation of traditional northern vernacular, leading seamlessly to the dock.

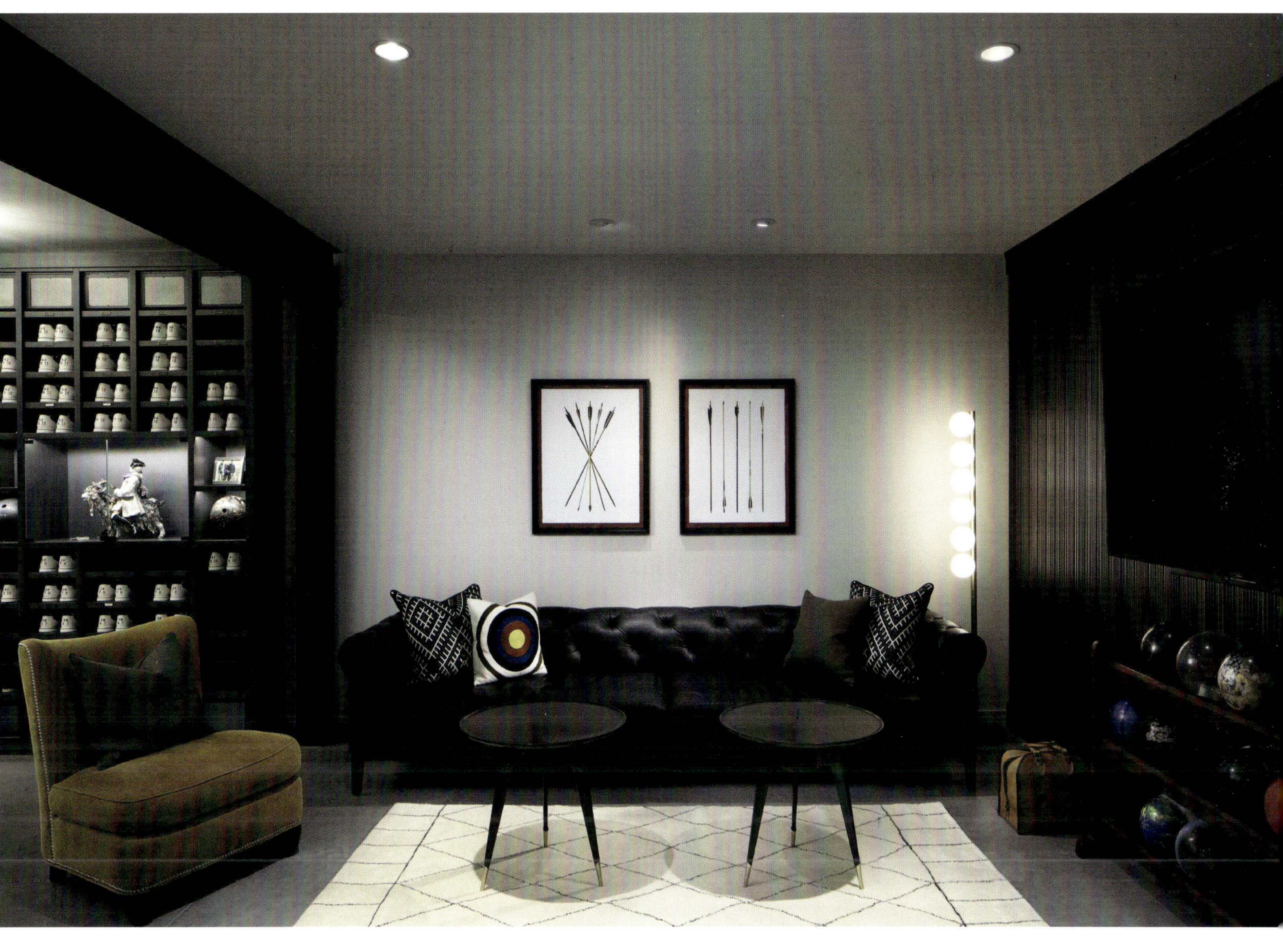

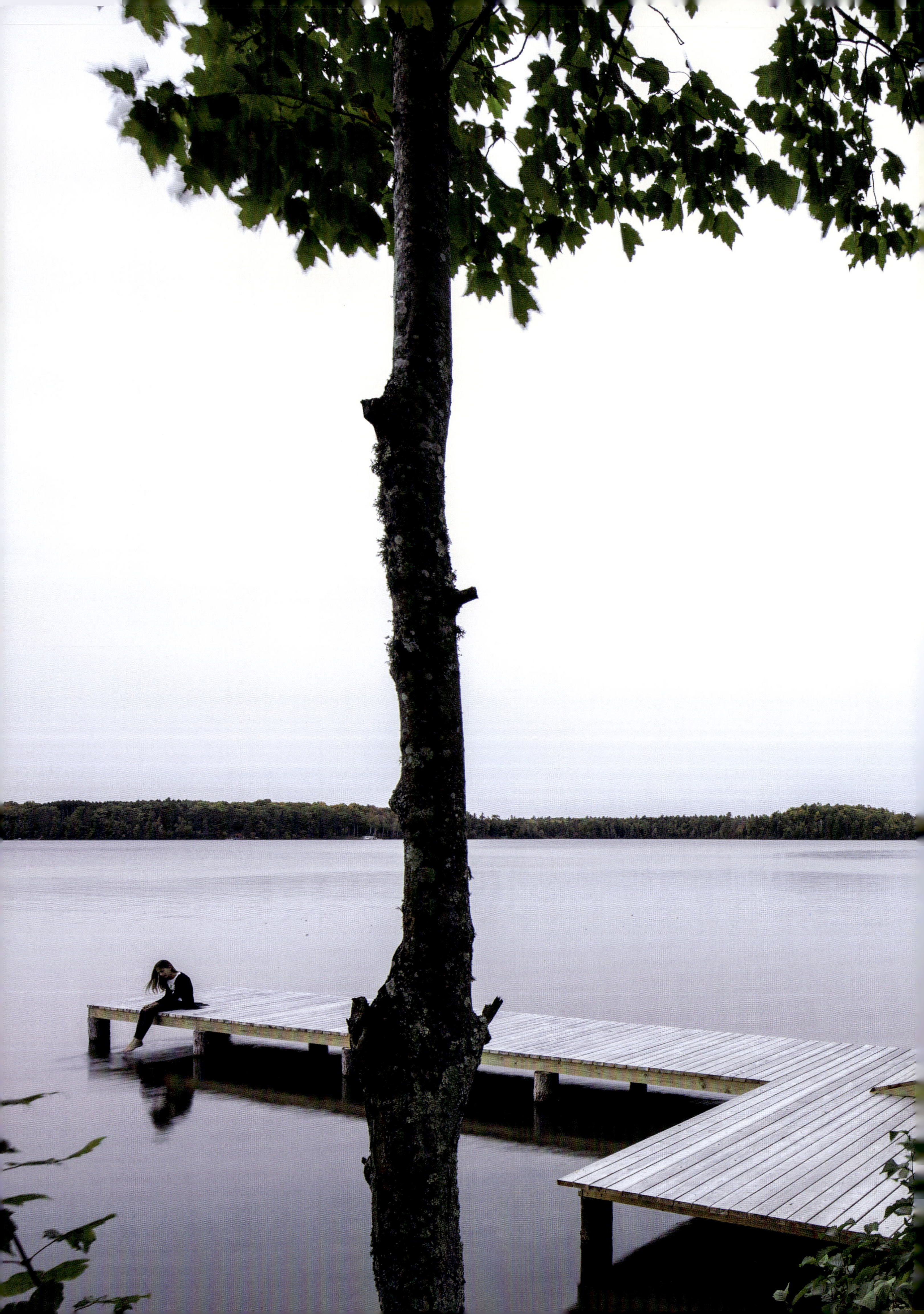

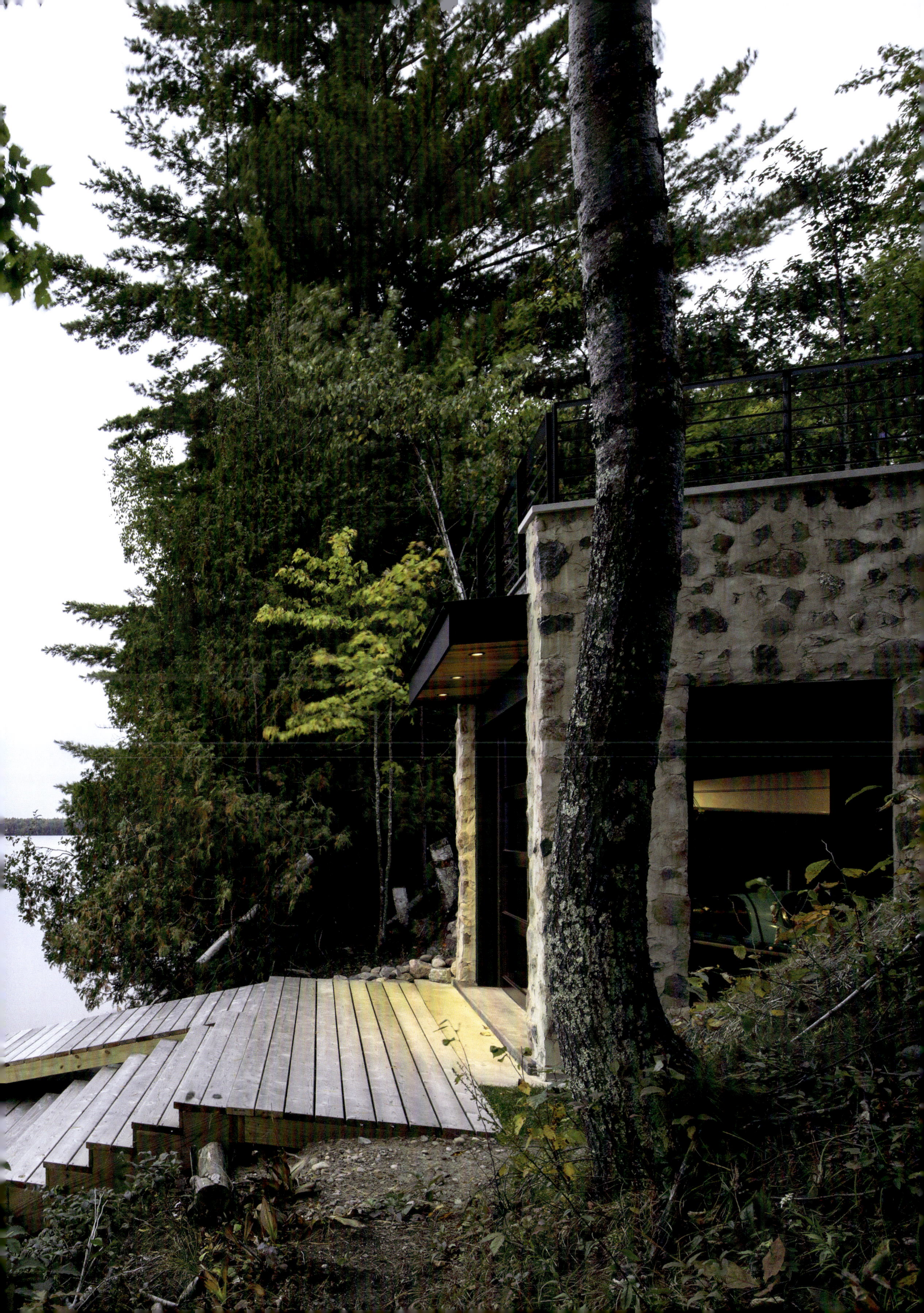

CONTRIBUTORS

ACKNOWLEDGMENTS

This book is the product of collaboration, a collective effort by many talented individuals, and I am deeply grateful to all who have helped bring it to life.

First, my deepest thanks go to the visionary interior designers whose work fills these pages. Your creativity, passion, and commitment continue to inspire me. I am proud to be part of the Midwest design community, and this book is a celebration of the many designers, artisans, and craftsmen whose hands and hearts bring these projects to life. Without you, this would not exist. I hope that by highlighting the wealth of talent within our community, this book elevates and honors everyone who contributes to shaping the spaces we inhabit.

A special thank-you to Carl Dellatore, who distilled the essence of each project with grace and insight and whose guidance shaped the book into what it is today.

I am also incredibly grateful to the team at Schiffer Publishing for believing in this project. To Peter Schiffer, thank you for seeing the vision and trusting in its potential.

And to wife, my family, and my friends—thank you for your love and encouragement. This book belongs to all of us. To everyone who made this possible, I am forever thankful.

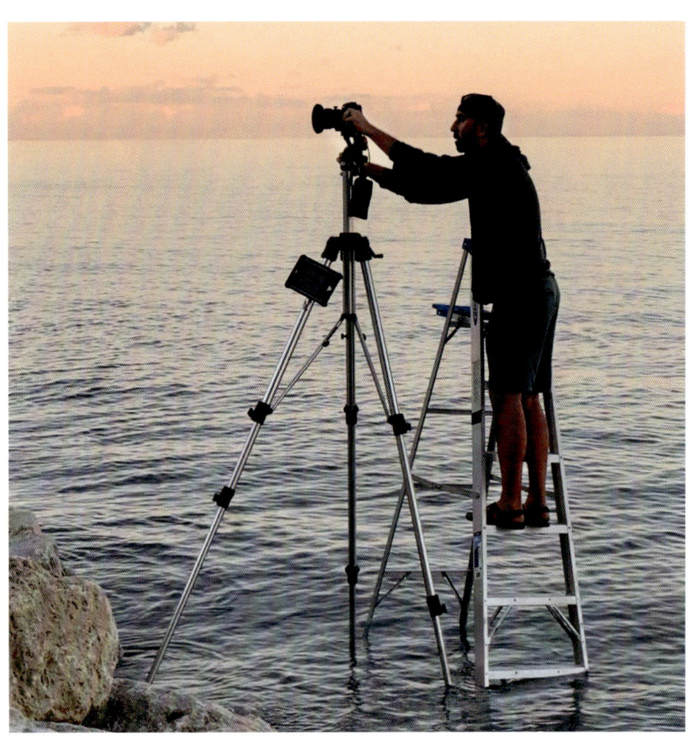

Photograph by Jenni Vetter

ABOUT THE AUTHOR

Ryan Hainey is from the Midwest. What started as a desire to leave turned into a deep appreciation for the land, the people, and the communities he's a part of.

Growing up, he was taught to respect the earth—its water, its soil, its quiet rhythms. His passions—fishing, watersports, cooking, photography, and woodworking—are expressions of that connection. Every interest reflects a relationship to place, an understanding of the importance of living with intention.

Ryan studied photography at the Milwaukee Institute of Art & Design and graduated in 2008 with a bachelor of fine arts. He began his career working with renowned sculptor Richard Edelman, but in 2013 he turned back toward his roots. After exploring abandoned spaces in his senior thesis, Ryan redirected his focus to interior design. He found inspiration in spaces that had stories to tell, and, in the process, he became deeply connected to the design community across the Midwest.

His work now lives in the pages of *Architectural Digest*, Luxe, and ArchDaily. The projects he captures—simple, authentic, and timeless—reflect his commitment to what feels real. His work has earned recognition and awards, but, for Ryan, it's never been about the accolades. It's about creating work that speaks without shouting.

At home, Ryan finds peace with his wife, their children, and their dog, embracing the Midwest's landscapes and finding quiet inspiration in the world around him.

In his work and life, Ryan is about honoring the past while creating with purpose. His photography is about telling stories—ones that linger and leave you with a sense of belonging.